MEDIA, FEMINISM, CULTURAL STUDIES

Stepping Forward: Essays, Lectures and Interviews
by Wolfgang Iser

Wild Zones: Pornography, Art and Feminism
by Kelly Ives

Global Media Warning: Explorations of Radio, Television and the Press
by Oliver Whitehorne

'Cosmo Woman': The World of Women's Magazines
by Oliver Whitehorne

Andrea Dworkin
by Jeremy Mark Robinson

Cixous, Irigaray, Kristeva: The Jouissance of French Feminism
by Kelly Ives

Sex in Art: Pornography and Pleasure in Painting and Sculpture
by Cassidy Hughes

The Erotic Object: Sexuality in Sculpture
From Prehistory to the Present Day
by Susan Quinnell

Women in Pop Music
by Helen Challis

Detonation Britain: Nuclear War in the UK
by Jeremy Mark Robinson

Julia Kristeva: Art, Love, Melancholy, Philosophy, Semiotics
by Kelly Ives

Luce Irigaray: Lips, Kissing, and the Politics of Sexual Difference
by Kelly Ives

Helene Cixous I Love You: The Jouissance of Writing
by Kelly Ives

The Poetry of Cinema
by John Madden

The Sacred Cinema of Andrei Tarkovsky
by Jeremy Mark Robinson

Disney Business, Disney Films, Disney Lands
Daniel Cerruti

Feminism and Shakespeare
by B.D. Barnacle

SEX IN ART

SEX IN ART

*Pornography and Pleasure
In the History of Art*

Cassidy Hughes

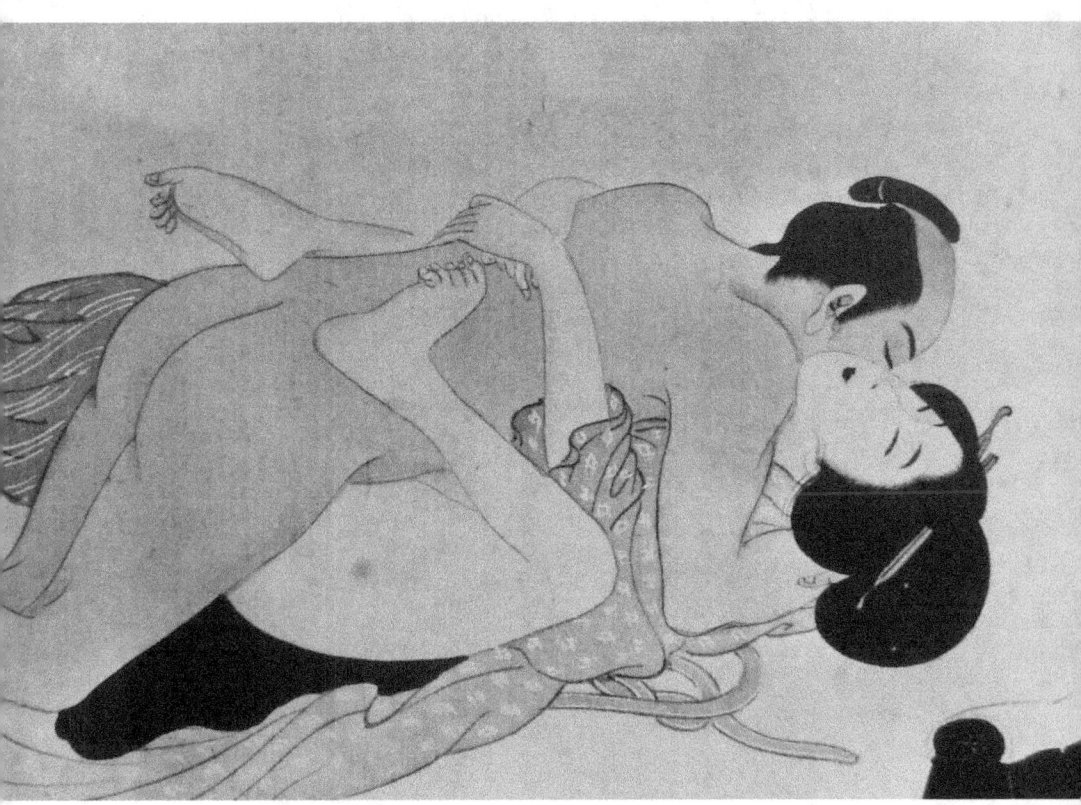

CRESCENT MOON

Crescent Moon Publishing
P.O. Box 1312, Maidstone,
Kent, ME14 5XU, U.K.
www.crmoon.com
cresmopub@yahoo.co.uk

First published 1998. Third edition 2012.
© Cassidy Hughes 1998, 2012.

Printed and bound in the U.S.A.
Set in Book Antiqua 10 on 14pt.
Designed by Radiance Graphics.

British Library Cataloguing in Publication data

Hughes, Cassidy
Sex in Art: Pornography and Pleasure In the History of Art
I. Title
704.9

ISBN-13 9781861713131 (Hbk)

ISBN-13 9781861713322 (Pbk)

CONTENTS

Part One: *Art, Pornography, Eroticism, Sexuality, Feminism*

1   The Pornography of Art/ The Art of Pornography;
     Pornography and Feminism/ Feminism
     and Pornography   23
2   Art, Sexuality, Eroticism, Pornography/ Pornography,
     Eroticism, Sexuality, Art   63
3   Sexuality, Art and Pornography   87

Part Two: *Prehistory, The Orient. Ancient Art, Renaissance*

1   Eroticism in Prehistoric Art   121
2   Oriental Eroticism   129
3   Eroticism in Ancient Art: Greece, Egypt, Rome   143
4   Sex in Renaissance Art   153

Part Three: *Modern Art, Symbolism, Expressionism, Surrealism,
     Eric Gill*

1   Symbolist and Decadent Art   253
2   Sex and Expressionism   265
3   Sex in the Great Moderns   289
4   Mad Love: Surrealist Sex   301

5   Eric Gill   309

Part Four: *Contemporary Art*

1   The Sexuality of Surfaces: Jasper Johns   319
2   The Sensuality of Surface and Abstraction in Contemporary
    Art   331
3   Contemporary Art   339
4   Eroticism in Contemporary Figurative Art   345

Part Five: *Sculpture, Brancusi, 'Women's' Art, 'Feminist' Art*

1   Sculpture   375
2   Constantin Brancusi   405
3   Women's Art, Feminist Art, Women Artists   419
4   Contemporary Feminist and Women's Art   433

Bibliography   447

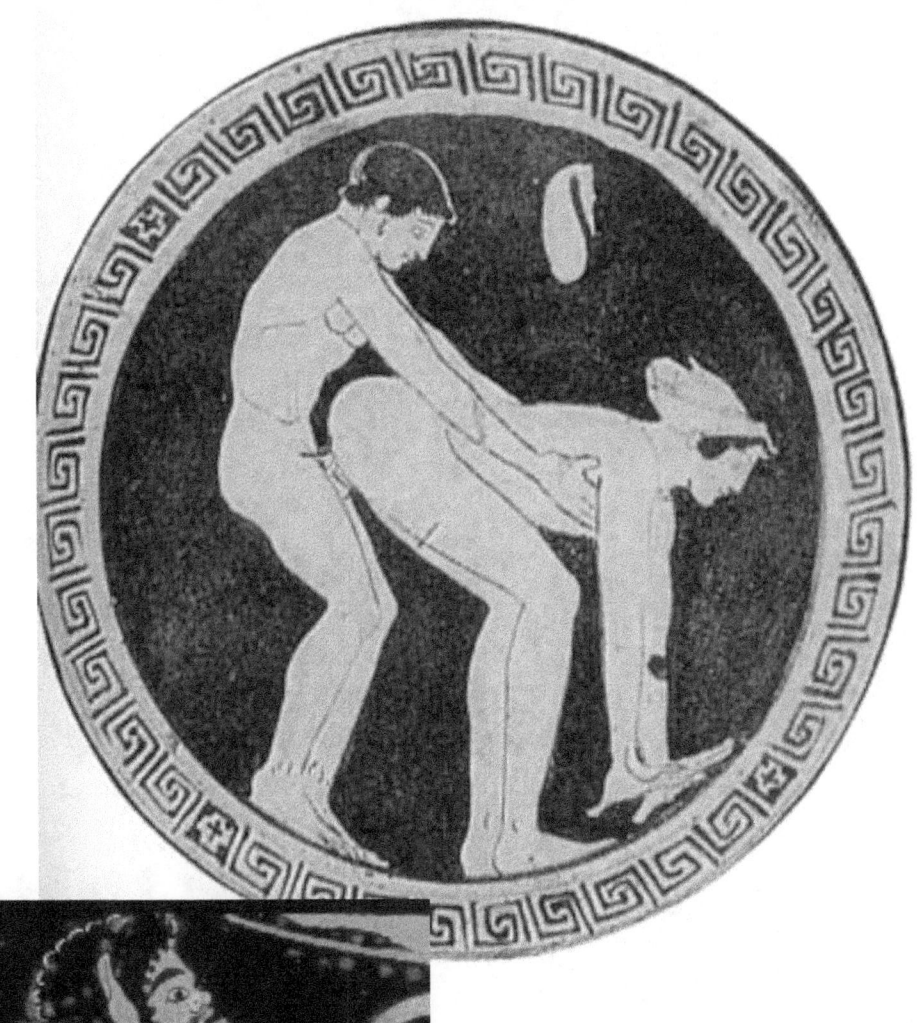

Art on ancient Greek vases

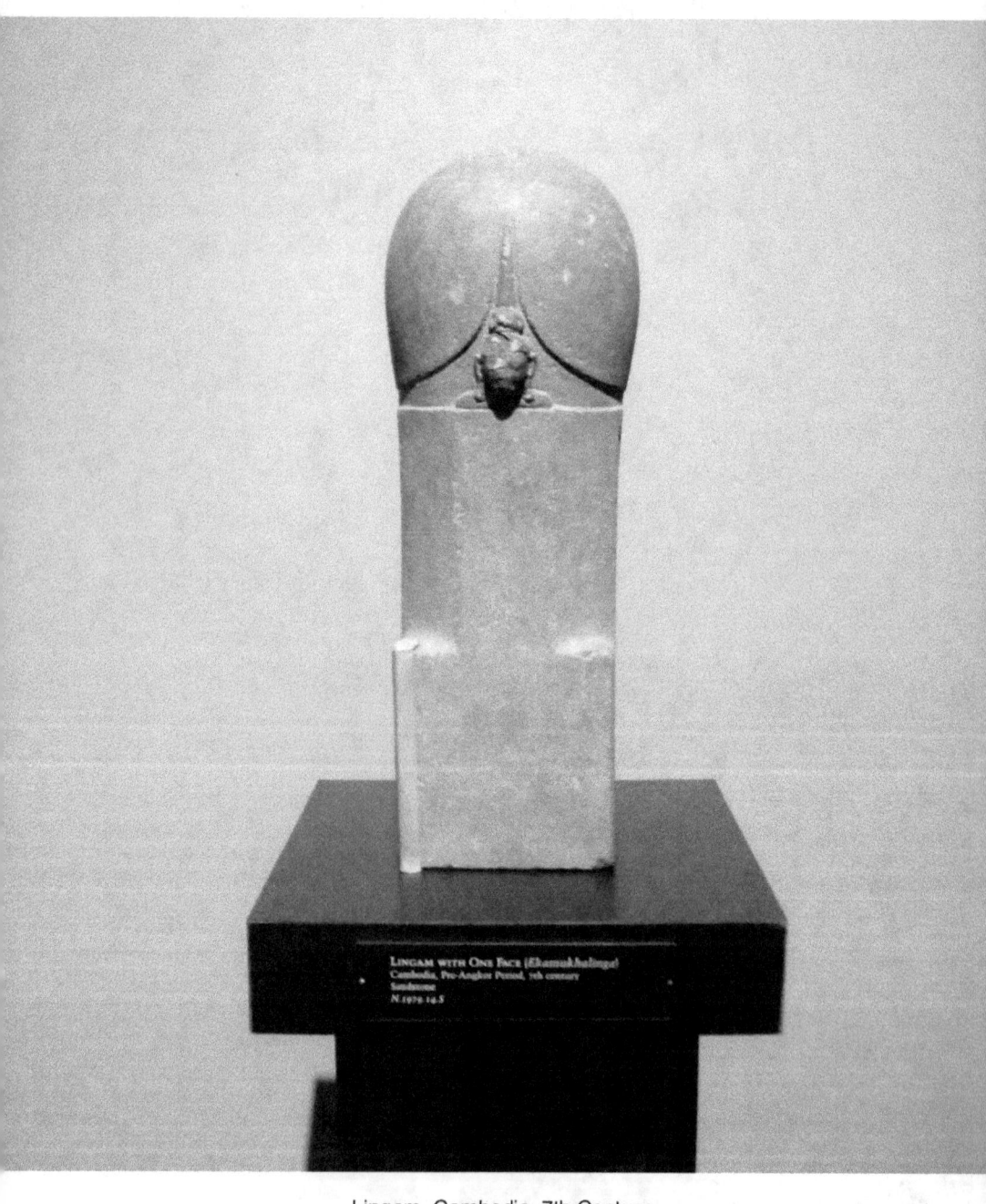

Lingam, Cambodia, 7th Century,
Norton Simon Museum, Pasadena, CA

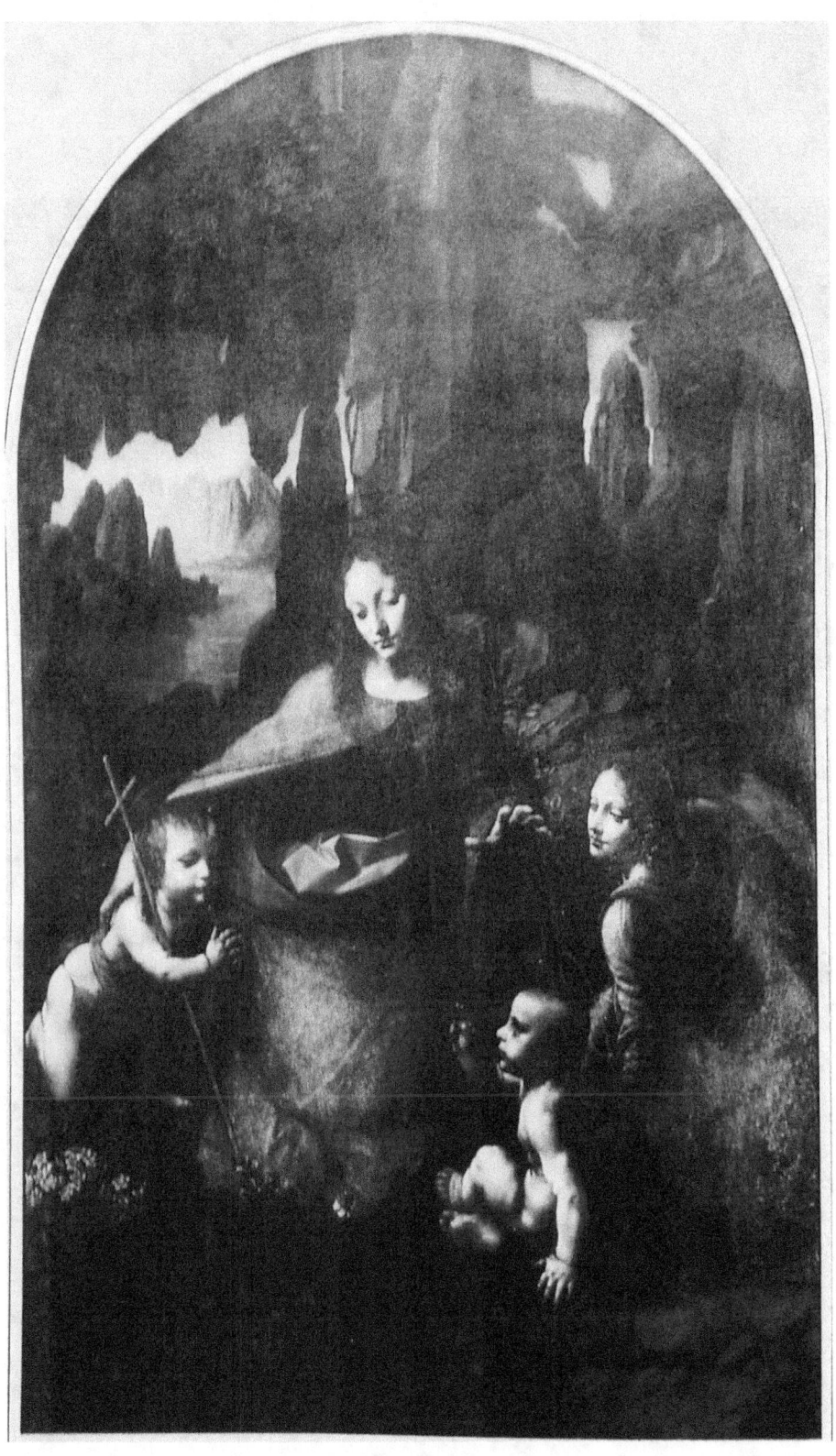

Leonardo da Vinci, The Madonna of the Rocks, London

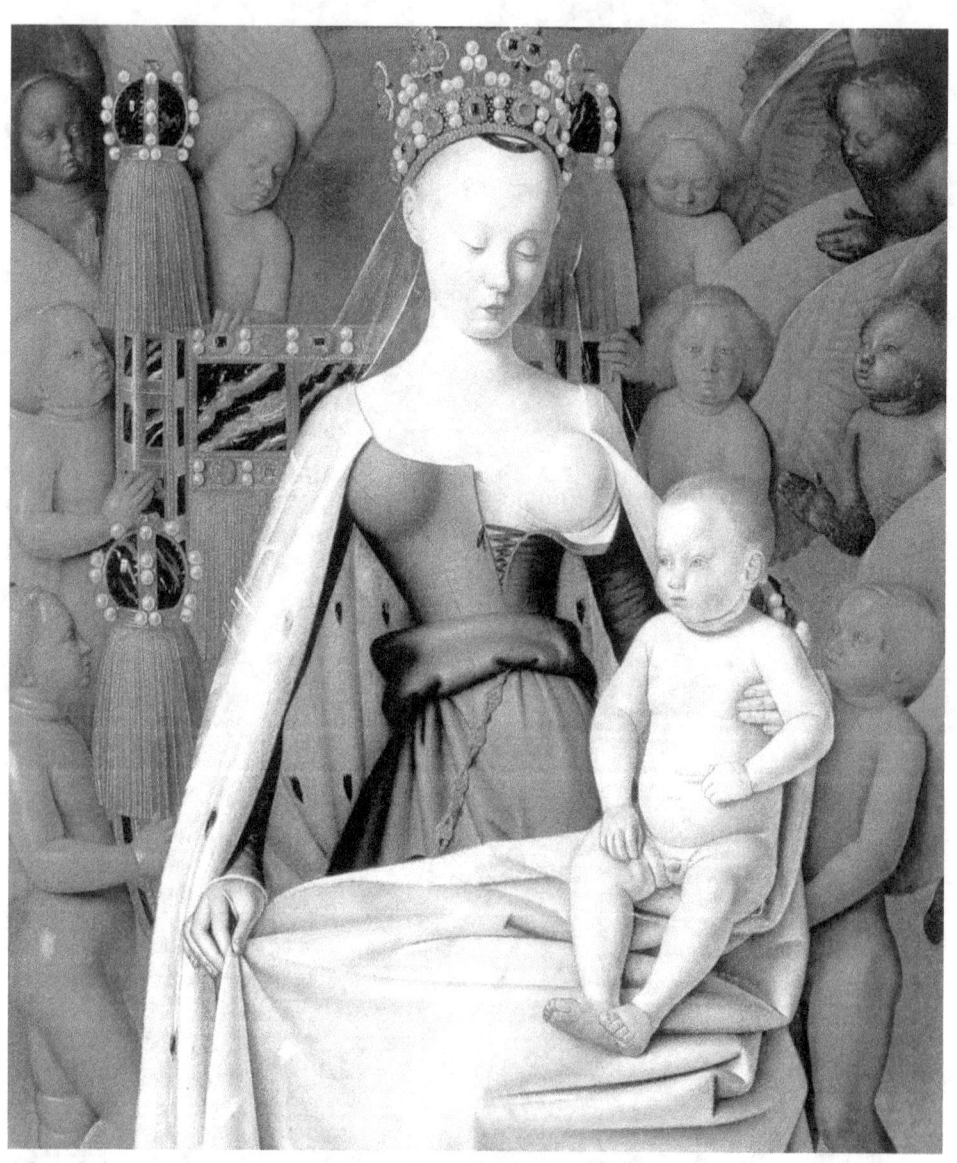

Jean Fouquet, The Melun Diptych, c. 1450

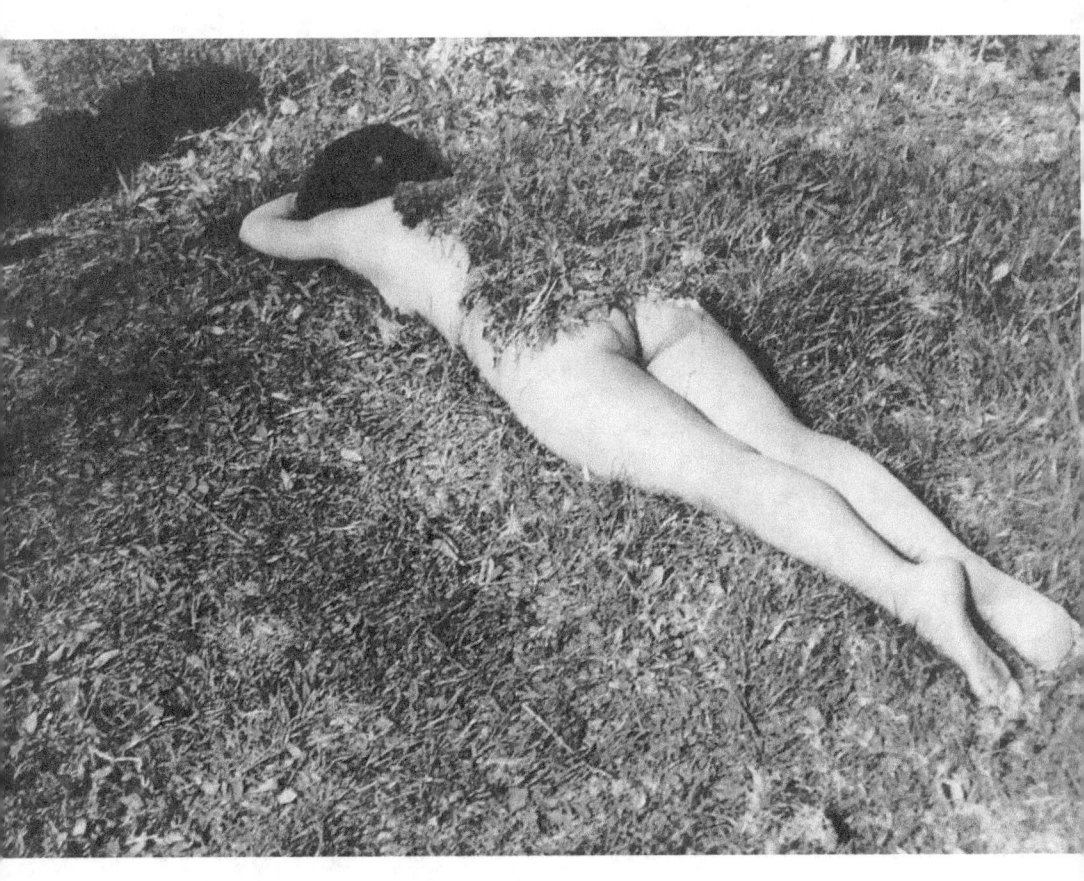

Ana Mendieta, Untitled (Grass On Woman), 1972

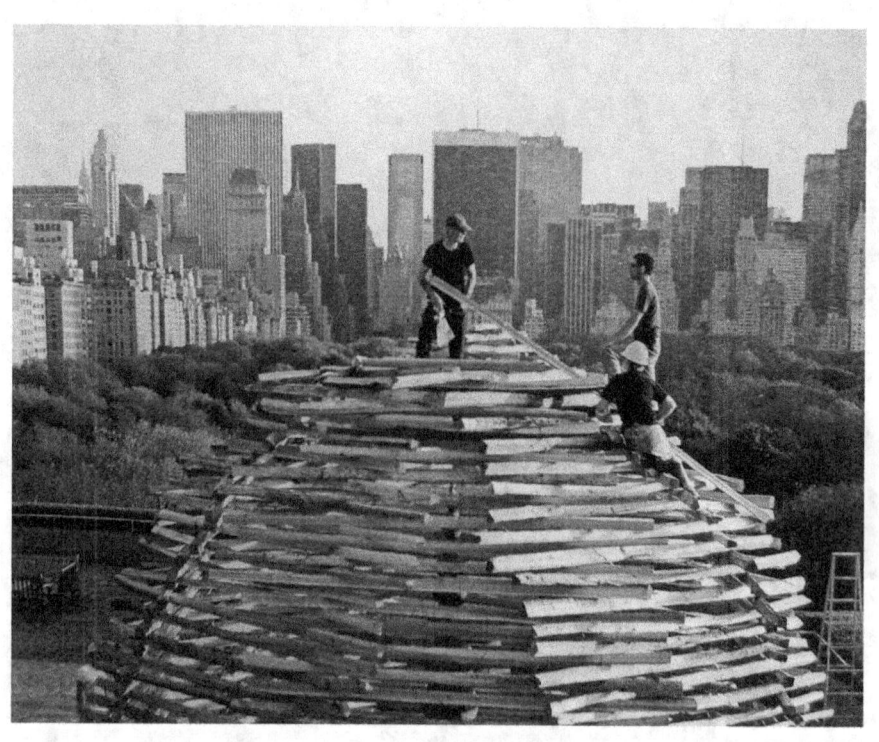

Andy Goldsworthy, Garden of Stones, New York City, 2003

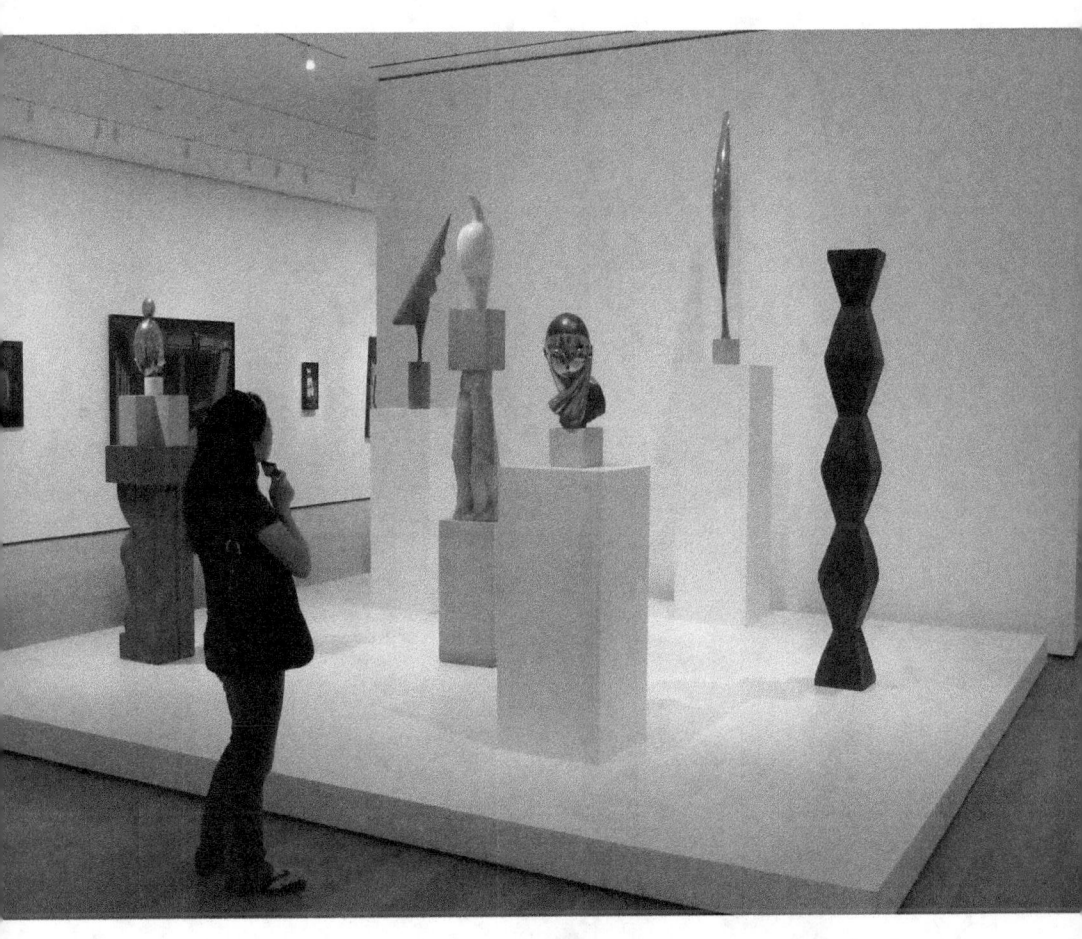

Constantin Brancusi display, Museum of Modern Art, Gotham

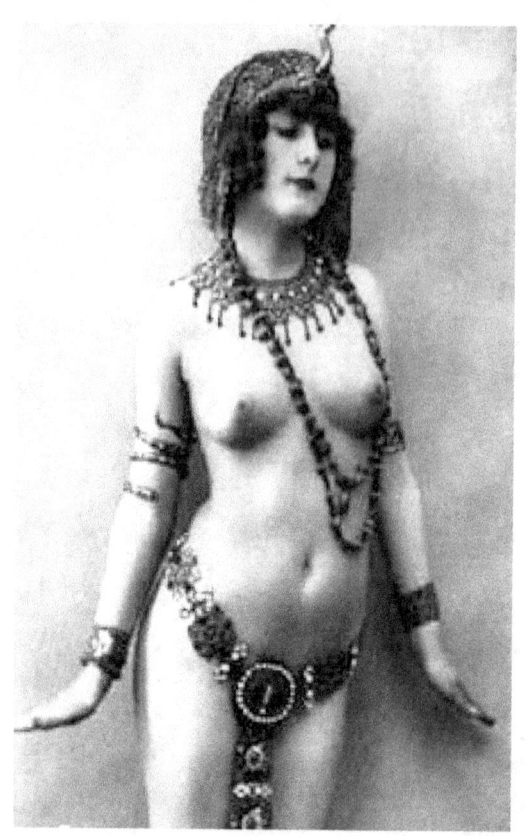

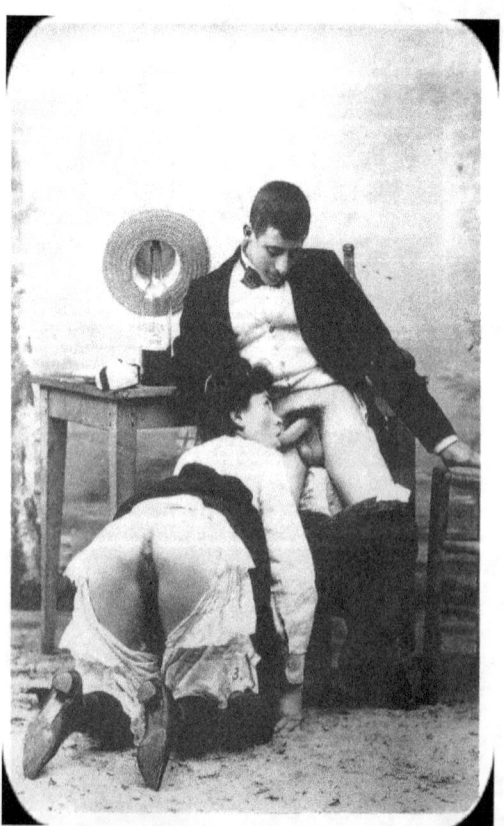

Late 19th century photographs, anonymous

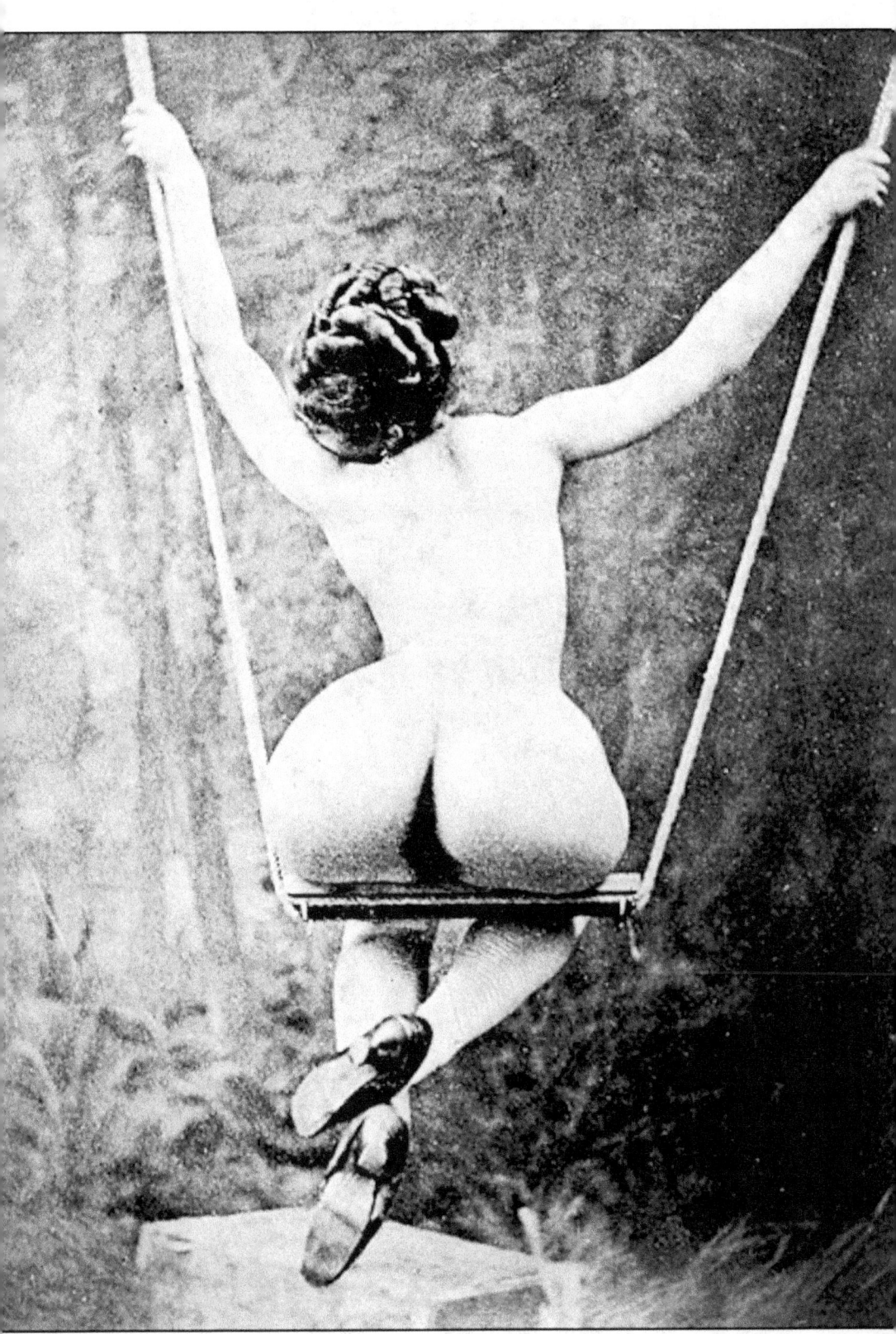

Pierre Louÿs

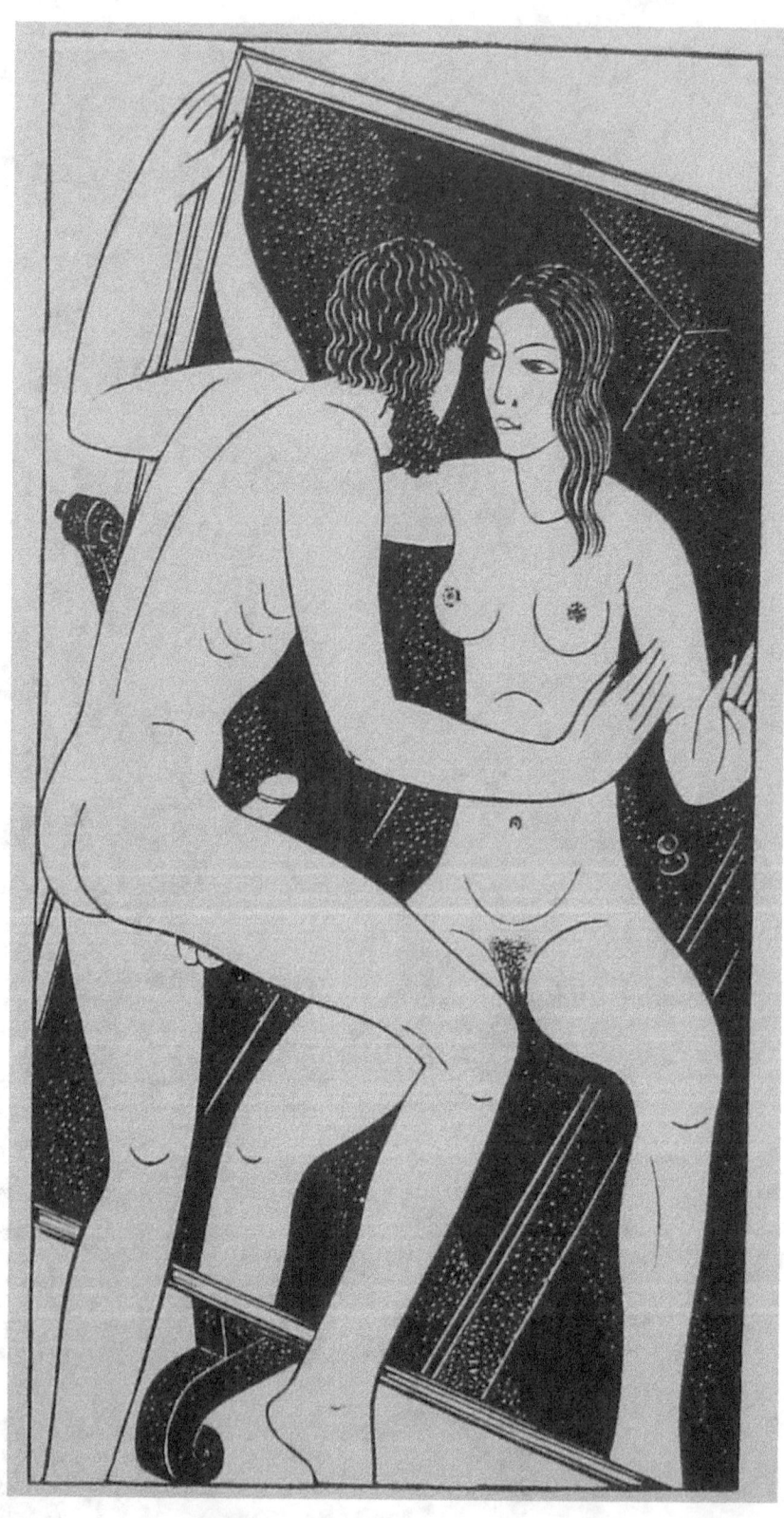

Eric Gill, Artist and Mirror, 1932

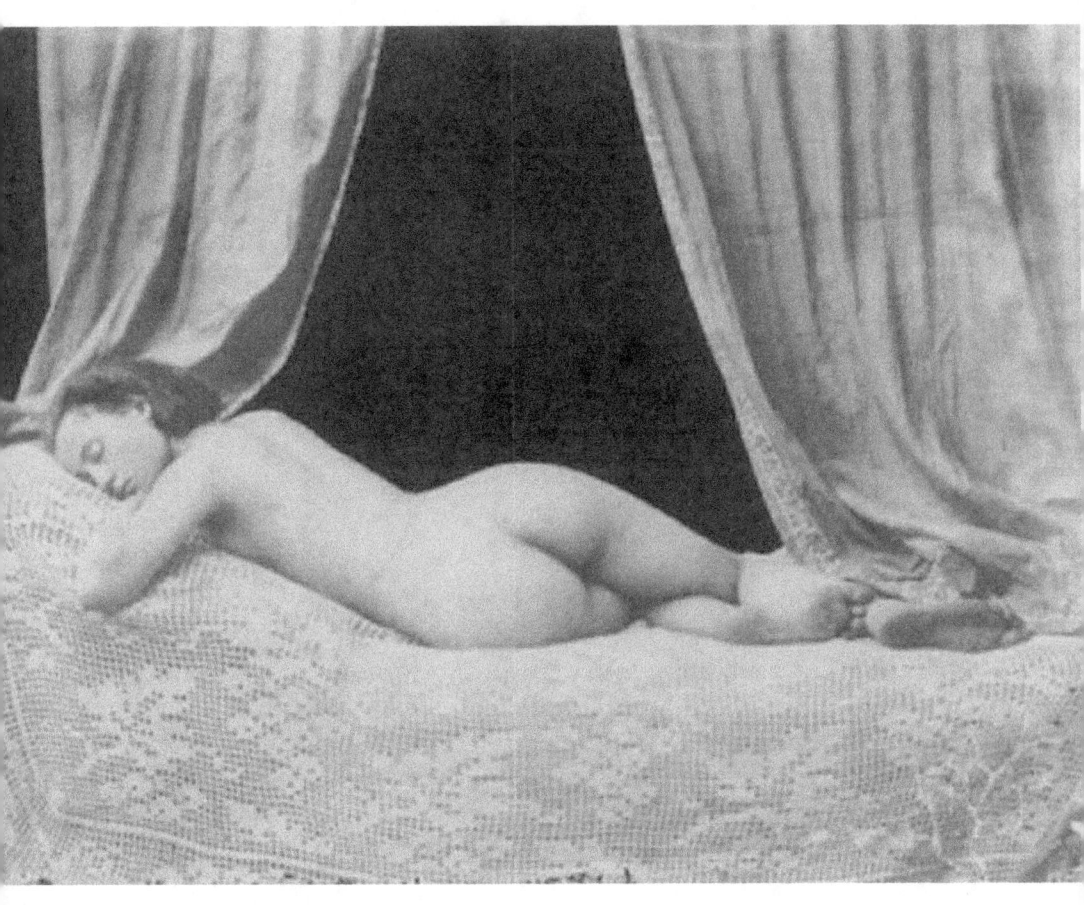

Anonymous, 19th century

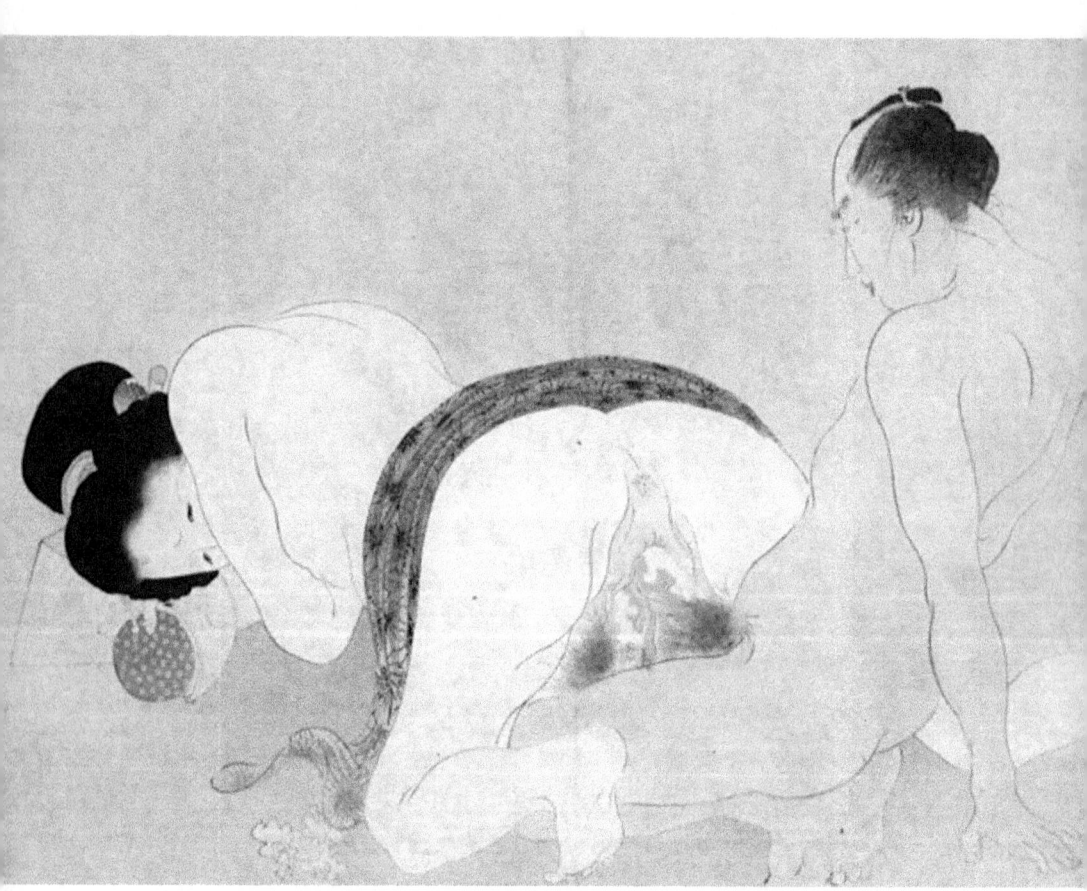

Shunga erotica, attributed to Tomioka Eisen (1864-1905)

Part One

ART

PORNOGRAPHY

EROTICISM

SEXUALITY

FEMINISM

1

THE PORNOGRAPHY OF ART/ THE ART OF PORNOGRAPHY: PORNOGRAPHY AND FEMINISM/ FEMINISM AND PORNOGRAPHY

This chapter looks at some of the discussions concerning porno-graphy, feminism and art. I present a variety of views on the issues, including summarizing many of the views of second wave feminism (particularly of the 1960s thru 1980s). Many of my ideas have changed since I wrote this book in 1998. The art vs. porno-graphy debate, for instance, is over, and porn is now accepted, far more than it has been for many years (though porn is still rejected in the places you'd expect). Porn and erotic art is simply no big deal anymore, but certain issues – religion and race to choose two of the hottest – are as controversial and explosive as ever.

In feminism, porn was a big issue, heating up to boiling point in the 1970s and 1980s (some of the key feminists in the debate were Andrea Dworkin, Mary Daly, Catherine MacKinnon, Susan Griffin, Hélene Cixous, Luce Irigaray, Susan Brownmiller and Robin Morgan). But as feminists at the time (and since) pointed out, the really important issues were not in the porn industry, but in culture and society at large – in the labour market, for instance, or in race relations, or in poverty, or in immigration. However, pornography and erotic art and the depiction of sexuality in art and the media was certainly fun for academics and critics and feminists to write about. But porn hasn't undermined civilization, in the East or West or North or South.

To begin: there are as many definitions of art and pornography as there are people (or more). Everyone has their own opinions, their own interests and agendas and realms to defend. There are the liberals who say that nothing should be censored, including pornography. Pornography is seen as part of artistic expression, and if people want to express themselves, they should, and if they want porn, they should have it. This is the view of liberals such as Peter Webb, who campaigned for freedom of expression, and an art that should celebrate eroticism.[1] It's a familiar viewpoint, which has been heard made many times. In the (male) liberal view, sex is OK, so sexual art must be OK, so that much of pornography must be OK. The 'experts' on sex, the so-called 'sexologists' (Fuchs, Krafft-Ebbing, Freud, Reich) argue that sex is a normal part of life, so it is logical that it should abound in art. Eduard Fuchs wrote; '[a]rt has treated erotic themes at almost all periods... [it] lies at the root of all human life.'[2]

Everyone seems to have their cut-off points, however, their 'standards' of 'taste' and 'decency'. It's a very subjective business, the debates between art and pornography, and between pornography and censorship. As Wendy Moore wrote: '[c]ensorship like freedom is an entirely subjective term'.[3] What you like defines yourself. As Pierre Bourdieu put it: '[t]aste classifies, and it

1 See P. Webb: *The Erotics Arts*, 1-9.
2 E. Fuchs: *Geschichte der Erotischen Kunst*, Albert Langen, Munich, 1912-26, I, 1.
3 W. Moore: There Should Be a Law Against It... Shouldn't There?", in G. Chester, 141.

classifies the classifier.'[4]

Taste, choice, categorization and classification, then, defines the viewer, the reader, the consumer. Censorship, one might say, defines a culture, and a culture's limits. And 'sensitive' novelists are wary of writing 'sex scenes', because they know that what they write defines themselves. Sex exposes them. Yet sex is crucial to art, many artists say. As Gertrude Stein remarked: '[l]iterature – creative literature – unconnected with sex is inconceivable.'[5]

What emerges from the left-liberal, patriarchal view of art and pornography is that censorship is largely political: it is not concerned so much with 'taste', 'decency' and 'defending' people as with political control. The history of censorship bears this out. As Catherine Itzin wrote: '[t]he purpose of censorship from beginning to end has been *political*: suppression.'[6]

Some things still shock people, upset them, disturb them. A survey for London's Royal College of Midwives of November, 1993 found that half of the men interviewed were opposed to breast-feeding in public.[7] Men don't want to see mothers breast-feeding in a restaurant, because it puts them off their food. They think it's 'embarrassing, unnecessary, exhibitionism, disgusting'. It's hard to believe, but men think breast-feeding is 'unnecessary'. 'Unnecessary'! To be 'disgusted' by breasts is very odd – even though plenty of heterosexual men adore them, make jokes about them, and put them in their newspapers and magazines. As Andrea Dworkin wrote in her novel *Mercy*: 'what's so dirty to men about breasts so they put tassles on them and have them swirl around in circles and call them the ugliest names; as if they ain't attached to human beings' (298).

Religious images when used blasphemously still shock some people. Salman Rushdie's *The Satanic Verses* and the death threat is one of the most notorious cases of religious intolerance of recent years. Seven people died in anti-Rushdie riots in Pakistan and India in February, 1989; ten people died in riots in Bombay; there

4 P. Bourdieu, 1984, 6.
5 G. Stein, in "A Conversation", John Hyde Preston, *Atlantic Monthly*, CLVI, Aug, 1935, 191.
6 C. Itzin: "Sex and Censorship: The Political Implications", in G. Chester, 41.
7 C. Mihill: "Breast-feeding falls foul of men", *The Guardian*, 6 Nov, 1993.

have been other deaths, all sparked off by a book being published in the late 20th century.[8] Andres Serrano's photograph *Piss Christ* created a lot of controversy, because it depicted (here we go again) a fusion of sex and the sacred, eroticism and Christianity.[9] Serrano said that he wanted to be 'descriptive or literal' in his use of bodily fluids.[10] The activist group Guerrilla Girls reminded viewers that 'the majority of exposed penises in major museums belong to the Baby Jesus.'[11]

The feminist Judy Chicago's *The Dinner Party* of the 1970s was reviled by critics because it focused on the vulva, what the art critic Robert Hughes called 'Chicago's relentless concentration on the pudenda'.[12] It's OK for male artists to paint the female genitals over and over (Pablo Picasso, Hans Bellmer, André Masson, Gustav Klimt, and Egon Schiele, for instance), but not for female artists. For Hilton Kramer, *The Dinner Party* was 'vulgar',[13] while Robert K. Dornan called it 'ceramic 3-D pornography'.[14]

When the American flag is burnt or used in a transgressive manner, some people get upset. Politically subversive acts disturb people, but when political art is combined with erotic art, the effect can be too much for the moral majority. Erika Rothenberg produced an art installation called *Have You Attacked America Today*, which contained a 'blonde couple' demonstrating how to use a DIY 'flag-burning kit'.[15] The Ridgeway Bennett group produced 'Cum Paintings', canvases shaped like triangles or

8 See W.J. Weatherby: *Salman Rushdie: Sentenced to Death*, Carroll & Graf, New York, NY, 1992; P. Theroux: "What About Rushdie?", *New York Times*, 13 Feb, 1992; "Islam zealots threaten Dante's tomb over Mohammed slur", *The New York Post*, 6 Mch, 1989; S.J.D. Green: "Beyond the Satanic Verses: Conservative Religion and the Liberal Society", *Encounter*, June 1990, 12-20; J.F. Baker: "A Rushdie Paperback?", *Publishers Weekly*, 13 Oct, 1989; S. Rushdie: "A Pen Against the Sword: In Good Faith", *Newsweek*, 12 Feb, 1990.
9 Andres Serrano: *Piss Christ*, 1987, Cibachrome photograph, Stux Gallery, New York.
10 A. Serrano, quoted in S. Dubin, 98. See M. Brenson: "Andres Serrano: Provocation and Spirituality", *New York Times*, 8 Dec, 1989, C1, 28.
11 Quoted in S. Dubin, 136.
12 R. Hughes: "An Obsessive Feminist Pantheon", *Time*, 15 Dec, 1980, 85-86.
13 H. Kramer: "Art: Judy Chicago's *Dinner Party*, Comes to Brooklyn Museum", *New York Times*, 17 Oct, 1980. And see C. Rickey: "Judy Chicago, *The Dinner Party*, The Brooklyn Museum", *Artforum*, Jan, 1981; R. Pedersen: "The Bitter Taste of the *The Dinner Party*", *Los Angeles Times*, 5 Nov, 1990; J. Rose Barras: "UDC's $1.6 million 'Dinner': Feminist artwork causes some indigestion", *The Washington Times*, 18 July, 1990; C. O'Neil: "House cuts D.C. funding over Judy Chicago display", *Outweek*, 15 Aug, 1990.
14 *Congressional Record*, 101st Session, volume 136, no. 98, 26 July, 1990.
15 See S. Dubin, 252.

crosses smeared with vinyl, wax and the sperm of the artists, spelling out the word 'cum'.[16]

Jean-Luc Godard's film *Hail Mary* (1985) created controversy when it depicted the Blessed Virgin as a gas station attendant.[17] There were bomb threats, 5,000 protesters reciting the rosary to cinema queues, and the 'film bears the distinction of being the first ever condemned by a pope (Pope John Paul II), and being the first instance in 400 years that a pope directly intervened in the suppression of a work of art', remarked Steven Dubin (93). But *Je Vous Salue, Marie* is a beautiful, original and very lyrical movie. It does feature a lot of nudity (from actress Myriem Roussel), and that means that the Virgin Mary is nude, and explicit sexual language, too. And *Hail Mary* is presented in Godard's trademark highly idiosyncratic style, which's not to everyone's taste.

Artistic transgressions of Christian religion upset people immensely, it seems. Witness, for instance, the complaints of the clergy and the church about women priests (a move that was resisted by the conservative – and largely male – priesthood). In 1984 an artwork of a crucified woman, *Christa*, was taken out of a church in New York because it was 'theologically and historically indefensible'.[18] A crucified *woman*, now there's a blasphemous image to conjure with. An artist superimposed the breasts and face of Marilyn Monroe over the Virgin of Guadalupe and there were threats to burn down the Museum of Modern Art in Mexico City.[19] The pop star Madonna fused the sensuality of pop icon Miss M with the untouchableness and sanctity of the Virgin Mary. Madge dances in a wedding dress in the video for *Like a Prayer*, and wrote the song *Papa Don't Preach*, attacking male authority figures. Her products *Erotica* and the book *Sex* flirt playfully with

16 E. Hess: "Gutter Politics", *Village Voice*, 3 July, 1990, 89.
17 J. Godard: *Hail Mary*, 1985, France. See J. Strong: "*Hail Mary* leaves council offended, box office booming", *Chicago Tribune*, 17 Apl, 1986; W. Smith: "Ecumenical crowd of protesters pans *Hail Mary*", *Chicago Tribune*, 5 Apl, 1986; M. Wilmington: "*Hail Mary*: A Godard Pirouette", *Los Angeles Times*, 20 Nov, 1985.
18 K.A. Briggs: "Cathedral Removing Statue of Crucified Woman", *New York Times*, 28 Apl, 1984.
19 L. Rohter: "Marilyn and Virgin: Art or Sacrilege?" *New York Times*, 2 Apl, 1988.

pornographic images.[20] Universal's *The Last Temptation of Christ* kicked up a fuss, with cinemas being set on fire, thousands of people protesting in the streets, and TV executives banning it, yet the film is clearly the work of a faithful Catholic, and director Martin Scorsese calls himself a believer in Christ as the Son of God.[21] Mel Gibson's *The Passion of the Christ* caused a similar controversy in 2004 (but not only about the depiction of Jesus, but also about possible anti-semitism. Gibson seems to have actively courted controversy with his political remarks – about homo-sexuality, for instance. Of course, a little controversy helps publicity, as Hollywood has known since the early 1900s).

So much art has to be censored, edited, screened, so that nothing offends anybody. The list of television shows that have not been broadcast because of their political or sexual or 'sensitive' content is enormous. Huge numbers of TV shows and document-aries have simply been ditched, often banned by governments.[22] Prime-time shows in the U.S.A. are pre-screened for executives and 'screeners', so that nothing offends.[23]

D.H. Lawrence is fairly typical among modern and *avant garde* writers in his view of pornography. For him, porn demeans sex, makes it 'dirty', squalid, limited: '[p]ornography is the attempt to insult sex, to do dirt on it,' he wrote in *Pornography and Obscenity*.[24] For Lorenzo, as for so many writers, poets, intellect-uals and philosophers, sex is something holy, sublime and central to existence. One must have 'a proper reverence for sex', Lawrence wrote in "A Propos of *Lady Chatterley's Lover*".[25] The problem with Lawrence, some commentators maintain, and one

20 See C. Philips: "Anger Over Madonna Single", *Los Angeles Times*, 4 Jan, 1991; "Clash Over Madonna", *New York Times*, 14 July 1990.
21 See J. Maslin: "*Last Temptation*: Scorsese's View of Jesus's Sacrifice", *New York Times*, 12 Aug, 1988; A. Harmetz: "7,500 Picket Universal Over Movie About Jesus", *New York Times*, 12 Aug, 1988; J. Casuso & C. Mount: "Protesters, fans flock to *Last Temptation*", *Chicago Tribune*, 13 Aug, 1988; B. Cronin & T. Gibbons: "600 Picket as Christ film opens", *Chicago Sun-Times*, 13 Aug, 1988; J. Caryn: "Paul Shrader Talks of *Last Temptation* and His New Film", *New York Times*, 1 Sept, 1988.
22 See J. Pilger: "Silence of the Lambs", *The New Statesman and Society*, 20 Aug, 1993, 14.
23 See B. Carter: "Screeners Help Advertisers Avoid Prime-Time Trouble", *New York Times*, 29 Jan, 1990.
24 D.H. Lawrence: *Pornography and Obscenity*, *This Quarter*, 1929, in *A Selection From Phoenix*, 313.
25 Lawrence, in *A Selection From Phoenix*, 331.

29

can say the same of Georges Bataille, Wilhelm Reich, Sigmund Freud, the Marquis de Sade, Henry Miller and others, is that he emphasizes sex too much; that, in *Lady Chatterley's Lover* especially, he reckoned a social revolution could only occur founded on a sexual revolution. Get right in your sex, Lawrence said, and everything else will fall into place. However, many feminists also place sexuality at the centre of the feminist debate. As Catherine MacKinnon said, in her manifesto of feminist theory: '[s]exuality is to feminism what work is to marxism'.[26]

Everyone who says anything about pornography and art and censorship usually states, either overtly or by implication, what *they* think is 'acceptable', and what is 'obscene' or 'unacceptable'. Steven Marcus offered a typical viewpoint: art is about 'the relations of human beings among themselves' while 'sex in pornography is sex without the emotions'.[27] The view is that 'true' art (or 'high' art) is emotional, and therefore justifies its existence. Deep feelings or emotions in art connote æsthetic and philosophical authenticity (or cultural value). As one of the founders of modern abstraction, Kasimir Malevich has it: 'the significant thing is feeling... Feeling is the determining factor',[28] while the prince of dreamy, escapist art, Odilon Redon, said: 'I speak to those who surrender themselves gently to the secret and mysterious laws of the emotions and the heart'.[29]

Pornography outrages some people, but it shocks people for different reasons. Benoîte Groult wrote that '[p]ornography has always existed and has never undermined anything. It has always given pleasure to the same men and the same women and shocked the same others.'[30] Speaking about porn, it seems, forces people to declare their political allegiances, their views on the quality of life, their philosophies, their fears. Pornography is an emotive subject – this partly explains the widespread debates about it in the modern era (the modern era which we might

26 C MacKinnon: "Feminism, Marxism, Method, and the State: An Agenda for Theory", in N.O. Keohane, *et al*, eds. *Feminist Theory: A Critique of Ideology*, Harvester, 1982.
27 S. Marcus: *The Other Victorians*, Corgi, London, 1969, 283-4.
28 K. Malevich: *The Non-Objective World*, tr. H. Dearstyne, Theobald, Chicago, IL, 1959, 67f.
29 Odilon Redon: *A soi même: Journal (1867-1915)*, Corti, Paris 1961, 115f.
30 B. Groult: "Le portiers de nuit", in E. Marks, 73.

define aptly as from the Marquis de Sade onwards).

It should be remembered, too, that when people speak about pornography they are not simply offering dispassionate, depersonalized, distanced accounts of something that is 'out there'. For porn to work, like any art or communication, it needs a reader, a viewer, a consumer. One can't, then, ignore the critic's own part in the discussion of pornography and feminism, for the critic, whether feminist or not, is also a consumer. Jennifer Wicke commented that

> it needs to be accepted that pornography is not 'just' consumed, but is used, worked on, elaborated, remembered, fantasised about by its subjects. To stop the analysis at the artifact, as virtually all the current books and articles do, imagining that the representation is the pornography in quite simple terms, is to truncate the consumption radically, and thereby to leave unconsidered the human making involved in completing the act of pornographic consumption.[31]

It is not simply a case of critics, feminists and consumers on one side and pornography, art and culture on the other. Critics pretend they coolly analyze texts from a distance, whereas they are involved with them at many levels. Subjectivity and objectivity merge, and there is not an area of neutral ground between the consumer and what is consumed. As Wicke put it:

> The academic market is hot for pornography because pornography is both the object and the subject of desire, the representation and the reader, the consumer and the consumed, one inextricable package. (ib, 79)

Feminists have many views on porn. Some feminists advocate the abolition of pornography, while others see the banning of pornography as more political suppression. On the one hand, there must be no censorship in a truly 'liberating' socio-political stance. On the other hand, some feminists see much of porn as violence against women. Probably the most powerful of commentators on pornography, and certainly the most incisive

31 J. Wicke: "Through a Gaze Darkly: Pornography's Academic Market:, in P. Gibson, 70.

and relentless in her analysis, is Andrea Dworkin, the New York feminist and ideologue. Her book *Pornography: Men Possessing Women* is a landmark in sexual politics debates. It is a work of rage, in which pornography is seen as a manifestation of the exertion by men of power over women:

> In the male system, women are sex; sex is the whore. The whore is *porne*, the lowest whore, the whore who belongs to *all* male citizens: the slut, the cunt. Buying her is buying pornography. Having her is having pornography. Seeing her is seeing pornography. (202)

Andrea Dworkin pinpoints the unceasing reductionism of patriarchy, where people are sexualized or reduced to their genitals. It's seen all the time in porn and culture. More controversially, Jenny Diski suggested that a rape 'victim's' life need not be utterly shattered after the rape, because it means society put too much emphasis on sexuality: '[e]very act of physical violence will have traumatic effects but what do we mean when we tell a young woman that her sense of self-esteem can be destroyed by an act of enforced penetration? Are we really meaning to say that a woman's central identity resides in her genitals?'[32] The genitals have replaced the soul as the site of a person's core or essence. Pornography, and art, adds to (or enhances, or reflects back) this psychosexual emphasis.

In the art criticism of the history of the painted nude, for example, attention is always drawn to the erotic nature of the naked body. David Hockney expressed a typical (patriarchal) view on this matter: 'Kenneth Clark points out in his book *The Nude* that there are bound to be elements of eroticism in any nude picture and I think he's absolutely right there.'[33] Kenneth Clark put it thus: '[a]ll good nude painting and sculpture is sexually stimulating'.[34]

Andrea Dworkin's point, and the opinion of many feminists, is that men reduce people to their sexuality, to penises and

---

32 J. Diski: "Double jeopardy of the victim victim", *The Guardian*, 27 Aug, 1993.
33 D. Hockney, in P. Webb, 376; K. Clark: *The Nude*, Penguin, London, 1960.
34 K. Clark: *The Nude*, John Murray, London, 1956, 6.

clitorises. As Dworkin asserted: '[t]he fact is that men can and do fetishize everything' (124-5). But this might apply to women too. So many writers are guilty of this incessant sexualizing of people, of seeing just the sexual aspect of someone, ignoring other aspects: D.H. Lawrence, Henry Miller, Dante Alighieri, Charles Baudelaire, the Marquis de Sade, Paul Éluard, etc. Many painters eroticize people, emphasizing the sexual element above all others: Pablo Picasso, Egon Schiele, Edgar Degas, Gustav Moreau, Hans Bellmer, Pierre Renoir, Eric Gill, Titian, etc. It seems male artists cannot make art without drawing attention at some time to a person's sexuality. Yes, but so do women artists.

Many modern thinkers have stressed sex above everything else: Georges Bataille, Sigmund Freud, Wilhelm Reich, Herbert Marcuse, etc. What happens is that people become genitals: women are reduced to 'cunt... our essence, our offense', as Kate Millet put it.[35] It's easier, feminists claim, for men to relate to a depersonalized, fetishized object, such as a vagina, a boot, a stocking, a woman's torso bereft of head and personality, than to relate to a real person, which is infinitely more complicated. Pornography reduces women to sex objects, much as men manufacture sex toys such as blow-up dolls, which are the ultimate, in one sense, of erotic reductionism. The sex doll doesn't moan she has a headache, she is 'always ready' for sex, so the adverts run. As Elizabeth Carola opined: 'sexually 'relating' to a fetishized image is far easier than sexually relating to another human being.'[36]

In some ways, then, pornography is the ultimate pleasure machine: it is a mirror, which reflects back the man's desire. The 'sex object', the woman, is a mirror, reduced, tailored and shaped to the consumer's needs, reflecting only what he desires: depersonalized sex, sex with no personality, no feedback, no empathy, no soul or emotion, no familial, social or political worries or responsibilities. Human-free sex, in other words,

35 K. Millet: *The Prostitution Papers*, Avon Books, New York, NY, 1973, 95.
36 E. Carola: "Women, Erotica, Pornography – Learning to Play the Game?", in G. Chester, 172.

machine-like sex, with no effort required, like vegging out in front of the TV, couch potato sex, computer sex, now called 'virtual reality' sex, sex without touching, without making contact with anything more demanding than a flickering computer/ digital/ internet/ video-generated image.

Benoîte Groult described the 'intellectual' books of high-class porn – by Miller, Bataille, de Sade:

> No matter what book it is, we always find the same male hero who, with the same arrogance, takes his pleasure in some creature who for him is reduced to two holes in the bottom of her body, plus a third on the bottom of her face... [37]

According to Andrea Dworkin, the way women are treated in pornography reflects the way they are treated in society. Pornography is the theory and social power is the reality, or as Robin Morgan put it: 'pornography is the theory and rape is the practice'.[38] For Dworkin, as for other radical feminists, such as Susan Griffin, Kate Millett and Susan Brownmiller, rape is sanctioned and sanctified in patriarchy.[39] Pornography helps to legitimize rape, to make it appear the norm, so that feminists see marriage as sanctified rape.[40] Dominique Poggi wrote: 'one of the principal functions of pornography: the purveying of an ideology of pleasure and enjoyment which urges rapelike relations, exalts rapists'.[41] But no, one of porn's principal functions is not to promote 'rapelike relations'. It's *fantasy*).

For Andrea Dworkin, porn is about male power: '[m]ale power is the *raison d'être* of pornography; the degradation of the female is the means of achieving this power' (25). This power is exerted, claims Dworkin, physically, economically, psycho-

37 B. Groult: "Les portiers de nuit", in *Ainsi soit-elle*, Grasset, Paris, 1975, and in E. Marks, 71.
38 See L. Lederer, ed. *Take Back the Night: Woman on Pornography*, William Morrow, New York 1980
39 S. Griffin: *Rape: the Power of Consciousness*, Harper & Row, New York, NY, 1979; S. Brownmiller: *Against Our Will: Men, Women and Rape*, Simon & Shuster, New York, NY, 1975; D. Rhodes & S.McNeil, eds. *Women Against Violence Against Women*, Onlywomen Press, London, 1985; J. Hammer & M. Maynard, eds. *Women, Violence and Social Control*, Macmillan, London, 1987.
40 See C. Kramarae & P. A. Treichler, eds. *A Feminist Dictionary*, Pandora Press, London, 1985.
41 D. Poggi: "Une apologie des rapports de domination", *La quinzaine littéraire,* Aug, 1976, in E. Marks, 77.

logically, philosophically, ideologically, politically and socially – in every sphere of life. Dworkin uses pornography as a way of showing just how men control so many aspects of life, and how men express their hatred of women.

For the establishment, Andrea Dworkin's cultural analysis goes too far. For some feminists, it doesn't go far enough. Some feminists have been critical of Dworkin, and of Dworkin's and Catherine MacKinnon's anti-pornography bill in the U.S.A..[42] The problems begin when anti-porn drives become as dogmatic and entrenched as pro-pornography agendas. The area is a minefield, continually paradoxical, with no clear dividing lines. There is massive confusion and ambiguity.

For some, Andrea Dworkin goes too far, or is too sweeping and generalized in her polemical statements. If Gillian Rodgerson and Linda Semple are right when they define the Dworkin-MacKinnon ordinance against pornography as being based on a view that 'basically any depiction of women in a sexual situation' was wrong or bad, then somebody is very mistaken here.[43] Dworkin and MacKinnon are not against *every* depiction of women as sexual beings. Dworkin is not 'against' sexual feelings. Rather, she despises those representations that damage, terrorize, debase and exploit women.

For Michael Moorcock, Andea Dworkin is an inspiration. She does not dictate, Moorcock says, but simply reflects what is already there in contemporary culture:

> Dworkin says her books are not prescriptive but descriptive. While continuing to expand the boundaries of feminism, she argues from a humanistic and idealistic perspective both intellectually stunning and stylistically eloquent.[44]

For some feminists, focusing on the porn issue means vital

---

42 See L. Duggan: "Censorship in the Name of Feminism", in G. Chester, 76-86; V. Burstyn, ed. *Feminists Against Censorship*, Douglas & McIntyre, Toronto, 1985; L. Kelly: "Feminists v Feminists – legislating against porn in the USA", *Trouble and Strife*, 7, 4-10
43 Gillian Rodgerson and Linda Semple: "Who watches the watchwomen?: Feminists against censorship", *Feminist Review*, no 36, Autumn 1990
44 M. Moorcock: *Casablanca*, Gollancz, London, 1989, 134-5.

energy is directed at only one issue, when there are many others that need attention. 'Porn is just one product in the big social supermarket,' wrote B. Ruby Rich.

> Why is pornography so important, finally? Is it important enough to be consuming all our political energy as feminists? ... whether symptom or cause, pornography presents an incomplete target for feminist attack. The campaign against pornography is a massive displacement of outrage that ought to be directed at a far wider sphere of oppression.[45]

The issue of pornography creates confusion and divides feminists as much as liberal intellectuals or politicians. As Julienne Dickey commented: 'why does the subject evoke on the one hand such passion, even hostility, and on the other hand an incapacitating confusion?'[46] Pornography is such a contentious issue, it seems no commentator can manœuvre through it without sinking into some bog or other of moral ambiguity or hermeneutic conflict. For feminists, the issue of porn often involves the most extreme emotions, from virulent hatred to passion. As Sue George remarked, '[f]or a feminist, therefore, to enjoy pornography is to feel doubly guilty.'[47]

There are many different kinds of pornography, as there are many different kinds of art or feminism. Seen through cultural or postmodern or deconstructionist or semiological theory, porn can be viewed as a realm of codes, meanings, contexts, signifiers, values, experiences and attitudes, which are politically controlled, manufactured by social, economic and political needs and demands. Pornography is thus the *representation* of... something; maybe certain kinds of sexuality, maybe somebody's thoughts on certain kinds of sexuality. Pornography is not *sexuality in itself*, it is mediation, representation, communication, a relic, a trace. Representations and mediations of sexuality feed back into

---

45 B. Ruby Rich: "Anti-Porn: Soft Issue, Hard World", *Village Voice*, 20 July 1982, in *Feminist Review*, eds., *Sexuality: A Reader*, 347-8, 350.
46 J. Dickey: "Snakes and Ladders", in G. Chester, 161.
47 S. George: "Censorship and Hypocrisy: Some Issues Surrounding Pornography that Feminism has Ignored", in G. Chester, 111.

people's actual sexual identities, in their actual sex 'acts', and vice versa, as Suzanne Kappeler noted (2). As a series of representations, then, porn can be seen as part of a *continuum* of other representations: TV, magazines, painting, writing, theatre, opera, cinema, the web, etc. Pornography is one area (one genre even) of representation, and is thus subject to the many mechanisms of idelogical, social, economic, metaphysical and physical pressures that influence other forms of representation.

Most commentators, of whatever ideological or political persuasion, agree that porn is full of conflict, hypocrisy and paradox, as well as heaps of desire, fantasy and pleasure. Catherine MacKinnon described sexuality in a way that might apply also to pornography:

> Sexuality is that social process which creates, organizes, expresses, and directs desire, creating the social beings we know as women and men, as their relations create society.[48]

For radical feminists, the West is a 'rapist' culture, a 'sadospiritual' society, as Mary Daly called it, using her new terms which she invented to describe the phallocentric nature of Western society.[49] 'The fact is,' claimed Daly, 'that we live in a profoundly anti-female society, a misogynistic 'civilization' in which men collectively victimize women, attacking us as personifications of their own paranoid fears, as The Enemy.'[50] Many feminists concur with Mary Daly's view of the West as phallocentric and violent. It seems to be 'us and them', as Ann Snitow noted: 'the brotherhood of the oppressors, the sisterhood of the victims'.[51] The problem with this view, of men against women, is that it reduces the conflicts too easily, too simply. Further, it ignores, as concentration on the pornography issue does, other issues, important issues of race, class, economy and

---

48 C. MacKinnon: "Feminism, Marxism, Method, and the State: An Agenda for Theory", op. cit.
49 M. Daly: *Pure Lust: Elemental Feminist Philosophy*, Women's Press, London, 1984.
50 M. Daly: *Gyn/Ecology: The Metaphysics of Radical Feminism*, Women's Press, London, 1978.
51 A. Snitow: "Retrenchment Verses Transformation: the Politics of the Anti-Pornography Movement", in V. Burstyn, op. cit., 113.

politics. Pratibha Parmar glossed Ann Snitow's comment thus:

> again this sisterhood of all women assumes that there are no
> significant differences between women, compared with the
> similarities of our experiences of pornography. I find such analysis
> both Eurocentric and nationalist. It is also insulting in its simplicity.[52]

For some feminists, the emphasis on the male-female
antagonisms obscures issues of race, for instance, which some
feminists regard as far more important than the usual issue of
men against women. As Audre Lorde, 'an Afro-American lesbian
poet and philosopher',[53] wrote: '[f]or then beyond sisterhood is
still racism.'[54]

When the establishment speak of feminism they usually
mean, without saying so, the white middle class feminism of
France or Anglo-America. It is important to remember that
however important issues such as porn and men-women conflict
are, the issue of racism is regarded by many feminists as much
more important to address.[55]

For Susan Griffin, pornography stems from body hatred, an
inability, found in many institutions, such as Christianity, to
accept wholeheartedly one's own body. Griffin argues that
'pornography is an expression not of human erotic feeling and
desire, and not of a love of the life of the body, but of fear of
bodily knowledge, and a desire to silence eros.'[56] Certainly one
finds a lot of body-loathing in erotic art – in Picasso, Schiele,
Bellmer, Toulouse-Lautrec, Magritte, etc. And Christianity is the
king of all body-hating religions. Pornography may be seen by
nay-sayers as an inability of the people who make porn to accept
fully the body in all its wildness and strangeness. Yeah, but
actually the opposite is also true: porn *celebrates* the body. Porn

52 P. Parmar: "Rage and Desire: Confronting Pornography", in G. Chester, 123.
53 Maggie Humm's description, in M. Humm, ed. *Feminisms: A Reader*, 137.
54 A. Lorde: "An Open Letter to Mary Daly", 1980, in *Sister Outsider*, Crossing Press, New York, NY, 1984.
55 C. Moraga & G. Anzaldúa, eds. *This Bridge Called My Back: Writings by Radical Women of Color*, Kitchen Table, New York 1983; B. Christian: *Black Feminist Criticism*, Pergamon, Oxford 1985; P.H. Collins: *Black Feminist Thought*, Unwin, London, 1990.
56 S. Griffin: *Pornography and Silence: Culture's Revenge Against Women*, Women's Press, London, 1981.

can also be seen as fantasy, as celebration, as *pure joy*. Porn is images of people doing what many people regard as the most fun you can have.

What happens, throughout history, is that wildness or madness is suppressed, repressed, sidelined and ignored, or, to use a term popular in contemporary cultural criticism, 'marginalized'. Wildness is marginalized, because it upsets the status quo; it usurps the societal and social norms. It is threatening. This is a continuing theme in the writings of Julia Kristeva. In "The True-Real" ("Le vréel"), Kristeva wrote:

> We know... how logic and ontology have inscribed the question of *truth* within *judgement* (or sentence structure) and *being*, dismissing as *madness, mysticism or poetry* any attempt to articulate that impossible element which henceforth can only be designated by the Lacanian category of the *real*. After the flowering of mysticism, classical rationality, first by embracing Folly with Erasmus, and then by excluding it with Descartes, attempted to enunciate the real as truth by setting limits on Madness; modernity, on the other hand, opens up this enclosure in a search for other forms capable of transforming or rehabilitating the statues of *truth*.[57]

When feminists discuss the body and sexuality, the results are just as controversial as discussions of art vs. porn. Many feminists speak of the sexual superiority of women. For instance, Xavière Gauthier says that

> ... witches [women] are bursting; their entire bodies are desire; their gestures are caresses; their smell, taste, hearing are all sensual. Their pleasure is so violent, so transgressive, so open, so fatal, that men have not yet recovered... Female eroticism is terrifying; it is an earthquake, a volcanic eruption, a tidal wave. It is disquieting and so is mystified. It is made a mystery.[58]

This transgressive, terrifying eroticism has not yet really been depicted for feminists in art or pornography. What's produced instead is men's version of it – male ideas of wild eroticism, and it

---

57 J. Kristeva, in *The Kristeva Reader*, 217.
58 X. Gauthier: "Pourquoi Sorcières?", in *Sorcières*, 1, 1976, in E. Marks, 201-2.

is for some feminists – and consumers – sometimes too reductive (and also has links to violence).

Women have an all-over, total body eroticism, claim writers such as Anaïs Nin, Peter Redgrove and Luce Irigaray. 'But *woman has sex organs just about everywhere*. She experiences pleasure almost everywhere', wrote Luce Irigaray.[59] Feminists have spoken of the wildness of women's eroticism and their fantasies. What this stance does is to uphold the eternal philosophical dualism of the West, setting women always against men, and using men to gauge women's sexuality. Feminists such as Hélène Cixous have argued, rightly, that masculine 'binary logic', which constantly opposes terms such as 'masculine' and 'feminine', is very limiting. It is two-term logocentrism, which reduces everything to 'yes' or 'no'.[60]

Julia Kristeva wrote in *About Chinese Women* that:

> no other civilization seems to have made the principle of sexual difference so crystal clear: between the two sexes a cleavage or abyss opens up… Monotheistic unity is sustained by a radical separation of the sexes: indeed, it is this very separation which is its prerequisite.[61]

The pornography issue emphasizes heterosexuality, whereas there are many forms of eroticism. Reducing erotic identities to male/ female or masculine/ feminine is limiting: eroticism is far stranger, more diffuse, more focussed and far wilder than genderized categories suggest.[62] Hence feminists' emphasis on *difference*: instead of always relating women's sexuality to men's: some feminists stress that it is *different* – not just sexually, but

---

59 L. Irigaray: "Ce sexe qui n'en est pas un", in *Ce sexe qui n'en est pas un*, Minuit, Paris, 1977, and in Marks & Courtivron, eds., 103. See also: Jane Gallop: "*Quand nos lèvres s'écrivent*: Irigaray's body politic", *Romantic Review*, 74, 77-83; E. Grosz: "Philosophy, subjectivity and the body", in C. Pateman & E. Grosz, eds. *Feminist Challenges*, Allen & Unwin, Sydney 1986, 125-43.
60 H. Cixous & C. Clément: *The Newly Born Woman*, 63f.
61 J. Kristeva: *The Kristeva Reader*, 141.
62 See E. Newton & S. Walton: "The misunderstanding: toward a more precise sexual vocabulary", in C.S. Vance, ed. *Pleasure and Danger*, Routledge & Kegan Paul, Boston, MA, 1984.

socially, economically, ideologically, racially.[63]

Pornography has its own 'genres' of sub-categories: there is S/M, hardcore, lesbian, gay, child pornography, soft core, and porn geared to any number of fetishes; rubber, leather, boots, large breasts, bondage, etc. These sub-genres are institutions in themselves, with their own codes and structures, but their institutionalized sexual images do not express the real eroticism that people experience (they suggest it, perhaps, or reflect parts of it).

Feminists such as Elaine Showalter and Jeanne Roberts propose that there is a female 'wild zone', as there is a male 'wild zone'. One knows about men's version of wild zone eroticism, what Hélène Cixous called 'glorious phallic monosexuality'.[64] The female wild zone is beyond patriarchal space, beyond patriarchal representations.[65] Julia Kristeva and Luce Irigaray, among other French feminists, have spoken of something in woman or the feminine that is 'unrepresentable', beyond art, beyond male culture. In *About Chinese Women*, Kristeva wrote of the women as a witch, someone outside of patriarchal discourse, or at least, thrown to the edge, the border between the known zone and the wild zone:

> ... woman is a specialist in the unconscious, a witch, a bacchanalian, taking her *jouissance* in an anti-Apollonian, Dionysian orgy. A *jouissance* which breaks the symbolic chain, the taboo, the mastery. A *marginal discourse*, with regard to the science, religion and philosophy of the *polis* (witch, child, underdeveloped, not even a poet, at best his accomplice).[66]

Victor Burgin, describing Julia Kristeva's philosophy, said that she positions

---

63 See M. Wittig: "The category of sex", *Feminist Issues*, vol. 2, no. 2, 1982, 63-8; A. Lorde: *Sister Outsider*, op. cit.; C. Guillaumin: "The question of difference", *Feminist Issues*, vol. 2, no. 1, 1982, 33-52.
64 H. Cixous, "The Laugh of the Medusa", in E. Marks, 254.
65 E. Showalter: "Feminist Criticism in the Wilderness", in E. Showalter, 1986, 262-3; J.A. Roberts: *The Shakespearean Wild: Geography, Genus and Gender*, University of Nebraska Press, Lincoln, Nebraska 1991, 1-5.
66 In J. Kristeva: *The Kristeva Reader*, 154.

the woman in society... in the patriarchal, as perpetually at the boundary, the borderline, the edge, the 'outer limit' – the place where order shades into chaos, light into darkness. This peripheral and ambivalent position allocated to woman, said Kristeva, had led to that familiar division of the field of representation in which women are viewed as either saintly or demonic – according to whether they are seen as bringing the darkness, or as keeping it out.[67]

Saintly woman (the Virgin Mary is a typical example) keeps the amazing energy of the female wild zone out of men's lives; the demonic woman (Mary Magdalene, the *femme fatale*, vampire, 'devil woman') is the one who brings the wildness with her. Patriarchy of course prefers bland, mute, passive door-stops in women, people who will stop the darkness from coming in, who will sit there and say nothing and get on with society's child-rearing and housework.

André Breton said the 'existence is elsewhere'. French feminists say that woman is elsewhere. 'She is indefinitely other in herself', wrote Luce Irigaray, maintaining that women

are already elsewhere than in the discursive machinery where you claim to take them by surprise. They have turned back within themselves, which does not mean the same thing as 'within yourself'. They do not experience the same interiority that you do and which perhaps you mistakenly presume they share.[68]

Here, perhaps, in the female wild zone, some of the wildness and strangeness and ecstasy of female eroticism may be experienced and depicted. Luce Irigaray also spoke in spatial terms of idealist feminism:

We need both space and time. And perhaps we are living in an age when *time must re-deploy space*. Could this be the dawning of a new world? Immanence and transcendence are being recast, notably by that *threshold* which has never been examined in itself: the female sex. It is a threshold unto *mucosity*. Beyond the classic opposites of love and hate, liquid and ice lies this perpetually *half-open* threshold, consisting of *lips* that are strangers to dichotomy. Pressed against one

67 V. Burgin: "Geometry and Abjection", in J. Fletcher, 115-6.
68 L. Irigaray: *Ce sexe qui n'en est pas un*, Minuit, Paris 1977, 28-29.

another, but without any possibility of suture, at least of a real kind, they do not absorb the world either into themselves or through themselves, provided they are not abused or reduced to a mere consummating or consuming structure. Instead their shape welcomes without assimilating or reducing or devouring. A sort of door unto voluptuousness, then? Not that, either: their useful function is to designate a *place*: the very place of uses, at least on a habitual plane. Strictly speaking, they serve neither conception nor *jouissance*. Is this, then, the mystery of female identity, of its self-contemplation, of that strange word of silence; both the threshold and reception of exchange, the sealed-up secret of wisdom, belief and faith in every truth?[69]

Many feminists suggest that women's eroticism cannot be represented, much as women themselves cannot be represented. Julia Kristeva wrote: '[i]n "woman" I see something that cannot be represented, something that is not said, something above and beyond nomenclatures and ideologies.'[70] Other feminists echo this idea, that women cannot be fully represented in the traditional media of patriarchy. As Hélène Cixous commented:

> It is at the level of sexual pleasure in my opinion that the difference makes itself most clearly apparent in as far as woman's libidinal economy is neither identifiable by a man nor referable to the masculine economy.[71]

The unrepresentable in art and pornography, according to some feminists, is women's eroticism, their *jouissance*, that 'explosive, blossoming, sane and inexhaustible *jouissance* of the woman', as Julia Kristeva described it.[72]

What occurs in most Western art, from Greek and Roman sculpture through the glories of the Renaissance to the latest porn, are male representations of female eroticism. Feminists say that there are no real depictions of female *jouissance* in art or literature. 'In my opinion,' wrote Marguerite Duras, 'women have never expressed themselves.'[73] What she means, perhaps, is that women

69 L. Irigaray: "La différence sexuelle", *Ethiope de la différence sexuelle*, Minuit, Paris, 1984, and in T. Moi, ed. *French Feminist Thought*, 128.
70 J. Kristeva: "La femme, ce n'est jamais ça", *Tel Quel*, Autumn 1974, in E. Marks, 135.
71 H. Cixous: "Sorties", in E. Marks, 95.
72 J. Kristeva: *About Chinese Women*, Marion Boyars, London, 1977, 63.
73 M. Duras, interview in *Signs*, Winter 1975, in E. Marks, 175.

have expressed themselves thus far in the terms and means and social structures defined by men. There is no feminine or 'women's' writing, according to some feminists. Hélène Cixous reckons she's found only three 'inscriptions of femininity' this century: Colette, Marguerite Duras and Jean Genet.[74]

Real sex, the French feminists argued, has not yet been represented. Women haven't done it because they work within the same patriarchal structures, codes and constraints as men. Men, generally, haven't got a hope of depicting authentic female eroticism, although the authors of millions of pornographic products would claim they know everything about female eroticism. On the other hand, in the mechanisms of cultural/ post-modern theory, *anyone*, male or female, should be able to create a truly feminine text. It *shouldn't matter* who the author is. If the French feminists are right, then nearly all of the art produced anywhere is orientated to the male, the masculine, the masculinist – even when it is created by women. Many women artists would dispute this. The notion of an 'authentic' 'women's'/ feminine art continues to be hotly debated.

According to French feminists, 'women's' or 'feminine' or female art is created in the gaps and silences of a text, but not in the intentional space of the artwork. Mary Jacobus explained the philosophy of French feminism:

> The French insistence on *écriture féminine* – on woman as a writing-effect instead of an origin – asserts not the sexuality of the text but the textuality of sex. Gender difference, produced, not innate, becomes a matter of the structuring of a genderless libido in and through patriarchal discourse. Language itself would at once repress multiplicity and heterogeneity – true difference – by the tyranny of hierarchical oppositions (man/ woman) and simultaneously work to overthrow that tyranny by interrogating the limits of meaning. The 'feminine', in this scheme, is to be located in the gaps, the absences, the unsayable or unrepresentable of discourse and representation.[75]

---

74 H. Cixous: "The Laugh of the Medusa", *Signs*, summer 1976, in E. E. Marks, 249.
75 M. Jacobus: "Is There a Woman in This Text?", in *New Literary Criticism*, Autumn, 1982, 14, 1.

For some feminists, philosophies based on the body are problematic, because to look for some essential nature of woman, some essence based in biology, is dubious, perhaps limiting, even damaging.[76] Indeed, Toril Moi claimed that 'to define 'woman' is necessarily to essentialize her.'[77] Elaine Showalter wrote of the biology and genderized views of feminism:

> Organic or biological criticism is the most extreme statement of gender difference, of a text indelibly marked by the body: anatomy is textuality... Simply to invoke anatomy risks a return to the crude essentialism, the phallic and ovarian theories of art, that oppressed women in the past.[78]

Biology, though, is crucial, the body is crucial. Hélène Cixous wrote: '[i]n censuring the body, one censures at the same time breathing and speech.'[79] But feminists such as Elaine Showalter are wary of biologist or essentialist philosophies. As Simone de Beauvoir put it, women are not born, they are made, meaning socially, culturally, politically, ideologically, psychologically.

In the view of second wave feminism, in pornography, the great signifier is the phallus, while the site of pleasure is the woman's body. Reclining on a million couches in artists' studios, the female nude offers itself up as a country to be colonized. It is both a pleasure machine and a fantasy. The orchestrator of pleasure in this pornographic scenario is that little slip of flesh, the penis. The phallus is good, whole, true, unifying, as opposed to the bad, fragmented, impure, chaotic vagina.[80] The phallus is the emblem of male power, as many commentators, not only feminists, note: '[t]he supreme power is the power that prevails

76 See S.R. Suleiman: "(Re)Writing the Body: The Politics of Female Eroticism", in Suleiman, 14f; E. Grosz: "Desire, the body and recent French feminism', *Intervention*, 21-2, 1988, 28-33; A.M. Jagger & S.R. Bordo, eds. *Gender/Body/Knowledge: feminist reconstructionsof being and knowing*, Rutgers University Press, New Brunswick 1989; N. Schor: "This essentialism which is not one: coming to grips with Irigaray", *differences*, 1 (2), 38-58.
77 T. Moi: *Sexual/Textual Politics*, 139.
78 E. Showalter: "Feminist Criticism in the Wilderness", in E. Showalter, ed. *the New Feminist Criticism*, Virago Press, London, 1986, 250.
79 H. Cixous: *Le Jeune Née*, Paris 1975, 179.
80 See T. Moi: *Sexual/Textual Politics*, 66f; S.M. Gilbert & S. Gubar: *The Madwoman in the Attic: The Woman Writer and the Nineteenth Century Literary Imagination*, Yale University Press, New Haven, CT, 1979.

over mortality', and this power is 'reasonably equated with the phallus'.[81] For feminists, the West is a phallic/ phallocentric/ phallogocentric society, where the phallus, the sublime signifier, the most censored in the West, is the beginning and the end of sexual pleasure. For Madeleine Gagnon, the phallus is an emblem of male narcissism:

> The phallus… represents repressive capitalist ownership, the exploiting bourgeois… The phallus means everything sets itself up as a mirror. Everything that erects itself as perfection.[82]

Whole philosophic systems are based on the phallus, yet, as Juliet Mitchell remarked:

> It's extraordinary what happens when you get rid of the centrality of the concept of the phallus. I mean, you get rid of the unconscious, get rid of sexuality, get rid of the original psychoanalytic point.[83]

If men reduce people to their sexual identities, as some feminists claim, then at the heart of this is the penis. Women are reduced to 'cunt', as Kate Millet put it, while men are all phallus. There are certainly no shortage of phallic symbols and artifacts about. The real thing, the real penis, is censored, carefully guarded – it's not much to look at anyway some say (though mine is very pretty) – so men displace their phallic sexuality onto thrusting cars, trucks, missiles, bombs, towers, cameras, computers, guitars, cigarettes, telephones, swords, guns, eyes, etc. These things abound in (patriarchal) art, and throughout the history of art (and porn adds a million further fetishes). The trouble is that the penis ain't much of a thing, after all. As Richard Dyer commented: 'the fact is that the penis isn't a patch on the phallus. The penis can never live up to the mystique implied by the phallus'.[84]

---

81 L. Steinberg: *The Sexuality of Christ in Renaissance Art and in Modern Oblivion*, Pantheon, New York, 1984, 90.
82 Gagnon: "Corps I", *La venue à l'écriture*, UGE, 10/18, Paris 1977; in E. Marks, 180.
83 J. Mitchell: "Feminine Sexuality: Interview with Juliet Mitchell and Jacqueline Rose", *m/f*, 8 (1983), 15.
84 R. Dyer: 'Don't Look Now", *Screen*, vol. 23, 3/4, 1983, and in A. McRobbie, 206.

The male nude can be seen as a phallus, as Gill Saunders pointed out:

> The male body, while not constructed as the site of sexual pleasure, is often symbolic of phallic power. The whole body, muscular, potent, active, may come to represent the phallus.[85]

The penis isn't a phallus, so, to make up for the disappointing insufficiency of the penis, macho masculinity is demonstrated by bulging muscles, clenched fists, sturdy poses. The male nude poses with a body of 'rippling muscles', bizarrely exaggerated, or gripping a gun, or standing next to a motorcycle, a car, a machine, something that can connote phallic power.

The male nude is uncomfortable. He doesn't like his photograph or painting or sculpture to be looked at like female nudes. He doesn't like it. He is used to being the one doing the looking. When the roles are reversed, ambiguity and confusion seeps in. The male nude is set up as spectacle, and as a passive object. To counter the awkwardness of this passivity, the male nude is shown *doing* something. Running, throwing a spear, fighting, etc. he tries to engage a position of activity, because to be the 'looked-at' one, the passive sex object, is very disquieting. Further, the activity of the male nude, which's seen everywhere – in photographs by Eadweard Muybridge,[86] in sculptures by Michelangelo, in films, in gay porn – aims at portraying phallic power. 'Even in an apparently relaxed, supine pose,' wrote Richard Dyer,

> the model tightens and tautens his body so that the muscles are emphasized, hence drawing attention to the body's potential for action. More often, the male pin-up is not supine anyhow, but standing taut ready for action.[87]

For men, according to feminists such as Andrea Dworkin, sex boils down to the penis, the penis rubbing up and down, which,

85 G. Saunders: *The Nude*, 26.
86 See L. Williams: "Film Body, an implanation of perversions", *Cinétracts*, vol. 3, no. 4, Winter 1981, 19-25.
87 R. Dyer, op.cit., 20.

Dworkin claimed, is the 'secret' and 'mystery' of sex:

> Commonly referred to as "it," sex is defined in action only by what
> the male does with his penis. Fucking – the penis thrusting – is the
> magical, hidden meaning of "it," the reason for sex... In practice,
> fucking is an act of possession – simultaneously an act of ownership,
> taking, force; it is conquering... In the male system, sex is the penis, the
> penis is sexual power, its use in fucking is manhood.[88]

Andrea GoodmanDworkin's analysis is representative of radical
second wave feminism: the penis is that magical signifier which is
always so curiously absent yet such an important component in
any pornographic situation or image. In the (second wave)
feminist view, the pornographer creates with his penis – the
paintbrush, camera, computer or pen – these things are called
'tools', a common euphemism for the penis (there are thousands of
other phallic control devices, such as game consoles, TVs, digital
cameras, hi-fis, cell phones, factory machinery, aeroplanes, etc).
The quill, stylus or 'sharp projective' is a crucial element in the
male's manufacture of art and pornography.[89] When Pierre Renoir
was asked how he painted when his hands were crippled by
arthritis he replied '[w]ith my prick'.[90]

In pornography, the eye becomes the phallus, and looking is
equated with caressing the obscure object of desire with the
phallus (in the Lacanian system). Throughout Western art the
phallus has been that visually absent but psychologically and
ideologically present object. It is central in erotic art. Look at the
Western art nudes – by Titian, Pablo Picasso, Egon Schiele, and
François Boucher: the phallus is there even though one doesn't
see it. It's the same in any number of books, poems, sculptures,
plays, operas, installations.

It is the same in aspects of homosexual eroticism, which is
defined in some ways, for feminists, by the phallus and the penis

88 A. Dworkin: *Pornography: Men Possessing Women*, 23.
89 See J. Derrida: *Spurs: Nietzsche's Styles*, tr. B. Harlow, University of Chicago Press, Chicago
1979, 37-9; on the penis as a paintbrush, see Carol Duncan: "The Esthetics of power in Modern
Erotic Art", *Heresies*, 1, 1977, 46-50.
90 In J. Hobhouse, 135.

thrusting. For Andrea Dworkin, the structure of the laws policing homosexuality can be seen as also controlling women's sexuality. For Dworkin, the sodomy laws protect men from being treated like women: '[t]he sodomy laws are important, perhaps essential, in maintaining for men a superiority of civil and sexual status over women. They protect men as a class from the violation of penetration; men's bodies have unbreachable boundaries.'[91] In Dworkin's view, men are never the one who's fucked: rather, they *always* do the fucking.

Lesbian sex is marked in contemporary cultural theory by the *lack* of the phallus. Hence, lesbian eroticism must always be 'deviant', because it departs from the patriarchal norms which exalt the phallus. Lesbianism must always be 'other', sexually, and many feminists note that the otherness of lesbian sexuality is one of the reasons that men and their patriarchal institutions are very threatened by lesbianism.[92] Lesbian identity attacks patriarchy at its powerbase. Men cannot control lesbians: '[l]esbians, by loving women and not men, pose a direct threat to the very basis of male supremacy', assert Alice, Gordon, Debbie and Mary.[93] The lesbian is crucial, argued Monique Wittig, because she 'is the only concept that I know of which is beyond the categories of sex (man and woman)'.[94] Wittig moved towards a view of culture that goes beyond gender, beyond 'biological dimorphism', and biology.

Lesbianism questions the prevalence of patriarchy and heterosexuality as the norms in a society. In her excellent essay "Compulsory Heterosexuality and Lesbian Existence", poet Adrienne Rich wrote: 'for women heterosexuality may not be a 'preference' at all but something that has had to be imposed,

91 A. Dworkin: *Intercourse*, 183.
92 T. Atkinson: *Amazon Odyssey*, Links books, New York 1974; Alice, Gordon, Debbie and Mary: "Separatism", in S.L. Hoagland & J. Penelope, eds. *For Lesbians Only: A separatist anthology*, Onlywomen Press 1988, 31-40; A. Rich: "Towards a woman-centred university", in *On Lies, Secrets and Silence*, Novotny, New York 1979; J. Johnston: *Lesbian Nation: The Feminist Solution*, Simon & Shuster, New York 1974; S. Rowbotham: *Beyond the Fragments: Feminism and the making of Socialism*, Merlin 1979.
93 Alice, Gordon, Debbie and Mary, op. cit., 31-40.
94 M. Wittig: "One is not born a woman", in Hoagland, op. cit., 446-7.

managed, organized, propagandized, and maintained by force'.[95]

Not all feminists agree about the revolutionary potential of lesbianism, if it is a lesbianism that keeps defining itself in terms of patriarchy. Elizabeth Mees reckoned that 'lesbianism, as an attack on hetero-relations, takes (its) place within the structure of the institution of heterosexuality. The lesbian is born of/ in it.'[96] There is no escape, it seems, from patriarchy and heterosexuality: the world is permeated with these ancient structures. As Sheila Jeffreys wrote: '[e]very woman grows up in a heteropatriarchal world',[97] while Ann Barr Snitow remarked:

> One of our culture's most intense myths, the ideal of an individual who is brave and complete in isolation, is for men only. Women are grounded, enmeshed in civilization, in social connection, in family and in love (a condition a feminist culture might well define as desirable) while all our culture's rich myths of individualism are essentially closed to them.[98]

In heterosexual porn, lesbian eroticism is often introduced, but always controlled by a patriarchal force. Typically, in a soft porn scenario, two bisexual women cavort on a bed overseen by a male ('I've always wanted to see ya with another woman', drools the man to his wife/ girlfriend; or, frequently, 'I got back from work an' saw my wife and her best friend writhin' on the bed'). Towards the end of the scene, the man makes love to both women. Why? Because they needed the phallus, they needed a man to be fulfilled. Variations on this scenario occur endlessly in pornography. The male presence (the phallus) is seen as necessary for the true satisfaction for women (for valorization, for authenticity: i.e., it's not *true* sex without the phallus).

Lesbian or women's porn, made by women for women, disappoints some feminists. Elizabeth Carola, who called herself a

95 A. Rich: "Compulsory Heterosexuality and Lesbian Existence", 1980, in E. Abel & E.K. Abel, eds. *The Signs Reader: Women, Gender and Scholarship*, University of Chicago Press, Chicago, IL, 1983.
96 E. Mees, in K. Jay & J. Glasgow: *Lesbian Text and Contexts: Radical Revisions*, New York University Press, New York, NY, 1990, 82.
97 S. Jeffreys: "The Censoring of Revolutionary Feminism", in G. Chester, 139.
98 A. Snitow: "Mass Market Romance: Pornography for Women is different", *Radical History Review*, no. 20, Spring/Summer, 1979.

'radical feminist lesbian', described magazines such as *On Our Backs, Bad Attitude, OW! - Outrageous Women: A Journal of Woman-to-Woman SM, Yellow Silk* and *The Power Exchange*:

> Like all porn, this new 'woman's' porn is neither about nor for women. Like all porn it is, in a most basic sense, *against* women and *about* male fantasy – the basic male fantasy of Woman as Wholly Sexual Object whose Purpose is To Be Fucked – which feeds men's egos, fuels their violence...

According to Elizabeth Carola, lesbian pornographic magazines are full of images and themes usually associated with male pornography:

> *On Our Backs*, in particular, is full of adverts for phalluses and endless verbiage about (and imagery of) extremely masculine 'Butches' introducing large objects – fists, bottles, phalluses – into the bodies of 'Femmes'... *On Our Backs* represents the 'middle range' of lesbian porn. The harder core publications like *The Power Exchange* feature half page adverts for surgical scalpels for 'unparalleled cutting and piercing' interspersed with litanies of young women being violently fist fucked, whipped and pierced and, of course, gratefully licking their 'mistresses' boots in return.[99]

If pornography is a contentious issue among feminists, then lesbian or 'women's' porn is extremely controversial, and feminists are very divided about it.[100] As Sue George noted: '[f]or a feminist, therefore, to enjoy pornography is to feel doubly guilty.'[101] Writers such as Pat Califa, Lisa Henderson and Sheila Jeffreys argue that sadomasochistic porn operating inside lesbian practice can be enriching.[102] For men it is clearly threatening,

99 E. Carola: "Women, Erotica, Pornography: – Learning to Play the Game", in G. Chester, 169-171. See S. Jeffreys: "Butch and femme: now and then", *Gossip,* 5, 1987.
100 See the essays in S. Munt's book; A. Koedt: *Radical Feminism*, Quadrangle, New York, NY, 1973.
101 S. George, in G. Chester, op. cit., 111.
102 P. Califa: "Feminism and Sadomasochism", *Heresies,* 12, 1981, *The Lesbian S/M Safety Manual*, Alyson, Boston, 1990, and "Unravelling the Sexual Fringe: A Secret Side of Lesbian Sexuality", *The Advocate,* 27 Dec, 1979; also: L. Henderson: "Lesbian Pornography: Cultural Transgression and Sexual Demystification", in S. Munt, 173-191; S. Jeffreys: "Sadomasochism: the erotic cult of fascism", in *Lesbian Ethics,* 2, 1, 65-82; M. Sulter: "Reviewing lesbian erotica", *Spare Rib,* 219, 1990-1, 42-4. See also, on sadomasochism: R.R. Linden *et al,* 1982; J. Jones: "Why I liked screwing? Or, is heterosexual enjoyment based on sexual violence?", in Onlywomen; K. Davis *et al,* 1983.

because it excludes them; it is made by women, for women: 'it is no longer for men alone to decide what is, or is not, exciting in pornography', as Linda Williams wrote in her book *Hard Core*.[103]

Men are excluded from lesbian porn: '[p]ornography for lesbians is unique in that it presumes a *female* gaze, and a lesbian one at that,' wrote Barbara Smith. But although 'lesbian' and 'women's' pornography is for made for and by women, it still works within patriarchy, within male-made structures, values, ideologies and attitudes, just as lesbianism itself, according to some feminists, is not truly 'outside' of heterosexuality and patriarchy. The view is that '[l]esbians who engage in consensual S/M are thus merely imitating and even colluding in patriarchal structures,' according to Clare Whatling.[104] Sheila Jeffreys claimed that '[s]m practice comes from nowhere more mysterious than the history of our very real oppression.'[105] Whatling suggests that lesbian S/M practice can parody and subvert patriarchal values and systems. She wrote:

> S/M is never *intrinsically* revolutionary. Like all sexual practice, it is a product of its time and context. As with other sexual practices, it may be oppositional under certain conditions, but it is never always so... S/M is constructed in relation to the society in which it is played out and cannot be understood without reference to the structures that exist there... Where S/M does perhaps differ from more conventional sexual practices is in the self-consciousness it brings to encounters. For S/M as a practice does much to foreground the constructedness of all sexuality.[106]

As Barbara Smith wrote: '[i]f heterosexual women fuck the enemy, then SM dykes fuck *like* the enemy.'[107]

One of the most contentious and fiercely debated aspects of

103 L. Williams, 1990, 264. See also A. Ross: "The Popularity of Pornography", in *No Respect: Intell-ectuals and Popular Culture*, Routledge, London, 1989, 171-208.
104 C. Whatling: "Who's read *Macho Sluts*", in J. Still, 193.
105 S. Jeffreys: "Sado-masochism", op.cit., 68.
106 C. Whatling, op.cit., 194.
107 B. Smith: "Sappho Was a Right-*Off* Woman', in G. Chester, 182-4. On sadomasochism, see T.S. Weinberg & G.W. Levi Kamel: *S and M: Studies in Sadomasochism*, Prometheus Books, Buffalo, New York, NY, 1983.

pornography is the issue of obscenity, taste and censorship. Throughout the history of art and porn, various individuals or groups of people have sought to defend certain territories, whether moral, psychological, emotional, spiritual, religious, philosophical, political or ideological. There is always some line between the 'acceptable' and the 'obscene'.

The history of censorship is long and complex. In the 20th century there have been many confrontations between artists and the establishment: with D.H. Lawrence's *Lady Chatterley's Lover*, with *Ulysses*, with films such as *Last Tango in Paris, Kids, Natural Born Killers, The Killing of Sister George, Performance, Trash, A Clockwork Orange* and countless others, with the *Oz* trials, with Senator Jesse Helms trying to stop NEA tax payers' money funding 'obscene' work, with reference to the photographer Robert Mapplethorpe (whose photos have created much controversy),[108] with internet porn, with punk rock and gangsta rap, and so on.[109]

The many debates concerning various Obscene Publications Acts and bills, the First Amendment of the American constitution, different regulatory groups, pressure groups, media organizations, publishers, and all manner of intellectuals and artists, have been intense, complex, protracted, and often a shambles. The confusions and ambiguities are at the centre of Western society. Pornography debates produce, very quickly, all manner of confusions and hypocrisies, of a moral, religious, psychological,

108 See M. Schoofs: "Robert Mapplethorpe: Exquisite Subversions", *Windy City Times*, 16 Mch, 1989; H. Kramer: "Mapplethorpe Show at the Whitney: A Big, Glossy, Offensive Exhibit", *The New York Observer*, 22 Aug, 1988; A.C. Danto: *Encounters & Reflections*, Farrar Straus Giroux, New York 1990; E. Kastor & Carla Hall: "Mapplethorpe Aftermath", *Washington Post*, 23 June 1989; T.A. Yasui: "The Mapplethorpe Bonanza", *Washington Post*, 21 Aug, 1989; P. Schjeldhal: "The Mainstreaming of Mapplethorpe: Taste and Hunger", *7 Days*, 10 Aug, 1988; R. Rooney: "The unambiguous stare of Mapplethorpe's lens", *Australian*, 25 Feb, 1986.
109 More Mapplethorpe articles: D. Dominick: "Robert Mapplethorpe's Proud Finale", *Vanity Fair*, Feb, 1989; "Robert Mapplethorpe: Aestheticizing the Perverse", *Artscribe International*, Nov/Dec 1988; J. Ribalta: "Decorative Heroism, The death of Mapplethorpe", *Lapiz*, Apl, 1989.

social and ideological nature.[110] For some, though, the censorship debate is 'in fact, a little internal quibble between sections of the bourgeois community' (according to Suzanne Kappeler).

Pornography goes to the heart of what people hold dear: their identities, their feelings, their philosophical, spiritual and political views, their view of the quality of life. Pornography unsettles these notions and structures. The fervour and uncertainty of the many attempts at legislation and policing show how problematic pornography is. In a case of recent years, five 'homosexual sadomasochists' were convicted in 1990 of inflicting 'injuries on each another's genitals during ritual sex' which involved 'cutting each other's genitals with surgical scalpels, sandpapering scrotums and pushing hooks into penises'. Their appeal was rejected by the courts.[111]

For law-abiding citizens, it seems, the 'line' has to be drawn somewhere. Somewhere between public and private, between sex and love, between visible and invisible, between freedom and control, between secrecy and publicity, between availability and censorship. Indeed, Walter Kendrick said the only definition of pornography is in terms of its forbidden or secret nature.[112]

Pornography brings the secret life of people out into the open. What the Western world holds most dear – the primacy and holiness of the individual, and the primacy and holiness of (heterosexual) love, of marriage, of the family – is cast into doubt by porn.

Hardcore pornography, in particular, tries to make everything as clear and as visible as possible, and is thus disruptive and unsettling for the establishment. There are, thus, many close-ups of genitals in hardcore pornography. Sex is ecstatic, so hardcore pornography has to show this ecstasy. It does

110 See *Art in America*, May 1990; C.H. Rolph: *The Trial of Lady Chatterley*, Penguin, London, 1961; G. Robertson: *Obscenity: an Account of Censorship Laws and Their Enforcements in England and Wales*, Weidenfeld & Nicolson, London, 1979; *The Attorney General's Commission on Pornography – the Meese Commission – Final Report*, US Government Printing Office, Washington DC, 1986; L. Lederer, ed., op. cit.
111 I. MacKinnon: "Lords reject appeals by sado-masochists", *The Independent*, 12 Mch, 1993.
112 W. Kendrick: *The Secret Museum: Pornography in Modern Culture*, Viking, New York, NY, 1987.

this by focussing on the genitals.

One mystery of sublime pleasure is the orgasm. Cameras look at the body from the outside, so to show orgasm they get as close as possible, to show quivering genitals, to achieve the 'come shot' or 'money shot', the ejaculation, and the 'meat shot' of penetration. In videos and films, a lot of groaning and gasping helps to sell the bliss of the orgasm. Typically, it is the woman who gasps loudest, for she is, as Virginia Woolf said, a mirror that enlarges what men do, that mythicizes their acts. Sexologists (Krafft-Ebing, Freud, Reich), have always emphasized the materiality of the orgasm, describing it in Newtonian, mechanistic terms, as it were something a machine does, as if science, by listing the physiological effects of the orgasm, could ever unveil its mysteries. Wilhelm Reich, for instance, described orgasm as electrical energy: '[t]he orgasm formula which directs sex-economic research is as follows: MECHANICAL TENSION › BIOELECTRICAL CHARGE › BIOELECTRICAL DISCHARGE › MECHANICAL RELAXATION'.[113]

It's also worth noting how humourless some porn often is, how dour and unsmiling and serious. Sex is taken very seriously by masculine culture. 'When one is making love,' wrote P. Piobb, 'one does not laugh; perhaps one may just smile. During the spasm one is as serious as death.'[114] Isn't this typical: during the greatest of pleasures known to 'humanity', one is not allowed to laugh. Typical of the patriarchal view of lovemaking. Solemn to the last gasp. How does Woody Allen put it? – the most fun you can have without laughing.

The female orgasm is 'anatomically invisible', as far as pornography is concerned. So the history of pornography, for some commentators, 'is the history of visual strategies to overcome the anatomical invisibility of the female orgasm'.[115] In porno-graphy, female orgasm is regarded with confusion and ambivalence. What actually is it? pornographers ask, what does it

---

113 W. Reich: *The Function of the Orgasm*, London, 1983, 9.
114 P. Piobb: *Venus, la déesse magique de la chair*, Paris, 1909, 80.
115 L. Nead, 98. See also L. Williams, 1990.

feel like? (Note that most pornographers throughout history have been men, forever excluded from experiencing the female orgasm). Thus the controversy over clitoral and vaginal orgasm, over female ejaculation, over multiple orgasms. Female ejaculation is 'visible evidence' of orgasm, yet it is censored by pornographers themselves at times.[116]

Pornography is the culture of eroticism in the West. There is sex on TV, in fiction, in blockbuster movies, in theatre, in pop music, but it is in porn that erotic feelings are most frequently communicated. Yet pornography is commodified sex, materialist sex, sex manufactured into particular types, genres, roles and modes. There are standard pornographic encounters, standard pornographic camera angles, standard pornographic orgasms. Eroticism, as Sigmund Freud knew, is powerful, whether emotionally, psychologically, culturally or politically. Pornography, then, deals with really wild eroticism by categorizing it, putting it into particular genres or narratives. The visual aspect of porn helps to deal with the wildness and passion of erotic feeling. Pornography produces images and representations, which are easier to deal with than the real thing. Jane Gallop wrote that the 'visual mode produces representations as a way of mastering what is otherwise too intense'.[117] Experiences such as orgasm and erotic desire can be too overwhelming to be communicated in words. Putting these experiences into visual representations enables them to be controlled, packaged, commodified. Yeah, 'cos porn's a business.

Pornography is *fantasy*, as well as genre, product, system, and materialism. Pornography (like all art) does not offer the consumer real people, but images, narratives, ideas, suggestions. The visual dimension of porn helps to create certain kinds of representations of erotic feelings which the consumer can deal with, because they are communicated in recognizable forms. So

116 See S. Bell: "Feminist Ejaculations", in Arthur and Marilouise Kroker, eds. *The Hysterical Male: New Feminist Theory*, St Martin's Press, New York, 155-169; also C. Straayer: "The Seduction of Boundaries: Feminist Fluidity in Annie Sprinkle's Art/Education/Sex", in Gibbons, ed., 168f
117 J. Gallop: *The Daughter's Seduction: Feminism and Psychoanalysis*, Cornell University Press, New York, NY, 1982, 35.

now we're in an S/M narrative – masters, mistresses and slaves Or, over here we're in the narrative where a sexually frustrated male picks up a female hitchhiker. Or, here we are in the 'bored housewife' scenario: sex-starved, she humps the plumber over the washing machine. The consumer always knows where she or he is with pornography.

Pornography delivers the goods.

It delivers the goods: which's why it's bigger than the movie or pop music industries (according to some reports – but in the world of billion-dollar businesses, *everyone* lies about the actual figures).

A traditional, left-liberal and conservative view is that pornography is *sex*, but art is *love*. Pornography trades in loveless sex, while art trades in sexy love. Each era, each generation, each culture redefines what sex and love are, what is acceptable and what is not. But 'love', as feminists say, is largely about power relations between people – relations that are dependent on and controlled by an array of factors: enculturation, social and economic pressures, political agendas, ethnicity, labour, place, classism, etc.

The general reactionary view is that pornography is depersonalized, dehumanized, unemotional, saccharine, synthetic, 'obscene' or 'dirty'. Art, meanwhile, is personalized, special, emotional, 'real' and sane. Yet art and porn are inter-changeable in many ways.

One of the most contentious of issues is the link between pornography and violence, where, according to Robin Morgan and many second wave feminists, 'pornography is the theory, and rape is the practice'. For some people, porn is criminal by its very existence. It invades the private sphere, as the Williams Committee of 1979 claimed,[118] and sex, the ultimate private 'act', becomes very public.

---

118 *Report of the Committee on Obscenity and Film Censorship,* Chairman, B. Williams, Her Majesty's Stationery Office, 1979, para. 7.6. See also, A.W. B. *Pornography and Politics: The Williams Committee in Retrospect,* Waterlow 1983; K. Ellis *et al,* eds. *Caught Looking: Feminism, Pornography and Censorship,* 1987; B. Brown: "Private Faces in Public Places", *Ideology and Consciousness: Technologies of the Human Sciences,* 7, Autumn, 1980, 3-16.

What all the debates around pornography demonstrate is that most people regard porn as amazingly powerful. Whatever their views on pornography, most people seem to agree that it has a massive influence, whether or not this influence manifests itself later as violence, coercion, exploitation, or servitude. Pornography, it seems, is the most powerful communication type of any communication type. Whatever form it takes – painting, video, website, phone sex, magazine, photograph, prose, performance – porn seems to be the most powerful kind of communication. The debates, about obscenity, censorship, regulation, policing, decency, etc, all acknowledge the power of pornography. Some feminists have made the point that if one agrees that pornography is influential and powerful, then one must also look at all other art in a similar way, whether high art (the fine art nude painting) or 'low art' (TV ads, billboards, tabloid newspapers, etc). Even unlikely candidates such as President Nixon realized this point. He commented on the American congressional report of the Commission on Obscenity and Pornography of 1970:

> The commission contends that the proliferation of filthy books and plays has no lasting harmful effect on a man's character. If that be true, it must also be true that great books, great paintings and great plays have no ennobling effect on a man's conduct. Centuries of civilization and ten minutes of common sense tell us otherwise.[119]

What follows from this is that, by extension, if one polices pornography one has to police all areas of artistic expression, all of culture. Andrea Dworkin's stance on this issue is firm: '[w]e will know that we are free when the porn no longer exists' (*Pornography*, 224). Feminists ask, is it simply porn that is the problem? Or is it the other institutions, such as education, or marriage? Is it not the whole of heterosexuality that is the problem? Or patriarchy, and the whole of Western culture? These questions are endlessly debated. Stephen Heath asked some of the basic questions:

---

119 R. Nixon, *New York Times*, 25 Oct, 1970, 71.

Is all pornography violent and offensive? Are there connections between pornography and sexual liberation that are important, progressive? Are men's and women's pleasures in sexual imagery bound up with or separate – separable – from pornographic representations and how? Are pornographic images for male arousal necessarily the reproduction of domination? What should be done about pornography and how?[120]

There are pertinent questions asked by feminists concerning porn. For instance, Rosalind Coward asked, does male sexuality always have a violent component?

Is it true that *any* public representation of sex is *only* for male sexuality and therefore male domination? Is it true that pornography is about violence against women or *necessarily* sustains violence against women.[121]

Is all pornography an incitement to violence? feminists ask. Elizabeth Sidney questioned the involvement of women in porn: '[w]hy do women help to create these materials?'[122] Some male feminists have explored their sexuality, debunking 'myths' about male ejaculation, orgasm, lovemaking, etc,[123] while other anti-sexist men have claimed that in pornography, men are shown, ultimately, in an inferior way to women: '[m]en might set the rules, but women are shown to come out 'enjoying it most'', wrote Andy Moye.[124] And of course female porn stars are the real stars in the industry (and are promoted as such), although there have plenty of stars among male performers.

Catherine MacKinnon suggested that porn helps to encode power relations between men and women by making the power relations seem 'sexy': 'male and female are created through the

---

120 S. Heath: "Male Feminism", *The Dalhousie Review*, and in A. Jardine and P. Smith, eds. *Men in Feminism*, Methuen, New York, NY, 1987.
121 R. Coward: "Sexual Violence and Sexuality", in *Feminist Review*, eds., 309.
122 E. Sidney: "Liberals, Feminism and the Media", in G. Chester, 208.
123 See J. Stoltenberg: "Refusing to be a Man", in J. Snodgrass, ed. *A Book of Readings for Men Against Sexism*, Times Change Press, New York 1977; J. Litewka: "The Socialised Penis", in Snodgrass, op. cit.; H. Brod, ed. *The Making of Masculinities*, Allen & Unwin, London, 1987.
124 A. Moye, "Pornography", in A. Metcalf & M. Humphries, eds. *The Sexuality of Men*, Pluto Press, London, 1985, 58.

eroticization of submission and dominance'.[125] The submission is made 'sexy', as is the objectification of women that occurs in pornography. So much of culture follows on from this eroticization. The world of fashion, design and style, for instance, comes straight out of the eroticization of women in pornography. Kathy Myers wrote that, though

> the fashion image and the pornographic image are in the first instance produced within quite distinct sets of social and economic circumstances... notions of hardcore pornography as mediated through auteuristic eroticism affect the form and presentation of certain up-market fashion images.[126]

Kathy Myers was referring to those *auteurs* of high fashion photography, David Bailey and Helmut Newton and their ilk. Their images take up the sadomasochistic and highly fetishized motifs of pornography and transplant them into the high fashion spreads of the glossy fashion magazines. Because these images are set in high fashion contexts, they are regarded as 'art' rather than pornography.

The economics of porn are straightforward: pornography operates on the basis of maximum capitalism, maximum 'market economy' and exploitation. Ann Snitow wrote that pornography 'is exploitation of *everything*'.[127] Pornographers pay very well for the 'services' of women models – hundreds and thousands of dollars per photo or video shoot. Pornography is big business. It is a bigger business than the many sectors of the entertainment industry – a four and a half billion dollar business in the U.S.A., according to Andrea Dworkin and Catherine Itzin (their estimates were from the early 1980s – nowadays, the porn industry is worth far, far more).[128] Elizabeth Sidney offered the following facts as an

---

125 C. MacKinnon: "Feminism, Marxism, method and the state: towards feminist jurisprudence", in S. Harding, ed. *Feminism and Methodology*, Indiana University Press, Indiana, 1987, 136.
126 K. Myers: "Passion 'n' Fashion: A Working Paper", *Screen*, vol. 23, no. 3/4, 1983.
127 A. Snitow: "Mass market romance: pornography for women is different", in Snitow *et al*, eds. *Powers of Desire: the politics of sexuality*, Monthly Review Press, New York, NY, 1983, 269.
128 A. Dworkin: *Pornography*, 10; C. Itzin, in G. Chester, 39.

indication of the mass consumption of porn:

> In America, according to NAPCRO the (U.S.A.) National Anti-Pornography Civil Rights Organisation, over 2 million households now subscribe to cable pornography and the magazines *Playboy*, *Penthouse* and *Hustler* each have a larger readership than *Time* and *Newsweek* combined.[129]

Women are involved in pornography for a number of reasons, many of them social, economic and political. Catherine Itzin wrote: 'pornography *is* violence. Against women by men. The violence is institutionalized and it is internalised (by women, which accounts in part for their 'tolerance' and sometimes 'participation' in it.)'[130] But the views of Itzin, Mackinnon, Dworkin and other feminists are not borne out by the facts: for many workers in the porn industry, it is not as exploitative and degrading as many feminists have suggested. It is labour, of course, but it's actually not so different from most other kinds of work. And those stigmas and demonizations attached to porn by second wave feminists have now largely been forgotten. Porn is not 'respectable', like being a lawyer, a priest or a doctor, but the aura of sleaze and exploitation has melted away.

The involvement of women in porn reveals again the power relations that operate within patriarchy and heterosexuality. The economics of pornography, like the economics of all of society, have tended to favour men. That is clear from any clutch of statistics (such as the comparison of salaries of men and women). Luce Irigaray said that the only kind of equality possible between the sexes was economic.

In pornographic production companies, whether of films, magazines, goods, etc, men still predominate in the important jobs – editor, art director, writer, manager, proprietor, CEO, photographer, cameraman, etc, while women are the models, the cleaners, the assistants and secretaries. The hierarchical

---

129 E. Sidney, writing in 1988, the early years of cable and satellite consumption, so the figures must be greater now, in G. Chester, 206.
130 C. Itzin, in G. Chester, 43.

organization of pornographic production emulates that of society as a whole, just as the ethics and attitudes and values of pornographic products emulate those of society as a whole. The economy of porn is not confined to sexism, to male-against-female issues, it is, for anti-porn feminists, also classist, and racist. Feminists note that despite so-called 'improvements' in race relations, it is still black people who are at the bottom of the societal pile, who do the menial jobs, such as cleaning. The economics of black labour helps institutions such as pornography – and art, medicine, education, government, etc – to thrive.[131]

For second wave feminism, the privileged person is white, middle class, First World, Anglo-Saxon, Protestant/ Christian – and male. Whoever may make pornography, pornography privileges a white, middle class, Anglo-Saxon, North American and European male viewpoint. Whoever the producers may be, porn, as a text, an experience, a system, is firmly located within white, middle class, Christian, masculinist discourse. Whoever the authors are, pornography ends up, textually, and contextually, as a white, middle class, Anglo-Saxon, Christian, male discourse. And at the bottom of the hierarchy of power are not white women, but black women.[132] The texts of porn, as well as the contexts, are white, middle class, Anglo Saxon and male. Or, in short, patriarchal, the term used as a shorthand in feminist theory for all that is masculine, aggressive, heterosexual, white, œdipal, bourgeois and First World.

One must always remember, feminists say, the racial and ethnic as well as the sexist implications of pornography. Not only it is produced by and for men, it is produced by white, bourgeois, Anglo Saxon, Christian men, but is 'for' anybody who will buy it. As Barbara Smith wrote:

131 See L. Rodgers, ed. *The Black Woman*, Sage, Beverly Hills, CA, 1989; G.T. Hull *et al*, eds. *All the Women Are White, All the Blacks Are Men, But Some of Us Are Brave: Black Women's Studies*, Feminist Press, New York, NY, 1982; B. Bryan *et al*, eds. *The Heart of the Race: Black Women's Lives in Britain*, Virago, London, 1985; Anima Mama: "Black Women, the Economic Crisis and the British State", *Feminist Review*, 17, 1984.
132 See A. Walker: "Coming apart", in L. Lederer, ed. *Take Back the Night: Women on Pornography*, Bantam, New York, NY, 1982, 84-93.

'Lesbian' pornography is not for or about lesbians and lesbian sexuality, so 'black' porn is not for black people, and 'kiddie' porn is not for children. Pornography does not describe sexuality, it describes sexual *acts*. It solidifies white, male, heterosexual fantasies, and the commodifies them.[133]

This chapter has sumarized some of the views on pornography and eroticism, including the general views of (mainly second wave) feminism, but there is plenty more to say on the issues. And I have altered my own take on the many of the topics. In short, porn is not the Nasty Evil Industry of Exploitation and Coercion (porn is ultimately no big deal – it's just another area of global capitalism). Instead, we have governments who take care of coercion and exploitation.

133 B. Smith: "Sappho Was a Right-*Off* Woman", in G. Chester, 179

2

ART, SEXUALITY, EROTICISM, PORNOGRAPHY/ PORNOGRAPHY, EROTICISM, SEXUALITY, ART

The age-old debate between art and pornography revolves around tired old questions: is art pornography? Is pornography art? Is consuming art therefore consuming pornography? Is there a set of attitudes, values, ethics and morals ascribed to art but not pornography? Is pornography any different, æsthetically, psychologically, physically, politically and morally from art? What is the boundary between art and porn? And who decides all these questions?

These questions, for feminists, become irrelevant beside debates of race, class, economics, political oppression, poverty, exploitation, war and violence. The art/ pornography debate is the game of bourgeois people, some feminists claim, who have nothing better to do. Instead of concentrating on porn, what about looking at other forms of oppression – racial, economic, political, ideological, heterosexual, familial, psychological, etc. This is the

64

question some feminists ask. B. Ruby Rich writes:

> If an analysis of porn were to confront its basic origin in the power relations between men and women, then it would have to drop the whole eroticism-versus-pornography debate and take on a far more complex and threatening target: the institution of heterosexuality.[134]

We know the male/ patriarchal view of the art versus pornography debate. Eroticism is justified and good because it is 'high art', it is superbly crafted, it is a 'work of art'. Thus the Kronhausens, the organizers of a major exhibition of 'erotic art',[135] write:

> one can perhaps distinguish between pornography and art. The criterion would be that the more a picture contains evidence of interpretative, creative elaboration, the closer it is to art.[136]

For Phyllis & Eberhard Kronhausens, as for so many artists and philosophers and intellectuals, erotic art is art because it is done well. Pornography is simply bad art.

Many guardians of æsthetics, many professors of art history and dons of 'the beautiful' go along with this view. Kenneth Clark is a typical establishment critic who puts forward the patriarchal view: nudes are OK provided they are æsthetically pleasing, provided they remain 'in the realm of contemplation', as he put it.[137]

The establishment art historical view of erotic art and porn is that true erotic or high art engenders quiet contemplation, a detached ravishing of the senses, a meditation on Platonic, Aristotlean and Kantian ideas of 'beauty' and æsthetics. 'High art', which is legitimate art, art which justifies itself by its 'genius' or obvious 'greatness', is about distance and disinterested pleasure. The high art nude, in painting or sculpture, in the

134 B. Ruby Rich: "Anti-Porn: Soft issue, Hard World", in Chester, 348
135 The 'first international exhibition of erotic art' was at the Museum of Art, Lund, Sweden, and Aarhus, Denmark, in 1968
136 Phyllis & Eberhard Kronhausen: *Erotic Art: A survey of erotic fact and fancy in the fine arts*, W.H. Allen, 1971, 3
137 Quoted in Lord Longford: *Pornography: The Longford Report*, Coronet, 1972, 99f

patriarchal view, justifies its existence by the brilliance of its production, the sumptuousness of its colour and form, the marvel of its human touches, the grandeur of its design, the loftiness of its ambition, the dynamism of its structures, and so on. As that producer of exquisite bodies, French Neo-Classical artist J.A.D. Ingres, wrote:

> There are not two arts, there is only one: it is the one which has as its foundation the beautiful, which is eternal and natural.[138]

The 'sublime' qualities of high art, to use one popular adjective of art criticism, are crucial to its success, as Carol M. Armstrong notes in her essay on Edgar Degas:

> One of the things any painted object does is to resist signification at some level because of its very objecthood. And the female nude – because of *its* objecthood may be seen as almost emblematic of that level of resistance. In fact, the female nude has been linked to that stratum of painting most in tension with the work of signification – the stratum we connect to what we call, inadequately, "abstraction"; facture, the handling of paint per se, foregrounded as an obvious fact of the painting. Femaleness and facture, facture and the female nude, they go together somehow. One need only think of Titian, the first great painter of the female nude in the Western tradition.[139]

Much as worshippers properly gaze at an icon or an image of a deity with wonder, the art critic and historian kneels before 'great art' and worships it.[140] The female nude is the highest form of non-religious art, and it confers a religious awe in its æsthete consumers. The emphasis is on Neoplatonic terms such as 'purity', 'beauty', 'form' and 'symmetry'. As Aristotle puts it: '[t]he chief forms of beauty are order and symmetry and definiteness.'[141]

In the Neoplatonic, Aristotlean, Renaissance view of the fine art establishment, there is good art and bad art, there is art of

138 J. Ingres, quoted in Goldwater, 216
139 Carol M. Armstrong; "Edgar Degas and the Representation of the Female Body", in Suleiman, 223
140 See Pierre Bourdieu, 1984
141 Aristotle: *Metaphysics*, book XIII, in Albert Hofstadter & Richard Kuhns, eds. *Philosophies of Art and Beauty: Selected Readings in Aesthetics From Plato to Heidegger*, Random House, New York 1964, 96

'taste', 'decency', 'refinement', 'purity' and 'civilization', and there is the vulgar, the uncouth, the disrespectful, the unornamental, the unlearned. Pornography falls into the latter category. In mediæval culture, there is Sacred and Profane love, drawn from Plato's *Symposium*, and the Venus Vulgaris (Earthly Venus) and Venus Coelestis. The Heavenly Venus is the one to aspire to, even though the Earthly Venus may be much more exciting.

These dichotomies are found throughout art. There is the chaste, passive, motherly Virgin Mary and the sexual, active, lascivious Mary Magdalene.[142] There is good and evil. There is Heaven and Hell. There is male and female. Throughout the history of Western culture we come across the same dualities, in one form or another. The female is clearly on the 'left' side, on the wrong side of the 'right' way. Women are the 'second sex', 'second class citizens': Sherry Ortner writes there is an opposition between culture and nature, and women are lower down in the male-made hierarchy:

> my thesis is that woman is being identified with – or, if you will, seems to be a symbol of – something that every culture devalues, something that every culture defines as being of a lower order of existence than itself.[143]

Women are imprisoned, as Hélène Cixous notes, in masculine binary logic, which is the 'classical vision of sexual opposition between men and women', as Verena Conley writes in her book on Cixous.[144] For Luce Irigaray, this duality is called 'the recto-verso structure that shores up common sense'.[145]

A list of these oppositions is useful, because they can be applied to every area of culture, from colonialism and racism, to science and medicine, from legislation of any kind to art of any kind:

---

142 See Marina Warner: *Monuments and Maidens*; Kenneth Clark: *The Nude*; Lynda Nead, 19;
143 Sherry B. Ortner: "Is Female to Male as Nature is to Culture", in M. Evans, ed. *The Woman Question*, Fontana 1982
144 Verena Andermatt Conley: *Hélène Cixous: Writing the Feminine*, University of Nebraska Press, Lincoln, 1984, 129
145 Luce Irigaray: *The Irigaray Reader*, 127

male	female
right	left
Heaven	Hell
positive	negative
speaking	silence
good	evil
us	them
rationality	irrationality
reason	intuition
science	religion
patriarchy	matriarchy
self	other
capitalism	communism
precision	imprecision
active	passive
subject	object
viewer	observed
high art	low art
bourgeoisie	proletariat
mind/ soul	body

It's no exaggeration to say that by and large men have created the æsthetics of art throughout Western culture. It is men, largely, who have defined what is and is not 'acceptable', what is to be applauded and what is to be ignored, outlawed or suppressed. And the producers of art that have been acknowledged publicly are (mostly) male. The artists of the West, like the pornographers, are mainly men. This fact explains a lot. The basic fact of Western art, which we shall keep returning to, is that, as Mary Ann Caws notes, 'the woman's body has been presented for the man's erotic pleasure'.[146] Throughout Western art, it seems, the scenario has been: *man looking, woman being looked at*; man creating representations of women to be looked at; men creating

---

146 Mary Ann Caws: "Ladies Shot and Painted: Female Embodiment in Surrealist Art", in Suleiman, ed. 267-8. See also Linda Nochlin, ed. *Woman as Sex Object: Studies in Erotic Art 1730-1970*, Newsweek, New York 1973

the economies and modes of representations within which everyone must operate.

Depictions of the female nude and of erotic gestures or 'acts' or whatever can be problematic. The female body, for instance, is already 'objectified' even before it is painted or represented. Once painted, it becomes a cultural artifact, a mass of codes, meanings, signs and values, none of them fixed, all of them dependent on the context of consumption, dependent on the socio-political make-up of the viewer, and so on.

Context is crucial in matters of eroticism and pornography. An image that is seen as 'erotic' in one context can easily be seen as 'pornographic' in another context. Take an image out of context, and soon a new, often ironic set of meanings are set in motion. Jacques Derrida has shown that a text may have many contexts, and is not fixed in one context forever.[147] Feminist artists have explored meanings and contexts, by placing traditional images in new contexts. Meanings are constantly in a state of flux. Nothing is fixed anymore. As Catherine Belsey writes: 'meanings circulate between text, ideology and reader' (144). Roland Barthes wrote that '[a]ll images are polysemous... they imply, underlying their signifiers, a floating chain of signifieds'. The consumer has the ability to 'choose some and ignore others'.[148] The cultural environment, socialization, economy, power relations, education, any number of factors can influence the meanings drawn from an image. With the female nude, in painting or pornography, the meanings are contextualized as erotic. As Anne Hollander notes, the nude always has a sexual dimension to it.

For instance, men can 'possess' and yet never 'possess' a female nude painting. It remains an image. The 'possession' or consumption is of a cerebral order, which is why critics and professors such as Kenneth Clark, Bernard Berenson, Jacob Burckhardt, Walter Pater, John Ruskin, Aby Warburg, Roger Fry, Ernst Gombrich and other art critics emphasize the *intellectual* nature of enjoying art. Art for the head, not the body, art for the

---

147 Jacques Derrida: *Eperons. Les styles de Nietzsche*, Flammarion, Paris 1978, 103f
148 Roland Barthes: *Image-Music-Text*, Hill & Wang, New York 1977, 39

eyes, not the full five senses. Françoise Parturier writes:

> With sex now subject to the exercises of thought, sexuality can no longer be sublimated in love, but rather in eroticism, which in the West is much more a philosophy, a cerebral enterprise, than an art of pleasure. Because it is founded on the theorem that woman is an object, that love and pleasure are two distinct realities which are naturally harmful, eroticism can only be misogynous.[149]

The establishment view of art and porn, then, is full of ambiguities, which many intellectuals have tried to resolve. Art critics, for instance, find themselves sinking in philosophical quagmires when they start to rave about depictions of the body, because they start to reveal their erotic arousal, their sexual identity; their lust, in short. There is always the chance that in talking of the eroticism of an artwork the critic will move unconsciously into pornography. It is a slip many art critics are aware of, but many, despite themselves, do it. They do not like to admit the amount of sex there is in art, the amount of erotic energy there is in creativity. The (male) critics don't like to acknowledge what (male) artists know, that sex, for men, is primary. As Carol Duncan writes: '[m]ore than any other theme, the nude could demonstrate that art originates in and is sustained by male erotic energy.'[150]

The female nude is the apotheosis of 'high art', yet it constantly wavers around the borderline between art and porn. The female nude is erotic *and* obscene, in the male system, both desired and loathed, both representable and un-representable.

With the rise of cultural or postmodern theory, which sees artworks as 'texts', the body has become a 'text'. The body, that thing that people thought was fixed and always in one place, is in motion. It is as fluid as emotions. For centuries, (male) critics and artists thought the nude was either a model in a studio or in a

---

149 Françoise Parturier: *Lettre ouverte aux hommes*, tr. Elissa Gelfand, Albin Michel 1968, in Marks, 63
150 Carol Duncan: "Virility and Domination in Early Twentieth-Century Vanguard Painting", in N. Broude & M.D. Garrard, eds. *Feminism and Art History: Questioning the Litany*, Harper & Row, New York, 306

painting on a gallery wall. Not so. Feminism has shown that the body itself is a site of social, racial, moral, æsthetic and political debates. The body, in fact, is central to feminism, as much as sex is. Elizabeth Grosz writes that the body's

> form, capacities, behaviour, gestures, movements, potential are primary objects of political contestation. As a *political* object, the body is not inert or fixed. It is pliable and plastical material, which is capable of being formed and organized in other, quite different ways or according to different classifactory schema than our binarised models.[151]

When feminists speak of 'rewriting the body', or of 'reclaiming' the body, they do not mean simply physically reclaiming the body, they mean reclaiming it politically, ideologically, psychologically, morally and artistically. The body is where everything happens: acts, thoughts, experiences, desires, they are all sited in the body. So feminism has to address the body and body politics, because the body is crucial. Similarly, pornography is powerful (partly) because it so powerfully deals with the body.

Lynda Nead writes in *The Female Nude* (71):

> The body is, therefore, central in the formation of individual identity and is the site of the subject's desires and fantasies, actions and behaviour. Once one rejects the perception of the body as a biologically determined and pre-cultural given and moves towards the conception of 'embodied' subjects, the way is opened for feminist interventions within the definition of the female body.

In art and porn, in fashion and manufacture, down the ages, the female body has been defined largely by men. If not by men, then by male-made ideas, male notions of what is 'beautiful', what is desirable, what is erotic, what is *de rigeur*. Feminism seeks to rewrite men's definitions of the body and eroticism.

The art-pornography debate centres around power, politics,

---

151 Elizabeth Grosz: "Corporreal Feminism", in *Australian Feminist Studies*, 5, Summer 1987, 3; also "The Body of Significance", in John Fletcher & Andrew Benjamin, eds. *Abjection, Melancholia and Love: The Work of Julia Kristeva*, Routledge 1990, 80-103

acceptability, philosophy and pleasure. The proper response to high culture is a detached enjoyment; pornography is disruptive, disturbing, debasing. Looking at a piece of high art, the pornographic response is lust while the high art response is rarefied contemplation. When pornographic responses to high art occur, the result is indignation from the art establishment. There are famous incidences of the 'debasing' of high art, as when a youth was so obsessed with a statue of Aphrodite of Cnidos that he masturbated on it, leaving a stain, as recorded in Pliny's *Natural History*; then there is the myth of Pygmalion, later reworked by William Shakespeare in *The Winter's Tale*, where the statue is sensually responsive; then there was Henry George Quinn who sneaked into the Uffizi Gallery to 'fervently kiss' the Medici Venus all over.[152]

Throughout history, female nudes of the high art type have been made for clients and connoisseurs – Titian made many nudes for such private, privileged consumption. Pornography too has been manufactured for the same clients and connoisseurs. When does a refined, rarefied enjoyment of erotic art become the vulgar, debased gratification of pornography? When does the connoisseur become the pornographic consumer?

Erotic art may defined as simply 'æstheticized sexual representation' (L. Nead, 103), that is, erotic feelings processed through the mechanisms of 'high culture'. For some feminists, there is no doubt that the enjoyment of the female nude is pornographic, and is largely inseparable from the lustful consumption of porn. The boundaries between art and pornography are being constantly blurred, constantly reset and rewritten. For instance, Louise O'Murphy, the model for Boucher's famous nude *Mademoiselle O'Murphy*, became King Louis XV's personal prostitute (his 'mistress', as critics call them) after the King saw Boucher's painting. The high art 'possession' or pleasure of the female nude in Boucher's painting became the real

---

152 Nicholas Penny: "Goddesses and Girls", in *London Review of Books*, 2-29, December 1982, 20; Simon Wilson: "Short History of Western Erotic Art", in Robert Melville: *Erotic Art of the West*, Weidenfeld & Nicolson 1973, 16

'possession' of Louise O'Murphy's body. Clearly, kings can buy what they like: they can have the best art, and have the best women.

The high art nude, then, is a site of political and economic manipulation, an expression of the power relations between patron and painter, between connoisseur, artist and model. In the trinity of people linked by the painting – patron, painter and model – the model is clearly at the bottom of the pile. She is dependent on both painter and patron. She has to please both of them to be successful. The relation of artist to model thus is another manifestation, for feminism, like that of husband and wife, of male power, of patriarchal culture in action, of the sexual economics which are at work everywhere in the world, and everywhere in history.

For Andrea Dworkin, 'erotic art' is simply high class pornography:

> ...erotica is simply high-class pornography: better produced, better conceived, better executed, better packaged, designed for a better class of consumer... Intellectuals, especially, call what they themselves produce or like "erotica," which means simply that a very bright person made or likes whatever it is. (*Pornography*, 10)

Andrea Dworkin is spot-on here. This is exactly what erotic art is, among other things. This view can be proved by any example from the history of art. (Male) power and money buys high class porn. The Emperor Tiberius had pornography hung on his walls at his villa at Capri, while the Emperor Nero had his Golden Palace decorated with pornography. Power and pornography have always gone together. Pornographic images themselves are expressions of power relations – social, political, racial, classist, economic and sexist power.

'High class' pornography (a.k.a. erotic art) is thought to be 'revolutionary' and 'rebellious'. But it is not. Benoîte Groult writes, voicing the opinions of many feminists:

I'm sick and tired of these same old obsessions that never change, even in "modern style" without punctuation. I'm sick and tired of the way eminent philosophers and sociologists put forth as "free," "new," and "revolutionary" those same old perverse scripts which do nothing but try, unsuccessfully, to stage the little sadist's timeless repertory in a new way: the same old shit, pus, blood, sperm (oh! come on!), whips, and chains are dressed in smart new clothes... That's revolution? That's subversion? To be precise, it's an extension of the bourgeois world, that world in which a few males obsessed with virile violence and convinced they are prophets shit on women, rip apart their vaginas, and kill them while fucking them – all because they hate women so for being desirable.[153]

Context, then, is crucial, as Julia Kristeva notes. If pornography is displayed in certain contexts it can seem to be erotica, or high art. If it is consumed in other contexts, it can seem to be nothing but porn.[154] 'What some call 'erotica' others call 'pornography',' as Lizbeth Goodman writes.[155] While Joanna Russ remarks: '[m]aybe Gloria Steinem can tell the difference between pornography and erotica at a single glance. I can't'.[156] Pornography is what *other* people do or consume, it seems.

It's a question of levels, areas, boundaries. The 'acceptable' becomes nothing more than the consensus but, as any study of the media shows, 'consensus' is created not by a nation or a mass of people, but by a very small group of particular sorts of people (in American broadcasting, mainly white, middle-aged males).

The context of consumption of art, the media, pornography and any kind of communication determines much. For instance, both porn and art are consumed in particular socio-political environments. For pornography, like art, is expensive, and requires a certain amount of money to be able to be consumed, whether this means buying magazines, or possessing a satellite dish and decoder, etc, at a banal, materialistic level; at a deeper level, the consumption of art and pornography is determined very much by the strictures of class, race, economy, privilege,

---

153 Benoîte Groult: "Les portiers de nuit", in Marks, 72
154 See also Rosalind Coward: "Porn: what's in it for women?", *New Statesman*, 13 June 1986
155 L. Goodman: "The Pornography Problem", in Booner, 279
156 Joanna Russ: "Being against Pornography", in C. Kramarae, re. Steinem: "Erotica and pornography: a clear and present difference", also in Kramarae

place and politics.

Art is, typically, for the 'privileged', for the select few, while porn is mass culture. As Joel Jovel wrote: 'pornography is the captivity of the erotic within mass culture.'[157] Artists continually defend their right to make erotic art. There must be no censorship whatsoever, say artists (and many feminists agree with them. There are feminists groups who are anti-censorship, such as Feminists Against Censorship, Feminist Anti-Censorship Task Force, Campaign Against Pornography and Censorship). Censorship of/ in pornography will not, feminists believe, lead to a better, freer culture: Marianne Hester commented:

> Lack of censorship against pornography is therefore highly unlikely to lead to lack of censorship against other areas of publication. Instead, it is the publication of oppressive material, such as pornography, which is likely to increase. (70)

André Masson said: 'censorship enforces a sort of involuntary hypocrisy of the artist'. The artist censors her/ himself, says Masson: s/he knows there are certain images that cannot be shown in a gallery.[158] A familiar argument, which allows for total subjectivity, the individuals rights of freedom of expression. The view is backed up by any number of artists. One of the most consistently pornographic of modern artists, Hans Bellmer, said: '[t]he idea of eroticism is an essential part of life, so it's right that artists like me should devote themselves to exploring that idea.'[159] The argument is also used by film directors when asked about violence in the cinema. Life is violent, they say, so we have to reflect that in our movies.

The erotic experience is a part of life, say artists, so we must be erotic in our works. What happens with porn is that sex becomes everything, and everything is subsumed to sex. The protagonists of pornography tumble into bed at every oppor-tunity. There are none of the usual structures of the traditional

157 Joel Kovel: "The Antididactic of Pornography", in Michael Kimmel, ed. *Men Confront Pornography*, Crown Publishers, New York, 1989
158 André Mason, quoted in Phyllis & Eberhard Kronhausen, op. cit., 42
159 Interview, 1972, in Peter Webb, 369

novel or fiction in pornography. The aim is simply to create as much sex as possible. Every other consideration – of personalities, of feelings, of social, political and economic obligations, of familial and societal responsibilities, etc – is forgotten. The protagonists simply get on with sex, and nothing but sex. Everything is padding in pornography. If there's no sex occurring, pornography has failed: there must always be sex, and lots of it. It's part of the escapism, of the fantasy.

It is the same with erotic and pornographic visual art and sculpture. Nothing else must get in the way of the sexual aspects. Thus, the female nude is not a part of some larger picture, of a city, a landscape, a group portrait, a political statement (although it is political); it is simply a nude, in the foreground, on some couch, openly displaying, even if coyly, her body. Some female nude paintings do include landscapes, cities or background interest, as in Bernardino Luini's *Nymph of the Spring*, but the real point of the picture is the nude, which dominates it.[160] The female nude is, simply, right in front of the viewer, despite the distantiation of the mechanics and politics of representation. There's the nude, upfront, much as in porn, there is the sex act, right on page one.

Pornography, like art, pivots around *desire*. And desire, as Hélène Cixous notes, is something that never dies: '[d]esire never dies', she says.[161] Pornography is about 'having' something *now*. Not in ten minutes, not next year, but *now*. Erotic art is about anticipation, about desire, about longing for 'the moment', the moment of pleasure. Pornography clears away all that stuff, and presents the Freudian primal scene now. Right now.

If some work is erotic – a scene on TV, a photo, a sculpture, a dance – it's because, in the opinion of some people, you don't 'see' everything. Something is hidden. The erotic experience in art is about anticipation, waiting, yearning. It's about potential and possibility, hidden but not hidden, partially clothed. As the

160 Bernardino Luini: *Nymph of the Spring*, c. 1525, oil on wood, 107 x 136cm, National Gallery of Art, Washington DC
161 H. Cixous and Catherine Clément: *The Newly Born Woman*, University of Manchester Press 1985

photographer Grace Lau, who has made many pictures of fetishism, commented: 'I prefer images that conceal, rather than those that reveal all.'[162]

Pornography, meanwhile, has people doing it now. They undress, and immediately get freaky. There's nothing to get in the way, not contraception, not fear, not aversions, not menstruation, not impotence, not interruptions, not anything. In short: it's *fantasy.*

Pornography turns 'what if?' into a reality. What if somebody took their clothes off in this train carriage and started having sex? is a typical question that erotic art suggests but porno answers. What if this woman at home turns out to be a nymphomaniac and this repair guy turns out to be a superstud? What if the wedding guest who just smiled at you turns out to be the fuck of a lifetime? In pornography, people *do* rip their clothes off and start doin' the dirty.

Pornography presents as a normal, everyday occurrence what is hidden away, what is desired but unspoken. Porn is the ultimate in fantasy, for in the fairy tale world of porn, every dream comes true. And it is not only 'true', it is 'real'. And it is not only 'true' and 'real', it hurts. For pain is a part of pornography for some critics. As Andrea Dworkin writes: '[p]enetration was never meant to be kind. In pornography, scissors, razors, knives, and daggers are poised at the entrance to the vagina, cuts evident on the delicate skin of the pubic area, often shaved...'[163] But pain is also a large part of Western culture.

Pain is good, because it means you are fully alive. This is the Existential view of patriarchal culture. 'Sensual pleasure is agony in the strictest meaning of the word', says C. Mauclair in a Freudian tone.[164] Suffering is holy, in the Christian tradition. The journey from martyrdom to sainthood and beatification is swift. The West exalts pain. Christ *suffered,* say theologians, so he must have been right, he must have lived hard, because he died hard.

162 Grace Lau: "Confessions of a Complete Scopophiliac", in Gibbons, 195
163 A. Dworkin: *Intercourse*, 223
164 C. Mauclair: *Magie de l'amour*, 145, quoted in Julius Evola, 84

Death becomes heroic. Death transfigures people. Suicide is even better, if you can manage it. Hence Marilyn Monroe, Vincent van Gogh, Johann Wolfgang von Goethe's Werther, Virginia Woolf. Die young, and become famous (many artists have followed this equation: Egon Schiele, Frédéric Chopin, Wolfgang Amadeus Mozart, Georges Seurat, James Dean, Paula Modersohn-Becker, D.H. Lawrence, Jimmy Hendrix, Jim Morrison, Arthur Rimbaud, Raphael, John Keats, Percy Shelley, and Novalis).

In the male system, sex and death are entwined. Further, death and the feminine, death and women are combined. Further, pain and sex are combined. Painful sex must be good sex, according to the patriarchy. If it hurts, it works is a typical adage often bandied about. Pain is good, because it cuts through everything and makes acute the transitoriness and bliss of the human condition, according to the (male) Existential view.

A lot of art of any kind comes out of agony, according to men. Love poetry flows from the emotional pain of being left by the lover. Thus, love poetry, from Sappho to the latest pop song, is a cry of pain from a bereft soul. Love songs come from loss, from losing the object of bliss, the beloved. Like babies, love poets sob forlornly.

Love is pain, death, sin, vice and fornication in the Christian view. Love poets transform the agony into art, as do creators of erotic art. There is a masochism at the heart of Western art, as there is at the core of Christianity. Christ on the Cross is the supreme example of masochistic suffering in the West, and is the most painted image, apart from the Madonna and Child, in the Western world.

There is a link here: the Crucifixion is the end of life, the painful letting go, while the child in the Madonna's arms is the beginning of life, swathed in the softness and care of the mother figure. The two images, Virgin and Child and the Crucifixion, form the twin poles of Western art. Both images are dominated by the feminine, for the Cross in the Crucifixion is the Mother, the Goddess, the Cross being part of the Earth from which Christ is later reborn – the second, spiritual birth echoing his first, earthly birth, depicted in so many Nativity scenes and Madonna and Child images.

It is noble to suffer, say male poets and artists and theologians and philosophers. As Joseph Campbell put it in *The Power of Myth*:

> Love is the burning point of life, and since all life is sorrowful, so is love. The stronger the love, the more the pain… Love itself is a pain, you might say – the pain of being truly alive. (205)

In porn, you simply change the word 'love' for 'sex'. Thus, to rewrite Joseph Campbell: 'the stronger the sex, the more the pain'. Good sex, in patriarchy, is strong sex. The greater the experience, the better the sex. This is the formula behind some of pornography not only exemplified by sadomasochistic sex, but also by soft core porn, and by bourgeois conceptions of love and marriage.

The male equation is sex = pain = life. Notions of woman and the feminine are bound up in this formula. Indeed, they make carrying out the formula possible. The emphasis on suffering in sex comes from any number of sources. The Marquis de Sade is a famous one. He inaugurates the modern age of pornography, and the age of intellectual sex, mental or head sex, sex without touching, sex for pornographers, the philosophical sex as espoused by Georges Bataille, Charles Baudelaire, Guillaume Apollinaire, Friedrich Nietzsche, Henry Miller, Sigmund Freud and Jean-Paul Sartre.

The Marquis de Sade is quite astonishing. As Andrea Dworkin writes: 'Sade's work is nearly indescribable. In sheer quantity of horror, it is unparalleled in the history of writing.' (*Pornography*, 92) De Sade is the high priest of metaphysical eroticism, as championed by Baudelaire, Jean Cocteau, the Surrealists, Algernon Swinburne, Lautréamont, Fyodor Dostoievsky and John Cowper Powys. Among visual artists, the inheritors of the Sadeian pornographic ethic include Pablo Picasso, Hans Bellmer, Cocteau, Max Ernst, Allen Jones, and David Salle.

The Sadeian philosophy of sex is fiercely heterosexual and heterosexist, with woman definitely the object of male lust. The history of the arts is also Sadeian and pornographic. Look at the poems of William Shakespeare, Dante Alighieri, Francesco Petrarch, Paul Éluard, Robert Graves, Maurice Scève, Torquato Tasso, John Donne, John Skelton, etc. Women – 'woman' – are the object of male desire in these poems. The poets emphasize the *pain* of love, the agony of desire. How I suffer for love of you! they cry, so many times – in Petrarch's *Rime Sparse*, Dante's *Vita Nuova*, Shakespeare's *Sonnets* or Robert Graves' *Collected Poems*. Some male poets tried to stylize the pain of love, but agony is inescapably a part of their form of erotic desire, as Dante shows time and time again in his *Divina Commedia*, as this extract from the *Paradiso* reveals:

Then Beatrice looked at me, her eyes
sparkling with love and burning so divine,
my strength of sight surrendered to her power –

with eyes cast down, I was about to faint.[165]

In the male, Sadeian view, only painful sex is authentic (or sex. This view is found in the major works of high class or literary porn: *The Story of the Eye, The Story of O, The Image, Tropic of Cancer, Lady Chatterley's Lover, The 120 Days of Sodom*, etc.

Georges Bataille's *The Story of the Eye*, acclaimed by intellectual luminaries such as Jean-Paul Sartre, Susan Sontag, Michel Foucault and Peter Brook, is typical amongst intellectual porn. The ethics it proposes – not secretly, not between the lines, not in the silences and spaces of the text, but upfront, in every sentence – are explained accurately by Andrea Dworkin: '[d]eath is the stunning essence of sex. The violence of death is the violence of sex and the beauty of death is the beauty of sex and the meaning of life is only revealed in the meaning of sex which is death.' (ib, 174-5). *The Story of the Eye* is famous for its depictions of anal, oral and genital sex, with a distinctive use of analogies

165 Dante: *The Divine Comedy: Paradiso*, tr. Mark Musa, Penguin 1986, IV: 139-142

and tropes which run together: eggs, eyes, mouths, balls, vulvas and anuses.

In high class porn, sex leads to death. The orgasm is the 'little death' (*petit mort*) and the most blissful way to die is at orgasm, where sex and death fuse rapturously and most poetically of all. The '*raptus*' of sex, the 'spasm', as men insist on calling the orgasm, is the experience that 'kills', and people 'die' in orgasm. As Andrea Dworkin explains, the stylization and so-called lyricism of high class porn hides the real violence underneath. It is already about power – power over other people, and the ultimate expression of power is killing someone (as countless Hollywood films show). Dworkin writes:

> What matters is the poetry that is the violence leading to death that is the ecstasy. The language stylizes the violence and denies its fundamental meaning to women, who do in fact end up dead because men believe what Bataille believes and makes pretty: that death is the dirty secret of sex. (ib., 176)

THE HISTORY OF PORNOGRAPHY

The history of pornography, then, is also the history of attitudes, values, morals and politics in the Western world. The history of pornography is also the history of art. Porn and art go together. They both contain the same tenets of sex = pain, of sex = death, of male power being exerted over 'victims' or inferiors, of whatever race, class, age, economy or nationality. The history of porn is largely the history of power. We are still summarizing feminist views here – battles that are over now and some of those conflicts were actually no big deal in the first place.

Pornography, like art, is born from a white, middle class, Christian, First World experience. Pornography's religious background, like that of art, is Judæo-Christian. Religious imagery itself features in pornography (nuns, monks, the bishop and the actress, Regan in the 1973 film *The Exorcist* masturbating with a crucifix, Mary Magdalene masturbating in front of a crucified penis in Félicien Rops' drawing, etc).

In the patriarchal view, religion is sexy, and sex is religious. Artists such as Eric Gill and Egon Schiele have combined sexual and religious imagery. Western art, like pornography, draws on of the Judæo-Christian insistence on sin, death, vice, fornication, dirt and suppression. The father of Christianity is not Jesus but St Paul. Jesus wrote nothing; St Paul wrote everything, setting down the views of Christianity in that fanatical prose in the *Corinthians* and *Galatians* and *Romans*, which gets so many things wrong about flesh and spirit and marriage. Michael Foucault writes of some of the strictures of Christianity:

> Christianity associated it ['the sexual act'] with evil, sin, the Fall, and death, whereas antiquity invested it with positive symbolic values.[166]

In Christianity, women are the 'gateway to Hell' as the early theologian Tertullian poetically put it; women are evil, sinful, lustful ('the Devil is a woman' is a common theme in mediæval philosophy as well as pop songs). From Eve in the Old Testament to the Virgin and Magdalene in the New, women are definitely second class citizens in the eyes of Western religion. Women-hating is startling in its violent manifestations – not just in wife-beating, which occurs everywhere and, one supposes, at every moment of human history, but also in the mass movements, such as the fight against witchcraft in the Middle Ages and later, when, armed with the *Malleus Maleficarum*, the Witchfinder Generals hunted down and tortured and killed hundreds or thousands, some say millions, of women.

In Christianity, chastity, abstinence, purity, virginity, mono-gamy, negation and suppression are exalted. Pornography reverses Christianity's strictures, it turns them upside-down, it lets

---

166 M. Foucault: *The Use of Pleasure*, 14

chaos loose, as in the Dionysian orgies, in the Greek bacchanales, in the Roman Saturnalia or 'time of chaos', a Twelfth Night of the senses, in which a Trickster God, Pan or Dionysus, usurps the norms and lets wild desire rage forth.

Pornography subverts the laws of Christianity, but it is based on the same laws. Porn comes out of the same world as Christianity. Not only is there much of Christianity in pornography, there is much of pornography in Christianity. For instance, Christian history is a catalogue of sadomasochistic events and acts, some really horrific scenes of torture and oppression. More acts of terror have been carried out in the name of God than in the name of 'freedom' or 'truth' or 'honour'.

Painters throughout Western history have reflected the violent acts of Christianity, portraying them as heroic gestures: Sandro Botticelli painted the massacre of the Innocents; Nicolas Poussin depicted St Erasmus having his entrails pulled out by a winch, many painters portrayed St Sebastian full of arrows (Andrea Mantegna, Antonella da Messina, Pietro Perugino, Henrick Terbruggen, and, more recently, Eric Gill and Egon Schiele), Francisco de Zurbarán painted a saint being crucified upside down (1629).[167]

A good bout of flagellation goes down well with Christians too, and many Renaissance painters painted Christ being whipped or tortured by the guards, and being crowned with thorns. Examples include Titian's two *Christ Crowned with Thorns* paintings, which make suffering a sublime, heroic experience,[168] or the ritualized whipping in Piero della Francesca's *The Flagellation of Christ*, a much-discussed Renaissance painting, or Luca Signorelli's more staid approach to the torture.[169]

167 Nicolas Poussin: *The Martyrdom of St Erasmus*, 1628, Pinacoteca Vaticana, Vatican, Rome; Hendrick Terbrugghen: *St Sebastian Tended by St Irene and the Maid*, 1625, Allen Memorial Art Museum, Oberlin College, Oberlin, Ohio; Antonello da Messina: *St Sebastian*, c. 1475, oil on panel, 67.4 x 33.5in, State Picture Gallery, Dresden; Andrea Mantegna: *St Sebastian*, c. 1470, tempera on canvas, 101.2 x 55.8in, Louvre, Paris, Pietro Perugino: *St Sebastian*, c. 1495, panel, 170 x 117cm, Louvre, Paris; Francisco de Zurbarán: *The Apostle Peter Appearing to St Peter Nolasco*, 1629, oil on canvas, 5ft 11 x 7ft 4in, Prado, Madrid
168 Titian: *Christian Crowned with Thorns*, mid-1450s, panel, 303 x 180cm, Louvre, Paris; *Christ Crowned with Thorns*, c. 1570-6, canvas, 280 x 181cm, Alte Pinakothek, Munich
169 Piero della Francesca: *The Flagellation of Christ*, c. 1450, panel, 59 x 81.5cm, Ducal, Urbino; Signoreli: *Flagellation*, c. 1480, canvas, 80 x 60cm, Brera, Milan

Not to be out-done, Vittore Carpaccio painted a bizarre picture: the crucified Jesus sitting on a throne, dead, with his eyes closed, with two semi-naked old men sitting on either side of him. The title is *Meditation on the Passion of Christ*.[170] There's the Saviour, looking very dead, on a throne, in a ruined landscape, while two old men sit right next to him and muse upon his death. Bizarre.

Sebastiano del Piombo goes even further: his *The Martyrdom of St Agatha* depicts the saint, *nude of course*, being tortured by a bunch of men, fully clothed of course.[171] They are applying gigantic metal pliers to her nipples. This is a depiction of sadism (in Christianity the euphemism is 'martyrdom'). Naturally, it seems, this is *sexual* torture, painted in such a straightforward fashion, the woman centre frame, the men surrounding her intent on brutalizing her. The rape, which must follow this torture, is not shown, and it is never shown in Renaissance art, and rarely in Western art. When rape occurs, as it must have done millions of times through the Christian era, men dragging away women are depicted, or Jupiter as a swan screwing Leda, but not the rape itself.

Not all of Christianity is suppression and chastity. In Christian mysticism there is wildness and ecstasy, in mystics such as Jan van Ruysbroeck, St Theresa, Meister Eckhart, Richard Rolle, Richard of St Victor, Catherine of Siena, John of the Cross, etc. Mysticism is the centre of any religion. It is the record of moments of revelations. Mystics speak of the amazing bliss which is surely the goal of religion. Yet institutionalized religion constantly moves mysticism to the fringes. Hence many of those wonderful ecstasies of the mystics – of any religion – are regarded with suspicion by the establishment, and are suppressed.

One such ecstasy in Christianity, of St Theresa, was the subject of Giovanni Lorenzo Bernini's famous 1640s statue.[172] More than a

170 Carpaccio: *Meditation on the Passion of Christ*, c. 1505, panel, 70 x 86cm, Metropolitan Museum of Art, New York
171 Sebastiano del Piombo: *The Martyrdom of St Agatha*, 1520, 31 x 175cm, Pitti Palace, Florence
172 Giovanni Lorenzo Bernini: *The Ecstasy of St Theresa*, 1645-52, S. Maria della Vittoria, Rome

few commentators have noted that Bernini's saint is in orgasm. Jacques Lacan writes that 'you only have to go and look at the Bernini statue in Rome to understand immediately she (St Teresa) is coming'.[173]

Parts of Christianity are pornographic, then, just as parts of Western culture are pornographic. There is nothing new about this view. The central image and meditation of Christianity, Christ on the Cross, is a pornographic image in itself. The pain Christ experiences is both fleshy and spiritual, both masochistic and glorified. Like religion, porn makes a cult of out pain, makes pain an essential ingredient in authentic living. Philosophies such as Existentialism bear this out.

What this means is that the creators of philosophy, religion, politics, art and culture see suffering as an essential component in life. Life without suffering is not quite an authentic life, in the male view. In the realm of sexuality, of which pornography and art are expressions, suffering is also regarded as important. This is where things get controversial. Saying that suffering or pain is essential in art or pornography or culture is one thing, saying it is essential in people's lives and in their sexuality is another. Some radical feminists make the connection between theory and practice, between representations and realities, between culture and people, so that what happens in porn happens in real life. Andrea Dworkin writes:

> Pornography reveals that male pleasure is inextricably tied to victimizing, hurting, exploiting; that sexual fun and sexual passion in the privacy of the male imagination are inseparable from the brutality of male history. The private world of sexual dominance that men demand as their right and their freedom is the mirror image of the public world of sadism and atrocity that men consistently and self-righteously deplore. (*Pornography*, 69)

Andrea Dworkin touches on one of the major hypocrisies surrounding pornography; that, while publicly deploring it,

---

173 Jacques Lacan in *Feminine Sexuality*; also Mervyn Levy, 32; also Président des Brosses, quoted in Howard Hibbard: *Bernini*, 1965, 241-2: 'If this is divine love, I know what it is'

people secretly consume it. There is one rule for the public domain, but another for the private realm. In second wave feminism, the personal is political, private and public are identical. Patriarchal people, however, like to keep the public and the private quite separate. Thus, while voting for political parties which deplore pornography, people in private consume it. After all, somebody must be consuming porn somewhere. If the pornography industry is bigger than the movie or record industry, then there must be a *lot* of people consuming it.

Art and porn alike, then, are founded on patriarchal, white, bourgeois, First World, Imperialist and male tenets. Whoever the audience of pornography is – gay, straight, bi, feminist, Marxist, capitalist, communist, A, B, C1, C2, D, E, bourgeois, proletariat, etc – the content and views of pornography are white, bourgeois, First World, and male. Pornography is founded, like art and religion, on the tenets of patriarchy, where heterosexual sex is both a metaphor and a method of enforcing male power over others. 'The foundation of the family in which men are served emotionally, economically and through domestic labour, is sexual intercourse', writes Sheila Jeffreys.[174] For feminists, the sex act is an expression of power, one of the methods which men use to assert their supremacy over others. In violent situations, sex is clearly a weapon: the invading forces of many an army in history, up to and beyond Vietnam, have raped the women after slaughtering the men. Rape surrounds us, all the time: in the newspapers we read that an unnamed Dublin man raped his daughter, made her pregnant, 'hit her fingers with a hammer and slashed her stomach with a knife in separate incidents over a 16-year period'.[175]

In violent situations, it is easy to see where the power lies. In psychological or cultural realms, it is more difficult. But products such as pornography clearly reflect what people are thinking. Other forms of communication, such as newspapers and TV, also reflect what people are thinking and feeling, but pornography

174 Sheila Jeffreys: "The Censoring of Revolutionary Feminism", in Chester, 138
175 Joe Joyce: "Dublin acts after rapist father jailed for 7 years", *The Guardian*, 6 March 1993

shows vividly the desires of people. And the desires that abound in porn revolve around power, around sex without any strings attached, around objectification and control.

3

SEXUALITY, ART AND PORNOGRAPHY

What is the 'erotic' element that art and pornography claim to
describe? What is sexuality? What is the relation of sexual feelings
to their representation in art and pornography? Sexual feelings
seem to be very subjective, something experienced by individuals
in their own way. Cultural theorists and feminists have shown
that sexual feelings, which form part of sexual identities, are
shaped, influenced and controlled by cultural and political forces,
as well as by personalities and personal experiences. How we
think about our bodies and our sexuality, say feminists, is very
much dependent on our cultural environment, as well as our
experiences in childhood. As Gayle Rubin wrote: '[s]ex as we
know it – gender identity, sexual desire and fantasy, concepts of
childhood – is itself a social product.'[176] Further, there is no 'fixed'
kind of sexuality: the sexual identities of people are always

---

[176] Gayle Rubin: "The Traffic in Women: Notes on the "Political Economy" of Sex", in M.Z.
Rosaldo & L. Lamphere, eds. *Women, Culture and Society*, Stanford University Press, Stanford
1974

changing, as the cultural environment changes. The personal is political, so what happens in the sociopolitical world affects the individual's sexuality directly, according to some feminists.

When anybody tries to define or describe their sexuality, things can get very confused. For a start, there are areas or causes which people seek to advertise or defend. Christians have their view of sex, while Marxists have another view. Lumping all Christians or all Marxists together is plainly ridiculous. Yet debates on sexuality are full of such problems of generalizing and stereotyping. The problem of language, of naming and describing, is central to any debate on sexuality. People can't agree on what colour something is, or what something smells like, and they have no hope of communicating their differences, because there is no really sophisticated language of colour or smell. If people can't even describe colours fully, there seems little hope of them really describing their sexual feelings.

Many people have tried, however, to describe sex. Most of the known examples are by men. So we know what men feel during sex, or what men have tried to describe. All we get in mainstream culture are men's descriptions of sexuality.

You can find men's depictions of sexuality everywhere. It is men, for instance, who invent terms such as 'the sex act'. It is actions that patriarchal culture exalts, not states of being. As Valerie Traub puts it:

Eroticism itself is increasingly being defined less as a fixed identity dependent on the gender of one's partner, and more as a dynamic mode based on the sum of one's erotic *practice*.[177]

Sexuality can therefore be seen as not what you *are*, but what you *do*. It is not *who* is fucking *whom* (that's gossip), but *how*.[178] The question is *how is this fucking being done?* Not *why* (we know why!), *but* always *how*.

For patriarchal people, of either/ any sex, it seems it is

177 Valerie Traub: "Desire and the Difference It Makes", in Valerie Wayne, 88
178 See Valerie Traub, in ib., 83

essential to know *who* is speaking about sex. Is the author male or female (or some other gender)? What is her/ his sexual identity? Patriarchal people are disturbed when their expectations of gender are disrupted. When, say, a male author writes of lesbian sexuality as if from the 'inside', as if in the 'character' of a lesbian. For example, who is the speaker and who is the subject of this poem:

> First, I want to make you come in my hand
> while I watch you and kiss you...
> I want to make you come
> in my mouth like a storm.[179]

It seems the speaker (Marilyn Hacker) is female and she is describing lesbian sex. But the words could just as apply hetero- sexual or homosexual eroticism. Only when parts of the body are mentioned – clitoris, nipples, penis, breasts – is it possible to decipher the gender of speaker, text or subject, and sometimes not even then.

Knowing what male sexuality is like – aggressive, quick, superficial, self-centred are some of the adjectives some feminists employ – we might look at some descriptions of female sexuality. Many feminists and women artists speak of female sexuality as wild, terrifying, shocking, open, transgressive, fatal. For some feminists, female sexuality is beyond description, because it is beyond patriarchal language, which is the only language around. Men cannot control female sexuality, feminists claim, so they try to suppress it. They mystify it, they ignore it, they mock it. Men, say feminists, are scared of women and their sexuality, so they suppress women and their thoughts, feelings and acts. Or they get violent. Hélène Cixous writes:

> Men say that there are two unrepresentable things: death and the feminine sex. That's because they need femininity to be associated with death; it's the jitters that give them a hard-on! for themselves!

---

179 Marilyn Hacker: 'Noces', from *Love, Death and the Changing of the Seasons*, Arbor House 1986

They need to be afraid of us.[180]

Luce Irigaray in her famous description of women's sexuality says women have an all-over eroticism, a total body sensuality, where the whole of the skin is alive to touches. 'The whole of my body is sexuate. My sexuality isn't restricted to my sex and to the sexual act (in the narrow sense)', writes Luce Irigaray (*Je, tu, nous*, 53). Critics of Irigaray's view of women's eroticism as two lips continually embracing say: '[a]ll that 'is' woman comes to [Irigaray] in the last instances from her anatomical sex, which touches itself all the time. Poor woman.'[181]

Some feminists argue for multiple sexualities, for a plurality of sexualities, as against the standard, traditional notions of hetero-sexuality, homosexuality, lesbianism and bisexuality. Some feminists argue for the use of erotic feeling as a political weapon. Instead of denying eroticism, some feminists propound an ethics of glorifying sexuality. The body becomes then the centre, the subject, instead of being merely the object of male lust. Eroticism then becomes a source of power, as Audre Lorde explains:

> The erotic is a resource within each of us that lies in a deeply female and spiritual plane, firmly rooted in the power of our unexpressed or unrecognized feeling.[182]

Women speak of their eroticism in fiction and fantasy as being multi-sensual, not simply a matter of the visual or haptic senses, but of every sense, and more, in a synæsthetic experience.

> In those early mornings it all tasted of sex after a few moments... The whole room seemed full of our commingled, complicated smells. And over and over again I'd come, sometimes still nearly asleep

writes Sue Miller,[183] while Summer Brenner said: 'our bodies

180 H. Cixous: "The Laugh of the Medusa", in Marks & Courtivron, 255
181 Monique Plaza: '"Phallomorphic power" and the psychology of "woman"", *Ideology and Consciousness*, 4, Autumn 1978, 32
182 Audre Lorde: *Sister Outsider*, Crossing Press, New York 1984, and in Humm 1992, 283
183 Sue Miller: *The Good Mother*, Harper & Row, New York 1986

made light in a soft room'.[184] Susan Griffin has written powerfully of lesbian eroticism:

>...my most profound longings and desires, for intimacy, to know, to touch and be inside the body and soul of another, becoming and separating from, devouring and being devoured, that wild, large, amazing, frightening territory of lovemaking belongs for me not with men, but with women.[185]

Nancy Friday has collected women's fantasies in a number of books: *My Secret Garden, Women On Top* and *Forbidden Flowers.* The fantasies involve lesbianism, group sex, sex with animals, sex with pop and movie stars, rape, anal sex, domination, S/M and all manner of erotic activities. Women's fantasies, like their fictions, are wilder, larger, more amazing and more frightening, to use Susan Griffin's words, than male fantasies and fictions, some feminists claim. The books of erotic fiction and fantasy by women[186] demonstrate something of the erotic ecstasy of women which, as Xavière Gauthier writes 'is so violent, so transgressive, so open, so fatal, that men have not yet recovered.'[187] Camille Paglia has written of a new form of sexuality which is not afraid of being extraordinary:

>Neo-Sexism, or the New Sexism [is] a progressive feminism that embraces and celebrates all historical depictions of women, including the most luridly pornographic. It wants mythology without sentimentality and every archetype, from mother to witch and whore, without censorship... The New Sexism puts sensuality at the centre of our responsiveness to life and art.[188]

One aspect of art, the media, sexuality and porn is common to

184 Summer Brenner: *The Soft Room*, Figures 1978
185 Susan Griffin: *Viyella*, in Laura Chester, ed. *Deep Down*, 326
186 See, for instance, Lonnie Barbach, ed. *Pleasures: Women Write Erotica*, Doubleday, New York 1984; Laura Duesing: *Three West Coast Women*, Five Fingers Poetry, 1987; Clayton Eshleman, ed. *Caterpillar Anthology*, Anchor 1971; Summer Brenner: *The Soft Room*, The Figures 1978; Lynne Tillman: *Weird Fucks*, 1980; Jane Hirshfield: *Of Gravity and Angels*, Wesleyan University Press 1988; Jayne Anne Phillips: *Black Tickets*, Delacorte Press 1979; Marilyn Hacker: *Love, Death and the Changing of the Seasons*, Arbor House 1986; Nancy Friday: *Forbidden Flowers: More Women's Sexual Fantasies*, Arrow 1993
187 Xavière Gauthier: "Pourquoi Sorcières?", in *Sorcières*, 1, 1976, in Marks, 201-2
188 Camille Paglia: "New Sexism for women", *The Guardian*, 30 September 1993

all of them: looking. In cultural/ postmodern/ post-Lacanian theory there is a politics and a psychology of looking. It is central to art and pornography. In the Lacanian system, desire, loss, seeing, language, expression and early psychosexual conflicts are all bound up together. Art and pornography are founded, on wanting to 'have' something, but the object remains 'other' and unattainable. In art, you can repossess something that was lost – some memory, or feeling. Jacques Lacan explains how desire is based on loss:

> Desire is that which is manifested in the interval that demand hollows within itself, in as much as the subject, in articulating the signifying chain, brings to light the want-to-be, together with the appeal to receive the complement from the Other, if the other, the locus of speech, is also the locus of this want, this lack.[189]

For French feminists such as Hélène Cixous, this philosophy of 'the lack' of Lacan is ridiculous. As she writes in "The Laugh of the Medusa": '[w]hat's a desire originating from a lack? A pretty meagre desire' (in E. Marks, 262). And Luce Irigaray and other feminists have criticized the Freudian-Lacanian emphasis on the phallus as the 'transcendental signifier', as the measure of authentic sexual pleasure.[190]

The Lacanian Look emphasizes eroticism. Seeing is erotic, the eye becomes a kind of phallus, caressing the obscure object of desire, which it can never 'possess'. As the poet Rainer Maria Rilke wrote: '[g]azing is a wonderful thing.'[191] The act of looking eroticizes the object. Jack Zipes describes it thus:

> For him [Lacan], seeing is desire, and the eye functions as a kind of phallus. However, the eye cannot clearly see its object of desire, and in the case of male desire, the female object of desire is an illusion created by the male unconscious. Or, in other words, the male desire

189 J. Lacan: *Ecrits: A Selection*, tr. Alan Sheridan, Tavistock 1977, 263
190 Luce Irigaray: *Speculum of the Other Woman*, tr. Gillian C. Gill, and *This Sex which Is Not One*, tr. Catherine Porter, both Cornell University Press, New York 1985. See also: Dorothy Leland: "Lacanian psychoanalysis and French feminism: toward an adequate political psychology", *Hypatia*, 3 (3), Winter 1989, 81-103
191 R.M. Rilke, letter to Clara Rilke, 8 March 1907, in *Gesammalte Briefe 1892-1926*, Insel Verlag, Leipzig 1940, II, 279f

for woman expressed in the gaze is auto-erotic and involves the male's desire to have his own identity reconfirmed in a mirror image.[192]

The look is an assertion of male power and sexuality. For the gaze is male, and feminists have grappled with the notion of a 'female' gaze, whether there can be such a thing as a female or feminine gaze.[193] 'Male desire is presented as a response to female beauty' writes Andrea Dworkin.[194] Margaret Whitford glosses Luce Irigaray's work thus:

> Western systems of representation privilege *seeing*: what can be seen (presence) is privileged over what cannot be seen (absence) and guarantees Being, hence the privilege of the penis which is elevated to the status of the Phallus.[195]

In the Jungian system, Beatrice, Laura, Cleopatra, Isolde, Eurydice, Ariadne and all those women of myth, poetry and legend, are incarnations of the *anima*, which is, as Carl Jung explains, something all males possess: '[e]very man carries with him the eternal image of woman, not the image of this or that particular woman, but a definitive feminine image.'[196] The *anima* is 'a personification of the unconscious in a man, which appears as a woman or a goddess in dreams, visions and creative fantasies', write Emma Jung and Marie-Louise von Franz, glossing Jung's *anima* concept.[197]

Male painters throughout history have depicted their version of the *anima*, it seems. Each (male) painter has a version of the

---

192 Jack Zipes: *Don't Bet on the Prince: Contemporary Feminist Fairy Tales in North America and England*, Gower, Aldershot 1986, 258
193 Maggie Humm: "Is the gaze feminist? Pornography, film and feminism", *Perspectives on Pornography*, eds. G.Day & C. Bloom, Macmillan 1988; Lorraine Gamran & Margaret Marshment, eds. *The Female Gaze*, Women's Press 1988; E.D. Pribram, ed. *Female Spectators: looking at film and television*, Verso, 1988
194 A. Dworkin: *Intercourse*, 114
195 Marget Whitford: *Luce Irigaray: Philosophy in the Feminine*, 1991, 1990, 30
196 C. Jung: *The Development of Personality*, vol. 17, Routledge, 1954, 198; Marie-Louise von Franz: *The Psychological Meaning of Redemption Motifs in Fairy Tales*, Inner City Books, Toronto 1980, 39f
197 Emma Jung & Marie-Louise von Franz: *The Grail Legend, tr.* Andrea Dykes, Sigo Press, Boston, Mass., 1980, 64

'inner feminine figure', as Carl Jung calls it.[198] For painters, this idealized *anima* figure seems to be another manifestation of that obscure object of desire, the eroticized woman, a mirror for male lust. The equation is: the more sublime and voluptuous the woman is painted, the more sublime and voluptuous is the artist's desire. The artist's model, then, can be seen as a Jungian *anima*, heavily eroticized, a Lacanian phallic mirror.

Further; in Lacanian psychology, desire, which is the foundation of the system, is enmeshed with speaking, with creativity and art. The œdipal crisis and the repression of the desire for the mother occurs with the entry into the Symbolic Order, and the entry into language. As Toril Moi crystallizes Lacan's thought so concisely: '[t]o speak as a subject is therefore the same as to represent the existence of repressed desire.' (*Sexual/ Textual Politics*, 99-100) The links between seeing and erotic pleasure, between the eye and the phallus, are found in much of Western high culture: not only in the history of painting, but also in the great works of poets such as Dante Alighieri, Francesco Petrarch, William Shakespeare and the troubadours. In a classic text of porn, Georges Bataille's *The Story of the Eye*, there are eyes placed in mouths, vulvas and anuses. Bataille takes the Sadeian ethic of the pornographic Look to its logical, literal extreme.

Men gaze at women and manipulate them into erotic poses according to feminists. Larysa Mykyta writes that:

> The sexual triumph of the male passes through the eye, through the contemplation of the woman. Seeing the women ensures the satisfaction of wanting to be seen, of having one's desire recognized, and thus comes back to the original aim of the scopic drive. Woman is repressed as subject and desired as object in order to efface the gaze of the Other, the gaze that would destroy the illusion of reciprocity and oneness that the process of seeing usually supports. The female object does not look, does not have it own point of view; rather it is erected as an image of the phallus sustaining male desire.[199]

---

198 C. Jung: *Memories, Dreams, Reflections*, Collins 1967, 210-1
199 Larysa Mykyta: "Lacan, Literature and the Look", *SubStance* (39), 1983, 54

The pleasure of the text, whether the text is a painting, film, magazine, photograph, piece of theatre, etc, comes, according to Roland Barthes, when the Look of the spectator is aligned with that of the author.[200] What feminist criticism has done is to question the masculine 'pleasure of the text', arguing for a feminist reading of the traditional masculine or patriarchal view of texts. For some feminists, however, there can be no true 'feminist gaze', because the Look is always masculine, ultimately. If the spectator is a 'gendered object', suggests Annette Kuhn, then 'masculine subjectivity [is] the only subjectivity available'.[201] The politics of representation, which are central to the consumption of pornography and art, are weighted firmly in favour of men and patriarchy. As John Berger writes: 'men act and women appear'.[202] As Catherine King notes: 'most images in masculine visual ideology are created to empower men as spectators – that is, to see themselves as endlessly important with things laid out for their desire'.[203] Clearly, porn is a series of texts or representations that maximizes the pleasure of the male spectator. The female nude painting does the same.

This chapter has further summarized (mainly second wave) feminist views of representation of sexuality, and how those representations and images relate to pornography. Again, the issues require further analysis. And I've changed my ideas since writing this – my opinions on many of these issues have altered. For instance, when many feminists took on the issue of the exploitation of women in pornography, they were really talking about the exploitation of labour and workers in a late capitalist system (in which sexuality and erotic art has little to do with it). And if they were looking at the issues of negative images and representation of women, and the 'objectification' of women in porn and erotic art, they were really talking about issues of

200 See Laura Mulvey: "Visual pleasure and narrative cinema", *Screen*, vol. 16, no. 3, 1975, 6-19
201 Annette Kuhn: *Women's Pictures: Feminism and the Cinema*, Routledge & Kegan Paul 1982, 63
202 John Berger: *Ways of Seeing*, 1972, 47
203 Catherine King: "The Politics of Representation: A Democracy of the Gaze", in Bonner, 136

representation in general – in every media and artform, not just the narrow area of videos, magazines and photos in the porn industry.

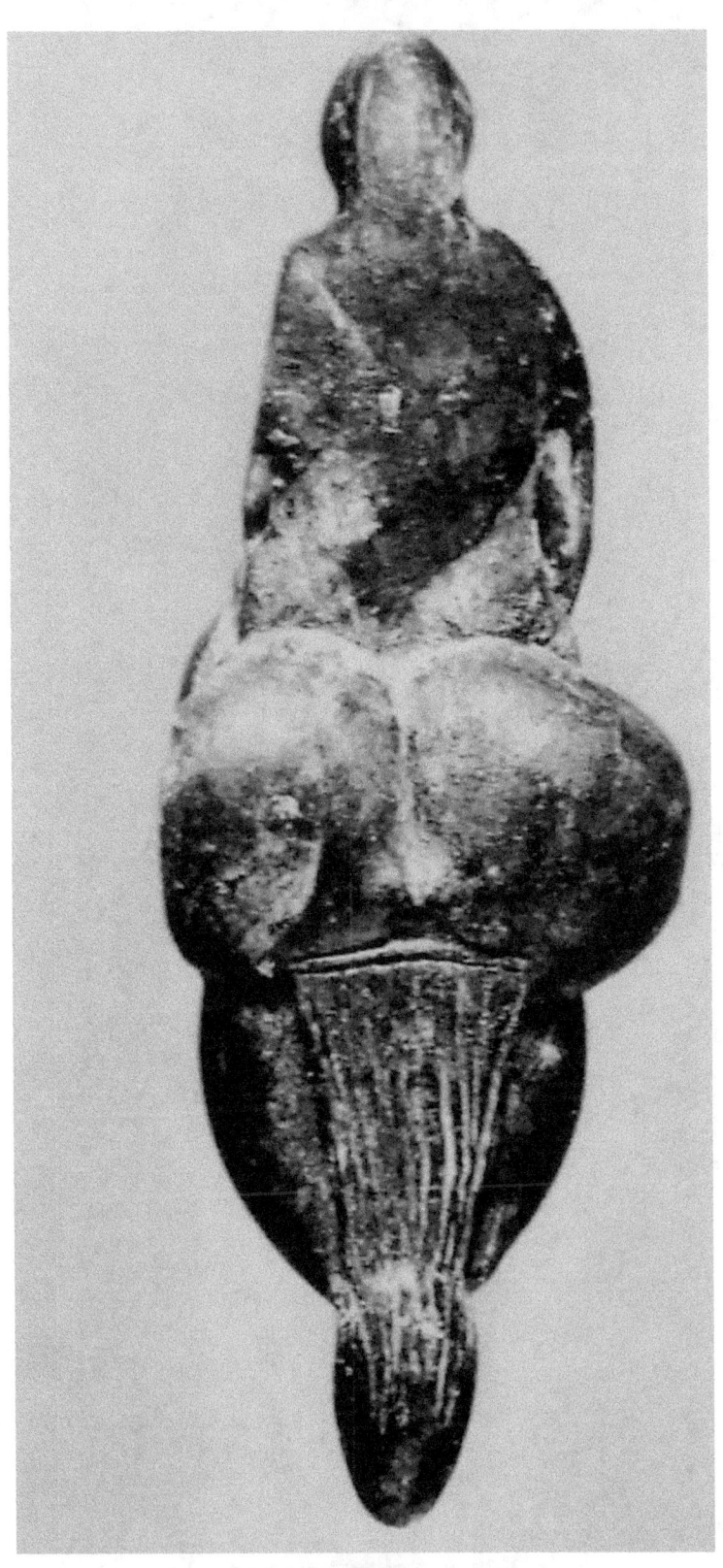

Venus of Willendorf, prehistoric, Vienna

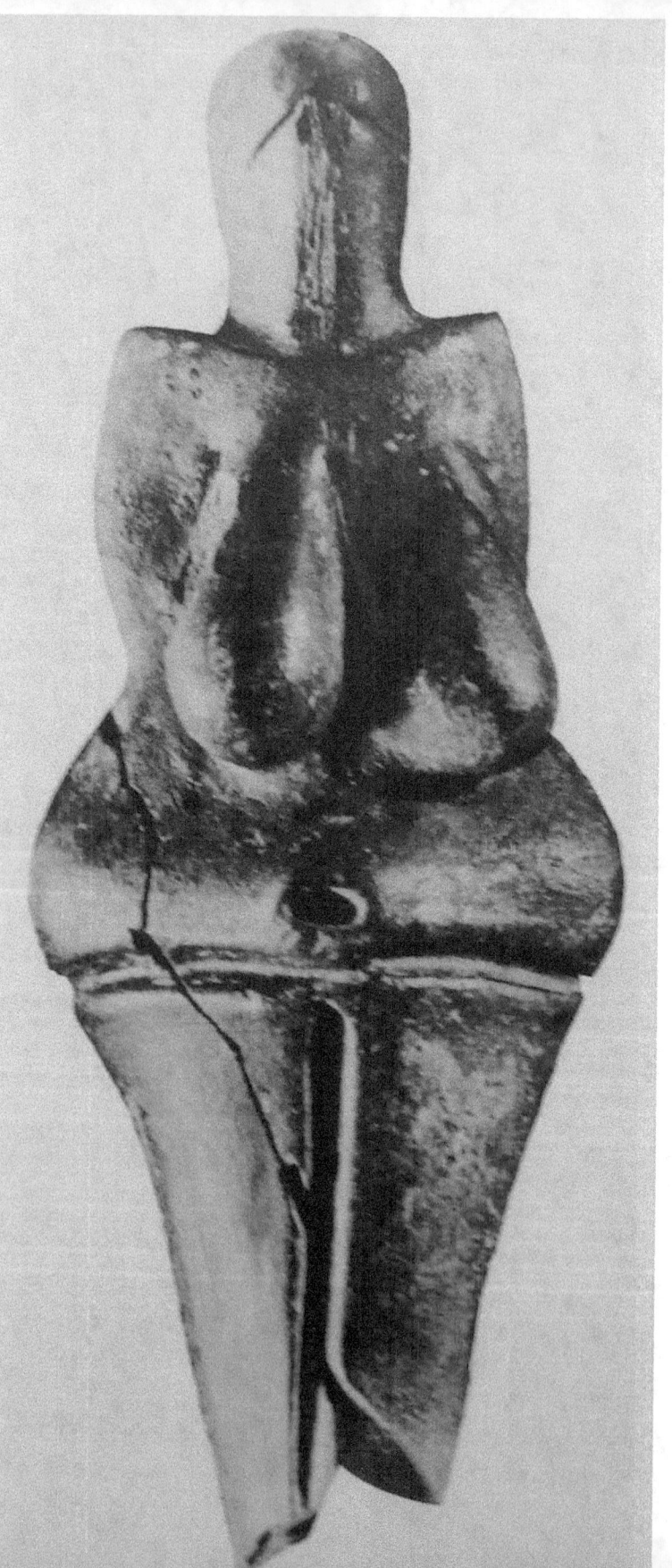

Stone Venus,
prehistoric.

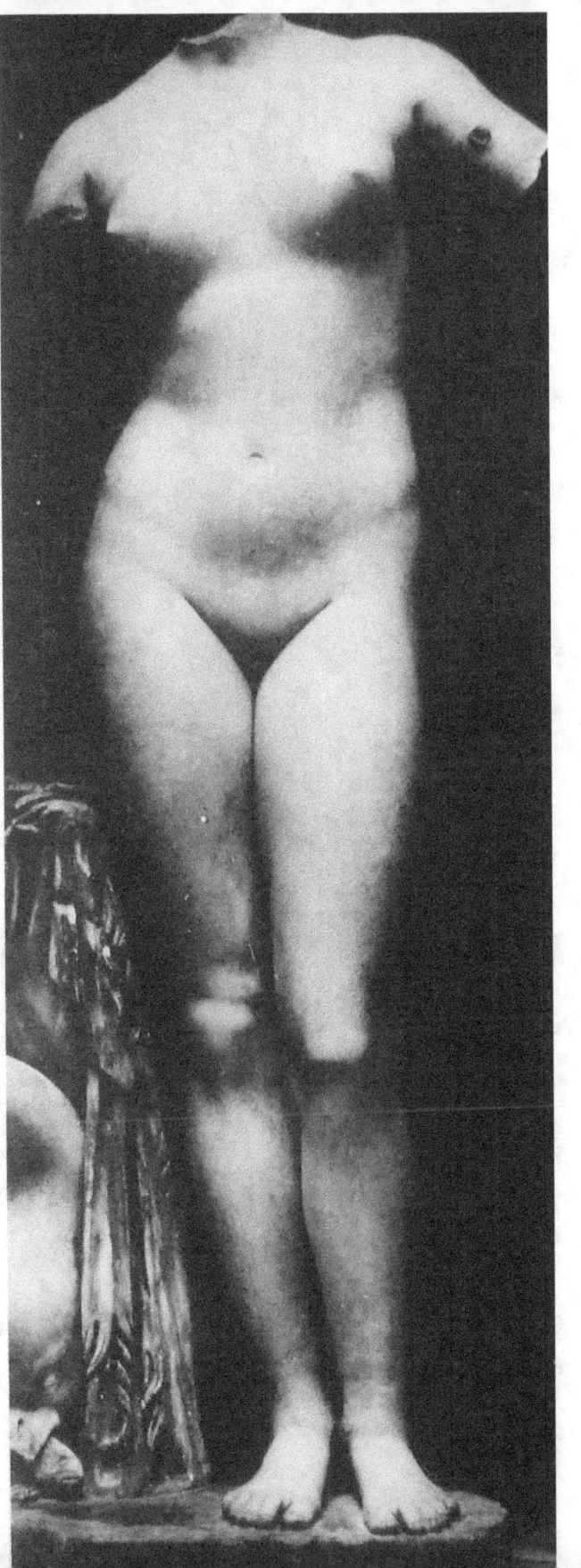

Aphrodite of Cyrene

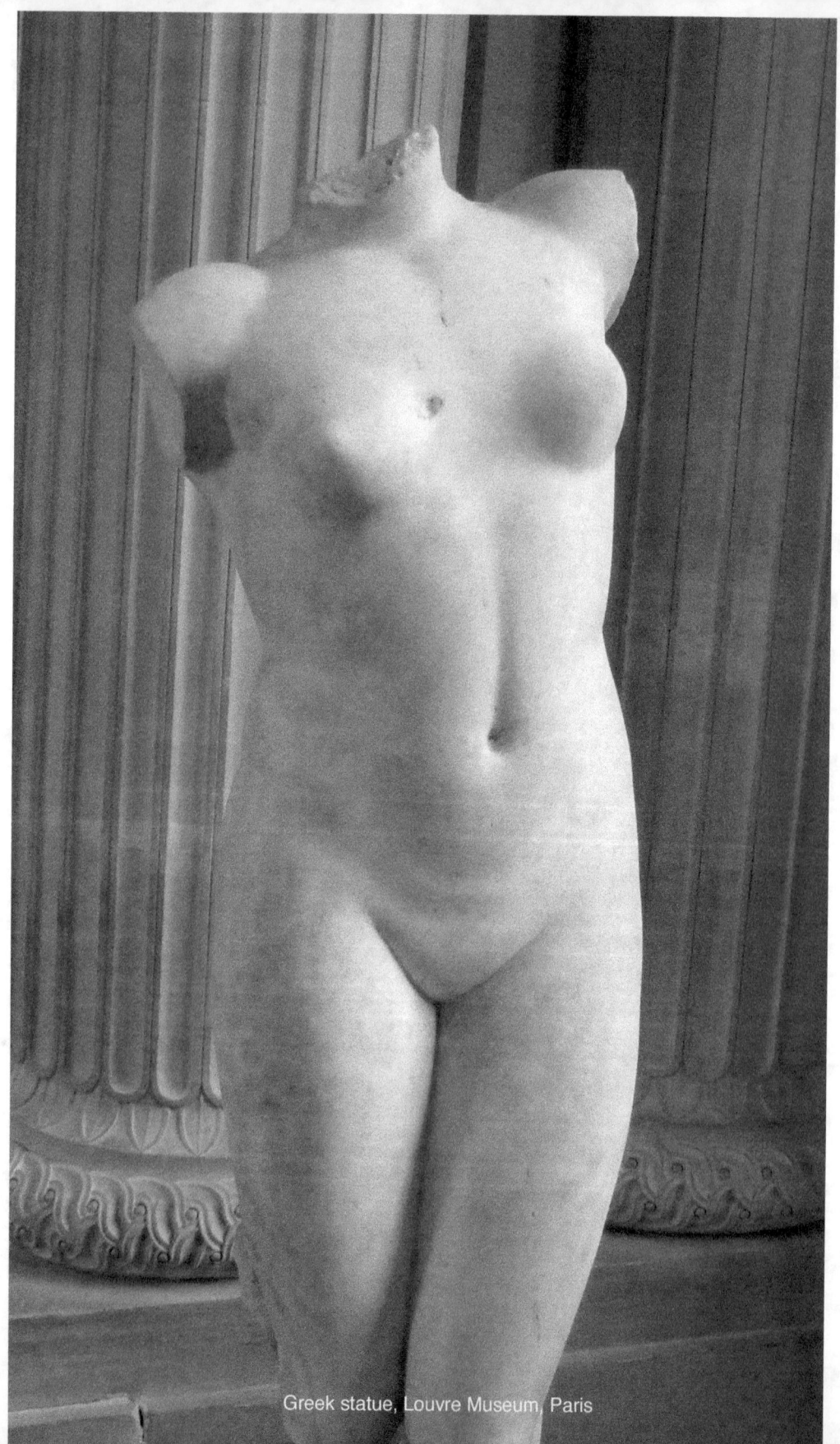

Greek statue, Louvre Museum, Paris

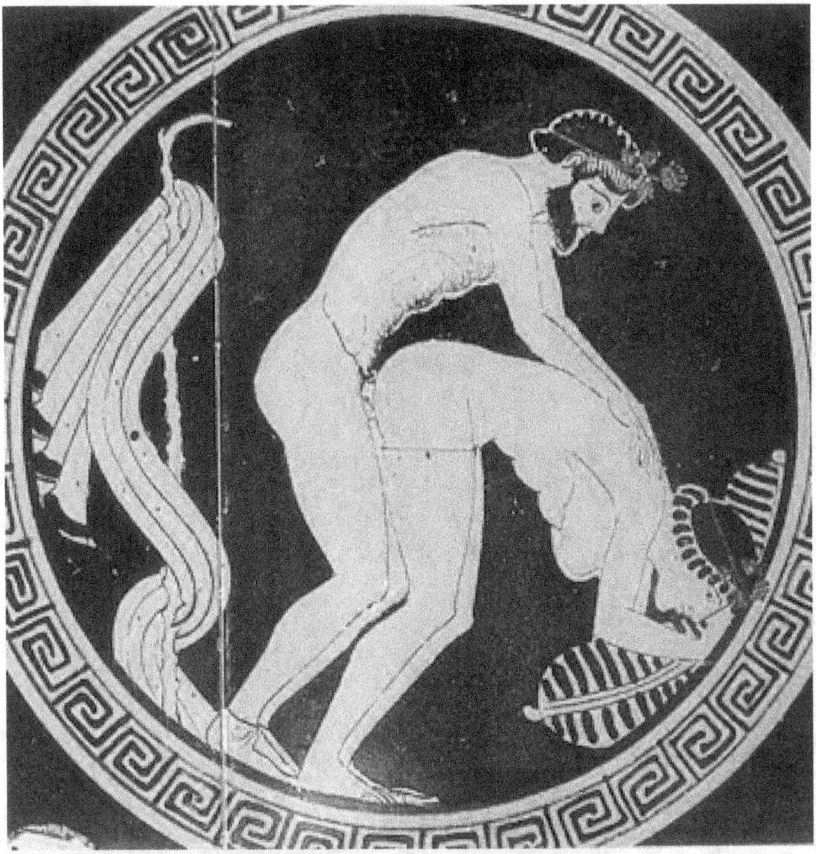

Greek vases,
5th century B.C.

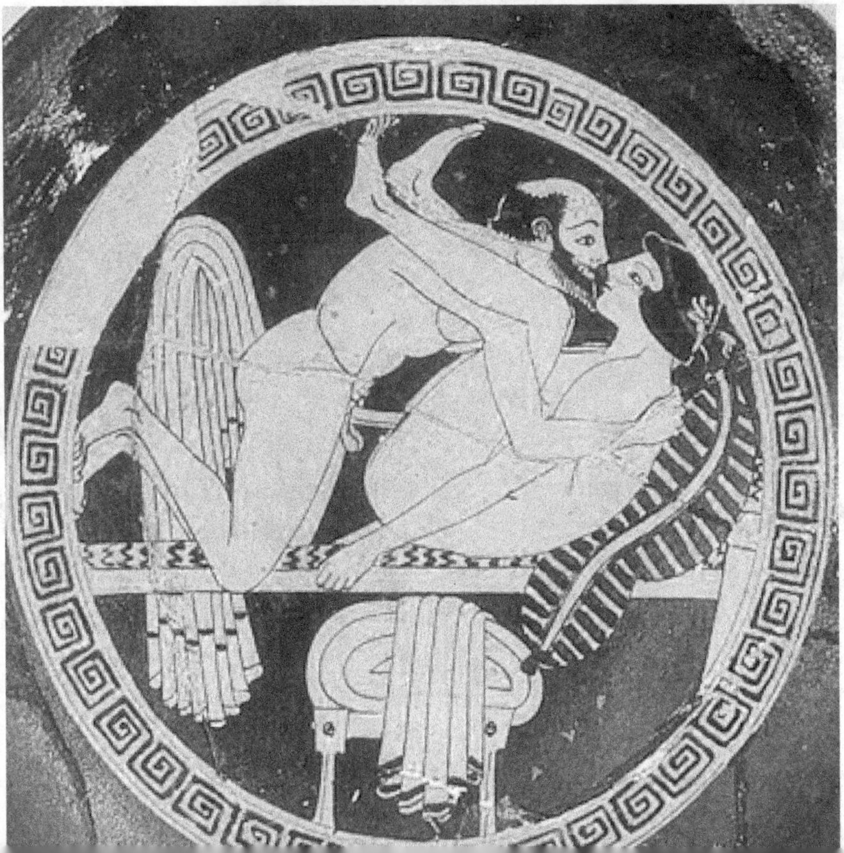

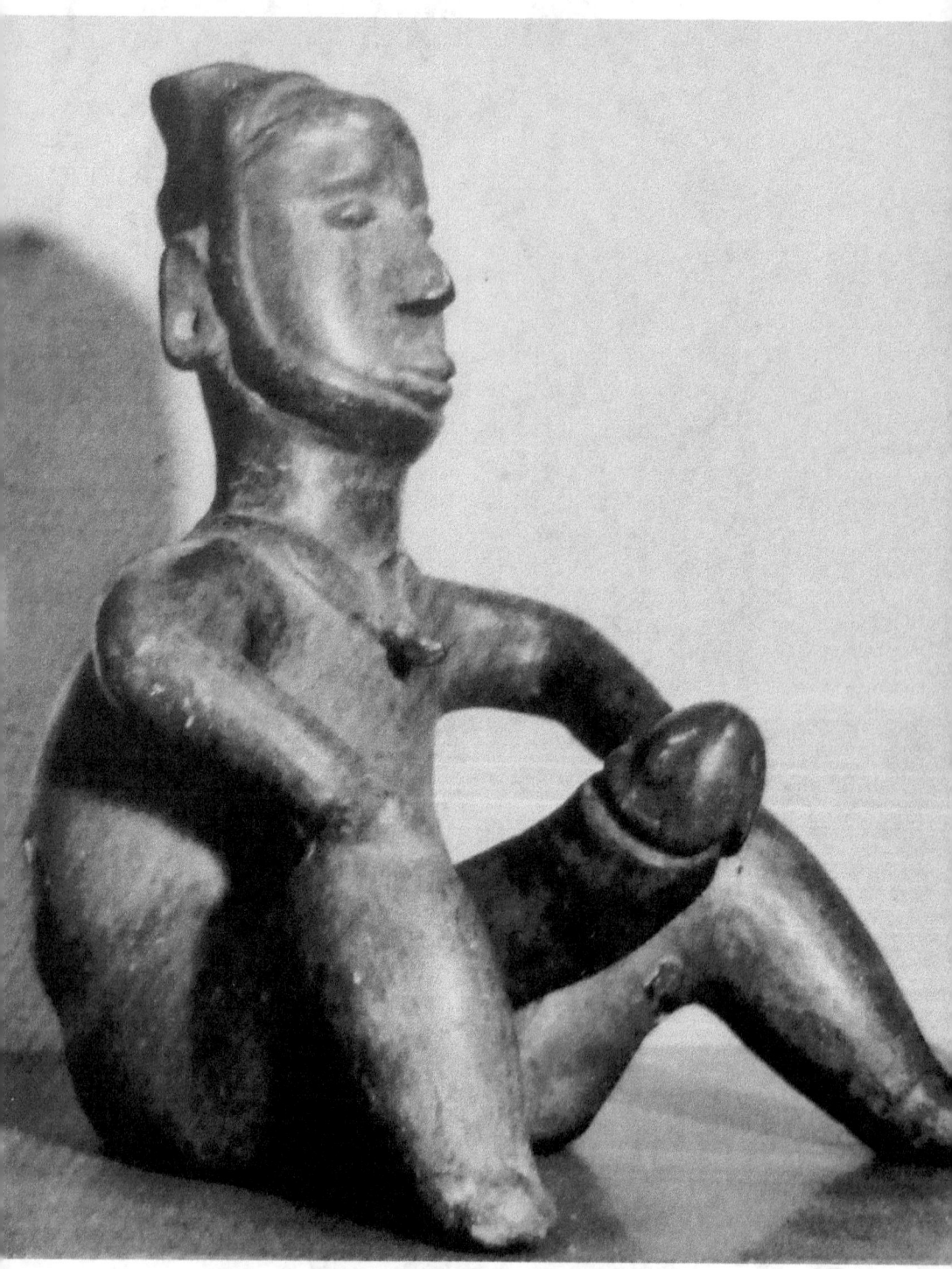

Terra cotta figure, 3rd century BC. Mexico

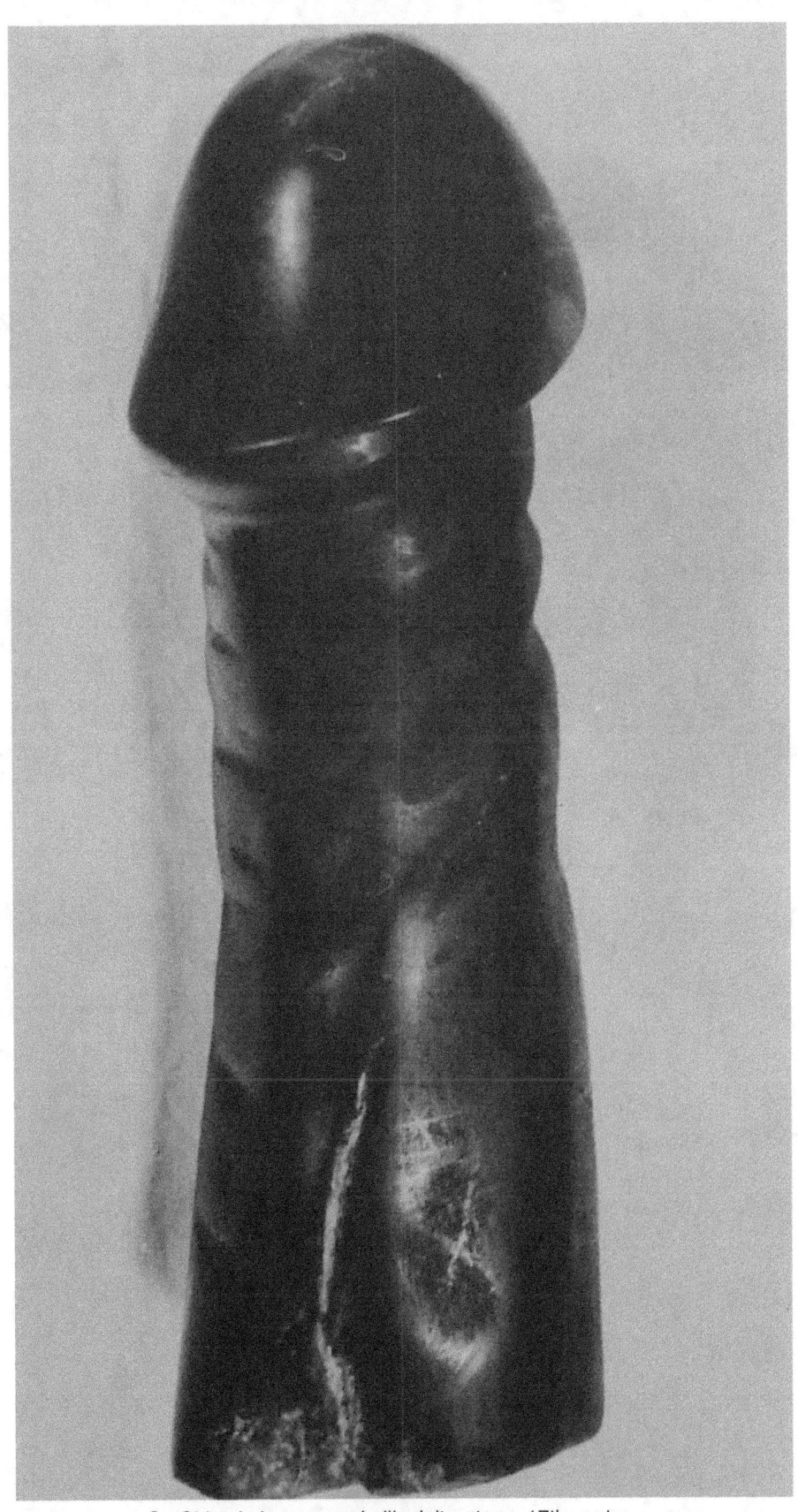

Go-Shintai, Japanese phallic deity, stone, 17th century

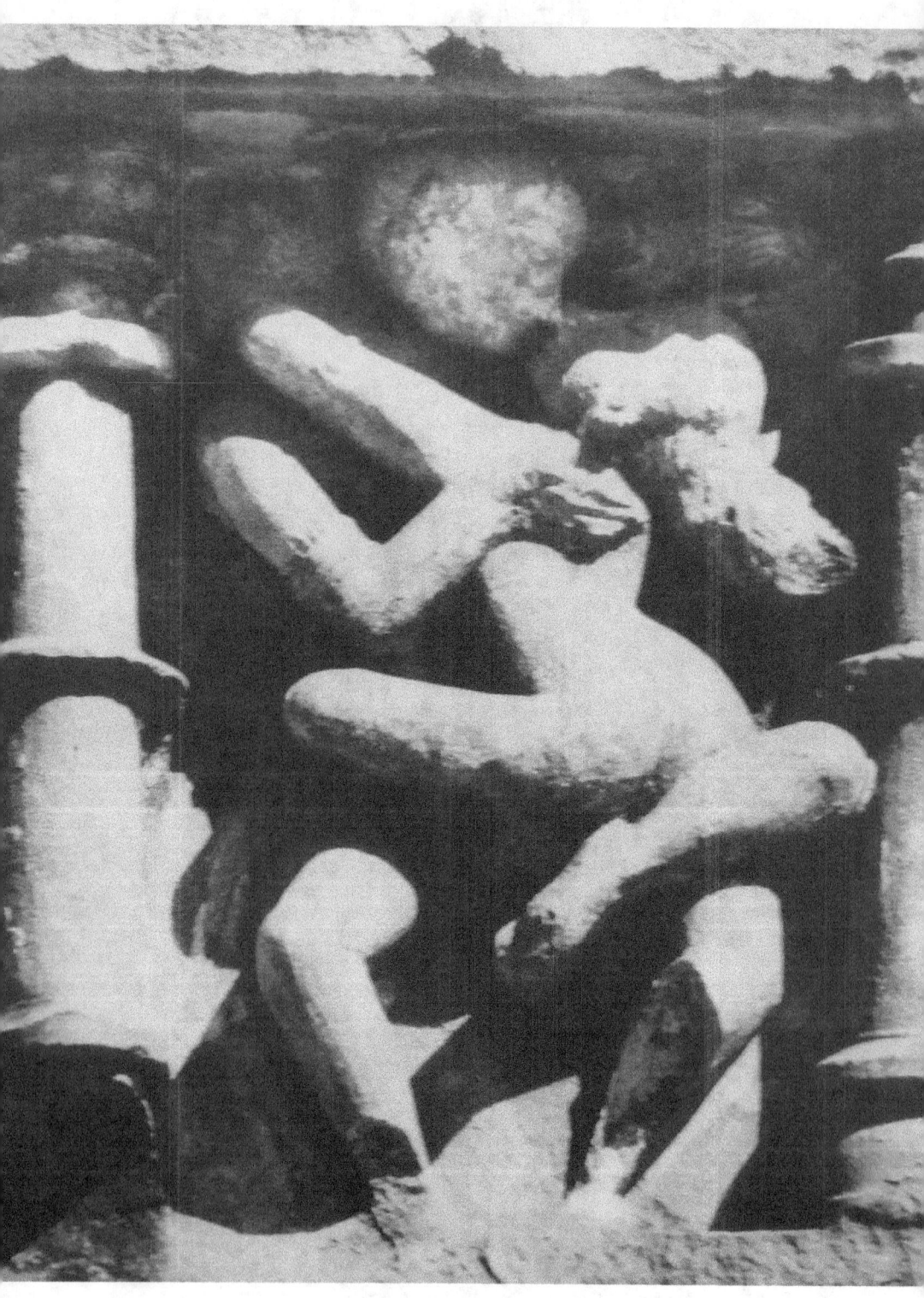

Khajuraho temple, 9th-11th century, North India

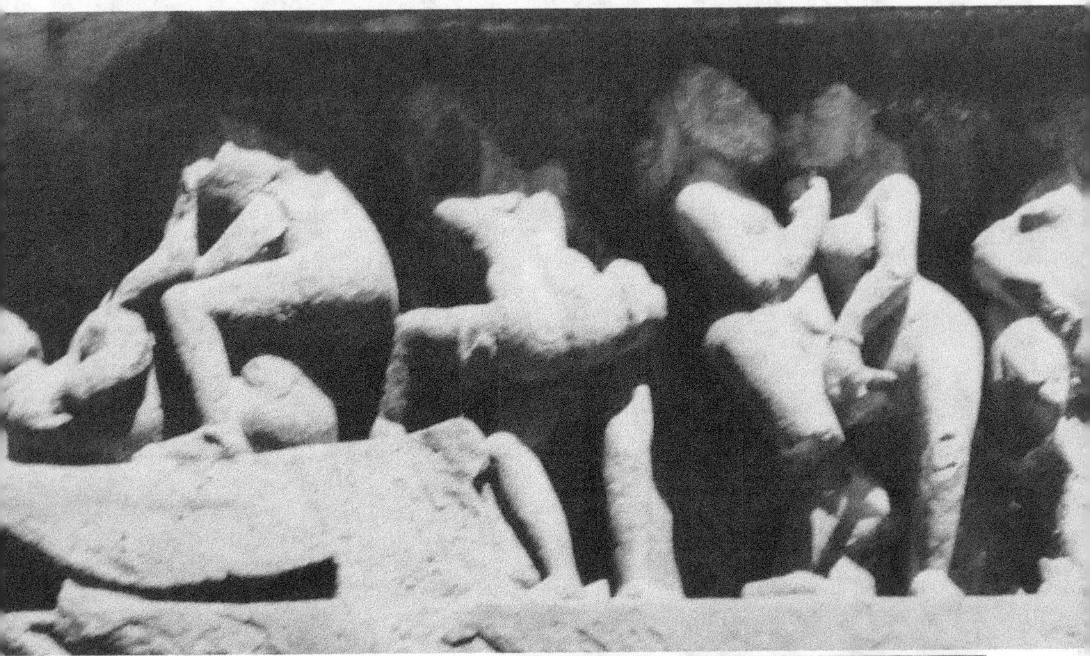

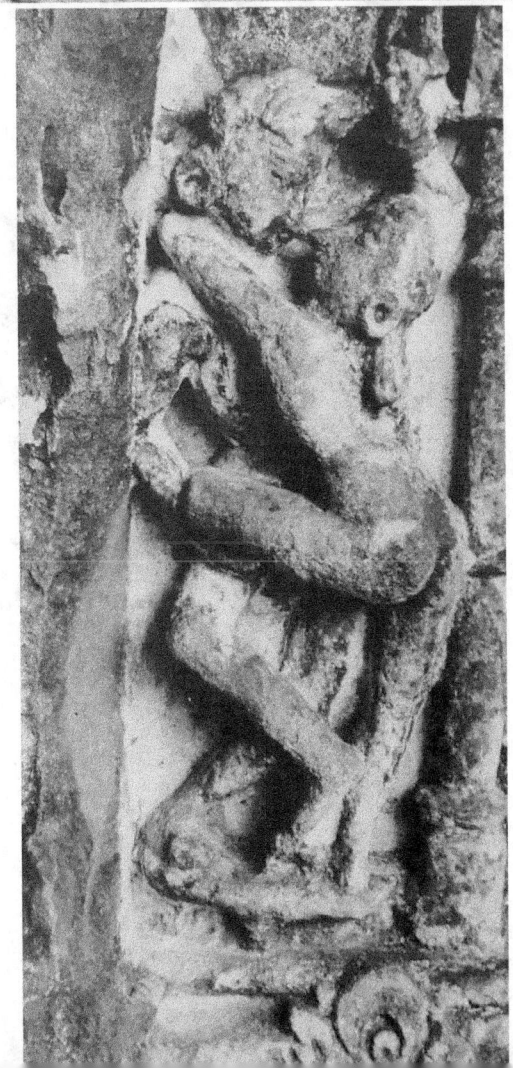

Khajuraho temple, 9-11 century,
Northern India, right.

Temple, 11th century, Mount Abu
area, Northern India

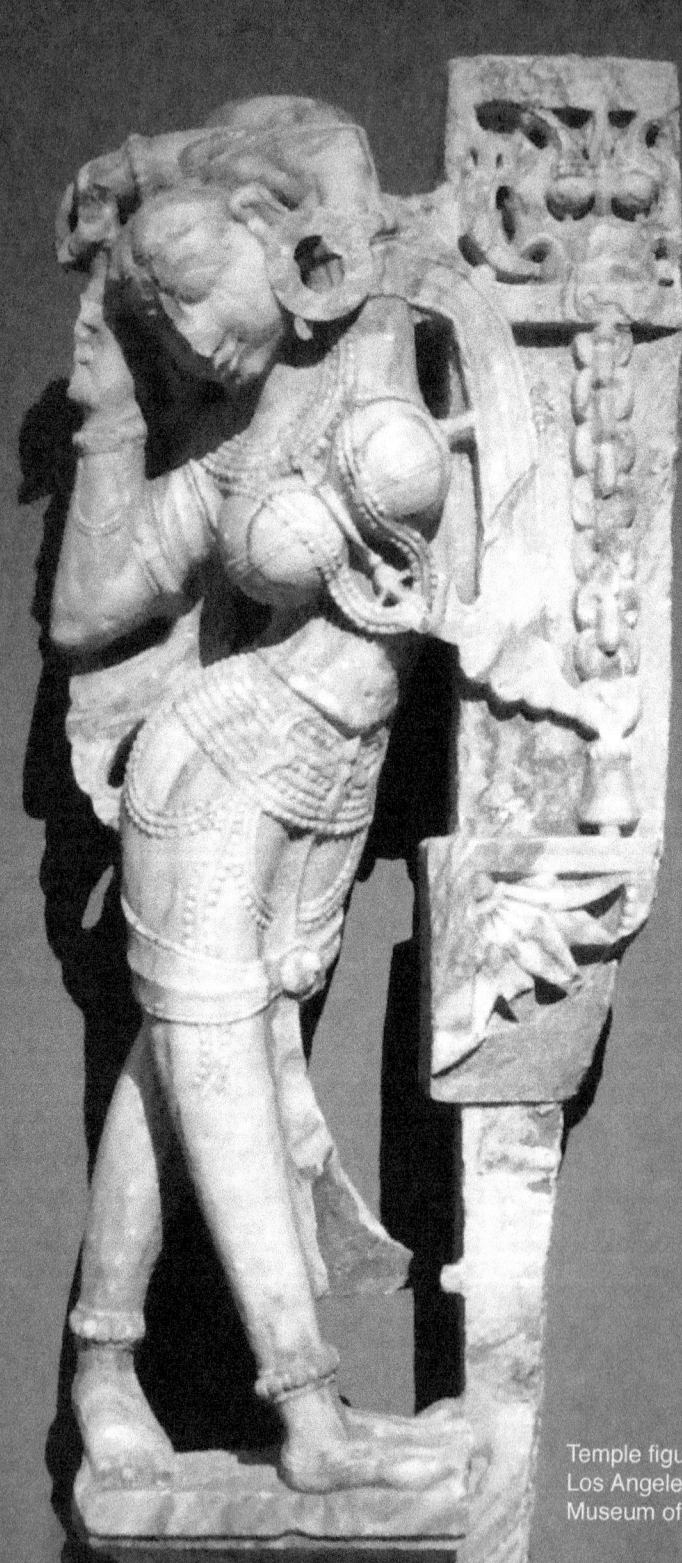

Temple figure, Indian,
Los Angeles County
Museum of Art

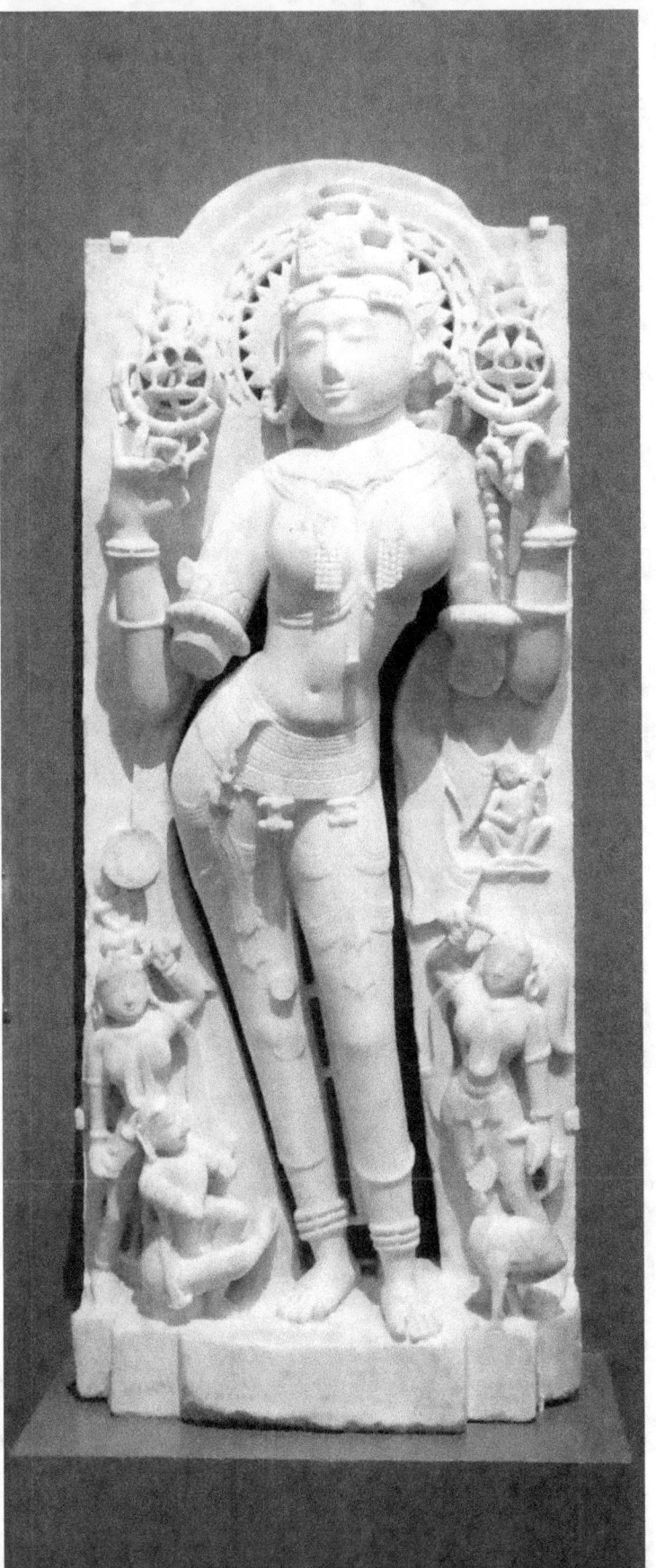

Indian temple figure,
Norton Simon Museum,
Pasadena, CA

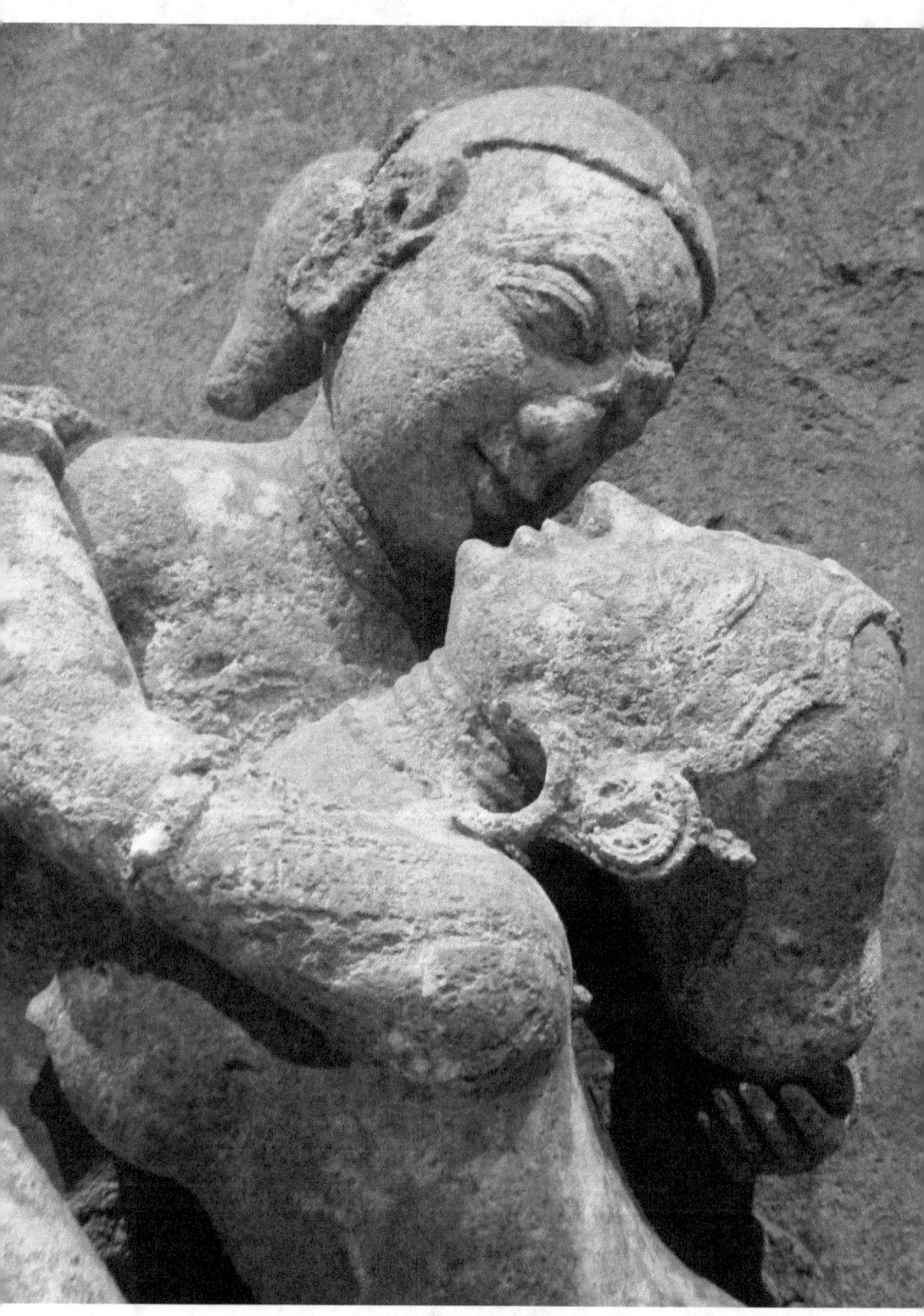

Temple figures, Indian, Norton Simon Museum, Pasadena, CA

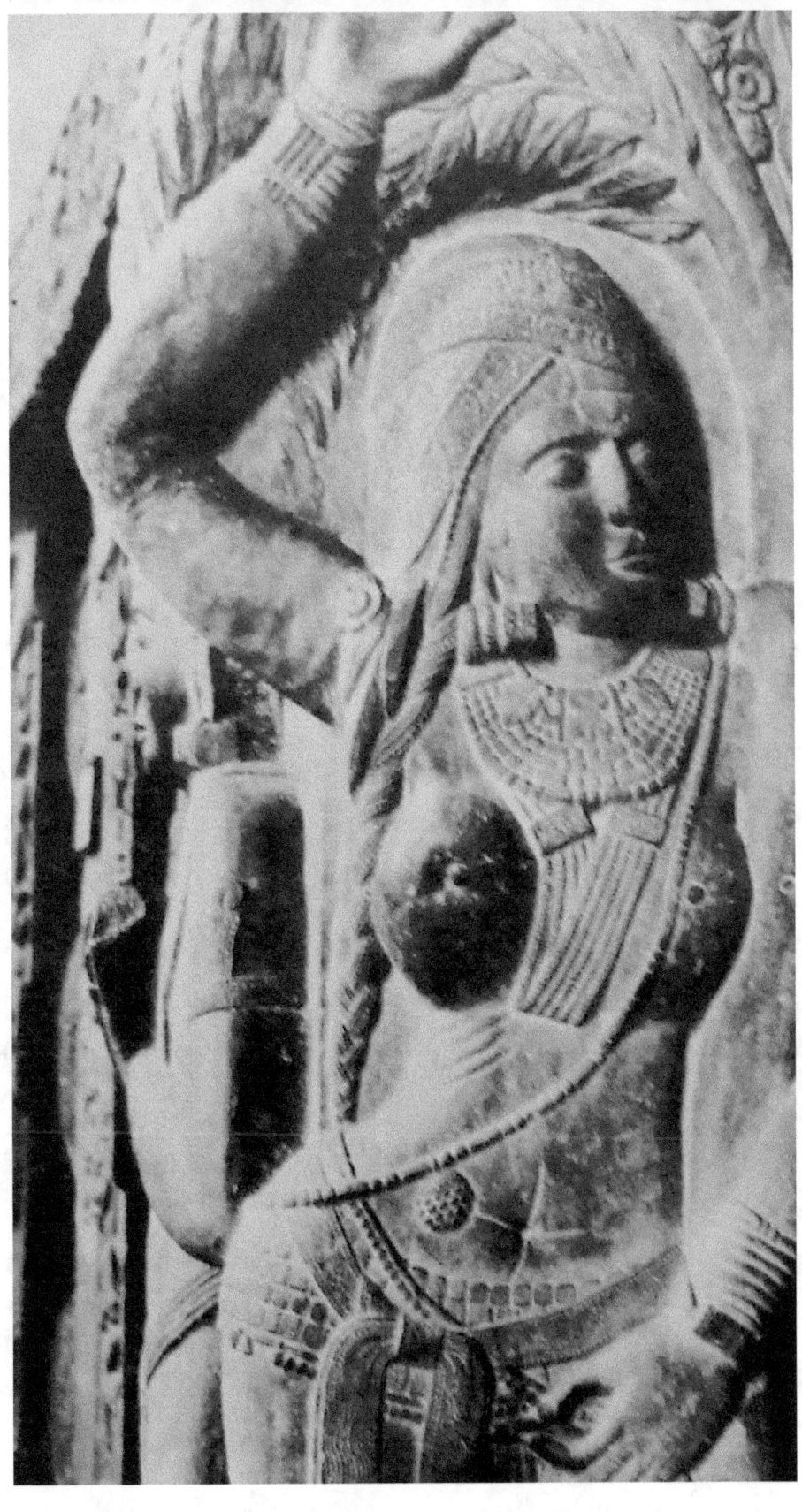

Yakshi figure, Indian Museum, Caluctta

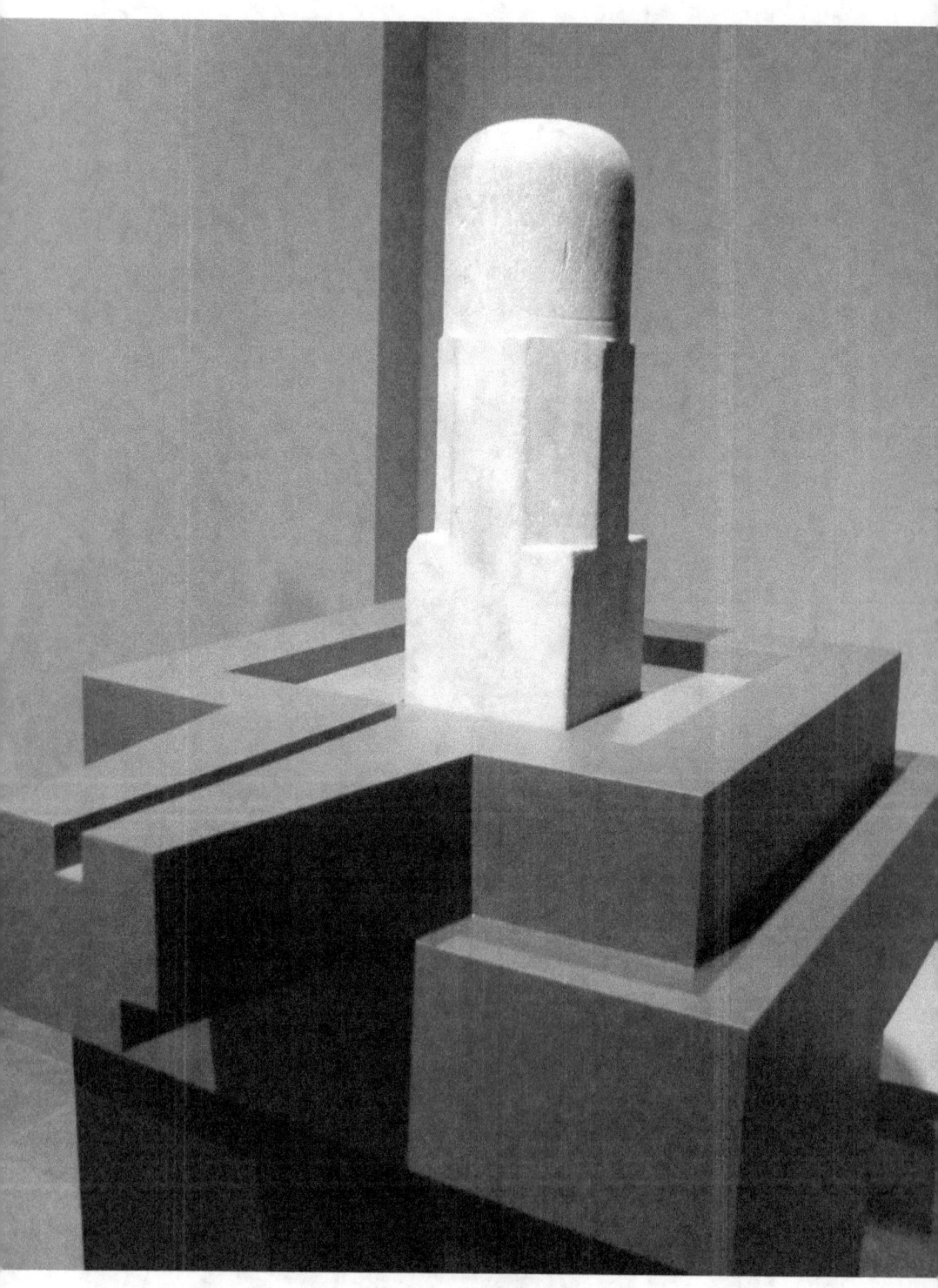

Lingam and Yoni, Cambodian, Norton Simon Museum, Pasadena, CA

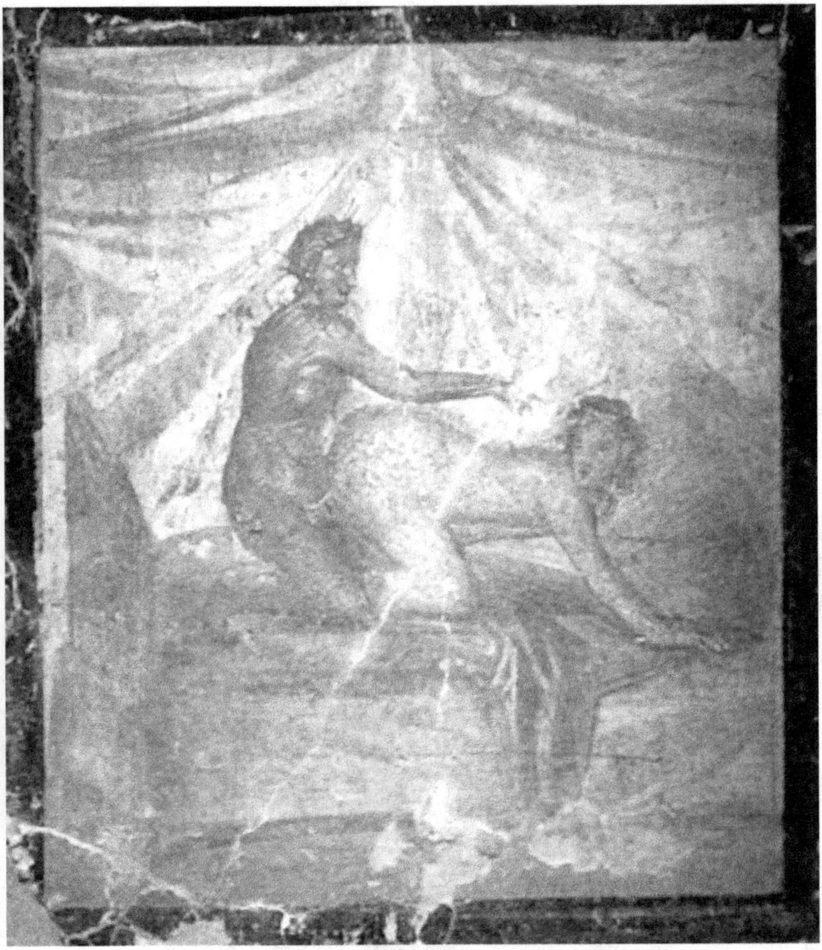

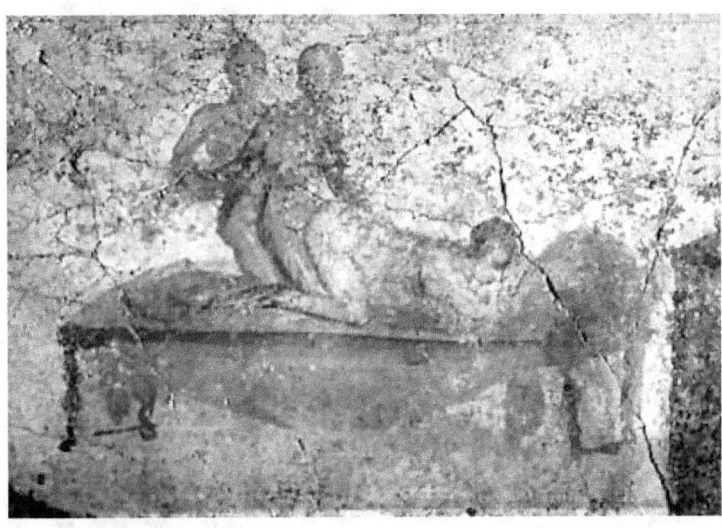

Ancient Roman art, Pompeii

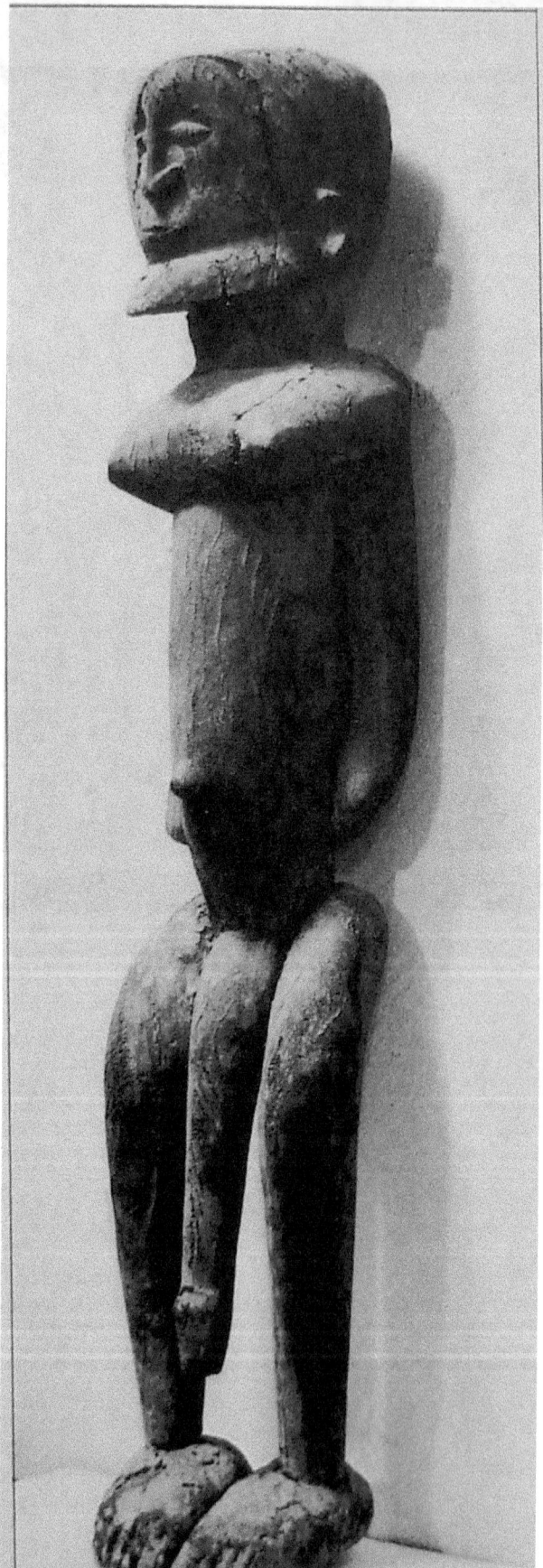

Wood figure, Ivory
Coast

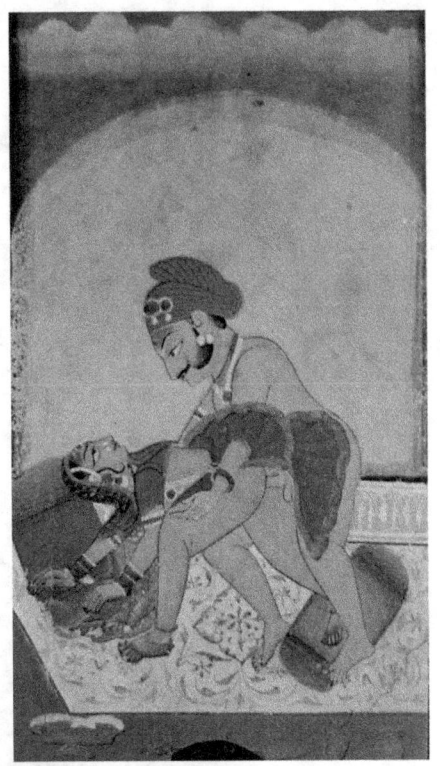

Indian erotic art:
Rajput, late 18th century, above.
Mogul style, 18th century, below.

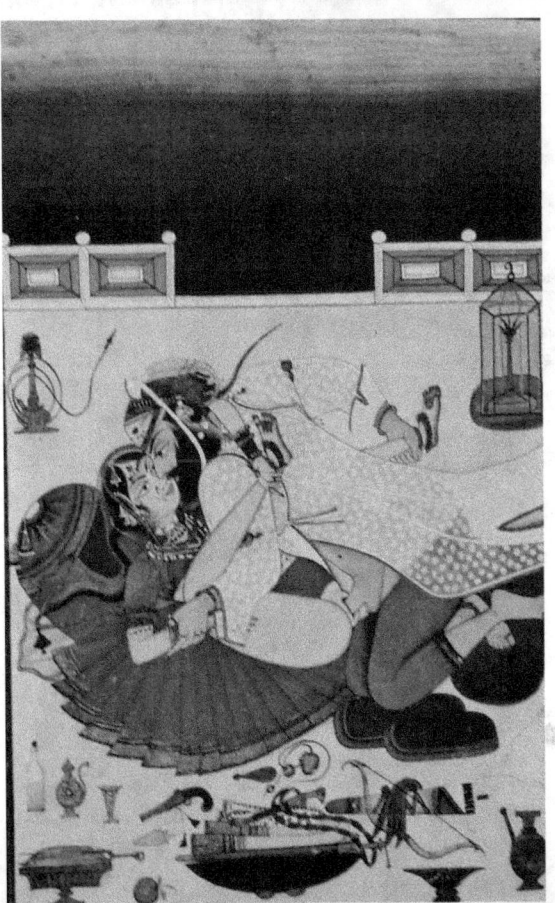

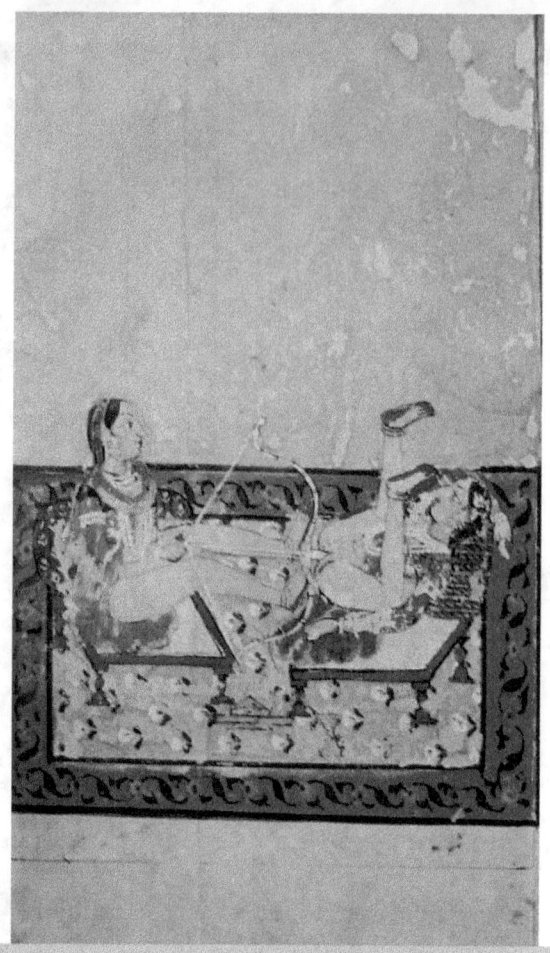

Indian erotic art:
mid-18th century, below.
Rajput miniature, 17th
century, above

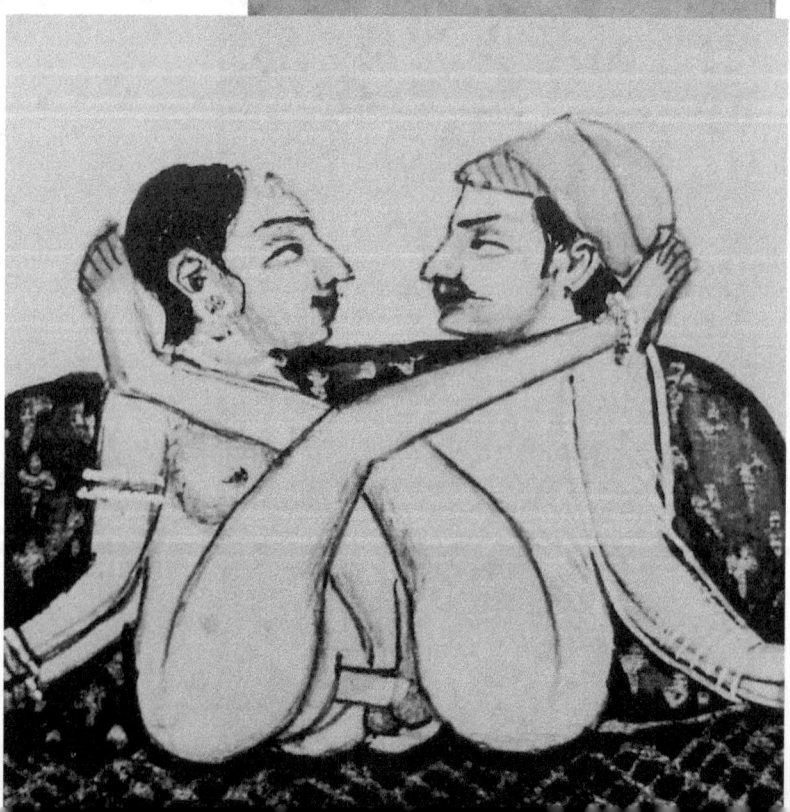

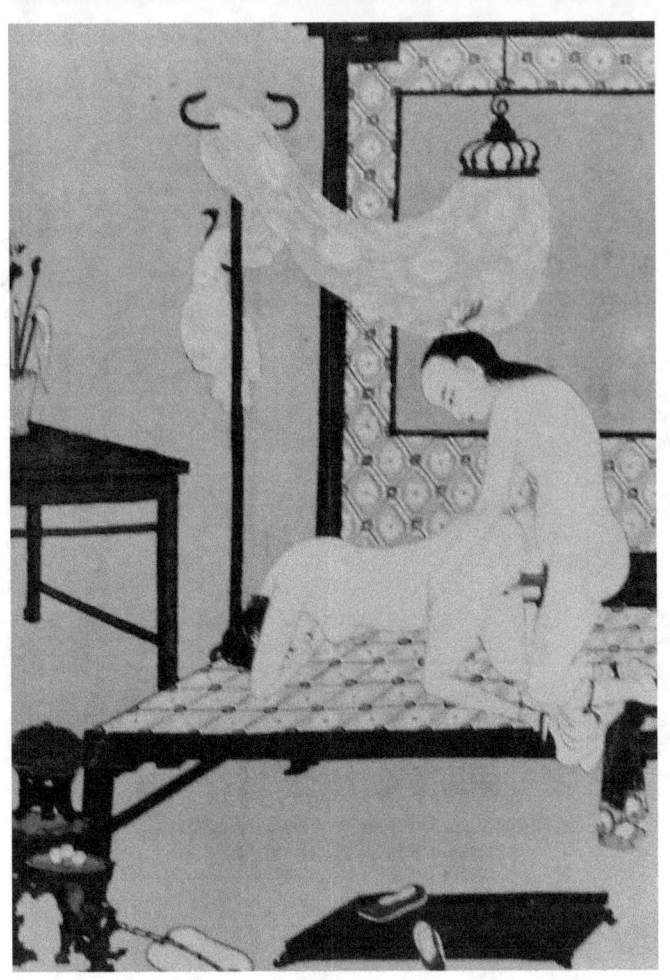

Chinese erotic art: erotic album, above.
Painted scroll, ukiyo-e school, c. 1640, below

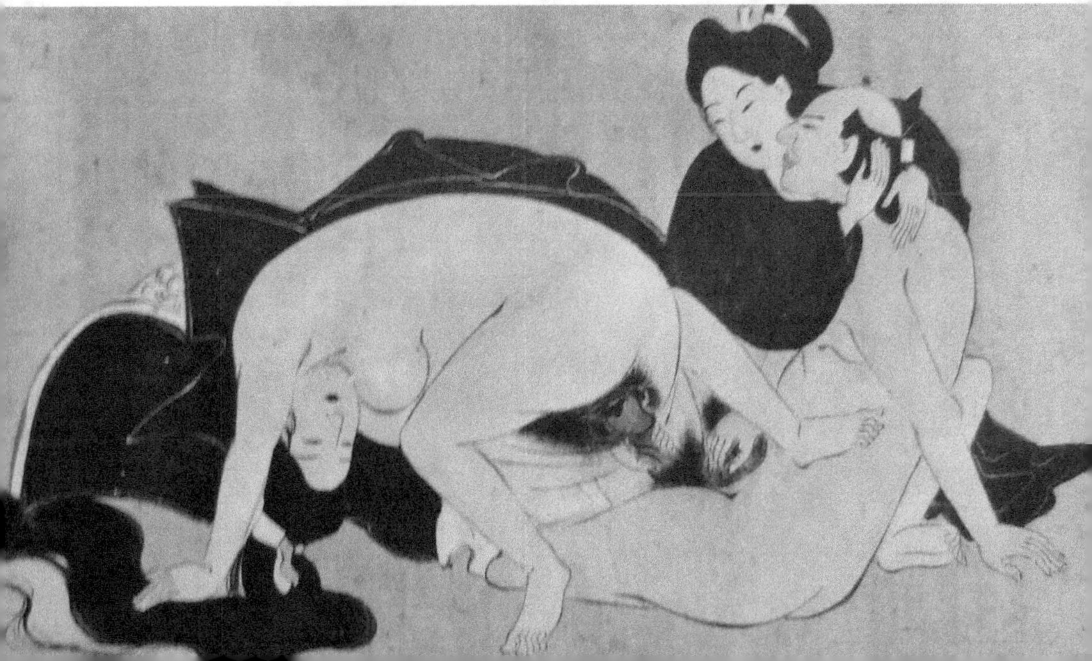

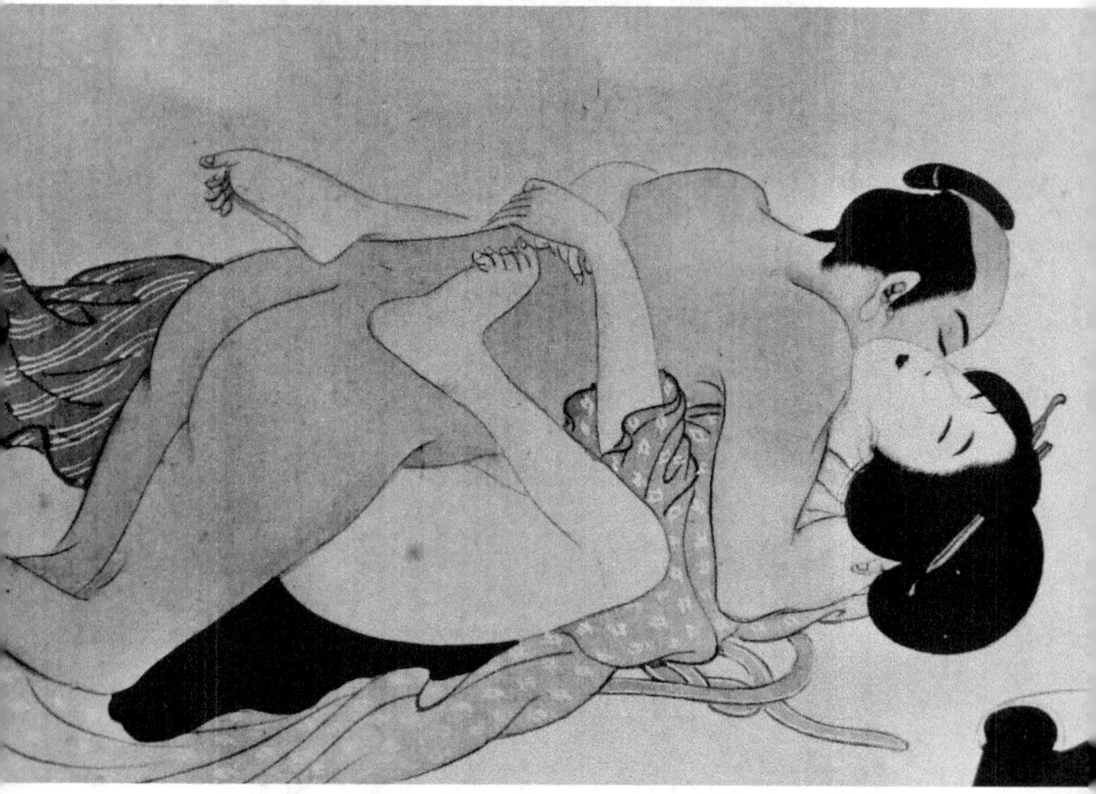

Two Hokusai school pictures: woodblock, 19th century, below.
Hokusai school, c. 1830, above.

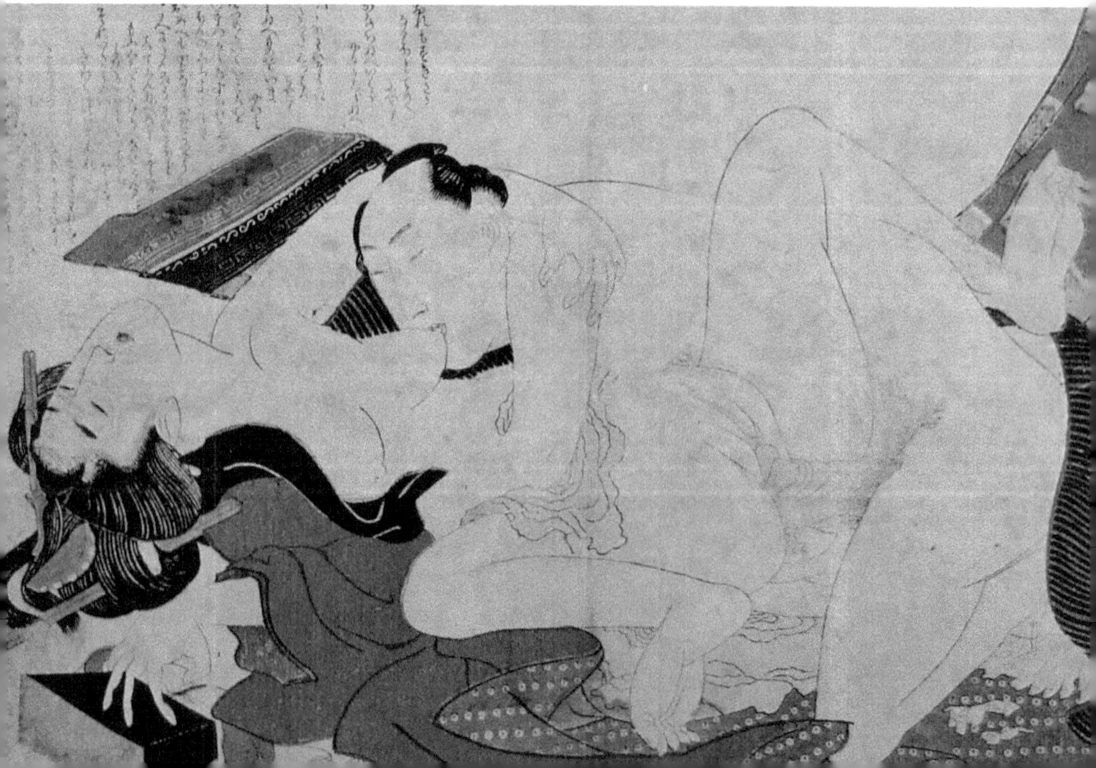

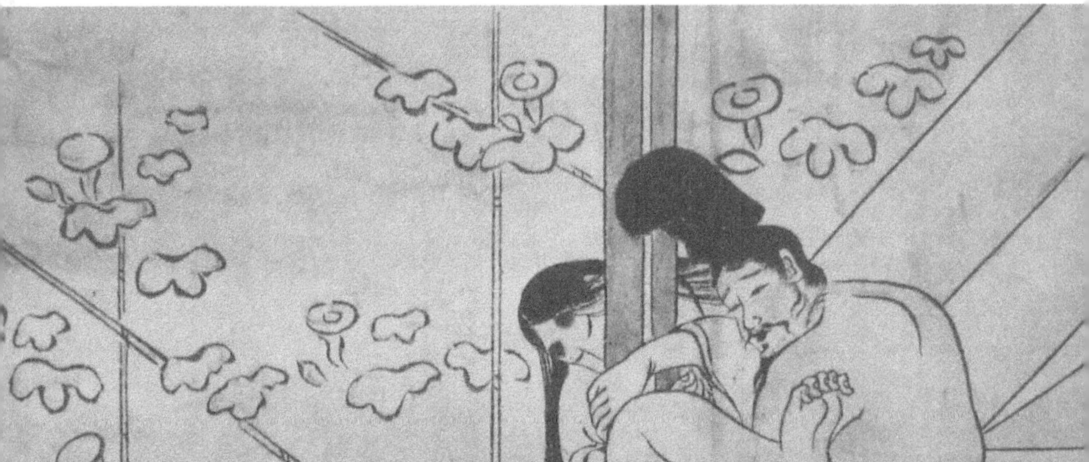

Japanese erotic art. Brushwood fence scroll, 1800s, above. Woodblock, below

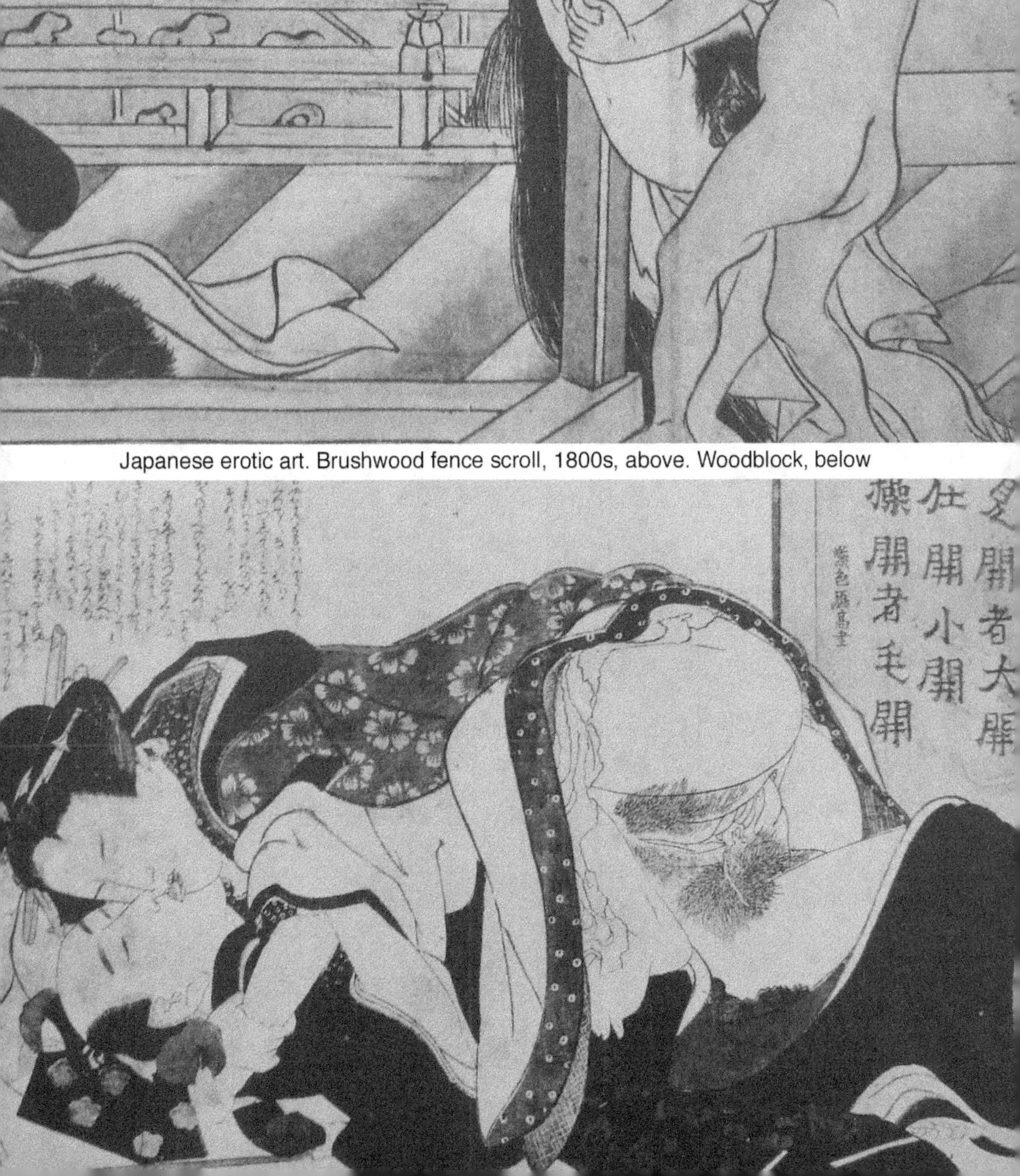

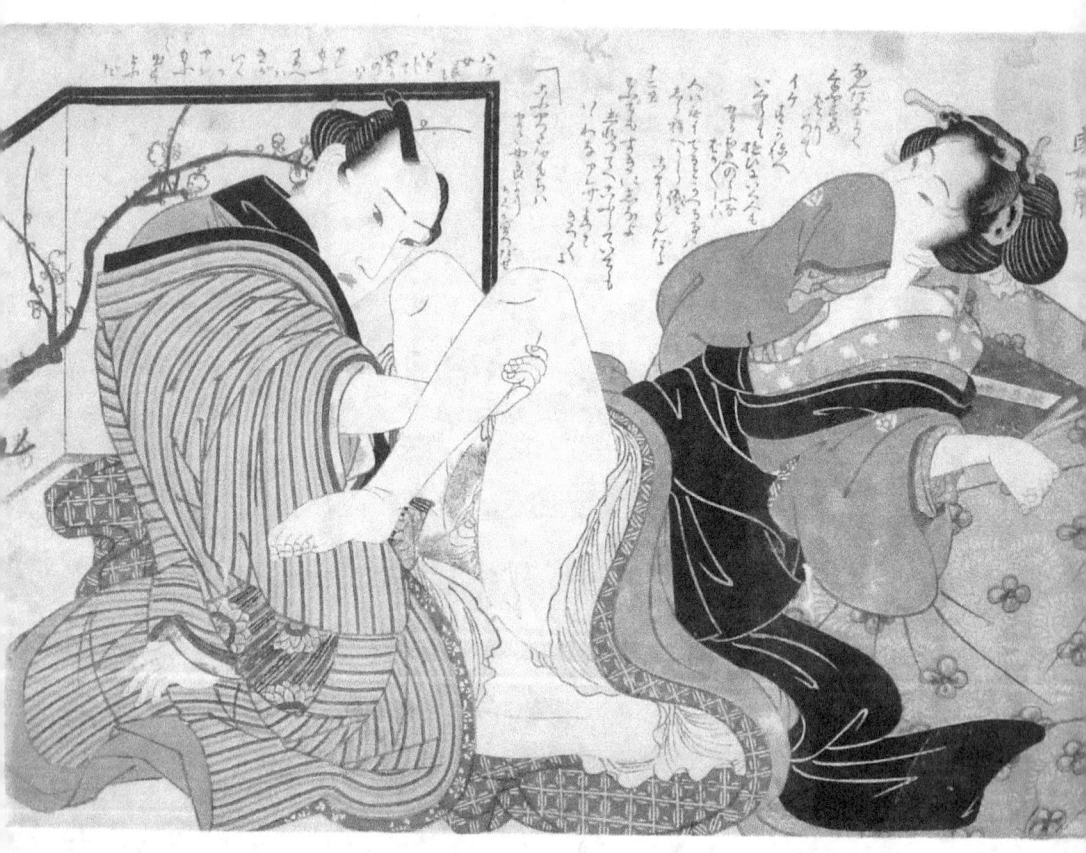

Japanese print, by Eizan

Part Two

PREHISTORY

THE ORIENT

ANCIENT ART

RENAISSANCE

1

EROTICISM
IN PREHISTORIC ART

It would be possible to argue that prehistoric art is patriarchal and masculine in nature, with its images of hunting and killing animals, its emphasis on death and survival (masculine, Existential concerns, from Charles Darwin to Jean-Paul Sartre), and the harshness of its environment. A discourse of heroic survival against the odds, against a hostile and unforgiving natural world. In fact, there is a mass of feminine mystery and imagery in prehistoric art: for instance, in the many statues or figurines of nameless Goddesses, known as "Stone Venuses",[1] which have been found.[2] There is a widespread acceptance of Goddess worship as being older than God worship. The Goddess, wrote Robert Graves, is 'immortal, changeless, and omnipotent'.[3]

1 *Venus of Willendorf*, Austria, limestone, palæolithic (end of Gravettian); *Venus of Kostenki*, Moravia, mammoth ivory, palæolithic (Gravittian)
2 The modern artist Louise Bourgeois has produced sculptures that are very much like the "Stone Venuses": her *Stake Woman* is a rounded, headless, armless form, with two prominent 'breasts' and the overall shape of a vessel(*Stake Woman*, c. 1970, pink marble, 11.4cm high, private collection).
3 Robert Graves: *The Greek Myths*, I, Penguin 1948, 13

In the beginning, it seems, was the Mother, not the Father. As Robert Briffault remarked: '[t]he All-Mother is older than the All-Father'.[4] Some commentators extend Goddess religion back beyond the cults of Classical and ancient Goddesses – before the era of ancient world deities such as Isis, Ishtar, Aphrodite, Diana – to prehistoric times.

Of course, no one can say for certain that prehistoric people believed this or that. We do not have any writing from the prehistoric period. We have artifacts and buildings. These are largely to do with death – all those tombs and graves filled with objects, the bones smeared with red ochre (perhaps alluding to the (menstrual) blood of life), and so on. Thus, anthropologists conclude that death was a major factor in prehistoric religion, for death was a primal certainty, inescapable, always there, always having to be dealt with.[5] A host of writers and thinkers have suggested that the 'eternal feminine' – variously termed the Earth Mother, the Mistress of All, the *plenum*, the *mater*, the Lady of Wild Things, the Magna Mater, Matrix, Ma-Gog, the Great Round, the Primum Mobile, the Tellus Mater – was the Goddess, a female deity who presided over all life and death.[6]

There is a widely held belief that in prehistoric times the mysteries of life – birth, growth, love and death – were bound up with the feminine. The Goddess is thus the manifestation of a relation with the world, the expression of a 'mystic solidarity' with the earth, with agriculture, with animals, with survival. Any number of commentators have noted the connections between women, wombs, fertility, growth, agriculture, sexuality, death, and religion. Mircea Eliade voices the typical view:

> The sacrality of sexual life, and first of all of feminine sexuality, becomes inseparable from the miraculous enigma of creation. Parthenogenesis, the *hieros gamos*, and the ritual orgy express, on

4 Briffault: *The Mothers: A Study of the Origins of Sentiments and Institutions,* Allen & Unwin 1927, III, 180

5 See Weston La Barre: *The Ghost Dance,* Allen & Unwin 1972

6 See Marija Gimbutas, Monica Sjöo, Shirley Nicholson, Ean Begg, Robert Graves, Elinor Gadon, Merlin Stone, Esther Harding, Peter Redgrove, Marina Warner, Barbara Walker, J.G. Frazer, Erich Neumann, Joseph Campbell, Geoffrey Ashe, Robert Briffault and Bachofen, who have all written about the Goddess

different planes, the religious character of sexuality. A complex symbolism, anthropocosmic in structure, associates woman and sexuality with the lunar rhythms, with the earth (assimilated to the womb), and with what must be called the "mystery of vegetation."[7]

If you want to see evidence of the feminine or the Goddess everywhere, you can. It's easy. Take the circular shapes of Avebury or Stonehenge, Britain's two great stone circles: these have to do with the ancient symbolism of the circle, with time, seasons, cycles, infinity, the 'great round' of life: this is the Goddess. The circle becomes a womb, if you like, the circular space in which the mysteries of life are experienced, and later are ritualized. The circle is female, if you want.

One can see the Goddess or the 'eternal feminine' in those "Stone Venus" figurines, and, later, in the Neolithic stones or menhirs, the standing stones, some of which had Goddesses carved onto them.[8] One can see the feminine in the long uterine passages and entrances to tombs, so that the poetic connection of womb = tomb has an ancient dimension, as well as occurring in Elizabethan poetry, for instance (William Shakespeare in particular was fond of the womb/ tomb trope, later taken up by Samuel Beckett). Thus, the bones covered in red ochre are put back into the 'womb' of the Earth, and bodies in burial lie in the foetal position.

Female eroticism plays a large part in prehistoric art. Women, in the carved figurines are mothers, and birth and motherhood are exalted. Hence some people think women were at the centre of prehistoric life in some places. Women, some thinkers reckon, held positions of power: they controlled 'trade' in sexual pleasure, for instance; they could withhold pleasure, and thus, with their knowledge of the menstrual cycle, they could exert power over men.[9] Eventually, men took over most forms of 'trade', until, as French philosopher Luce Irigaray pointed out in *Ce sex qui n'en*

7 Mircea Eliade: *A History of Religious Ideas*, 40-1
8 Menhir statue of a woman, sandstone, St-Sernin, France. Neolithic, c. 2000 BC, Musée des Antiquités
9 See Chris Knight: *Blood Relations*, Yale University Press 1991; Peter Redgrove: *The Black Goddess*; Penelope Shuttle & Peter Redgrove: *The Wise Wound*

est pas un: '[t]he trade that organizes patriarchal societies takes place exclusively among men. Women, signs, goods, currency, all pass from one man to another'.[10] Mary Jane Sherfey has written this of the controversial matter of sexual politics in the prehistoric era:

> There are many indications from the prehistory studies in the Near East that it took perhaps five thousand years or longer for the subjugation of women to take place. Data from the 12,000 to 8,000 B.C. period indicate that pre-civilized woman enjoyed full sexual freedom and was often totally incapable of controlling her sexual drive. Therefore, I propose that one of the reasons for the long delay between the earliest development of agriculture (c. 12,000 B.C.) and the rise of urban life and the beginning of recorded knowledge (c. 8,000-5,000 B.C.) was the ungovernable cyclic sexual drive of women. Not until these drives were gradually brought under control by rigidly enforced social codes could family life become the stabilizing and creative crucible from which modern civilized man could emerge.[11]

Whatever the conflicting views on prehistoric sexuality, it is always seen as heterosexual. Fiercely heterosexual. It is never homosexual – and as for lesbian, no way. As for any other kinds of sexuality, no way. Only when one reaches the ancient Greek era do you find modern thinkers acknowledging homosexuality or anything other than heterosexuality. But homosexual sex, lesbian sex, bestiality, necrophilia – every sex act imaginable has probably been practised since the beginnings of humanity.

It is the *representations,* the *discussions,* the *thoughts* about and of sexuality that are heterosexual. In other words, what is known about prehistoric sexuality comes from depictions of certain kinds of sexuality. And we know that pictures often have little to do with realities. For instance, a picture of a kiss has hardly anything to do with the actual *experience* of a kiss. So those prehistoric images of men hunting, or of animals, or of squatting women giving birth, or of faceless Goddesses, probably have little to do

10 Luce Irigaray: *Ce sexe qui n'en pas un*, Minuit 1977, in Marks, 107
11 Mary Sherfey: "A Theory on Female Sexuality", in S. Cox, ed. *Female Psychology: The Emerging Self*, Science Research Associates, Chicago 1976

with the *realities* of prehistoric life, which we can know very little about now.

The views on prehistory, then, say more about the people who are propounding the views than about prehistory itself. Views on prehistoric eroticism say more about the psychologists, anthropologists, biologists, historians and thinkers who make those views, than about prehistoric eroticism itself.

Those images of fertility magic or hunting magic form only a tiny part of what palæolithic people got up to. You can only draw so many conclusions from such images. There is a gulf, as artists know, between realities and representations. You might have all manner of feelings about something – sexuality, say – but your representations of those feelings only form a tiny part of what you really feel. What's on paper, or in a painting, or in a performance, is only a tiny aspect of all you feel. Artists know the limitations of representations. Some artists spend their lives hacking away at the same basic feeling or image (J.M.W. Turner with his skies, Mark Rothko with his abstract colourfields, Samuel Beckett with his ever-reduced texts, and Francesco Petrarch writing the same basic sonnet of lost love), but still feel they have only partially addressed what they really wanted to do or express.

So those prehistoric images of animals on cave walls, or anonymous women in stone figures, probably have little to do with the *reality* of prehistoric life. We can only infer a little back from those images. And what is inferred, by anthropologists, historians, psychologists, etc, is that prehistoric was largely hetero-sexist. All those Goddess images, for instance, are more than counterbalanced by images of death and killing of hunting and sacred animals, of a very patriarchal view of life. Men still celebrate hunting, and it seems it was no different ten thousand years ago. During and after the last Ice Age, life was probably as fiercely male-dominated, culturally as well as physically, as it is now. Things haven't changed that much.

While it's nice to think of the "Stone Venuses" as proof of the religious significance of women in the palæolithic era (c. 30,000-

10,000 BC), they are stereotypes too. Stereotypes of woman as divine nurturer and carer. Prehistoric representations, then, can be seen as pornographic, in the sense that pornography objectifies people sexually, reduces them to genitals. There are a lot of genitals in prehistoric art, as in Neolithic art. There are the usual phalluses and wombs, men dressed in animal skins, with the phallic horns or antlers on their head, men as ithyphallic hunters or shamen. Phallic cult are found everywhere, in all times of history, in one form or another. During the ancient Roman honeymoon, for instance, the bride was expected to sit on the erect phallus of a statue of the god Tutinus, before going to the marriage bed.[12]

One thing is certain: art was, originally, religious. It had a religious function. Modern commentators sexualize prehistory, so that everything connotes sexuality in one way or another. So that, according to the modern view, people in ancient times were rutting away madly, emulating and far surpassing the animals they hunted in terms of sexual appetite. The modern view promotes, in fact, the male idea of paradise: when not eating or hunting (hunting being a synonym for men's violent 'games', such as war), people were tupping like mad things. This is a patriarchal paradise, a golden age when only a bearskin stood between people and pleasure.

Art critics and historians look back fondly on erotic primitive art, for there was a time, it is felt, when sexuality was freely expressed in art, without the 'hang-ups' of the modern era. Clearly, art critics, sociologists, historians and psychologists look back at prehistoric and primitive art nostalgically, in their search for a 'sexually liberated' space, to use that telling 1960s term. Depictions of sex abound, or seem to, in prehistoric and ancient art. A 2000 B.C. terracotta relief from Babylonia shows two people making love from behind; a Libyan demon makes love to a woman, in a 5000 B.C. engraving; someone sucks someone else's penis on a ceramic vessel from 500 A.D. Peru; two animals

12 See Julius Evola, 174; A. De Marchi: *Il Culto Privato in roma Antica*, Milan 1896

copulate in a 300 B.C. Peruvian caring.[13] Figures with over-size erections are commonplace – they are fertillity figures, aids in magical rites, talismans and fetishes. J.G. Frazer prudishly writes in *the Golden Bough*: 'ruder races in other parts of the world have consciously employed the intercourse of the sexes as a means to ensure the fruitfulness of the earth.[14]

In prehistoric art, sexuality is associated with religion; sexuality is religious, and the religious dimension has an erotic element in it. Notions of fertility, magic, sexuality, agriculture and so on are entwined. The obviousness of such statements needs to be remembered constantly, especially since our era is so unmagical.

---

13 *Terracotta relief depicting copulation from behind*, Mesopotamia, Babylonian period, c. 2000 BC; *Semi-human sexual demon*, rock engraving, Ti-n-Lalan, Libyan Fezzan, c.5000 BC, Fabrizio Mori, Rome; *Ceramic Vessel*, Mochica Culture, Peru, c. 500 AD, Institute for Sex Research, Indiana University
14 Frazer: *The Golden Bough*, abridged edition, Macmillan 1959, 136

2

ORIENTAL EROTICISM

Hindu, Tantric, Taoist and Chinese erotic art is founded in a religion quite different in some key areas from Western religion. There seems to be less guilt, sin, body-hating and repression in Indian, Japanese and Chinese erotic art (this discussion will focus primarily on erotic art in India, Japan and China). The cosmic energy of life has a sexual dimension which is gloriously celebrated. Indian, Japanese and Chinese erotic art may be just as sexist and patriarchal as Western erotic art, but it is also freer, more exuberant, and more joyous.

In Oriental erotic art, sexuality is a cosmic energy, an essential part of an authentic religious worldview. Indian, Chinese and Japanese erotica is thoroughly sexist, though. As with witches' covens and Western magic, erotic energy manifests itself in men and women in erotic pairings, in heterosexual components, and the symbols of the *lingam* and *yoni* are, yet again, the penis and vagina.

Maithuna, the figures of lovemaking couples, are found on Indian temples; though, again, it is nearly always men and women that are depicted writhing together. Lesbian and gay and other forms of sexual identity and practices are rarely depicted. There are renditions of lesbian and gay 'sex acts', in the Moghul Indian erotic manuals, for instance, and in the Turkish Khamas poems.[15]

In Indian religion there are *shiva and shakti* as the cosmic forces; in China it is the *yin* and *yang*. Always there is an emphasis on the masculine and the feminine, and the union of the two. As the *I Ching* puts it: '[s]exual union of man and woman gives life to all things.'[16]

What one notices, though, is the sense of humour and joy in Oriental erotic art. People *smile*, and *laugh*. This sense of joy is what is missing from so much of Occidental erotic art, which is shot through with Judæo-Christian feelings of sin, guilt, shame and death-awareness. Sex is a serious business in much of Western erotic art, but participants in Asian erotic art are allowed to be seen to be enjoying themselves.

Those figures on the temples of Khajuraho or in Rajasthan, they're having a great time. They make love and they *smile*. Hey! sex is fun – and those carvings on the Indian temples show lovemaking as intimate, sensual pleasure, unblemished by death-consciousness or sin or guilt.[17] (A view regularly trotted out by modern writers is that sex is actually difficult, smelly, rough, dirty, nerve-wracking, etc. Oriental erotic art shows that there are other forms of sexual behaviour).

The carvings on the temples of India, such as Khajuraho temple, are among the most celebrated examples of erotic art from the history of art, and rightly so. The images of a woman climbing up a man's body, thighs spread, with him deep inside her, and the two of them kissing, are rapturous and totally unforgettable. These stone couplings are among art's most ecstatic images – and the effect is greatly enhanced by the frieze format,

15 *Lesbian scene*, 17th century, Koka Shastra, Bibliotheque Nationale, Paris; *Homosexual scene*, Khamsa poems, Ata'i, Turkey, 19th century, Museum of Turkish and Islamic Art, Istanbul
16 *I Ching*, tr. James Legge, Dover, New York 1963, 1
17 Couple from the heaven bands of a temple, Rajasthan, 13th century, sandstone, 11in high; naked ascetic coupling with a Yogini, from Laksmana temple at Khajuraho

by collecting so many figures into the same space. And all of them are making love, or standing there exuding infinite desire.

Oriental erotic art is famous for its 'athletic' sexual positions – i.e., sex that goes beyond the missionary position or woman on top position of so much of Western erotic art. The variety of sexual positions are propounded in Oriental texts such as *The Perfumed Garden*, *Ananga-Ranga*, or the *Kama Sutra*, which demonstrates 64 ways of fucking. The positions themselves have a religious aspect, being associated with yoga, with meditation and with sex magic. The positions of the body echo or are manifestations of cosmic, religious energy. (Focussing on other sexual positions is partly a graphic function, too: it's easier to depict sexual positions outside of the missionary position if you want to concentrate on genitals touching. The missionary position hides everything. Which's why it's used as the main position in commercial cinema, for instance).

Chinese/ Taoist eroticism features quaint titles for sexual positions: *Two Fishes Side-by-Side*, *Turning Dragon*, *Leaping Wild Horses*; there are types of thrusting (for example, nine shallow, one deep); cute names for orgasms ('the bursting of the clouds'); the penis is the 'Jade Stem'; and the vagina is the Palace, or Gateway of Jade, or the Peach.

Some Eastern erotic art is based in sex magic, which is a broad term covering many kinds of controlling of sexual energy, involving yoga, meditation, ritual, *mantras* and *yantras*. Typical is the conservation of orgasmic energy, where the man does not ejaculate. As Philip Rawson put it in *The Erotic Art of the East*, '[t]o every Oriental mind, mere orgasm is never the goal of love'.[18]

Oriental sex magic is, as in Western sex mysticism, a male-made construct, built around masculine notions of sexuality. The emphasis on not ejaculating is but one indication of the male-favoured slant of sex magic. The vulva or *yoni* is glorified: there are images of *yonis* everywhere in India – in Hyderabad, as a woman lying back with her legs spread wide open, in holy water containers, in *coco-de-mer* shells split open to serve as a *yoni* image,

18 Rawson: *The Erotic Art of the East*, Weidenfeld & Nicolson, 1973, 29

etc.[19]

Although the vulva is revered – there is a sculpture showing a man worshipping the *yoni* of the Yogini as Goddess[20] – the phallus is the essential component in sex magic. The central image – of the *yoni* and *lingam* – requires the fire, the creative spirit of the male phallic element to set the cosmic, divine energies alight. The vulva or feminine principle on its own its not enough. In Tantra, the female creative aspect is exalted, either depicted as the *yoni*, or a Goddess, as Philip Rawson explained in *The Art of Tantra*:

> Hindu Tantra proclaims everything, the crimes and miseries as well as the joys, to be the active play of a female creative principle, the Goddess of many forms, sexually penetrated by an invisible, indescribable, seminal male. In ultimate fact He has generated Her for his own enjoyment.[21]

Philip Rawson's last sentence gives the game away: the god creates the Goddess for his own pleasure. The man has his mistress – this is a common set-up, the men who keep women for sex. Everything, it seems, reverts back to the male. Tantric and Taoist sex magic, which aims for multi-orgasmic sex for both partners, reverts back in the end to the man. The male becomes the measure for everything, as in human-(man)-centred Renaissance philosophy, which is the basis of Western philosophy.

Hindu Tantric sex magic is very sensual, with its rites using meat, wine, butter, etc. There is an 'extreme' version of Tantric sex magic, the so-called left hand ritual, where sex is practised when the woman menstruates. The aim, again, is to harness and channel wild sexual energies. The 'left hand' paths of Eastern sex magic were fascinating for groups of Western artists and writers, who were interested in gaining power over the world.

Western sex magic veers from the notorious and violent – as

19 Coco-de-mer, South India, 19th century, 17in high; Icon, 11th century, Hyderabad, stone, from a temple; Holy water container, Bengal, 18th century, copper, 12in long
20 At Madura, South India, 17th century
21 P. Rawson: *The Art of Tantra*, 11

practised by the Beast himself, Aleister Crowley – to the gentle and dreamy, as practised by the novelist John Cowper Powys. Crowley went much further in the (sex) magical quest than A.E. Waite, W.B. Yeats, Madame Blavatsky, S.L. MacGregor Mathers, and the Golden Dawn. Aleister Crowley's sexploits are well-known; he sodomized Victor Neuberg in Paris as part of a ritual; he was into S/M, drugs, group sex, etc; he made a number of women pregnant, etc.[22] 'Do what you like' was Crowley's dictum, or, to put it another way, 'have as much sex as you like and don't bother about consequences'. Crowley was, like the Marquis de Sade, the ultimate libertine. Anything goes, as long as you don't get caught doing it (as de Sade and Crowley were).

The cult of sex magic in the works of Aleister Crowley, the Marquis de Sade, Georges Bataille, and even in seemingly peace-loving types such as Wilhelm Reich and D.H. Lawrence, was essentially the creation of a mythology of magic and religion that could justify a culture that exalted men, male sexuality, while diminishing women and female sexuality. It is astonishing how little these 'high priests' of modern sex took the other person, the partner, into consideration. If the woman was clitorally aroused, Lawrence reckoned, she should be suppressed, while in Crowley's output there is not much about the other person. She is an anonymous, nameless, characterless person. Her feelings are not consulted.

'Operation prolonged and intense; orgasm multiple... the gods clearly visualized and alive,' as Aleister Crowley put it.[23] The goal in Crowleyan sex mysticism was ecstasy via 'death in orgasm', the age-old masculine fusion of sex and death, a mix of alchemy, Tantrism, Gnosticism, Western magic and Hermet-icism.[24] Crowley's sex magic turns out to be virulently patriarchal, sexist and misogynist, as well as crude and violent. The Russian Georg Gurdjieff, another powerful magus revered by a circle of devotees (though less notorious than Crowley), could apparently

---

22 See Colin Wilson: *The Occult*, Granada 1973, 457-491
23 quoted in J. Symonds: *The Great Beast: The Life of Aleister Crowley*, 1952, 135
11 Richard Cavendish: *The Magical Arts*, Arkana 1984, 38-42; C.R. Cammell: *Aleister Crowley*, Richards Press, 1952; Evola, 264-7

make a woman have an orgasm by looking at her and breathing in a particular way.[25]

There are any number of other manifestations of sex magic and erotic rituals in the Occident: in the Greek Eleusian Mysteries, for instance, where the *hieros gamos* or sacred love-making occurred in total darkness; in the secretive, supposedly homosexual rites of the Knights Templar, who worshipped the blasphemous deity Baphomet; in the so-called 'obscene kiss' of the mediæval witches at 'Black Masses', and copulation with the Devil; in 'Dianic' sex at Sabbats; and in the 'Great Work' of mediæval and Renaissance alchemy.[26]

Witchcraft and witches, the witch hunts and trials, have been examined by a number of feminists, and the lies, hypocrisy and sexism, both blatant and hidden, of texts such as the notorious *Malleus Maleficarum*, have been studied.[27] Witches have long been regarded as practising dubious sexual rituals, and there are many examples in the history of the visual arts (perhaps the witches' sabbaths or orgies are the most notorious).

The British novelist John Cowper Powys created his own form of sex magic, based on an ethereal lovemaking without touching, a form of sex magic found in Tantrism and some Western sex magic. Powys called it 'cerebral lust', a way of loving that is essentially that of courtly love or Renaissance sonnets, a loving from afar, over distances, a spiritual, ghostly form of love. He explained it in his book *In Defence of Sensuality*:

> It is not absolutely necessary for the two lovers to be together. If the mystic-sensuous element in their love be really strong, neither fate nor destiny can undo what the First Cause, through the medium of pure chance, has done. Time and space, in fact, have no longer any power

25 See Colin Wilson, op.cit., 524
26 See Julius Evola, 79, 193; 206; E.J. Martin: *The Trial of the Templars*, Allen & Unwin 1928
27 'In the notorious *Malleus Maleficarum* of the late fifteenth century, sexism was explicit. Women, the *Malleus* claimed to demonstrate at length, were more likely than men to be witches because they were weaker, more stupid, superstitious, and sensual.' Jeffrey B. Russell, *A History of Witchcraft*, Thames & Hudson 1981, 68-9; Marianne Hester, 107-204; Mary Daly: *Gyn/Ecology*, 178-222; Andrea Dworkin, 1974, 118-150; H.R. Trevor-Roper: *The European Witch-Craze of the Sixteenth and Seventeenth Century*, Harper, New York 1969; A.L. Barstow: "On studying witchcraft as women's history: a historiography of the European witch persecutions", *Journal of Feminist Studies of Religion*, 4, 1988

to separate them when once they have met. This is no fantastic, idealistic, romantic moonshine. It is a law of living consciousness, a psycho-chemical law. All lovers will bear witness to this... Real lovers... go to and fro over the face of the earth, in a delicate and delicious trance. Each of the two of them can eat nothing but the other eats too – can drink nothing but the other eats too. They can breathe no air, however far-travelled it may be, but the spirit of the other is diffused throughout its undulating presence... it follows that each of them will share the other's contemplations, and have thoughts, fancies, feelings, and sensations in common with the other.[28]

John Cowper Powys' highly idiosyncratic vision of super-spiritual love is still that of Western patriarchy. Western sex magic hardly ever produces important visual or sculptural art. Powys may create amazing images in prose with his seemingly bizarre mysticism of masturbation, and Aleister Crowley may prate manically of loving as one wishes, but Western sex magic did not produce many really important artworks. There are marvellous passages in sex magic literature about 'astral light', the 'subtle body', the 'Magickal Child' and transcendent union, but rarely were any decent artworks created.

The goals of Western sex mysticism are similar to those of Oriental sex magic, as found in Taoism and Tantrism: to harness the energies of the orgasm, to 'make cosmic' life, to unite macro and microcosm, inner and outer, near and far, above and below, Heaven and Earth, to reintroduce the sacred into life, to turn profane time and space into sacred time and space. Ritualized sex has a mythic, religious component, which in Tantrism and Taoism, is uppermost. Mircea Eliade wrote that 'in the case of ceremonial sexual union, the individual ceases to live in profane and meaningless time, since he is imitating a divine archetype ("I am heaven, thou art Earth," etc)'.[29]

Tantrism is a life-affirming cult, with pleasure as a goal. But sexual practise is always contextualized within a cosmic, religious, and philosophical framework. It is never pleasure for pleasure's sake, never simply a series of multiple orgasms, so the text books

28 John Cowper Powys: *In Defence of Sensuality*, Village Press 1974, 144-5
29 Eliade: *The Myth of the Eternal Return*, Princeton University Press, New Haven 1971, 36

say, although sex magic, East or West, is about cultivating the energies of the orgasm. As John Mumford commented: '[s]ex magic operates upon the premise that whatever is held in the imagination at the moment of orgasm will come to pass.'[30] Orgasm is that prime mystical state, the *jouissance* at the heart of mysticism. As Mumford wrote: '[o]rgasm is the only spontaneous, natural experience of a deathless, breathless, timeless, sorrowless dimension.'[31]

Mystical orgasm is the ecstasy at the heart of Western as much as Oriental mysticism. Catholic mystics, especially, experienced blinding, burning, tumultuous, orgasmic mystical ecstasies. St Theresa experienced some of the most intense religious blisses in the history of mysticism, and her swooning was caught in Giovanni Lorenzo Bernini's famous statue (1645-52). The eroticism of female mysticism is apparent in so much of women mystics' writings. Marie of the Incarnation (1566-1618) wrote: '[i]t owes its origin to the mutual embraces of the soul and this most adorable Word who by the kisses of His divine mouth fills her with His spirit and with His life.' Later, she noted: '[h]er being is entirely penetrated and possessed by Him. It is consumed by caresses and acts of love which cause it to expire in Him by suffering deaths the most sweet'.[32]

For mystics of the mediæval and early modern era, God is the ultimate Divine Lover, much as Christ is regarded as the bridegroom who 'marries' the bride, the church. The New Jerusalem, in the *Revelations,* comes down arrayed 'as a bride'. Nuptial imagery – that is, thoroughly erotic imagery – occurs throughout Judæo-Christianity, from the sensual *Song of Songs* onwards. Indeed, the more ascetic and austere the mystic, the more erotic and joyous the mystical outpourings. Burning with the fire of love, pierced hearts bleeding the blood of life, the imagery of mysticism is drenched in eroticism. It is all about, like Tantrism or Taoist sex magic, desire. St John of the Cross wrote in his *The*

---

30 John Mumford: *Ecstasy Through Tantra*, Llewellyn Publications, St Paul, Minnesota 1988, 93
31 J. Mumford, op.cit., 33
32 *The Autobiography of Venerable Marie of the Incarnation, O.S.U., Mystic and Missionary*, tr. J.J. Sullivan, Loyale University Press, Chicago, 1964, 56f

Dark Night of the Soul: 'love is like fire, which ever rises upward with the desire to be absorbed in the centre of its sphere.'[33] Even seemingly unbudgably ascetic mystics such as the Arabic, Persian and Sufis, Al-Hallaj, Rumi, Jami, Al-Ghazzali, Rab'ia and Hafiz wrote incredibly erotically of being God-intoxicated, and Allah was seen often as the Divine Lover in whose arms the mystic desired to be extinguished in an excess of rapture that is clearly sexual.

Tantric and Taoist sex magic has become popular with Westerners, with New Age, hippy and holistic folk, the sort who go in for neo-pagan weddings at Avebury stone circle, or who start up vegetarian cafés in San Francisco. For Taoist and Tantric sex magic provides a justification for sexual liberation; a religious context is found for multi-orgasmic sex, which is not found in Christianity. The interest in Oriental sex magic, then, can be seen as part of the general flight to the East of many a bourgeois Westerner in the modern era. Even seemingly perspicacious minds such as the French feminist Julia Kristeva, such an incisive and ironic voice in contemporary culture, has found a new and nourishing eroticism in China. As Kristeva noted in *About Chinese Women*, the Chinese way of loving is not centred in the Western œdipal, ego-centred way. 'They impress us with their positivity, their attitude towards sex as 'normal': nothing is sinful in this refined quest for pleasure.'[34]

Other feminists might point out that China, and India, are fiercely patriarchal societies, despite their fondness for matriarchies and the Great Goddess. In China, too, as Mary Daly and others have pointed out, there is the practise of foot-binding, in which 'women were grotesquely crippled', Daly wrote.[35] Kristeva, though, is convinced of the Chinese non-egoistic erotic union:

---

33 St John of the Cross, *Dark Night of the Soul*, tr. E.A. Peers, Doubleday, New York 1959, 175
34 Kristeva's *About Chinese Women*, Marion Boyars 1977, in Mary Eagleton, ed. *Feminist Literary Criticism*, 80
35 Mary Daly: *Gyn/Ecology*, 135. See also Andrea Dworkin: *Women Hating*, Dutton, New York 1974, Howard S. Levy: *Chinese Footbinding: The History of a Curious Erotic Custom*, Walton Rawls, New York 1966

Whatever the reasons, though, the psychosomatic result of this kind of *jouissance* is that the woman does not consider herself as 'inferior', 'devalued' and desirable only at that price – which is the case in sexual economies dominated by the phallus. Furthermore, because the man is neither the master nor the active, inducing the principle of the orgasm, but rather one of the two who are each two in themselves (each partner being both *male* and *female*, the difference between them being a matter of degree), the sexual act becomes a mutual exchange: what is missing in the one is offered by the other.[36]

The erotic art of a culture is one thing, but the actual experiences are another. In Indian, Japanese and Chinese erotic art, people are shown gleefully and gymnastically contorting and entwining around one another. On hammocks, swinging from trees, on balconies, beds, cushions, tables, beside lakes, they copulate anywhere and everywhere. The depictions, by many anonymous artists, and also by people such as Katsushika Hokusai, Utagawa Kunisada, Kitagawa Utamaro, Nishikawa Sukenobu and Torii Kiyonobu, show all manner of sexual activities, including a woman being licked by an octopus, rape by demons, and a blowjob while waiting in line at Burger King (just kidding). Chinese erotic drawings and Japanese *shunga* prints, especially, depict lovemaking as an innocent, pleasurable activity. The couples tup amidst serene Eastern landscapes, with vases filled with flowers, little fences, beautiful gardens, bo trees, lakes and streams. It all seems so pastoral and sublimely tranquil.[37]

In Indian erotic art, the participants have a wonderfully serene temperament: in sets of miniatures and paintings, the couples go through every variety of sexual position, while calmly smiling to themselves or to each other. It's explicitly erotic art, with the genitals on display: the thighs of men and women are bent right back, to reveal the penis entering the vagina.

The people are *types*, as they are in contemporary porno. They are not individualized: they are simply *a* man and *a* woman. It

36 Julia Kristeva: *About Chinese Women*, in Eagleton, 80
37 Harunobu: *A Fantasy*, late 1760s, anonymous: *Trio in a Garden*, 18th century, China; *The Attack from the Rear, or 'The Leaping White Tiger'*, painting on silk from an album of the K'ang-hsi period, 1662-1722, C.T. Loo Collection, Paris; *In the Garden on a Rocky Seat*, painting on silk, K'ang-his period, C.T. Loo Collection, Paris

doesn't really matter *who* they are. They are, though, definitely the leisure class, aristocrats and the bourgeoisie. Indian erotic art includes depictions of tupping on the back of an elephant, love-making during a tiger hunt, a woman using a bow to fire a phallic arrow into a woman, and an antelope mounting a woman.

The other striking thing about Indian, Chinese and Japanese erotic art is how *decorative* it is, how much the artists are concentrating on patterns, on shapes, on the props and furniture in the pictures. The world of Oriental erotic art is certainly visually stunning, and luxurious, with its couches and hangings, its large windows opening onto pleasure gardens, its rich carpets and furnishings, and the lavish costumes (the patterned kimonos, for instance). There is little modelling: rather, the pictures, prints and scrolls are flattened visually, with line and colour doing all of the work (shadows, textures, and modelling are dispensed with).

The goal is immortality, oneness, meditation. Sperm, associated with *yang* energy, is believed to rise up the spine to the brain in Chinese sex magic, as in Indian *kundalini* yoga. The imagery and meanings are masculinized: jade, the petrified sperm of the celestial dragon, is associated with the phallus, while *yang* energy is thoroughly phallic. In Japanese Shinto religion there was a gigantic Phallus of heaven, a celestial pillar; giant phalluses were carried in processions, as in ancient Greece; phallic symbols were common, often as talismans for good luck, as in Roman times.

While some Japanese erotic art is grotesque – the exaggeration of the genitals, for instance, where a penis and a vulva are masses of folds of skin – in Indian culture there is a flipside to the phallic *shiva-shakti, yoni-lingam* scenario of mystical lovemaking, and that is the Great Goddess Kali, probably the wildest Goddess in history, in East or West, North or South. The Goddess Kali stands, not sits, on the corpse of the god Shiva. She looms over his erect phallus, brandishing in her many arms a sword to behead and castrate Shiva. As she makes love to him, she kills him. She is the phallic, devouring, terrible Mother.[38] It's easy to see the Goddess Kali in her 'terrible' aspect as yet another example of male projection of male fear of women, of women as creators and destroyers, as mothers or whores, birthers or murderers.

Chinese and Japanese erotic art is distinctive in its portrayal of the human figure, the elegant flowing lines, with the clothes and furnishings and bedding mirroring the curves of the bodies. Genitals are greatly enlarged – penises are hugely engorged, poised at the entrance of swollen, wide-open vulvas, with clitorises aroused and prominent. It's common in this kind of erotic art to see men walking around with gigantic cocks, sometimes a few feet long, with the men supporting them with their hands. In humorous erotica, men balance fans on their schlongs, or carry buckets, or ride their members on wheels, as cannons. In satirical scrolls, by Jichosai (18th century), men battle with their phalluses like swords.

The sense of play and fun is readily apparent in amongst the scenes of fucking. But the tupping is only one element in amongst the visual richness on display: just as significant are the patterned clothes, the flowery, printed textiles, and the rich colouring of reds, greens and blues. The bodies in Chinese and Japanese erotic are usually partially naked, and show up as pale cream (the artists use the base, the paper or the scroll itself, as the basis for colouring the bodies).

Sometimes the lovers have people to help them – a 17th century Japanese scroll depicts a friend helping to guide a penis into a courtesan's vagina. In a Kangyo 19th century drawing, two women mount a man. The lovers support themselves with a sling around their necks in an early 17th century Japanese scroll. In a late 18th century drawing, two men make love to a woman, all of them smiling. In a Moroshige painting (17th century), a couple watch themselves masturbating each other in a mirror. In a late Ming/ early Ch-ing dynasty scroll, a woman sits in a swing on a

38 *Goddess Kali*, Orissa, 19th century, gouache on cloth, 15 x 13in, collection: Ajit Mookerjee, New Delhi; *Icon of the Terrible Goddess Seated in Intercourse on the Corpse of Siva*, Rajasthan, 18th century, brass, 5in high, collection: Ajit Mookerjee

tree while her lover enters her. In later Chinese art, people fuck wherever they can – on chairs, on tables, hanging from a wooden post, in gardens. Orgies were sometimes depicted, as in the late Ming dynasty painted scroll.

The inheritance of Japanese erotic art is the *manga* and *animé* tradition of contemporary Japan, in comics, comicbooks and animated movies. Among the most famous of these is the *Legend of the Overfiend* series of animated movies, which draws inspiration from many sources, but also from Japanese erotic art, particularly in its more eccentric (and violent) aspects (other famous *hentai* comics and *animé* include *La Bleu Girl, Cream Lemon, Plastic Little* and *Bible Black*). *Manga, hentai* and *animé* comics and cartoons also use the human types of Japanese erotic art, and exaggerate them even further. The emphasis on young women (*shojo*), for instance, with their huge eyes, tiny mouths, large breasts and voluptuous bodies, are notorious (in the West) – not only because of their sexual objectification, and the violence in many of the situations (with rape a favourite), but also because they are very young.

3

EROTICISM IN ANCIENT ART: GREECE, EGYPT, ROME

Ancient Greek culture is everywhere celebrated as the one of the foundations of Western culture. So much of ancient Greek culture – the arts, politics, philosophy, writing, structures and ideas – is found throughout Western culture. Ancient Greek art remains the highpoint of Western art. You name it, the ancient Greeks did it – and much better than just about all the artists that followed them. Poetry, sculpture, architecture, philosophy, mathematics, science, political systems, erotic art – the ancient Greeks were brilliant at everything, it seems. The great leap in art made by the ancient Greeks from what had gone on before seems much larger than the 'improvement' of the Renaissance compared to mediæval art, or the emergence of abstract art at the beginning of the 20th century. What the ancient Greeks did overshadows the Renaissance, and modern art. Art may have had its true highpoint 2,000 years ago. Ancient Greek art is truly 'beautiful', to use the most apposite of all Neoplatonic terms. Look at Greek

144

sculpture, from the female figures of Auxerre (*c.* 625 BC) to the
wonderful *Victory of Samothrace* (*c.* 200 BC).[39]

Here, in ancient Greek art, one finds the birth of modern
æsthetics, modern notions of beauty, of ideal form and of the
stature of high art. In ancient Greek art, one finds the
amalgamation of art and philosophy – that 'great' art must be
produced from a 'great' philosophy – which has remained with
high art ever since.

When you look at Greek mythology you see a wild,
unrestrained celebration of the central'mysteries or experiences of
life; birth, growth, love, sex, death, violence, desire, loss,
departure, confusion, etc, all those great subjects at the centre of
patriarchal culture. For, despite its exaltation of Goddesses –
Athena, Hera, Aphrodite, Diana, Artemis, Kore, Persephone –
Greek culture is supremely masculinist and patriarchal. Zeus, for
instance, is astonishing in his wildly phallic, hungrily sexual
exploits. He seems to have fucked every Goddess in Greek
mythology. He thunders about the sky, raging like the most
macho instinct gone wild. He slept with Mnemosyne over nine
nights and she later gave birth to nine daughters, the Muses; he
raped Demeter in the form of a bull, and she bore Kore; he
married Hera; he pursued and had his way with Electra, Taygete,
Callisto (in the form of Artemis), Aegina, Antiope, Niobe, Mera,
Leto, Danaë, Semele, Europa, Leda, Hesione, Elara, Naerea,
Protgenia, Thalia, and many others. Zeus had everybody, it
seems. He appeared to Semele in all his thunderous majesty, but
the sight killed her. Nevertheless, he took the child in her womb,
hid it in his thigh, and later it became Dionysus, the wild god of
wine.

There are many other phallic gods in Greek mythology –
Pan, for instance, often depicted in statues as an ithyphallic
seducer, or Dionysus, the god of the cult of the maenads, as
sculpted by Scopas.[40] These gods do what they like. They are the

39 *Female Figure*, from Auxerre, *c.* 625 BC, limestone, daedalic style, Louvre, Paris; *Victory of Samothrace*, *c.* 200 BC, marble, Louvre, Paris
40 Scopas: *Dancing Maenad*, 4th century BC

beings that transgress boundaries, that bring wildness back into the world. The deities are personifications of human feelings, on one level, and what is clear is that Greek mythology and art is a manifestation of mainly male or masculine emotions. And if feminine or female feelings or experiences are represented, they are usually male or masculine views of female emotions. For although we do not know *who* most of the sculptors and artists of ancient Greece (or Rome, or Sumer, or Egypt) were, they were probably mainly male. Even if women artists contributed, the results are still patriarchal. For this is the problem, always the problem: that, whoever the author is, most art is patriarchal. Because the codes, structures, contexts and representations are biased towards the masculinist or patriarchal viewpoint.

Greek mythology is very erotic, and for some it would be classed as pornographic. There is a violence to it which is expressed in matter-of-fact terms, as if violence with sex is inevitable (this is the view of some male writers). It's also in Homer, in *The Odyssey* and *The Iliad*. Rape is not uncommon in Greek mythology. Goddesses and gods express their sexuality openly. Who's sleeping with whom is a key element in Greek mythology. It's a kind of celestial gossip, the tittle-tattle of the heavens.

Nowadays royalty, movie stars and celebrities perform the functions of Greek deities, where the cavortings of the Kennedys or the Windsors absorbs much of the media. Thus, Marilyn Monroe is a modern-day Aphrodite, a 'holy whore' or sacred prostitute, who slept with the great men of the era.

Generally, Greek mythology follows the usual heterosexual pattern of masculine power and female submission, but with a few exceptions, such as Goddesses like Hera, Artemis, Athena and Diana, who were not always to be taken by any god that lusted after them. Gods take goddesses and women regularly, and to feminists the relationships are sometimes clearly rape. There are some powerful representations of women in ancient Greek art – of Athena as a warrior, with shield and spear, of Leto striding through the world carrying two children, of Persephone returning to her mother, the Corn Goddess Demeter, of Artemis setting the hounds on Actaeon. These are powerful images of women, set within patriarchal discourse, certainly, but at least they're not drudges, housewives or bimbos.[41]

The representations of the Olympians are some of the high-points of Greek art: Zeus, Poseidon, Hestia, Artemis, Athena, Apollo, Ares, Hera, Demeter, Aphrodite and Hermes. The statues, friezes and paintings of the Greek deities show them to be very confident beings, and often smiling. This is new: *smiling people in art!* Many of the statues, of Artemis, Athena, and others, are smiling, often softly, secretly, to themselves.[42] The softly smiling sculptures, such as the *Maenad with Goat*, a Graeco-Roman relief, the polychromed, exquisite marble *Kore*, the headless *Nike Untying Her Sandal*, the delicious *Aphrodite of Knidos*, are pure mystery, the artist lost to time.[43] The anonymous nature of Classical sculptures enables anybody to claim them (as indeed, everyone has grabbed their chunk of Graeco-Roman marble on their military conquests or colonial grand tours).

As Michel Foucault notes, Greek notions of sexuality identity and activity were different those of the modern Western world. Sex was more of a continuum, without the boundaries between normality and 'deviant' behaviour that are found everywhere in the West.[44] Greek sexuality is regarded as healthy and open, even though it was shaped by economy, class, status, place, gender, power and culture, as much as modern concepts of sexuality.

The depictions on vases in red and black are famous: people

---

41 *Artemis and Actaeon*, metope from Temple E, Selinus, National Museum Palermo; *Demeter and Persephone*, 5th century BC, Mansell Collection; *Athena*, from the temple of Aegina, Munich Museum; *Leto with Apollo and Artemis*, c. 600 BC, limestone; *Athena and Alkyoneus*, from the Altar of Zeus from Pergamon, marble relief, Hellenistic, c. 180 BC, State Museums, Berlin
42 *Artemis*, Greek, Pompeii, Mansell Collection; *Artemis Bendis*, relief sculpture, 4th century BC, Mansell Collection; *Marine Aphrodite*, late 1st century BC, British Museum;
43 After Praxiteles: *Aphrodite of Knidos*, c. 350 BC, marble, Roman copy of a lost Greek piece, Vatican Museum, Rome; *Maenad with Goat*, late 5th century BC, marble, Roman copy of a lost Greek work, Palazzo dei Conservatori, Rome; *Nike Untying Her Sandal*, c.410 BC, Classical Greek, Akropolis Museum, Rome; *Kore*, c. 530-520 BC, from the Athens Acropolis, marble, polychromed Greek, Acropolis Museum, Rome
44 'The Greeks did not see love for one's own sex and love for the other sex as opposites, as two exclusive choices, two radically different types of behaviour', wrote Michel Foucault (*The Uses of Pleasure*, 187).

being taken from behind while they suck someone's penis, a woman carrying a giant phallus, musicians with erections, a man balancing a wine jar on his wiener, etc.[45] The flowering of Greek art on vases – from around 600 BC – is remarkable. Ancient Greek vases are exquisite, and the erotic art depicted in red and black lines is some of the most lyrical and touching in the history of erotic art.

Ancient Greek and Roman art is described as a permissive, open sexual zone, a period in history when any kind of debauchery was permitted. 'Debauchery' is the right word for modern views of Roman 'excesses', the orgies of Emperors such as Nero, Caligula and Tiberius. It was the world of the phallus, we are led to believe by art critics and historians, a world in which phalluses were everywhere. On vases, in carved stone, in reliefs, on amulets, in mosaics. The Romans had phallic shrines; an erect wiener set in a miniature temple, like a god in a temple. The Romans had phallic figures: dicks with legs, the glans of the penis as someone's head. And so on.[46] The Roman world, even more than the Greek, was the supremely phallic/ ithyphallic era in history, in terms of art. The Roman warriors, the battle, the legions, the massive, monumental architecture, the erotic poetry, all of Roman culture is patriarchal and phallic. Anything went, it seems. There are statues of the goat-god Pan making love with a goat, and of copulation in brothels in frescoes, at Pompeii, one of the most famous of all ancient erotic art sites.[47] It certainly was a bawdy era, a priapic age. Or it was an era in which erotic art flourished in some areas (but that is true of any era: there probably *hasn't* been a time when people *haven't* made erotic art of some kind or another, since the origins of art-making).

Unlike the palæolithic or prehistoric eras, the ancient period was the time of the word, of writing. Thus, from Greek poets (in

45 *Orgy Scene*, Attic cup, Greece, attr. to Skythes, Louvre, Paris; *Naked Woman Carrying Giant Phallus*, Attic vase, Greece, Painter of Pan, Staatliche Museen, Berlin; *Revelling Seleni*, Attic vase, Greece, British Museum
46 *Roman phallic amulets*, Pompeii, Italy, 1st century AD, British Museum; *Roman Phallic Shrine*, Pompeii, Italy, 1st century AD, Naples Museum
47 Joseph Nollekens: *Pan and the Goat*, 1760s, terracotta, British Museum; *Brothel Scene*, Pompeii, Italy, 1st century AD, Naples Museum

the *Greek Anthology*, for instance) and from Roman poets (Ovid in his *Art of Love*, Petronius in his *Satyricon*, Catullus, Martial, Juvenal, Propertius, and Apuleius in his *The Golden Ass*), we know a lot about Greek and Roman sexual identities and practices.

Representations of sexuality in the prehistoric and ancient worlds, then, conform to (largely heterosexual and patriarchal) stereotypes. Women are depicted as mothers (there are countless images of women suckling babies), sometimes as warriors or angry wraiths (Artemis, Kali), sometimes offering their breasts, sometimes as passive virgins, or intercessors, or as sexual beings, either voraciously devouring men and beheading/ castrating them, or coupling with them in ecstatic/ spiritual union. Rare it is to find a depiction of eroticism that stands outside the accepted heteropatriarchal culture of the ancient worlds. But there is plenty of gay and lesbian art, of course.

One such non-orthodox image of eroticism is found in the relief of Lilith, four thousand years old, where the Goddess is the 'Lady of Beasts', the Queen of 'wild things', of nature in its unreigned state. Here, Lilith is the denied and suppressed aspect of patriarchal religion, the 'first wife' of Adam, the 'first man'; she is the 'negative' dimension of sexuality, the opposite of motherhood, nurturance and passivity, the opposite of the woman who stays in the home, who rules the domestic side of things. Lilith usurps that masculinist notion of women 'in their proper place', beside the hearth. Lilith is a Gorgon or Medusa figure, one of the originals of the witch figure.[48] Lilith throws her sexuality flagrantly into the face of the patriarchal establishment, as Mary Magdalene does later in Christianity.

In Indian religion there is the figure of the *yakshi*, found on many temples. The *yakshi* figure is supremely sexual, with her enlarged breasts, rounded hips and 'seductive' poses, her body slunk to one side, 'alluring', as art critics would have it. Indeed, the *yakshi* statue on a pillar of the court of the Emperor Kanishka,

48 *Lilith*, terracotta relief, Sumer, Larsa dynasty, c.2000 BC, Museum Antiker Kleinkunst, Munich

of the 2nd century A.D. has dark patches on the breasts and between the legs, where people have stroked the statue.[49] During the Christian era, female wildness and eroticism was suppressed, and focused onto one woman, the Magdalene. Statues of the Renaissance era depict her as a bedraggled, repentant sinner.[50]

In depictions of eroticism, such as that of the Indian Goddess Kali when she is in her devouring or deathly aspect, male fear of women reaches a peak. Kali is a Black Goddess who dances on top of men; she copulates with them and slays them at the same time.[51] Statues of Kali show her sucking the life or essence (sperm or *soma*) out of the male, while she brandishes a sword, fire, skulls and snakes in her many arms.[52] Kali is the 'dark one', the Queen of Blood, who presides over extraordinary blood sacrifices. She is the ultimate manifestation of the 'monstrous feminine', the Freudian 'Terrible Mother', the castrating, devouring, corpse-eating Goddess.[53]

Kali is the manifestation of excessive anxiety about sexuality and relations with women amongst patriarchal religions. What Western religionists did in the Judæo-Christian era was to suppress what Robert Briffault calls 'the chthonic aspects of the Queen of Heaven',[54] all of that wild sexuality, producing the Devil, notions of 'sin' and 'evil', witches, and any scapegoats they could muster. What patriarchal people (not always men) prefer is the homely, passive, nurturing woman, embodied in the personality of the Blessed Virgin Mary. Even here, though, in the cult of the Madonna, there are many vestiges of ancient Goddess worship. Beliefs, for instance, that somehow woman or the 'eternal feminine' encompasses everything. Whatever there is in the male

49 *Pillar with a yakshi*, 2nd century AD, Kushan period, red sandstone, Bhutesar, Mathura, Indian Museum, Calcutta

50 Gregor Erhart: *St Mary Magdalene*, early 16th century, polychromed wood, Louvre, Paris

51 Wendy O'Flaherty writes: 'The Goddess not only dominates her consort but kills him, cutting off his head. In this she resembles the female praying mantis, who bites off her consort's head... By eating his head, the mantis removes her consort's inhibitions and frees him to copulate more vigorously.' (*Women, Androgynes, and other Mythical Beasts*, University of Chicago Press, Chicago, 1980, 81.)

52 *Kali the Devourer*, copper casting, northern India, modern, Victoria & Albert Museum, London

53 See Heinrich Zimmer: "The Indian World Mother", in *The Mystic Vision*, *Eranos* Yearbooks, 6, Bollingen Series XXX, 1968

54 Robert Briffault: III, 183

world, it is enfolded in the female world, like the child is enfolded by the other in the womb, and, later, in her arms, sitting on her lap. In times of anxiety and trauma, people often return ('regress', Freudians would say) to primæval feelings and situations. The key image of a *regressus ad uterum* or return to the Mother, is the Madonna and Child, found throughout the history of world art, and everywhere: in Peru, in Sumer, Africa, Greece, in Aztec art, everywhere there are images of mothers and babies.

In Western art, one finds the *Madonna and Child* everywhere; but deeper, perhaps, are the (rarer) images of the primal matriarchal trinity, of child, mother and grandmother. In Catholic art, this means St Anne, the Virgin and Jesus. Leonardo da Vinci painted the trio of holy figures, and there was a cult of St Anne in the Netherlands.[55] Masaccio's image is probably the best known in Renaissance art.[56] But an artwork in Western art that shows just how much patriarchal religion still regards 'Woman' or the 'eternal feminine' or the Goddess as central and crucial to life are those sculptures of the seated Virgin which open up to reveal the Christian figures inside: God, crucified Christ and various saints.[57] Here, the Madonna envelops not only all of humanity, as in the *Madonna della Misericordia* paintings, where the Virgin shelters everyone under her cloak,[58] but also all the protagonists of Christian religion. All the mysteries of religion, including the Creator Himself, God, are contained within the body of the Madonna. Here, Mary is the Mother not only of Christ but of God, the Mother behind everything. She is also the church, the very building of the church. You enter her body when you enter a church. The cathedrals of the mediæval era were called 'Notre Dame', Our Lady, and they are explicitly wombs of the Goddess (inside they are hot and dark, and blood mysteries, such as the

---

55 see Leon Dresen-Coenders, ed. *Saints and She-Devils: Images of Women in the 15th and 16th Centuries*, Rubicon Press 1987; Margaret Whinney: *Early Flemish Painters*, Faber 1968; Jeremy Robinson: *Glorification*, 45f
56 Masaccio: *Madonna and Child with St Anne*, c. 1423, panel, 175 x 103cm, Uffizi, Florence
57 *"Vierge Ouvrante"*, 15th century, painted wood, France, Musée de Cluny, Paris; *Virgin*, c. 14th century, wood covered with linen, gesso and gilt, Germany, Metropolitan Museum of Art, New York
58 See Piero della Francesca: *Madonna della Misericordia*, centre of a polyptych, c. 1460?, 134 x 91cm, Town Hall, Sansepulcro, Italy

Mass or Eucharist, occur there, as in wombs. The entrances to cathedrals, those Gothic arches, can be seen as vulvas. The entrances to churches are often narrow slits, shaped like vulvas. The ribbed shapes around the pointed doorways echo the labia.)

The Christian view, then, echoes that of antiquity and prehistory; that, behind everything that male gods may create, is the Goddess. She is the primordial darkness of the universe behind everything, or, in ecological terms, she is the primal sea out of which life grew. These notions are found everywhere, in one form or another, in most ancient societies. 'Woman', the 'eternal feminine', the Goddess is exalted, but again, always in patriarchal terms. The Goddess is sexualized still, even in motherhood. As psychologists note, the mother-child relation is the first sexual relation in one's life, and Andrea Dworkin has brought attention to a 'pornography of pregnancy' (pregnant women are a sub-genre of commercial porn). It seems, then, that even in the seemingly positive exaltation of women in mothering, there is sexism, and porn. That, even in the glorification of women as Goddesses, as very space and time itself, as the universe behind God, Jesus, Zeus, etc, there is sexism, stereotyping and patriarchal control at work.

4

SEX IN RENAISSANCE ART

Imagine a nude painting of the Blessed Virgin Mary. The idea, to patrons, critics and consumers of Renaissance and mediæval art is shocking, as well as blasphemous. A naked Mother of God, it is unthinkable in terms of Renaissance and mediæval painting. There is a cult of the Virgin baring one breast, to suckle the baby Jesus. Here painters could depict breasts and nipples being sucked and it was all sanctified by the Catholic establishment. Anthony Van Dyck, Titian, Jan Gossaert (Mabuse), Hans Baldung, Joos van Cleeve, Rembrandt van Rijn and Peter Paul Rubens, among many others, painted the breasts of the Madonna.[59] The scene is usually a Holy Family, in Christ's childhood, with Jesus one or two years old, in some house, a room somewhere. Or the scene is a landscape in paintings entitled *The Rest on the Flight Into*

59 Titian: *The Virgin and Child*, c. 1570s, 75.6 x 63.2cm, National Gallery, London; Jan Gossaert: *The Virgin and Child*, c. 1530s, 47.7 x 38.2cm, Gemäldegalerie Staatliche Museen Preussicher Kulturbesitz, Berlin; Hans Baldung: *The Virgin and Child with an Angel*, 91 x 64cm, Gemäldegalerie Staatliche Museen Preussicher Kulturbesitz, Berlin; Anthony Van Dyck: *The Rest on the Flight into Egypt*, c. 1627, 134.5 x 114.5cm, Alte Pinakothek, Munich; Joos van Cleeve: *The Rest in the Flight into Egypt*, 54 x 67.5cm, Musées Royaux des Beaux-Arts, Brussels; Rembrandt van Rijn: *The Holy Family*, c. 1640, 41 x 34cm, Louvre, Paris; Peter Paul Rubens: *The Holy Family with the Apple Tree*, 1620-2, 353 x 233cm, Kunsthistorisches Museum, Vienna

Egypt. Here, Joseph, always depicted as an old man, looks on longingly as Jesus is breast-fed. Joseph is an onlooker, a way into the picture, for the (male) viewer looks at the mother and child through Joseph's eyes. (The viewer is assumed to be masculine in most Renaissance paintings). In one painting of the Virgin breastfeeding Christ, by Orazio Gentileschi, Joseph has fallen asleep.[60] We do not see the mother and child through his vision. Instead, Jesus looks directly out at the viewer while he sucks his mother's nipple. The viewer is thus embroiled in this erotic mother-child relationship.

An intriguing mix of the erotic and the spiritual, the sacred and the profane, occurs in Jean Fouquet's *The Melun Diptych*, where the Madonna bares her breast. This alone is not remarkable, although the breast is certainly more openly and erotically displayed, as spectacle, than in most Madonna art. The model for this voluptuous Mother of God, though, was Agnès Sorel, mistress of King Charles VII.[61]

But the sexualization of the Madonna occurred in a different way. The erotic feelings the Virgin aroused were sublimated, or directed at different targets, in particular the Goddesses of the Classic world: Venus, Diana, Aphrodite, Circe. Here, in the depiction of the Classic Goddesses, Renaissance painters could focus on the female form, and its nude, erotic aspects, justified by the subject being one from mythology.

Greek mythology enabled Renaissance artists to use images and themes of a wilder, stranger and more erotic nature than the images, themes and codes of Christianity. While Catholicism suppressed sex at every opportunity, only allowing it to express itself in figures such as Mary Magdalene, who had to be portrayed as an eternal penitent, Greek mythology was fully human. The Greek gods and goddesses are playful, stupid, silly, deceitful, jealous, angry, wily, poetic, ignorant and erotic, quite unlike Jehovah or Jesus. Greek myths were subjects in which

---

60 Orazio Gentileschi: *The Rest on the Flight into Egypt*, 175.3 x 218.4cm, Birmingham Museum
61 See Marina Warner: *Alone of All Her Sex*, 203

painters and sculptures could let themselves address erotic issues. The myths, drawn from Ovid, Plato, Apuleius and others, contain many erotic moments, such as Zeus/ Jupiter making love to Leda in the form of a swan, or Apollo pursuing Daphne – to escape him, she changed into a laurel tree (this was a favourite myth of Francesco Petrarch's), or Actaeon seeing Diana naked, or Pygmalion falling in love with his statue of Venus which comes alive, or the god Zephyr chasing Chloris: when he embraces her, flowers spill from her mouth, as depicted in Sandro Botticelli's famous *Primavera* (1478). Jean-Léon Gérôme painted an indubitably erotic depiction of Pygmalion: the statue comes alive and the sculptor embraces her passionately: the woman's legs are still white marble, but her upper body is already flesh. Typically, Gérôme makes sure that the groin and hips of the statue-becoming-woman are fleshly, for the woman is clearly destined to be the artist's whore, a statue made for sex.

The New Testament stories do not allow for such wild eroticism as the Greek and Roman myths. Artists went back to the *Old* Testament to find erotic themes. Eroticism is found in many of the depictions of Adam and Eve, for instance, which is of course that paradisal state where sexual awareness was absent. In Renaissance art, Adam and Eve coyly cover their genitals. In depictions of Adam and Eve – in the art of Lucas Cranach, Fra Angelico, Albrecht Dürer, Masaccio, Masolino da Panicale, Titian and others[62] - the genitals are covered or turned away from the viewer, yet that original Edenic state of pre-sexuality is the one state, surely, in which the body *could* be openly displayed. For the pre-sexual Paradise was where life was at its height, at its most holy, in the state God had planned.

The myth of Paradise is tied up with notions of childhood, of the Golden Age, that time, *in illo tempore, ab origine,* when everything was wonderful. Paradise is a state of pure desire and pure gratification, where nothing stop the flow of desire, no

62 Albrecht Dürer: *Adam and Eve,* 1504, engraving, 25.2 x 19.4cm, Victoria & Albert Museum, London; and *Adam and Eve,* 1507, Prado, Madrid; Masolino: *Fall,* 1427/8, fresco, 208 x 88cm, Santa Maria del Carmine, Brancacci chapel, Florence; Titian: *The Fall of Man,* c. 1570, oil on canvas, 114.2 x 73.2in, Prado, Madrid

responsibilities of any kind, the perfect state of childhood, free from social, familial, political, economic, racial and nationalist tensions. Interestingly, it is not usually Paradise that is depicted, as in Lucas Cranach's wonderful vision of Eden in his *The Golden Age* (*c.* 1530),[63] where the couples dance, swim, eat and make love, but the Fall, the moment when Adam and Eve eat the apple, as in Adriaen Isenbrandt's painting (1550-51), or the moment when they are expelled from Paradise by the Archangel, as in Masaccio's famous fresco (1427/28), where Adam and Eve sob and moan.[64]

Of course, there is deep sexism in the Judæo-Christian Fall, for it is the woman who picks the apple and offers it to Adam. From the beginning, in the Judæo-Christian tradition, it is the woman who makes men 'fall'. In some depictions, the sexism is doubled, by having the serpent shown as a snake-woman – the torso of a woman, the legs, like those of a mermaid, as in Michelangelo Buonarroti's *Temptation and Expulsion* (1508-12).[65] The symbol of the half-woman half-fish, still in use today,[66] is another manifestation of patriarchal people's projection of their sexual fears onto women, so that what lies 'below the waist' is feared and objectified as something slimy and fishlike, something dark, from the depths of the unconscious, which is the sea. The mermaid appears sculpted on mediæval churches, some of the mermaids expose their genitals, like the *sheila-na-gig* figure, which again fuses sacred and profane, spiritual and sexual, desire and fear.[67] The mermaid appears in much of Victorian art, as an image of men's ambivalent views of female sexuality – in E.M. Hale's *Mermaid's Rock* (1894), for instance, or John William Waterhouse's Pre-Raphaelite *A Mermaid* (1901).[68]

63 Lucas Cranach: *The Golden Age*, c. 1530, oil on wood, 75 x 103.5cm, Nasjonalgaleriert, Oslo
64 Masaccio: *The Expulsion of Adam and Eve*, 1424-5, fresco, 208 x 88cm, S. Maria del Carmine, Cappella Branacci, Florence
65 Michelangelo: *Temptation and Expulsion*, 1508-12, fresco, Sistine Chapel, Vatican, Rome
66 See the depiction of the Mary Magdalene in the wilderness sequence of Universal's film *The Last Temptation of Christ* (1988, USA)
67 See Anthony Weir & James Jerman: *Images of Lust: Sexual Carvings on Mediæval Churches*, B. T. Batsford, 1986, 48ff
68 John William Waterhouse: *A Mermaid*, 1901, 38.5 x 36.3in, Royal Academy of Arts, London; Edward Matthew Hale: *Mermaid's Rock*, 1894, 48 x 78in, City Art Gallery, Leeds

The strangest image of Paradise in Western art is undoubtedly Hieronymous Bosch's *The Garden of Earthly Delights*, a veritable banquet of fantasy, power, racism, sexism, Freudianism, death, violence and outrageous juxtapositions.[69] 'Art is never chaste', said Pablo Picasso, 'if it's chaste it isn't art'.[70] In Bosch's case, this is certainly true. There is nothing chaste about Bosch's vision of Paradise, no attempt at cloaking the explosion of desire. No wonder Bosch is a favourite of Surrealists, for they too allowed desire free rein (or tried to).

The *Bible's Old Testament* provides other opportunities for sensual scenes, among them Judith, who decapitated Holofernes after making love with him, Samson and Delilah, Sodom and Gomorrah, etc. Like Salomé with the head of John the Baptist, Judith and Holofernes was an opportunity for a bloody, sensual painting, as in Artemisa Gentileschi's brilliant painting (1615/20).[71] The head is where 'maleness' resides, where sperm and creative power are, where the essence of manhood is, as history shows. There have been many headhunting cults down the ages. Hernando Cortez saw 136,000 heads collected in Mexico's great Aztec temple, for instance, and the Celts had their prophetic head of Bran, while the Greeks had the singing, oracular head of Orpheus.[72] The symbolism of the skull can be sexual, and the head being cut off by Salomé or Judith is clearly a castration metaphor. In Lucas Cranach's painting of *Judith*, she poses with the green-skinned head in front of her, while brandishing a large castrating sword.[73]

The common subject of the Renaissance nude was Venus. As the Goddess of Love in mediæval and courtly love poetry, Venus, with her phallic assistant, Cupid, as the cherub armed with bow

69 Bosch: *The Garden of Earthly Delights*, 1503-4, oil on canvas, centre panel: 220 x 195cm, Prado, Madrid
70 Picasso, in Dore Ashton, ed. *Picasso on Art: A Selection of Views*, Viking Press, New York 1972, 15
71 Artemisa Gentileschi: *Judith*, 1615/20, Pitti Palace, Florence
72 See Weston La Barre: *Muelos*, Columbia University Press, New York, 1985, 13-64; T.G.E. Powell: *The Celts*, Praeger, New York 1958; B. R. Ortiz: "Counting Skulls: Comment on the Azec Cannibalism Theory of Harner-Harris", *American Anthropologist*, 1983, 82:2, 403-6
73 Lucas Cranach: *Judith with the Head of Holofernes*, panel, 33.8 x 23.4in, Kunsthistorisches Museum, Vienna

and arrow, presided over erotic experiences. The poetry of the troubadours was distinctly erotic and physical, despite its insistence on manners, etiquette and morals. The aim of courtly love poetry was to get into the bed of the beloved woman, basically. Venus was called upon to aid the lover in this pursuit of the Holy Grail, the mystic cauldron of Woman, her womb. Venus is both Holy Whore and chaste Mistress of 'Love'. She is Love personified. The Louvre birth plate, c. 1400, shows the Goddess Venus hovering over a Tuscan Garden of Love attended by two angels. Below are six famous warriors. All of them are staring intently at the genitals of the floating Goddess.[74] The lines of sight are marked on the painted salver. The Goddess is depicted in a mandorla, just like the Virgin Mary in *Assumption* images. The pictorial centre of the picture is Venus's vulva.[75]

Countless female nudes depict Venus in a variety of poses of shyness and abandonment. Giorgione's *Sleeping Venus* (c. 1508) makes the looking at the body easier, because she is asleep.[76] Yet this depiction is created very definitely for the pleasures of eroticism, made for the *jouissance* of looking. Other Renaissance Venuses, from Sandro Botticelli's *Birth of Venus* (c. 1482) to Titian's *Venus of Urbino* (1538), to the Master of Flora's *Birth of Cupid* (1540-60), are offered as gorgeous depictions of women, of mythical women painted sublimely, of women who expose their 'looked-at-ness' for all to see.[77] Even unusual visions of the female nude, such as the paintings of Lucas Cranach, come across, finally, as erotic art.[78] Titian's nudes are the highpoint of the high art nude; his nudes are as voluptuous as possible, for instance the woman reclining in bliss in the foreground right-hand corner of

74 See Paul Watson: *The Garden of Love in Tuscan Art of the Early Renaissance*, Associated University Press 1979, 17, 23
75 *The Triumph of Venus*, anonymous, birth plate, School of Verona (?), c. 1400, Louvre, Paris
76 Giorgione: *Sleeping Venus*, c. 1508, oil on canvas, 108 x 175cm, Staatliche Kunstsammlungen, Gemäldegalerie, Dresden
77 Titian: *Venus of Urbino*, 1538, oil on canvas, 119.5 x 165cm, Uffizi, Florence; Sandro Botticelli: *The Birth of Venus*, c. 1482, tempera on canvas, 173 x 279cm, Uffizi, Florence; Master of Flora: *Birth of Cupid*, c. 1540/60, oil on wood, 108 x 130.5cm, Metropolitan Museum of Art, New York
78 Lucas Cranach: *the Nymph of Spring*, Palitz Collection, New York; *The Judgement of Paris*, panel, 40.2 x 27.8in, Metropolitan Museum of Art, New York

Titian's *Bacchanal of the Andrians* (1523-24).[79]

Even in unexpected places, such as in Early Italian Renaissance art, such as in Pietro Lorenzetti, one finds erotic objectifications of women that look towards the high art nude. And otherwise chaste and sober painters, such as Giovanni Bellini, produced female nudes made to be looked at erotically.[80] Piero di Cosimo's Neoplatonic, mythological paintings are called 'mysterious' by critics, but they also contain female nudes that are distinctly erotic.[81] Antonio Pisanello's drawing of the person-ification of 'Luxury' undoubtedly depicts a prostitute: his drawing is a form of Renaissance porn, given 'high art status because Pisanello was a major artist.[82] Some images of the Renaissance and later nudes contain men in the picture, who modulate the viewer's gaze.[83] The man in the picture stands in for the viewer, and the gaze is distinctly erotic (and male, except in certain cases, such as Simon Vouet's image of Psyche and Amor (1626), where the female contemplates the male body).[84]

These high art depictions of Venus and the female nude were often produced as pornography has been produced throughout history: tailor-made, for male clients. The wealth of the patrons in high art somehow justifies whatever is portrayed in the art; similarly, because these nudes were high art, they justified their existence by their artistic genius. Yet the fact that they were produced for erotic reasons is clear, and is made even clearer when these nudes include a man staring at them. In some pictures of Venus and Cupid, the cherub and the Goddess of Love are shown embracing, again emphasizing the (heterosexual) erotic nature of the image, as in Agnolo Bronzino's famous picture

79 Titian: *Bacchanal of the Andrians*, 1523-24, canvas, 175 x 193cm, Prado, Madrid
80 Ambrogio Lorenzetti: *Peace*, in *Good Government*, c. 1338-40, Palazzo Publico, Sienna; Giovanni Bellini: *A Young Woman at Her Toilet*, 1515, Kunsthistorisches Museum, Vienna
81 Piero di Cosimo: *Simonetta Vespucci*, c. 1477, tempera on panel, 22.4 x 16.5in, Condé Museum, Chantilly; *Venus, Mars and Cupid*, c. 1490, panel, 72 x 182cm, Staatliche Museen, Berlin
82 Pisanello: *Allegory of Luxury*, drawing, Albertina, Vienna
83 Antonio Allegri de Correggio: *The Sleep of Antiope*, c. 1525, oil on canvas, 189.8 x 124.1cm, Louvre, Paris; Peter Paul Rubens: *Angelica and the Hermit*, c. 1625-8, oil on wood, 43 x 66cm, Kunsthistoriches Museum, Vienna
84 Simon Vouet: *Psyche Looking at the Sleeping Amor*, 1626, oil on canvas, 112 x 165cm, Musée des Beaux Arts, Lyons

(1545), or Paolo Veronese' *Venus and Adonis* (1580).[85]

With their hands on the woman's breasts, the males in these Venus pictures take possession of the woman's body. The high art depictions of Venus with a male character (Adonis or Cupid) are simply sophisticated versions of an image found throughout history, in folk pictures, in portraits, in woodcuts, in all manner of illustrations: the prelude to sex, or the suggestion of sex, is made by the man's hand on the woman's breast. One finds this image everywhere, and in much of high art (in the School of Fountainbleau's *Venus, Mars, and Cupid*, and in Rembrandt van Rijn's work).[86] It expresses, in blatantly sexual terms, the power relations between men and women. Man is the active one, the do-er, the toucher; woman is passive, the acted upon, the touched. See, for instance, Piero di Cosimo's *A Mythological Subject*, where a Pan-figure, a satyr, touches a sleeping woman, who is *naked, of course* (and in sculpture, too: see Antonio Canova's *Cupid and Venus*).[87] The images, with the woman being touched, however gently, suggest possession. In some Renaissance images, rape is depicted with no ambiguity, as in Albrecht Dürer's *Sea-Monster Abducting a Woman*, where a horned man drags along a naked woman, clearly for his own enjoyment.[88]

It is worth noting some of the elements of Neoplatonism in Renaissance art, because Neoplatonism is the magical and philosophical system that underlies the humanist renascence of Classical art. The hermetic doctrines of ancient Neoplatonism come through Gnosticism, and are expounded by Renaissance figures such as Marsilio Ficino, Cornelius Agrippa and Pico della Mirandola. The basic tenet is that 'all is one', that what happens on earth is reflected by what happens in the heavens, and vice versa, that everything is related by a system of correspondences.

85 Veronese: *Venus and Adonis*, oil on canvas, 68 x 52cm, Kunsthisorisches Museum; Agnolo Bronzino: *Venus, Cupid, Time and Folly*, 1545, oil on wood, 146 x 116cm, National Gallery, London
86 Rembrandt: *The Jewish Bride*, c. 1666, Rijksmuseum, Amsterdam; School of Fountainebleau: *Venus, Mars and Cupid*, panel, 38. 6 x 31.5in, Petit Palais, Paris
87 Antonio Canova; *Cupid and Venus*, marble, Villa Carlota, Lake Como; Piero di Cosimo: *A Mythological Subject*, panel, 65 x 183cm, National Gallery, London
88 Dürer: *Sea-Monster Abducting a Woman*, c. 1498, engraving, 25.2 x 19cm, British Museum

Humanity is at the centre of this new humanism, as the alchemist and philosopher Agrippa noted in his *De occulta philosophia*: 'Man has in himself All that is contained in the greater world'.[89]

The Renaissance and Neoplatonic humanist worldview has remained the basis for (Western) art since the Renaissance, and the basis for much of philosophy – certainly the philosophy of the Romantic, religious, subjective, emotional kind, as found in Friedrich Nietzsche, Immanuel Kant, Sigmund Freud, Carl Jung, Percy Bysshe Shelley, and most of the great art historians – Bernard Berenson, the Warburg school, John Ruskin, Walter Pater, Roger Fry, etc. Renaissance Hellenic hermeticism was a philosophy created for and by the educated upper classes, and man, i.e., the white bourgeois male, was at the centre of the new world system.

The rise of the popularity of Greek and Classical mythologies in the Renaissance epoch was both a cause and an effect of the new person-centred religion. God was displaced, though Catholic imagery lived side by side with pagan images. The Renaissance era, with its 'Neoplatonic mysticism and Aristotlean intellect-ualism',[90] paved the way for the movement into rationalism and the age of reason and'enlightenment. It allowed for an increasing prevalence in art for erotic imagery, so that high art could be more openly erotic in its treatment of high art subject matter. Depictions of the Goddess Venus are thus an indicator or barometer of the increasing eroticization of the nude in Western high art, from Antonio Correggio, through Titian and Paolo Veronese to Édouard Manet, and beyond Manet to Auguste Rodin, Henri Matisse, Pablo Picasso, and later, Allen Jones, Hans Bellmer and Tom Wesselman.

In the Renaissance representations of Venus, sacred and profane, private and public, fear and desire merge. On the one hand, Venus is depicted often with as much awe and slavish worship as the Virgin Mary. She is a Goddess, with her attendant cherubs, like the Madonna with her attendant angels. Cupid

89 quoted in Ferguson: *An Illustrated Encyclopaedia of Mysticism*, 9
90 E.H.Gombrich: *Symbolic Images*, 179

162

becomes Christ, echoing the tenet of Catholicism that *deus est caritas* ('God is Love'). But Cupid is often Venus's consort, not simply her messenger, much as Jesus and Mary were depicted as equals, if not lovers, crowned in a spiritual marriage in Heaven. The Goddess alone is not complete, if she is a Goddess of Love. A Goddess must have her consort, according to the male system. Women alone bemuse and infuriate men. Surely, men think, there must be some companion in the set-up. Thus figures such as Salomé, Joan of Arc, many saints (Hildegard of Bingen, Catherine of Siena, St Theresa, etc), Elizabeth I, and others are objects of fascination and ridicule for patriarchal people. Thus, the ancient deities, such as Ishtar, Isis and Venus, had their male lovers; the same emphasis on heterosexual pairings occurs in Renaissance art. Even in those depictions where Venus seems to be alone, such as Sandro Botticelli's *Birth of Venus*, have a male element orchestrating the action. In Botticelli's revered image, the god of the wind, Zephyr, blows Venus to the shore. The action of the wind is symbolically masculine, associated in mythology with the creative breath of the Hindu *Upanishads*, with the Word of God, with male procreativity, etc. Behind Botticelli's Venus, then, with her (for men) ambiguous sexuality, lies male power.

So Renaissance anthropomorphism is supremely patriarchal, for it is always man who is the measure of everything, not woman. This is true in Renaissance geometry and architecture as well as painting and sculpture: men are very definitely at the centre of the Renaissance (and hence the modern) conception of art and artistic philosophy.[91] You see this everywhere in Renaissance, but most powerfully in Leonardo da Vinci's famous depiction of universal or Renaissance man (*The Proportions of the Human Body*).[92] It would be subversive if a woman was at the centre of the

91 See Robert Lawlor: *Sacred Geometry: Philosophy and Practice*, Thames & Hudson 1982, 90f; Marilyn A Lavin: *Piero della Francesca's Baptism of Christ*, Yale University Press 1981; Erwin Panofsky: *Studies in Iconology*, Harper & Row, New York 1972; Fred Gettings: *The Hidden Art: A Study of the Occult Symbolism in Art*, Studio Vista/Cassell 1978; Matilda Ghyka: *The Geometry of Art and Life*, Sheed & Ward, New York 1946; Charles Bouleau: *The Painter's Secret Geometry: a Study of Composition in Art*, tr. Jonathan Griffin, Thames & Hudson 1963
92 Leonardo: *The Proportions of the Human Body*, after Vitruvius, pen and ink, c. 1492, Accademia, Venice

universe; Leonardo's cosmic man would not work; for woman lacks the 'transcendent signifier', the phallus.

The eroticism of the Greek and Classical Goddess and figures, then, clashes at times violently with the passivity and meekness of the Virgin Mary in depictions of femininity in Renaissance art. In the Vatican, for instance, which is the centre of world Christianity for many, there is a bathroom decorated with the *History of Venus*, by Raphael Sanzio. These rooms, however, are censored, and left out of the Vatican guidebooks.

The myth of Venus is based on that of the Greek Goddess Aphrodite. According to Homer, Aphrodite, the 'foam-born', was birthed from the severed, castrated genitals of the god Uranus, which were cast into the sea, creating white foam. The Goddess was blown ashore by the West wind, Zephyrus, to Cyprus, where she was greeted and covered by the Horae. This is the scene Botticelli depicts, and the sexual origin of Venus lies behind all those female nudes of the Renaissance.

Venus and the Virgin thus represent the twin poles of patriarchal culture: the sexual and asexual, the naked and the clothed, the lover and the mother, etc. The two merge, confusedly and ambiguously, in many Renaissance artworks. The Virgin is both Mother and Lover of Christ, just as, according to psychoanalysis, the mother is the child's first lover. The cults of the milk and breasts of the Madonna emphasize the erotic nature of the child-mother relation. The structure of the Madonna and Child image, with the child seated on the other's lap, echoes that of Osiris sitting on the 'throne' of his mother Isis, who is also his lover, in ancient Egyptian art.

Even such seemingly gentle occasions such as the Annunciation are not free of sexist, patriarchal and erotic/ porn connotations. For a start, Mary is simply living her life when the Archangel Gabriel rushes in and tells her she is to bear the Son of God. Mary replies: 'how can this be, seeing I know not a man' (*Gospel of Luke*). As soon as she accepts, in the very moment she assents, she conceives Christ in her womb. It is literally the Word become Flesh.

Renaissance painters, such as Fra Angelico, depict the Annunciation as a delicate, silent moment, the two figures, Gabriel and Mary, kneeling together in spiritual communion. Angelico's Virgins are shy, passive, sad creatures.[93] For Mary in the *Gospels* is a 'good wife'; she accepts the Word of God.

Yet the Annunciation is clearly also a spiritual coercion. The woman is passive and humble. Her opinion or sanctity or dignity is not taken into account: she is forced to accept God's seed inside her. She cannot refuse the Word of the Lord. So it is sex by force for some feminists, because it is sex without consent (but is it sex? Or is it conception? These are theological paradoxes which much concerned theologians in the mediæval era).

Further, it is the taking of an earthly woman by God. It is, in fact, another version of those lusty, phallic gods – Zeus, Apollo, Jupiter – who pursue women and seduce and rape them (Jupiter chasing Danaë or Leda, Apollo chasing Daphne, etc). The gods descend on women and impregnate them. Jupiter does it by a 'golden shower' (sperm from the sky) in the myth of Danaë. The Judæo-Christian God does it by his angelic messenger, Gabriel, and the 'Word of God'. The Annunciation is yet more of the 'pornography of religion', we might say, following a second wave feminist approach. And of course, theologians and Early Christian Fathers had many problems with the Virgin Mary being an *earthly*, not a divine being. Mary was flesh-and-blood, while Christ was sent by God. Many theological debates occurred throughout the history of Christianity trying to grapple with things such as the 'virginal birth' – birth without the real pains and ruptures of labour. Clearly, on the matter of the Virgin Mary's humanity and sexuality the theologians, from St Paul through St Augustine and Thomas Aquinas to Luther and up to the latest Popes, Christian thinkers had many problems, which they are still trying to resolve. It is only very recently in

93 Angelico: *The Annunciation*, c. 1440, fresco, San Marco Museum, Florence; *The Annunciation*, late 1440s, 194 x 194cm, Prado, Madrid; *The Annunciation*, c. 1443, fresco, 187 x 157cm, cell three, San Marco Museum, Florence

Christianity's history – 1950 – that the Madonna's Assumption into heaven, her *bodily* Assumption, has become dogma, declared by the Pope in 1950.

Some Renaissance painters depict the movement of the power of the Word of God in their *Annunciations*. In Simone Martini's Uffizi *Annunciation* (1333), Mary bends away from the words issuing from Gabriel's mouth, embossed in gold.[94] The string of Latin words are phallic, recalling the Lacanian link between language and sexuality. It is the very Word that changes itself into phallic power, into a spermatozoon, a seed.

One of the most violent representations of the Annunciation comes, surprisingly, from Sandro Botticelli. As in Botticelli's fresco of the Annunciation at San Martino, the Guardi chapel *Annunciation* (1481) depicts Gabriel full of power, his clothes billowing about him on the breath of God, the Word of God.[95] Again, we see the mythic, psychic connections between breath-wind-speaking-language-maleness-creativity. Robert Graves writes that in superstition it was believed that mares could be made pregnant by the wind blowing at them from behind.[96] Botticelli's art is full of rushing air and blowing drapery.

Fra Roberto Caracciolo organized the Annunciation into fifteen stages.[97] In the Colloquy, where the real drama occurs, the tensions move from *Conturbio* (disquiet) through *Humiliato* (submission) to *Meritatio* (merit). Botticelli's *Annunciation* clearly depicts a violent kind of *Conturbio*.

In the Guardi *Annunciation* by Sandro Botticelli, the Virgin bends away from the Archangel, her head lowered in humility. The picture revolves around the most dynamic of lines, the diagonal. On the diagonal one sees the faces and outstretched hands of Mary and the Angel. As she leans away from him, her blue cloak opens to reveal her red dress. So often in Renaissance paintings the Virgin wears a blue cloak which is slitted open to

---

94 Simone Martini: *The Annunciation*, 1333, panel, 184 x 114cm, Uffizi, Florence
95 Botticelli: *The Annunciation*, 1490, 150 x 156cm, Uffizi; *The Annunciation*, 1481, fresco, 243 x 550cm, Forte del Belvedere, Florence
96 Robert Graves: *The White Goddess*
97 Caracciolo: *Sermones de Laudibus Sanctorum*, Naples 1489, in Michael Baxandall: *Painting and Experience*, 51

reveal red underneath, such an obvious vulva image.

Sandro Botticelli's *Annunciation* is violent. It depicts an aggressive sexual approach of a woman, though the pressure here is psychological and spiritual: the Archangel, as in all other depictions of the Annunciation, does not touch the Virgin. That would be too lascivious, if the Archangel's hand were placed on the breast or belly of the Virgin Mary. That would be too direct. So Gabriel does not touch the Madonna, but makes love to her from a distance, as God makes love to the Virgin from a distance, from the privileged position of Heaven. God sits on his heavenly throne, spiritually penetrating and impregnating the Virgin, who remains a Virgin, despite the physicality and pain of pregnancy and labour. The Virgin is too passive, fatally passive, for feminists. *Ecce Ancilla Domina* she says: 'behold the handmaid of the lord' (J. Metford, 28). The Virgin Mary moves from being a virgin, from 'knowing not a man', to becoming pregnant, in one anguished moment. Like Tess Durbeyfield in Thomas Hardy's 1892 novel *Tess of the d'Urbervilles*, she knows little of men. Then, the first time she knows 'love' (i.e. sex) she gets pregnant. This, then, is for some feminists a vicious kind of possession, which has the blessing of the top guy in the West, God.

The *Annunciations* of painters such as Sandro Botticelli, Fra Filippo Lippi, Fra Angelico, Simone Martini and Leonardo da Vinci illustrate that eternal paradox, the seduction and possession which is not a seduction and possession, that impregnation which is not an impregnation, that power over women which is denied by patriarchal people.

One aspect of Christian imagery and Renaissance art that most Christian thinkers would not acknowledge is the eroticism of the Saviour's naked body. It is certainly a significant element in the celebrated depictions of Christ on the Cross: by Peter Rubens, Diego Velásquez and Andrea Mantegna, among many others.[98]

98 Mantegna: *Calvary*, 1459, 67 x 93cm, Paris, Louvre; Rubens: *Christ Between the Two Thieves (Coup de Lance)*, 1620, 429 x 311cm, Musée des Beaux Arts, Antwerp; Velásquez: *Christ Crucified*, 1630, 248 x 169cm, Prado, Madrid

Christ's nakedness sends conflicting signals. Clearly, nudity has a religious or mythic aspect, connoting nature/ naturalness, purity, birth, creation, renunciation, unveiled reality, truth.[99] In art, however, nudity is ambiguous: in religious contexts it is both spiritual and sexual.[100] Christ's body is often sexless, or androgynous, or feminized.[101] Christianity is an ambivalent cult; it has a clothed, virginal woman as the object of worship on the one hand, and a naked, equally virginal and chaste man on the other. In the most holy of churches, nudity is sanctified by the statues, icons and paintings of Christ on the Cross.

Christianity cannot deal with expressions of sexuality. It has a long history of suppressing sexuality, of body-hating, of repressing eroticism and erotic art. What Christianity does is to ignore erotic feelings, or to marginalize them in the outpourings of mystics. Other religions, such as Hinduism, acknowledge eroticism. There is room for the expression of sexual feelings in Hinduism; there are many gods, for a start. Such polytheism allows, as in the Greek pantheon of deities, for all manner of feelings. Renaissance painters understandably looked to the Old Testament, to historical figures and the Greek and Roman mythologies.

The dying or dead Christ, naked but for a slip of cloth and sometimes depicted entirely naked but with his legs bent to one side, hiding the 'transcendent signifier', the phallus, is an image of homoeroticism. Theologians and art historians down the ages did not or would not admit that Christ was or could have been an object of lust. Yet this is clearly the case in some depictions of the naked Saviour, such as paintings by Giovanni Battista Rosso, Michelangelo Merisi da Caravaggio, or Antonello da Messina.[102] These nude figures send a mass of signals, from the pathetic to the narcissistic, from the erotic to the spiritual.

As newspapers and TV moguls know, death is sexy: violent

99 See J.C. Cooper: *An Illustrated Encyclopaedia of Symbols*, 112-3
100 See Marina Warner: *Monuments and Maidens*, 304
101 See William Thompson: *The Time Falling Bodies Take to Light*, 109
102 Antonello da Messina: *Crucifixion*, 1475, 52.5 x 42.5cm, Musée des Beaux Arts, Antwerp; Caravaggio: *Entombment*, 1604, 300 x 203cm, Vatican, Rome; Rosso: *Dead Christ Supported by Angels*, c. 1524-7. Oil on wood, 133.6 x 104.4cm, Museum of Fine Arts, Boston

168

news is called 'sexy' news. And Christ dying on the Cross is the ultimate in 'sexy' news. It is the ideal news story: the death of an amazing individual, so much easier for the public to identify with than some complex ideological war on the far side of the planet (individuals are much easier to portray in the media – and in art – than issues). The (homo)erotic aspect of the nude Jesus plays a part in the eroticization of death and life that occurs in Renaissance painted *Crucifixions*. The homoeroticism of nude figures in other contexts – in mythology, naked Cupids, cherubs, Greek gods and the like – is OK, it is part of paganism, such as in Perugino's *Apollo and Marsyas* (*c.* 1496), or in depictions of dancing naked in bacchanales, for example).[103] Depictions of Greek or pagan mythology is deemed justifiably homosexual by establishment art critics, because ancient Greek culture was homosexual in part. But seeing Christ's phallus, now that is blasphemy, as the many cover-ups, done by artists or others, demonstrate. Eric Gill put the eroticism back into the crucified Christ by drawing his penis, and by drawing attention to the penis, by enlarging it, in many woodcuts and sculptures.[104] Gill's Christs are distinctly eroticized, as for Gill religion and sex were part of the same mystery.

More problematic are those Renaissance paintings of Christ that emphasize the physical agony of the Crucifixion. It is a gory event, and painters such as Peter Rubens feast on the blood gushing from the wounds, while Lucas Cranach's *Pietà* had Christ covered in cuts all over his skin. The most anguished Christ is undoubtedly that of Matthias Grünewald, whose Saviour figures curl up in agony, the body shrunken and exhausted, pitted, scarred, cut and beaten, the head fallen down, the ankles crushed together.[105] Grünewald's *Crucifixions* (in his *Isenheim Altarpiece* [1512-16], for instance) gets closest to making visual the agony at the heart of the sadomasochistic ritual at the heart of Christianity.

Patriarchal people (mostly male) protect their own interests. So

103 Perugino: *Apollo and Marsyas, c.* 1496, Louvre, Paris
104 Gill: *Crucifix with Crown of Thorns*, 1922, print, Victoria & Albert Museum
105 Grünewald: *Small Crucifixion*, 1520, 61.5 x 46cm, National Gallery, Washington; *Crucifixion*, c. 1510, 73 x 52.5cm, Öffenliche Kunstsammlung, Basel; *Christ on the Cross (the Isenheim Altarpiece)*, 1512-6, oil on panel, central panel: 269 x 307cm, Musée d'Unterlinden, Colmar

homosexual art is OK, because many male critics and artists appreciate homosexual representations or issues. The reality of lesbian art becoming part of the establishment in the arts is far off. Two of the greatest artists of the High Renaissance (and therefore of all Western culture, according to patriarchal critics) were homosexual: Leonardo da Vinci and Michelangelo Buonarroti.

MICHELANGELO BUONARROTI

Beside Michelangelo Buonarroti (1475-1564), the precocious, religious, obsessive hero of the era, other Renaissance sculptors often seem lightweight, insubstantial or hackneyed. Lucia della Robbia, Benvenuto Cellini, Baccio Bandinelli, Giambologna, Bartolommeo Ammanati and Donatello – every sculptor measures themself against Michelangelo, or is measured against Michelangelo by future generations. Michelangelo's sculptures are full of the spirit of life which is expressed with an assurance of touch and modelling that is in itself erotic. His sculptures assert their eroticism, whatever the subject, from the superb *Dawn* and *Dusk* of the Medici tomb, to the late *Pietà*.[106]

There is undeniably a vivacious enjoyment of the male form in Michelangelo's *Ignudi* in the Sistine Chapel,[107] for instance, while his *Dying Slave* is one of the most sensual images of eroticism combined with death in Western art.[108] Michelangelo's slave dies utterly voluptuously, his arms pulled up to expose his body. Michelangelo's figures are confident in their nudity and their sexuality. They exude confidence – too much, it seems, for the owners of the Sistine Chapel: figures in Michelangelo's *Last*

106 Michelangelo: *Tomb of Lorenzo de' Medici*, h. 173, Medici Chapel, Florence; *Pietà*, late 1550s, marble, 226cm high, Florence cathedral
107 Michelangelo: *Ignudi*, 1508-10, fresco, Sistine Chapel, Vatican, Rome
108 Michelangelo: *Dying Slave*, 1513, marble, 229cm high, Louvre, Paris

Judgement had drapes painted over their genitals during the Counter-Reformation.[109] And in 1970 the use of Michelangelo's *David* on a poster was banned.[110]

Michelangelo Buonarroti's figures add angst-ridden and 'modern' tensions – of self, identity, passion and Existential awareness – to the basically life-affirming gestures of ancient Greek sculpture. Michelangelo takes the anonymous, often indifferent eroticism of Greek statues and turns it into something modern or Renaissance, something decidedly individual and subjective. The anguish of (some of) Michelangelo's figures is that of a 'great' artist striving to achieve the Holy Grail or Philosopher's Stone of sculpture, the perfect form, that Neoplatonic impossibility. Beautiful as they are ('beauty' is precisely the right term for Renaissance's notions of perfection), Michelangelo's statues are not final, finished forms. They are fluid, aching for the touch of completion which nobody can give them. In Michelangelo's art, eroticism is passionately – sometimes desperately – asserted.

LEONARDO DA VINCI

The most erotic artist of the Renaissance, the one who created the darkest and the strangest images, who painted the most hypnotic smile in art, who took Western painting to the highest point it has reached, was not Michelangelo Buonarroti, Andrea del Sarto, Fra Angelico, Sandro Botticelli, Piero della Francesca, Andrea Mantegna, Giovanni Bellini, Raphael, Titian, Michelangelo Merisi da Caravaggio, Simone Martini, Fra Bartolommeo, Lucas Cranach

---

109 Michelangelo: *The Last Judgement*, 136-41, fresco, 1375 x 120cm, Sistine Chapel, Vatican, Rome

110 'In 1970, a bookseller in Sydney, Australia, was arrested for displaying a poster of the nude *David*, and the same happened in South Africa in 1973.' Peter Webb, *The Erotic Arts*, 4-5

or Masaccio, but Leonardo da Vinci (1452-1519).

Like Michelangelo Buonarroti, Leonardo da Vinci produced an erotic version of *Leda and the Swan*. Both Michelangelo's and Leonardo's images are lost. We know both, though, because they were copied.[111] Michelangelo's picture is explicitly erotic: the huge swan lies between the deity's legs, the feathers of his wing over her vulva, a touch that expresses male possession of the woman's sexuality.

Leonardo da Vinci made his *Leda and the Swan* as porn is made; at the request of a (male) client: 'I executed the painting... for a lover. He wished to see the features of his goddess mirrored so that he might kiss them without arousing suspicion', Leonardo wrote.[112]

Leonardo da Vinci is one of the most celebrated of artists, he's perhaps the most exalted artist in the West. He is the artist-as-hero, the artist-as-genius, undisputed genius (like William Shakespeare or Sophocles). Leonardo is enshrined for his amazing mind, his scientific curiosity, his ideas on botany, anatomy, architecture, weaponry, engineering, etc. But it is Leonardo's *sfumato* painterly technique, his brilliant manipulation of oil colours, that makes him so profoundly erotic. Stendhal wrote of Leonardo's 'soft, melancholy tones, full of shadows'.[113] The most common adjective applied to Leonardo's art is 'mysterious'. Walter Pater wrote famously of the *Mona Lisa*, in a way which says more about Pater and late Victorian and Decadent art than it does about Leonardo:

> She is older than the rocks among which she sits... [she embodies] the animalism of Greece, the lust of Rome, the mysticism of the Middle Ages with its spiritual ambition and imaginative loves, the return of the pagan world, the sins of the Borgias.[114]

Pater reinvents the *femme fatale* image of the *Mona Lisa* for his own Decadent age. Each era reinvents Leonardo da Vinci, or any

111 After Michelangelo: *Leda and the Swan*, 16th century, Royal Academy, London
112 quoted in Peter Webb, 112
113 Stendhal: *Histoire de la peinture en Italie*, 1877
114 Walter Pater: *The Renaissance*, Fontana 1964, 123

artist. The most astonishing mythicization of an artist is undoubtedly that of Vincent van Gogh, so that van Gogh's works sell for millions and millions of dollars, far exceeding (nearly) all other artists.

Leonardo da Vinci is and is not typical of the Renaissance. There is no one else quite like him, not before, and not since. His art transcends time and place, and becomes a symbol of all that is 'great' and to be strived for in art. His erotic *sfumato* technique stems from his manipulation of oil glazes, similar to those employed by the Early Flemish painters (Jan van Eyck, Rogier van der Weyden and Hans Memling, among others).

Leonardo da Vinci creates very deep space, deep shadows, sculptural forms, dark tones and glowing lights. His art is 'deep', one might say: artistically, psychologically, emotionally and spiritually and every which way. Like high or intellectual erotic art, Leonardo's art hides as much as it reveals. Leonardo's paintings are mysterious, difficult to penetrate. In the art of Leonardo, the visible is self-consciously obscured. There are veils which have to be lifted aside, to uncover the mysteries and beauties within. This is the process of eroticism – all tantalizing anticipations – while often porn shows everything at once ('cos who wants to wait?).

Leonardo da Vinci's art is *occult* in its eroticism: it hides its essence in cloaks of superbly-crafted presence. Something is there, the viewer knows, but it is not readily available, it is not presented in daylight. If the *manufacture* of high art is a crucial element in its power, then Leonardo's paintings are the most sublimely sensuous of all high art works. The skin on his figures – in the two *Virgin of the Rocks* paintings, for instance – is in one glance like cold marble, then in the next glance like snakeskin, then like living flesh, moving gently, reflecting back the light of the room.

In eroticism, *nearly* seeing the erotic is one of the key experiences. Eroticism trades on glimpses of the body, on fragments of scenes being revealed. Leonardo da Vinci is the master of such erotic glimpses. As Paul Valéry wrote of Leonardo da Vinci in a famous essay: '[h]e feels a desire to picture the invisible wholes of which he has been given some visible parts.'[115]

The figure of the angel is a key element in Leonardo da Vinci's depiction of the 'invisible'. The angel, as the German poet Rainer Maria Rilke noted, is that presence that can move between this and the Otherworld, between light and dark, between the living and the dead, between Heaven and Earth. Leonardo's angels are the most terrifying figures in Renaissance art. They are human and more-than-human, they are softly smiling, they are sunken in shadow, they are sumptuously androgynous, both male and female, and more than either, like the divine being of alchemy.

Leonardo da Vinci's angels are at the height of their mystery in *The Adoration of the Magi* (1480, Uffizi), a truly magnificent drawing, and so frightening in its inexplicableness, its miraculous ability to hypnotize the viewer, its astonishing power and frenetic energy.[116] Leonardo's angels move amongst humans in that shadowy zone below the tree. It is a vision of humanity in a whirlpool of religious energy, the focus of which is the epiphany of the Virgin and Child, who sit so calmly still in the centre.

In the two paintings of *The Virgin of the Rocks* (about 1483 and 1503-06), the Leonardoan angel appears at its most voluptuous.[117] The sketch of Leonardo's angel (1483-90) is extraordinary in itself,[118] but when Leonardo's unsurpassed graphic abilities are combined with his deeply erotic *sfumato* lighting and oil technique, the result is dazzling. Leonardo's painted angel is, to use Oswald Spengler's term, 'indescribable'.[119] So the art critic moves into superlative overload, as Walter Pater or John Ruskin

115 Paul Valéry: *An Introduction to the Method of Leonardo da Vinci*, 1894, in *An Anthology*, selected by James Lawler, Routledge 1977, 54
116 Leonardo: *Adoration of the Magi*, 1481-2, panel, 246 x 243cm, Uffizi, Florence
117 Leonardo: *The Virgin of the Rocks*, c. 1503-6, oil, 189.5 x 120cm, National Gallery, London; *The Virgin of the Rocks*, c. 1483-6, oil, 198 x 123cm, Louvre
118 Leonardo: *Study For the Head of an Angel*, 1483-90, silverpoint on light brown prepared surface, 18.2cm x 16cm, Royal Library, Turin
119 Oswald Spengler: *The Decline of the West*, Allen & Unwin 1961, 154

often did, and comes out with a load of over-lyrical hyperbole. The gushing style of some art historians helps to emphasize the erotic nature of art and art criticism.

Leonardo da Vinci's angels certainly have a 'terrifying ethereality', to use a term typical of the more Romantic branches of art criticism. Leonardo's 'genius' is more than a thaumaturgic ability to manipulate paint and tone and colour, but this does help. The American painter Adolph Gottlieb wrote: '[p]aint quality is meaningless if it does not express quality of feeling.'[120] Gottlieb announces again the connection between the materiality of painting and the emotionalism of it. Certainly Leonardo knows how to modulate expressiveness and feeling through paint and line. Nowhere is this more apparent than in the famous Leonardo Smile.

Many pages have been written about the enigmatic Leonardo da Vinci Smile, which at once inviting and repelling, at once mysterious and joyful, complex and simple, timeless and evanescent, so transient yet always fixed. The Leonardo Smile is the apotheosis of ambivalent emotion. For European intellectuals, the Gioconda Smile is the cruel smile of the Medusa, the Fatal Woman, the eulogized Black Venus.[121] In fact, the Leonardo Smile is the most transparent of all images, for its reflects the emotions of whoever is looking at it. Leonardo's art is more like a mirror than most other painter's works, except perhaps Andy Warhol. Warhol, like Leonardo, is one of those artists who creates a myriad of responses, from disbelief through jealousy to admiration. As Nico in Warhol's Velvet Underground sang, 'I'll be your mirror'. Warhol's art is a mirror, as is Leonardo's, a carefully controlled, stylish reflector. The Gioconda Smile of the *Mona Lisa* is at the heart of the Leonardo cult (and the screenprints of Marilyn Monroe are at the heart of the Warhol cult).

The Leonardo da Vinci Smile appears in *The Adoration of the Magi*, the two *Virgin of the Rocks*, the *Mona Lisa*, *Lady with the*

---

120 Gottlieb in *The New Decade*, Whitney Museum of Art, New York 1955, 36
121 See Mario Praz, 320; and D'Annunzio's poem 'Gorgon' in M. Praz, 50; also, Charles Baudelaire's 'Les Phares', in *Flowers of Evil, ed.* M. & J. Matthews, New Directions, New York, 1958, 12-13

Ermine, St John the Baptist and, most powerfully, perhaps, in *The Virgin and Child With St Anne*.[122] Sigmund Freud has his opinions on the Leonardo Smile: for him, Leonardo was recapturing his mother's smile.[123] In his art, Freud suggests, Leonardo triumphed over 'the unhappiness of his erotic life' (ib., 162). The source of the Leonardo Smile may not be in Freudian conflict and taboo: instead, it may be an attempt on Leonardo's part to express an inexplicable joy, the kind of joy one feels sometimes at simply being alive. Like the joy of suddenly feeling a ray from the sun on one's face after hours of cloud. Whether such joys are erotic in motive, cause or nature is debatable. What is certain is that Leonardo's smiling people are mesmerizing. As Rudolf Otto writes, the experience of the Numinous (which he terms the *mysterium tremendum*) 'may become the hushed, trembling, and speechless humility of the creature in the presence of – whom or what? In the presence of that which is a *mystery* inexpressible and above all creatures.'[124]

The presence in Leonardo da Vinci's art is distinctly female and feminine. For him, the mystery of life is embodied best in women, in Goddess figures. Leonardo's women are simultaneously objects of awe and veneration, as paintings, and producers of awe and veneration, as Goddesses. Many elements in Leonardo's are feminized or feminine: not only the androgynous or feminized males, such as the Baptist or St Jerome, but also the profusion of flowers, for instance, in the two *Virgin of the Rocks*. These flowers symbolize the Virgin Mary (carnation, iris, lily, etc) but also they point towards woman as the Goddess of Flowers and Plants, as the Earth Mother, the fertile Mother of all. The Madonnas are depicted in caves, again an explicit female symbol ('the Great Earth Mother is the mother of stones' writes a Jungian, Erich Neumann [261-2]).

Leonardo da Vinci's Madonnas are Queens of the

---

122 Leonardo: *Lady with the Ermine*, c. 1485-90, oil on panel, 54 x 39cm, Czartoryski Museum, Cracow; *St John the Baptist*, c. 113-6, panel, 69 x 57cm, Louvre, Paris; *Virgin and Child and St Anne*, c. 1510, oil on panel, 168 x 112cm, Louvre, Paris
123 Sigmund Freud: *Leonardo da Vinci*, tr. Alan Tyson, Penguin 1963,
124 Rudolf Otto: *The Idea of the Holy*, Oxford University Press, 1958, 13

Underworld, presiding over the unconscious, unborn underworld states of being. The Louvre *Virgin of the Rocks is* particularly rich in floral imagery. At Christ's feet, for instance, is *cyclamen purpurascens*, which symbolizes love and devotion.[125] All the signifiers in Leonardo's portrayals of the Madonna are of an abundant world, of flowers and plants, in which life is thriving. Leonardo's vision of a vegetative, organic Goddess emphasizes that the authentic *participation mystique* with the Earth is feminine.

In *The Virgin of the Rocks* there is the suggestion of an immense, holy touch, a miraculous touch which heals, like the 'laying on of hands' in Jesus' life. The Madonna raises her hand, which is stretched out, foreshortened, towards the viewer, at once blessing the Christ child and encouraging him. The upraised hand of the Virgin is a gesture of power, for at the heart of Leonardo da Vinci's world is not the Judæo-Christian male God or Jehovah, but a Goddess who has more in common with ancient deities such as Isis or Inanna than with the relatively recent phenomena of the Virgin Mary.

Indeed, Leonardo da Vinci can be seen to be obsessed with the ideas of female power and motherhood. Two works depict the trinity of matriarchy, the powerful bonding of child, mother and grandmother, embodied in the Louvre *Virgin and Child with St Anne* and in the London or Burlington 'Cartoon', *St Anne with the Virgin, Child and Baptist.*[126] It is St Anne who is the power behind Leonardo's Goddess figures. She is the crone, the wise old woman, later depicted as a 'witch' in mediæval culture. She is an incarnation of the Black Goddess, the occult deity of secret energies and mysteries. Black Goddesses include the Gnostic Sophia, Diana and Isis (later Goddesses of witches), Hecate, Medusa, Circe, Lilith (Adam's first lover), and the Indian Kali.[127]

The Black Goddess appears in Tantrism, Taoism, Catharism, alchemy, witchcraft, Neoplatonism and other occultisms. The *Tao*

125 See William A. Emboden: *Leonardo da Vinci: On Plants and Gardens*, Christopher Helm, Bromley, Kent, 1987, 116

126 Leonardo: *St Anne, the Virgin and Child with the Baptist* c. 1498, black chalk and white on paper, 141.5 x 104.6cm, National Gallery, London

127 See Monica Sjöö, 210; Peter Redgrove; Ean Begg; Robert Graves: *Mammon and the Black Goddess*, Cassell 1965

Te Ching speaks of 'knowing the male, but keeping to the role of the female': '[k]now the white, but keep to the role of the black'.[128] For some, the black Mother is the origin of humanity; we are all descended from one African woman (Sjöo, 32). Peter Redgrove writes that the Black Goddess is the deity of the invisible, of the unconscious, of second sight and 'supersensible' eroticism (137). This is Leonardo's world, this dark, hyper-sensitive, erotic environment.

Leonardo da Vinci's Goddesses are dark, fecund, mythic types, figures of mystery and power. His St Anne trades in the mediæval and Renaissance cult of St Anne, especially prevalent in Northern European art. St Anne becomes another represent-ation of primæval nature, of the Goddess as Earth Mother. Leonardo's Dark Moon or Negative Goddess is a Renaissance version of woman as origin of life, of woman as nurturer and carer. In one sense, the St Anne pictures are nostalgic, looking back on the happy unity of childhood. Indeed, Leonardo's Marys are – rarely in Renaissance art – shown smiling. Probably the most inscrutable smile in Western art is not that of the *Mona Lisa*, but of St Anne in the Louvre *Virgin, Child and St Anne*. Here, St Anne is the rock, the roots, the pivot, the foundation of life. She smiles softly at the Virgin pulling the child away from the lamb. The two Mothers, St Anne and the Madonna, merge together, physically. Their limbs entwine.

St Anne is at the back of everything. From her body grows the Madonna, and then the child. St Anne melts into the darkening blue of the landscape, while the Madonna stands out in vermilion. The pyramidal structure of Leonardo's *St Anne, Virgin and Child* is surmounted by St Anne' face.

Leonardo da Vinci's *Holy Families* do not pivot around the so-called 'nuclear family': father, mother and children; they centre on the grandmother, mother and child. Naturally, psychologists see in Leonardo's images the tensions of incest, of childhood sexuality, of emotional traumas and the complications

---

128 *Tao Te Ching*, tr. D.C. Lau, Penguin, 1963, 85

surrounding mother-child relationships. Fred Gettings sees
Leonardo's *Burlington Cartoon* as a depiction of *two* Jesuses, a
fusion of the celestial and earthly ones.[129] In mythology, twins are
common – Osiris and Set, Castor and Pollux (whom Leonardo had
depicted in his lost *Leda and the Swan*). The idea of the two Jesuses,
also put forward by Sigmund Freud, expresses the ancient
conflicts between the god and his rival for the Goddess's love. In
ancient mythology, there is a god of the waxing year who is
usurped by the god of the waning year. There is always, it seems,
a rival in the heterosexual relations of gods and goddesses.

The theme of the rival is taken up by William Shakespeare in
many plays: in *The Tempest*, for example, where Prospero, the
banished Duke, has a political rival and a magical/ spiritual one,
Caliban. Again, the feminine mysteries dominate Shakespeare's
last play; Caliban, Prospero's rival, takes his magical power, as
Prospero does, from the Witch Sycorax.[130] The world of *The
Tempest*, then, like that of Leonardo da Vinci, is pervaded by
feminine mysteries.[131] (There are many other similarities between
Leonardo and Shakespeare; not just that both artists are regarded
as geniuses, the very apotheosis of their artform, but also in their
use of androgynous figures. Shakespeare wrote parts of women
that were played on stage by men, and characters such as
Rosalind, Viola, Portia and Julia have ambiguous sexual
identities).[132]

In Leonardo da Vinci's paintings, the myths and conflicts of
matriarchal incest are questioned, the mother-son paradox in
which, symbolically, the son is simultaneously father, husband
and child. The religious dimension of incest is noted by some
critics in Egyptian religion, for instance. C.G. Jung wrote that

129 Fred Gettings: *The Hidden Art*, 54-5
130 See Ted Hughes: *Shakespeare and the Goddess of Complete Being*, Faber 1992
131 See B.D. Barnacle: *Shakespeare: Love, Magic and Poetry in the Sonnets and Plays*, Crescent
Moon 1993
132 See Marjorie Garber: "The Transvestite's Progress", in Jean L. Marsden, ed. *The
Appropriation of Shakespeare: Post-Renaissance Reconstructions of the Works and the Myth*,
Harvester Wheatsheaf 1991, 145-6; Alan Bray: *Homosexuality in Renaissance England*, Gay
Men's Press, 1982; Jean Howard: "Crossdressing, the theatre and gender struggle in early
modern England", *Shakespeare Quarterly* (39), 1988, 432; Stephen Orgel: "Nobody's perfect: or
why did the English stage take boys for women?", *South Atlantic Quarterly*, (88), winter 1989,
7-28

'usually incest has a highly religious aspect'.[133]

Leonardo da Vinci's art allows for a multiplicity of readings. It is distinctly non-didactic, non-monoscopic. Sigmund Freud, for instance, analyzed the Louvre *St Anne, Virgin and Child* as an expression of childhood emotional conflicts: the smile in both figures, says Freud, is 'the blissful smile of the joy of motherhood' (*Leonardo*, 157). But Leonardo's Two Mothers defy a final, standard analysis. They remain a mystery. For in Leonardo's art, as in so much of art, the opposite is also true. As Tom Chetwynd writes: 'in symbolism, as in life, everything is continuously changing into its opposite' (268-272). This is true too of pornography and eroticism: what is sublimely erotic and 'high art' may just as easily be seen as lowest art and pornography. Leonardo's figures, like the statues of Michelangelo or the nude Christs of Diego Velásquez, Peter Paul Rubens, Rogier van der Weyden or Juseppe Ribera, might be seen as expressions of conflicts between sexuality and spirituality, or culture and nature, or the visible and the invisible, or any manner of dichotomies.

RENAISSANCE EROTIC ART

After the astonishing output of Leonardo da Vinci and Michelangelo Buonarroti, Renaissance art lost some of its passion, although it became increasingly openly erotic. Images such as Peter Lely's *Nymphs by a Fountain*, anything by Peter Paul Rubens, Jean Honoré Fragonard's *Bathers*, Jacques-Louis David's *Cupid and Psyche*, and Jean Auguste Dominique Ingres' study for *Ruggiero and Angelica* are openly erotic, displaying the body as a

---

133 C.G. Jung: *Memories, Dreams, Reflections*, 152, 191

sensual object.[134] Myths such as that of the Judgement of Paris and the Three Graces allow ample opportunity for painting acres of quivering female flesh, as in paintings by Raphael, with his Neoplatonically idealized figures, or in the work of Rubens, Lucas Cranach and Hans Baldung Grien.[135] Artists such as Tintoretto, Paolo Veronese, François Boucher, Giovanni Tiepolo, Jean-Antoine Watteau, Guido Reni, Rembrandt van Rijn, Guercino, Correggio, Baron Antoine-Jean Gros, Anne-Louis Trioson-Girodet, Théodore Géricault, and Eugène Delacroix do not hide their depictions of erotic bodies behind mythological narratives. Their images often put eroticism in the foreground: the pretence at mythological or historical painting is not longer upheld, and the nude form becomes primary. See, for instance, the voluptuous nude in Correggio's *Jupiter and Antiope* (c. 1525), the acres of female flesh in *The Three Graces* by Tintoretto (1540), or in his *Susannah and the Elders* (1560),where the image of a woman admiring herself in a mirror occurs, to shift the focus from masculine vanity, or the ample back view of a woman, *nude of course*, stared at by two men, clothed of course, or luminous skin of the women, *nude of course*, in Hans Baldung's *Sacred and Profane Love* (1523), where it is not clear after all which is which, which is 'sacred' and which 'profane'.[136]

The Romantic and Decadent *femme fatale* is nothing new in the 19th century: earlier paintings such as Guido Cagnacci's *Lucretia* is explicitly erotic; Lucretia stabbing herself sublimely merges sex and death in an image of the feminine.[137] One mythic image

---

134 Peter Lely: *Nymphs by a Fountain*, c. 1650-5, canvas, 129 x 144.8cm, Dulwich Picture Gallery, London; David: *Cupid and Psyche*, 1817, canvas, 184.1 x 241.6cm, Cleveland Museum of Art; Jean-Honoré Fragonard: *Bathers*, canvas, 64 x 80, Louvre, Paris; Jean-Auguste-Dominique Ingres: *Study for Ruggiero and Angelica*, c. 1819, canvas, 84.5 x 42.5cm, Musée Ingres, Montauban
135 Rubens: *The Judgement of Paris*, c. 1638-9, Prado, Madrid; Lucas Cranach: *The Judgement of Paris*, 1530, Staatliche Kunsthalle, Karlsruhe; Hans Baldung Grien: *The Three Graces*, c. 1540, Prado, Madrid; Raphael: *The Three Graces*, c. 1504, panel, 6.6 x 6.6in, Condé Museum, Chantilly
136 Hans Baldung: *Sacred and Profane Love*, 1523, panel, 25.6 x 18.2in, Städel Institute, Frankfurt; Tintoretto: *Susannah and the Elders*, c. 1560, oil on canvas, 76 x 95.6in, Kunsthistorisches Museum, Vienna, *The Three Graces*, 1578, oil on canvas, 57.5 x 61in, Ducal Palace, Venice; Correggio: *Jupiter and Antiope*, c. 1525, oil on canvas, 74.8 x 48.8in, Louvre, Paris
137 Guido Cagnaci: *Death of Lucretia*, canvas, 87 x 66cm, Musée des beaux Arts, Lyons

allowed for artists to paint a scene that depicted nudity and eroticism, magic and heterosexual love, the myth of Danaë. She was imprisoned in a tower by her father, who was warned by an oracle that she would bear a son that would murder him. The god Jupiter (Zeus) saw her, lusted after her, and descended to her in a shower of gold, which she caught between her legs; the result was Perseus. Painters depict the moment when the golden semen of the phallic deity falls on the nude Danaë, as in the versions by Correggio, Titian, Rembrandt and Mabuse.[138]

The sexploits of phallic deities such as Zeus/ Jupiter, whether he's chasing Leda as a swan or impregnating Danaë as a golden shower, provide many opportunities for artists to make erotic art which is justifiably 'noble' because it comes from Classic mythology. Thus, one finds Guilio Romano depicting Jupiter with an erect penis about to tup Olympia,[139] while in Antoine Coypel's (?) picture of Leda and the Swan (c. 1750), Jupiter's genitals are again the focus of the image, as the woman sits astride his legs.[140]

As I've noted above, many of the great artists of Renaissance and post-Renaissance art have produced erotic art, erotic art meant for selected clients, not for mass consumption, in addition to the eroticism in their 'great' works. Thus, the great Rembrandt van Rijn drew a couple copulating on a bed, Henri Fuseli drew a woman sucking the nipples of a woman, her hand on her clitoris, François Boucher drew half-naked people groping each other, Francesco Parmigianino drew a hilarious Witches' Sabbath, featuring a witch astride a gigantic phallus, Francisco de Goya drew two people sucking each other's genitals, Nicholas Géricault painted two people writhing under Caravaggesque drapes, and

138 Rembrandt van Rijn: The Danaë, 1636, oil on canvas, 186 x 201cm, Hermitage St Petersburg; Titian: Danaë, 1553-4, oil on canvas, 128 x 178cm, Prado, Madrid; Mabuse (Jan Gossaert): Danaë, 1527, Alte Pinacothek, Munich; Correggio: Danaë, 1531/2, canvas, 161 x 193cm, Borghese Gallery, Rome
139 Guilio Romano: Jupiter and Olympia, 1525-35, Mansell Collection, London
140 Antoine Coypel (?): Jupiter with Leda and the Swan, from Histoire Universelle, c. 1750, British Museum

William Turner sketched people lovemaking.[141]

Painters such as Peter Paul Rubens do not hide their interest in the eroticism of art. Rubens' paintings are wild romps through fields of nakedness, through acres and acres of flesh.[142] When you see a large number of Rubens' paintings together, the effect is overwhelming: no other painter created such a shivering, trembling vision of shivering, trembling flesh. Among other post-Renaissance painters, there is a wealth of eroticism in Michelangelo Merisi da Caravaggio, Juseppe Ribera, Bartolomé Murillo, Giovanni Tiepolo, Artemisia Gentileschi, Francisco de Zurbarán and Paolo Veronese.

In the art of Titian, as in Leonardo da Vinci, the sensuality of the paint surface is primary in the 'genius' of the art, in the critical acclaim the art generates. Whatever the subject, Titian manages to produce marvellous paintings.[143] Titian's soft colouring, his blurring of forms, his use of luminous lighting and his open use of paint look towards Impressionism and modern painting. Paintings such as *Venus Anadyomene* (*c.* 1520) can stand happily beside Pierre Renoir as a modern depiction of a woman, a typical representation of woman as erotic object, of woman as Goddess and earthbound, flesh-and-blood being.[144]

These are typical views of the feminine' Titian's work, like that of any of the post-Renaissance 'great' artists – Rembrandt, Velásquez, Tintoretto, Veronese, Goya – trades in archetypical representations of women. J.A.D. Ingres' art, for instance, contains many voluptuous female nudes, where there is no attempt whatsoever at pretending that the goal of the painting is anything

---

141 Henry Fuseli: *Lesbian Couple,* c. 1815-20, Edward Croft-Murray, London; François Boucher: *Pastoral Scene*, c. 1750s, Cary von Karwath, Vienna; Francisco de Goya (?): *Sixty-Nine*, c. 1790s, G. Lo Duca, Paris; Rembrandt: *Ledakant*, c. 1646, British Museum; J.M.W. Turner: *Sheet of Sexual Drawings*, c. 1820s, British Museum; Théodore Géricault: *Lovers*, 1815-6, oil on canvas, 24 x 32.5cm, private collection, Geneva; Francesco Parmigianino: *Witches' Sabbath*, 1530s, British Museum
142 See for instance his *Diana and Her Nymphs Surprised by Fauns*, oil, 50 x 124in, Prado, Madrid
143 Titian: *The Pesaro Altarpiece*, 1519-20, canvas, 478 x 268cm, Santa Maria Gloriosa dei Frari, Venice; *Christ Crowned with Thorns*, mid-1540s, 303 x 180cm, Louvre, Paris; *Pietà*, up to 1576, 353 x 348cm, Galeria dell' Academia, Venice
144 Titian: *Venus Anadyomene*, c. 1520, canvas, 76 x 57.3cm, Duke of Sutherland Collection, on loan to the National Gallery of Scotland, Edinburgh

other than the avid contemplation of female flesh and eroticism.[145] By the time of Pierre Renoir, there is no mythological or religious counterpoint to the pornographic approach to the female nude, there is simply the nude itself, depicted in poses which reveal and conceal, which titillate and tantalize, as in Renoir's *Grandes Baigneuses* (1884-87), which is an idealized vision of an erotic paradise of sexually available women.[146]

One of the strangest of all Western painters is Nicolas Poussin. He produced a few distinctly erotic works, the usual drawings of erect penises, nude women and copulation.[147] His major art, the mythological paintings, sends conflicting signals of eroticism and revulsion. So many of his paintings depict Greek orgies, often presided over a statue of Pan, a madly-grinning Pan with no arms or legs, just a torso and a head. In *Triumph of Pan* (1636) the sovereign overseeing the Bacchic frenzy is not a demure and enigmatic Venus, as in Sandro Botticelli's *Primavera*, but a red-faced goat-god, Pan.[148]

In the art of Nicolas Poussin, as in Peter Rubens, there are endless displays of naked bodies, but they are painted in a cold, matter-of-fact style, quite unlike the sensuality of, say, Titian or Michelangelo Merisi da Caravaggio. Poussin's mythological scenes are friezes, in which all the actors are frozen. They are stiff with the awareness of their own monumentality. With their over-emphasized gestures, Poussin's people seem caught in an act, in a drama or a masquerade they would rather not join. They are personifications and victims of primal urges of greed, jealousy, vengeance and lust. They are subject to the ravages of time and the cycles of life, as depicted in Poussin's *A Dance to the Music of Time*.[149]

In pictures such as *A Bacchanalian Revel Before a Term of Pan* (1635-38), the figures, the men with their red-hued skin, the

145 See Ingres' *The Turkish Bath*, 1859-63, Louvre, Paris, for example, or *Odalisque with Slave*, 1842, Walters Art Gallery, Baltimore
146 Pierre-Auguste Renoir: *Grandes Baigneuses*, 1884-7, Philadelphia Museum of Art
147 For instance, the ithyphallic satyr in a drawing in the Musée Condé, Chantilly, and a drawing in the Louvre, called *Acis and Galatea*
148 Poussin: *Triumph of Pan*, 1636, canvas, 52 x 57in, National Gallery, London
149 Poussin: *A Dance to the Music of Time*, canvas, 84.8 x 107.6cm, Wallace Collection, London

women pale like the moon, cavort with limbs entwined in pagan rites that seem both innocent and sinister, harmless and violent, erotic and desexed.[150] For all their wild movement, Nicolas Poussin's paintings are monolithic and static, like stones. The figures are expressions of some deep anxieties and ambiguities, for Poussin's art is ever one of unease and anxiety. He depicted some brutal acts – a man being strangled by a snake, for instance., or a saint having his entrails pulled out by a winch. The brutality is æstheticized, as sex is, producing that bizarre *frisson* of violence mythicized and æstheticized, where revolting acts of terror become objects of painterly forms, where violence is subjected to formal considerations – in the slow motion of contemporary cinema, for instance, or in the huge works of Rococo and Baroque art (in Charles Le Brun, for instance).

Two of the most famous female nudes in the whole history of art, Diego Velásquez's *Venus* (1649-50)and Francisco de Goya's *Naked Maja* (1900-05), offer views of women as voluptuous sites of pleasure.[151] These are images of pure desire, pure wish-fulfilment, pure pleasure, which are also pornographic. There is no doubt that the painted high art female nude, as an image, is very like the pornographic image, which offers women as sexualized objects of male lust. They are part of a continuum of representation. What differentiates 'high culture' nudes from the nudes in porn is largely to do with context, with the sociopolitical environment in which the nudes are consumed. You can put Goya's *Naked Maja* into a soft core pornographic context and it would send only a few conflicting signals with the rest of the photography there. Fashions change – in costume, hair, make-up, pose and props – but it is startling how similar the nude, female or male, is in art. The fundamental relation, of sexualized women being offered up to be looked at and lusted over by desirous males is remarkably similar the world over, and through history.

---

150 Poussin: *A Bacchanalian Revel Before a Term of Pan*, c. 1635-8, National Gallery, London.
151 Diego Velásquez: *The Rokeby Venus*, 1649-50, oil on canvas, 122.5 x   , National Gallery, London; Francisco de Goya: *Naked Maya*, 1800-5

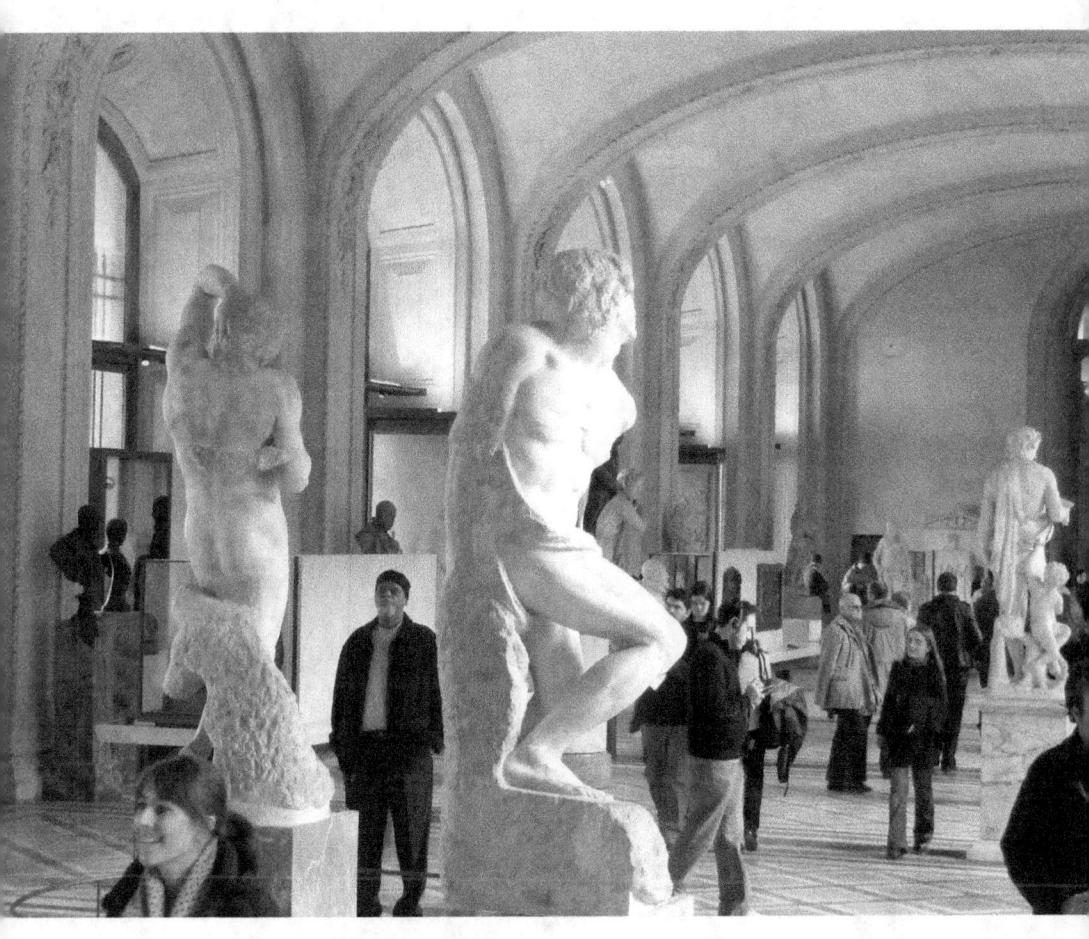

Michelangelo Buonaroti, Dying Slaves, Louvre, Paris
(This page and over)

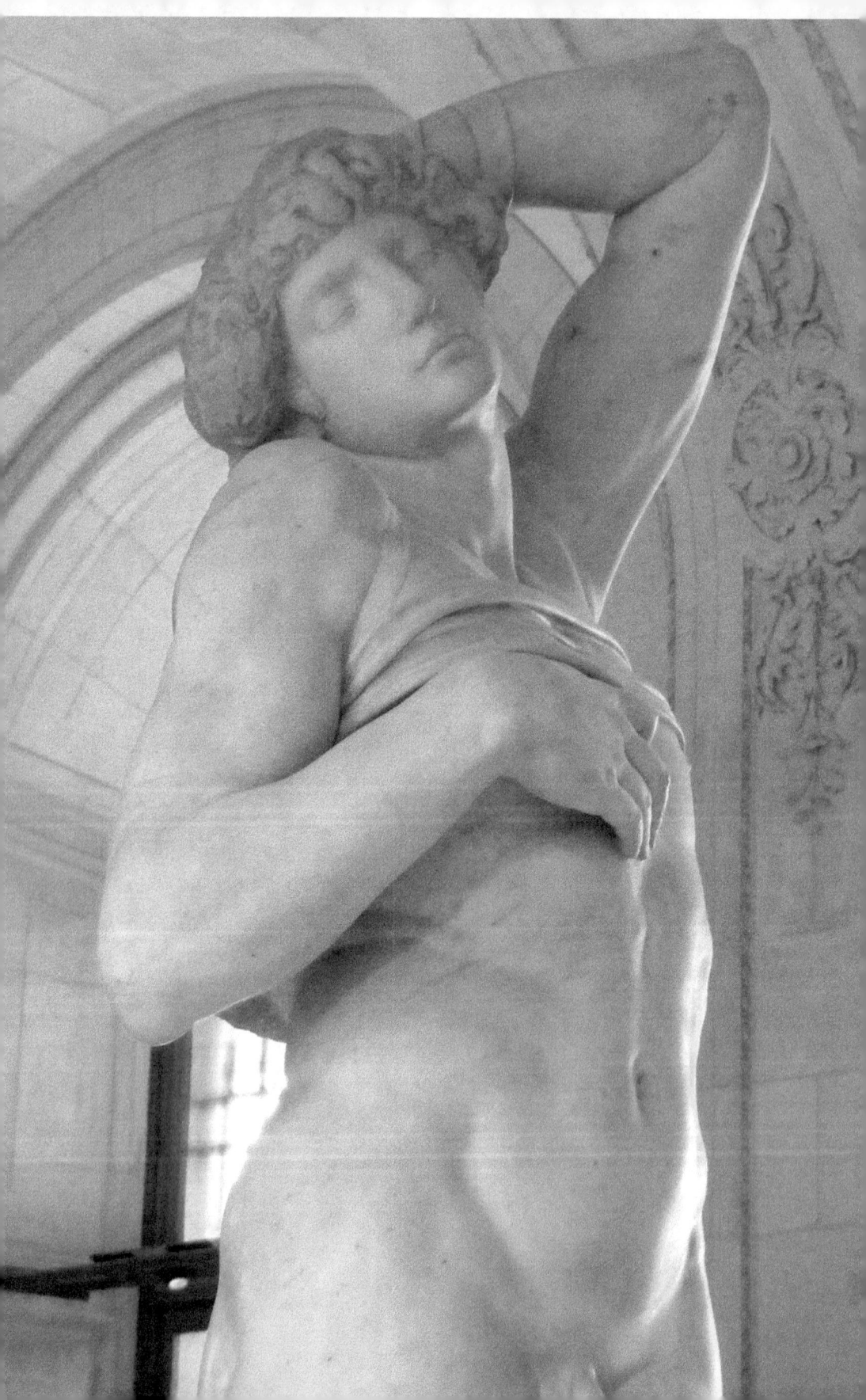

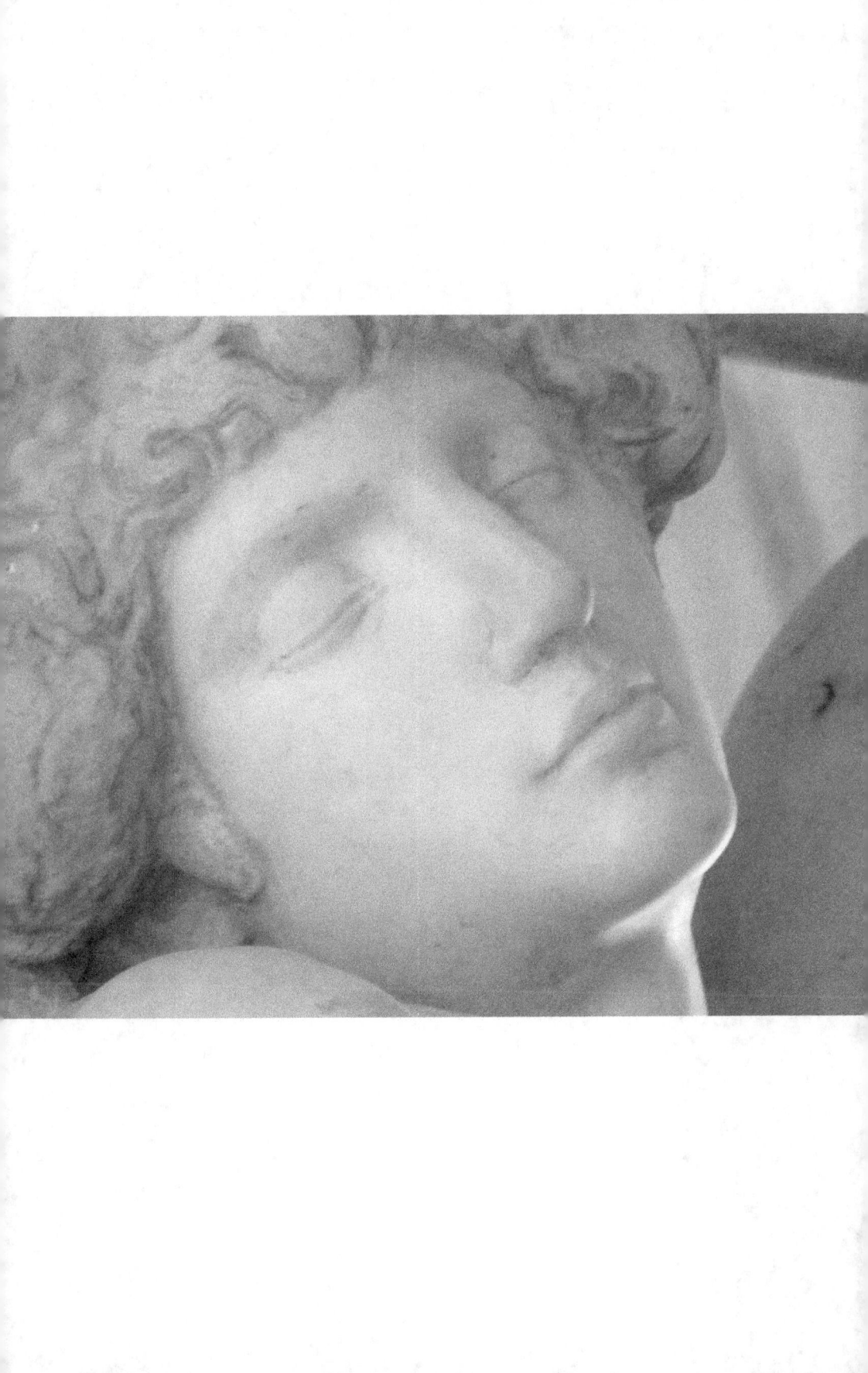

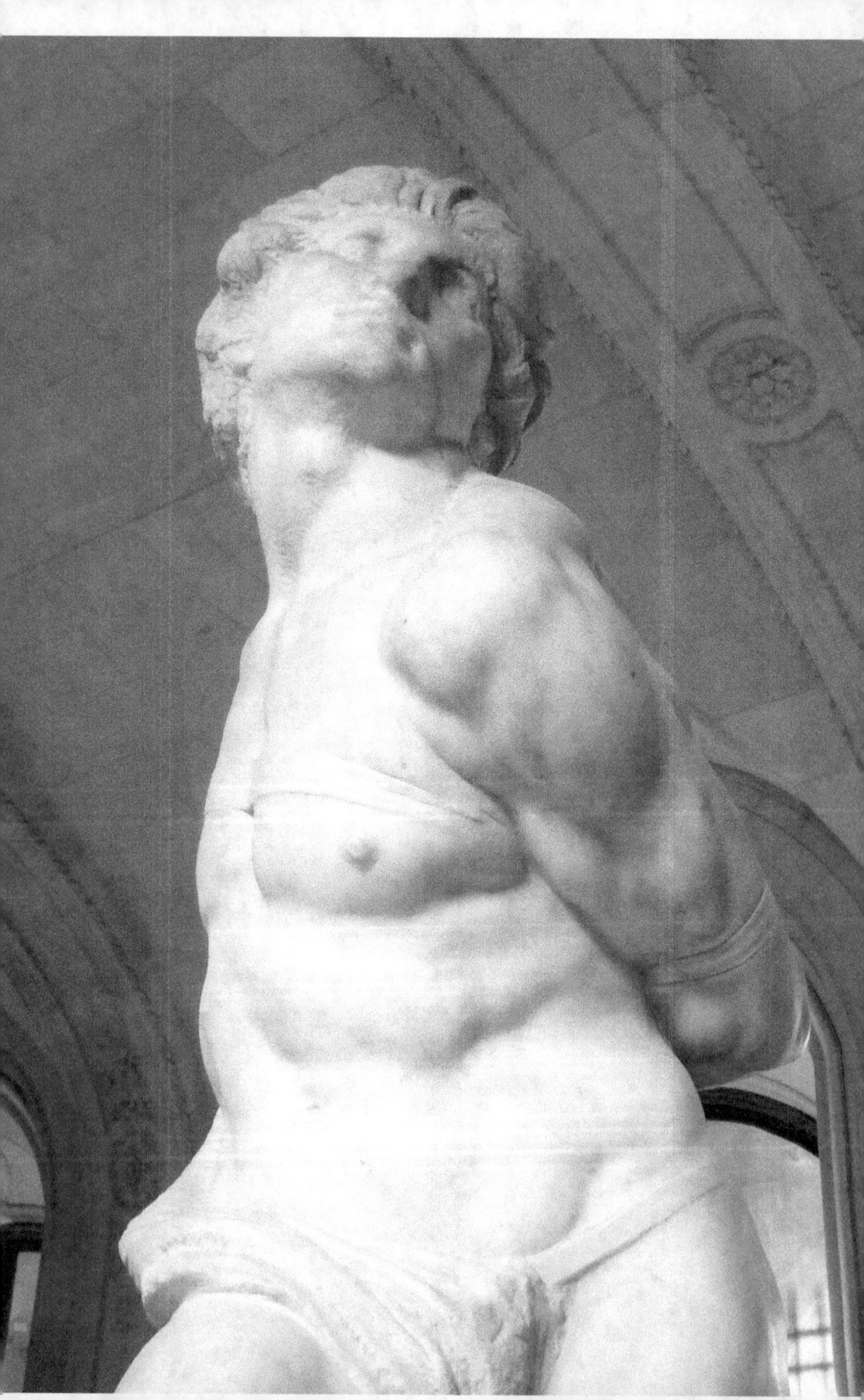

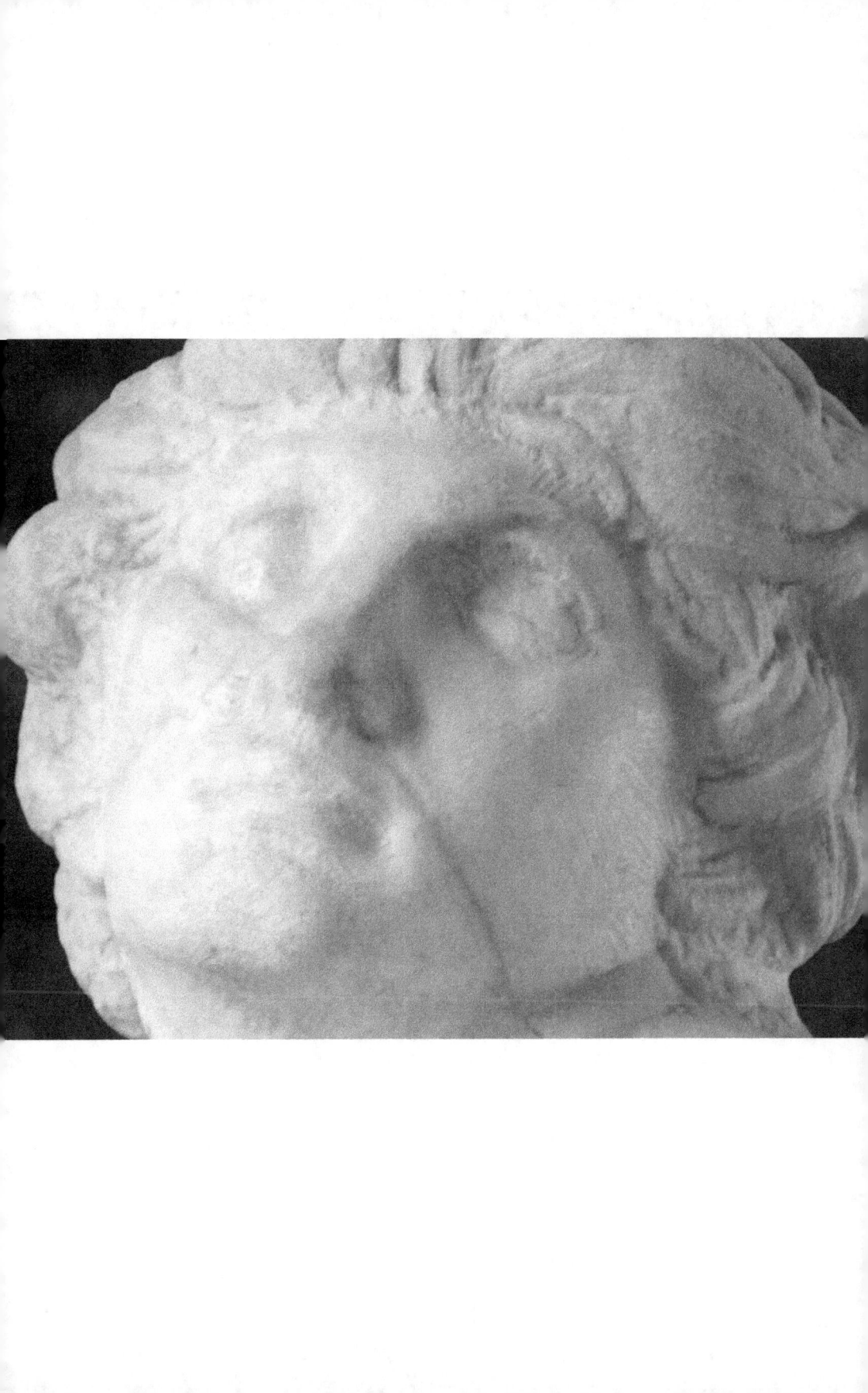

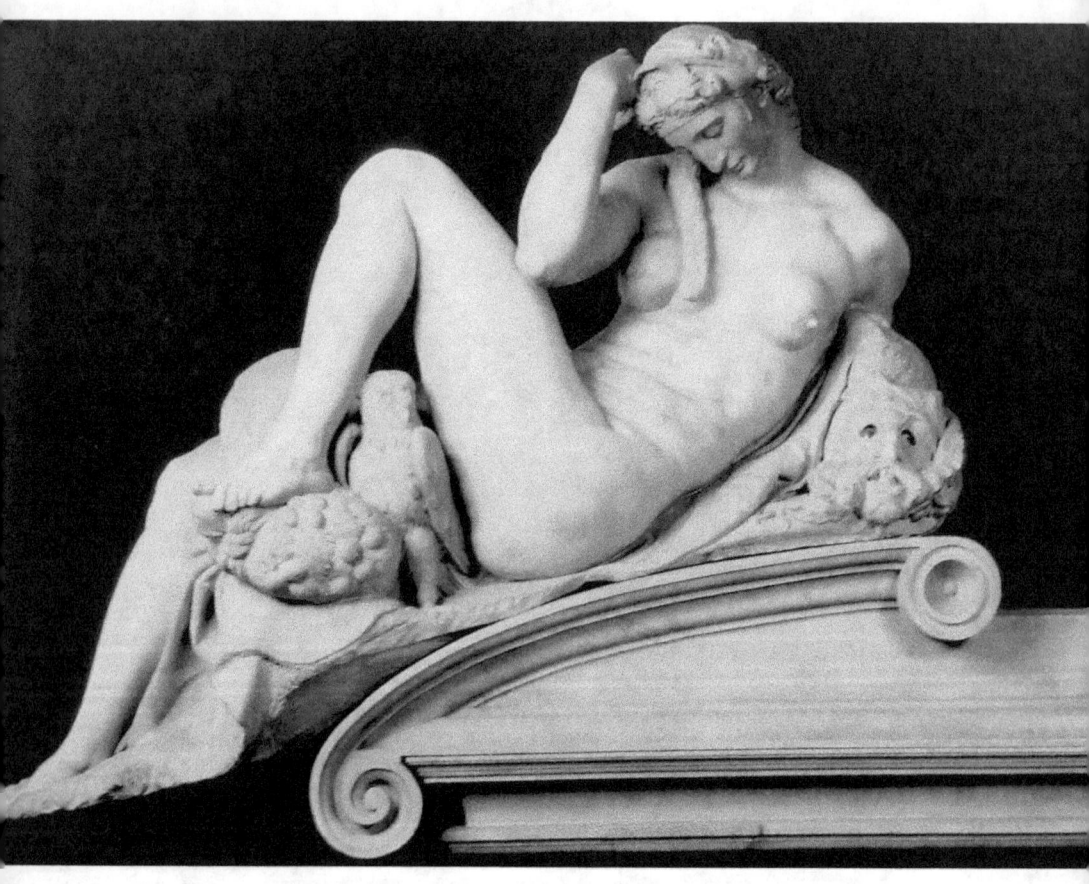

Michelangelo, Night, Medici Chapel, Florence

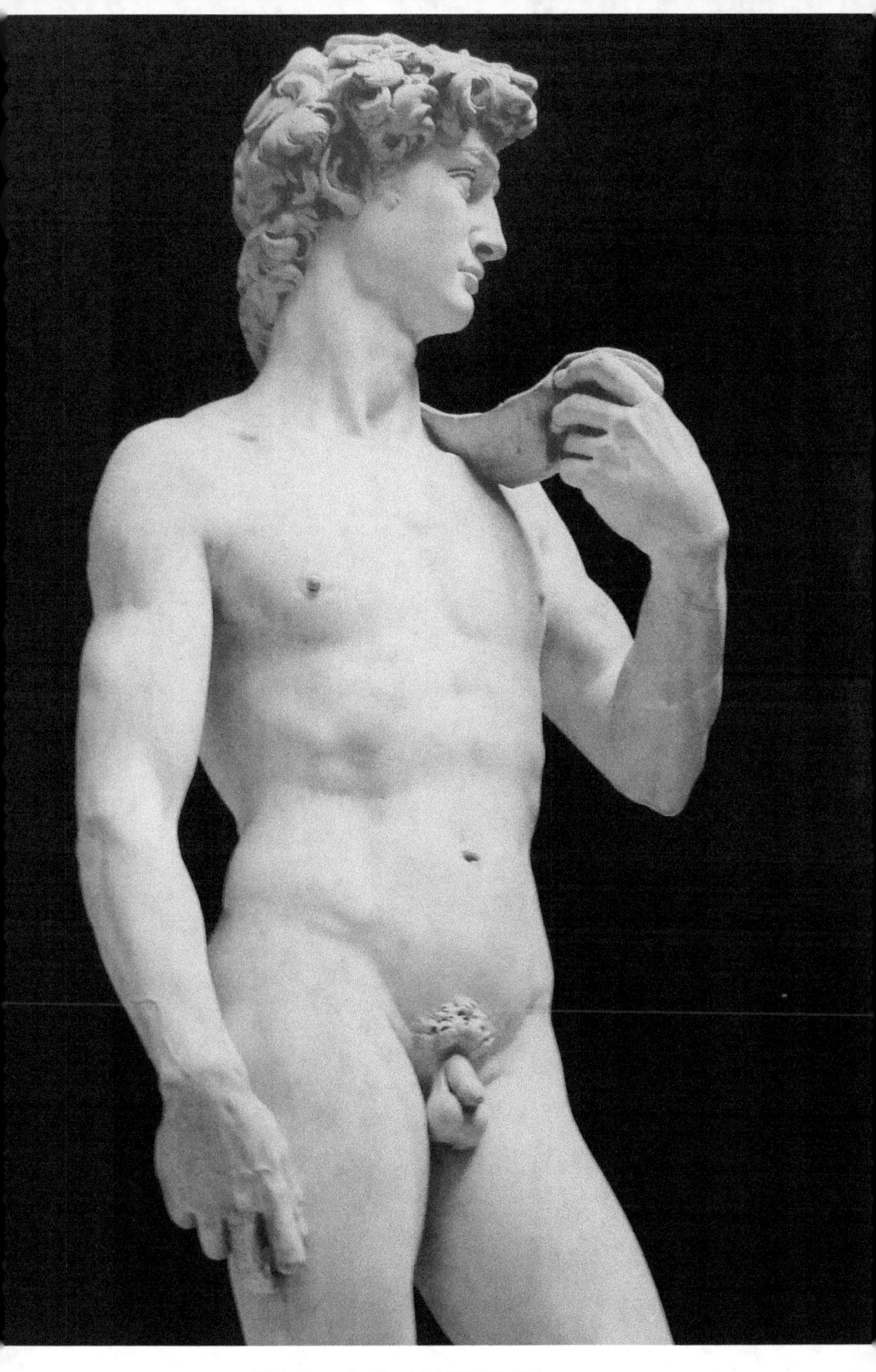

Michelangelo, David, 1501-04, Florence

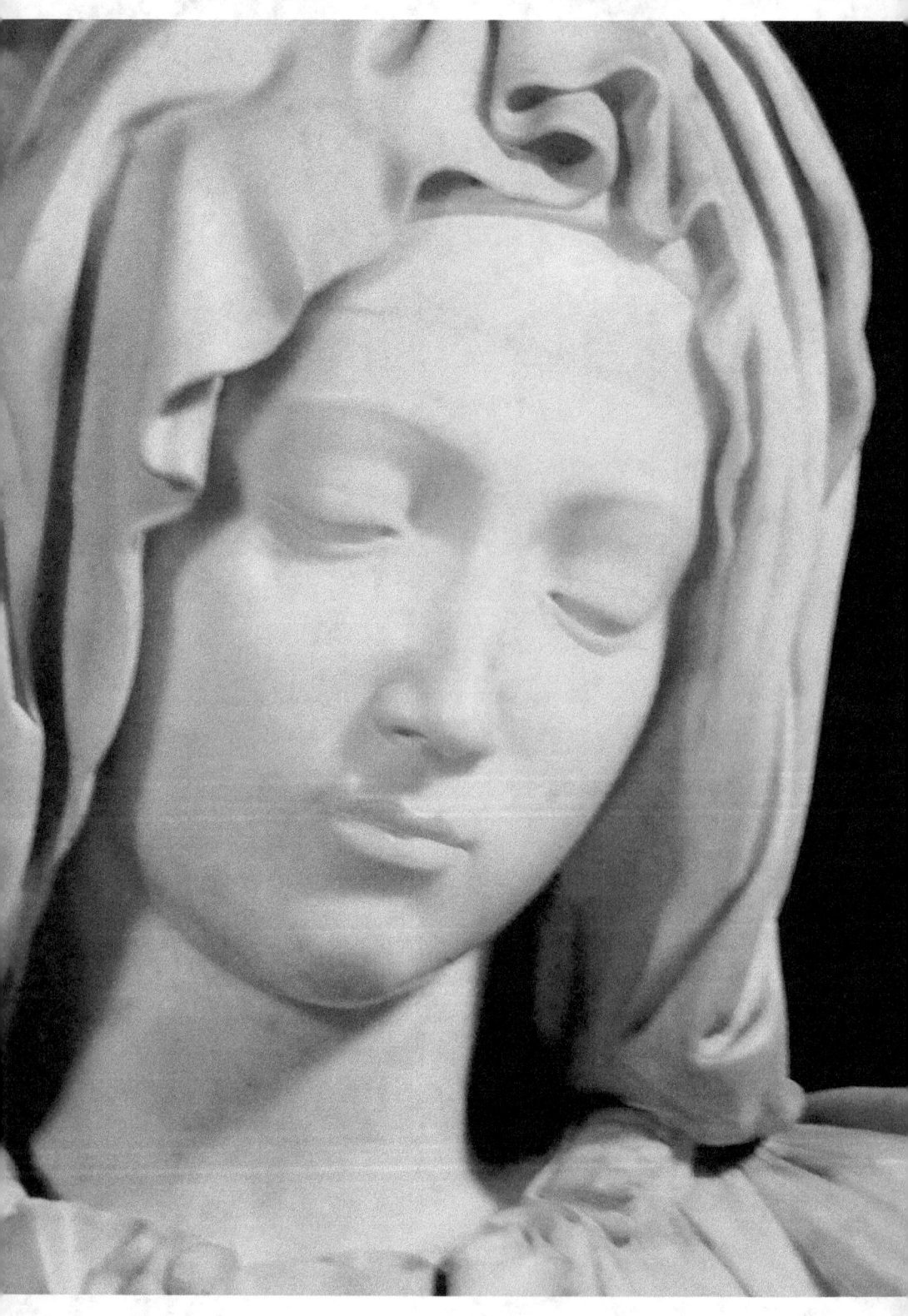

Michelangelo, Pietà, detail, Vatican, Rome

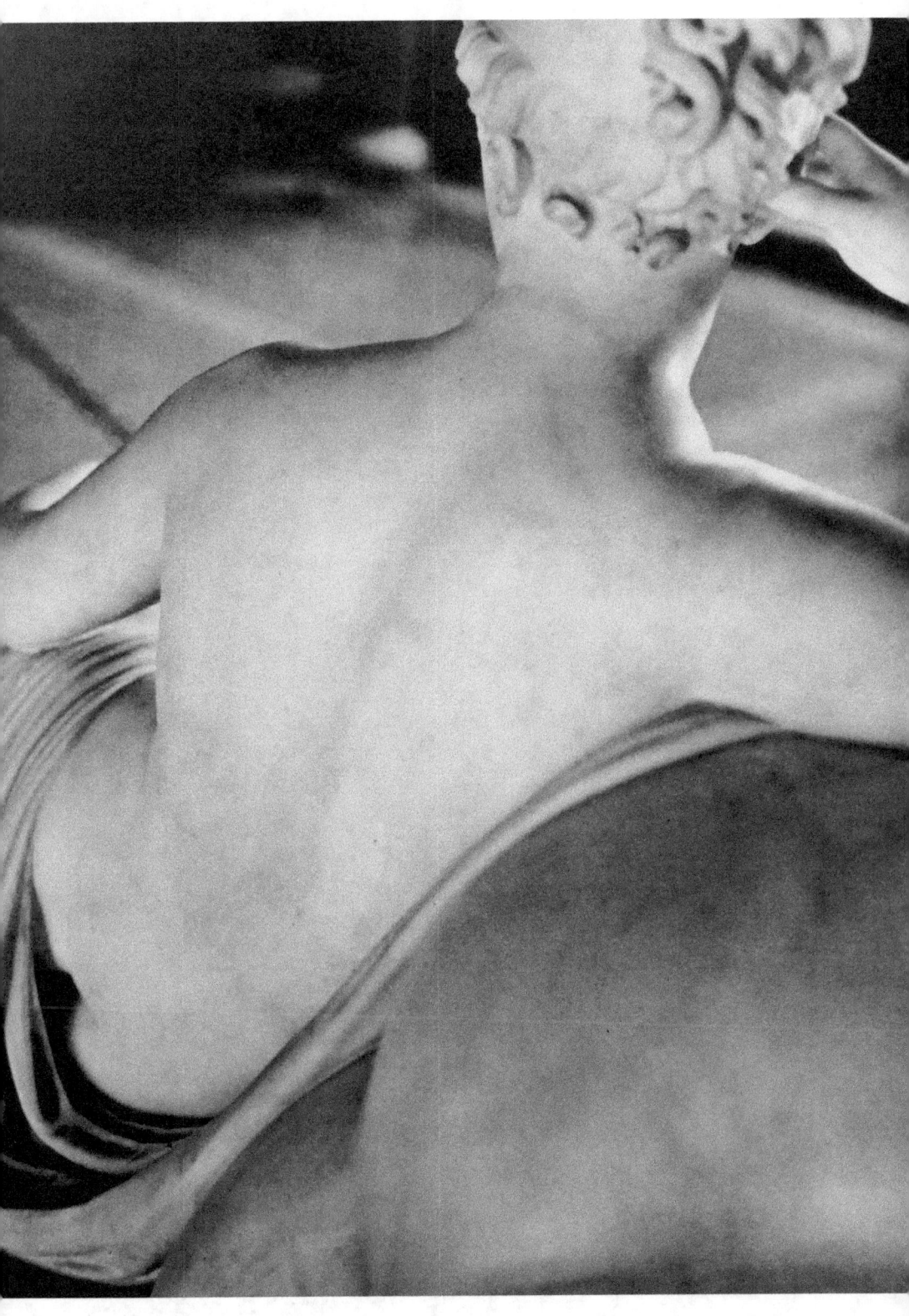

Antonio Canova, Venus Victorious, 1808

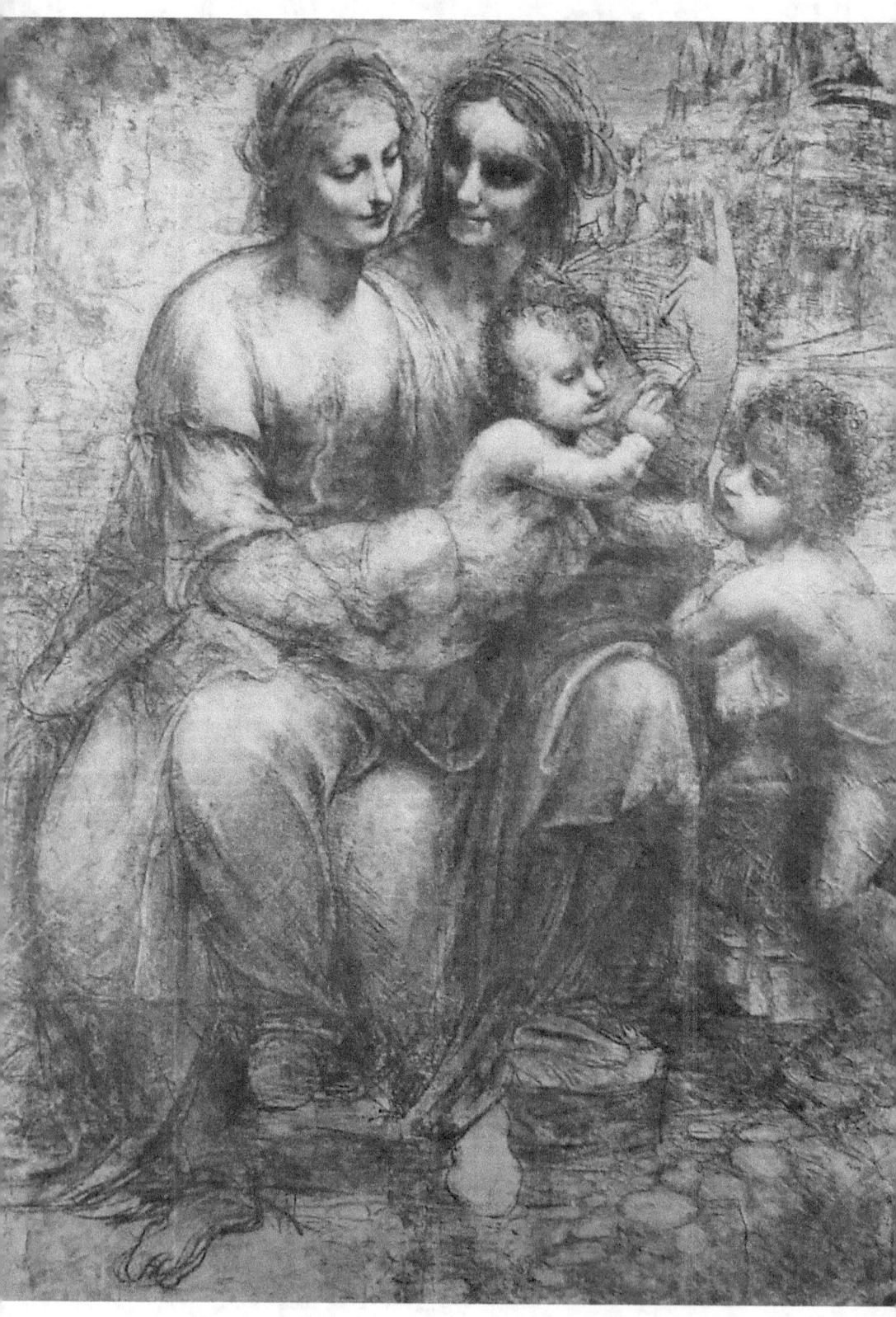

Leonardo da Vinci, The Virgin and Child With St Anne, London

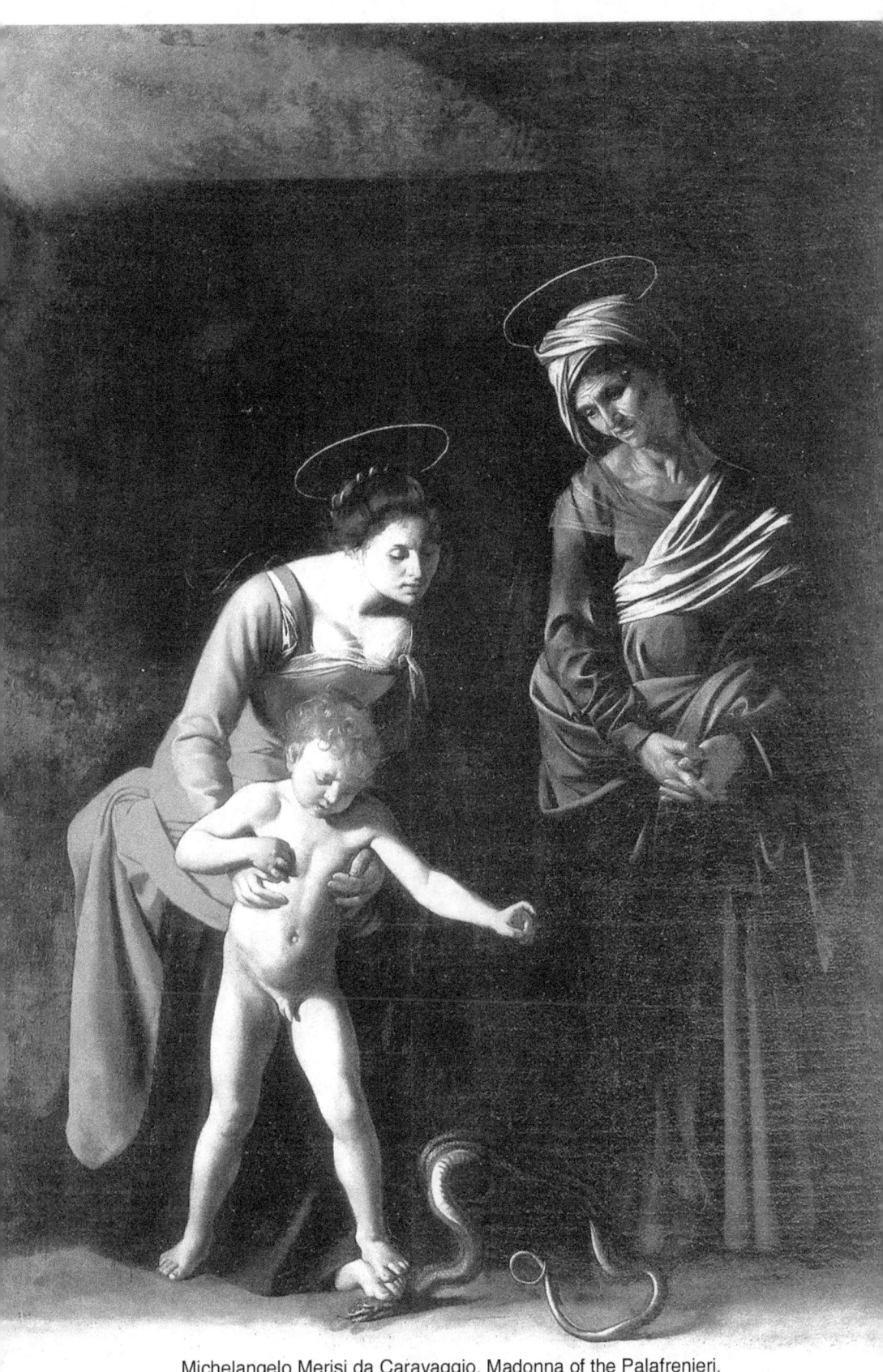

Michelangelo Merisi da Caravaggio, Madonna of the Palafrenieri,
1605-06, Galleria Borghese, Rome

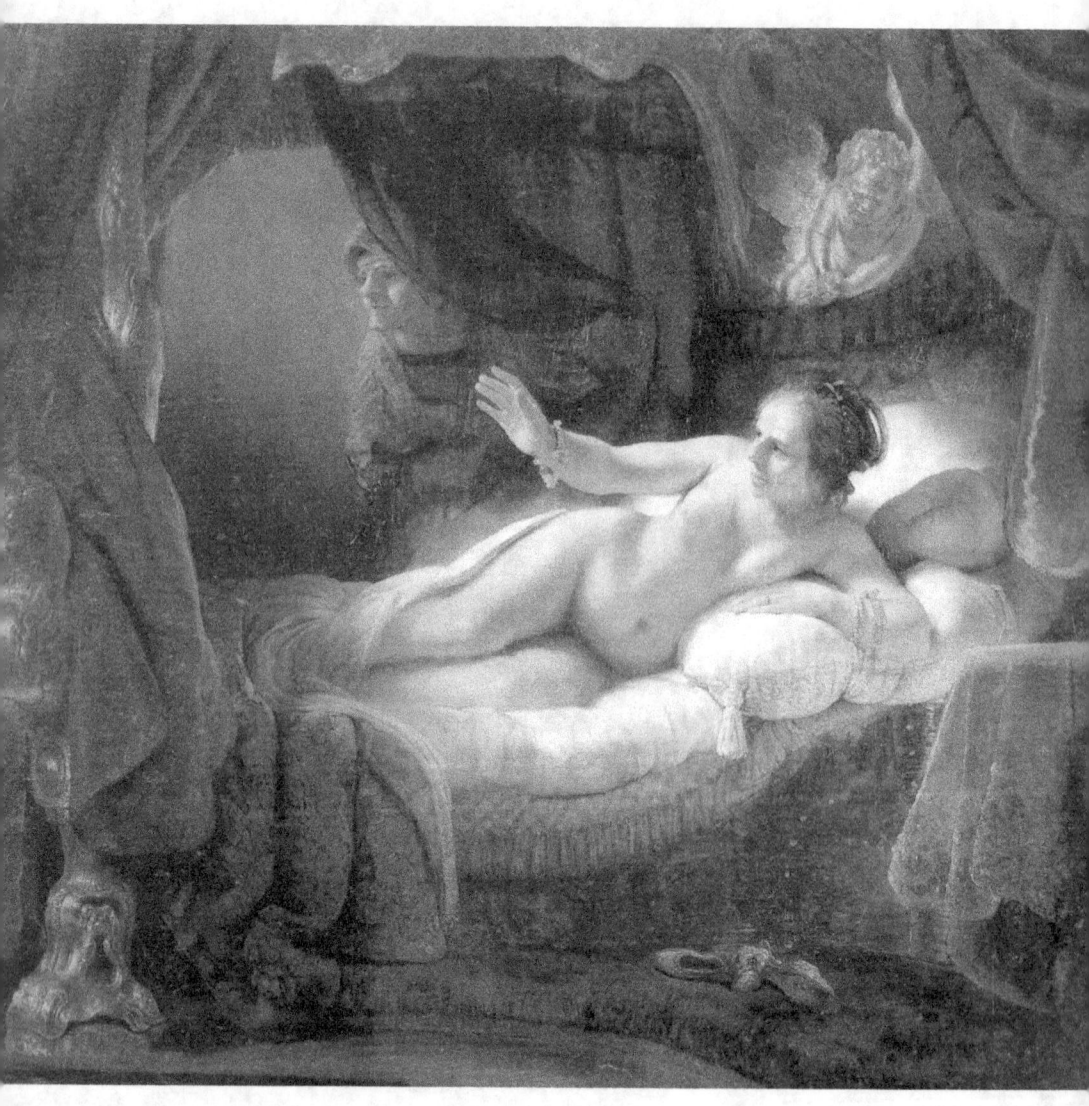

Rembrandt van Rijn, Danae, 1636, St Petersburg

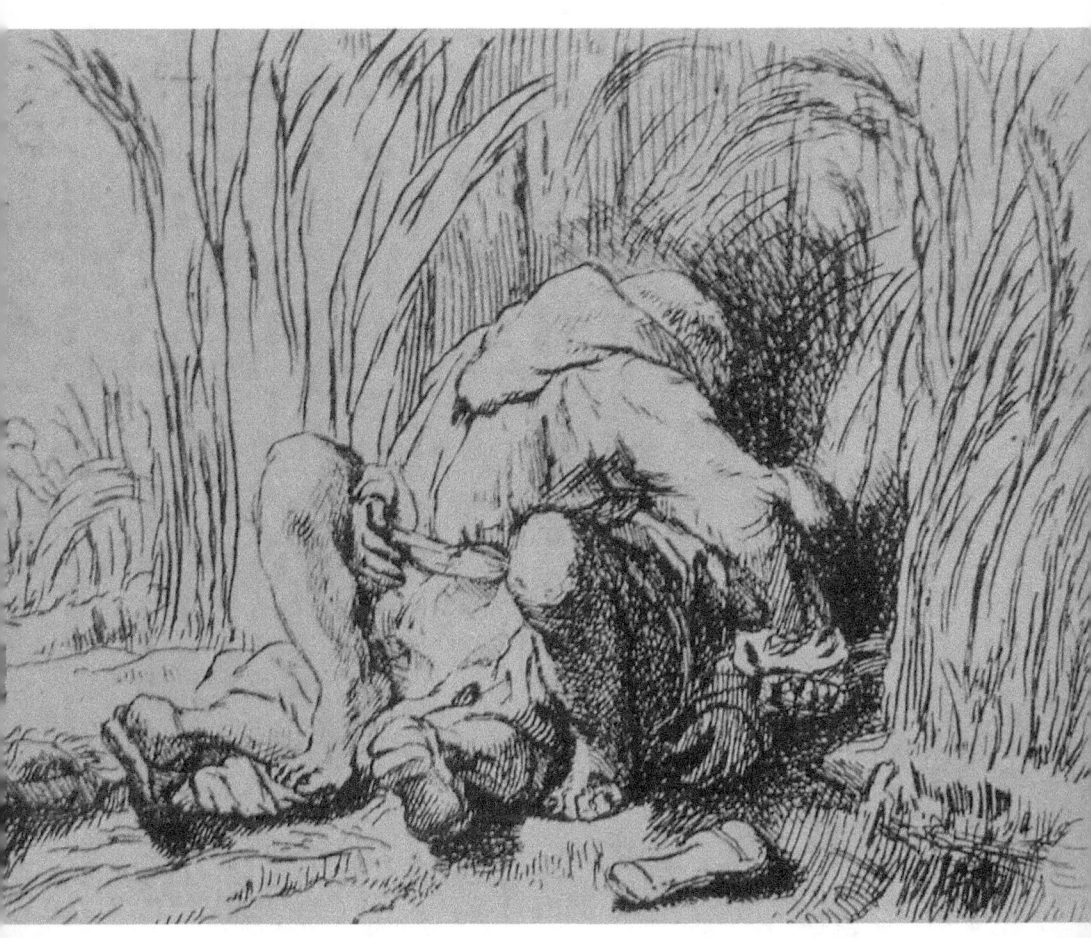

Rembrandt van Rijn, The Monk In the Cornfield

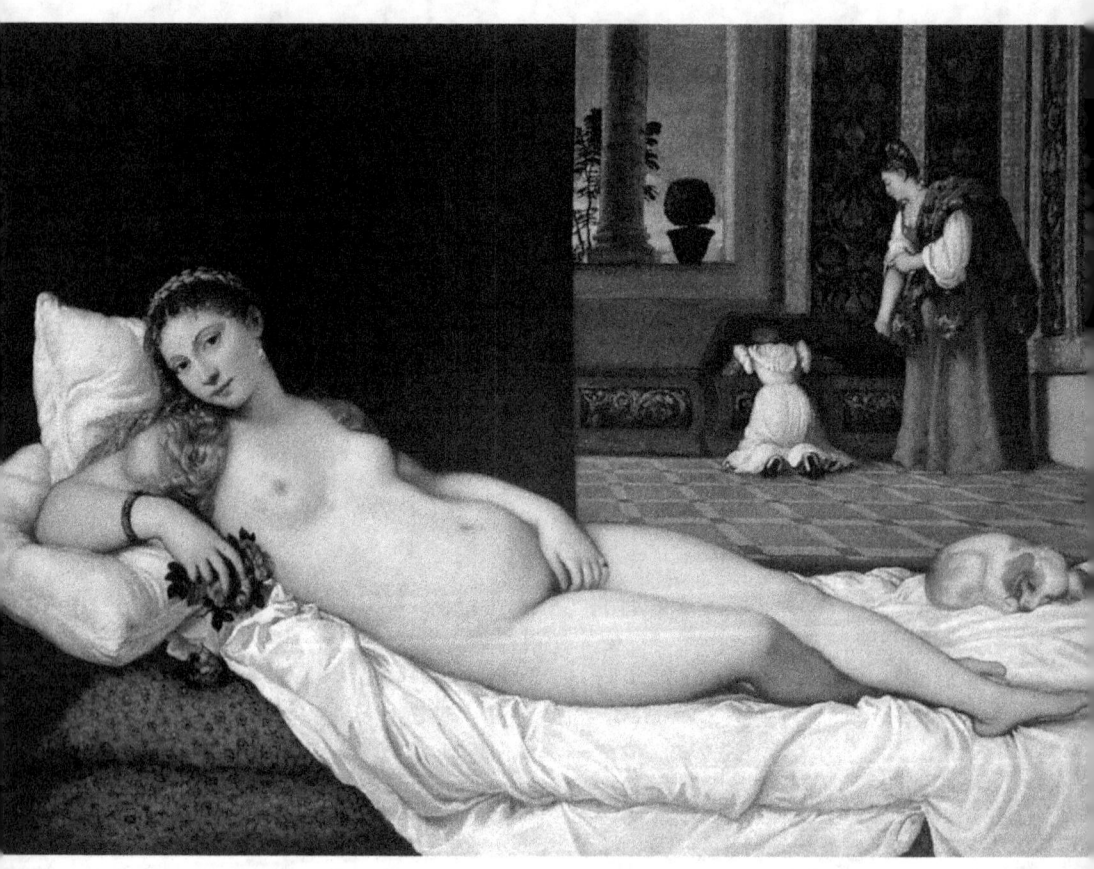

Titian, The Venus of Urbino, 1538, Uffizi, Florence

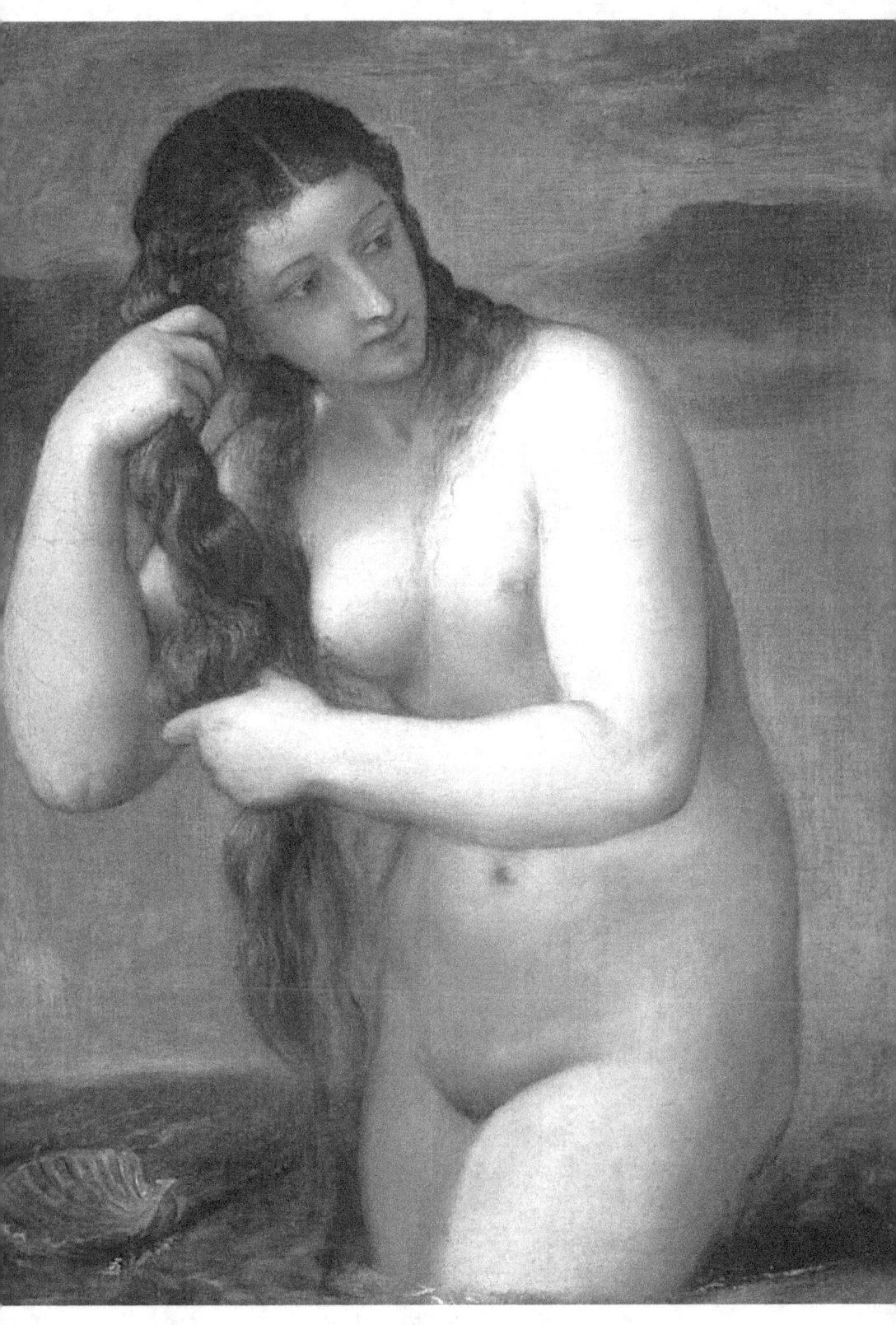

Titian, Venus Rising From the Sea, 1520, Scotland

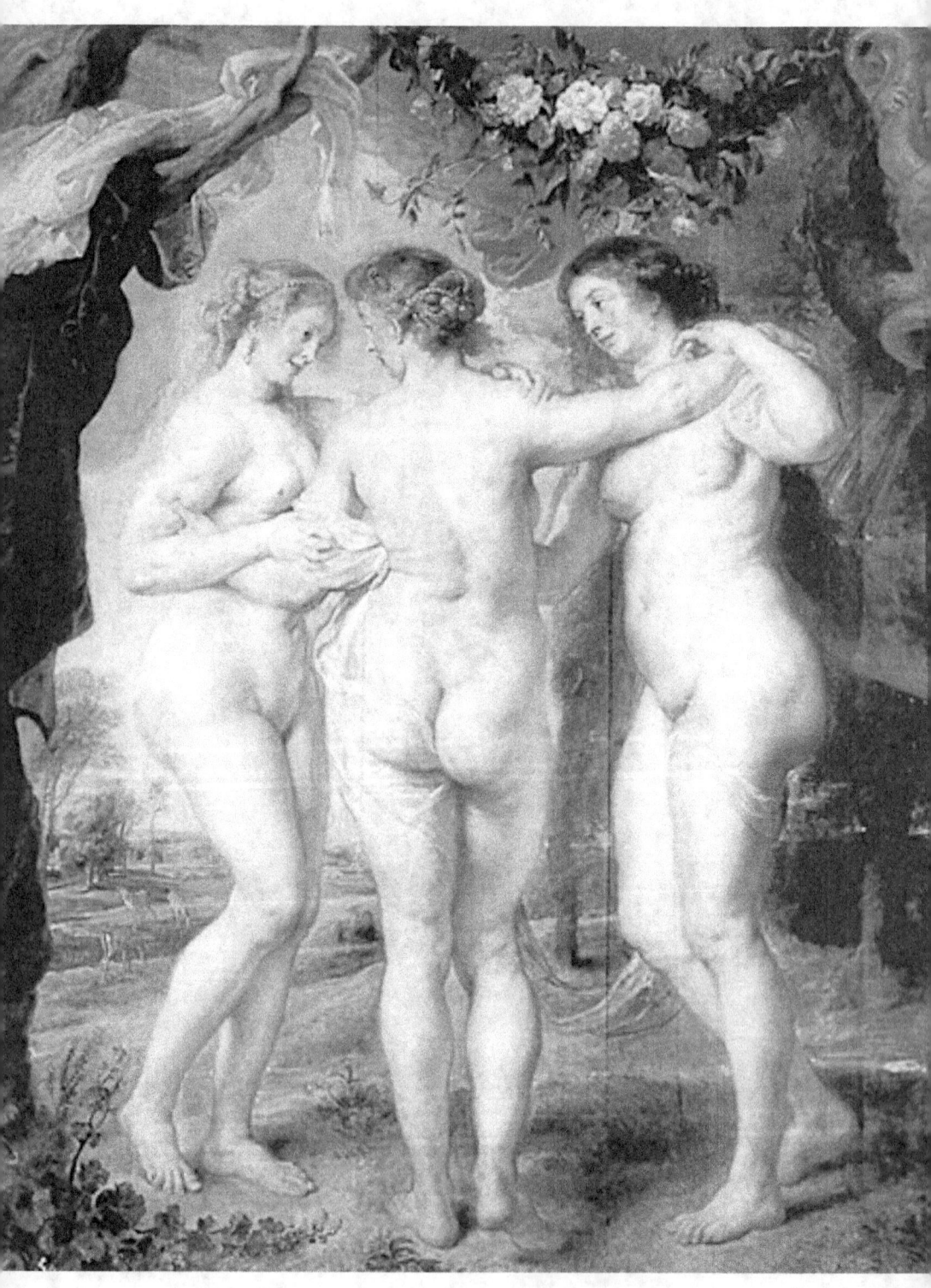

Peter Paul Rubens, The Three Graces, 1638-40, Prado, Madrid

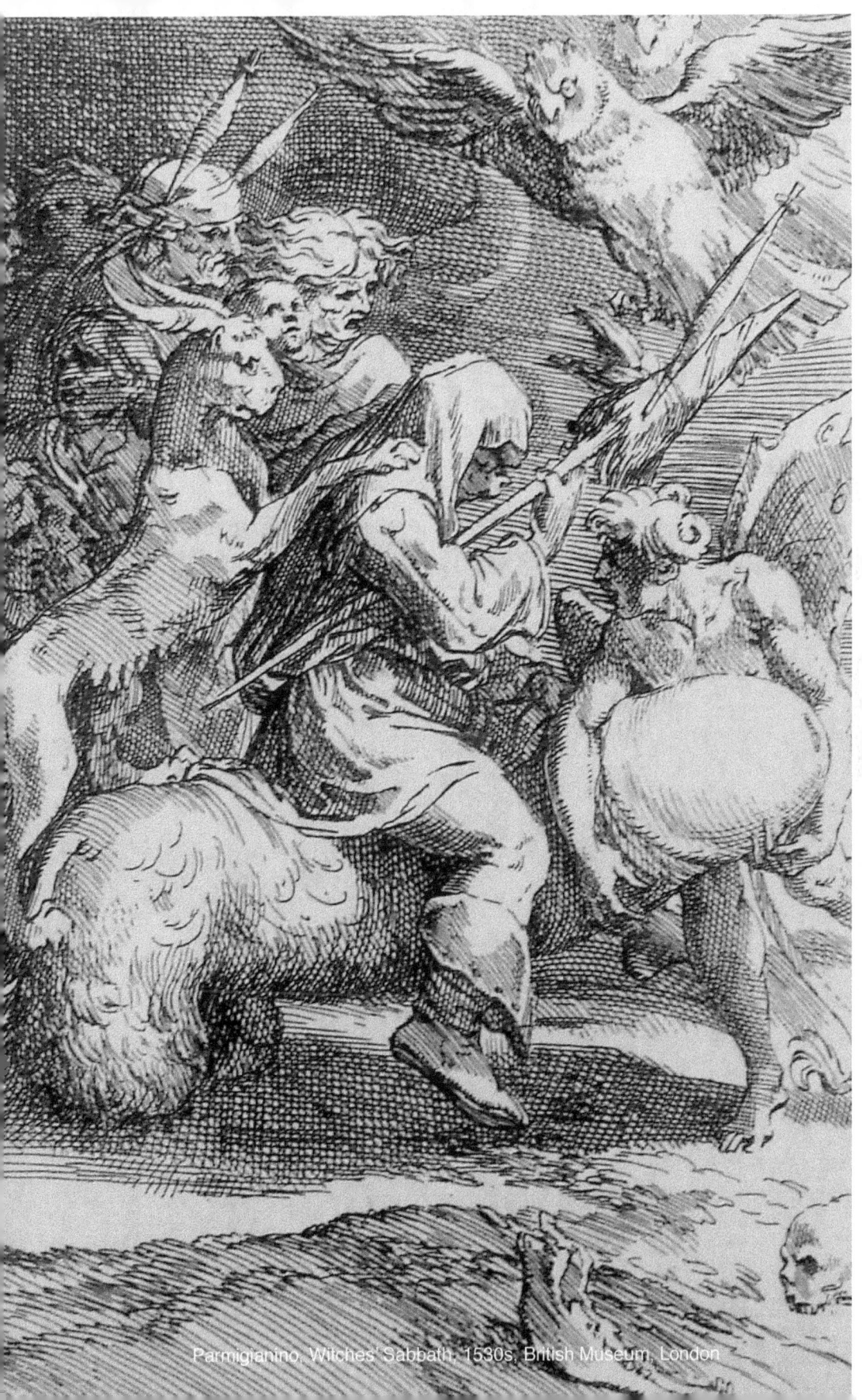

Parmigianino, Witches' Sabbath, 1530s, British Museum, London

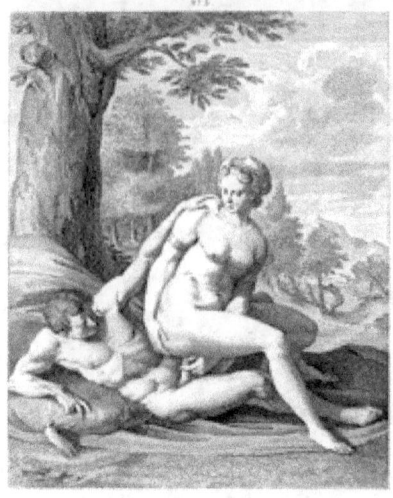

ANGELIQUE ET MEDOR

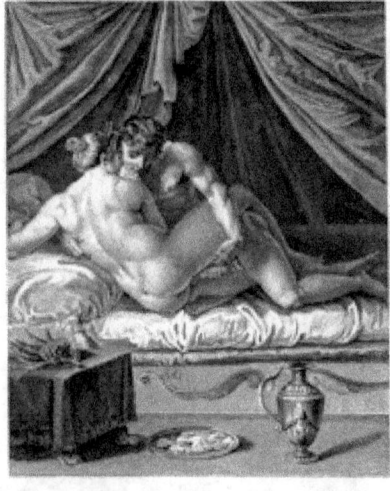

ANTOINE ET CLÉOPATRE

Agostino Carracci, I Modi, 1524
(this page and following pages)

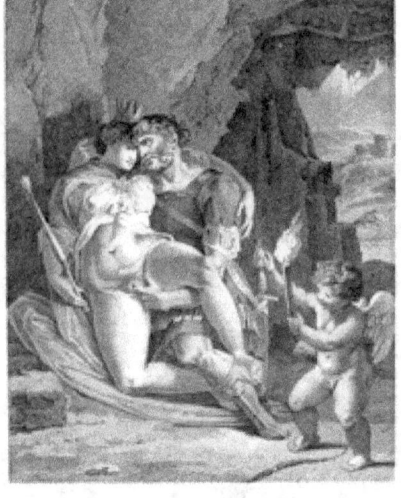

ENÉE ET DIDON

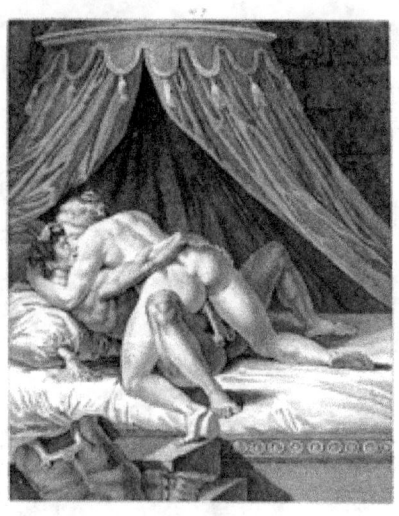

MARS ET VENUS

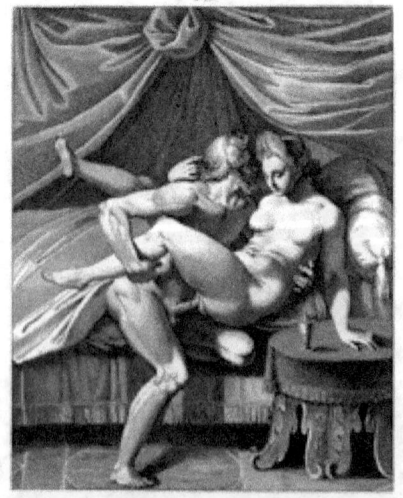

JUPITER ET JUNON

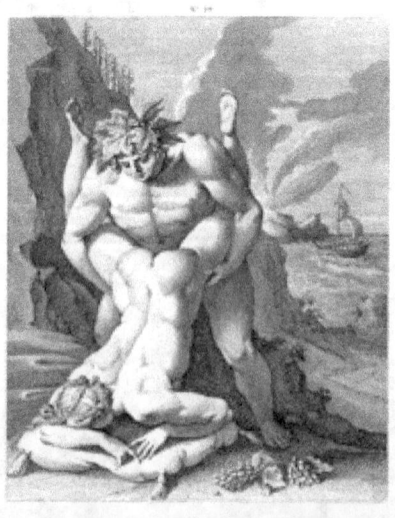

BACHUS ET ARIANE

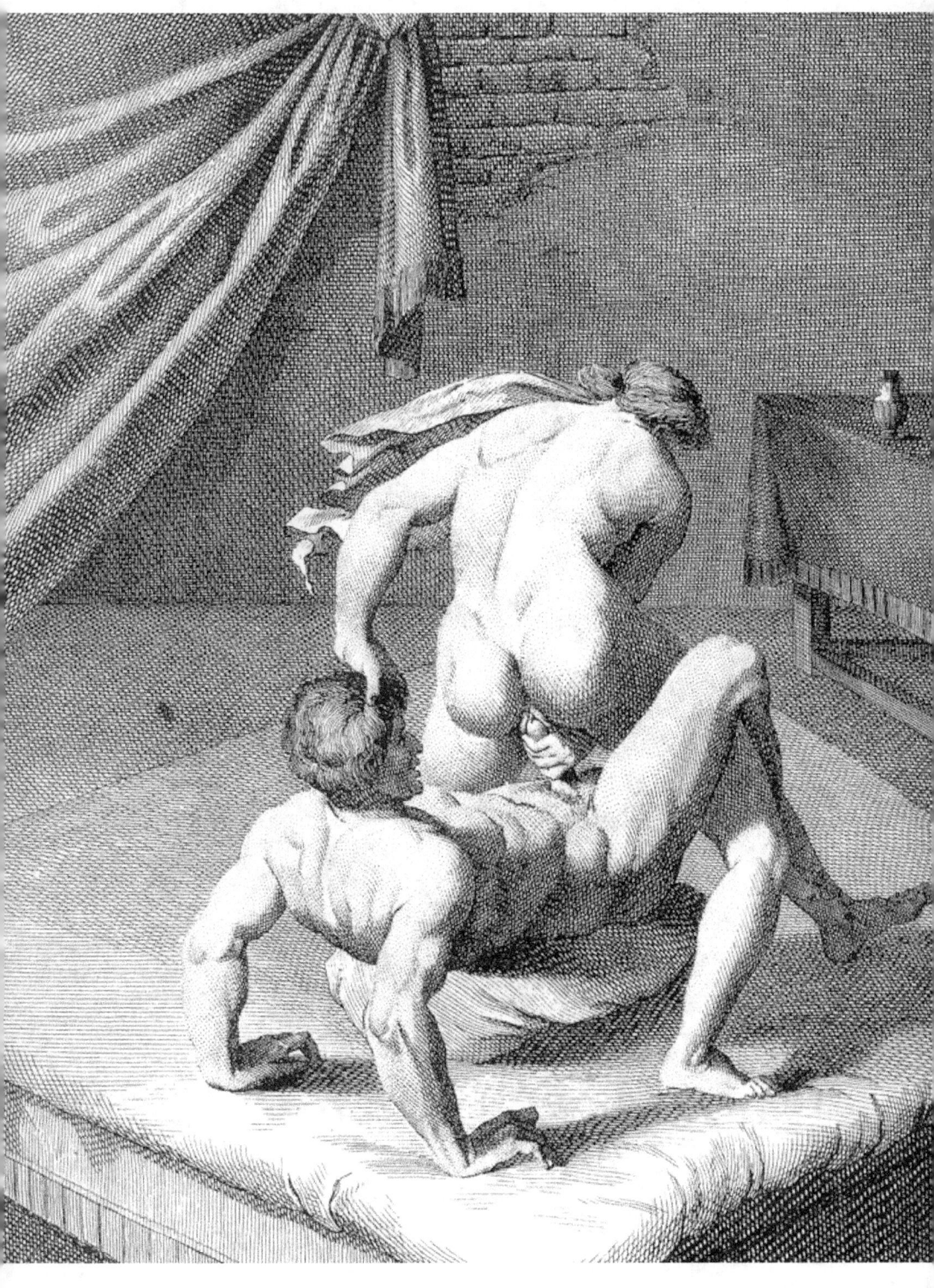

POLYENOS ET CHRISIS

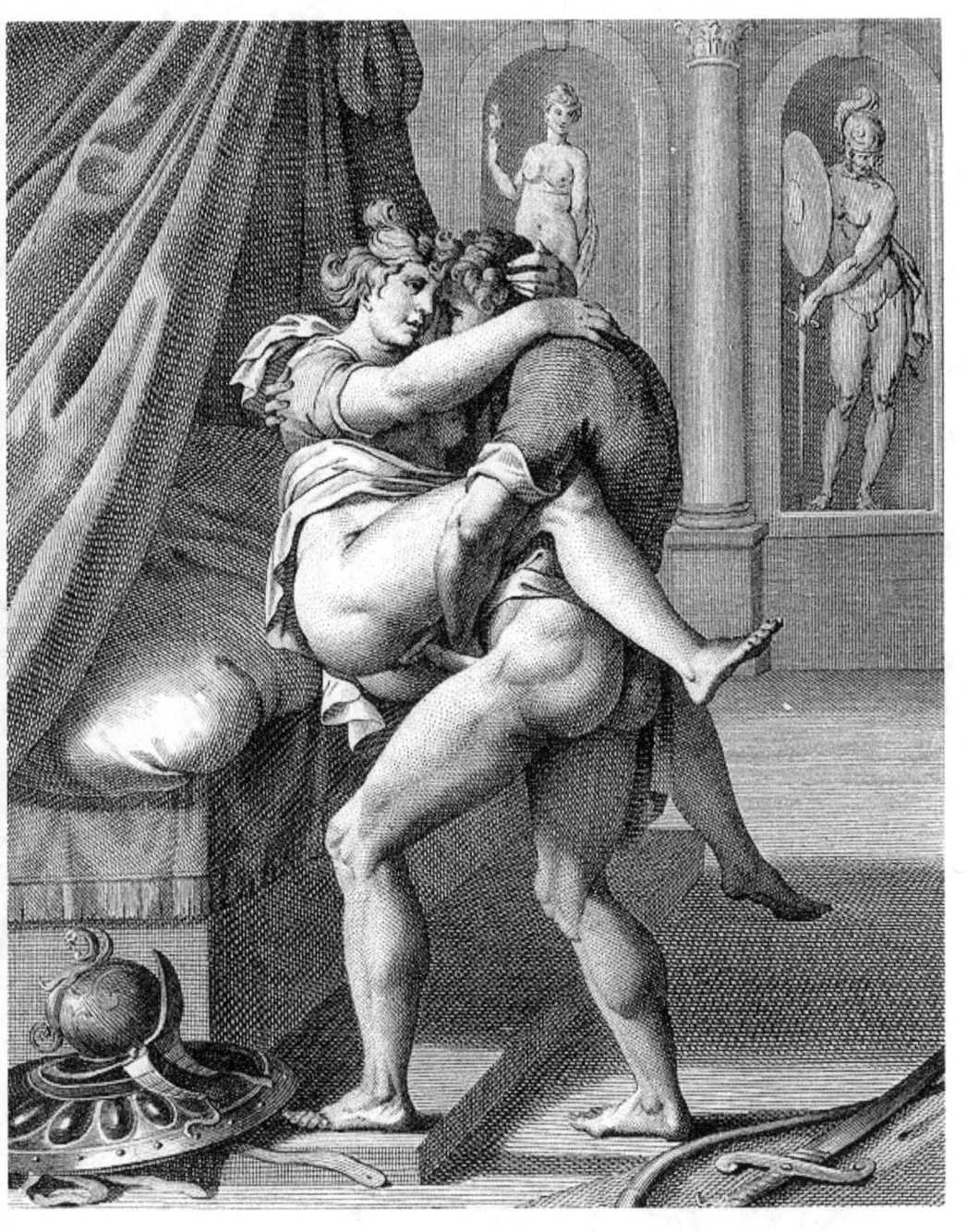

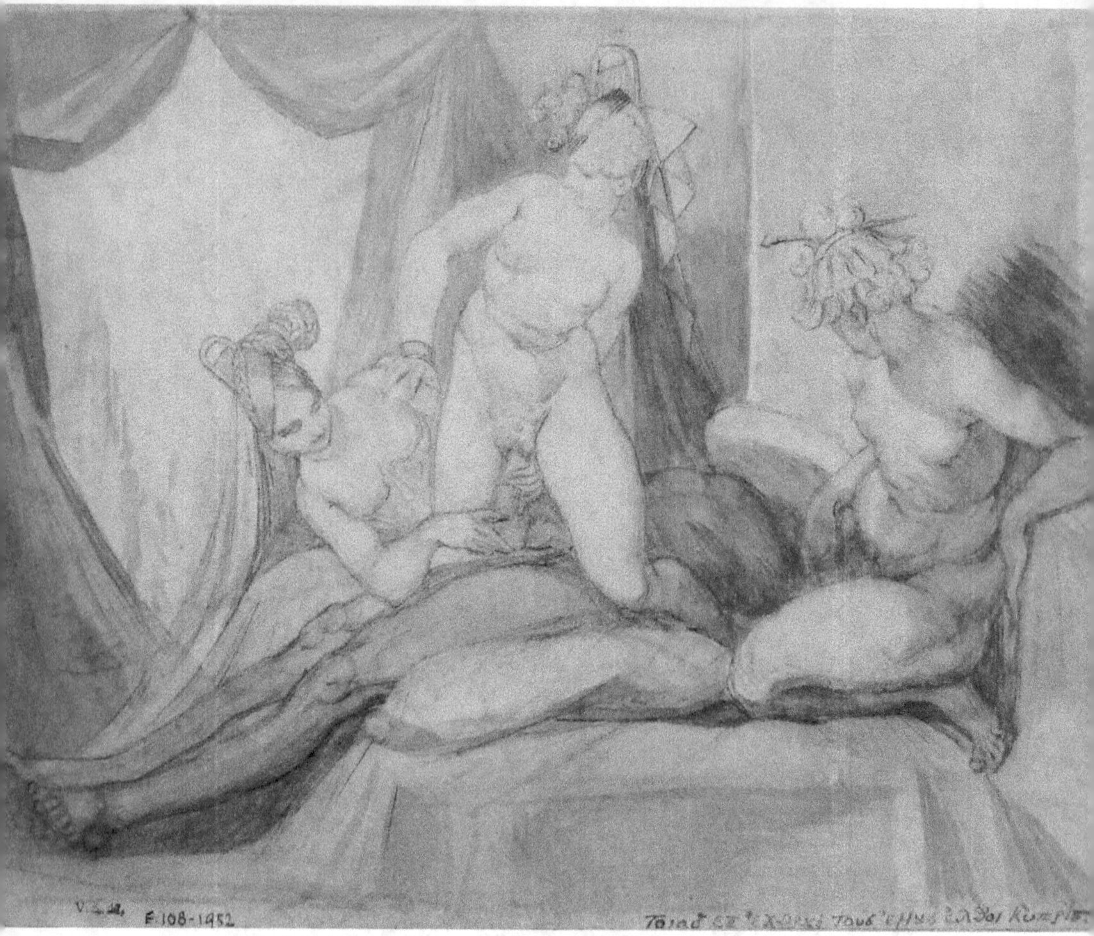

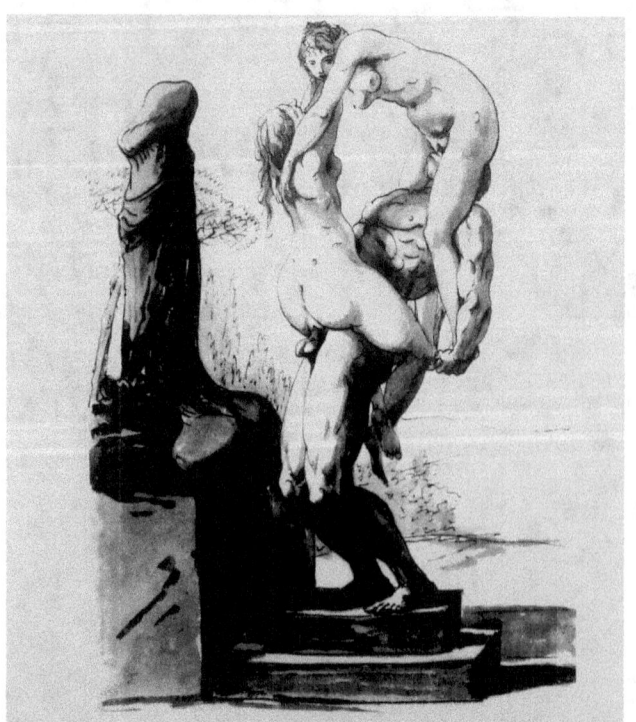

Henry Fuseli, Orgy Scene, 1809-10, Victoria & Albert Museum, London, above.

Jean-Baptiste Regnault, left.

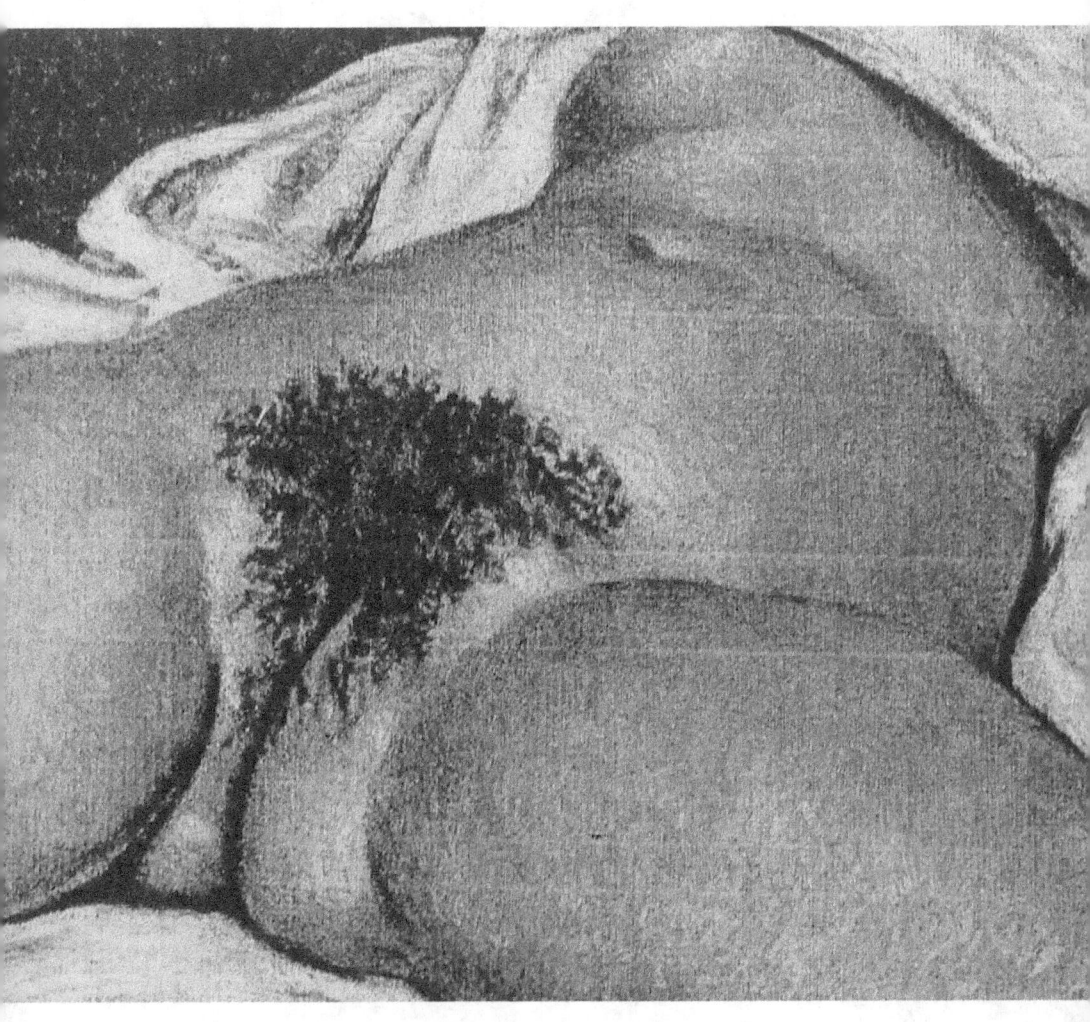

Gustave Courbet, The Creation of the World

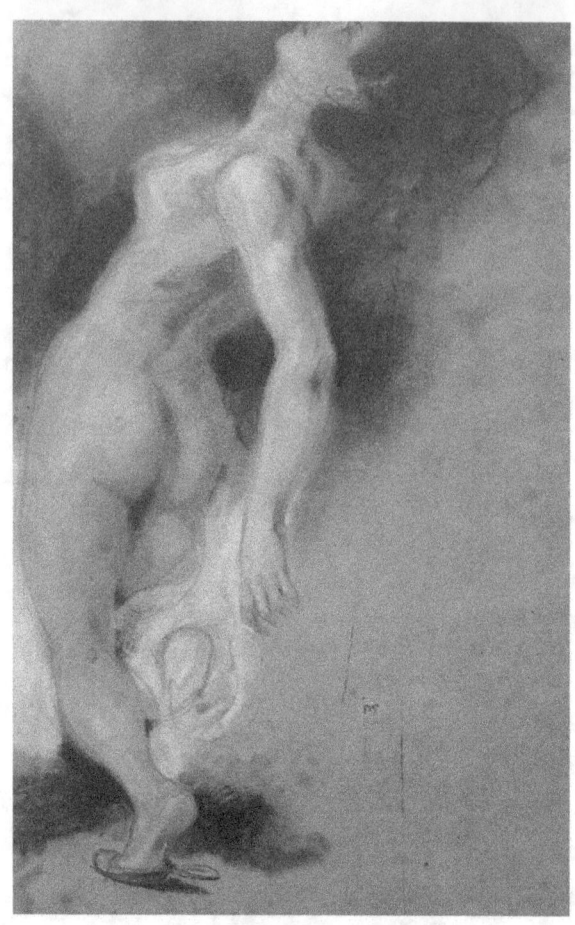

Eugene Delacroix, sketch, above.
Anonymous, Leda and the Swan, below.

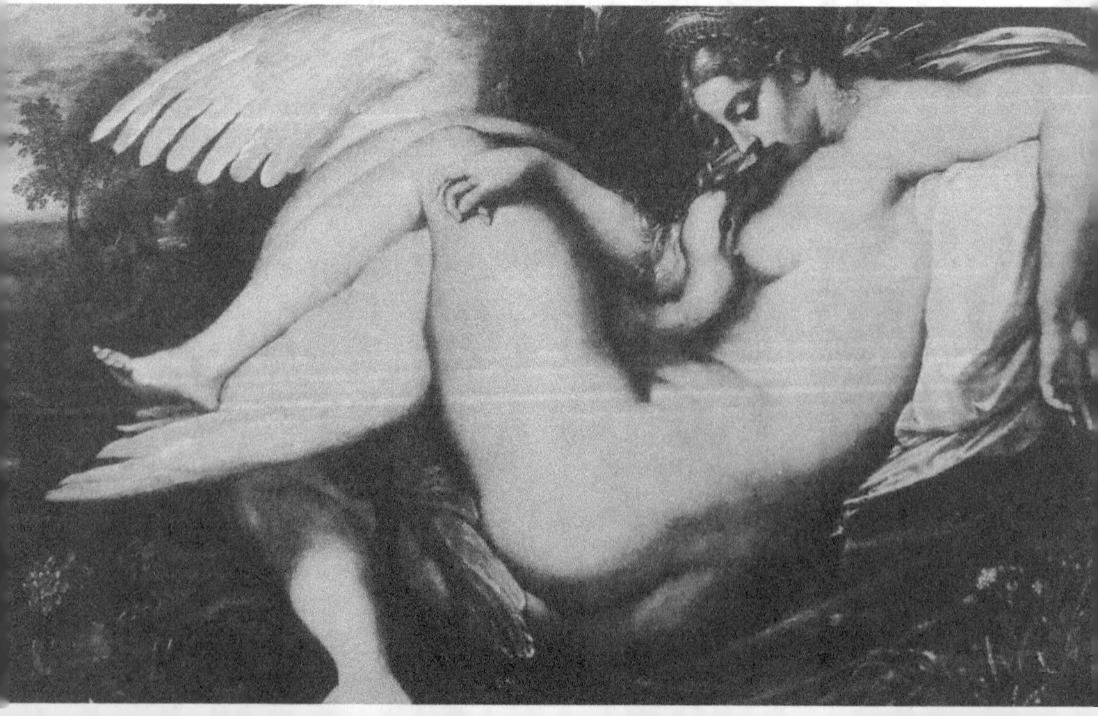

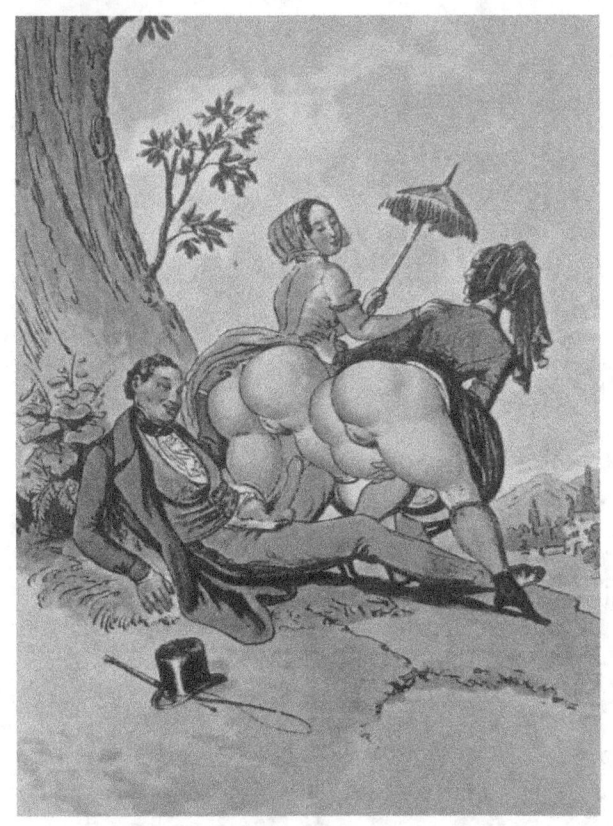

Peter Fendi, above.
Thomas Rowlandson, below.

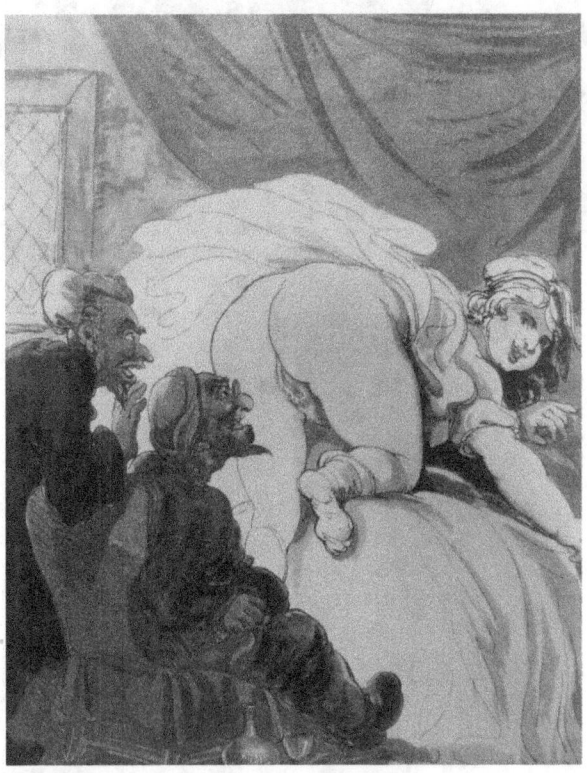

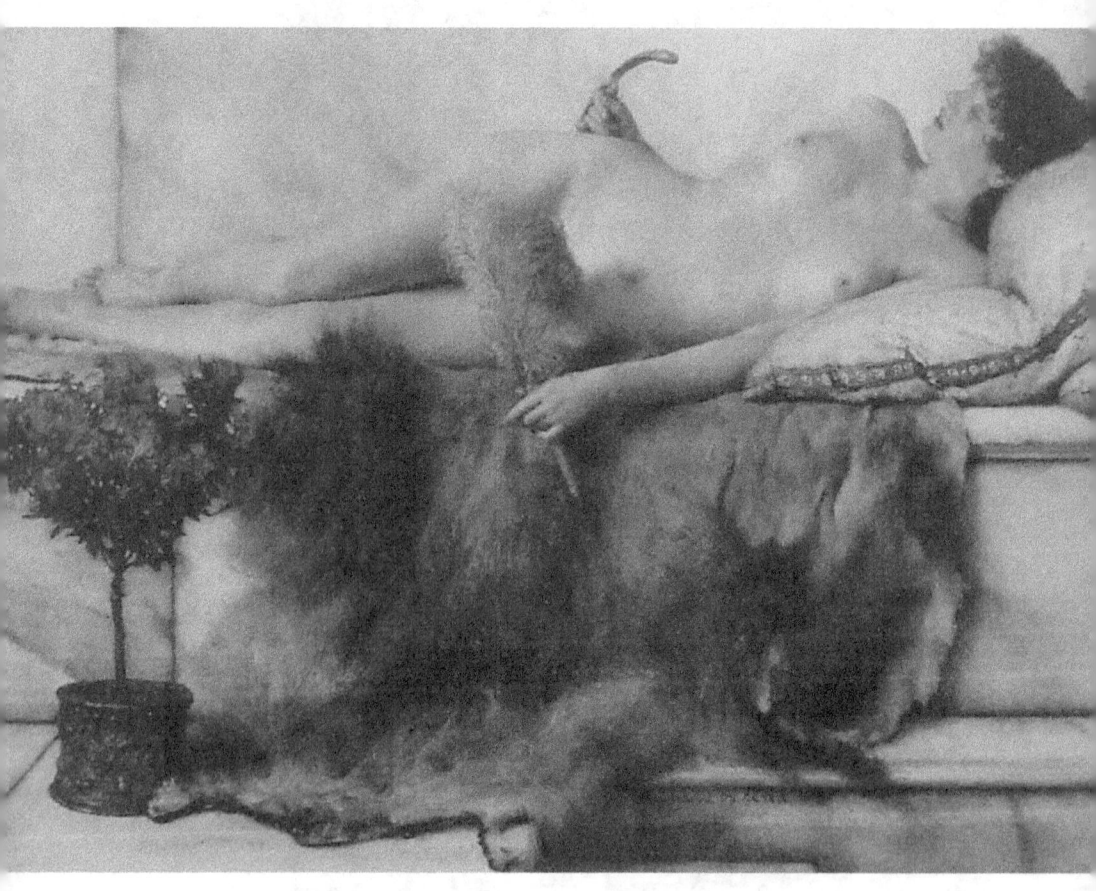

Lawrence Alma-Tadema, In the Tepidarium, 1881,
Lady Lever Art Gallery, Liverpool

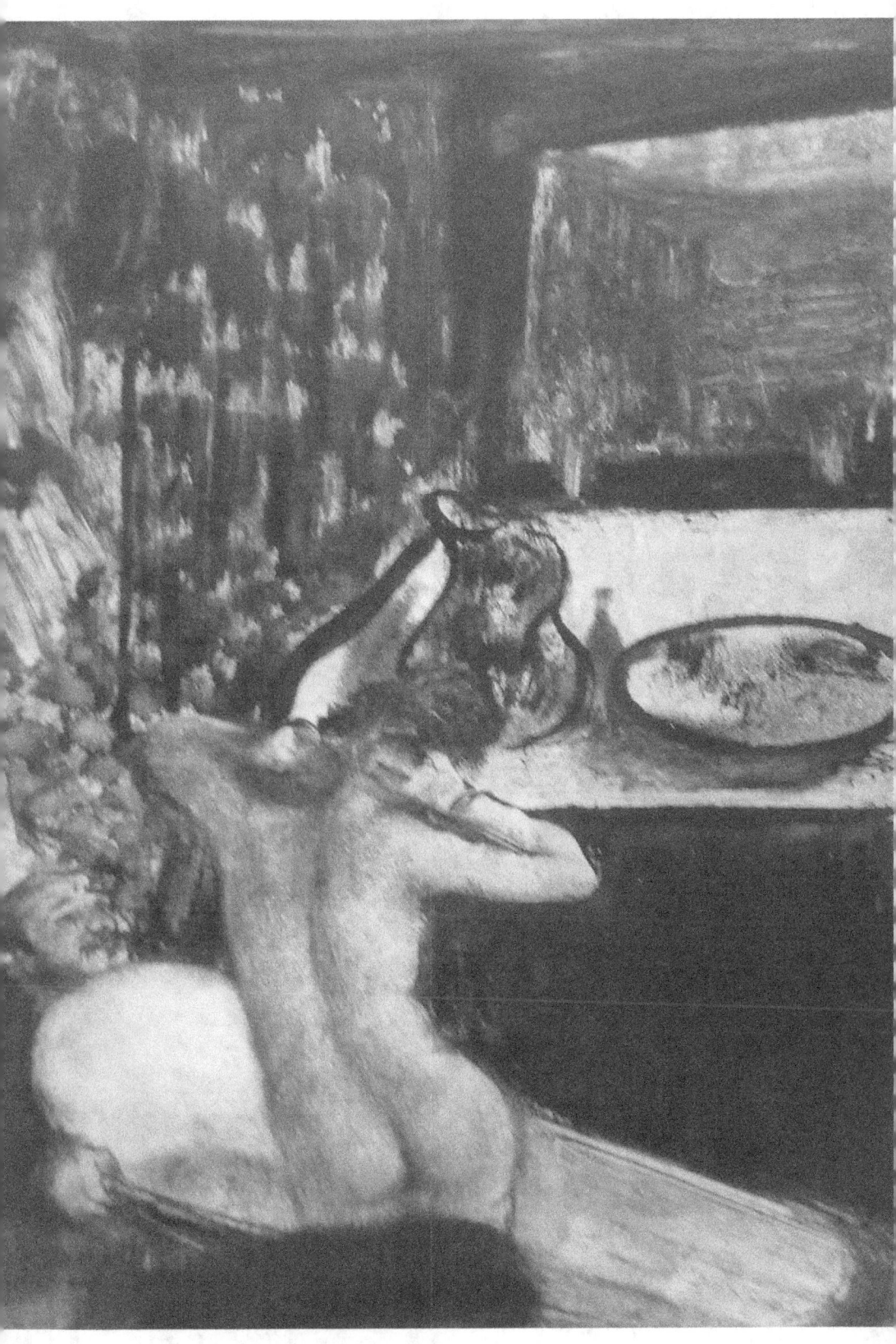

Edgar Degas, The Bath

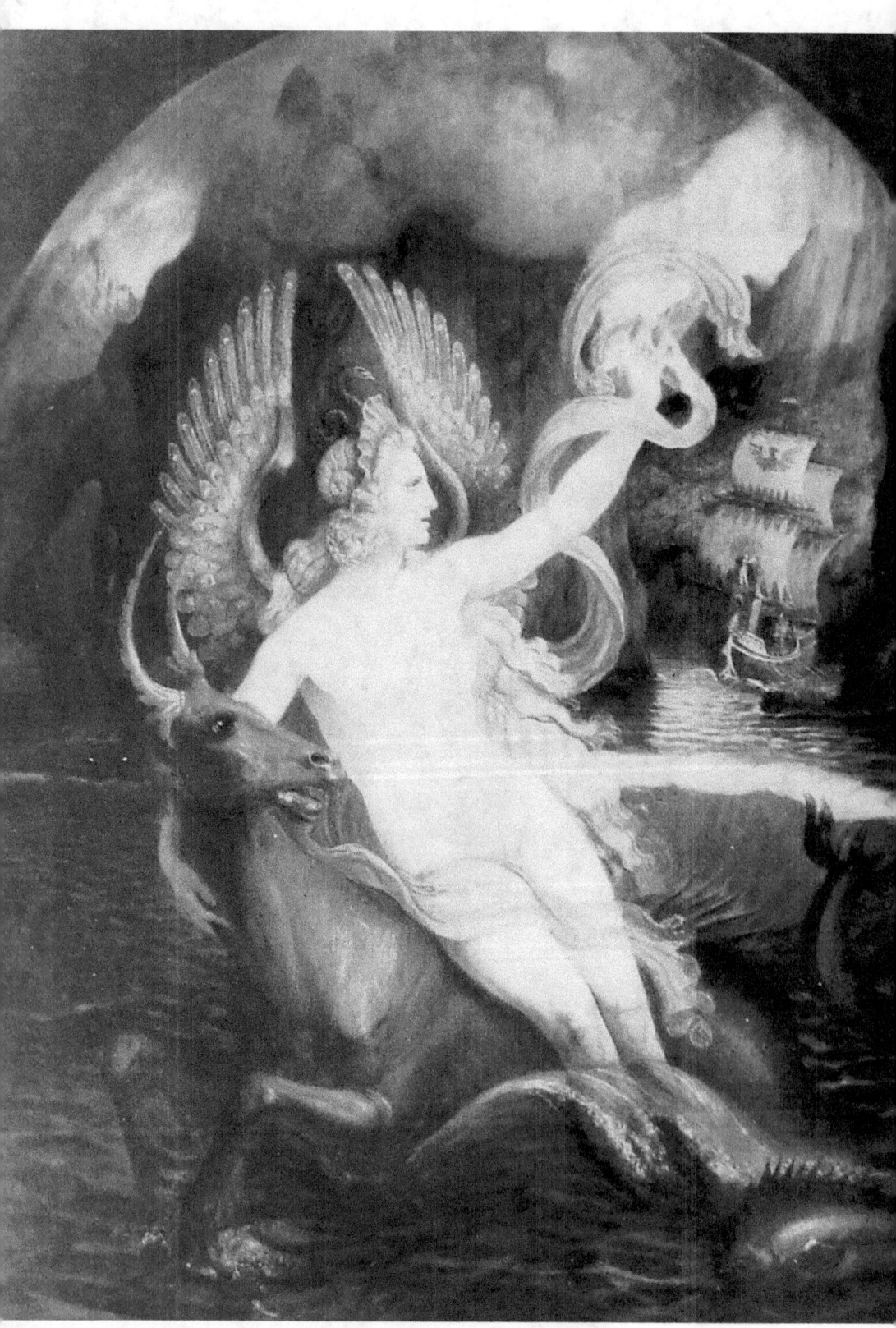

Armand Point, The Siren, 1867

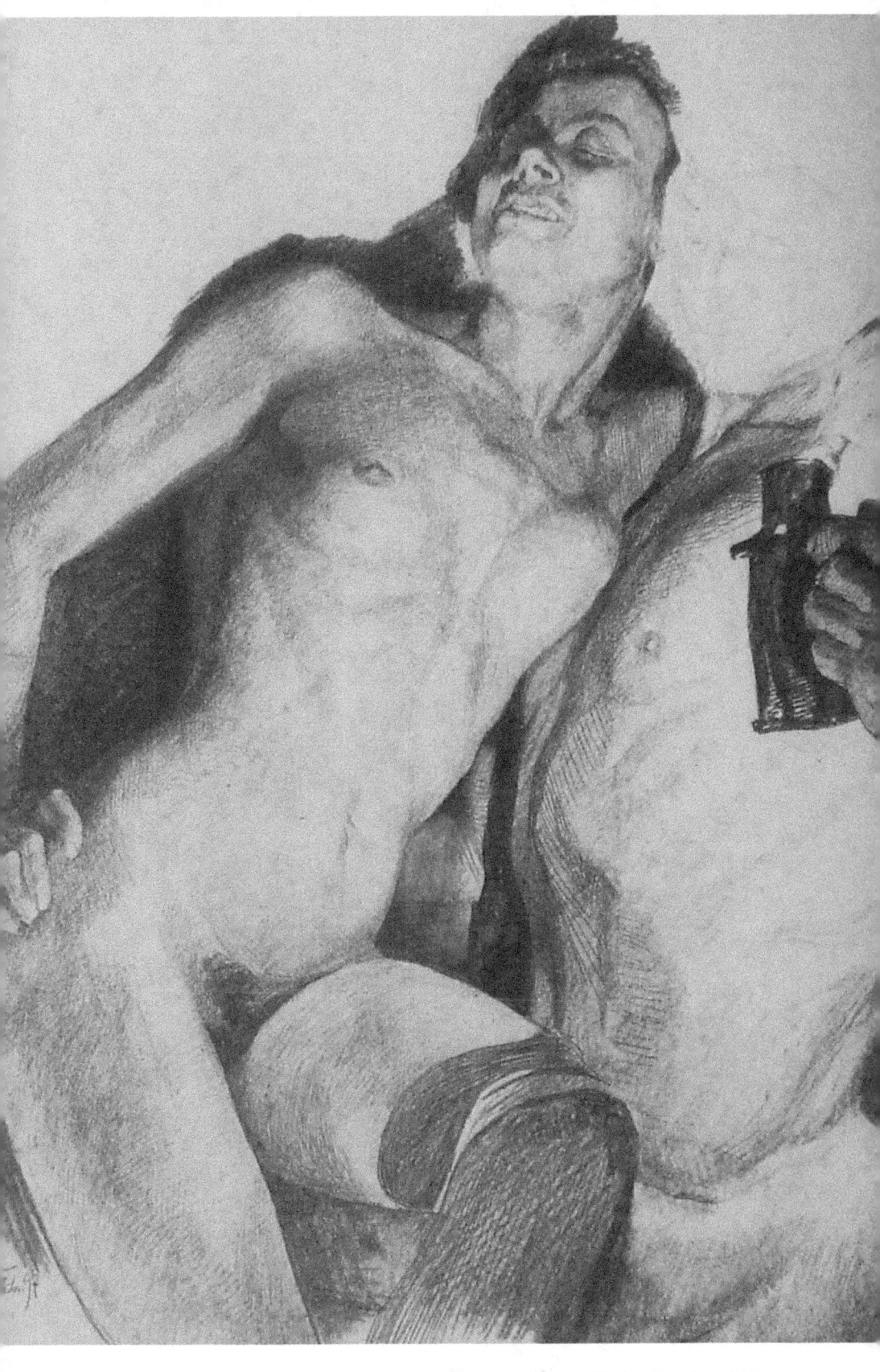

Otto Grenier's truly extraordinary The Devil Showing Woman To the People, 1897

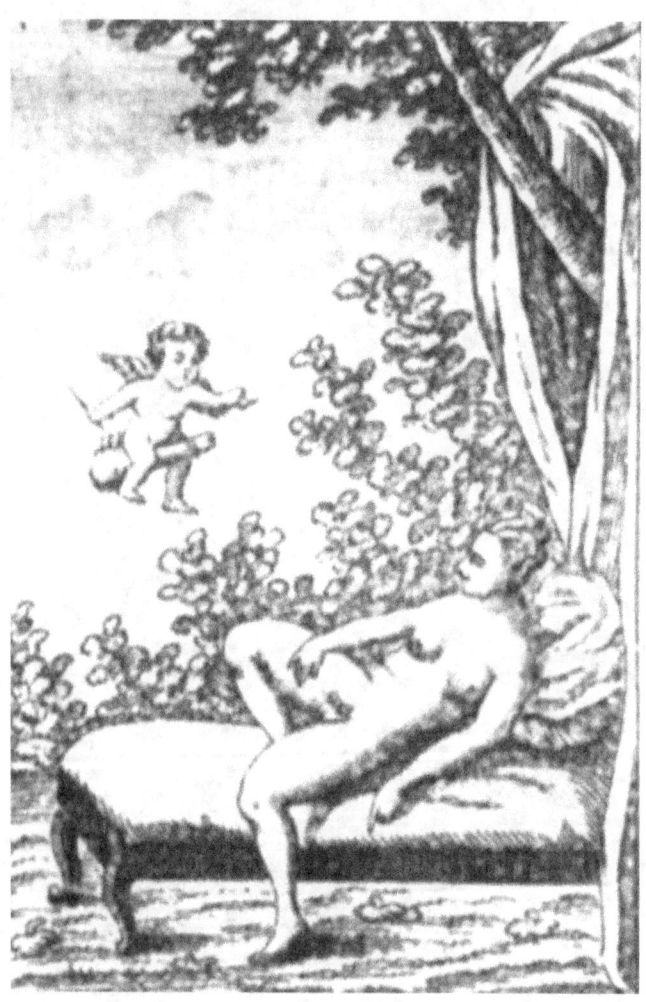

Anonymous, from Memoires de Suzon

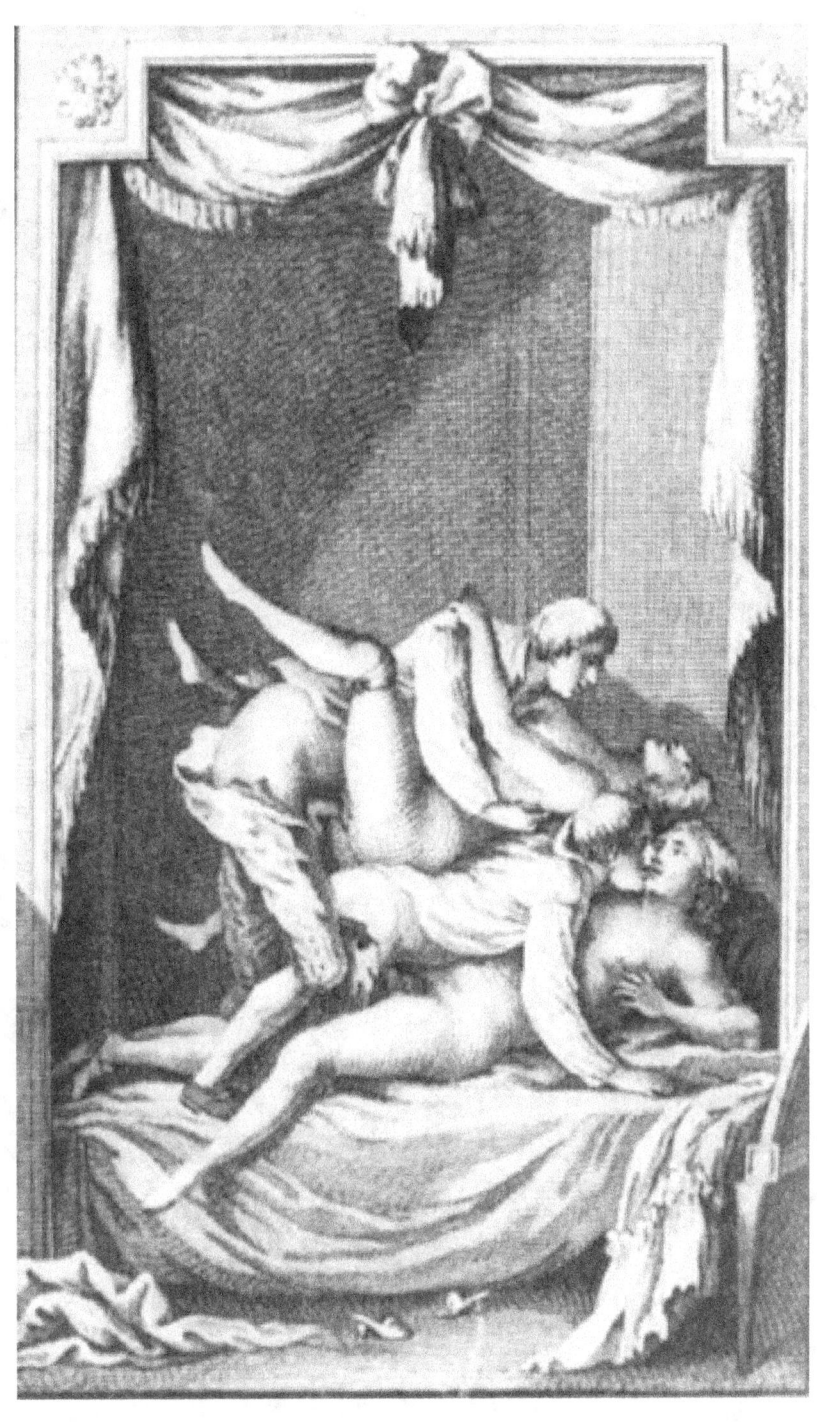

Antoine Borel, illustration for Mémoires de Saturnin,
by Jean-Charles Gervaise, 1787

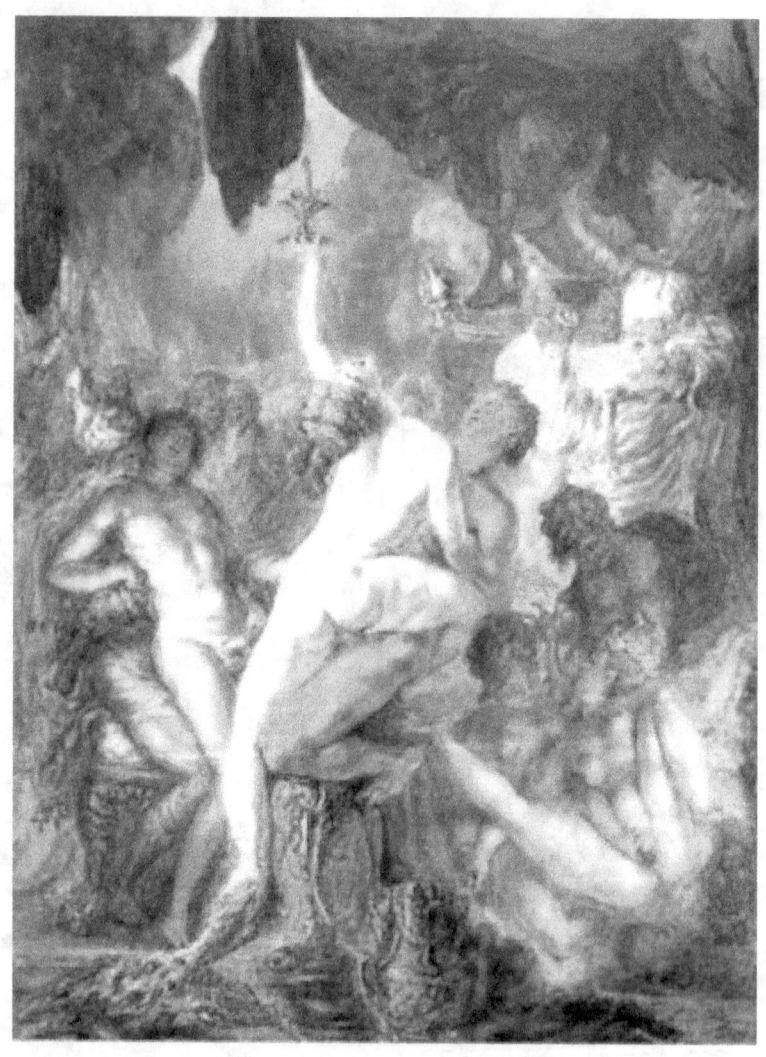

Anonymous, from Histoire Sainte, Adorazione del vitello d'oro

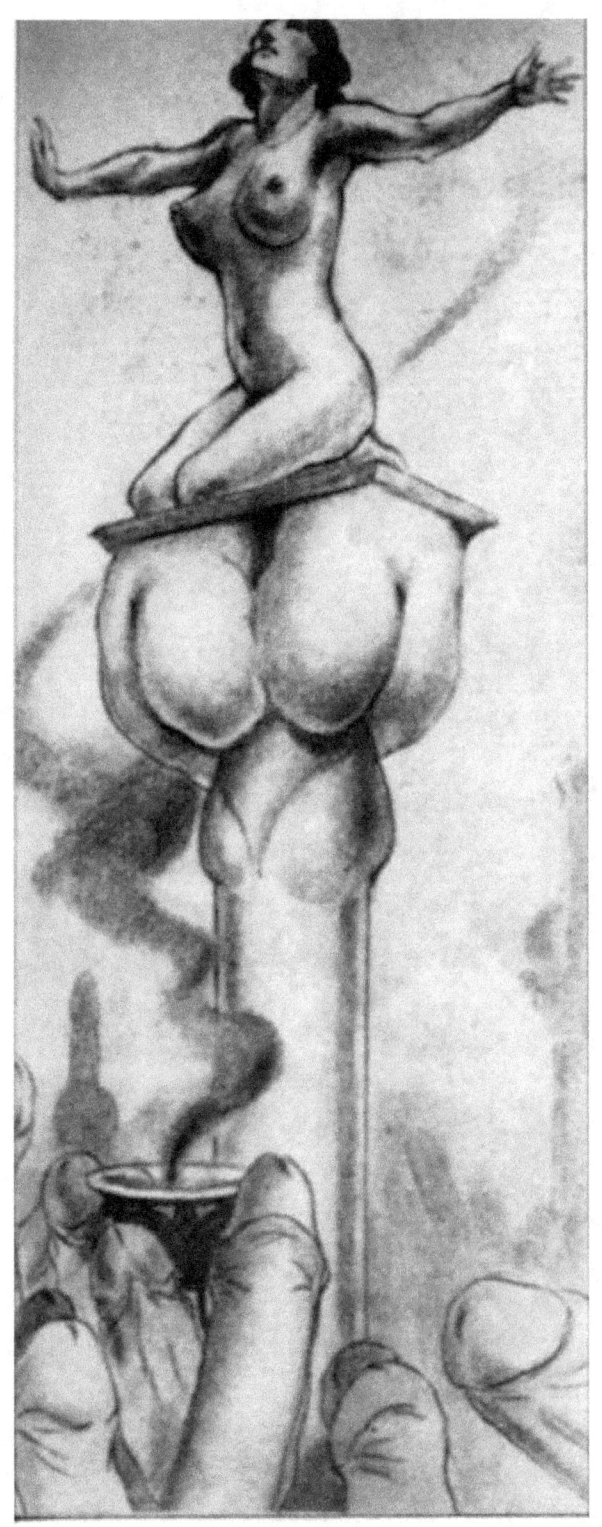

Anonymous, 19th century

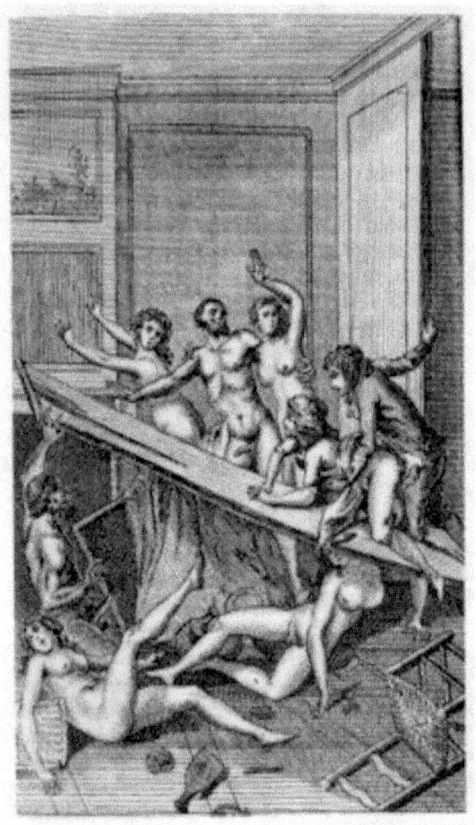

Illustration from Histoire de Juliette,
Marquis de Sade, 1797

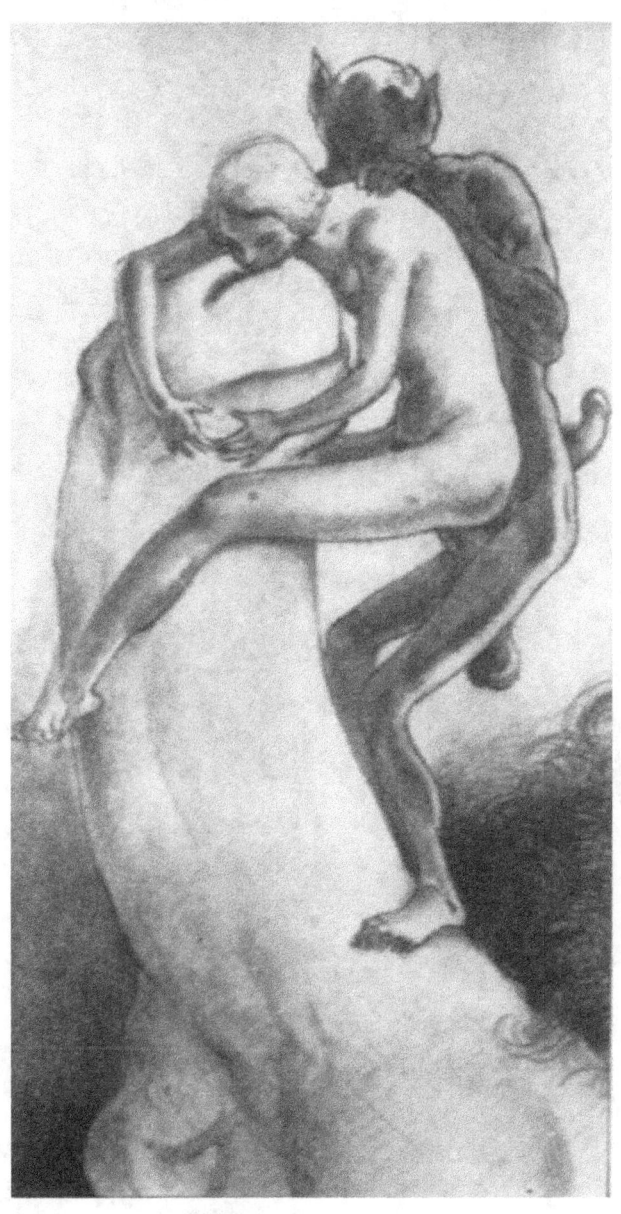

Anonymous, 19th century

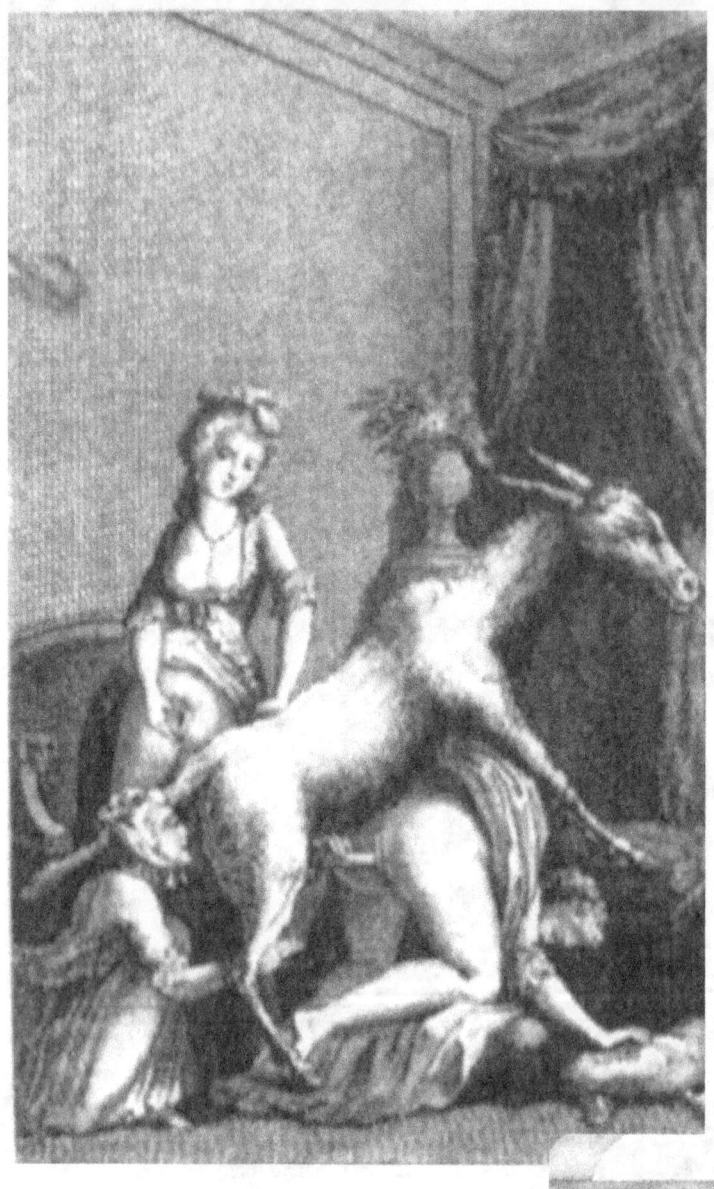

Anonymous, from Le Diable
(this page and over)

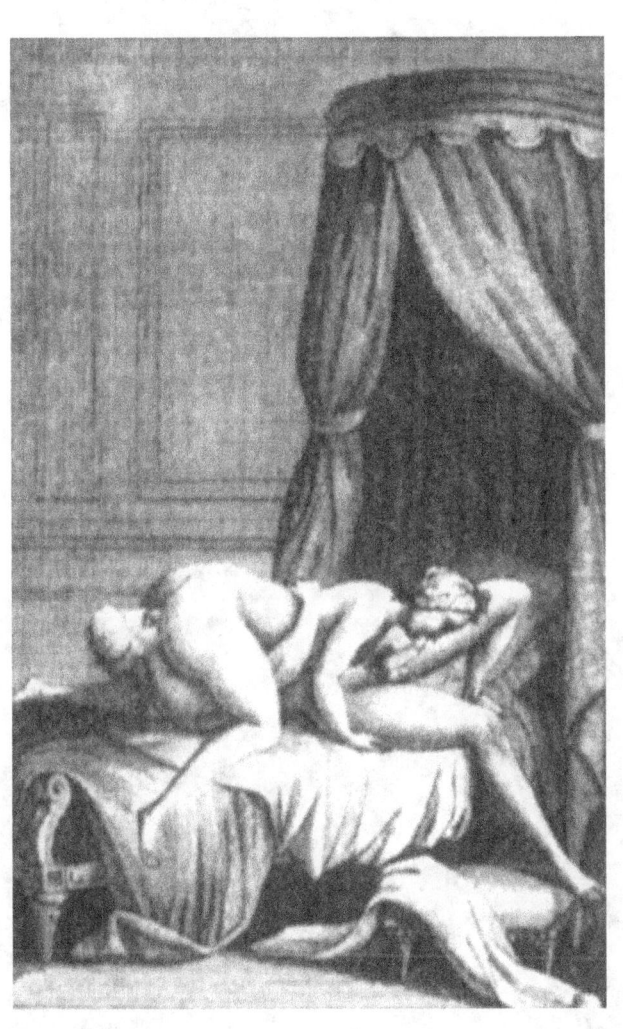

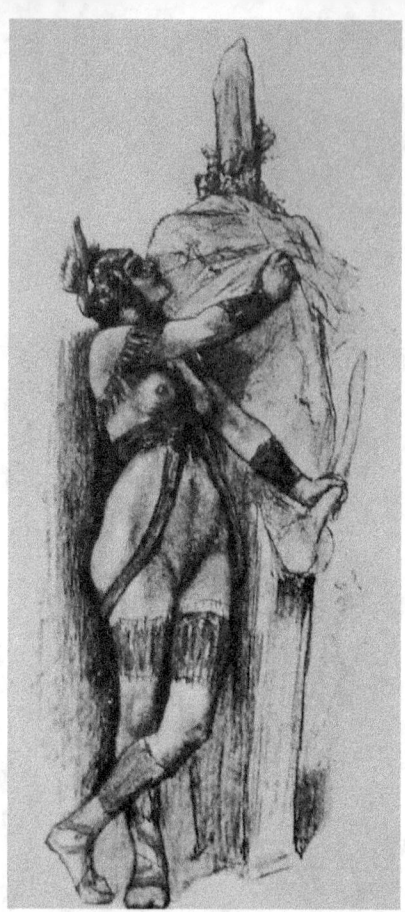

The inimitable Félicien Rops, French fin-de-siècle Decadence at its most extreme.

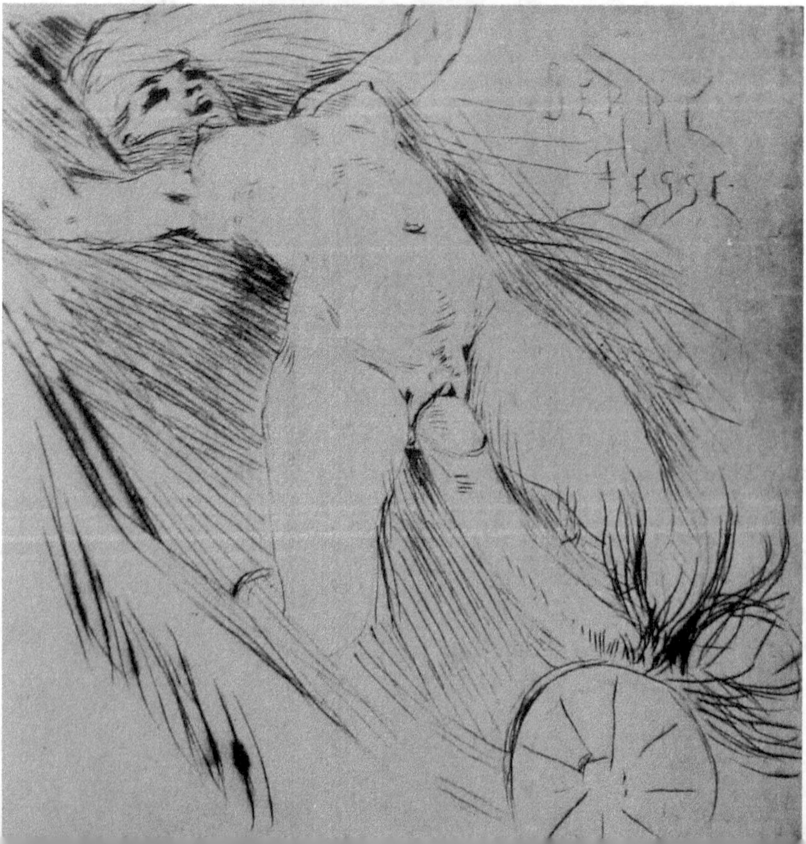

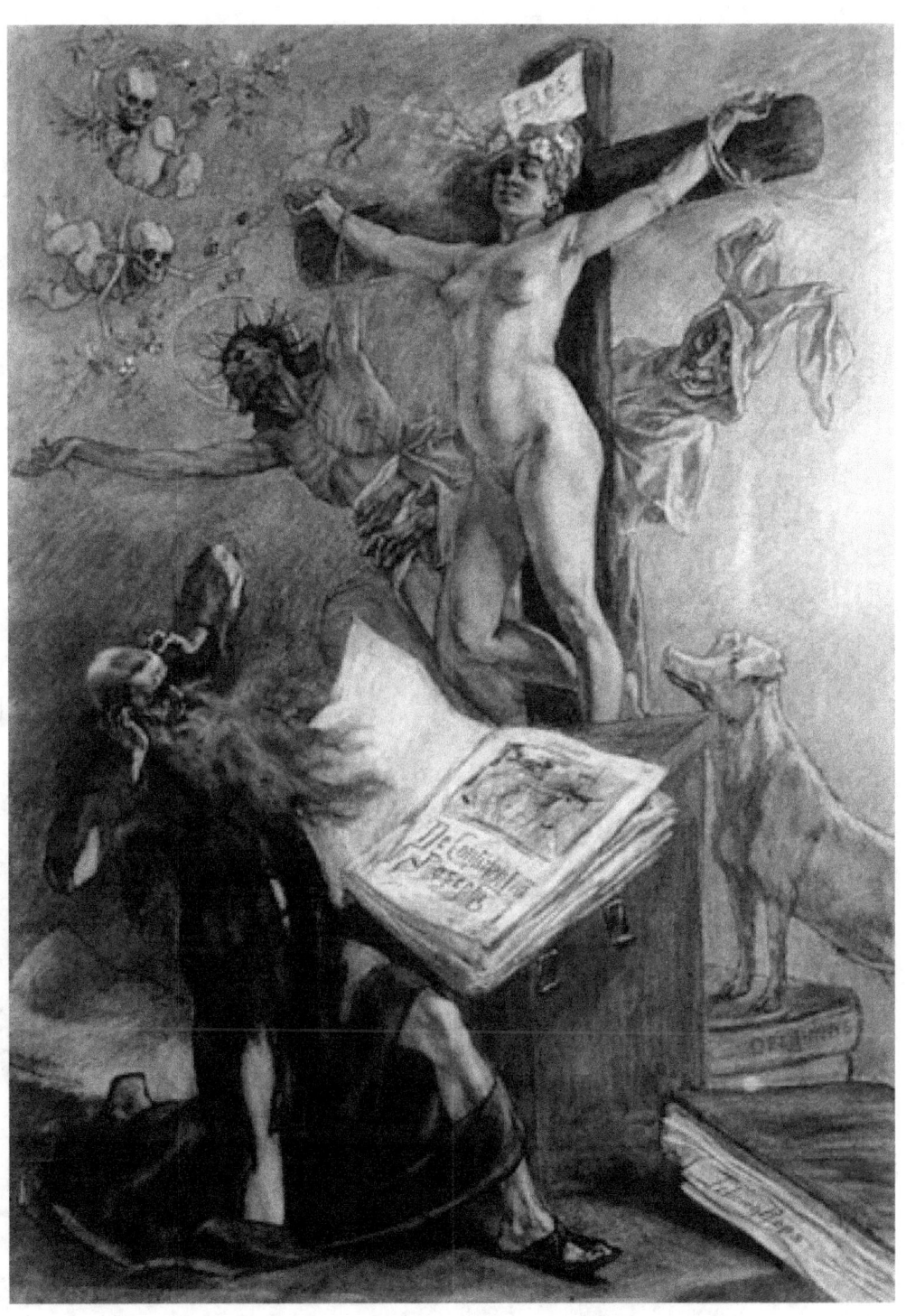

The Temptation of St Anthony, a popular subject of the era, by Félicien Rops

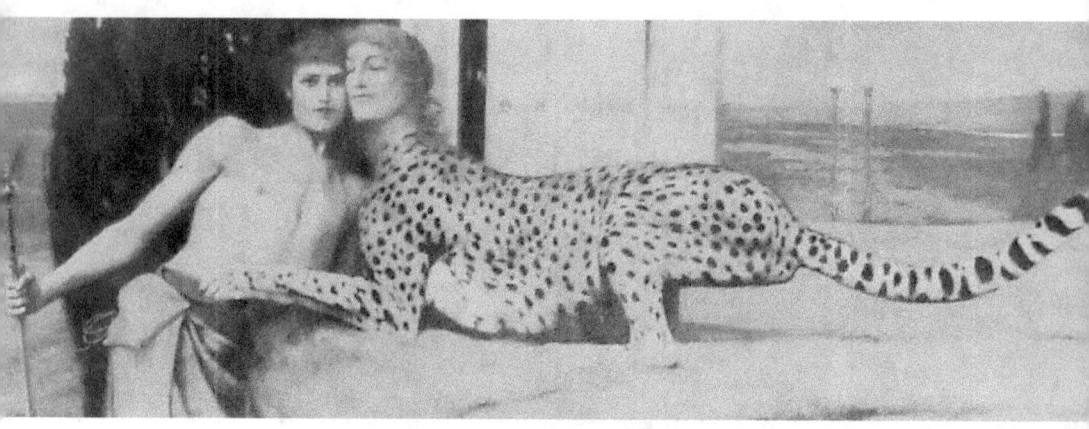

Franz Knopff, Caresses of the Sphinx, 1896, above.
Gustav Klimt, The Bride, 1917-18 (unfinished), below.

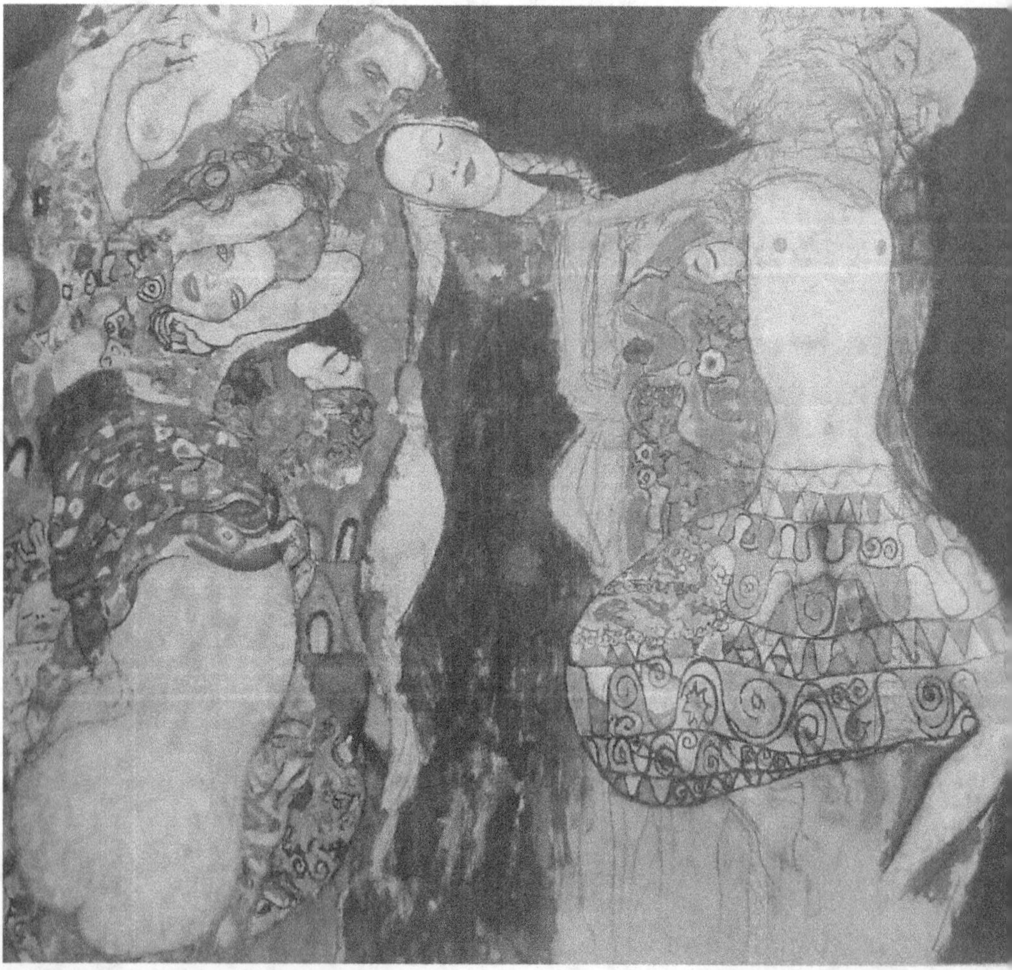

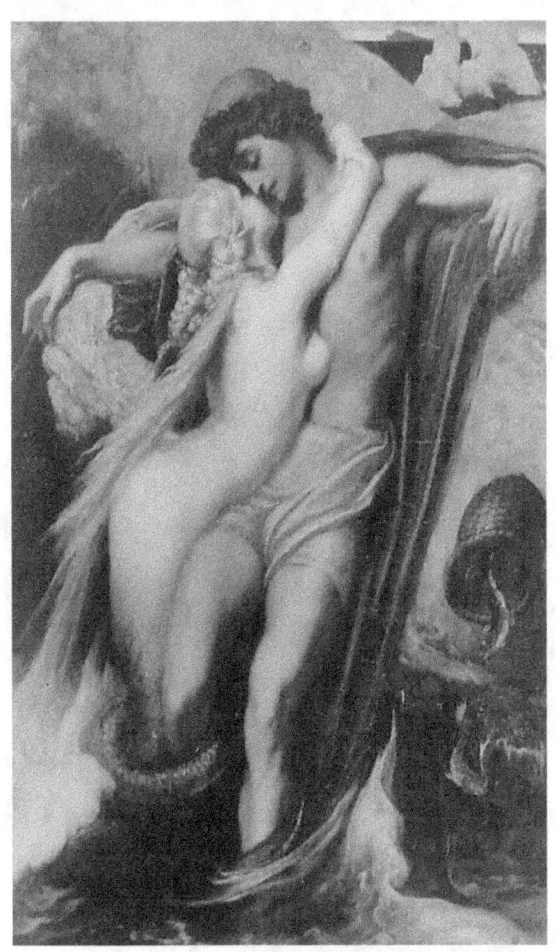

Classic Victorian nude imagery, by Lord Leighton: The Fisherman and the Siren, 1858, Bristol, above; and Actaea, the Nymph of the Shore, 1868, Ottawa, below.

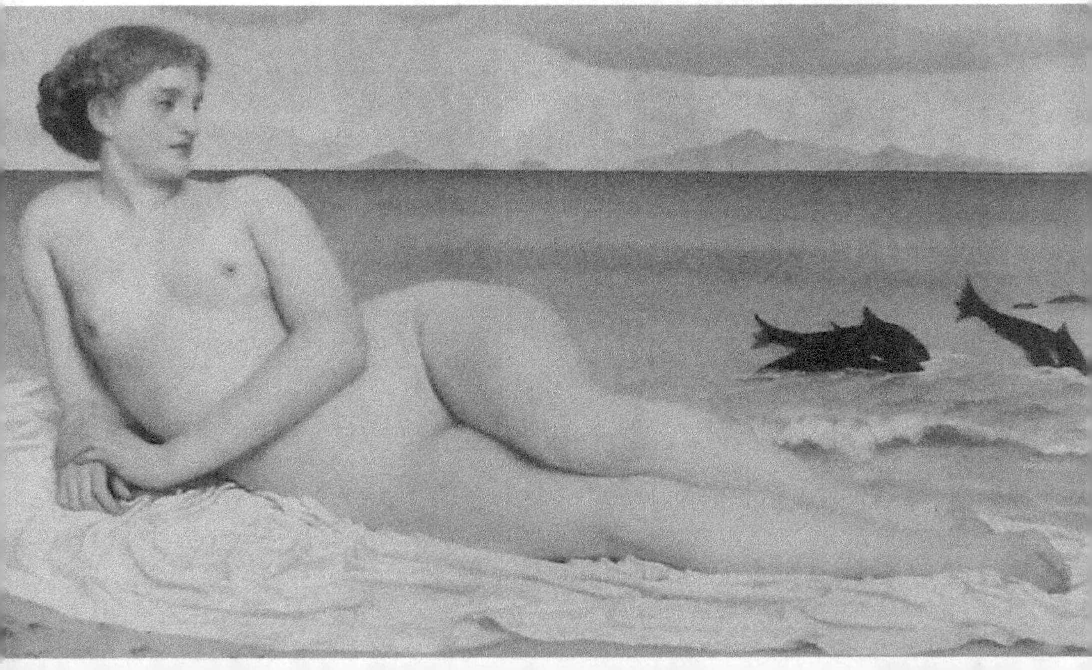

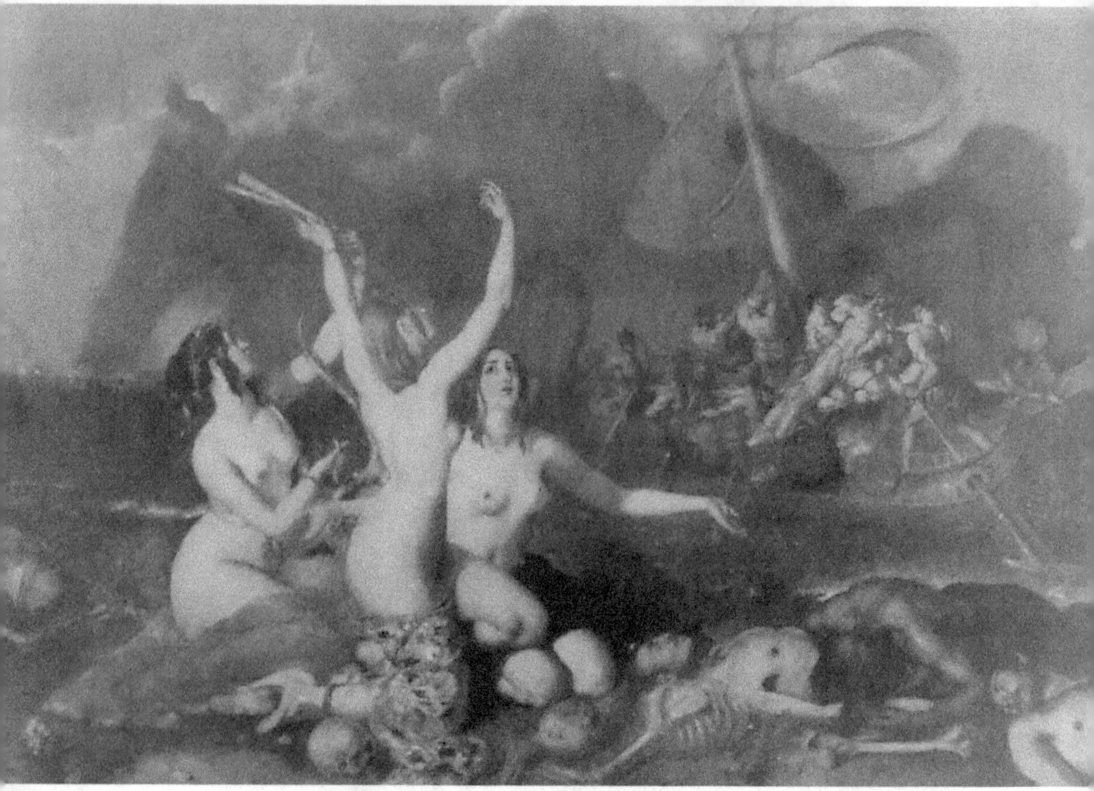

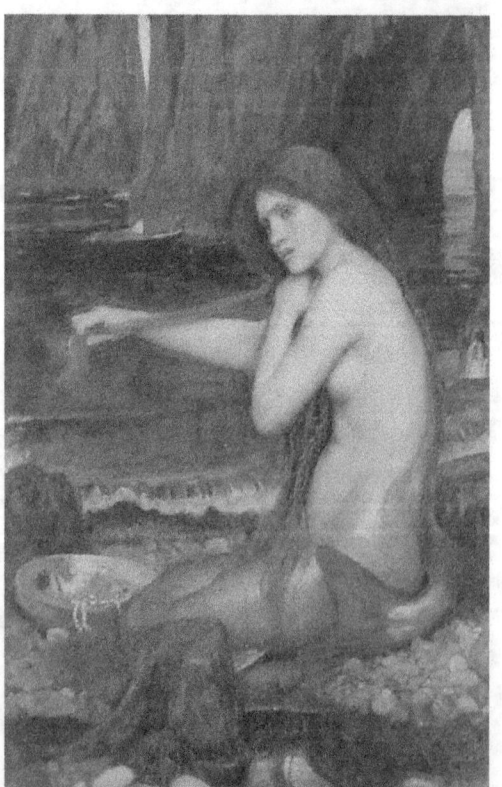

A favourite theme in 19th century
painting: sex, death, nudity and
the sea.
William Etty's The Sirens and
Ulysses, 1837, Manchester.
above.

J.W. Waterhouse,
A Mermaid, 1901, Royal Academy,
London, below.

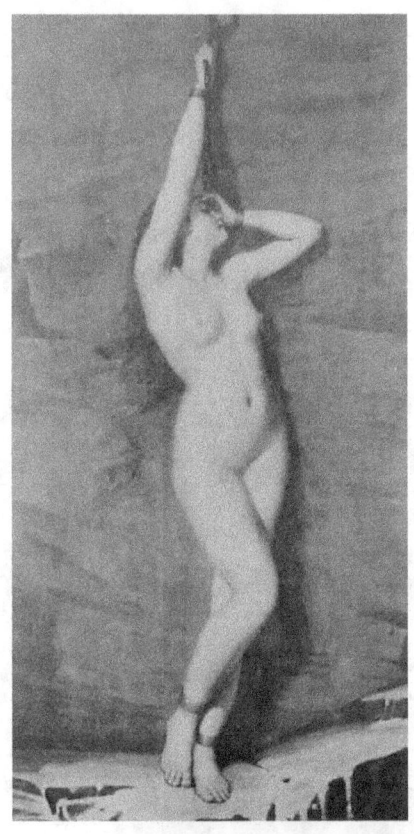

Two views of Andromeda chained to the rock in Victorian art, a good excuse for nudity.
By Edward Poynter, 1870, below.
And Arthur Hill, 1875, Russell-Cotes Art Gallery, Bournemouth, below.

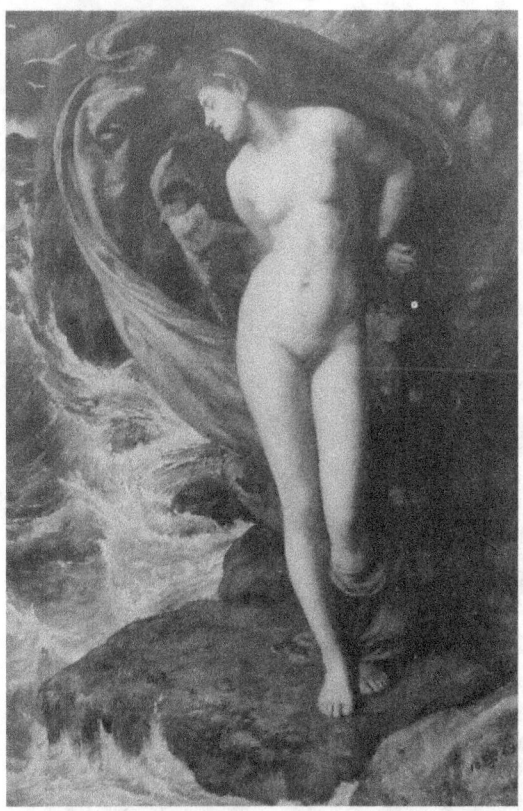

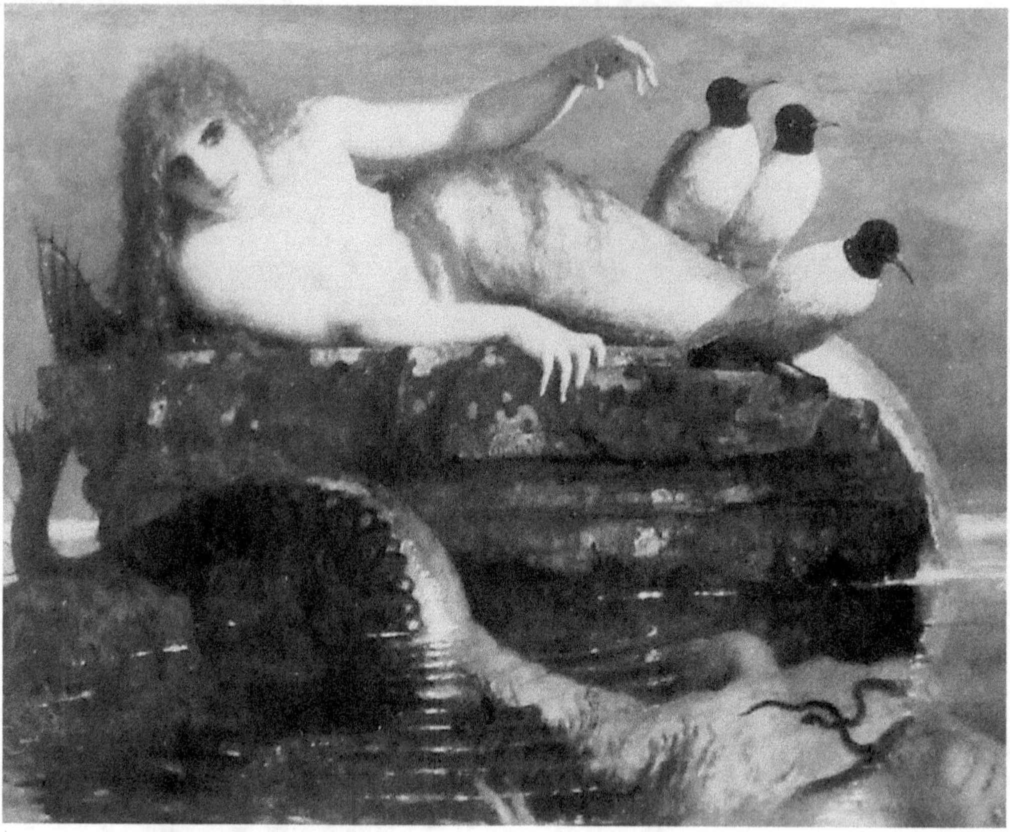

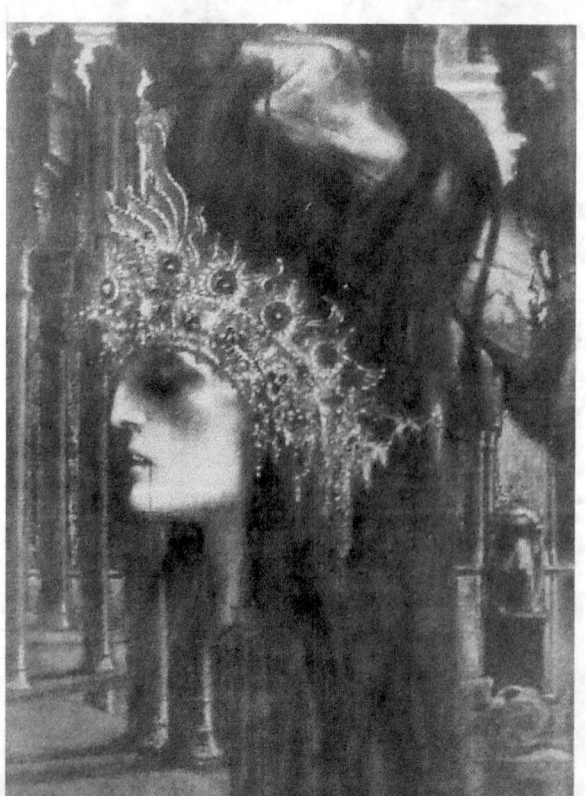

Arnold Böcklin, Calm Sea, 1887, above

Jean Delville, Orpheus, 1893, below

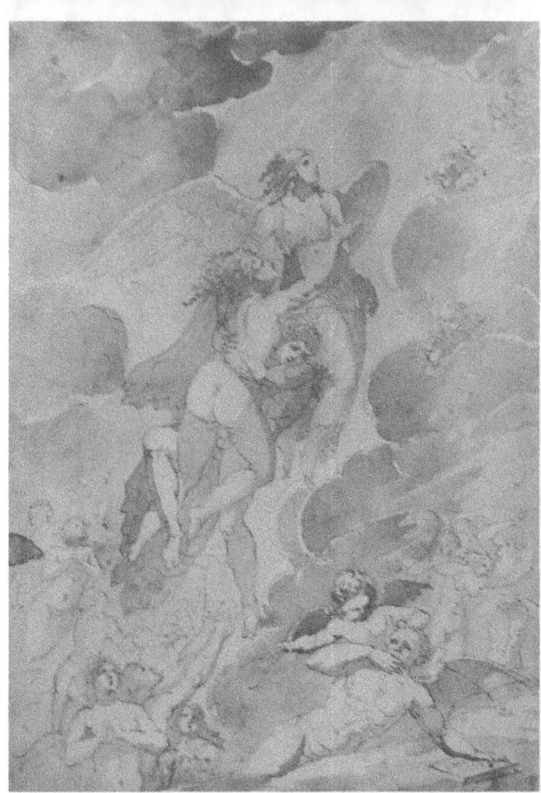

Two drawings by
Johan Tobias Sergel,
Sweden, late 18th century

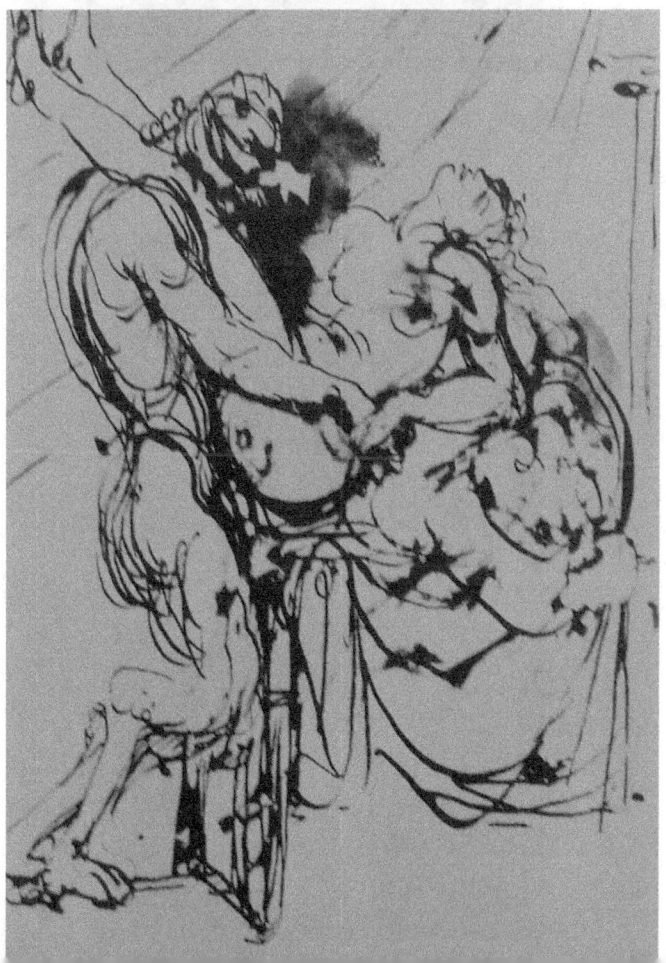

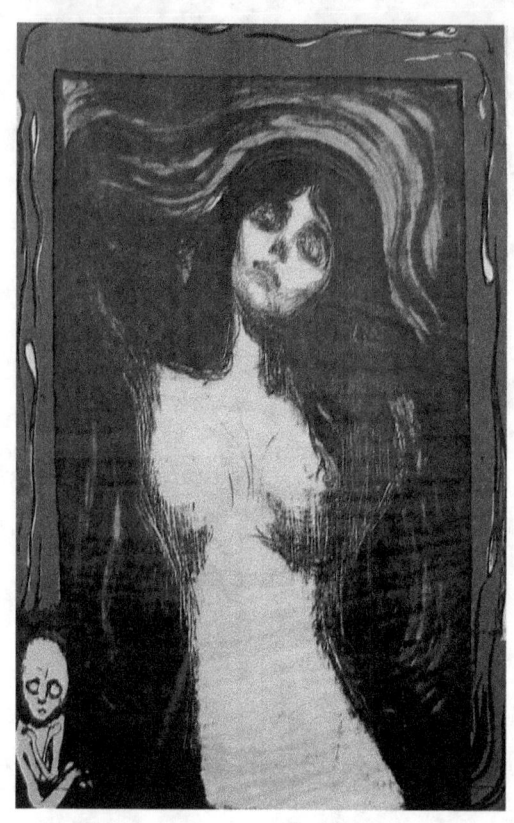

Sexuality in the tortured Scandinavian manner:
Edvard Munch's The Kiss and The Madonna

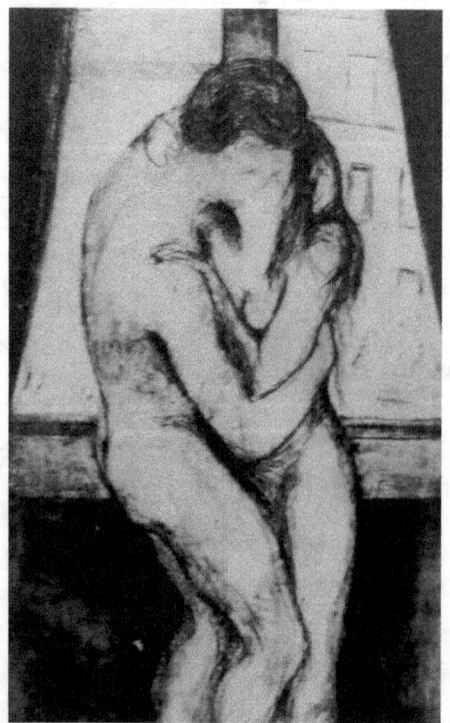

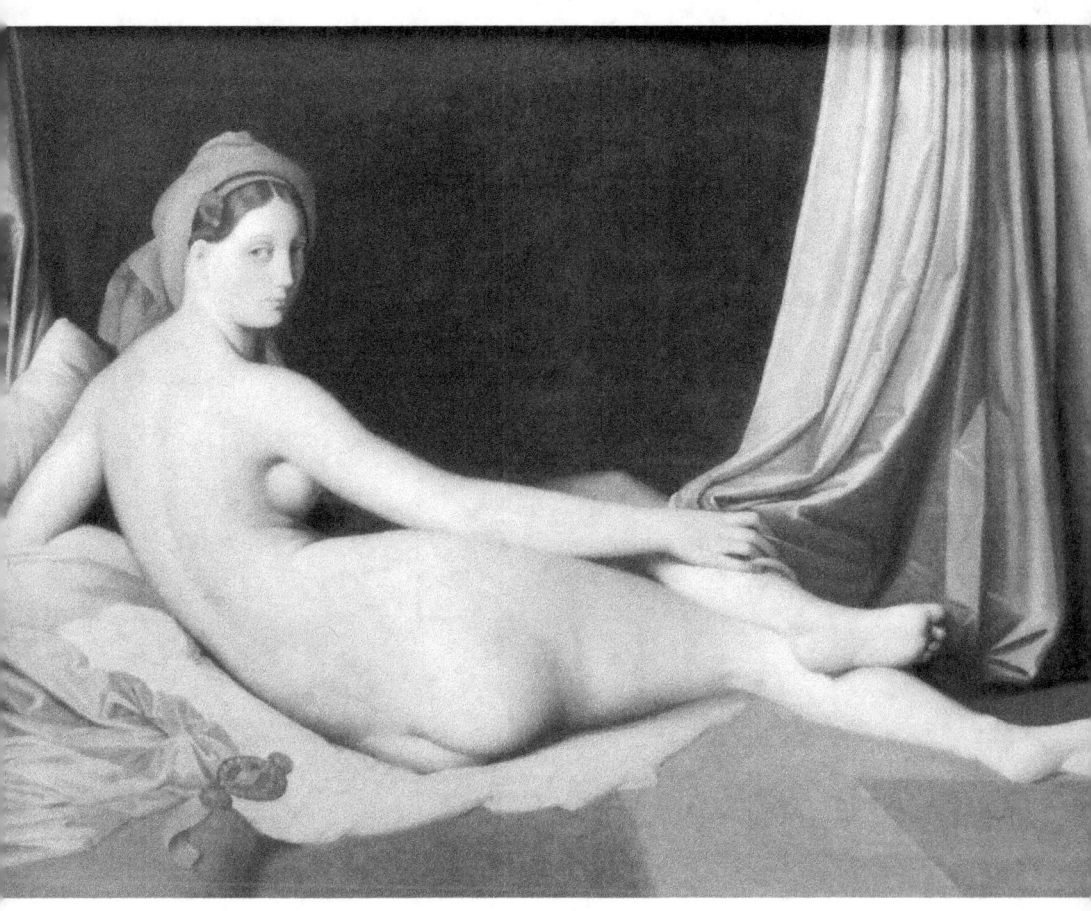

Jean Dominique Ingres

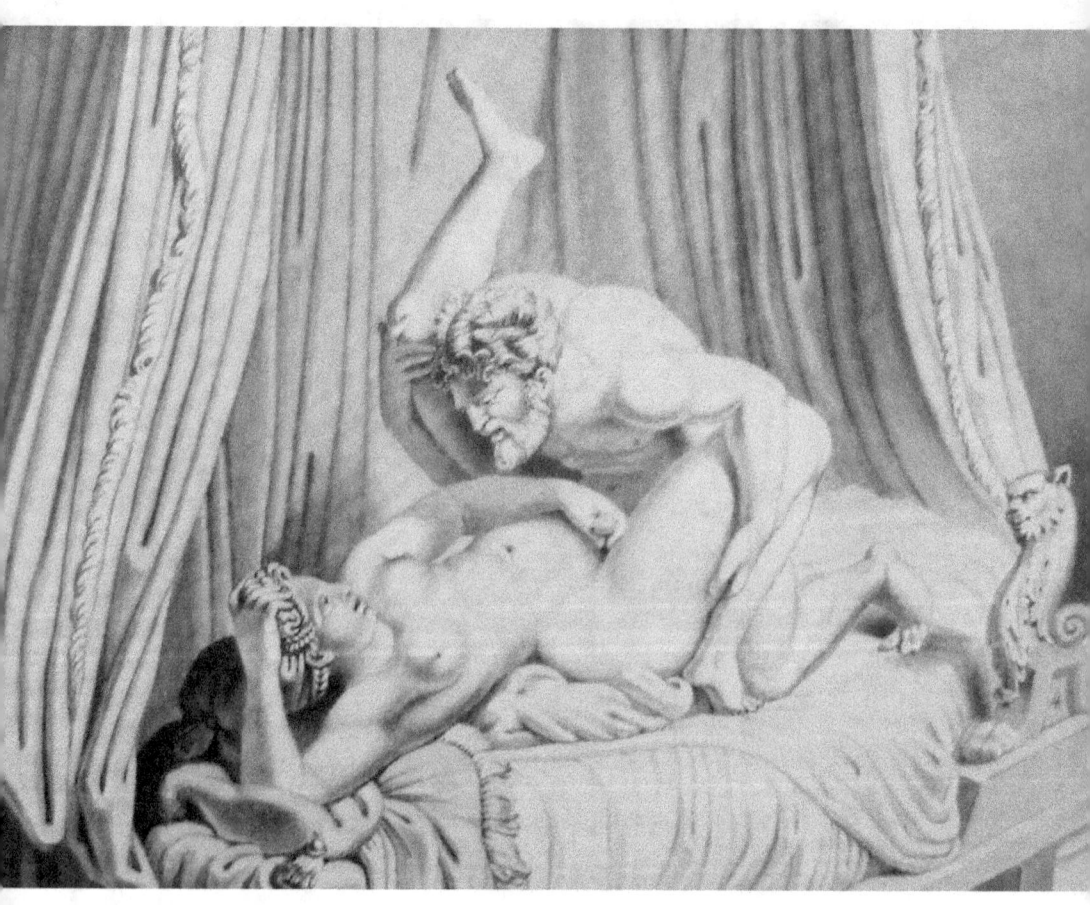

Friedrich von Waldeck, from Postures, c. 1858

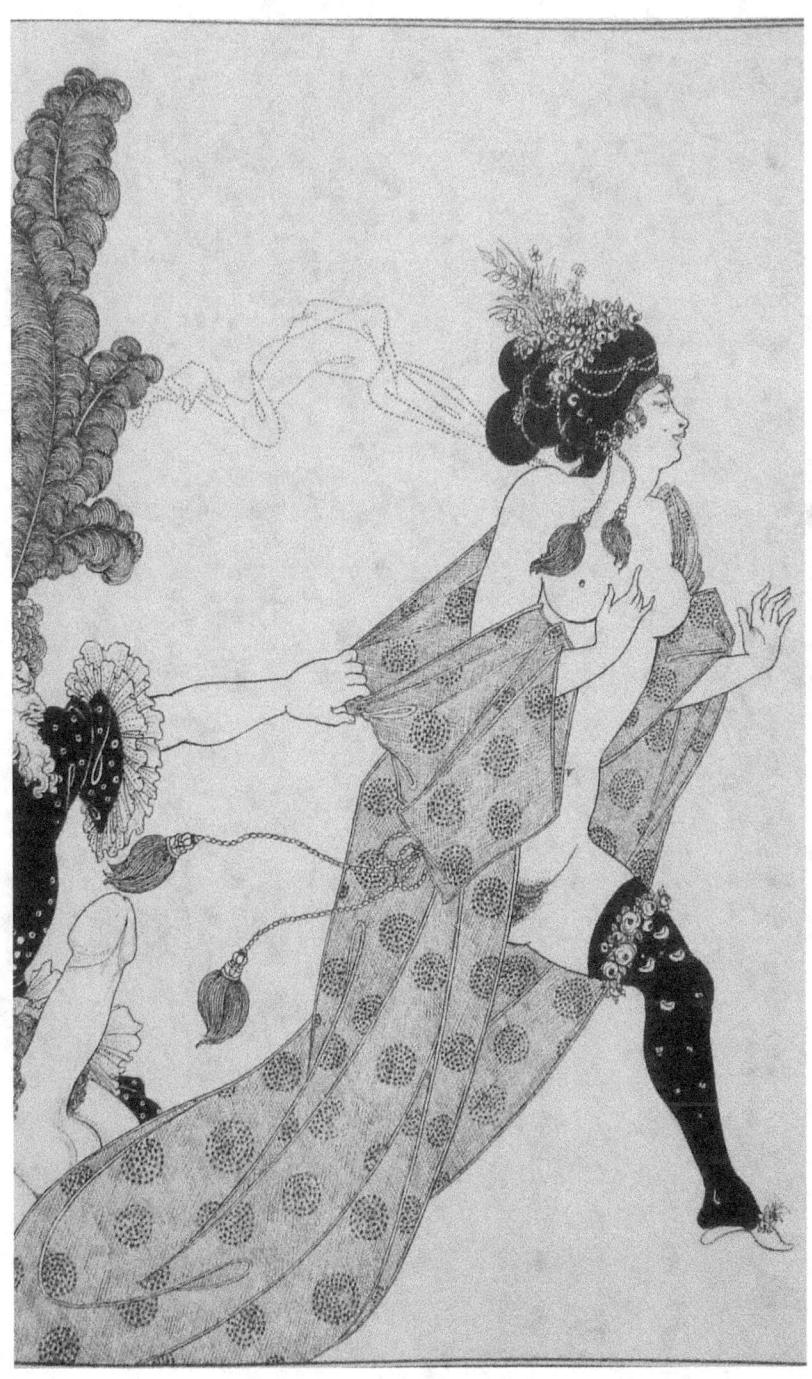

Aubrey Beardsley

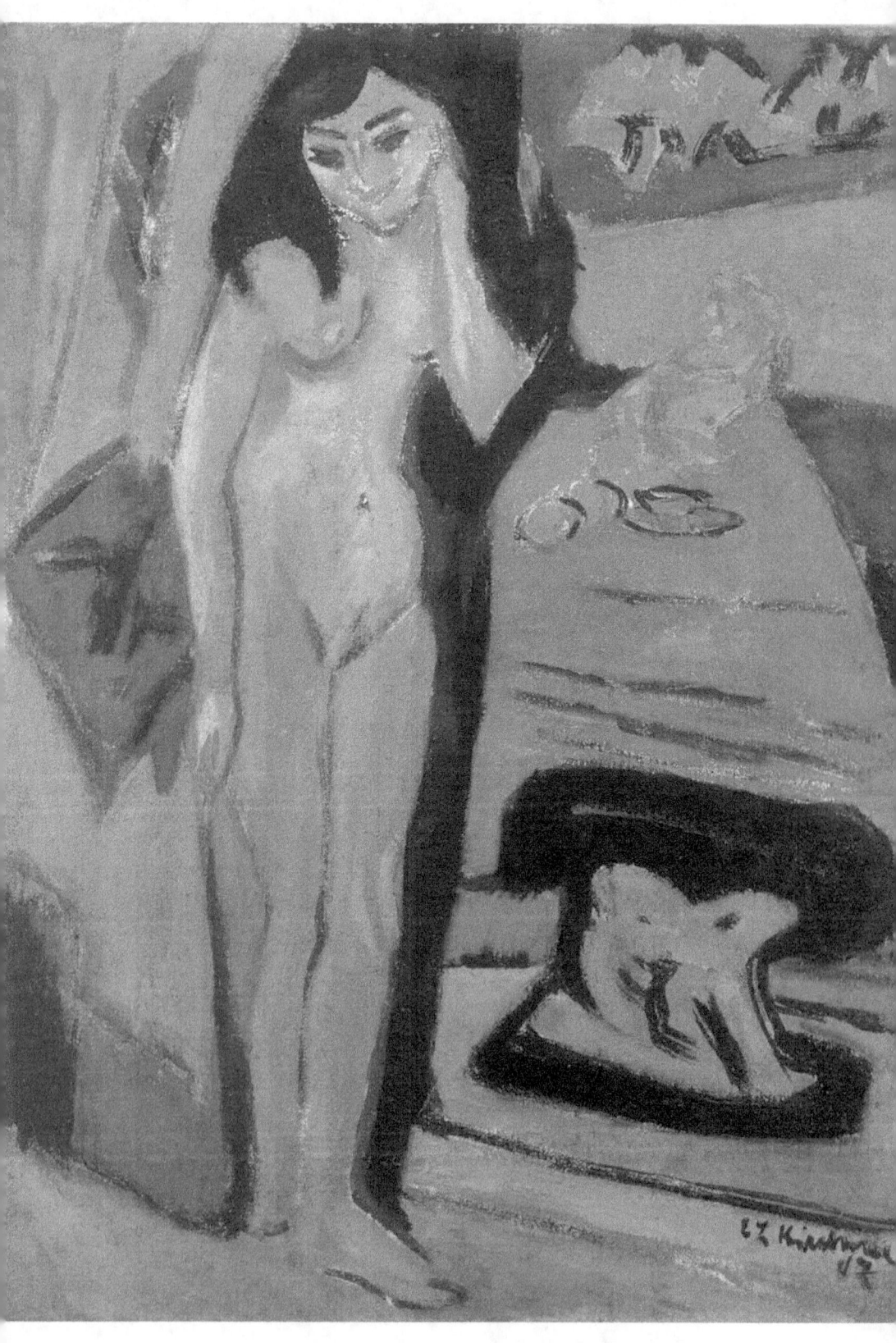

Ernst Ludwig Kirchner, Naked Woman, 1910/ 26, Amsterdam

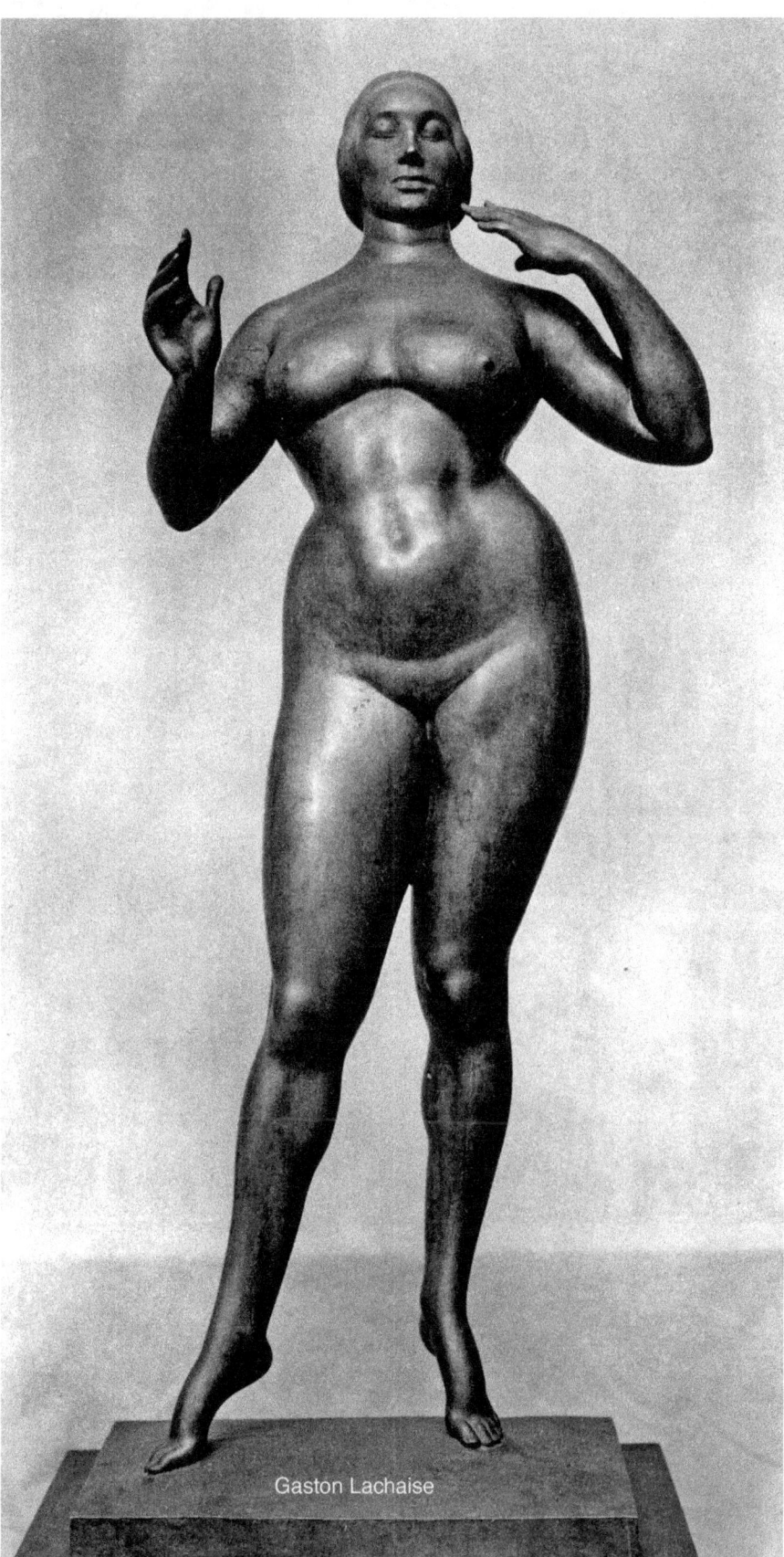

Gaston Lachaise

Egon Schiele, Girl With
Black Hair, 1911 (right).

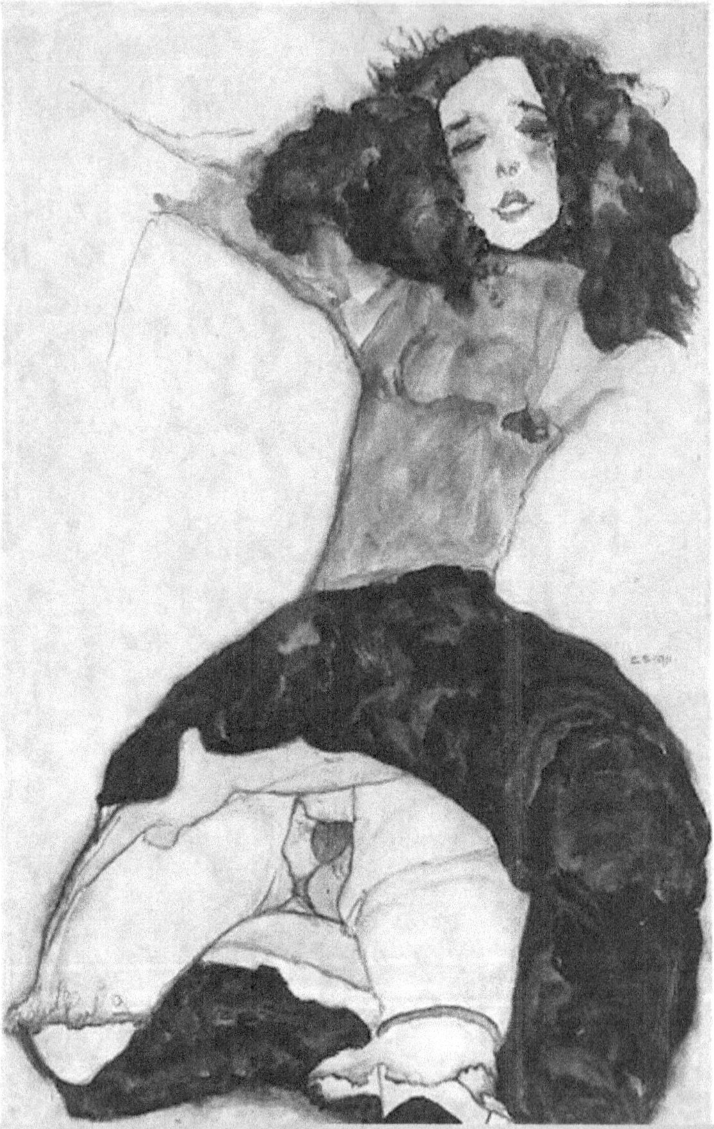

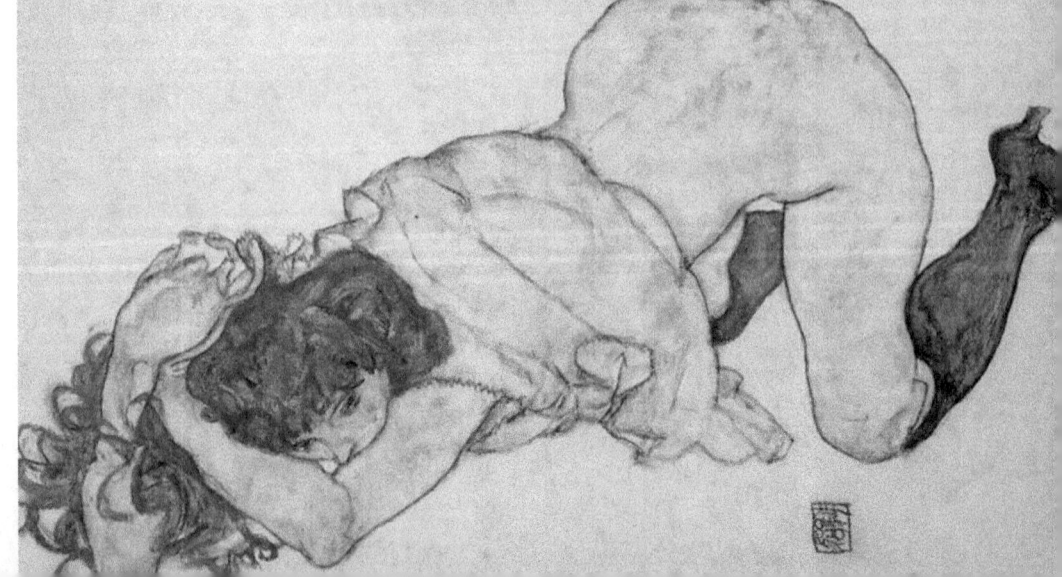

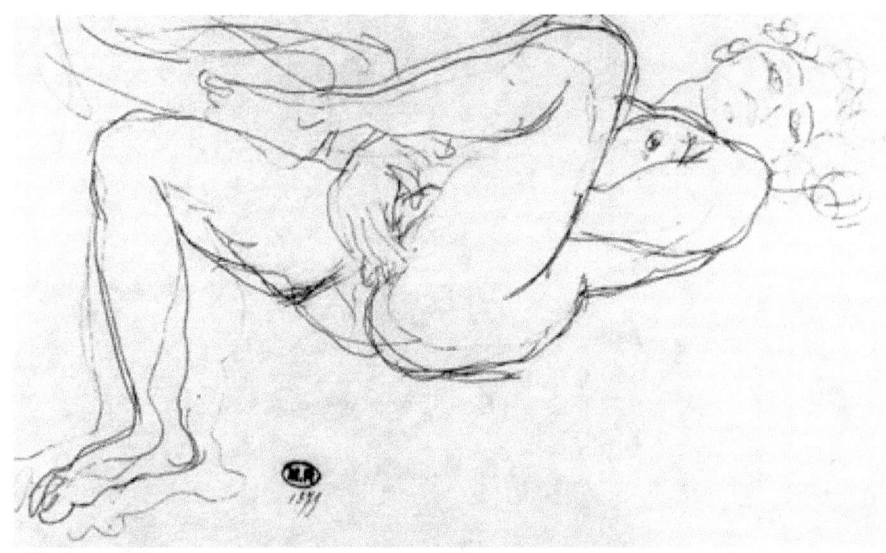

Auguste Rodin, drawings

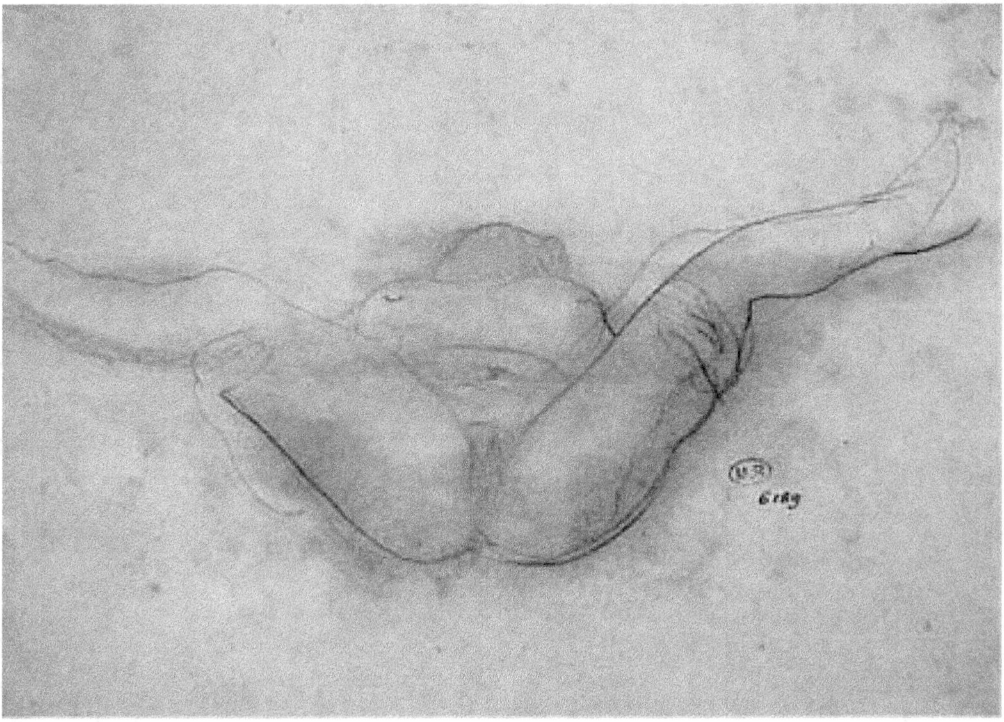

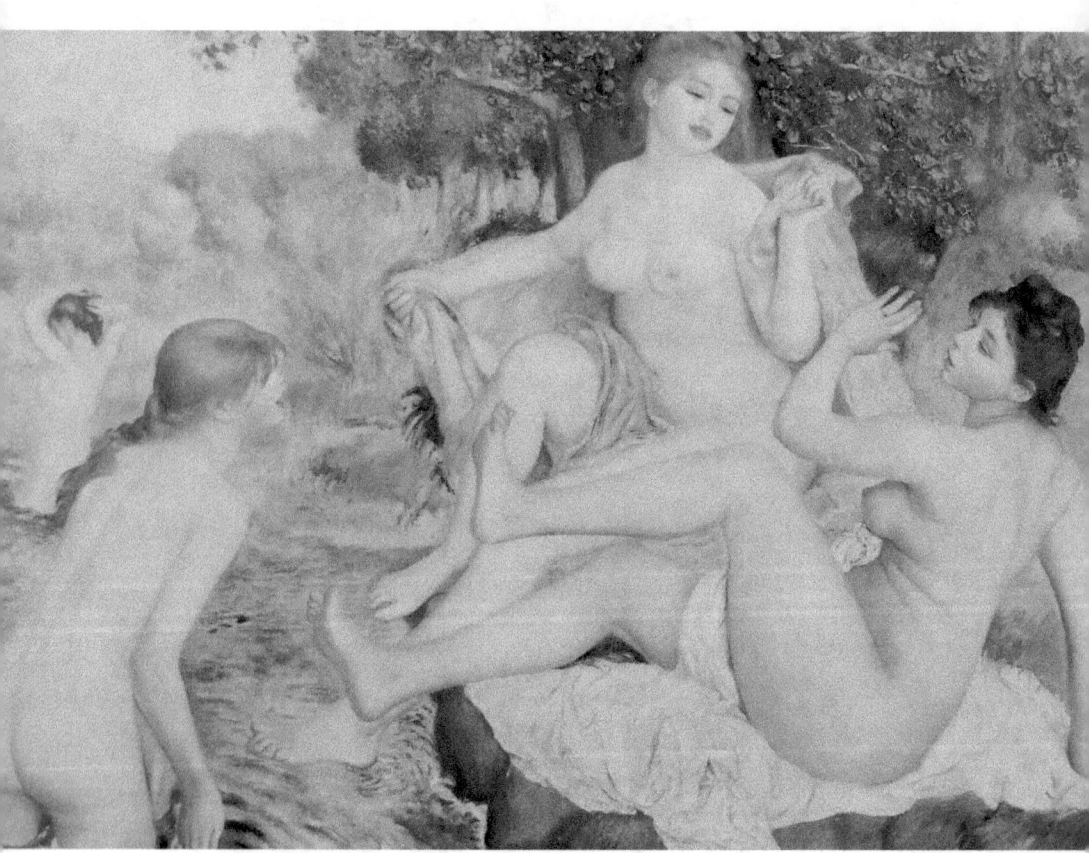

Pierre Renoir, The Bathers, 1887, Philadelphia

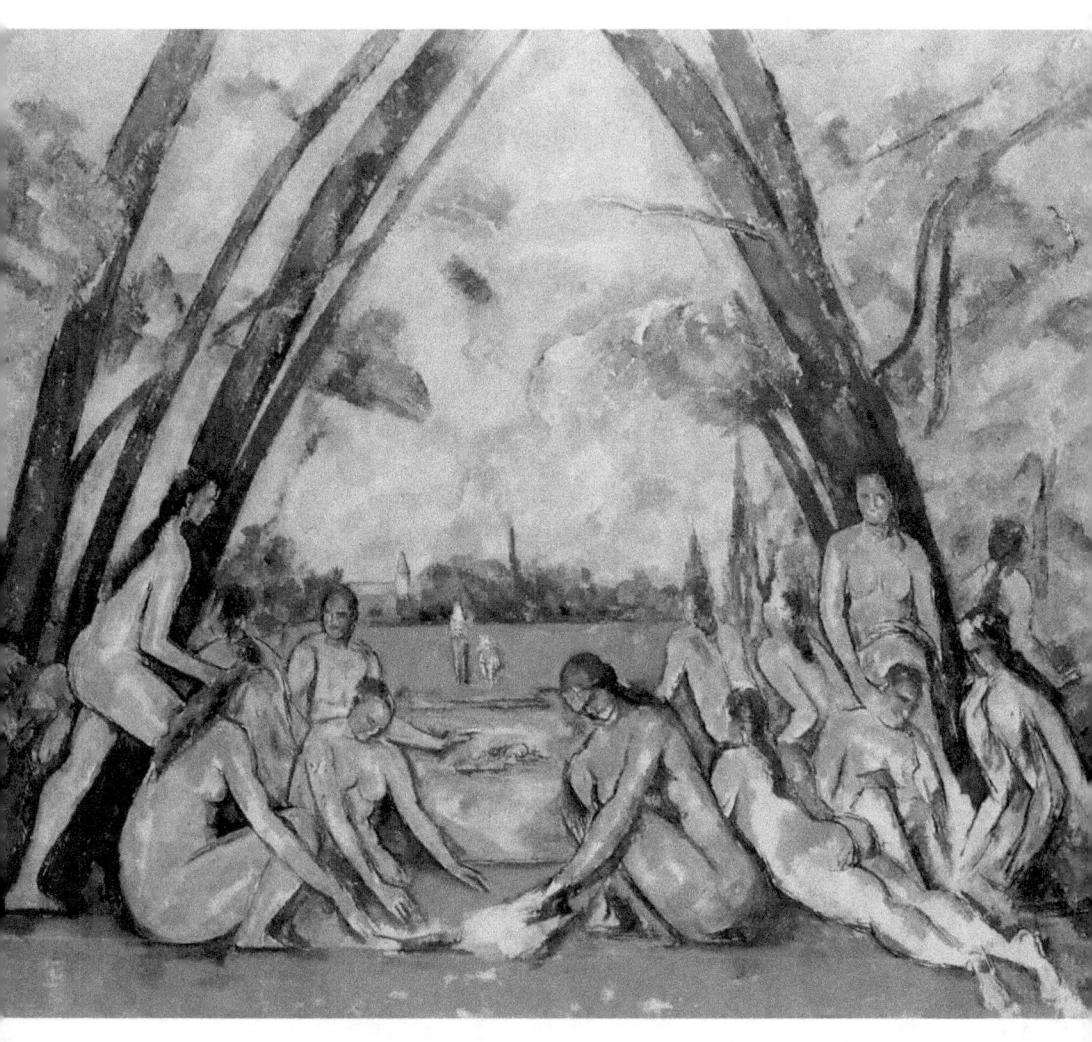

Paul Cézanne, Large Bathers, 1906,
Philadelphia Museum of Art

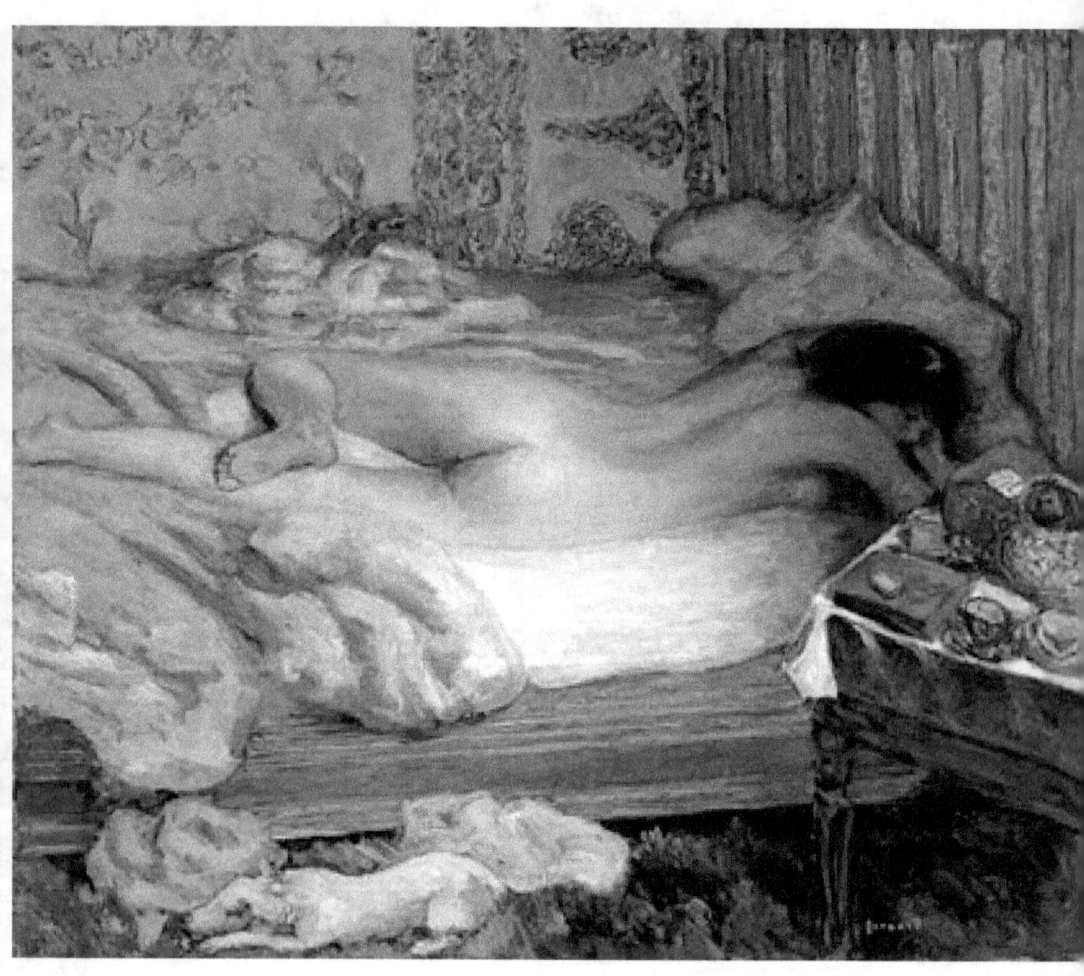

Pierre Bonnard

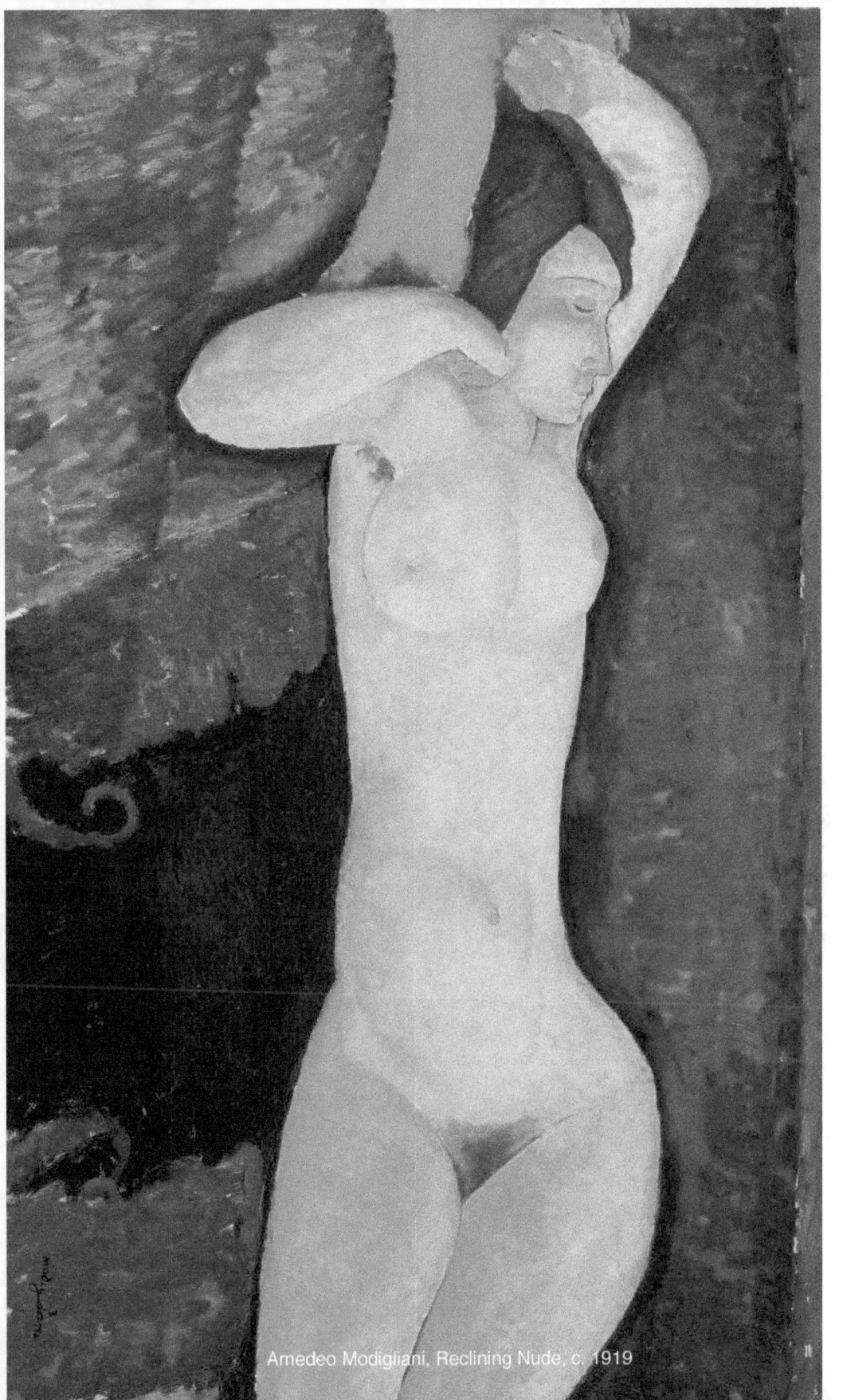

Amedeo Modigliani, Reclining Nude, c. 1919

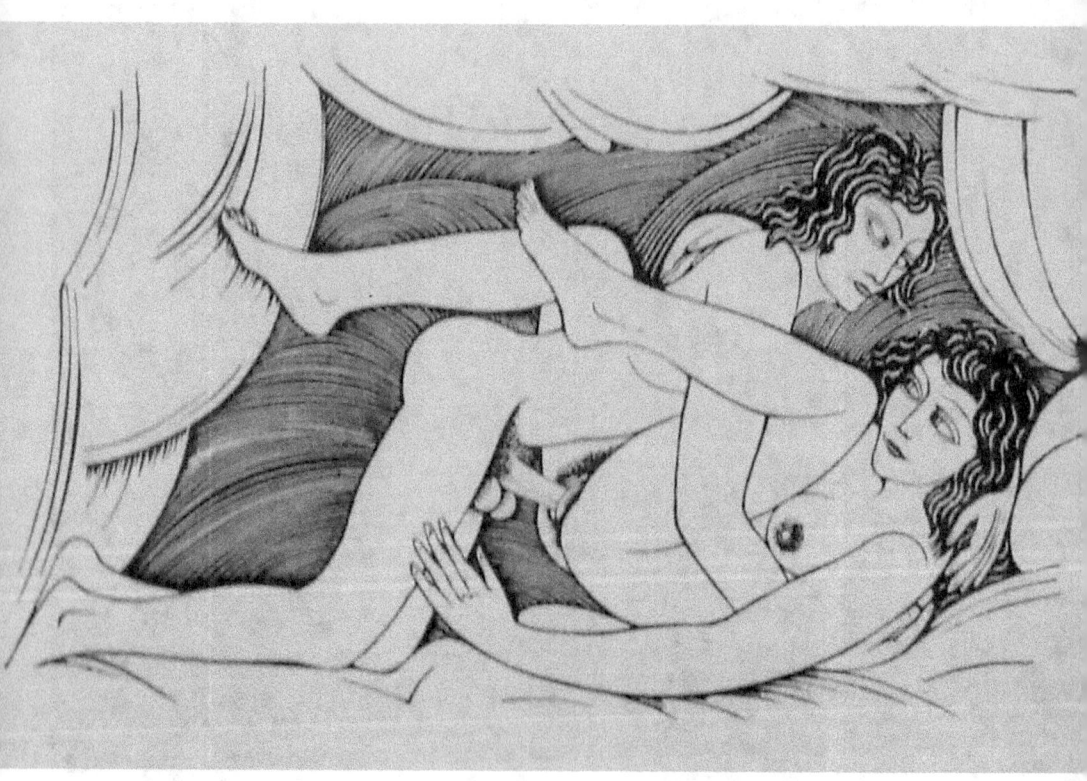

Eric Gill, Lovers (The Raised Bottom), 1934

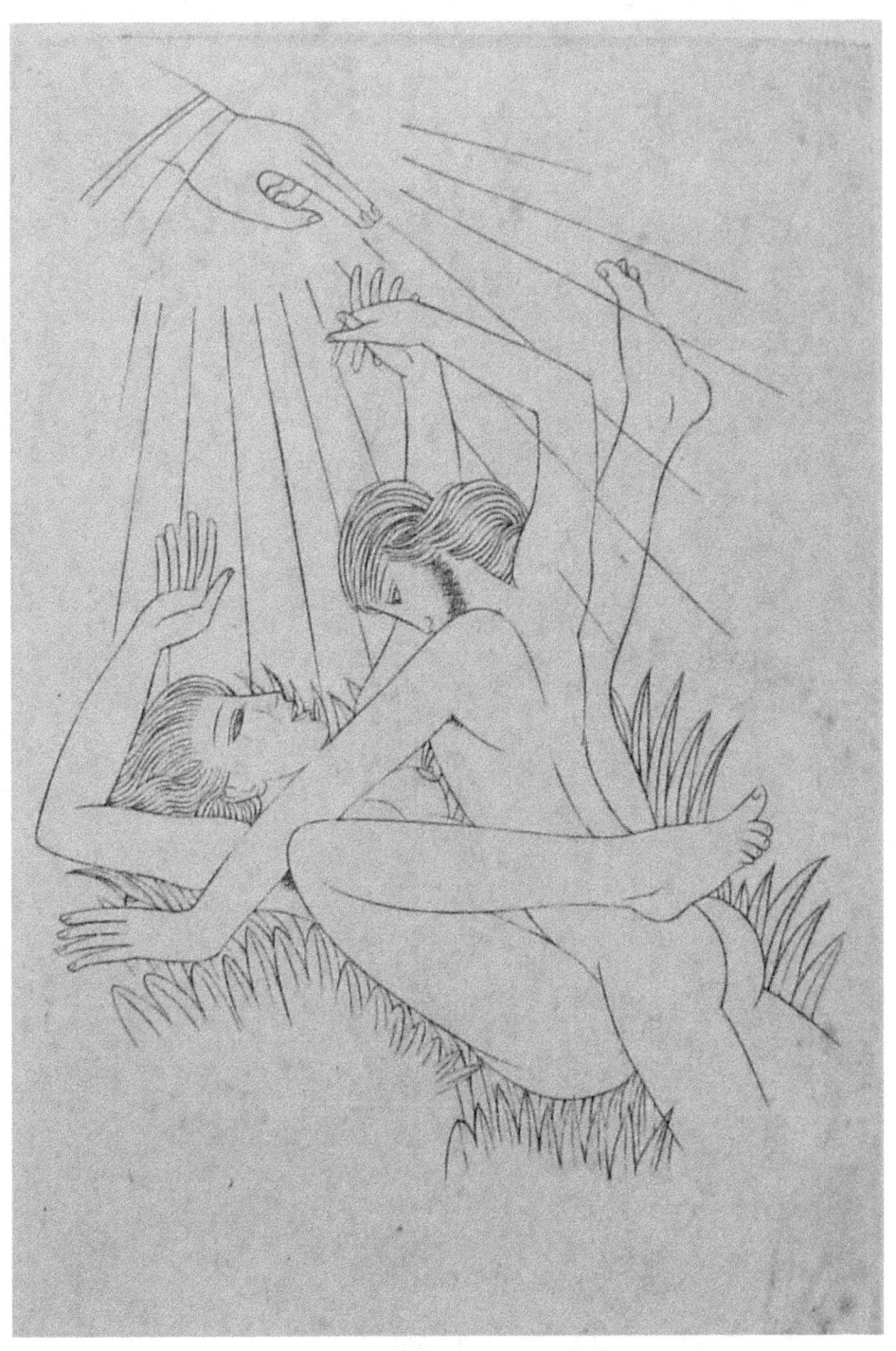

Eric Gill, Earth Receiving, 1926

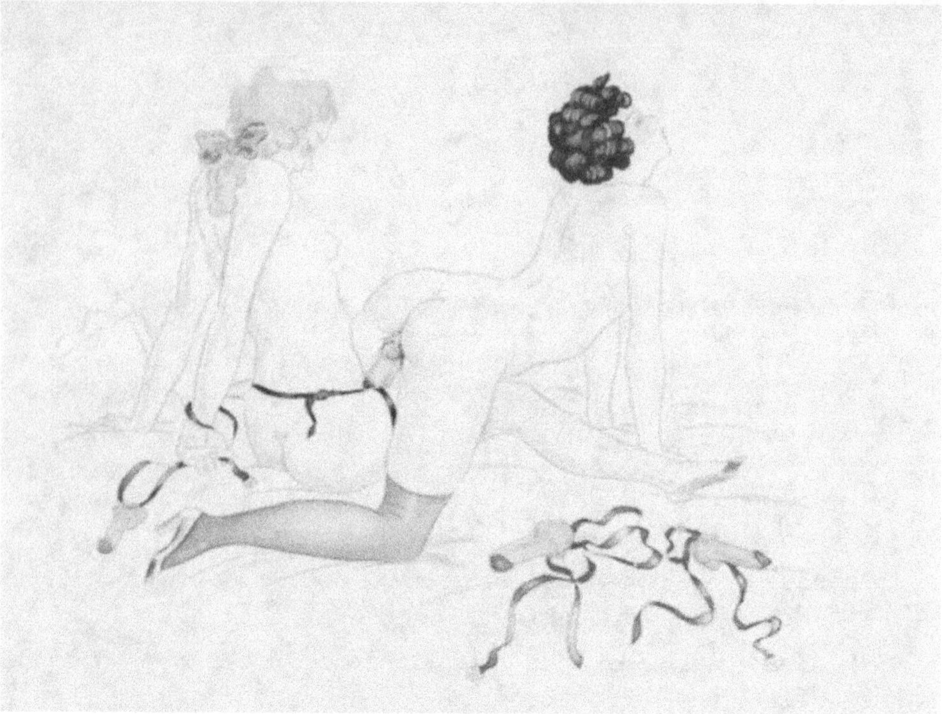

André Collot

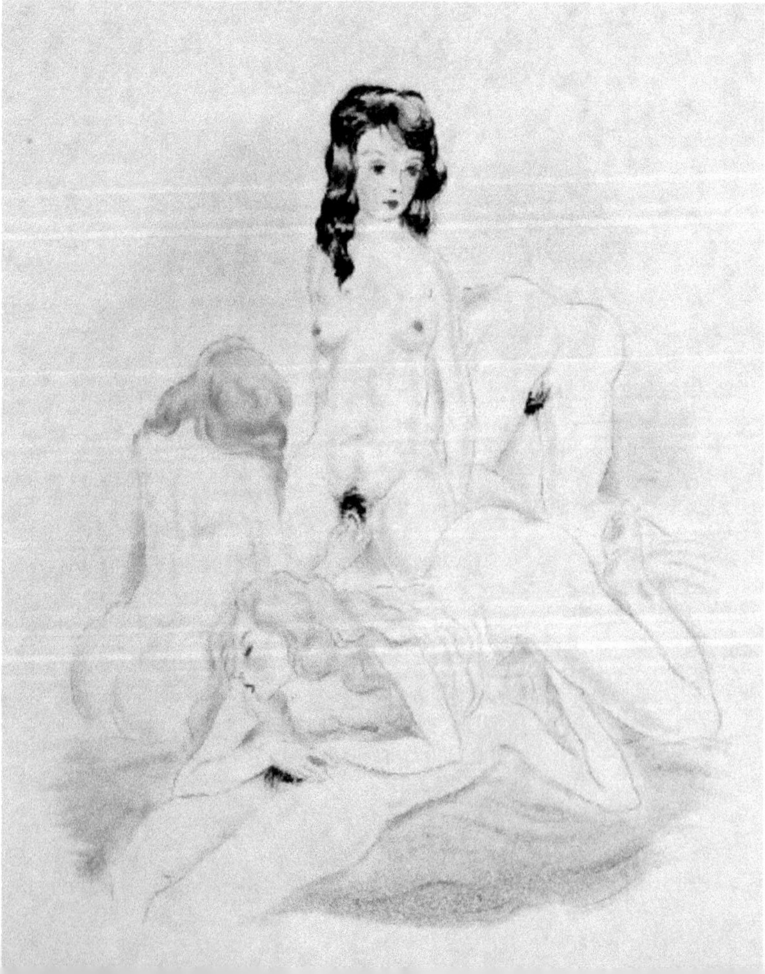

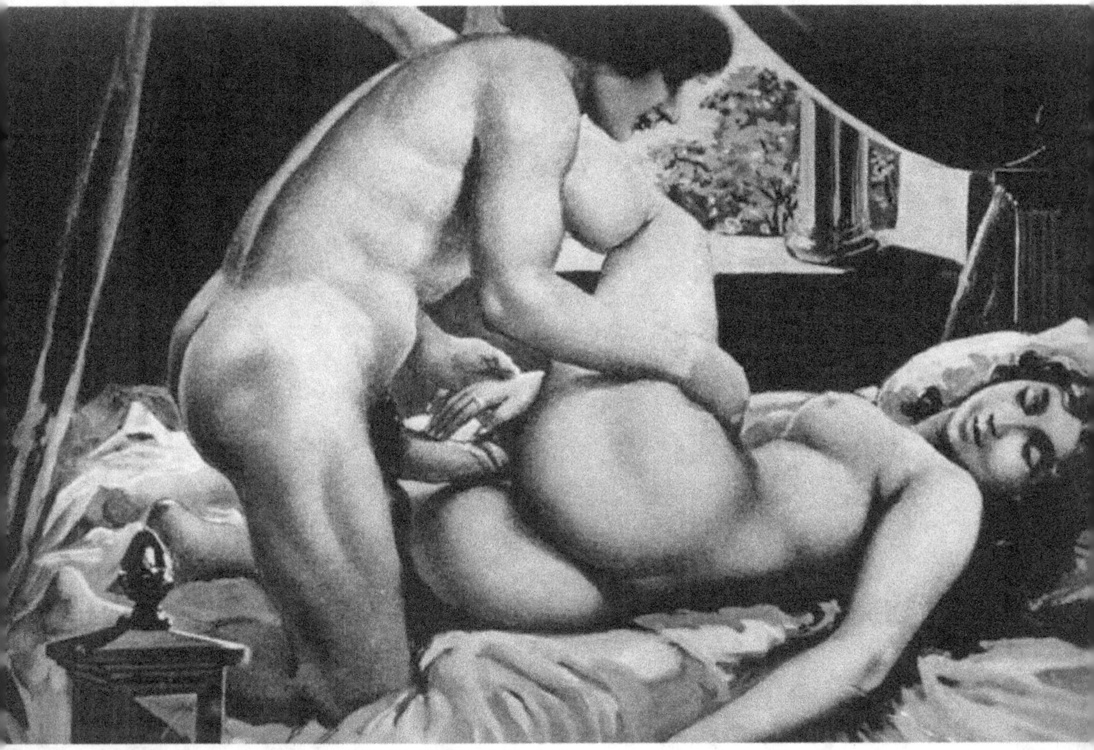

Paul Avril

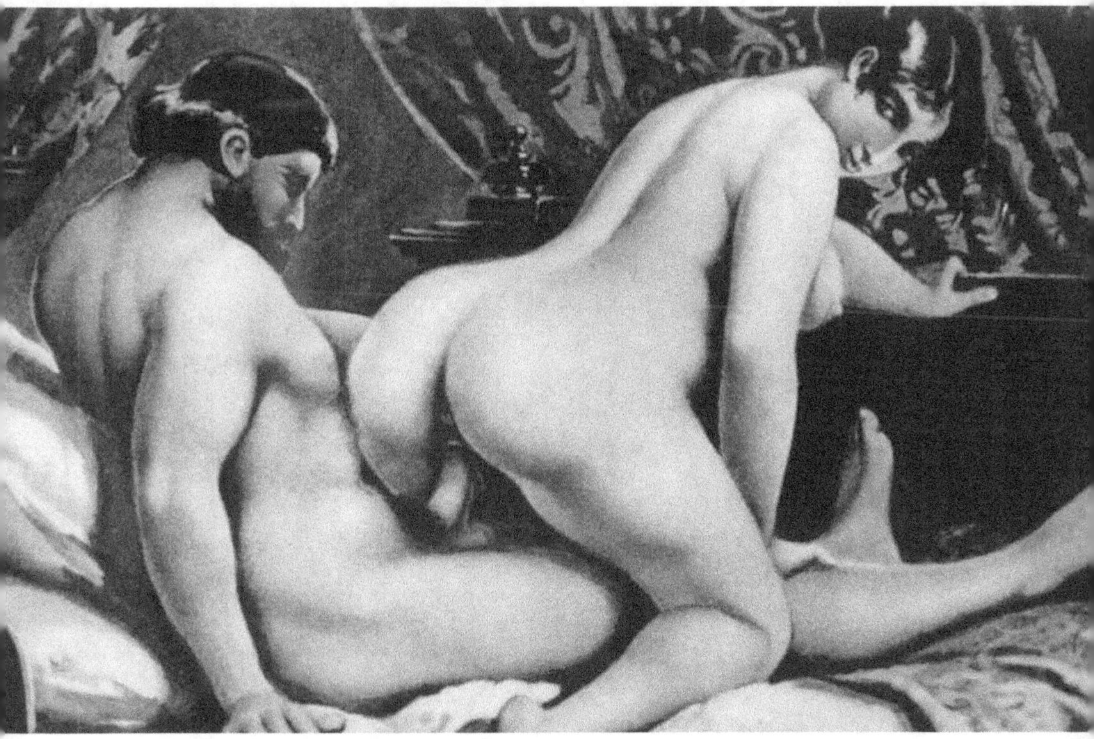

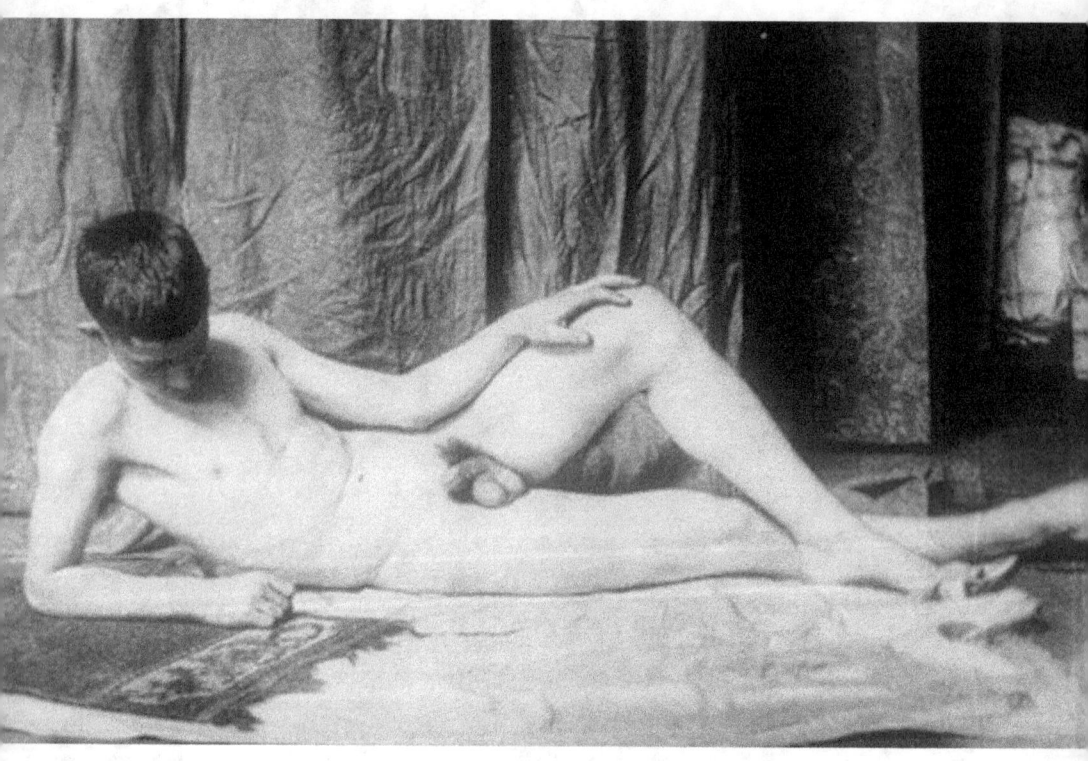

Reclining Male Nude, 1887–92,
Thomas Eakins, platinum print

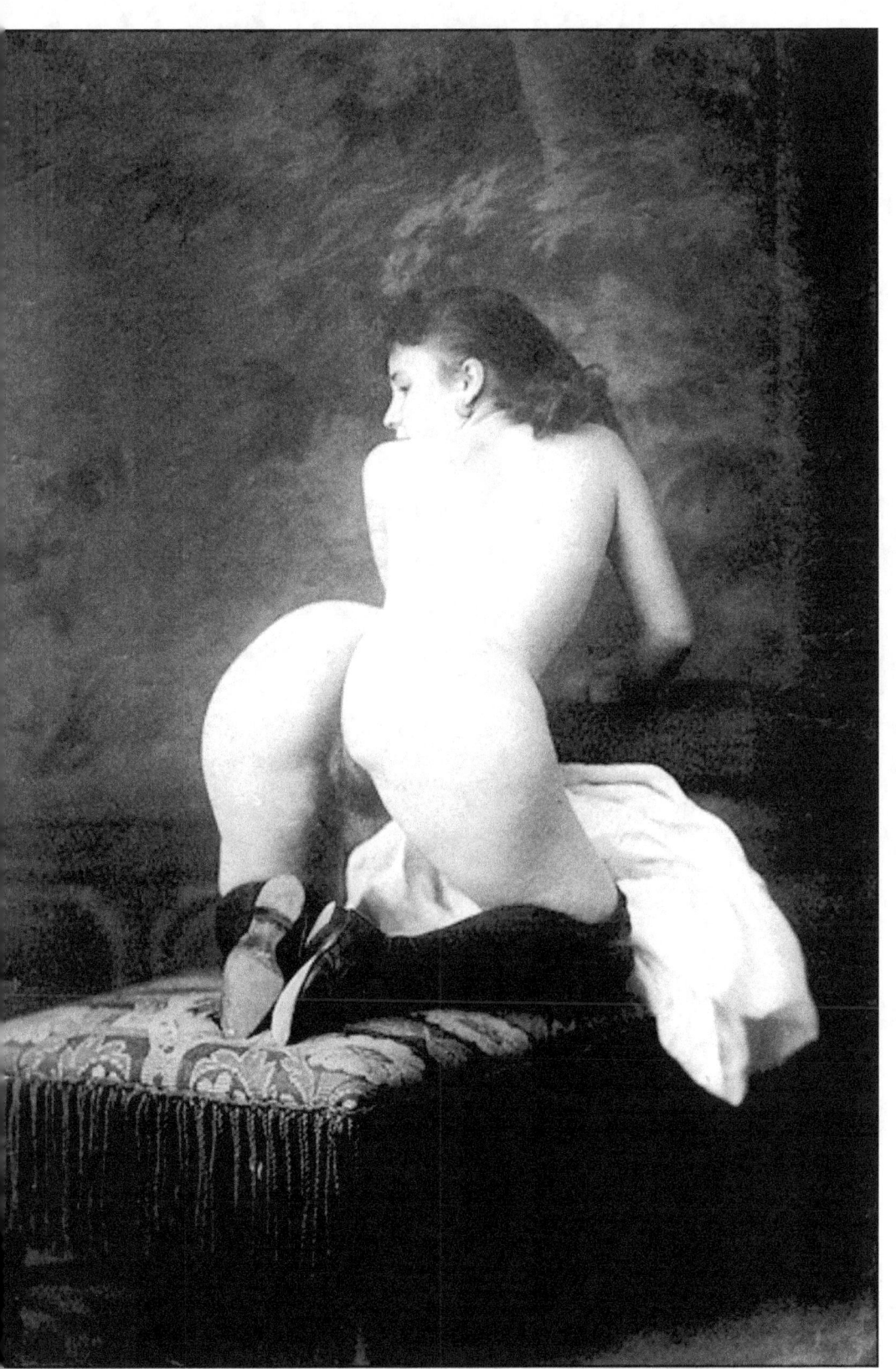

Pierre Louÿs

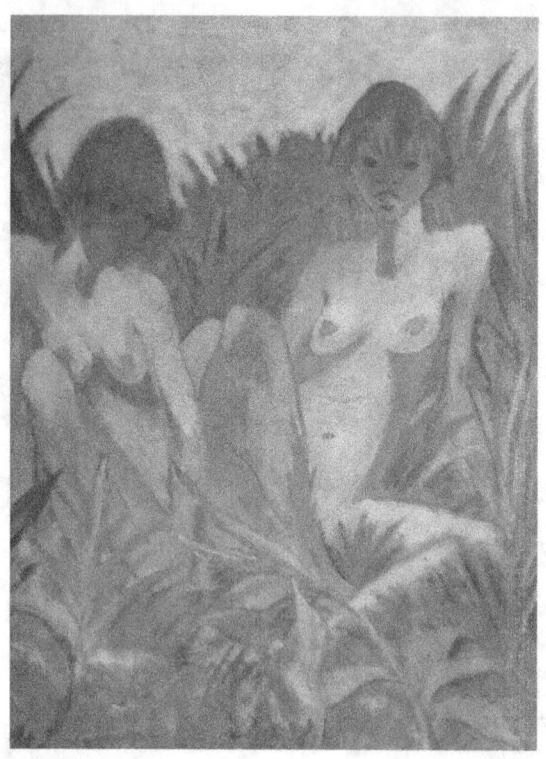

Expressionist sex: Otto Mueller, Two Girls In the Grass, above.
Ernest Ludwig Kirchner, Semi-Nude Woman With Hat, below.

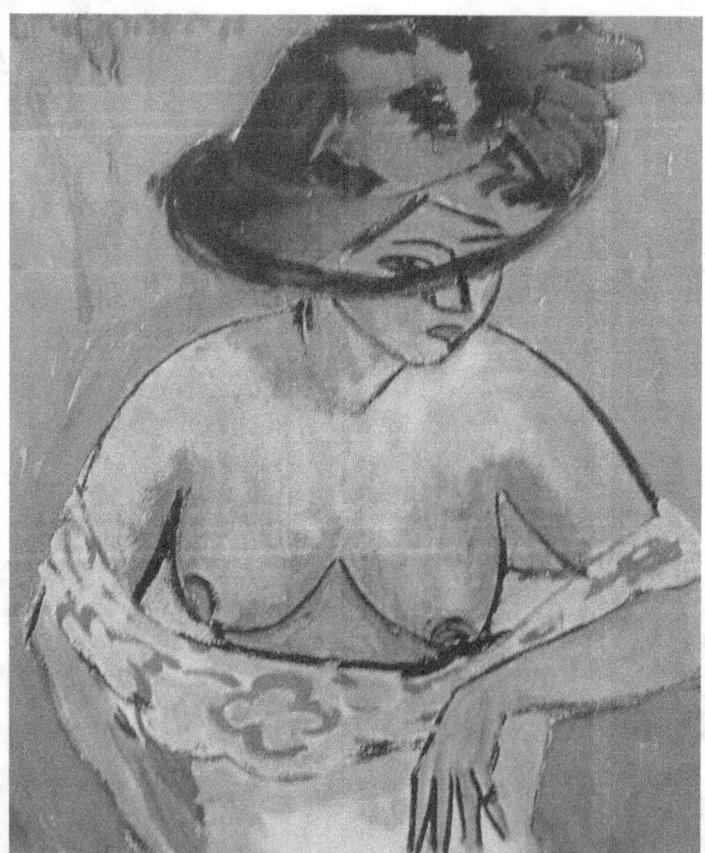

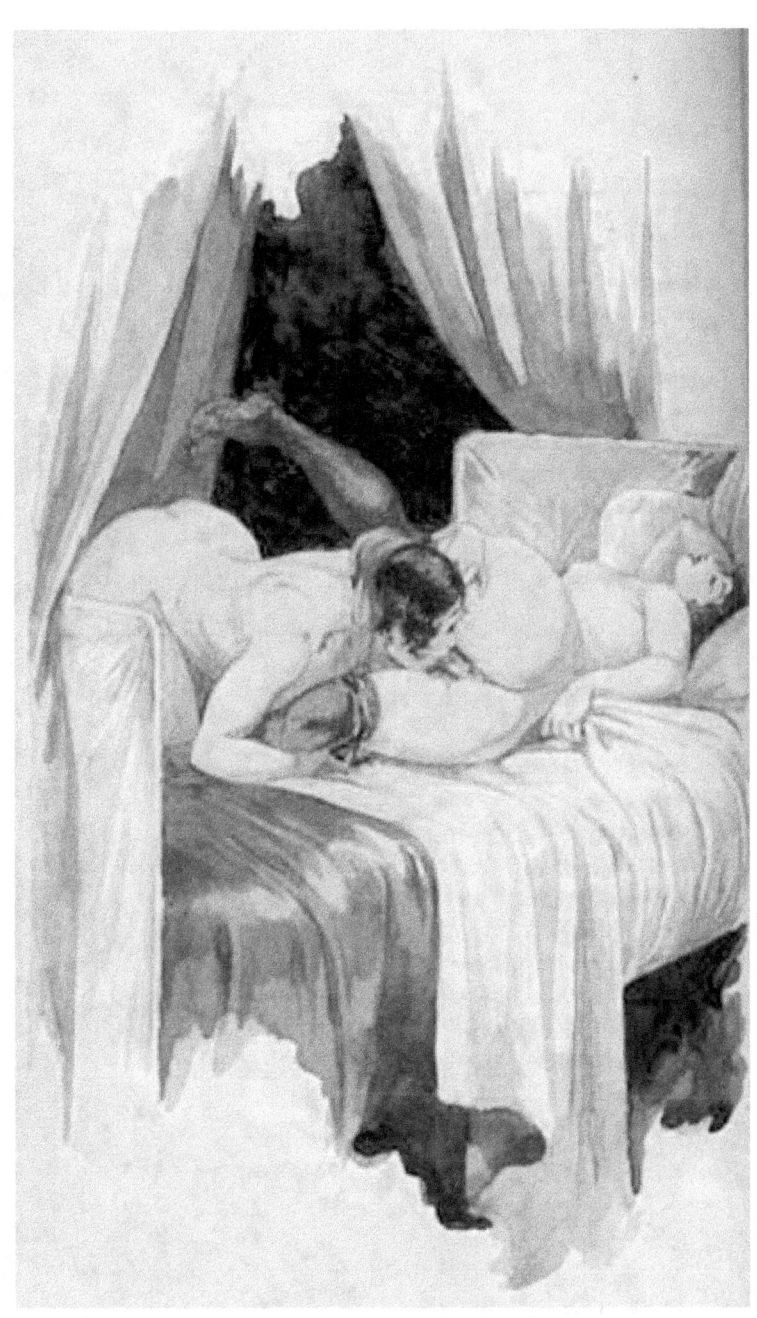

Martin van Maele

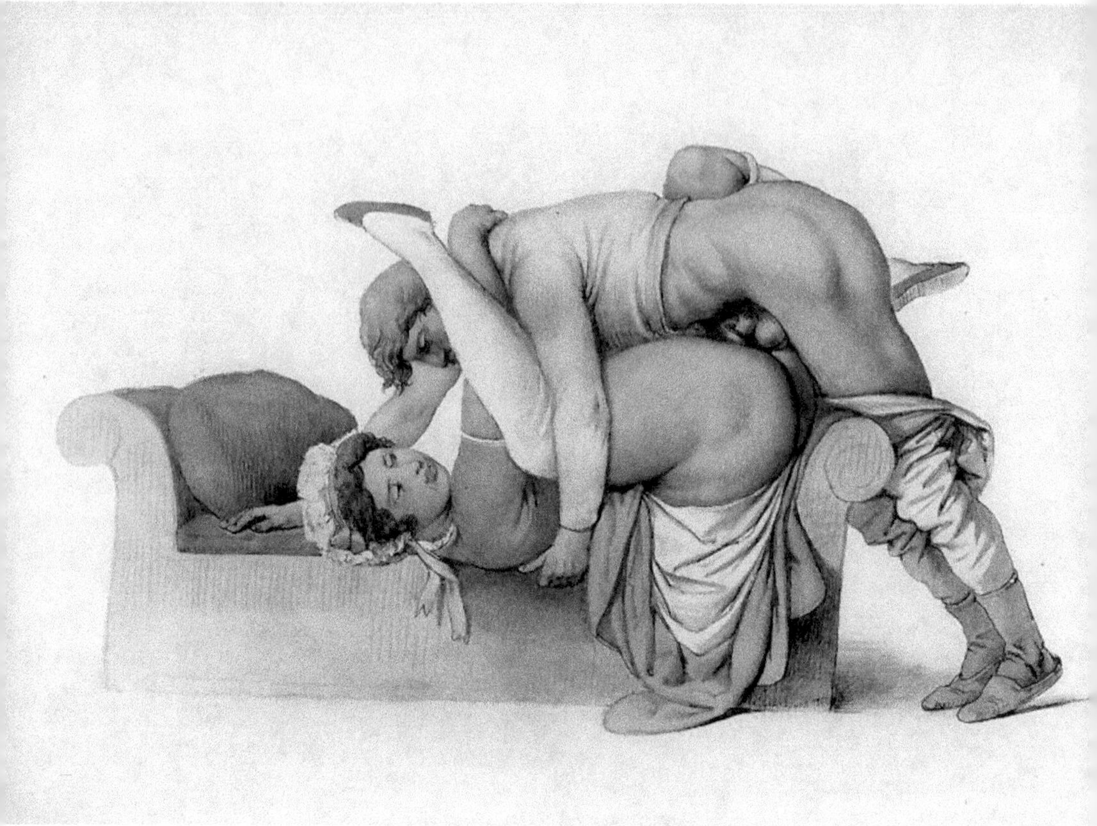

Johann Nepomuk Geiger

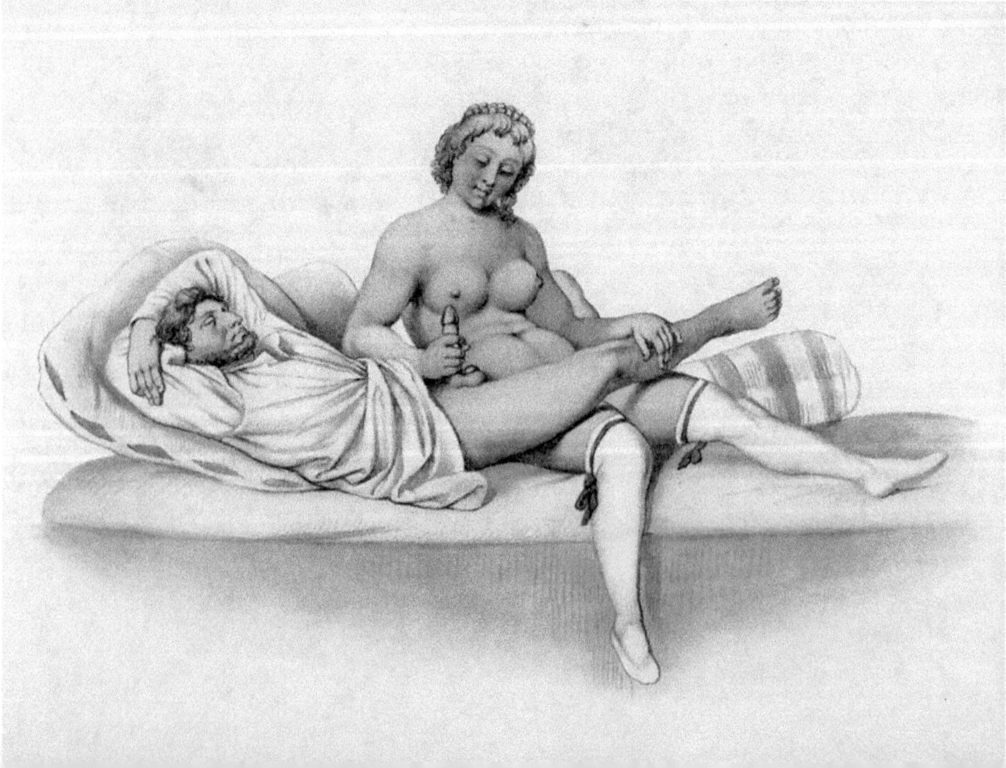

Part Three

MODERN ART

SYMBOLISM

EXPRESSIONISM

SURREALISM

ERIC GILL

1

SYMBOLIST AND DECADENT ART

Symbolist art, Decadent art, *fin-de-siècle* art, whatever you want to call it (we're talking mainly 1880s and 1890s, but also earlier and later, into the 20th century), is the most blatantly erotic of 'high art'. Other art movements that followed Symbolism – Surrealism, for instance, or Pop Art – simply improvize on the excesses of Symbolist art. For in artists such as Gustave Moreau, Edvard Munch, Félicien Rops, Odilon Redon, Jean Deville, Franz von Stuck – one discovers figurative art at its most excessive. The high priest of the Symbolist era is undoubtedly Gustave Moreau. His images make the Pre-Raphaelites in Britain seem positively watered-down, and the Pre-Raphaelites themselves are as contrived, luxuriant, and mythical as any group of artists.

The Symbolist and Decadent age is marked by 'gory exoticism', as Mario Praz puts it (289), by mysticism and black magic, the macabre, the aestheticism of 'beauty', opulence and indulgence, where the key phrase is from Paul Verlaine: 'Je suis l'Empire à la fin de la décadence'.[1] The Symbolist age was summed up by works of literature such as Arthur Rimbaud's *Une Saison en Enfer*, Lautréamont's *Chansons de Maldoror*, Edgar Allan Poe's horror stories, Charles Baudelaire's *Flowers of Evil*, *Salambô*, J.-K. Huysmans' *À Rebours*, Joséphin Péladan's *Le Vice suprême* and *Parsifal*. Some of the key artists of the Decadent and Symbolist age include Richard Wagner, Honoré de Balzac, J.-K. Huysmans, Jean Moréas, Albert Aurier, Octave Mirabeau, Walter Pater, Gustave Flaubert, Jan Troop, Gustave Moreau, Oscar Wilde, Pierre Louÿs, Arnold Böcklin, Pierre Puvis de Chavannes, and Stéphane Mallarmé. Rimbaud argued for a 'rational derangement of all the senses', and showed how marvellous poetry could be when it was unfettered and wild, in his *Les Illuminations*. Rimbaud's tenets, of the 'seer' poet, of madness, of magic, of rebellion, provide the basic ground for many art 'movements', from Symbolism through Surrealism to Pop Art (and rock music – such as The Doors and Patti Smith).

The representation of women is central to Symbolist and Decadent art, as it is to 19th century art as a whole. The result is a misogynism which is often fierce and vicious. Edward Burne-Jones, the most celebrated of the Pre-Raphaelites, wrote: '[t]iresome the modern woman is. I like women when they're good and kind and pretty – agreeable objects in the landscape of existence – give life to it'.[2] This is a typical sexist comment of the Victorian age. John Burgan, a professor of divinity at Oxford, said: '[w]oman's strength lies in her essential weakness'.[3]

Some late 19th century paintings appropriate women's mysteries, such as childbirth, as in Giovanni Segantini's *The Evil Mothers* (1894), which depicts women tied to trees by their own hair in a wilderness, punished for rejecting motherhood.[4] Many images of the 19th century often objectify women sexually, depicting them as sex objects: many artists did not hide their lust;

1 Verlaine: *Selected Poems*, tr. Joanna Richardson, Penguin 1974, 180
2 Burne-Jones: "Conversations", in Kestner, 107
3 Burgan, 1884, in Joan Burstyn: *Victorian Education and the Ideal of Womanhood*, Croom Helm 1980, 33
4 Segantini: *The Evil Mothers*, 1894, oil on canvas, 120 x 225cm, Kunsthistorisches Museum, Vienna

their women are openly displayed, legs akimbo, spines arched, heads thrown to one side, as in standard porn. The women in many images of 19th century art pose in a pornographic fashion: in Henri Gervex's *Rolla* (1878), in many works by Félix Vallotton, in Rodin's' frenetic sculptures of kisses, in the artworks of Rops, Moreau, Delville, etc.[5]

Symbolist and Decadent art is marked by an obsession with eroticism, an eroticism that is soaked in ancient Greek and Egyptian mythology, in the visions of 'evil' of de Sade, Baudelaire and Poe, in Catholic 'sin', in death, in all things Gothic and Arthurian, in Oriental, Arabic, Hindu worlds, in style and fashion and costumes, in 'perverse' forms of sexuality, such as androgynism. In art of the 19th century there is an abundance of depictions of the naked human body. It is very noticeable, far more than in art of the Renaissance, or of the mediæval era. Yet it is quite a different obsession with the body from that of the ancient Greeks. The nude is usually female. If male, then it is subjected to a similar eroticization, though, as with Renaissance nudes, the male nude is 'justified' by being part of a mythological or historical context.

When one looks at late 19th century art, in particular that of the Symbolist and Decadent type, one is struck by the explicit identification of women with death, with decay, perversion, sin, evil, pain, violence, excess and terror. All the things usually associated with men are projected onto women. This sounds like simplistic Jungian psychology, but it applies in most cases. Such as Frank Kupka's fantastic winged deity, her breasts bare and her eyes ablaze, presiding over defeated armies of naked bodies: this is an archetypical Decadent image of women.[6]

The image of woman is central to 19th century art, and particularly the naked woman, which we find in profusion in the work of Gustave Moreau, Jean Delville, Félicien Rops, Franz von Stuck, etc. In the manifesto of the revival of Rosicrucianism, the

5 Gervex: *Rola*, 1878, oil on canvas, 175 x 220cm, Musée des Beaux-Arts, Bordeaux; Félix Vallotton: *The Spring*, 1897, oil on board, 48 x 60cm, Musée du petit Palais, Geneva
6 F. Kupka: *The Conqueror Worm*, print, Bibliothéque Nationale, Paris

Salon de la Rose + Croix, Joséphin Péladan wrote: '[t]he nude made *sublime*'.[7]

There are women as sphinxes, as eternally mysterious, simultaneously loathed and lusted after beings, as in Franz von Stuck's *The Sphinx*, where a nude woman is thoroughly eroticized, the emphasis being on her voluptuously painted body rather than her sphinx-like pose, raised on her elbows.[8] In Stuck's *The Kiss of the Sphinx* (c. 1895), sex and death are melted together in a *mors osculis*, the 'kiss of death' of occultism.[9] In Lucien Levy-Dhurmer's *Salomé*, the woman kisses the severed head of the Baptist on its platter, effortlessly creating that familiar fusion of sex and pain, castration and masochism, found in much of male art. (Marquis von Bayros drew John the Baptist sucking Salomé's nipples[10])

This is a common theme in patriarchal or male art: dying at orgasm, orgasm as the 'little death' (*petit mort*). For patriarchal people (mainly male artists), bliss is dying at orgasm. The Goddess Kali beheads her consorts during sex, and women in Decadent art kiss their partners to death. The kiss is but a stylized and uncensorable way of depicting fucking. Women suck the life out of you, so patriarchal people say; the vagina is thus the 'gateway to hell', as Christian theologians put it, the vagina is the road to oblivion. That other kind of 'kiss', of the vampire sucking blood from the neck, is another form of masculinized eroticism. Women are 'vamps' or 'nymphos' (familiar types in porn – the unsatisfied housewife, the woman who 'couldn't get enough').

The vampire neatly summarizes the patriarchal love of the Gothic, of sin, blood mysteries, and masochism (masochism in the voluptuousness of the victim, who lays himself down for the vampire's attack). All these notions are found in Edvard Munch's *Vampire* (1895), one of those cold but crazed depictions of lust and terror quite particular to Munch.[11]

The *femme fatale* is one of the main types of painted and

7 Joséphin Péladan: *L'Art idealistique et mystique*, Paris 1909, in Edward Lucie-Smith: *Symbolist Art*, 112
8 Stuck: *The Sphinx*, Hessisches Landesmuseum, Darmstadt
9 Stuck: *The Kiss of the Sphinx*, c. 1895, oil on canvas, Museum of fine Arts, Budapest
10 Marquis von Bayros: *Salomé with the Head of John the Baptist*, c. 1900, private collection
11 Edvard Munch: *Vampire*, 1895, coloured lithography and linocut, Munch Museum, Oslo

sculpted women in 19th century art: there are other incarnations or versions of the same basic type; the woman as death, as a prostitute, as a dominatrix, a temptress, a queen, a warrior, an Amazon, etc. In Giulio Aristide Sartorio's *Gorgon and Fallen Heroes* (1893-98), the woman stands triumphant literally on the broken heroes' heads: *naked, of course*, with her hair, ginger-red, of course, swirling about her, she is at once pin-up pornography and hated 'Woman', at once desired and loathed.[12] Another woman triumphant over the male occurs in Arnold Böcklin's *Calm Sea* (1887), where a mermaid on a rock coils her tail around a drowning man, his eyes wide open in the throes of death. The mermaid, like the vampire or the sphinx, combines woman and animality, woman and otherness, woman and primæval, primitive, earthy/ earthly instincts, below the belt, down there, the dark zones of sex.[13]

Edvard Munch takes the domineering female figure to an extreme, in images such as his *Madonna* (1895-1902), where the naked Goddess looks scornfully down on a shrivelled male figure, while sperm wriggle hopelessly around the frame. Munch's *Madonna* is an expression of male angst, male anxiety about (sexual) impotence, about the masochistic relation with women.[14] Other images by Munch – his *Vampire, Three Stages of Woman* (1902), and *Puberty* (1893) – reveal his deeply anguished and ambivalent attitudes towards women and sexuality.[15]

The *femme fatale* type neatly melds sex and death, desire and fear, contact and loss, for the (male) artist. She appears in Medusa, Salomé, Delilah, Jezebel, Judith, Lilith, Ninuë (the lover of Merlin), Venus, Helen of Troy, La Belle Dame Sans Merci, and Cleopatra. These female types combined beauty with death, immense power and all manner of sadistic, masochistic and fetishistic fantasies. These are the women who will whip you to death, if you wish, as in Leopold von Sacher-Masoch's *Venus in*

12 Sartorio: *Gorgon and Fallen Heroes*, 1893-8, oil on canvas, 305 x 421cm, Galerie Nazionale d'Arte Moderna, Rome
13 Böcklin: *Calm Sea*, 1887, wood, 200 x 100cm, Musée d'Art Moderne, Paris
14 Munch: *Madonna*, 1895-1902, lithograph, 60.7 x 44.3cm, Nasjonalgalleriet, Oslo
15 Munch: *Three Stages of Woman*, 1902, oil on canvas, 162 x 252cm, Munch Museum, Oslo; *Puberty*, 1893, Nasjonalgalleriet, Oslo;

Furs. Figures such as Cleopatra provided the longed for combination of socio-political, religious sovereignty, wild eroticism, intrigue, magnificent settings and gory love-deaths. As Max Lake informs us:

> The amatory skills of Cleopatra passed into legend while she lived. Apart from the rapid seduction of both Julius Caesar and Mark Antony, she is reported to have fellated one hundred noblemen in a single evening. Her Greek nickname was *meriochane*, 'she who parts wide for a thousand men.'[16]

The flipside of the holy whore figure of Cleopatra, Medusa, Venus and Salomé is the passive virgin type: in Symbolist art she is pale, drowned Ophelia,[17] or the wistful madonnas of Pre-Raphaelite art (particularly in Dante Gabriel Rossetti, an artist with the silliest name in British art history), and in Gustave Moreau's softly dreaming watercolour *Sappho.*[18]

The depictions of women as mythical beings in Symbolist and Decadent can be seen as misogynistic, often extremely so. If the 'holy whore', whether Aphrodite, Cleopatra or the Sphinx, is the Queen or Goddess of Symbolist, Satan is undoubtedly the hero, which is only right for a culture founded on the Marquis de Sade and Charles Baudelaire. Women and death are merged throughout Western art. In many Symbolist pictures, for instance, the figure of death with the sickle is a woman,[19] while in Otto Greiner's *The Devil Showing Woman to the People* (1897), Satan holds up a woman, *naked of course*, in stockings, of course, as a sex object.[20] Indeed, much of Symbolist art, and modern art, can be seen as 'the Devil showing woman to the people'. The Devil is the artist, showing women in various forms of sexual

16 Max Lake: *Scents and Sensuality: The Essence of Excitement,* John Murray 1989, 58
17 John Everett Millais: *Ophelia,* 1851-2, Tate Gallery, London
18 Gustave Moreau: *Sappho,* watercolour, 18.4 x 12.4cm, Victoria & Albert Museum
19 in Odilon Redon's *Death: My Irony Surpasses All Others,* 1889, lithograph, 26 x 19cm (from Flaubert's *The Temptation of St. Anthony,* another key work of the Symbolist/Decadent era), Bibliothèque Nationale, Paris; Félicien Rops: *Mors Syphilitica,* Bibliothèque Nationale, Paris; Alfred Kubin: *The Best Medicine,* 1901-2, pen and India ink, 17 x 29cm, private collection; Gauguin: *Madame La Mort,* 1899, charcoal and India ink, 24 x 29cm, Musée d'Orsay
20 Otto Greiner: *The Devil Showing Woman to the People,* 1897, chalk on paper, 39 x 29cm, Art Gallery of Ontario, Toronto

objectification, from high art nudes to hardcore porn.

In Félicien Rops' art, Satan appears as an ithyphallic wraith, like Pan gone Gothic, brandishing his erect penis as an image of terror. Erotic art centres on the hard dick, as we have seen – psychologically and politically as well as physically. In *Les Sataniques* (1884), a series of fantastical etchings, Rops fuses sex and death and religion: Satan is shown on the Cross, a blasphemous image in itself, for nowhere else in Western high art do we see Satan on Christ's Cross. Satan is strangling a woman (*naked of course*) with her own hair. Lovely stuff.

Félicien Rops' etchings are all cock, all phallic energy gone wild. A woman impales herself on the phallus of a statue of a crazily grinning Pan or Satan, flanked on each side by bizarre dwarf-like beasts, each holding up six-foot erect penises. In another image, Satan appears as a ram's skull, a familiar motif (deriving again from Pan, perhaps). The phallus this time is a massive snake-like thing which curls downwards and enters a woman, who's *naked of course*.[21] The phallus becomes a ridiculous motif or image all too quickly.

Félicien Rops' images of torture and eroticism (erotic torture, or torturous eroticism), are also ridiculous. His image of Mary Magdalene (*c.* 1885) masturbating in front of a little wooden cross upon which a phallus is crucified is hilarious.[22] She stares up at the crucified prick as she rubs herself between her legs. Great fun.

Pre-Raphaelite art hides its misogynism under a surface of mediævalism, Gothic imagery, Arthurian motifs and a breathless romanticism. But the images of women are stereotypical, reductive, eroticized: there is the purer-than-pure woman, with her unreal, pale skin, who bends wistfully like the Madonnas in Renaissance *Annunciations* (in Burne-Jones' *The Baleful Head*, 1885-87)[23] or they are conniving, nefarious witches (as in the *Morgan Le Fay* painting (1864) of Frederick Sandys).[24]

21 Rops: *Les Sataniques*, 1884, Piccadilly Gallery, London
22 Rops: *Mary Magdalene*, *c.* 1885, collection: Simon Wilson, London
23 Burne-Jones: *The Baleful Head*, 1885-7, oil on canvas, 155 x 130cm, Staatsgalerie, Stuttgart
24 Sandys: *Morgan Le Fay*, 1864, oil, Birmingham Art Gallery

British 19th century painters sometimes rival even Gustave Moreau, the most exotic of figurative visionaries, in the depiction of really bizarre and misogynistic scenes. Frederic Leighton, for instance, painted a very voluptuous mermaid coiling her tail around a drowned sailor (1858). It is a variation on the theme, depicted by Félicien Rops, Eric Gill and Auguste Rodin, among others, of a nude, long-haired woman, a Mary Magdalene figure, embracing a swooned, seemingly passive male.[25] Frederick Sandys' *Danaë* (1867) depicts a dreamy Goddess raising her arm to reveal her body. This painting is clearly erotica, right down to the thin dress she wears, revealing her breasts in a manner similar to women's wet T-shirts contests.[26]

Nothing disguises the obvious erotica of much of British Victorian art. The artists may set their nude women in historical or mythical settings, but, really, nothing hides the fact that these (male) painters wanted to paint nude women as objects of lust. Arthur Hacker produced an image of the goddess Circe in a classic pornographic pose, arms raised, nude, surrounded by a horde of (male) admirers; Hacker's *Syrinx* (1893) and *Daphne* (1895) are similar pictures of women exhibiting their naked bodies for the delectation of men.[27]

A number of Victorian painters seized on the scene of Andromeda chained to the rock, moments before her hunky hero charged in to thrust his phallic spear into the gullet (vagina) of the sea serpent. Here was a good opportunity for an erotic image, for the chained woman added a fetishistic aspect, as well as enabling the raised arms to expose that all-important thing, the (female) body of pleasure.[28]

Any number of Victorian painters can be cited as producing

---

25 Frederic Leighton: *The Fisherman and the Syren*, 1858, 26.5 x 18.5in, Bristol Art Gallery
26 Frederick Sandys: *Danaë in the Brazen Chamber*, 1867, chalk on paper, 26 x 17in, Bradford Art Gallery
27 Arthur Hacker: *Circe*, 1893, 46 x 71in; *Daphne*, 1895, 73 x 27in; *Syrinx*, 1892, 76 x 24.2in, Manchester City Art Gallery
28 Arthur Hill: *Andromeda*, 1875, 35.5 x 17.5in, Russell-Cotes Art Gallery, Bournemouth; Frank Dicksee: *Andromeda*, 1890, private collection; Edward John Poynter: *Andromeda*, 1870, 19.5 x 13.5in, private collection; William Blake Richmond: *Perseus and Andromeda*, 1890s, 88 x 44in, private collection; Frederic Leighton: *Perseus and Andromeda*, 1891, 91.5 x 50in, Walker Art Gallery, Liverpool

misogynist, sexist, patriarchal and degrading images of women. Albert Moore with his *A Venus*, George Story and his *Circe*, John William Waterhouse's *Echo and Narcissus*, to mention some of the lesser-known examples.[29]

GUSTAVE MOREAU

However astonishing the fantastical paintings of the Pre-Raphaelites or any 19th century artist may be, those of the French master Gustave Moreau (1826-98) out-do them all. He is the supreme champion of fantasy art, of any kind. His paintings are the richest imaginable, in terms both of content – in the exotic, Byzantine architecture, the incredibly ornate costumes, the flamboyant gestures – and of physicality and technique.

For Gustave Moreau's paintings, when he finished them, are extraordinarily densely painted. Layers of oil are laid upon each other, so that the surface of the amazing *Jupiter and Semele* (1896) is actually jewel-like.[30] You have to see this painting in the flesh in Moreau's house in Paris to believe it. *Jupiter and Semele* is an image of pure sex: it is manufactured deliberately to be an orgasmic and orgiastic feast for the eye, where the pleasure of looking causes multiple orgasms. Moreau's painting is as voluptuous as painting can get. It is a multiple voluptuousness, because the form and the content breed continuously, creating myriad pleasures. The painterly technique, the drawing, the colours and the forms combine with the images of Greek, Byzantine, Roman and Oriental architecture to create a marvellous vision of phallic and female power. For Jupiter (or

29 John William Waterhouse: *Echo and Narcissus*, 1903, 43 74.5in, Walker Art Gallery, Liverpool; George Story: *Circe*, 1909, 18 x 26in, private collection; Albert Moore: *A Venus*, 1869, 63 x 30in, York City Art Gallery
30 Gustave Moreau: *Jupiter and Semele*, 1896, oil on canvas, 213 x 118cm, Musée Gustave Moreau, Paris

Zeus) is the supreme phallic god of antiquity – he lusts after and takes just about every Goddess he can, as we have seen. Jupiter is surrounded by half-naked figures, angels, and demons. Sitting on his throne, Jupiter in Moreau's last completed painting is the erotic man, adored by the woman swooning in orgasm beside him.

Gustave Moreau's world is supremely sexual, and for feminists it would be sexist. Women conform to stereotypes, to whores, witches, virgins, maidens, etc. Semele swoons over the radiance of the god Jupiter. Moreau's painting is the apotheosis of the religious cult of Symbolism and Decadence, which makes a religion of æsthetic depictions of sex and death and decadence. The word, *decadence*, from Paul Verlaine, connotes profuse amounts of eroticism, debauchery, declining state power, Imperialism and 'perversions'. Moreau's painting captures this decadence perfectly.[31]

Gustave Moreau's is the poet's painter, the painter of poetic visions, someone whom J.-K. Huysmans praised in the *Bible* of the Decadent era, *À Rebours* (*Against Nature*). Moreau is the painter of pure emotion: 'I only believe what I do not see and uniquely what I feel', he remarked.[32] Moreau's art brings together all the crucial elements of Symbolist art; the mysticism, eroticism, nostalgia (for Byzantium, Greece, Rome), Imperialism, romanticism, decadence, occultism and dreams.

Gustave Moreau's paintings are soaked in dream imagery – not the hallucinatory sort that people think can only be obtained from by use of LSD – but by the visions of poets have in their dreams. Dreams of ancient and timeless worlds, where rituals or mysterious scenes, such as Salomé dancing, or Hercules amongst Thespius' daughters, occur endlessly and statically.[33] Moreau's world is of an eternal Orphic dreaming: he painted Orpheus'

---

31 It's a pity Moreau sometimes falls back on having his figures open their eyes so widely. The idea is to indicate a spiritual awakening, but his wide-eyed people look like they've just sat on something sharp. The humour is unintentional.
32 Moreau, quoted in José Pierre, 134
33 Moreau: *Salomé Dancing Before Herod (Tattooed Salomé)*, 1876, oil on canvas, 92 x 60cm, Gustave Moreau Museum, Paris; *Hercules Among the Daughters of Thespius*, begun 1852, oil on canvas, 258 x 255cm, Gustave Moreau Museum, Paris

head on the lyre, as did Odilon Redon, who is even dreamier than Moreau, if that is possible.[34] Moreau's people seem to be asleep, when they are not wide awake with religious enlightenment. Salomé in many drawings and paintings dances with eyes closed.[35]

The half-asleep figures emphasize the passivity and interiority of Gustave Moreau's mythopoeic world. There is little confrontation, although there is anguish and pain aplenty. Salomé dominates his art. She is the ultimate castrating force. For Freudians, Salomé in Moreau's art is the return of the castrating mother. Moreau's famous *The Apparition* (1876) orchestrates in the most decorative and stylized manner, more mannered than Mannerist art, more baroque than Baroque art, more romantic than Romantic art, the anguish of fear and desire, the fear of rejection and loss, the craving for contact and sublimation.[36] In Moreau's art, eroticism is suppressed, repressed, sublimated, interiorized, so that it comes out all the stronger at key points, concentrated into orgasmic moments which, in formal terms, have to do with repetition, rhythm, architectonics, space, colour and style. But if you look at what actually goes on in Moreau's art, you find a world where women, though cast in powerful roles, as Goddesses, are often actually passive and meek. When eroticism does appear clearly, it is heterosexual – as in the drawing called *Lust*, where a phallic deity, Pan, looms sternly behind a recumbent woman (who is *naked, of course*).

But Gustave Moreau's eroticism is also sublimely ambiguous, and multi-sexual: Moreau's figures, like those of Leonardo da Vinci (his hero), are not confined to being wholly male or wholly female: not only are they in-between, or combining both genders, like hermaphrodites or transsexuals, they are also different genders, beyond male and female.[37] Two genders, plus a gender

34 Odilon Redon: *Orpheus*, c. 1913-6, pastel, 70 x 57cm, Cleveland Museum of Art; Moreau: *Thracian Girl Carrying the Head of Orpheus*, 1866, oil on canvas, 154 x 99.5cm, Louvre, Paris
35 Moreau: *Salomé Carrying the Head of St John the Baptist*, pencil and ink, 30 x 19cm, Gustave Moreau Museum, Paris; *Salomé*, study, oil on wood, 23 x 33cm, Gustave Moreau Museum, Paris; *Salomé*, pencil, 60 x 36cm, Gustave Moreau Museum, Paris
36 Moreau: *The Apparition*, 1876, watercolour on paper, 106 x 72cm, Louvre, Paris
37 Moreau: *Lust*, 24.8 x 32cm, Gustave Moreau Museum, Paris

that's in-between, simply isn't enough for Moreau – and I agree with him: there should be more genders, to accurately reflect what sexual and genetic identity actually is.

Only Jean Delville, with the exception of Félicien Rops, comes closest to Gustave Moreau's extravagant vision. Painters such as William Blake, Henry Fuseli and John Martin had depicted phantasmagorical vistas, but Moreau's art is the apotheosis of visionary art. Delville, like Odilon Redon and Moreau, painted Orpheus' head, and emphasized the dreaming nature of art (floating heads were popular in Symbolist art).[38] It was Delville who created that archetypical image of *fin-de-siècle* occultism, the bizarre portrait of the wife of the Symbolist poet Stuart Merrill (1892).[39] Like Fernand Khnopff's *I Lock the Door Upon Myself* (1891), Delville's image is marked by haunted eyes, weirdly bright eyes which stare at the viewer.[40] These eyes are possessed, perhaps by spirits, born from some ectoplasmic Spiritualist evening session in Paris.

It is Jean Deville who provides the wildest depiction of the King of late 19th century art, Satan, in *Trésor de Satan*, where the fiery archangel dances manically over a flow of nude bodies writhing in a Rubens-like manner at the bottom of the sea.[41] More writhing nude bodies occur in Delville's *L'Amour des Ames*, where the lovers are rising amidst swirls of fire and light above the sea. It is a cosmic image, with its stars and planets in the background, reminiscent of theosophical imagery, the pictures done under hypnosis, like those of A.E. Waite and the Golden Dawn artists.[42] But Delville's most powerful image is that of the extraordinary Goddess in the aptly titled *Idol of Perversity* (1891), which is a phrase that could apply to much of Symbolist and Decadent art, which made idols out of perversity.[43]

38 Jean Deville: *Orpheus*, 1893, oil on canvas, 79 x 99cm, collection: Mme Gilléon-Growet, Brussels
39 Deville: *Portrait of Madame Stuart Merrill*, 1892, coloured chalk, collection: E. Jannss-Junior
40 Khnopff: *I Lock the Door Upon Myself*, 1891, oil on canvas, 72 x 140cm, Neue Pinakothek, Munich
41 Delville: *Trésor de Satan*, Musées Royaux des beaux-Arts, Brussels
42 Delville: *L'Amour des Ames*, lithograph, Bibliothéque d'Art et d'Archélogie, Paris
43 Delville: *Idol of Perversity*, 1891, private collection

2

SEX AND EXPRESSIONISM

SCHIELE, KLIMT, BECKMANN, NOLDE, KOKOSCHKA, KIRCHNER, MODERSOHN-BECKER, KOLLWITZ, MUELLER, HECKEL, SOUTINE, ROUAULT

GUSTAV KLIMT

Gustav Klimt (1862-1918) is one of those 'acceptable' erotic artists, whose art is consumed these days as mild erotica, regularly appearing in prints and posters and calendars, next to Henri Matisse, Claude Monet and Vincent van Gogh. Klimt never strays from the heterosexist norm of softcore pornographic consumption. Klimt is vigorously heterosexual in his art. He passionately adores women, and is a modern summary of all male artists who have loved and painted women. In paintings such as *Danaë* (1905), *The*

Kiss (1907-08) and *Woman* (1913), Klimt produced luxuriant, post-Symbolist, post-Byzantine icons of femininity in the Art Nouveau style of Vienna termed 'Secessionstil'.[44] Decadence or over-indulgence is one of Klimt's hallmarks. At times, only Gustave Moreau seems more luxuriant. Klimt depicts naked or half-naked bodies flowing over each other, entwined and writhing but also half-asleep, their eyes closed or half-open, as if stuck in some slow motion opium orgy.[45]

Gustav Klimt flattens every element of his representations onto one picture plane, and turns the image into pure ornamentation and decoration. He is supremely stylish, and rarely allows any evil serpent to slither in and spoil his basically tame nostalgic paradise. In his friezes, one sees the epic grandeur asserting itself.

Gustav Klimt's art is exuberantly ornamental. He dispenses with three dimensionality, and goes for an abstract flatness, as in *The Fulfilment* (1905-09) – which features an erotic embrace like that depicted in *The Kiss* – where the background is a mosaic of swirls.[46] Klimt's art is utterly sensual, in its intent, and the signals it gives off: the lush colours, the profuse use of gold, the swirling shapes, the intricate patterns, flowing lines and the exaltations of the human form. In portraits such as that of Adele Bloch-Bauer (1907), Klimt's paintings are as voluptuous as paintings get, with their profusions of gold, acres of gold, walls of gold.[47]

In the drawings the eroticism is more specific: Gustav Klimt drew women reclining, legs drawn up, masturbating, their hands moving dreamily over their vulvas and clitorises as they look at the viewer. They have titles such as *Reclining Woman* (1912-18), or *Seated Woman, With Open Legs*.[48] Auguste Rodin was the immediate precursor of Klimt's masturbating nudes: Klimt had seen Rodin's erotic drawings (1900), and they inspired him.[49]

44 Klimt: *Danaë*, c. 1905, 77 x 80cm, Galerie Weltz, Salzburg; *The Kiss*, 1907-8, 180 x 180cm, Österreichische Galerie, Vienna; *Woman*, 1913, pencil 56 x 35cm, Vicktor Fogarassy Collection,
45 See, for instance, Klimt's *The Virgin*, 1912-3, Narodny Galerie, Prague
46 Klimt: *The Fulfilment*, c. 1905-9, Muséedes Beaux Arts, Strasbourg
47 Klimt: *Adele Bloch-Bauer*, 1907, Österreichische Galerie, Vienna
48 Klimt: *Reclining Woman*, 1912-8, pencil, 37 x 56cm, Grapische Sammlung Albertina, Vienna
49 Rodin: *Reclining Female Nude*, c. 1900, pencil, 12.2 x 8in, Musée Rodin, Paris

As with the images of pornography, these are anonymous women, any women, with faces but no names, no characters.[50] These are orgasmic images, celebrating female orgasm. This form of eroticism is not confined to the private drawings, drawings which can be seen as a private form of porn: Gustav Klimt's famous *Judith* (1901) stares voluptuously at the viewer with her eyes half-closed, in a orgasmic state.[51] It is a pose cultivated by Hollywood stars, the seductive, luscious look to camera.

The drawings of women lying back with their legs spread are pure erotica – the *Seated Nude* (1913), for example.[52] *Goldfish* (1901/02) depicts in oil a woman, *nude of course*, squatting, buttocks prominent.[53] Women are seen as water, the symbolic feminine element, in *Flowing Water* (1898).[54] *Water Serpents I* (1904-07) is the usual Gustav Klimt offering,[55] a semi-nude woman sliding down the picture, eyes closed, dreamy, asleep perhaps, or blissed-out, her hair, long of course, flowing around her. So many of Klimt's figures are elongated, slipping vertically down the painting, caught in a cascade of ornamentation. This is the standard Klimtesque scenario, this dreamy nude slipping past the viewer, as in his university pictures and large-scale paintings: *Philosophy* (1899-1907), *Medicine* (1900-07) and *Jurisprudence* 1903-07).[56]

Gustav Klimt's depictions of women are archetypical, absolutely at the centre of mainstream Western art. His lesbian imagery, for instance, is, essentially, that of porn. When he paints pregnant women, as in the great *Beethoven Frieze* (1902), or in

50 Klimt: *Seated Woman, with Open Legs*, 1916/7, pencil, 57 x 38cm; *Recumbent Semi-Nude*, 1914/5, blue crayon, 37 x 56cm, Historical Museum, Vienna
51 Klimt: *Judith I*, 1901, Österreichische Galerie, Vienna
52 Klimt: *Seated Nude with Closed Eyes*, 1913, pencil, 57 x 37cm; *Reclining Semi-Nude Woman*, 1913, pencil, 56 x 36cm, both Historical Museum, Vienna
53 Klimt: *Goldfish*, 1901/2, oil on canvas, 150 x 46cm, Dübi-Miller Foundation, Kunstmuseum, Solothurn
54 Klimt: *Flowing Water*, 1898, oil, 52 x 65cm, St Etienne Gallery, New York
55 Klimt: *Water Serpents I*, 1904-7, oil, gold leaf, mixed media on parchment, 19.6 x 7.8in, Österreichische Galerie, Vienna
56 Klimt: *Philosophy*, 1899-1907, oil on canvas, 430 x 300cm, destroyed; *Medicine*, 1900-7, oil on canvas, 430 x 300cm, destroyed; *Jurisprudence*, 1903-7, oil on canvas, 430 x 300cm, destroyed

Hope II (1907-08), he uses a much censored image in Western art.[57]
The nude pregnant woman still provokes controversy when it is
displayed in the popular media or in art today. Klimt's pregnant
women, though, are simply part of his overall exaltation of
women.

The sexuality depicted in Gustav Klimt's art is fully in tune
with the art of, say, Titian, J.-A.-D. Ingres, or the anonymous
Greek sculptors of Classic times. His painting *The Three Ages of
Woman* (1905) celebrates 'the feminine principle' in a time-
honoured but essentially reductive and stereotypical fashion.[58] It's
the old, old image of woman as child, mother and grandmother,
distinctly eroticized (the women are nude). Women are often
shown as passive (some would say gormless) figures, one leg in
front of the other like a fashion model, their heads on one side, as
in *Adam and Eve* (1917-18), or *Water Serpents* (1904-7).[59]

Gustav Klimt's drawings circulated as soft porn in *fin-de-siècle*
Vienna among the art collectors and *cogniscenti*. The city is often
marketed now as a seething cauldron of decadence and style, the
End of the Empires, the heady years before the First World War,
like Berlin before the Second World War, when Vienna was a
fevered mass of eroticism, death, art and culture. This mythic
Vienna is the over-romanticized *mittel European* city, the city
where Sigmund Freud was opening up the unconscious with the
publication in 1899 of *The Interpretation of Dreams*, where the
Vienna Secession and Wiener Werkstäte produced amazing
graphic and fine art. Names such as Robert Musil, Ludwig
Wittgenstein, Karl Kraus, Freud, Gustav Mahler, Kolo Moser,
Oscar Kokoschka, Arnold Schoenberg, Otto Wagner, Josef
Hoffmann, Josef Stalin, Adolf Hitler, Leon Trotsky and Arthur
Schnitzler are all associated with the Vienna of the turn-of-the-

---

57 Klimt: *Beethoven Frieze*, 1902, casein, gold leaf, semiprecious stones, mother-of-pearl,
gypsum, charcoal, pastel and pencil on plaster, 216 x 636cm, Österreichische Galerie, Vienna;
Hope II, 1907-8, oil and gold on canvas, 110.5 x 110.5cm, Museum of Modern Art, New York.
See Marian Bisanz-Prakken: "The Beethoven Exhibition of the Vienna Secession", in Erika
Nielsen, ed. *Focus on Vienna 1900*, Houston German Studies, no. 4, Fink, Munich 1982; Peter
Vergo: "Gustav Klimt's Beethoven Frieze", *Burlington Magazine*, 115, no. 839, 1973, 109f
58 Klimt: *The Three Ages of Woman*, 1905, Gallerie Nazionale d'Arte Moderna, Rome
59 Klimt: *Water Serpents*, c. 1904-7, Österreichische Galerie, Vienna; *Adam and Eve (unfinished)*,
1917-8, Österreichische Galerie, Vienna

century era, making it a cultural centre to rival the best. Vienna was the city of sex and death, of pornography and prostitution, as critics attest.[60]

EGON SCHIELE

Egon Schiele (1890-1918), Gustav Klimt's disciple, is the embodiment of *fin-de-siècle* Vienna, the decadent *zeitgeist* of the 'city of dreams' which was obsessed with itself, which psychoanalyzed itself endlessly, which simultaneously celebrated and suppressed eroticism.

Egon Schiele, like Pablo Picasso or Eric Gill, is one of the great modern erotic artists.[61] He is dæmonic compared to Gustav Klimt.[62] His view of sex is the usual male bourgeois one that sex = pain and pain = being truly alive. He said: 'I am a human being. I love death and I love life.'[63] Schiele wrote from prison in 1912: 'I believe that man must suffer from sexual torture as long as he is capable of sexual feelings.' Schiele's poetry is a mass of Expressionist meditations on the painful moments of life – sex, death, birth, violence:

> An eternal dreaming
> full of the sweetest overabundance of life –
> restless – with heavy pangs within, in the soul. –
> It blazes, burns, yearns for battle, –
> spasm in the heart
> Calculating – and madly alert with excited lust.
> (from 'Self-Portrait')[64]

60 See Frank Whitford: *Egon Schiele*, Thames & Hudson 1981, 92f
61 See Alessandra Comini: *Egon Schiele*, Braziller, New York 1976; Jane Kallir: *Gustav Klimt, Egon Schiele*, Galerie St Etienne, Crown, New York 1980; Rudolf Leopold: *Egon Schiele*, Phaidon 1973; Peter Selz: "Egon Schiele", *Art International*, 4, no. 10, 1960, 39f
62 Otto Benesch: *Egon Schiele als Zeichner*, Vienna 1950, "Egon Schiele", *Art International*, II, 1958-9, no. S 9-10
63 quoted in Whitford, 193
64 quoted in Schiele: *I, Eternal Child*, 44

Egon Schiele's art is characterized by his nervy, stark line. He
was not a painter in the richly sensuous tradition of Peter Rubens
or Eugène Delacroix. Schiele's oil paintings are like coloured
drawings. His drawings, though, are viciously realist and
incisive. He does not miss a single blemish or irregularity of
bone, skin, muscle or hair. Drawings such as *Recumbent Woman*
are ruthless realistic: the sagging flesh of the woman, the
blemishes on the skin, the hairy armpit and the indifference of
the model are all recorded with a forensic, pathological intensity.[65]
This sort of picture is a far cry from the chaste images of
traditional, male, academic art. Schiele's' drawings do not
romanticize or soften the subject, as Gustav Klimt or Georges de la
Tour do. Schiele's thin, spindly figures have something in
common with those of Alberto Giacometti (in the latter's *Diego*, for
instance).[66]

There are a number of elements in Egon Schiele's art which
are the hallmarks of erotic art. Firstly, there is the massive
emphasis on sexuality. Always the observer's aware not only of
the body, but of the erotic nature of the figure in Schiele's work.
Like Gustav Klimt, he produced endless drawings of women in a
variety of poses, most of them characterized by twisted limbs,
spread legs, heads thrown to one side, hands splayed across
thighs or torsos. While Klimt's recline in comfort, luxuriantly,
Schiele's women are distinctly uncomfortable, restless, itchy,
twitchy, dissatisfied. Schiele did produce erotic drawings that
were seemingly direct copies of Gustav Klimt, such as the
Reclining Woman of 1911.[67] The pose is pure erotica: on thigh
drawn up, the woman lies back, breasts exposed, her mouth
pouting and her eyes half-closed. This pose can be seen in
millions of softcore porn images.

The *Reclining Girl*[68] of 1910 shows a young woman lying back
with her finger on her clit, emulating Gustav Klimt's images of

65 Egon Schiele: *Recumbent Woman*, 1914, pencil and gouache, 30.4 x 47cm, Graphische
Sammlung Albertina, Vienna
66 Giacometti: *Diego*, 1953, oil, 100 x 81in, Guggenheim Museum, New York
67 Schiele: *Reclining Woman*, 1911, pencil and gouache, 31.5 x 44cm, Fischer Fine Art, London
68 Schiele: *Reclining Girl*, 1910, pencil, 55.7 x 37cm, Neue Galerie am Landesmuseum
Joanneum, Graz

woman masturbating. Egon Schiele plays with expectations however, for his model is young, under-age perhaps, something of a Lolita figure. Many of Schiele's women are like this: young, underdeveloped, thin, boyish, to use the terms of patriarchy. Schiele favours women that are 'boyish', yet he emphasizes vulvas and breasts. His models are androgynous, both feared and desired, both male and female. Schiele appropriates the androgyny theme in Symbolist art and infuses it with his own tortured form of eroticism. As Frank Whitford writes, expressing the paradoxical fear and desire theme of art and pornography:

> Physically immature, thin, wide-eyed, full-mouthed, innocent and lascivious at the same time, these Lolitas from the proletarian districts of Vienna arouse the kind of thoughts best not admitted before a judge and jury. (82)

This is what Egon Schiele's art does, and what most erotic art does. It invites consumption and looking and simultaneously repels it. Schiele invites looking then shows how horrible it is to look. His models are deeply eroticized but, as one gets closer, one realizes that there is as much repulsion and disgust in Schiele's art as there is desire. It is another manifestation of the age-old dichotomy in patriarchal art of sex and death. Sex is the invite, the seduction, the promise of pleasure; death is the repulsion, the decay, the denial of pleasure.

Another aspect of Egon Schiele's art that is found in both porn and art is fetishism. So many of Schiele's models wear stockings – striped stockings or purple stockings.[69] Schiele has one of the sharpest eyes for a startling graphic image. All of his art is very *stylish*, very fashionable. It always *looks good*, as fashion photography can. The dresses and stockings are part of the stylistic design, integrated as ornament, as in the work of Gustav Klimt, and are as crucial as the angular limbs or looks of complicity.

The 1911 drawing of a semi-nude woman lying on her front is

---

69 Schiele: *Girl with Striped Stockings*, 1910, gouache, 31.5x 44cm, private collection; *Nude with Purple Stockings*, 1911, watercolour, 45 x 31.4cm, private collection

typical of Egon Schiele's stylish erotica.[70] She lies with eyes closed, her legs are apart, to reveal her vulva, which Schiele has, as usual, coloured red with watercolour over his pencil drawing. This is usual enough in erotica, and in Schiele's art, this focusing on the woman's genitals. What is unusual, perhaps, is the fashionable items that Schiele clothes his model in: a stripey skirt, the stripes are very colourful: light blue, red, dark blue, orange, black, purple. She wears a check shirt, the colours here again are bright: green, red, orange, black and white squares. The overall effect is a combination of porn and fashion. In Schiele's drawings, everything in the picture is fetishized, not just the model. The nude woman is clearly a sex object, but so is the arrangement of the clothes, the colours used, the graphic quality of the lines. Andrea Dworkin writes of fashion and pornography:

> The fact is that men can and do fetishize everything and no woman can possibly know how to match up any given man with any given fetish, nor how to anticipate, nor how to avoid, "provoking" sexual arousal due to a fetishized desire. What women can know, but do not sufficiently appreciate, is that common male fetishes determine female fashion... "Women's fashion" is a euphemism for fashion created by men for women; the failure to follow the dicta of this fashion has severe economic repercussions for any woman.[71]

Egon Schiele will dress a woman in stockings very often, or sit her with a yellow towel, as a fashion accessory, as in *Reclining Nude With Yellow Towel*, or with high heeled shoes, as in the *Seated Nude In Shoes and Stockings*, or with stockings and high-heeled shoes in one of his pictures of lovers embracing, the man, as often, looking like a puppet.[72]

Egon Schiele's eye for style and fashion and the choice prop is mirrored by the photographer Robert Mapplethorpe, who also explored the boundaries between erotic art and porn. Schiele and

---

70 Schiele: *Reclining Nude, Half Length*, 1911, pencil & watercolour, 18.8 x 12.4in, private collection, New York
71 Dworkin, *Pornography*, 125-6
72 Schiele: *Reclining Nude with Yellow Towel*, 1917, tempera and black chalk, 12.2 x 19in, private collection; *Seated Nude in shoes and Stockings*, 1918, charcoal, 18. x 11.8in, Metropolitan Museum of New York; *Man and Woman*, 1913, pencil, watercolour and tempera, 31 x 18.8in, private collection

Mapplethorpe argue for a detached, cool approach to eroticism, so that a tree can be drawn with the same detachment or love as a naked body. The two things, body and tree, are explored with equal fervour or dispassion by the artist. Or, as Mapplethorpe put it:

> I don't think there's that much difference between a photograph of a fist up someone's ass and a photograph of carnations in a bowl.[73]

And, again, Mapplethorpe says: '[w]hether it's a cock or a flower, I'm looking at it in the same way',[74] and Egon Schiele would agree with this statement. Flower or flesh, cock or carnation, it is treated with same artistic rigour. But this approach neatly sidesteps the issue of *what* is depicted. For all their coolness, Schiele and Mapplethorpe, like Pablo Picasso, Hans Bellmer, Titian, Thomas Rowlandson, Auguste Rodin and any other erotic artist, know very well that they love depicting eroticism and the body. They *know* that the subject they chose to portray – the naked human body – is a contentious subject for some people. They *know* that erotic art creates controversy. And if we can't say exactly what the artists' intentions are, we know that, even now, nudity still upsets, disturbs and annoys some sectors of society.

Egon Schiele arranges his models with meticulous care, like the photographers Robert Mapplethorpe or Edward Weston, artists who, like Schiele, straddle the borderline between art and pornography. There are no poses before the modern era like the woman's in Schiele's *Nude with Violet Stockings*.[75] She sits with her knees drawn up, facing the viewer, her right arm wrapped around her neck, her other arm stretched out. Only the right eye is visible, for she lowers her head. It is a pose at once withdrawn and exhibitionist. It is a pose of studied maleficence.

Egon Schiele's erotic art is a catalogue of erotic props, fetishes and kinks. He produced archetypal images of lesbianism, the two

73 quoted in Parker Hodges: "Robert Mapplethorpe, Photographer", *Manhattan Gaze*, 10 December 1979, 5
74 Mapplethorpe in Lawrence Chua: "Robert Mapplethorpe", *Flash Art*, Jan/Feb 1989, 103
75 Schiele; *Nude with Violet Stockings*, 1910, watercolour, 45 x 31cm, private collection

women embracing each other but not for their own pleasure. They embrace and pose for the artist's gaze, for the Look of the voyeur, the pornographer, the (male) consumer.[76]

There is a series of images of women embracing each other where one looks like a doll,[77] has those idiot, blank eyes of the puppet, a Schielean motif that crops up in other works, such as in the *Embrace* of 1915, where the man is a limp doll being propped up from behind by the woman, a pose that recalls the dead Christ collapsed in his mother's arms in so many Renaissance paintings (in Sandro Botticelli's two famous *Pietàs*, for instance, where the dead God is embraced by the Virgin Mary and Mary Magdalene. Both of Botticelli's paintings are highly erotic).[78]

Egon Schiele in fact fancied himself as Christ, as many a (male) artist has done. Schiele used for a poster one of the most voluptuous occurrences in all of Christianity, apart from the Crucifixion itself: the martyrdom of Saint Sebastian. This is another sex-and-death experience, the glorification of pain so it becomes holy. Schiele depicts himself as Sebastian being pierced by huge arrows – more like harpoons.[79] In Schiele's art, as in most artists, sexuality and religion are entwined. Thus, many of his depictions of love, of two people embracing, or of the family, are treated simultaneously as religious and erotic works. He made a series of pieces fusing the sacred and the profane: *Death and the Maiden, Cardinal and Nun, Pregnant Woman and Death, Holy Family, Dead Mother* and so on.[80] These are Schiele's strangest images, bringing together the family, loss, death, desire and religion. Cardinals or monks embrace women, or death embraces women, or mothers hold dead babies, or living babies are swathed in cloth

76 Schiele: *Two Girls Embracing Each Other*, 1915, pencil and gouache, 48 x 32.7cm, Museum of Fine Arts, Budapest
77 Schiele: *Two Girls Lying Entwined*, 1915, pencil and gouache, 33 x 49.7cm, Graphische Sammlung Albertina, Vienna
78 Botticelli: *Pietà*, c. 1495, 107 x 71cm, Museo Poldi Pazzoli, Milan; *Pietà*, c. 1495, 10 x 207cm, Pinakothek, Munich
79 Schiele: poster for the Arnot Gallery exhibition, 1914, 67 x 50cm, Historisches Museum der Stadt Wien
80 Schiele: *Death and the Maiden*, 1915, oil on canvas, 150.5 180cm, Österreichische Galerie, Vienna; *Cardinal and Nun*, 1912, oil on canvas, 70 x 80.5cm, private collection; *Holy Family*, 1913, pencil and gouache on transparent paper, 47 x 36.5cm, private collection; *Pregnant Woman and Death*, 1911, oil on canvas, 100.5 x 100.5cm, Národní Galerie, Prague; *Dead Mother*, 1910, oil on wood, 32 x 25.7cm, private collection

by dead mothers, or pregnant woman sleep beside monks. The poses are the same as those of lovers making love.

In the art of Egon Schiele, lovers seem to fall into each other, grappling each other around the waist. His depictions of fucking focus on the visceral physicality of sex. In Schiele's world, lovers contort around each other, legs open, not kissing, bodies askew, as in *Embrace*,[81] a much more frenetic and vicious depiction of lovemaking than Gustav Klimt's softly-drawn couple.[82] Their clothes are half-off, they are tangled in cloth and limb, yet they stare silently outwards, away from other. In the 1914 *Man and Woman (Liebespaar)*, the man stares at the viewer in that peculiar gaze which Schiele makes his own, a look that is both arrogant and melancholy. The woman, meanwhile, kneels beside the man, her head buried in her arms. It is a painting of dejection.[83]

Entwined in each other, Egon Schiele's lovers are not 'together' at all. They are not by any means the two halves of a soul made one, as in Platonic theory. Yet there is a tenderness that redeems so much of Schiele's art, for he is not totally vicious in his realism This tenderness is embodied in Schiele's famous *Embrace* of 1917, which Simon Wilson describes as 'one of the great images in art of human sexual love' (52).[84] There is empathy and pathos in his depictions of eroticism. The heroic element, the martyrdom and sainthood, the pain and pathos save Schiele's art, in a traditional (i.e. patriarchal) reading of his work. In fact, he was supremely self-obsessed, as few artists have ever been.

We come to perhaps the most instantly accessed aspect of Egon Schiele's art: its self-reflexivity. He was preoccupied with himself above everything. This is expressed in many aspects of his work, from the photographs he had taken of himself,[85] to the long series of self-portraits. These images are startling. Schiele draws himself grimacing at the viewer/ artist, or pulling his cheek down self-consciously, or staring malignantly, or splaying

81 Schiele: *Embrace*, 1913, watercolour, private collection
82 Klimt: *Recumbent Lovers*, c. 1908, 35 x 55cm, Historical Museum, Vienna
83 Schiele: *Man and Woman (Liebespaar)*, 1914, oil on canvas, 46.8 x 54.8in, private collection
84 Schiele: *Embrace*, 1917, oil on canvas, 110 x 170cm, Österreichische Galerie, Vienna
85 photographs by Anton Trcka and Johannes Fischer, 1914-5, Graphisches Sammlung Albertina, Vienna

his fingers in that characteristic way (second and third fingers open), or screaming.[86] Schiele's self-portraits have something of the neurotic quality of Vincent van Gogh's paintings, but the poses are far more tortured and incisive. Schiele concentrates on his whole body. His self-portraits are often nude, and often emphasize explicitly his sexuality. The self-portraits explore aspects of his sexuality, from vulnerability to orgasm. There are self-portraits where Schiele is masturbating, and other self-portraits where he places his hands over his genitals as if masturbating, but also as if signifying the shape of a vulva.[87] The images of Schiele gesturing towards the feminine are further examples of his exploration of gender issues, of masculinity and femininity.

Sex is the key for Egon Schiele, the way into the world of self, identity, psychology and desire. Schiele's erotic self-portraits examine the mythicizing forces in the realms of gender and sexuality. The result is an eternal confusion. Even as he exposes or exhibits his body, Schiele wants to cover it up. He contorts himself, conjuring up evermore intricate forms of self-torture. He is all ambiguity and ambivalence. There is no simple resolution, no unification, no stasis, no harmony.

In the wildly ithyphallic image *Eros* Egon Schiele holds out an enormous erect penis.[88] Men've been seen with erect phalloi before, since time immemorial. In the modern era, there are many images of men wielding their phalloi in the art of Eric Gill, Aubrey Beardsley, Félicien Rops, etc (in Beardsley's fantastical illustration of a scene from Aristophanes' lusty Athenian comedy, *Lysistra*, for instance – *Cinesias Entreating Myrrhina to Coition*).[89] In the *Standing Male Nude, Back View*, Schiele emphasizes the

86 Schiele: *Self-Portrait, Nude Facing Front*, 1910, pencil, watercolour, gouache, glue, white body-colour, 55.7 x 36.8cm, Graphische Sammlung Albertina, Vienna; *Self-Portrait with Hand to Cheek*, 1918, black chalk and gouache, 44.3 x 30.5cm, Graphische Sammlung Albertina, Vienna; *Self-Portrait*, 1912, pencil, watercolour, gouache, 46.5 x 31.5cm, private collection; *Self-Portrait with Black Vase*, 1911, oil on wood, 27.5 x 34cm, Historische Museum der Stadt Wien, Vienna; *Self-Portrait Screaming*, 1910, watercolour, collection: Viktor Fogarassy, Graz
87 Schiele: *Self-Portrait Masturbating*, 1911, pencil and watercolour, 47 x 31cm, Graphische Sammlung Albertina, Vienna.
88 Schiele: *Eros*, 1911, watercolour and gouache, collection: Victor Lownes
89 Aubrey Beardsley: *Cinesias Entreating Myrrhina to Coition*, 1896, pen and ink, 26 x 18cm, Victoria & Albert Museum, London

buttocks and testicles.[90]

Egon Schiele's *Eros* is strange, because the phallus is pink and orange, while the rest of the body is brown and grey. Schiele looks up at the viewer with a morose, hang-dog expression, looking like a little schoolboy who just wet his underwear. As Erwin Mitsch describes Schiele's studied melancholy: '[t]he cry of affliction is followed by an exhausted collapse. The picture-frame has become a prison from which there is no escape.'[91] This facial expression, combined with the twelve-inch penis, is indeed a bizarre combination. Schiele cannot decide whether he fears sex or desires sex.

Egon Schiele was one of the few artists (in the modern era) who went to prison for making erotic art. The police confiscated a hundred erotic drawings of his and he was accused of having sex with a minor.[92] The general critical opinion on Schiele is that he was not a pornographer, but a highly individual artist. According to his friend, Arthur Roessler, Schiele created out of fear as well as desire: '[w]hat drove him to depict erotic scenes from time to time was perhaps the mystery of sex… and the fear of loneliness which grew to terrifying proportions.'[93]

The most telling image in all of Egon Schiele's art is the stylized version of the ubiquitous *Artist and Model* scenario, the scenario Pablo Picasso drew many a time,[94] *Self-Portrait Drawing a Nude Model Before a Mirror*.[95] This is Schiele's most deeply erotic image, and one of the most erotic of all modern images, because it satisfies all the criteria of art and pornography, and also psychology and cultural theory criticism. Firstly, it depicts a beautiful woman, posing arrogantly and self-consciously in front of a mirror, a scenario explored by Picasso in his melancholy *Girl*

90 E. Schiele: *Standing Male Nude, Back View*, 1910, chalk, watercolour and gouache, 17.6 x 12.2in, private collection
91 Erwin Mitsch: *The Art of Egon Schiele*, 1975
92 See F. Whitford, 115; Alessandra Comini: *Schiele in Prison*, New York 1973
93 Arthur Roessler: *Errinnerungen an Egon Schiele*, Vienna 1948
94 P. Picasso: *Le Peintre et Son Modèle*, V, coloured pencil on cardboard, Musée National d'Art Moderne, Paris
95 E. Schiele: *Self-Portrait Drawing a Nude Model Before a mirror*, 1910, pencil, 55.2 x 35.3cm, Graphische Sammlung Albertina, Vienna

Before a Mirror.[96]

Secondly, the picture satisfies the voyeuristic demands of porn, for the artist, shown in the picture sketching the model, lets the viewer in on his gaze. The viewer looks with the artist at the model, and is thus justified in her/ his perusal of the woman's body. It is the woman's body that is on view here, as in all those other (male) *Artist and Model* paintings, such as Gustave Courbet's gigantic canvas *The Studio of the Painter* (1855), those by Pablo Picasso, or in the odd photograph of Henri Matisse with his model, taken by Brassai, where the old master, bearded, bespectacled, in a white coat (looking like Sigmund Freud) stares at his model, nude, standing before him; Matisse looks at her indifferently as she poses for him; he is staring not, of course, at her face, but at her pubis.[97]

Thirdly, Egon Schiele's drawing sets up a network of looks beloved of post-Lacanian theorists: the model narcissistically looks at herself in the mirror;[98] the artist looks to one side; the viewer unites these Looks with a gaze that is contextualized as voyeuristic. Schiele constructs his *Artist and Model* so that the viewer is forced to look at the image voyeuristically, erotically. The pose of the model, hand on hip, is distinctly sexual: the picture becomes a mirror maze of eroticism.

Strangest of all, perhaps, in Egon Schiele's weird *œuvre*, are the depictions of the family he never had. He had set monks or figures of death next to pregnant women or mothers, or he pictured babies alive inside their dead mother's wombs. Strange indeed. The oil painting *The Family*, is one of his most finished paintings, showing the artist crouching behind a woman. Between their legs sits a small child with large, black eyes. It is one of Schiele's most accomplished works.

Egon Schiele's figures nearly always exist in empty space. He draws the figure and nothing else. In the oil paintings, he creates

96 Picasso: *Girl Before a Mirror*, 1932, oil on canvas, 63.8 x 51.2in, Museum of Modern Art, New York
97 Courbet: *The Studio of the Painter*, 1855, oil on canvas, Louvre, Paris; Brassai: *Matisse With His Model*, gelatin silver print, Victoria & Albert Museum
98 See Martha J. Reineke: "Lacan, Merleau-Ponty and Irigaray: reflections on a specular drama", *Auslegung: a Journal of Philosophy*, 14, winter 1987, 67-85

a darkened space around the figures, which are luminous. The cardinals, nuns, pregnant women and lovers kneel or lie on sheets or ruffled material, or in dark places. Schiele is interested in the figures' relation *to each other*, not to the spaces they inhabit. The shapes of his figures are related to the edges of the frame or the piece of paper, but, apart from that, their main spatial relation is with each other. It is, indeed, relationships that Schiele investigates in the late works. Relationships between a blind mother and her children, or between two lovers, or between two monks. The relationships veer from fear to desire in Schiele's art. In the late works, he is more inclined towards affection, compassion and love. The couples kneel together. They do not rut away at each other. They kneel, much as Lou Andreas-Salomé spoke of enjoying a 'kneeling together' with the poet most like Schiele in many ways, Rainer Maria Rilke.[99]

It is wrong, then, to see sadness in Egon Schiele's imagined pictures of the family he never had. He was only 28 when he died. He would probably have gone on to have children and a family. Besides, these are idle, biographical speculations; gossip merely.

ERNEST KIRCHNER, OTTO MUELLER, ERICH HECKEL

Other Expressionists employ a similar approach to erotic art. Like Egon Schiele, artists such as Ernst Ludwig Kirchner, Max Beckmann, Erich Heckel and Emil Nolde use the thick black outline to define the body in space. The black line carves out figures in space with a self-confidence, a roughness, a macho display of technique. Expressionist art – the term 'Expressionist' is

---

99 See B.D. Barnacle: *Rilke*, Crescent Moon 1993

used in its widest sense here, to include many different artists – is characterized by its emotional intensity brought into focus by the black line. Instead of softening everything into pure light and colour as the Impressionists had done, the Expressionists made art jagged, restless, urban and anguished. The Expressionists are deeply unhappy artists. As Henri Matisse wrote: 'I too have said one wouldn't paint if one were happy. I'm in agreement with Picasso on that one. We have to live over a volcano.'[100]

Agony is one of the hallmark of Expressionist art, and this is true in the depictions of sexuality. Again, it is women who dominate the sexual discourse of the Expressionists. As with the Symbolists and the Viennese Secessionists and New Artists, the Expressionists use women as subjects and sexual objects, as sites of fears and desires about sexuality and life, as vehicles of lust and despair. The emotional and moral ambiguity is apparent in so much of Expressionist art. In Ernst Kirchner's art, for instance, we find simultaneous love and hate of his subjects, which he communicates with his vigorous descriptive lines and his offbeat use of colour, such as in *Five Women in the Street*.[101] Kirchner's portrait of a woman with her blouse pulled down to show her breasts is essentially no different from softcore porno images.[102] For art historians, Kirchner's eroticization of his subject is redeemed because of its 'artistic merit'. But no amount of art historical discussion of Kirchner's innovative colouration[103] obscures the fact that his painting objectifies women sexually.

The Expressionist style turns the world into a mass of angular planes edged with black lines. Nudes become integrated into a series of subjects: landscapes, street scenes, clowns, religious figures, men playing cards at a table. The sexual dimension is put alongside everyday occurrences – people bathing in a lake is a typical scene. Erich Heckel's Brücke-style interlocking planes turn the nude woman in *Glassy Day* into an abstract form amidst other

---

100 Matisse, quoted in Pierre Schneider: *Matisse*, Rizzoli, New York 1984, 734

101 Ernst Ludwig Kirchner: *Five Women in the Street*, 1913, 120 x 90cm, Wallraf-Richartz Museum, Cologne

102 Kirchner: *Semi-nude Woman With Hat*, 1911, 76 x 70cm, Wallraf-Richartz Museum, Cologne

103 See Wolf-Dieter Dube: *The Expressionists*, 42f

abstract forms.[104] Even so, despite the planar, geometric abstraction, this is an image that does not flatten out the eroticism of the situation – a woman paddling in a lake.

Otto Mueller's motif is a group of young women sitting in long grass. He painted variations on this theme many times.[105] The women are nude, have sallow eyes but no individual personality. They are types, with their pointed knees and elbows. They are made up of straight lines, and painted in a style that is deliberately 'primitive' or crude. Mueller's nude women are clearly erotic for him, though they are anonymous, abstracted, curiously bland, as if, once he had painted them, Mueller was scared by what he had created. So he takes all the individuality out of them, and turns them into a series of shapes. Pablo Picasso did this with his Avignon women, though they are have more personality, more of a sense of self than Mueller's nude women.[106]

EMIL NOLDE

Eroticism in the art of Emil Nolde (1867-1956), as in Georges Rouault's output, is subsumed into a really intense exploration of religious imagery. Rouault and Nolde are two of the best of modern figurative religious artists. In their work, as in that of Max Beckmann and Marc Chagall, the full pain and ecstasy of the human condition is brilliantly depicted. Nolde is rarely erotic in the way of the art of Ernst Kirchner or Egon Schiele. In his *Golden Calf Dance*, however, Nolde captured some of the wildness of wild dancing.[107] It is a depiction of ecstasy and celebration that is far wilder than, say, Henri Matisse's *The Dance*.[108] While Matisse's

104 Erich Heckel: *Glassy Day*, 1913, 120 x 96cm, Staatsglerie moderner Kunst, Munich
105 Otto Mueller: *Two Girls in the Grass*, 1905, tempera, 141 x 110cm, Staatsgalerie, Munich
106 Picasso: *Les Demoisels d'Avignon*, 1907, MOMA, New York
107 Emil Nolde; *Golden Calf Dance*, 1910, 88 x 105cm, Staatsgalerie, Munich
108 Matisse: *The Dance*, 1910, oil, 260 x 391cm, Hermitage Museum, St Petersburg

282

painting exudes joy, Nolde's Old Testament dance offers up a wild abandon that comes close to the fervour of lovemaking. Like Paul Klee's *Blossoming*,[109] Emil Nolde's *Golden Calf Dance* is a portrayal of ecstasy that goes beyond sex or religion. It is a non-institutionalized ecstasy, a bliss transcending gender or politics. As Nolde wrote in 1909, he worked in a state close to religious bliss as he painted: '[t]hen again I went down to the mystical depth of human divine existence'.[110]

But the most erotic of Emil Nolde's works are his watercolours, the landscape studies of his homeland, North Schleswig (erotic though without a human body in sight). Nolde's luminous colours are brighter than Ernst Kirchner at his most garish, or Henri Matisse during the height of his Fauvist period, or Vincent van Gogh in his late, mad year, or Pierre Bonnard in the late pictures of his wife.

In watercolour paintings such as *Marshy Landscape* or *Freislandische Landschaft*, Emil Nolde achieved a truly sublime and pulsing sense of colour and light.[111] His colours are extraordinary, the richest in art in terms of saturation and sheer hedonism. The thunder-dark clouds look forward to the sensuous, misty canvases of Mark Rothko. Nolde turns landscape into an eternal purple twilight that melts in on itself in the most voluptuously colourful manner. Nolde depicts the end of the sunsets that J.M.W. Turner painted when the sun was still high in the sky. In Nolde's landscapes, it is nearly night, pure darkness.

Emil Nolde's landscapes are deeply feminine, then, for as we have seen, the feminine, night, the Goddess and darkness are concepts or experiences that have been complexly entwined since earliest times. The Egyptians depicted night as the Goddess Nut, bending over the Earth, the 'Great Lady who gives birth to the gods,' as Plutarch described her, identifying her with Rhea.[112] Arching over the Earth, the Goddess Nut, like Kali or Isis, is the

109 Klee: *Blossoming*, 1934, oil, 91 x 80cm, Kunst Museum, Winterhur
110 Emil Nolde: *Jahre der Kampfe*, Rembrandt, Berlin 1934, 103f
111 Emil Nolde: *Marshy Landscape*, 1916, Kunstmuseum, Basel; *Freislandische Landschaft*, watercolour, 30 x 44cm, private collection
112 C.T. Hopfner: *Plutarch über Isis und Osiris*, Prague 1940, I, 81f

cosmic night behind everything; she is all space and time, as Joseph Campbell said. Here, in Nolde's sensual, darkening skies, the Goddess appears again. The symbolism may be archaic, but the sensuality of night falling is as piquant now as it has ever been. (Night is always falling somewhere on Earth – the real night, and the symbolic, ecstatic and agonizing night).

The Expressionists' worldview seems more authentic, closer to real life than, say, that of the Impressionists or the Neo-Classicists. In Expressionism we get a sharp sense of the harshness of existence. There are few smiles or laughs in Expressionist art – think of the art of Karl Schmidt-Rottluff, Max Pechstein or Alexander Kanoldt – yet their view of life seems closer to the real thing than that of many other artists. But in amongst the apparently sombre or dour images there are many wild colours and much exuberance – especially in the art of Ernst Kirchner, Alexei von Jawlensky, Kees van Dongen and Gabriele Münter.

If you take the European intellectual view on eroticism of the Marquis de Sade, Charles Baudelaire and Georges Bataille as being true – that sex signifies the highpoint of life, the apotheosis of being alive, the most intense experience there is, in opposition to death (but also related to death) – then the Expressionists must be the most successful of modern artists, because they, more than the Symbolists, Impressionists, Neo-Classicists or Surrealists, show humanity at its most intense. The Existential, intellectual view of life is that life is painful, and that sex and death are two parts of the same ontological mystery. If this is so, and it is very much a masculinist viewpoint, then Expressionist art captures this intensity more successfully than almost any other artform. True, there have been countless images of suffering in the Renaissance – all those crucifixions (most dramatically, perhaps, in Mathias Grünewald's masterpiece, which is a forerunner of the Expressionist stance). And there have been images of pain in artists such as Artemisia Gentileschi, Francisco de Goya, Titian, Guiseppe Ribera, etc. But only with the Expressionists does this acute, angst-ridden view of life infuse every aspect of art, and every kind of subject, from landscapes to domestic scenes, from portraits to flowerpieces. In the male view, life is about pain, so the Expressionists are the supreme celebrants of this view.

MAX BECKMANN

German artist Max Beckmann (1884-1950) is best-known for his series of triptychs produced in the 1930s and 1940s. this was art in the grand, tragic manner, taking on big themes with self-confidence Expressionist gestures. There is no glamour in Beckmann's art. His early major painting *Night* seethes with tragic pain.[113] Beckmann does not veer away from pain. Indeed his ambition, like so many of the Expressionists – like Lovis Corinth, James Ensor, Georges Rouault, Chaim Soutine – is to intensify it.[114] In Beckmann's art one finds many of the typical Expressionist motifs – of clowns, dancers, masks, acrobats. These motifs are deployed with bitter irony in Beckmann's mythicizing drama of life, which aims to get at the 'magic of reality', as he called it.[115]

Max Beckmann's sense of sexuality is integrated into his ironic, often savage view of life. For him, modern life was mostly made up of suffering. The great triptychs of mythic events focus on the savagery of mid-20th century life. In *Temptation* there are the extraordinary images of the cage, the primitive and Classical gestures and faces, the brutal slavery and the bizarre huge blue and red bird.[116]

Max Beckmann's triptychs assault the viewer with violence,

113 Max Beckmann: *Night*, 1918, 134 x 156cm, Kunstsammlung Nordrhein-Westfalen, Düsseldorf
114 'I shall never, I know, abandon the fullness, the roundness, the pulse of life, on the contrary, I should like to intensify it more and more', he wrote to his wife in 1915 (quoted in Dube, 164)
115 Max Beckmann, lecture, 1938, quoted in Chipp, 188
116 Max Beckmann: *Temptation*, 1937, oil, triptych, 200 x 170cm, side panels, 215 x 100cm, Bayerische Staatsgemaldesammlungen, Munich

285

violence that goes on all the time. Beckmann, cleverly, isolates the violence and injustice, thus magnifying it. It is not lost in a blur of gloom, it is depicted under bright blue skies, against bright seas. The result mythicizes human gestures and actions, so that a triptych like *Departure* can get closer to the realizing on canvas the 'atrocity exhibition' of modern life more successfully than most other attempts.[117]

Max Beckmann's *Departure* and other triptychs brilliantly capture the pornography of modern life, the inhuman yet so human (and mostly male) traumas, battles, murders, injustices and tortures that occur throughout the modern era, and throughout all eras. Two figures, one upside down, are bound together; another is tied to a pillar, gagged; her hands are severed; axes are wielded; a trumpet is blown; all is brutality, gruesome horror. The central panel opens onto a wide seascape: the dream of escape and release from the horror (the 'horror' of Joseph Conrad's *Heart of Darkness* and Francis Coppola's film *Apocalypse Now*).

Max Beckmann has an epic sense of humanity and history, and depicts it in a deceptively simple manner in his canvases. Beckmann's art presents a carnival of horror, enacted in a timeless, mythic space that is at once everyplace and noplace. What is shocking about the work of Beckmann, as about George Grosz, is not the savagery of their satire and irony, but the fact that what they depict is true. Worse, what they paint only contains a million millionth of the true horror and pain that is going on around us *all the time*. Beckmann, like Georges Rouault, Lovis Corinth and Emil Nolde, shows the viewer that people are horrible to each other. It's a simple message, but the Expressionists really emphasize it by exaggerating what they see. Yet their exaggerations are not fantasies but truths, and we know that the real situation is much worse. When you go to the Impressionists, say, after the Expressionists, you see a bunch of bourgeois goofs painting cosy little domestic and countryside

117 Max Beckmann: *Departure*, 1933, oil, 215 x 115, 215 x 99cm, MOMA, New York

scenes which are pure escapism. The Expressionists, at least, try to depict some of the agony and horror of being alive. Painters since then have gone further on the road of ontological extremism (the Surrealists, for instance, or the Pop artists), but few have equalled the convulsive impact of the Expressionists, and in particular painters such as Max Beckmann and Emil Nolde.

The heroic, epic quality of the Expressionists is supremely masculinist, and women are definitely relegated to an inferior position in the manly mediations on big themes such as war, politics, nationalism and tragedy. Thus, Max Beckmann's treatment of love was often harsh and patriarchal, as in the painting *Brother and Sister*.[118] Some of the madness of the incestuous love between the Teutonic siblings is exacerbated by the violence of the colour scheme, which juxtaposes stained-glass crimson with yellow hair and the black sword. Beckmann's painting brutally conveys the powerful taboo of incest, a central theme in world culture from Egyptian religion (Isis and Osiris) through Elizabethan drama (in *'Tis Pity She's a Whore*, for instance) to Thomas Hardy and Lawrence Durrell.

WOMEN EXPRESSIONISTS

In the art of women Expressionists, such as Paula Modersohn-Becker and Käthe Kollwitz, tenderness is uppermost. The feverish self-criticism and patriarchal political satire of the art of Max Beckmann and George Grosz gives way in the work of Modersohn-Becker and Kollwitz to a human-scale depiction of tragedy and pain. In Kollwitz's (1867-1945) output, people clutch each other affectionately and desperately, as in her woodcut *Mary and Elizabeth* or her sculpture *Twins*, which shows a squatting

---

118 Max Beckmann: *Brother and Sister*, 1933, oil, collection: Stephen Lachner, California

mother enfolding two children tightly in her arms.[119] Kollwitz's art is marked by an empathy for people who suffer the trials and tribulations of modern living. Her concerns are political: against war, and for the proletariat ('I was gripped by the full force of the proletarian's fate', she wrote).[120]

In Paula Modersohn-Becker's (1876-1907) work there is a tenderness of approach that aims to get at the individual, not to make heroic painterly gestures. Modersohn-Becker's art is highly emotional; 'what counts are my personal feelings', she said, echoing the thoughts of many an Expressionist artist.[121] In images such as *Mother and Child*, where two nude people cuddle on a rug,[122] we see that solidarity of emotion, of two people bonding strongly, that is an important aspect of Kollwitz's art, and of other women Expressionists, such as Marianne Werekin and Gabriele Münter. In her self-portraits, Modersohn-Becker looks directly and clearly at herself. Again, the heroic and self-aggrandizing gestures of male self-portraits (those of Vincent van Gogh, Jacques Louis David and Egon Schiele, for example) are not there. When Modersohn-Becker paints herself nude, as in the self-portrait of 1906 when she is holding a flower, there is none of that insistent emphasis on sexuality that one sees in Schiele's work.[123]

119 Käthe Kollwitz: *Mary and Elizabeth*, woodcut, San Francisco Achenbach Foundation for Graphic Arts, *Twins*, 1935, bronze, Staatliche Museen zu Berlin
120 *The Diary and Letters of Käthe Kollwitz*, ed. Hans Kollwitz, tr. R. & C. Winston, Genry Regnery Co., Chicago 1955, 43
121 in *Briefe und tagebuchblätter von Paula Modersohn-Becker*, Kurt Wolff, Berlin 1920, 177
122 Modersohn-Becker: *Mother and Child*, 1907, Roselius collection, Bremen
123 Modersohn-Becker: *Self-Portrait*, 1906, Kunst Museum, Basel

3

SEX IN THE GREAT MODERNS

MATISSE, PICASSO, DEGAS, MODIGLIANI, MOORE, GAUGUIN, PASCIN, MAILLOL, RODIN, COURBET, MANET, RENOIR, BONNARD

Eroticism in the great painters of the modern era, those artists who command millions of dollars when their major works appear at international auctions, is thoroughly conventional, according to the rules and structures of patriarchal culture. From the mid-19th century onwards, the nude becomes increasingly eroticized. Nudes are always in part erotic. Even in nudes which consciously negate any inkling of eroticism – as in the mediæval images of Death and the Maiden, or Adam and Eve – there is always an element of eroticism. In the modern era, an emphasis on the sexuality of the body becomes more and more apparent.

Many major artists have produced erotic art, from Titan to

J.M.W. Turner. Titian drew in charcoal and chalk two people having sex, the woman (as ever) underneath, the man on top (as ever), while Turner made a (rare) sketch of people making love – the people are anonymous and faceless, while the genitals, as in all good erotica, are emphasized.[124] Even that ascetic and detached painter, the rigorous formalist Paul Cézanne, is not beyond emphasizing heterosexuality in art: take his *The Bathers*,[125] always a subject in which lots of flesh can be on display, and (nearly) always the results portray men and women differently, as also in interpretations of the subject of *Bathers* by Henri Matisse, Ernst Kirchner, Pablo Picasso, etc.

In 1867 Gustave Courbet painted a woman's torso, seen from below. With her legs spread, the picture is really a close-up of a vagina, and is clearly pornographic. Maxime Du Camp described how Courbet's painting presented pornography as high art:

> In the dressing room of this foreign personage [the Turkish collector Khalil Bey] one sees a small picture hidden under a green veil. When one draws aside the veil one remains stupefied to perceive a woman, lifesize, seen from the front, moved and convulsed, remarkably executed, reproduced *con amore*, as the Italians say, providing the last word in realism. But, by some inconceivable forgetfulness, the artist, who copied his model from nature, had neglected to represent the feet, the legs, the thighs, the stomach, the hips, the chest, the hands, the arms, the shoulders, the neck, and the head.[126]

It has cosmic aspirations, for the title is *The Origin of the World*, again echoing the mythology of the Goddess, and woman as the site of all time and space.[127]

Personal, private erotic art became increasingly public. Thus, Édouard Manet's *Déjeuner sur l'Herbe* (1863) puts the nude into a contemporary setting.[128] The picture is not idealized, the woman is not on a pedestal, the intention is not to be timeless and ethereal,

124 Turner: *Sheet of erotic drawings*, c. 1820s, pencil & wash, 10.5 x 14.5in, British Museum, London; Titian: *A Couple in Embrace*, c. 1750, charcoal & white & black chalk on blue paper, 25.1 x 26cm, Fitzwilliam Museum, Cambridge
125 Cézanne: *The Large Bathers*, 1906, oil on canvas, 82 x 90in, Philadelphia Museum of Art
126 Maxime Du Camp: *Les Convulsions de Paris*, Hachette, Paris 1889, II, 189-190
127 Courbet: *The Origin of the World*, 1867, now in the Musée d'Orsay, Paris
128 Manet: *Déjeuner sur l'Herbe*, 1863, Louvre, Paris

as in so many nudes. Manet's approach is to be direct, to move towards naturalism, as in his infamous *Olympia* (1863).[129]

Édouard Manet is often described as the founder of modern art, and one can see why, for in the art of Manet the seamlessness of the picture surface breaks down, and painting becomes increasingly a matter of marks on a canvas. The naturalism/ realism, the everyday subject matter, the indifference to the painting-viewer relation, make Manet 'modern'. A case could be made for many other painters – such as J.M.W. Turner, or Eugène Delacroix, or Jacques-Louis David, or Titian, or Giotto – as being the 'founder' of modern art. It doesn't really matter. But Manet's straightforward treatment of sexuality is powerful. Not necessarily 'new', but new in Western painting. Manet's *Olympia* broke and reworked the traditional relations between female sexuality, representation, 'high' art, and consumption.[130]

Many artists love their subjects. Their paintings are acts of love. As Alfred Sisley says, speaking of landscape, but his notion also applies to the human figure: '[e]very picture shows a spot with which the artist himself has fallen in love'.[131] On canvas, they try to recreate their love of their subject. We see this especially in the nude, whether the male or female nude. Artists such as Pierre Renoir said they painted with their penis (when Renoir had arthritis). The paintbrush becomes a phallus, gilding and caressing the (obscure) object of desire. The painter creates the Jungian *anima*, the beloved woman, the soul-mate on the canvas.

Seen in Lacanian theory, the female model becomes the 'obscure object of desire' feared and desired, ever unreachable, the manifestation of eternal loss.[132] We can see elements of the Lacanian lack, desire, repression, mirror stage, Symbolic Order and œdipal anxiety in the modern artists who create specifically erotic images. In the output of artists such as Pierre Renoir, Henri

129 Manet: *Olympia*, 1863, Louvre, Paris
130 See T.J. Clark: "Preliminaries to a Possible Treatment of *Olympia* in 1865", *Screen*, 21:1, Spring 1980, 18-41, and T.J. Clark: *The Painting of Modern Life: Paris in the Art of Manet and His Followers*, Thames & Hudson 1985, 79-146
131 In R. Goldwater, 309.
132 Toril Moi: *Sexual Textual Politics*, 99f; Anika Lemaire: *Jacques Lacan*, Routledge & Kegan Paul 1977; Elizabeth Wright: *Psychoanalytic Criticism*, Methuen 1984

Matisse, Jules Pascin, Aristide Maillol, Auguste Rodin, Gustav Klimt, Amedeo Modigliani and Pablo Picasso, one finds loss, desire, repression and anxiety quite clearly. The art they produce is fiercely heterosexual, glorifying women, even as, in some cases (Picasso) the paintings seem to denigrate women. Renoir, in paintings such as *Bather Arranging Her Hair*, Pascin in *The Prodigal Son*, and Lawrence Alma-Tadema in *In the Tepidarium*, produce works that exalt women as sexual objects. The soft flesh is available but also distinctly not available; there is acres of skin, especially in Pascin's painting, but it is not touchable either.[133] These nude paintings remain chimeras, never to be possessed, always to be yearned for. As Nicolas Poussin wrote of painting: '[p]ainting is nothing but an imitation of human actions, which alone are, properly speaking, inimitable'.[134] Poussin recognizes that painting is always an imitation, a mirror; the real thing can never be possessed in art. It is the same in erotic art – indeed, it is most dramatically expressed in erotic art – this paradoxical fear and desire, this simultaneous desire and loss, this ambiguous conflict between possession and dispossession.

There are a number of renowned modern artists who are unrestrained in their exaltation of women. Auguste Rodin is a typical example. Of the *Venus de'Medici* Rodin wrote: '[n]otice all the voluptuous curvings of the hip... And now, here, the adorable dimples along the loins... It is truly flesh... You would think it moulded by caresses!' Rodin is the classic womanizer artist, who made love to his models physically as well as psychologically and æsthetically. His models became his mistresses (such as Camille Claudel). Like many artists, he produced erotica for private consumption.

But enthusiastic eroticism infuses everything Auguste Rodin created. Sculptures such as *The Metamorphoses of Ovid* is typical – it depicts two lovers embracing.[135] The sculpture *Christ and the*

133 Pierre Renoir: *Bather Arranging Her Hair*, 1885, canvas, 92 x 73cm, Sterling and Francis Clark Institute, Williamstown, Mass.; Lawrence Alma-Tadema: *In the Tepidarium*, 1881, wood, 24 x 33cm, Lady Lever Art Gallery, Port Sunlight; Jules Pascin: *The Prodigal Son*, 1928, oil on board, 15 x 18in, private collection, Switzerland
134 In R. Goldwater, 154.
135 Rodin: *The Metamorphoses of Ovid*, plaster, height 13in

Magdalene is more controversial, for it depicts Mary Magdalene sexually embracing the crucified Christ.[136] The image is blasphemous, fusing sex and religion in age-old fashion. This eroticization of Mary Magdalene occurs also in the art of Félicien Rops and Eric Gill.

Love infuses every gesture Aristide Maillol makes. There are no blemishes, no irregularities, no awkward poses in Maillol's city of women. Each figure is softly rounded, softly drawn or sculpted. It seems as if make artists have loved creating rounded forms in women since time immemorial – large-hipped women appear not only throughout Western art (in the art of Peter Rubens, Titian, Rembrandt van Rijn, and Henri Matisse), but also in prehistoric imagery, in the faceless "Stone Venuses". These large women are less like potential lovers than mothers. They seem to conform to the Freudian and Lacanian emphasis on the mother as the male's first lover. The large women in the works of Picasso, Matisse, Rodin, Maillol and Gauguin are motherly, so clearly the mother figure of psychoanalysis, and the Goddess of ancient mythology.

For Henri Matisse, art is a celebration of life. No other of the great modern artists is as joyful as Matisse, except perhaps Paul Klee. Matisse exudes joy, throughout the phases of his art, from paintings such as *The Joy of Living*[137] which is a modernist pastoral scene, with people dancing, kissing, playing music, to the late cut-outs, which are really joyful, really exuberant.[138]

For Henri Matisse, eroticism is a part of life that is not, as in Pablo Picasso or Egon Schiele, exaggerated. Matisse's art is erotic in the sense that being out in the open air is erotic. His art is erotic in the sense that swimming can be erotic, or dancing, or playing music. Simple pleasures, these, pleasures that are culturally-conditioned but also occur everywhere. Activities such as swimming, playing music and dancing go beyond cultural boundaries, and beyond sexuality. One might see Matisse's joyful

---

136 Rodin: *Christ and the Magdalene*, 1894
137 Matisse: *The Joy of Living*, 1905-6, oil, 175 x 240cm, Barnes Foundation, Merion, Pennsylvania
138 Matisse: *Nude With Flowing Hair*, 1952, paper cut-out, 108 x 80cm, private collection, Paris

art as religious as well as erotic. That joy, seen in Existential terms, is both religious and erotic. As Matisse wrote: '[a]ll art worthy of the name is religious. Be it a creation of lines and colours; if it is not religious it does not exist.'[139] The erotic-religious view of existence is found in the philosophies of Friedrich Nietzsche, André Gide, D.H. Lawrence, Eric Gill, Anaïs Nin, Paul Éluard, Robert Graves, and in any number of modern artists.

For Henri Matisse, the site of this religious view is the human figure, and in male art that means the female figure. Matisse wrote: '[w]hat interests me most is neither still life nor landscape but the human figure. It is that which best permits me express my almost religious awe towards life.'[140]

Henri Matisse pinpoints the role of the (female) figure in much of art: it is the site of religious feelings, as something to worship. Clearly, this worshipping of the (female) figure is deeply sexist. It defines the dualities and paradoxes of art: consisting for feminists of the male artist, the female model; the male gaze, the passive female; the male manipulator, the female victim. See, for instance, Matisse's The Blue Nude.[141]

Many forms of sexuality are based on the heterosexual notions of active and passive. Women's passivity mythicizes men, as Valerie Traub notes '[m]en desire women because their gender role positions them as active; women desire men because their own 'lack' must be filled.'[142] In the patriarchal system, which is our own and has been for thousands of years, everyone, including men, are 'victims'. Not only is the 'system' to blame, as Simone de Beauvoir commented:

> it is too abstract to say... that only the system is to blame. Men are to blame, too. The man of today did not establish this patriarchal regime, but he profits by it, even when he criticizes it. And he has made it very much a part of his own thinking. One must blame the system, but at the same time be wary of men, and not let them take

139 Matisse, 1951, in Jack D. Flam: Matisse on Art, E.P. Dutton, New York 1978, 140
140 Matisse: "Notes of a Painter", in Flam, 38
141 Matisse: The Blue Nude (Souvenir of Biskra), 1907, oil on canvas, 36.2 x 55.1in, Baltimore Museum of Art; The Pink Nude, 1935, oil on canvas, 26 x 36.5in, Baltimore Museum of Art
142 Valerie Traub:"Desire and the Difference It Makes", in Valerie Wayne, ed., 89

over our activities, our potentialities. The system and men both must be attacked.[143]

Christine Jackson is more certain about who does what who:

Boys, not girls, are filling remand centres. Men, not women, batter their partners, abuse children and fight on the football terraces.[144]

Aristide Maillol, Auguste Rodin, Jules Pascin and Henri Matisse are relatively unambiguous in their adoration of the female form. Their art is partly an expression of male lust, and it admits its own lust. More problematic is the art of Egon Schiele, Pablo Picasso, Pierre Bonnard, Edgar Degas and Amedeo Modigliani. Vincent van Gogh, in his very few nudes, had shown a deep ambivalence towards eroticism (in his strangely pathetic *Sorrow* for instance).[145] In the art of Pierre Bonnard, the ambivalence, the simultaneous fear and desire, appears heightened by a fevered application of colour, far more obsessive than anything in van Gogh's work. Like Egon Schiele and Andrea del Sarto, Bonnard painted the same woman over and over again – his wife. Bonnard's works often depict in a tender manner intimate, domestic scenes.[146]

But what strikes the viewer the more s/he looks at Pierre Bonnard's works of his wife are some strange facts. Firstly, she is often nude, and eroticized. The whole thrust of the paintings, with their intensely saturated colours and richly worked surfaces, is of veneration. At the same time, there is a disgust in Bonnard's works, a repulsion which he cannot disguise, as in Pablo Picasso's late erotic drawings. Bonnard exalts his wife but gives her no personality. She has no face. So many of Bonnard's nudes have the face in deep shadow. While other elements in the room or bath or wherever are sharp, the face is left blurred, or it is in shadow, as in *La toilette*, which is odd, because the rest of room

143 Simone de Beauvoir: interview in *Ms*, July 1972, in Marks, 144-5
144 Christine Jackson, letter, *The Guardian*, 6 March 1993
145 Van Gogh: *Sorrow*, 1882, black chalk, 4.5 x 27cm, collection: Garman Ryan, London; *Reclining Nude*, 1887, Vincent van Gogh Museum, Amsterdam
146 Bonnard: *Nude in Front of the Fireplace*, 1917, Musée de l'Annonciade, St-Tropez

and the rest of the painting is painted in vibrant reds, pinks and oranges.[147] In *Mirror in the Dressing Room*, Bonnard concentrates on the woman's body – *nude, of course* – reflected in the mirror. He paints her back and buttocks, as he has done so many times, and cuts off her head in the top of the mirror's frame.[148]

The blurred faces occur, as we saw, in Egon Schiele's art, when Schiele painted either himself or a woman as a puppet, with sockets or points for eyes. The effect is unsettling. Pierre Bonnard seems to be reverting to the standard practices of some porn, which cuts off faces, or renders people anonymous, much as so much of pornography is produced by people who prefer to call themselves 'Anonymous', or give themselves silly names.

Pierre Bonnard's paintings mythicize the intimate day-to-day activities of his beloved, as art has always done, so that drying the body after a bath becomes a religious ritual. The same thing happens in the art of Edgar Degas. In both Degas' and Bonnard's works, the voyeur is built into the image. One is always aware of looking. One is always aware that the image is constructed for the pleasure of the artist. The viewer is a voyeur in Degas' art, in so much of art. As Degas said: '[i]t is as if you looked through a keyhole.'[149] This is emphasized in Degas' art by the studied indifference to the viewer, when the women turn their backs to the viewer, and in Bonnard's art one often looks through doorways or mirrors or frames of some kind. Both artists, as in late Pablo Picasso, emphasize the act of looking, the pleasure, of seeing.

Edgar Degas' nudes, with their gorgeous pastel colours, spatial flatness, ritualized poses and gestures are brilliant graphic orchestrations, and seem at first to be simply formal explorations, as the poet Paul Valéry maintained.[150] These are the images, of

---

147 Bonnard: *La Toilette*, 1914, oil, 119 x 79cm, Musée National d'Art Moderne, Paris; *The Bath*, 1925, oil on canvas, 33.8 x 47.5in, Tate Gallery, London
148 Bonnard: *Mirror in the Dressing Room*, oil, 120 x 97cm, Pushkin Museum, Moscow
149 quoted in P.A. Lemoine: *Degas et son œuvre*, Paris, 1946-9, I, 107
150 'All his life, Degas sought in the Nude, observed from all sides, in an unbelievable quantity of poses... the unique system of lines that would formulate any given moment of the body with the utmost precision and the utmost generality", wrote Paul Valéry (*Degas Danse Dessin*, Gallimard, Paris 1938, 59).

nude bathing women, that Degas is famous for.[151] In fact, Degas' nudes have much to do with voyeurism, with scopophilia, with framing the obscure object of desire, so that the woman retains her 'looked-at-ness', to use Laura Mulvey's term from her key essay on visual pleasure.[152] Degas' nudes rewrite the relation between body, space, artwork and viewer, as Carol M. Armstrong notes.[153]

Edgar Degas' tender, sensual and tightly-controlled images try to erase the artist's viewpoint. Degas would like us to believe that he wasn't really there, drawing those women crouching on bathroom floors. They turn away from the artist, and Degas denies his interest in them, which is obviously erotic. But Degas cannot erase his erotic looking, his pleasure in brushing over with pastels every inch of skin of these anonymous women. For instance, Degas so often draws the hips, buttocks and back, and the women, bent over, are like the women of erotica, who always show off their bodies, and often their asses and hips.[154]

Although Edgar Degas' nudes can be seen as detached and aiming for a cool objectivity, Degas is drawing, time after time, nude women, who go about their tasks of cleaning and washing, and sit, like cats, self-absorbed. Degas heavily invests in his subjects, in these nude women. He is very interested in them, it seems, despite his professed detachment. His interest has an erotic component which if *he* can deny it, his art cannot deny it. Degas' nudes, then, can be seen as celebrations of the female nude, which turn out to be sexist, such as those of Giorgione in his *Concert Champêtre*, J.A.D. Ingres in his *A Sleeping Odalisque*, Jacopo Tintoretto in his *Susannah and the Elders*, Pierre Renoir in his *La Nymphe de la Source*, Leon Kroll in his *Nude*, or John Everett

151 Degas: *Woman Drying Herself*, c. 1890-5, pastel, National Gallery of Scotland, Edinburgh; *The Tub*, c. 1885, pastel and gouache, 71.1 x 71.1cm, Hillstead Museum, Farmington, Connecticut
152 Laura Mulvey: "Visual Pleasure and Narrative Cinema", *Screen*, 16, 3, 1975
153 Armstrong, in Suleiman, ed., 225: 'Degas's nudes may be seen as a deliberate revision of the syntax of the female body and of the structure of viewing in which it as traditionally situated; that they may be seen as describing a relationship between viewer, space, and body that speaks to the traditional positioning of the *male* body, the meaning of its exteriority, its projection into a field of vision, and ultimately into disembodiment and invisibility; finally, that they problematize the formalism of the female nude, and the meaning of its apprehension through form and facture.'
154 See Degas' *The Tub*, c. 1891, pastel on paper, Burrell Collection, Glasgow; *Après le Bain*, charcoal on paper, Victoria & Albert Museum

Millais in his *The Night Errant*.[155] Peter Rubens' *Three Graces* features three heavily sensualized women, their hips and buttocks emphasized, as in Degas or Maillol.[156]

For, again, as with Pierre Bonnard and so much of art, Edgar Degas' models remain 'models'. That is, just women, without names or personalities. Degas tries, as Paul Valéry pointed out, to produce universal and individual art, both everyday and mythic, but produces only universal art freighted with individual touches. But the real touch, the real individual gestures of the women, are not there in his works.

Some of Edgar Degas' images are specifically voyeuristic, such as *The Admiration* (*c.* 1880), which depicts an old man kneeling at the side of a bathtub in which a woman washes herself. The man is clearly the worshipper abasing himself before the Goddess, much as in Greek mythology Actaeon saw Diana bathing (Titian painted the consequences of Actaeon seeing the Goddess naked).[157] The brilliant handling of *chiaroscuro,* line and shape in Degas' *The Admiration* does not obscure the fact that this is an image that trots out the conventions of pornography: men looking at women, women objectified sexually, the artist controlling the network of looks: from viewer to the kneeling man in the drawing, and from the man to the woman. *The Admiration* is supremely an image of women being looked at, of women as sites of (sexual) pleasure.

Amedeo Modigliani's nudes seem to be the archetypical 'modern master' nudes, with their sleek bodies at once 'pure', like Classical sculpture or the cool, sleek lines of Jean Dominique Ingres, yet also quite definitely sensual-sexual. Modigliani's nudes are – apart from being women (of course) – available, passive, relaxing back for the viewer's enjoyment, just like

---

155 John Everett Millais: *The Night Errant*, oil on canvas, Tate Gallery, London; Jacopo Tintoretto: *Susannah and the Elders*, 1555-6, oil on canvas, Kunsthisorisches Museum, Vienna; Ingres: *A Sleeping Odalisque*, oil on canvas; Giorgione: *Concert Champêtre*, oil on canvas, Musées Nationaux, Paris; Leon Kroll: *Nude*, 1933-4, oil on canvas, 48 x 36in, Metropolitan Museum of Art, New York
156 Rubens: *Three Graces*, 1638-40, oil on panel, 7ft 3in x 5ft 11in, Prado, Madrid
157 Degas: *The Admiration*, c. 1880, monotype, black ink on paper, 21.5 x 16cm, Bibliotheque d'Art et d'Archæologie de France, Paris

women in pornographic magazines.[158] Their eyes are closed, their arms are open, they show their bodies to the viewer, not always sad, but often smiling mysteriously (with what pornographers call a 'come on' look on their faces). 'Come and get me', these nude women in the art of Modigliani say, really, just like the women in the art of Titian, Ingres, and Jean-Honoré Fragonard ('come and get me, but don't really touch'). And if the models or figures do not state it as boldly as that, it is implied in their passive pose, and in the relation between viewer and subject. The *connection* between viewer and subject in the art of Modigliani, as in the work of Pablo Picasso, Henri Matisse, Pierre Bonnard, Edgar Degas, Egon Schiele, Gustav Klimt, Titian, J.A.D. Ingres, François Boucher, and other high art painters, is erotic.

Pablo Picasso's late erotic drawings are marked by a frantic energy and the all-seeing presence of a Tiresias-figure, who looks on as various beings copulate. Picasso's people always have clearly marked genitals. However he arranges the bodies on the paper, Picasso always makes sure the genitals are thrust forward, onto the frontal picture plane, as in *Raphael and La Fornarina*, in which a painter makes love to his model while Picasso draws himself as the Tiresias-like old man observing the Freudian primal scene.[159]

In the art of Pablo Picasso, sexual acts can be tender, as some commentators have noted,[160] but more typically they are brutal, and, in the late drawings, desperate. Picasso's treatment of women is often savage: there is as much loathing as there is love in many of his depictions of women[161] – not only in his drawings and paintings, but in his sculptures too.[162] In Picasso's erotic art, one finds the age-old connections that men make between sex and

158 Amedeo Modigliani: *Recumbent Nude*, 1917-8, private collection; *Seated Nude*, c. 1917, Courtauld Institute of Art, London
159 Pablo Picasso: *Raphael and La Fornarina*, 1968
160 Robert Rosenblum: "Picasso and the Anatomy of Eroticism", in Studies *in Erotic Art*, Basic Books, New York, 338
161 See, for instance, Picasso's *Woman Dressing Her Hair*, 1940, oil on canvas, 51.3 x 38.3in, collection: Mrs Bertram Smith, New York, or *Nude Under a Tree*, 1959, oil on canvas, 182.9 x 244cm, Art Institute of Chicago
162 Picasso: *Woman in Garden*, 1929-30, bronze, 210cm high, Picasso Collection; *Woman's Head*, 1931, iron painted white, 10cm high, Picasso Collection

death, between women and sex and death, as Janet Hobhouse observes. [163] For Picasso, then, as for Egon Schiele, Gustave Moreau, Leonardo da Vinci, Auguste Rodin and any number of artists, women are the site, the vehicle, the vessel or the space where sexuality, death, being, desire and fear meet and merge. In Picasso's late work, as in the late work of Schiele, Bonnard and Matisse, women predominate; they are exalted, they become Goddesses, loathed and loved in turn.

---

163 'The output and intensity of Picasso's late work have often been attributed to the artist's notorious fear of death. If so, the image he contacted again and again as a source of energy and safety from mortal threat was emphatically female and sexual. The erotic content is unlike anything else in his art, in its insistence, urgency and power. All reference to himself and his work is made in terms of the female, who seem to be endowed with the properties of creativity and immortality.' (J. Hobhouse, 133)

4

MAD LOVE: SURREALIST SEX

The Surrealists seemed to approach sexuality in a new way, but their concepts of *l'amour fou*, of sex and death, of æsthetics and poetry, turn out to be as patriarchal, as sexist and routinely heterosexual as the rest of Western art. As André Masson wrote, 'eroticism and death are always coexistent.'[164] Typical among Surrealist images and philosophies is Salvador Dali's *Phenomenon of Ecstasy*, showing various photos of women (supposedly) in orgasm, a collage that targets the main areas of Surrealist discourse which are always connected: eroticism, death and the feminine.[165]

The Surrealist artists did not seriously alter notions of sexuality, although they did question them. Indeed, Surrealism focused on sex obsessively, as obsessive as Symbolism, from which it derives much. If a book prints a still from the key Surrealist film, Luis Buñuel's and Salvador Dali's *Un Chien Andalou*, it is always the image of the man's hands pressed

164 André Masson: *Entriens avec Georges Charbonnier*, Paris 1958, 138
165 Dali: *Pheomenon of Ecstasy*, in *Minotaure*, nos. 3-4, 1933, 77

against the woman's breasts, or the image of the woman's being cut (or maybe it was just that someone from the film's distributors thought those were the best images to sum up the movie).

Nearly all the major Surrealist artists made erotic art, or included erotic elements in their art: René Magritte produced the *Rape*, showing a woman's body as a face, with breasts for eyes and the vagina for the mouth,[166] Salvador Dali drew many erotic pictures, including bizarre moustachioed men being sucked off by prepubescent girls entitled *Choice Treats for Children* (child abuse images which are distinctly un-PC), Man Ray produced films that evoked pornography, and Ernst Fuchs made Hieronymous Bosch-like visions of sex and death.[167]

The Surrealists rewrote the human body, and the territory was, again – whaddya know? – the female nude. The Surrealist artists added humour in their remaking of the body, and of representations of the body, if you find Man Ray's *Violin d'Ingres* funny, where a woman's back has violin holes drawn on it, so that her body becomes a 'violin', in the manner of Jean Auguste Dominique Ingres.[168] The Surrealists, for all their polemical thinking and manifestos, were – for feminists and sceptics – once again men lusting after women, men desiring and loathing women, men controlling, manipulating and exploiting women in photographs, paintings, collages, films, sculptures, etc. As Mary Ann Caws writes:

> The Surrealist body represented, taken (in) by the gaze and glance of the spectator, presents no margin of interpretation unless the female – for it is usually *she* – submits actively to such a stare, giving what is in any case taken by the male, she will have no role except enforced submission.[169]

The Surrealists appropriated psychoanalysis, occultism, *avant*

---

166 Magritte: *The Rape*, 1934, pencil drawing, 14 x 9.5in, Menil Foundation Collection, Houston, Texas
167 Fuchs: *Die Hochzeit von Unicorn*, 1952-60, 28 x 14in, collection: the artist, Vienna; Man Ray: *Return to Reason*, 1923
168 Man Ray: *Violon d'Ingres*, 1924, photograph, 16 x 12in, Galeria Arturo Schwarz, Milan
169 Mary Ann Caws: "Ladies Shot and Painted: Female Embodiment in Surrealist Art", in Suleiman, 270

garde art and thinking, societal rebellion, dream theory, etc, but they came up with the old essentialist and idealized views of women and eroticism, the same old reduction to genitals.

The high priest of Surrealism, André Breton, defined the terms, the ancestry and the goals of the new artistic cult. Symbolism was a key element in Breton's philosophy of Surrealism, in particular Gustave Moreau. Breton wrote:

> The discovery of the Musée Gustave Moreau, when I was sixteen, conditioned my way of loving for ever. Beauty and love came as revelations to me there through some of the faces and the attitudes of some of the women... I was completely spellbound.[170]

I'd definitely agree with Breton about Moreau's museum in Paris, a completely extraordinary place, and maybe the Global Headquarters of Surrealism.

André Breton defined the history and ancestry of Surrealism: from Lautréamont, Arthur Rimbaud, Paul Valéry, Edgar Allan Poe, J.-K. Huysmans, Marquis de Sade and Charles Baudelaire among writers; from Gustave Moreau, Hieronymous Bosch, Henry Fuseli, William Blake and Giorgio de Chirico, among painters. The tenets of Surrealism are now familiar to all, as are the leading lights among its practitioners: Joan Miro, Pablo Picasso, Salvador Dali, René Magritte, Yves Tanguy, Max Ernst, Man Ray, André Masson, Hans Bellmer, Marcel Duchamp, Louis Aragon, Breton and Paul Éluard.

The gestures and productions of Surrealism seem tired and worn-out by now: Salvador Dali's soft clocks and dreamy desertscapes (Dali is still very popular in museums), Yves Tanguy's even dreamier landscapes full of unreal junk, René Magritte's oh so clever juxtapositions, and André Masson's bizarre transfigurations. The Surrealists were in fact profoundly mistrusting of women and the feminine at times, producing dubious images as a matter of course. They are of the Georges Bataille and the Marquis de Sade school, the European intellectual

---

170 Breton: "Hommage", in *Le Surréalisme et la peinture*, in Paladilhe, 165

tradition that fuses sex and death, love and pain, in images such as Dali's *Young Virgin Sodomized by Her Own Chastity*, an image that plays with porn, depicting the limbs of the woman, who is *naked of course*, fragmenting and changing into a phallus, aimed at the woman's buttocks. Despising the idea of someone remaining a virgin, that is, someone who chooses not to be fucked by a man, Dali has her sodomized. It is an image of unadulterated violence.[171] (Is sodomy true sex? One of Samuel Beckett's derelict characters wonders just that: is it true love in the ass?).

The chauvinism, racism, elitism, intellectualism and mediocre technique produces many bad paintings in Surrealism. The attempt to shock is all too contrived, all too determined, all too self-conscious, too self-consciously ironic (as in Max Ernst's *The Virgin Punishing the Infant Jesus in the Presence of Three Witnesses: Breton, Éluard and the Artist*).[172]

Sexuality in Surrealism is deeply ambivalent and problematic.[173] Many Surrealists exalted women and the feminine, but ended up as sexist as other artists. André Masson's automatic drawing entitled *La Terre* depicts Mother Earth as a woman, *naked of course*, lying back with her legs spread, revealing her vagina and anus.[174] It is a (yawn) typical male image of female sexuality. Even seemingly innocuous painters, such as Paul Delvaux, produced tormented images. His women, *naked of course*, stare into space, lost in reveries, as in Gustave Moreau or Giorgio de Chirico. But Delvaux's women are marked by an emphasis on pubic hair (as in the art of Eric Gill). Delvaux, like so many Surrealists, creates a world of simultaneous desire and revulsion. His images invite then repel.[175]

Some of André Masson's images look like rapes. He shows bodies torn to shreds by tumultuous forces, as in *Metamorphosis of*

171 Dali: *Young Woman Self-Sodomized*, 1954, Alemany Collection, New York

172 Ernst: *The Young Virgin Punishing Christ*, 1928, 195 x 130cm, Krebs, Brussels

173 See Xavière Gauthier: *Surréalisme et Sexualité*, Paris 1971; Robert Benayoun: *Erotique du Surréalisme*, Paris 1965; Whitney Chadwick: "*Eros* or *Thanatos*: The Surrealist Cult of Love Reexamined", *Artforum*, 14, Nov 1975, 46-56

174 André Masson: *La Terre*, 1939, sand and oil on wood, 17 x 20.9in, Musée National d'Art Moderne, Paris

175 Delvaux: *Hands*, 1941, private collection

Gradiva and *There is no perfect world*.[176] Victor Brauner produced similar transmogrifications of the human form, so that a vulva appears in one image in the usual place on a 'body': it expands in the following two images, and in the fourth, it is wrapped around the woman's shoulders.[177]

The women Surrealists created their own form of erotic art, and are so much more interesting than the male Surrealists (Frida Kahlo, Dorothea Tanning, Remedios Varo, Leonora Carrington and Léonor Fini). They are discussed in the chapter on women artists. Some female Surrealists produced wholly patriarchal or masculine art, art which did not veer at all from the masculinist norms: Nusch Éluard with her photographic collages, or Léonor Fini's nude drawings.[178]

Surrealism is a violent art movement, in which the body is cut up in a thousand different ways. The object of all this lust and penetration and transformation is the female body, *naked of course*. If the phallus is the great, transcendent signifier, the naked female body is the great, immanent object, that which is signified, the site of æsthetic explorations, the ultimate pleasure machine. The female form is attacked ruthlessly in some Dada and Surrealist art. The titles of the artworks reveal much: *The Bride Stripped Bare By Her Bachelors Even, Young Virgin Auto-Sodomized By Her Own Chastity, The Rape,* and so on.

The most bizarre Surrealist artist, and the most violent without a doubt, is Hans Bellmer. His *Doll* series are deeply disturbing images of the female body which the artist delighted in wrenching into all sorts of impossible contortions. Bellmer wrote, in *The Doll*, a veritable summary of the erotic pleasure of the artist and viewer, the consumer who sucks up lasciviously the object:

---

176 Masson: *Metamorphosis of Gradiva*, 1939, oil on canvas, 38 x 51in, Paris; *There is no perfect world,* drawing, 1938
177 Brauner: *Little Morphology*, 1934, oil on canvas, 21 x 25in, collection of André-François Petit, Paris
178 Léonor Fini: *Female Nude*, 1947, charcoal on paper, whereabouts unknown; Nusch Éluard: *Photo-collage*, c. 1935, postcard, 5.4 x 3.5in, private collection

To adjust the joints to each other, coax the limbs, head and torso into winsome poses, then run the eye and hand over these softly dipping vales, relish the pleasure of the shapely curves, give them a pretty turn or with blood-rousing gusto wrench them out of shape.[179]

Hans Bellmer's *Doll* is the ultimate sex object, the ultimate fetish, a precursor of the blow-up doll of sex toys. Bellmer speaks of penetrating through layers until some core or womb is reached. His drawings and photographs are full of fingers or penises being thrust into different orifices, into mouths, vaginas, anuses. Bellmer is obsessed with penetration. He drew penises entering vaginas many times.[180] Bellmer's art is the ultimate Surrealist trans-formation, as vulvas turn into penises, and buttocks become the glans of the wiener. Bellmer's drawings depict a continuous orgy, utterly pornographic, a feast of penetration and pleasure.[181] (The multiple penetrations look forward to the art of H.R. Giger (in the film *Alien*), and the 'tits and tentacles' movies in Japanese animation).

Faces are often left out: Hans Bellmer's drawings create a frenzy of limbs and torsos, sometimes just buttocks and groins. 'All my work is erotic – it always has been', said Bellmer.[182] He is distinctly a part of that European intellectual tradition stemming from the Divine Marquis and Charles Baudelaire. In Bellmer's art, the Sadeian ethic of sex = death is exploited in endless variations. As Géza Roheim wrote, '[d]eath is coitus and coitus is death'.[183] This psychotic view, so mistaken, is central to much of modern culture, from the Marquis de Sade to Jean-Paul Sartre. Bellmer's art, and that of René Magritte, Salvador Dali, Max Ernst, André Breton, Paul Éluard and Pablo Picasso, ascribes to this view of sex = death.

Hans Bellmer depicts nothing but the sex act. He is unusual in this. Other artists produced erotic art as part of their whole art:

179 Bellmer: *The Doll*, 1934, in Picon, 153
180 See Bellmer's *A Sade*, etchings, 1961
181 Bellmer: *A Woman From the Back*, coloured pencils, 30 x 37cm, private collection; *Traite de la Morale*, 1968, etching, collection: the artist, Paris
182 quoted in Peter Webb, 369
183 G. Roheim: *Animism, Magic and the Divine King*, quoted in P. Webb

Eric Gill, David Hockney, Félicien Rops, Bill Turner, but Bellmer focuses entirely on genitals and sex. Very few artists have been so determined in their depiction of eroticism. It permeates every aspect of Bellmer's art. And it is a pornographic art. Bellmer's art, like the major erotic text of Surrealist or modern European art, Georges Bataille's *The Story of the Eye*, is pornography masquerading as erotic or high art.

5

ERIC GILL

Eric Gill (1882-1940) is one of the major erotic artists of the 20th century. For him, eroticism was a vital part of life, and should be openly displayed in art. He moved from nudes to Madonnas easily and simply: sex and religion were part of the same mystery for him. He built eroticism into most of his depictions of people. He continually drew attention to a figure's genitals. He was obsessed, for instance, by pubic hair. He was also fascinated by the penis, particularly his own.

Despite being open about sexuality, Eric Gill did keep some of his art secret. There are private drawings in the collections of the Victoria and Albert Museum and the British Museum in London, which depict, for instance, some seventy drawings of penises. The drawings are careful anatomical studies, complete with measurements. Some of the phallic drawings show Gill masturbating, or on a bed, or in a mirror. Sometimes the drawings of penises enter the critically acceptable arena, as in the prints entitled *The 'Most Precious Ornament'*.[184]

Eric Gill was meticulous in his recording of sexual activities.

184 Gill: *The 'Most Precious Ornament'*, 1937, print, Victoria & Albert Museum

310

His private writings reveal a secret code for acts such as anal intercourse. He also experimented with dogs, incest (with daughters and sisters) and group sex.[185] So many male artists have drawn, painted or sculpted their penises: Jasper Johns, Egon Schiele, Pablo Picasso, Hans Bellmer, Robert Rauschenberg, Salvador Dali, and Tom of Finland. Men love their dicks. As did the ancients: from the Cerne Giant in Dorset, with its 30-foot long dick, to ithyphallic cave paintings of the palæolithic era.

In Eric Gill's art one finds all the usual tensions of Western art: the relation between women and fertility, agriculture, nature and nurture; the constant eroticization of people, the reduction to sexual identities; and the idea that sex can instigate a social and spiritual renewal or revolution.

Eric Gill's sense of sexuality is distinctly heterosexual, as with other campaigners for sexual liberty, such as D.H. Lawrence. Like Lawrence, Gill exalted women and the idea of woman; like Lawrence, Gill secretly admired the male form: in the work of both Gill and Lawrence there is an emphasis on the phallus, the symbolic erect phallus, which meant religious rebirth, as Lawrence showed in *The Escaped Cock*, a novella of the 'phallic' man, the new Adam. Lawrence's testament of erotic revolution, *Lady Chatterley's Lover*, was admired by Gill, and Gill illustrated it, depicting Mellors and Connie making love, kneeling on grass.[186] (There is also a bisexuality, or multi-sexuality, in Gill's art – or in his life, rather, than in his art. And he also experimented with sex with animals).

Like D.H. Lawrence, Eric Gill believed in the holiness of sex and the holiness of art. Sex, art and religion were a continuum for Gill, as for Lawrence and others, such as Gustav Klimt, Michelangelo Buonarroti and Pablo Picasso. For Gill, as for so many artists, making art was a holy activity. Gill espoused the tenets of William Morris and the Arts and Crafts movement, maintaining that craftsmanship was sacred. 'The point is that human works should be holy, for holiness is properly their

185 See Fiona MacCarthy: *Eric Gill*, Faber 1989
186 Eric Gill: *Lady C*, 1931, print, 2nd state, Victoria & Albert Museum

311

criterion', wrote Gill in a late essay. The Word of God was the first creative act, Gill said, and writers such as André Gide concur with this view. Eric Gill wrote:

> What is a work of art? A word made flesh. That is the truth, in the clearest sense of the text. A word, that which emanates from the mind. Made flesh; a thing, a thing seen, a thing known, the immeasurable translated into terms of the measurable.[187]

In many images, Eric Gill depicted sex in sacred ways, either by giving his pictures of copulating couples a religious context – a title, perhaps, as in *Earth Wrestling*, or he puts the hand of God above the lovers, and rays of light emanate from the hand, blessing the sex act, as in *Earth Receiving*.[188] The image of the couple making love below the hand of God perfectly summarizes Gill's view of sex, of sex as a religious experience.

In most of his religious-erotic images, Eric Gill is wildly phallic and heterosexual. The woman is definitely 'passive' and the male is 'active'. The woman, as Earth, 'receives', while the man does the fucking. The woman gives herself, gives of herself, in Eric Gill's art, as in his series of erotic prints illustrating the most sensual poem in the *Bible*, the *Song of Songs*, where the woman offers her breasts to the man.[189] According to Marina Warner, the *Song of Songs* is immensely erotic: '[t]here has never been a more intense communication of the experience of desire.' (*Alone*, 126) Maybe: a lot of poets would disagree about that! The *Cantia Canticarum* allows for depictions of unbridled sensuality within a Christian/ religious context, however. The nuptial imagery allows for artists to be as sensual as they dare in a religious setting. Gill's merging of eroticism with Catholicism operates within the mystical tradition of Catholicism, as espoused by St Bernard, Jan van Ruysbroeck, St Theresa and St John of the Cross. It is a wild and ecstatic mysticism which describes religious bliss in very sensual terms.

187 Gill: "The Priesthood of Craftsmanship", *Blackfriars*, in Goldwater, 456-7
188 Gill: *Earth Wrestling*, 1926, engraving on copper, Victoria & Albert Museum; *Earth Receiving*, 1926, engraving on copper, 12.4 x 8.8cm, University of Texas, Austin
189 Gill: *Ibi Dabo Tibi*, 1925, Victoria & Albert Museum

In the art of Eric Gill, eroticism veers from moments of tender affection, as in *Approaching Dawn*, from an illustration of Geoffrey Chaucer's *Troilus and Creseyde*, to undiluted porn, such as in *The Chinese Maidservant*, which shows a woman bending over, revealing her buttocks. The aim of such images is to sexualize the female body, to make it available to the (male) gaze.

In other images, such as *Lot's Daughter*, Eric Gill depicts two people making love in a picture employing plain, unadorned marks,[190] as found in Taoist sex manuals,[191] or in the fucking of *Lovers in Tent* or *Lovers, the Raised Bottom*, which depicts two people making love,[192] and, as so often in erotica, focuses on the penis and vagina, as if that was all there was to sex (Andrea Dworkin writes that sex means 'penile intromission followed by penile thrusting, or fucking').[193] This is clearly the case in Eric Gill's works, where the phallus is at the centre of pleasure and power. Sex in his works means penile thrusting. The man is on top, the woman is underneath, accepting everything. Gill's art reveals the same power relations as depicted in high art, low art, porn, advertizing, TV and the media: male power is dominant, and sex revolves around the phallus.

There is no clitoris in Eric Gill's art. Similarly, D.H. Lawrence condemned those 'cocksure' women who took control and employed clitoral sex, as in his *The Plumed Serpent*. It's only the vulva. For Gill, the phallus is the 'transcendent signifier', as in the print *Eve* which shows a female nude with a snake between her legs, curling towards her groin, clearly the snake here is the penis, as so often in patriarchal art.[194]

Often, Eric Gill's ithyphallic imagery is laughable, as in his *God Sending*, which shows Jesus flying towards the Earth with an erection, his head beaming with light, God's hand behind him, in

190 Gill: *Lot's Daughter*, 1926, pencil and watercolour, 13.5 x 1.6cm, University of Texas, Austin
191 *The Leaping White Tiger*, album leaf in ink and colours on silk, Chinese K'ang-hsi period 91622-1722), C. T. Loa collection, Texas
192 Gill: *Approaching Dawn*, 1927, in *Troilus and Cresseyde*, Golden Cockerel Press; *Lovers, the Raised Bottom*, 1934, Victoria & Albert Museum
193 Dworkin: *Pornography*, 23
194 Gill: *Eve*, 1926, print, Victoria & Albert Museum

Heaven, sending Christ on his way.[195] Here is that most blasphemous of images: not only an erotic Christ, but Christ with an erection! In Gill's art it's very silly, but D.H. Lawrence was deadly serious about *his* ithyphallic Christ, when he wrote of the resurrected Saviour making love with a priestess of Isis in *The Escaped Cock*. D.H. Lawrence's novella argues for a regeneration of the world through a full 'awakening' of the body.[196] Gill proposes the same thing.

In one of Eric Gill's 'humorous' drawings, a man dressed as flower holds out his penis, which also has a flower on it.[197] The rider reads; 'the domestic hose comes out well in time of drought'. Gill means that the penis can 'water' the world in drought. The implication, as ever in Gill's art, is that the penis can rejuvenate life, that the penis is at the centre of life, that the penis helps everything to grow, to achieve itself.

What's limiting about Eric Gill's art, as about some porn, is that it emphasizes the genitals, leaving so much out (but that is of course one of porn's strengths too). It's the same with Gill's sculptures – his acrobats, for example, are women holding their legs wide open, exposing their vulvas.[198] Indeed, the very reason that Gill turned to sculpture, so he says, was sexual: his wife was pregnant with their third daughter, Joanna, and because of the 'enforced abstinence', i.e., no sex during pregnancy, Gill turned to stone carving.

Some of Eric Gill's best works are sculptures: in *Divine Lovers* he produced an image of two people clasping each other in an embrace of complete closeness. There is no space between the lovers: Constantin Brancusi had done the same thing in his *Kiss* sculptures, which flattened the two bodies so they could be merged together completely. Brancusi recognized the anatomical problem, saying that kissing upright is difficult, because of the nose. His lovers are noseless: they simply kiss, eternally joined

195 Gill: *God Sending*, 1926, engraving on copper, Victoria & Albert Museum
196 D.H. Lawrence: *The Complete Short Novels*, Penguin 1982. 596
197 Gill: *The Domestic Hose*, 1929, woodcut, Victoria & Albert Museum
198 Gill: *Splits II*, 1923, bath stone with added colour, Harry Ransom Humanities Research Center, University of Texas, Austin

together, veritably an expression in stone of the Platonic concept of two-as-one, of twin souls joined as one.[199]

It seems, then, that there is nothing blasphemous about Eric Gill's art, no matter how erotic it seems. All he does is juxtapose sex and religion in a way that people have been doing for millennia. What's astonishing is that anybody nowadays thinks Eric Gill's erotic art is shocking. For Gill clearly creates establishment art that only mildly questions patriarchal notions of the erotic and the mystical. Besides, Gill's fusion of the mystic and the erotic is sanctioned in high or intellectual art – in artists such as Hans Bellmer, Georges Bataille, the Marquis de Sade, Charles Baudelaire, Henry Miller, Egon Schiele, etc.

199 Constantin Brancusi: *The Kiss*, 1907-8, stone, 11in high, Museum of Art, Craiova, Romania. See also Eric Shanes: *Brancusi*, 19f

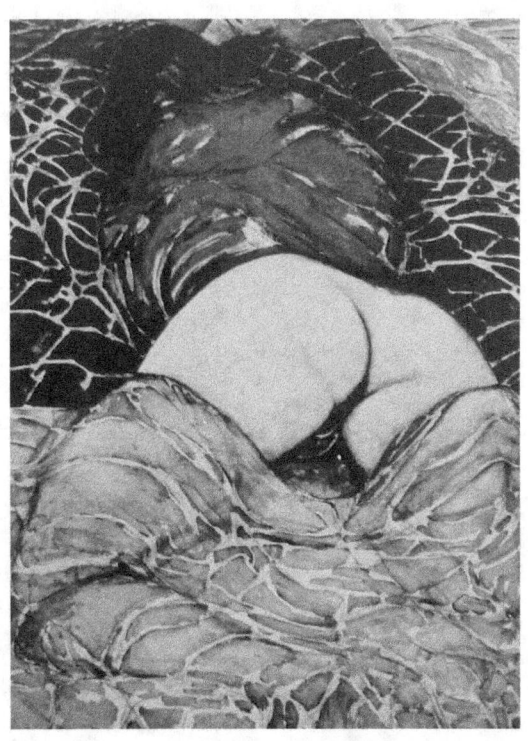

Arturo Carmassi, above,
Cesare Peverelli, Italy, below

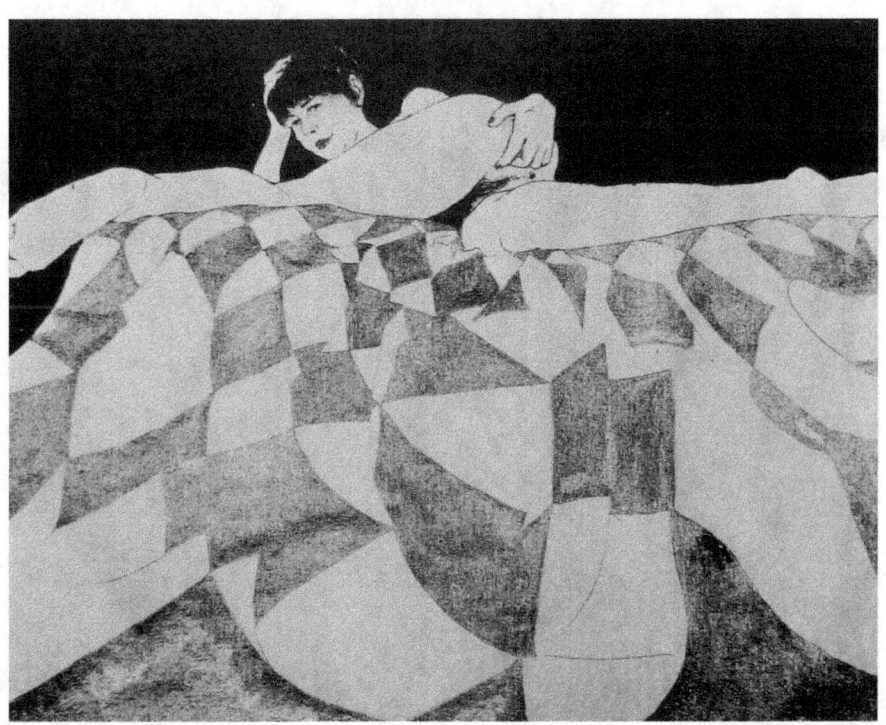

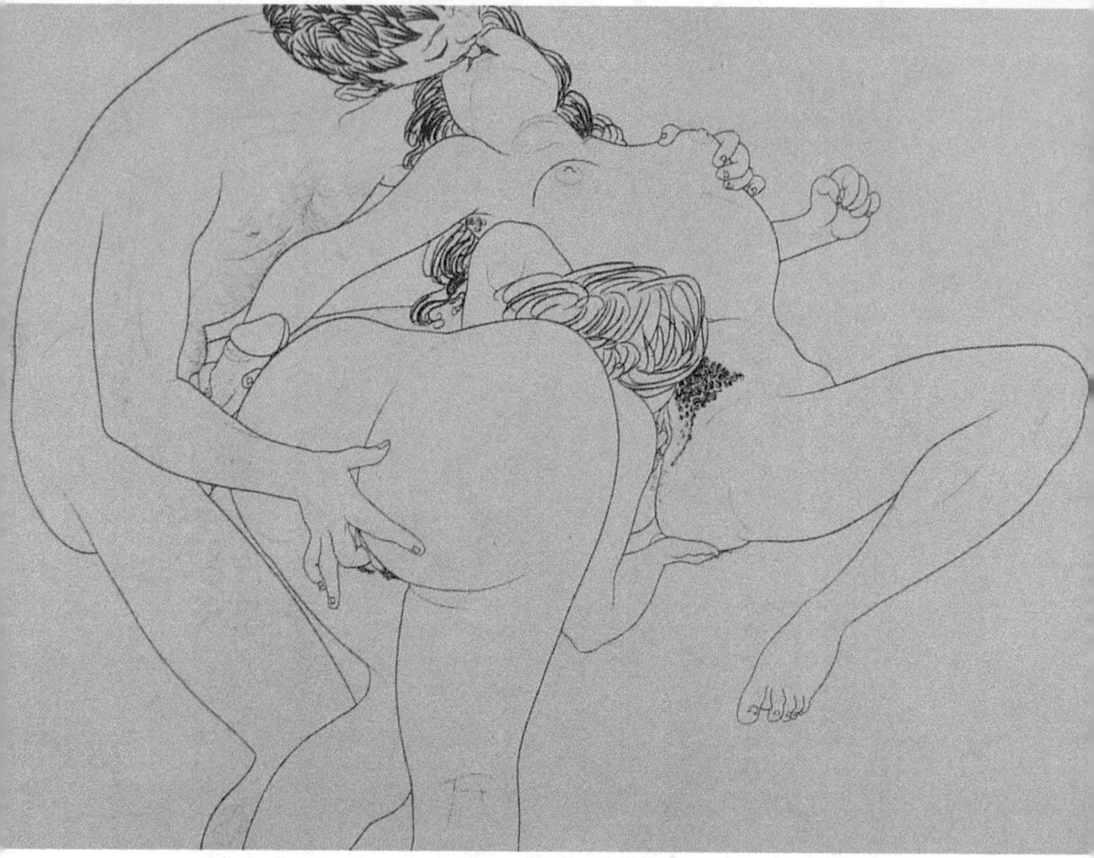

Mario Tauzin (French), above. Robert Stanley (American), below.

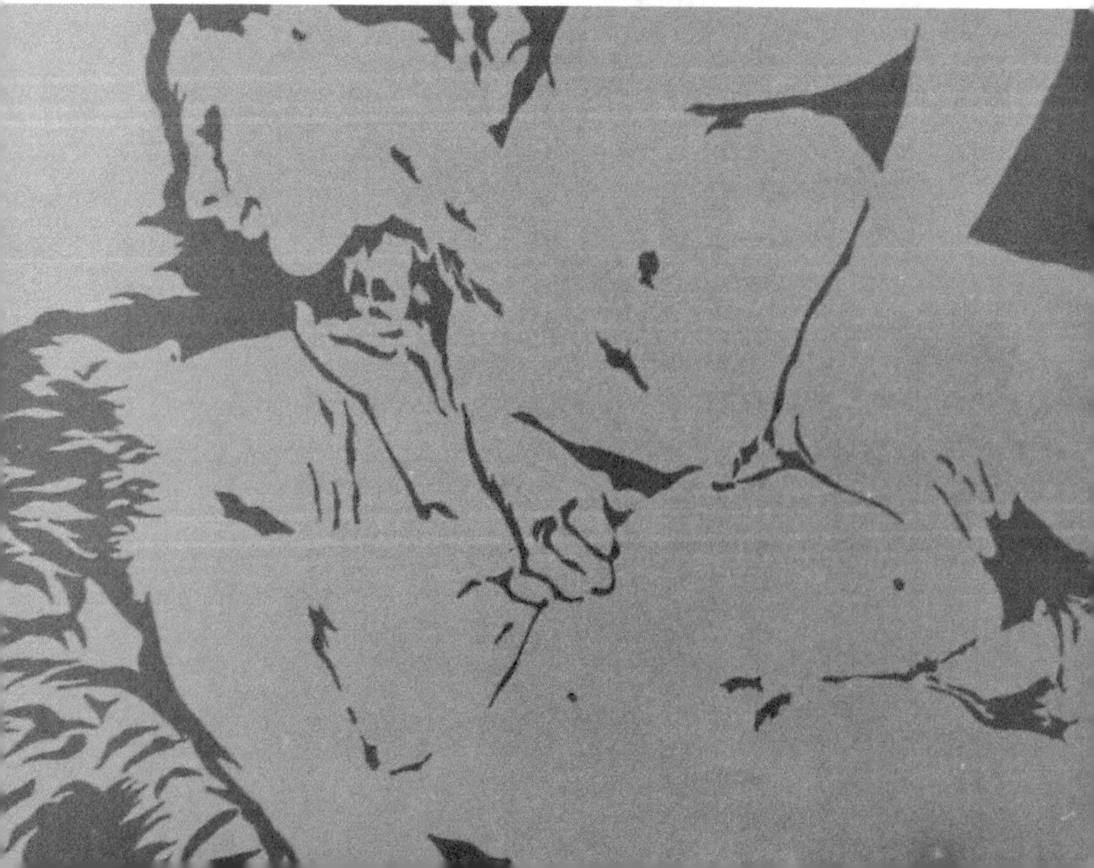

Part Four

CONTEMPORARY ART

JASPER JOHNS

1

THE SEXUALITY OF SURFACES

JASPER JOHNS

I think that one wants from a painting a sense of life. The final suggestion, the final statement, has to be not a deliberate statement but a helpless statement. It has to be what you can't avoid saying.

Jasper Johns[1]

The problem is not doing something, the problem is knowing what one wants to do.

Jasper Johns[2]

An American artist who is probably the most erotic of all contemporary artists in his manipulation of paint and texture and surface is Jasper Johns (b. 1930). Johns does not depict naked women or the usual trappings of erotic art. In fact, there are no

---

1 Johns, quoted in David Sylvester: "Interview", *Jasper Johns Drawings,* Museum of Modern Art, Oxford 1974, 14
2 Johns, quoted in Daniel Wheeler, 139

naked women or men in his art. Bits of bodies, yes – a handprint, the cast of a leg, masks, critics' mouths – but not the usual sex objects of Western art. (However Johns did make an image of his own 'genitalia and buttocks' in *Skin I* and *Skin II*.)[3]

Instead, the eroticism of Jasper Johns' works comes from his incredible surfaces, which are made of oil and wax or encaustic, spread thickly on the canvas. Paintings such as *White Flag, Highway, Canvas* and *Scent* are really exquisite works, so intensely tactile and sumptuous.[4] Johns' drawings with ink are just as luscious – ink on plastic, so the colours swirl and merge into each other.[5]

The sensuality of surfaces, of textures, of brushwork, of the artist's sense of touch, is crucial to the greatness of art, as Lynda Nead writes: 'the artist's subjectivity that is registered by the brushwork and surface is sexualized. Art criticism writes sex into descriptions of paint, surface and forms.' (58) Paul Gauguin wrote of the sensual primacy of painting in the familiar terms of late 19th century 'theory of correspondences', which was used by many poets, painters and dramatists:

> Painting is the most beautiful of all arts. In it, all sensations are condensed... A complete art which sums up all the others and completes them. – Like music, it acts on the soul through the intermediary senses: harmonious colours correspond to the harmonies of sounds.[6]

Frank Stella wrote of the space a painting creates, and how this space can envelop the viewer, sensually:

3 Johns: *Skin I,* 1973, charcoal on paper, 25.5 x 40.25in, collection: the artist; *Skin II,* 1973, charcoal on paper, 25.5 x 40.25in, collection: the artist. See Rosenthal, 18
4 *White Flag,* 1955, encaustic and collage on canvas, 199 x 307cm, Collection: the artist; *Highway,* 1959, encaustic and collage on canvas, 190.5 x 154.9cm, Collection: Mrs Leo Castelli, New York; *Scent,* 1973-4, oil and encaustic on canvas, 182.9 x 320.6cm, collection: Ludwig Aachen; *Canvas,* 1956, encaustic and collage on canvas with objects, 76.2 x 63.5cm, Collection: the artist. See Robert Bernstein: *Jasper Johns' Paintings and Sculptures 1954-1974,* Ann Arbor, Michigan 1985, Richard Francis: *Jasper Johns,* New York 1984, Max Kozloff: *Jasper Johns,* New York 1969
5 Johns: *Untitled,* 1983, ink on plastic, 24.8 x 36.2in, Museum of Modern Art, New York; *Perilous Night,* 1982, ink on plastic, 31.6 x 40.8in, collection: the artist; *Untitled,* 1983-4, ink on plastic, 26.2 x 34.5in, collection: the artist
6 Gauguin: "Notes Synthetiques", in *Paul Gauguin: A Sketchbook,* tr. Raymond Cogniat, Hammer Galleries, New York 1962, 57f

An effective painting should present its space in such a way as to include both viewer and maker each with his own space intact. It is not that this experience should be literal; it is simply that the sense of space projected by the painting should seem expansive: expansive enough to include the viewing and the creation of that space. (*Working Space*, 9)

Other artists have spoken lovingly of the loving nature of the canvas itself, the beauty of the art object. Maurice Denis wrote: '[t]he emotion – bitter or sweet, "literary" as the painters say – emerges from the canvas itself, a plane surface covered with colours.'[7]

A sense of space is crucial for Jasper Johns. 'As well as I can tell,' he says, 'I am concerned with space. With some idea about space. And then as soon as you break space, then you have things.[8]

Jasper Johns works very closely with his paintings, becoming absorbed totally in the surfaces, as a critic wrote:

when he is working, Jasper is totally concentrated on those surfaces. He lives in those surfaces. The surfaces are his whole world, they are everything. He loses himself in them. They are everything.'[9]

Jasper Johns' tactile surfaces are built up using wax – the thick impasto of oil and wax is one of the keys to his textures, because when the wax cools, one can paint on top of it very soon, instead of waiting for the paint to dry.[10] Johns used encaustic and oil because he wanted evidence of the gestures he made *before* and *after*, that is, a finished painting which would reveal its making. He said:

It was very simple. I wanted to show what had gone before in a picture, and what was done after. But if you put on a heavy brushstroke in paint, and then add another stroke, the second smears

7 Maurice Denis: "Definitions of neotraditionism", 1890, in *Théories: 1890-1910*, Rouart et Watelin, Paris 1920, 5f
8 quoted in Peter Fuller: 'Jasper Johns Interviewed", *Art Monthly*, no 18, July 1978, 12
9 quoted in Michael Crichton: *Jasper Johns*, 21

10 Johns, quoted in Crichton, 28

the first under the paint unless the paint is dry. And paint takes too long to dry. I didn't know what to do. Then someone suggested wax. It worked very well, as soon as the wax was cool I could put on another stroke, and it would not alter the first.[11]

These are the seemingly simple and obvious techniques and stratagems that concern artists, this dealing with such simple but important processes such as drying paint. Artists are, typically, humble, and Johns here says it 'was very simple', yet it is also crucial.

Marcel Duchamp and Kurt Schwitters are usually cited as precursors of Jasper Johns' mixed media explorations. Robert Rauschenberg and Johns rewrote the notion of painting-as-object by sticking objects onto it. Kurt Schwitters is often cited as a major exponent of multi-media formalism. Schwitters explained how he came to do it:

> I simply could not see any reason why old streetcar tickets, driftwood, coat checks, wire and wheel parts, buttons, junk from the attic and heaps of refuse should not be used as material for paintings, any less than colours made in a factory.[12]

Jasper Johns was concerned with doing something different from other artists. He is a 'radical conservative', quite self-consciously reactionary. As he said:

> I had a feeling that I could do anything... But if I could do anything I wanted to do, then what I wanted to do was find out what I did that other people didn't, what I was that other people weren't... It was not a matter of joining a group effort, but of isolating myself from any group.[13]

The Johnsian motifs – the targets, flags, numbers, maps – are merely patterns or shapes which free the artist to explore other things. He is not interested in maps or flags or ale cans or numbers but in plasticity, surface, colour, texture, form and other

11 Johns, quoted in Daniel Wheeler, 134-5
12 Schwitters, quoted in Roh, 133
13 Johns, quoted in Wheeler, 143

painterly concerns. As Johns says:

> Take an object
> Do something to it
> Do something else to it
> " " " " "₁₄

The motifs take care of certain elements in a work, so that the artist is free to look at other aspects. The aim is to create 'things which are seen and not looked at', Jasper said, and explained further:

> Using the design of the American flag took care of a great deal for me because I didn't have to design it. So I went on to similar things like the targets – things the mind already knows. That gave me room to work on other levels.₁₅

The flags and targets are disarmingly simple forms, a formal reductionism that allows æsthetic expansion in other areas. As the critic Max Kozloff wrote, the flags and targets were

> merely so many abstract forms upon which social usage has conferred meaning, but which now, displaced into their new context, cease to function socially. From this tremendous insight alone have sprung the momentum of Pop Art and the huge quantities of abstraction that is emblematic in character.₁₆

Jasper Johns' famous American *Flag* is a complex work that opens up the way into Pop Art. *Flag* can be read in a number of ways, which seemingly conflict with each other. Johns explores the notions and relations between presentation and representation, between image and actuality, between iconography and abstraction. Johns' *Flag* is at once a banal icon (though for the America of the 1950s, feelings of US nationalism, embodied in the American Stars and Stripes, were running high, as they still are),

---

14 Jasper Johns: "Sketchbook Notes", in *Art and Literature*, 4, Lausanne, Spring 1965, 192
15 in Leo Steinberg: "Jasper Johns: The First Seven Years of His Art", in *Other Criteria: Confrontations with Twentieth-Century Art*, Oxford University Press, New York 1972, 31
16 Max Kozloff: "Pop Culture, Metaphysical Designs and the New Vulgarians", *Art International*, March 1962, 34-6

and a complex piece of formal abstraction. With Johns' *Flag*, everyday signs and images, taken for granted, are treated with a grandeur of style and technique formerly employed by the great painters, the Old Masters. Johns uses the gestures of Abstract Expressionism, which aspire for grandeur and monumentality in painting, and gives them an ironic, self-reflexive twist. Johns produced a new sense of space which the art object inhabits. Rosalind Krauss writes:

> Johns's *Targets* or *Ale Cans*, in negating the internality of the abstract-expresionist picture, simultaneously rejects the innerness of its space and the privacy of the self for which that space was a model. His was a rejection of an ideal space that exists prior to experience, waiting to be filled, and of a psychological model in which a self exits replete with its meanings prior to contact with its world. (259)

The key to Jasper Johns' reworking of formalism and abstraction in the flags, targets, numbers and alphabets was precisely the sensuality of his art. It was the way he so powerfully employed the techniques of the Old Masters, of great art, that made his flags and targets so successful. For critics could not see Johns' banal signs culled from popular culture as trivial art, because Johns used one of the key elements in high art, the sensual, heavily impastoed surface. Johns' art could not be dismissed by critics, then as now, because its surface is as sensual and painterly as Rembrandt van Rijn, Diego Velásquez, Édouard Manet or Titian. In *Working Space*, Frank Stella discussed Michelangelo Mersisi de Caravaggio's art, but he could just as well be speaking of Jasper Johns:

> The second miracle of Caravaggio is the miracle of surface. Skin, flesh, and pigment blend into reality. Painting is acknowledged as an act and as a physical fact, but immediately afterward, almost simultaneously, the presence of the human figure is felt as real, touchably there. (1)

Paintings such as *White Flag* ('the most blatantly sensuous

canvas Johns has ever produced' writes Michael Crichton[17]) or
Good Time Charley,[18] are full of an erotic pleasure in surface, a
feeling for touch that surpasses that of any other contemporary
artist. The later works are full of sensual pleasures.[19] Pieces such
as *Book*, a real book covered in a thick layer of wax and oil, are
positively voluptuous in their haptic sensibility.[20] When Jasper
Johns folds or mixes in bits of newspaper or stencils or various
objects – such as rulers, wires, frames, cups or casts – the result is
even more extraordinary. Works such as *Untitled* mesh a number
of panels with sticks of wood and other objects which are stuck
directly on top of the canvas.[21] As with Robert Rauschenberg,
these stuck-on objects set alight the painting. Jasper explains why
he uses 'real objects' stuck onto his paintings:

> My thinking is perhaps dependent on a realization of a thing as being
> the real thing... I like what I see to be real, or to be my idea of what is
> real. And I think I have a kind of resentment against illusion when I
> can recognize it. Also, a large part of my work has been involved
> with the painting as object, as real thing in itself. And in the face of
> that 'tragedy,' so far, my general development... has moved in the
> direction of using real things as painting. That is to say I find it more
> interesting to use a real fork as painting than it is to use painting as a
> real fork.[22]

Much of Jasper Johns' art explores æsthetic issues in a
seemingly naïve manner. As Johns talks about using oil and wax
because it dries quickly, so he explored colour and the relation of
colours to their names. He was interested in the *idea* of colour, of
colour as a means of communication, and how it is conditioned by
cultural factors. In *False Start*, Johns painted splodges of yellow
and stencilled the word WHITE over it.[23] He stencilled ORANGE in

17 Michael Crichton: *Jasper Johns*, 31
18 *Good Time Charley*, 1961, encaustic on canvas with objects, 96.5 x 61cm, Collection: the artist
19 Johns: *Dancers on a Plane*, 1979, oil on canvas with objects, 78 x 64in, private collection, New York
20 *Book*, 1957, encaustic with objects, 25.4 x 33cm, private collection, New York
21 *Untitled*, 1972, oil, encaustic and collage on canvas with objects, 183 x 487.7cm, Museum Ludwig, Cologne
22 quoted in David Sylvester, op. cit 15-16
23 Johns: *False Start*, 1959, oil on canvas, 5.6 x 4.4ft, collection: S.I. Newhouse, Jr., New York

white letters over a patch of bright red. His aim, he said was to find other ways of using colour:

> The flags and targets have colors positioned in a predetermined way. I wanted to find a way to apply color so that the color would be determined by some other method.[24]

The result is a painting that aims to go beyond visual pleasure, to become an ironic comment on perception and conceptualization.[25] Jasper creates, as critic Barbara Rose notes, a metaphysics of art, which does not separate art from life, or æsthetics from experience.

Jasper Johns' late works excite critics such as Robert Rosenblum, who was greatly impressed with Johns' series of paintings, *The Seasons*.[26] Rosenblum writes of Johns' paintings:

> The Johns' paintings, the quartet of the cycle of the four seasons are just heart-breakingly intimate tragic comments on the passing of time, nature, personal biography and so on. As such they really seem to extend the great tradition of the history of Western art, in particular of romantic identity with nature... They [the paintings] seem to be personal projections of his own life viewed against the passing seasons. That's a traditional theme, God knows, in Western art. The pictures not only have that universal aspect of going from spring to winter but also all kinds of cryptic as well as decipherable references to his own art, biography, and past. They're very meditative, they're like the works of some late great poet who is contemplating his life, his career, his future against the aspect of eternity. They really are very directly moving in the grand old tradition...

There are works where Jasper consciously addresses erotic issues, such as in the *Skin* drawings, mentioned above, where he takes an image of his own genitals. In his famous *Target with*

---

24 Johns, quoted in Wheeler, 136
23 See Barbara Rose: "Decoys and Doubles: Jasper Johns and the Modernist Mind", *Arts*, May 1976, 68-73; "Jasper Johns: Pictures and Concepts", *Arts*, November 1977, 148-153.
26 Johns: *Spring, Summer, Autumn, Winter*, 1985-6, each encaustic on canvas, 75 x 50in, collection: S.I. Newhouse, New York; collection: Philip Johnson; collection: the artist; collection: Asher B. Edelman and Mildred Ash. See John Russell: "The Seasons: Forceful Paintings from Jasper Johns", *New York Times*, 6 February 1987; Barbara Rose: "Jasper Johns – The Seasons", *Vogue*, January 1987, 192f; Judith Goldman: *Jasper Johns: The Seasons*, Leo Castelli Gallery, New York

Plaster Casts of 1955,[27] Johns placed under the little trapdoors parts of the human (male) body including, of course, the penis. The *Painting with Two Balls* of 1960 is just that: a canvas split across its width with two balls stuck in the crack.[28] In a later piece, the *Tantric Detail* drawing of 1980, Johns placed a pair of testicles in the same place as the two balls in the 1960 *Painting*. There is an undercurrent of homoeroticism in Johns' art which critics have only rarely addressed fully (Johns is homosexual, and lived with Robert Rauschenberg in the Fifties).[29]

Later works of Jasper Johns' playfully stuck on genitals to paintings, such as the 1980 *Dancers on a Plane*.[30] Johns said he was influenced by 'Tantric paintings in which Shiva and Shakti copulate, representing the interpenetration of destructive and creative forces.'[31] One might see Johns' 'crosshatch' paintings, with their energetic, mobile and very painterly marks as a form of a cosmic, religious dance. Dancing itself is course profoundly erotic. As the glib Frank Sinatra puts it, 'what is dancing but making love set to music?'

Jasper can be as stunning and erotic in his pencil drawings and lithographs as in his painting.[32] Few contemporary works of art are as thrilling as those densely-shaded sketches, where the crosshatching is thick and makes deep black squares and rectangles, as in *Coat Hanger*, *Flag* and *Device Circle*.[33] These deeply dark squares and shapes are exquisite – their total presence is simultaneously religious and erotic. They recall the

27 Johns: *Target with Plaster Casts*, 1955, encaustic & collage on canvas with objects, 51 Finlain, collection: Leo Castelli, New York
28 Johns: *Painting with Two Balls*, 1960, encaustic and collage on canvas with objects, 65 x 54in, collection: the artist
29 See James Cuno: "Jasper Johns", *Print Quarterly*, vol. 4 no. 1, March 1987, 92; Roni Feinstein: "New Thoughts for Jasper Johns' Sculpture", *Arts Magazine*, vol. 54, no. 8, April 1980, 139-143; Rosenthal, 48f
30 Johns: *Dancers on a Plane*, 1980, oil on canvas with painted bronze frame and objects, 200 x 162cm, Tate Gallery, London
31 Johns in 1987, quoted in Mark Rosenthal, 44
32 See Riva Castleman: *Jasper Johns: A Print Retrospective*, Little, Brown, New York 1986; Richard Field: *Jasper Johns: Prints 1960-1970*, Praeger 1970; Christian Geelhaar: *Jasper Johns: Working Proofs*, Peterborough 1980; Schapiro: *Jasper Johns, Drawings*, Abrams, New York 1984; Judith Goldman: *Jasper Johns: Prints 1977-1981*, Thomas Segal Gallery, Boston
33 *Coat Hanger I*, 1960, lithograph, 91.4 x 67.9cm, edition of 35, Universal Limited Art Editions; *Flag*, 1957, pencil on paper, 27.6 x 38.9cm, collection: the artist; *Devive Circle*, 1960, pencil on paper, 38 x 37cm, Collection: Ronald S. Lauder.

magic squares of Robert Fludd, the 17th century alchemist, such as the small black square, a mass of lines and crosshatching which has *Et sic infinitum* written along each of the four sides. Fludd's magic square is an alchemical statement on the original chaos before life began, but it is also a beautiful object, that drawing, whose impact stems from a tactile presence and sense of pleasure.[34] It is the same with other alchemical texts which depict primal chaos, as in the entropy image of Coenders van Helpen.[35]

These alchemical visions of primal matter, the *nigredo* or blackness of the *opus alchymicum*, are clearly related to womb imagery, to the great cosmic darkness of the Goddess as Great Mother, the *regressus ad uterum* which is a primal desire in Jungian psychology, to get back to the womb.[36] These black magic squares are seen now by critics as forerunners of modern abstraction – as precursors of Kasimir Malevich's red and black squares, or the five foot black squares of Ad Reinhardt and other Abstract Expressionists.[37]

The whole of Jasper Johns' work can be viewed as sculpture, as an exploration of the relation between real objects and their representation, an exploration of the links between imagination, fantasy, memory, image, representation and perception. The late works quote from earlier works, in complex ways. In a number of late works, Johns places a plaster cast of an arm, his arm, the artist's arm, reaching for the artist's tools, perhaps.[38] The arm – the hand especially – connotes the creative ability of the artist, the human touch, the creative Hand of God, in effect, which, as it reaches down from the top of Johns' mixed media paintings, is clearly a controlling force. Yet, at the same time, the arm is

---

34 Robert Fludd: *Utriusque cosmi maioris scilicet et minoris metaphysica, physica atque technica historia*, Oppenheim 1617, I, 26
35 Coenders van Helpen, Barent: *Trésor de la philosophie des ancients*, Cologne 1693, 29
36 See Johannes Fabricus: *Alchemy: The Medieval Alchemists and Their Royal Art*, Aquarian Press, 1989, 98f
37 See Hugh Cumming: "Abstract Painting and the Spiritual" and "The Spiritual in Art: Abstract Painting: Charles Jencks interviews Maurice Tuchman", in A.C. Papadakis, ed. *Abstract Art and the Rediscovery of the Spiritual*, 19f, 42
38 Johns: *In the Studio*, 1982, encaustic and collage on canvas with objects, 72 x 48in, collection: the artist; *Perilous Night*, 1982, encaustic on canvas with objects x 5in, collection: Robert & Jane Meyerhoff, Phoenix, Maryland; *Untitled*, 1983, encaustic and collage on canvas with objects, 48.2 x 75.2in, collection: S.I. Newhouse, Jr., New York

dismembered, fragmented, a sign pointing towards a reality of creativity and humanity that is elsewhere.

The late works of Jasper Johns that quote earlier works explore the relation between personal history and art history, between notions of an artistic career and its representation, between the poetics of memory and the memory of poetics, art as mnemonic poetry.[39]

Jasper Johns' bronze 'sculptures', echoing the work of Marcel Duchamp, Kurt Schwitters and Max Ernst, re-present real objects – ale cans, lightbulbs, shoes.[40] Whatever the æsthetics of the 'sculptures' – with their complex explorations of the relations between reality, image, form and space – they are sumptuous objects. Johns' bronze sculptures are even more exciting, in terms of texture and touch, than his paintings: his bronze *Flag* is crushingly beautiful, as juicy a work of art as was ever produced by anybody anywhere.[41]

---

39 Johns: *Racing Thoughts*, 1983, encaustic & collage on canvas, 48 x 75.2in, Whitney Museum of American Art, New York; *Ventriloquist*, 1983, encaustic on canvas, 75 x 50in, Museum of Fine Arts, Houston
40 Johns: *Ale Cans*, 1964, painted bronze, 3 x 6 x 2in, Leo Castelli Gallery, New York; *English Lightbulb*, 1968-70, metal, wire, polyvinylchloride, 5 x 3in, Leon Castelli Gallery, New York; *High School Days*, 1964, 12in, collection: the artist
41 *Flag*, 1960, bronze, 31.1 x 47.6cm, collection: the artist

2

THE SENSUALITY OF SURFACE AND ABSTRACTION IN CONTEMPORARY ART

There are many other contemporary artists who have developed an acute sense of surface and texture, among the more successful are painters such as Christopher Le Brun, Anselm Keifer, Thérèse Oulton, Lance Smith, Hughie O'Donoghue, R. B. Kitaj, Jim Dine and Richard Diebenkorn. Among contemporary artists, however, Jasper Johns seems to be the king of surface. He can handle any medium. It seems he can apply anything to his works and remain dazzling. Very few artists are as sexy in their use of materials.

FRANK STELLA. One thinks of Frank Stella (b. 1936), who since the 1970s and his *Indian Birds* series has been building his paintings out from the wall, so that they become deliriously three-dimensional, though Stella claims they remain 'paintings', not sculptures. Stella's new works are as exuberant and as colourful as art can be. They are so startling in their sheer pleasure and enthusiasm that some people must be put off by them, observing them with suspicion. Works such as *Thruxton 3X* are explosions of light, colour, texture, shape, pattern, volume, space and multi-media extravagance.[42] Pieces like *Diavolozoppo* (1984) are constructed out of as many materials as the painter can get his hands on.[43] *The Try Works* employs huge slabs of aluminium pressed into elaborate French curves, layered over each other, painted in wild red, blues and pinks.[44] Works of joy – with no angst, no suffering, no grappling with big issues – just the beauty of beauty.

Paint has been laid on thickly for a long time – think of J.M.W. Turner's late oils, or Vincent van Gogh in canvases such as the famous *Wheatfield with Crows* or *The Starry Night*.[45] Certainly van Gogh's painterly surfaces, like those of, say, Henri Matisse or Pierre Bonnard, are very erotic, with their feverish brushmarks laid on top of each other. Perhaps the eroticism of van Gogh's paintings plays a part in the fact that his works command higher prices than any other artist: $53.9 million for *Irises*, and 82.5 million dollars for *Portrait of Dr. Gachet*.[46]

But Frank Stella's massive mixed media structures are truly wild, wild, wild, like raptures of paint, metal, fibreglass, ink and crayon. No one can deny that Stella has very decisively and joyfully exploded the traditional easel kind of painting, where everything sits neatly within a box-like frame, on a flat, illusionistic surface. Stella's later works systematically demolish the traditional, academic notion of painting as a rectangle of illusion. For there is no illusion in Stella's works: they are not depicting anything other than themselves, with their squiggles

42 Frank Stella: *Thruxton 3X*, 1982, mixed media on etched aluminium, 75 x 85 x 15 in, Shindler Collection, Honolulu
43 Frank Stella: *Diavolozoppo*, 1984, oil, urethane enamel, fluorescent alkyd, acrylic, and printing ink on canvas, etched magnesium, aluminium and fibreglass, 139 x 170 x 16in, collection: the artist
44 Stella: *The Try Works (B-6, 2X)*, 1988, mixed media on cast aluminium, 281.3 x 235 private collection
45 Vincent van Gogh: *Wheatfield with Crows*, July 1890, oil on canvas, 50.5 x 103cm, Rijksmuseum Vincent van Gogh, Amsterdam
46 See Suzanne Muchnic: "N.Y. Art Auction Scene: A Still Life", *Los Angeles Times*, 17 November 1990, F1, 11

and zigzags patterns, their fluorescent pinks and lurid greens, their splotches and dabs and overpainting. Stella says:

> My painting is based on the fact that only what can be seen there *is* there. It really is an object... All I want anyone to get out of my paintings, and all I ever get out of them, is the fact that you see the whole idea without any confusion... What you see is what you see.[47]

Frank Stella dislikes the flatness of modern painting, and of abstraction in particular: the smooth flatness of Barnett Newman or Jules Olitski or Morris Louis. Much as he admires other abstract painters, Stella aims to move beyond them by destroying the solemnity of the flatness of modern painting. He writes in *Working Space*, his major artistic credo:

> The result of modern painting's restrictive view of flatness has been a negative reaction to the yielding surface of painting. Painting today is trying to be deliberately messy in order to deny the fragility and limits of the surfaces available to art. (51)

Many contemporary painters are self-consciously messy – for example John Walker, Michael Porter, Amat, K.H. Hödicke, Enzo Cucchi and Francis Bacon. Freudians have things to say about artists who are deliberately messy – for them it all goes back to anal psychology, toilet training and constipation. Aesthetically, the explosion into chaos and mess helps to renew the connection, as Frank Stella says, with the eroticism of texture, with the sexuality of texture and the sensuality of surface, which has always been a large part of art. For instance, Greek sculpture: the smoothness of the marble and stone is crucial to the overall experience of the statue. Similarly with Italian Renaissance painting, with all its punched and embossed gold, which provides the spaceless, divine background to Jesus and the Virgin in so

---

47 Stella, radio broadcast, 1964, in Gregory Battock, ed., 158. See Robert Rosenblum: *Frank Stella*, Penguin 1971, William S. Rubin: *Frank Stella*, New York Graphic Society, Greenwich, Conn., 1970, ff: "Frank Stella: Portrait of the Artist as an Image Administrator", *Art in America*, Feb 1985, 94-107, Frank Stella and the Simulacrum", *Flash Art*, Feb-March 1986, 32-5,

many altarpieces and panels.

It is this sexuality of surface that artforms such as photography and digital art lacks. Graphic art and illustration, too, like advertizing, are too clean, too slick and polished. Digital art, Photoshop art, computer art, like Superrealism, is clinical and artificial. And computers and cell phones and TV screens still cannot reproduce the gloriously sensual surfaces and textures of painting and sculpture. Digital art is too clean, too slick, which suits advertizing – which aims to create a world of lies and delusions. Advertizing promises a world swept clean of complication and mess, and the world certainly is complicated and messy. Contemporary painting, then, counters this false purity in late consumer capitalism and digital art by loading its canvases with thick paint and impasto marks, and with all manner of materials, from plants to metal to wood to paper. As with Stella's riotously colourful paintings/ reliefs/ objects, much of contemporary painting moves towards the condition of sculpture.

ROBERT RYMAN. Other artists who have explored the sensuality of surfaces include Robert Ryman (b. 1930), with his really sumptuous white squares. As Ad Reinhardt painted black-on-black squares, so Ryman explores the mysticality of white-on-white, as Kasimir Malevich had done.[48] Paintings such Untitled, a small painting by contemporary standards (53.5 inches square), or the very small Untitled of 1961 (12 inches square), display a sense of the tactile to rival Jasper Johns. Ryman's art, like Jasper Johns', is founded on the sensuality of paint, of surfaces, of the eroticism of texture. We come back to this again and again in art criticism, this sensualism of surface. As Lynda Nead writes of Kenneth Clark: 'Clark reads brush marks and lines as though they are part of a symbolic language of sensual impulses, telling traces of sexual desire.'[49]

---

48 Ryman: Department, 1981, oil on aluminium, 60 x 60in, collection: Rhona J. Hoffman, Chicago. See Carlo Huber: Robert Ryman, Kunsthalle, Basel; Nancy Grimes: "Robert Ryman's White Magic", Art News, Summer 1968, 86-92; Carter Ratcliff: "Robert Ryman Making Distinctions", Art in America, June 1986, 92-97
49 Lynda Nead: "Getting down to basics: art, obscenity and the female nude", in Isobel Armstrong, ed., 206

By limiting himself to white, Robert Ryman frees himself up for an exploration of different media, for he paints in white on many kinds of material: canvas, linen, cotton, wood, paper, steel, copper, aluminium, mylar, fibreglass, Plexiglass, cardboard, etc, and with different sorts of media: oil, baked enamel, paper, vinyl acetate emulsion, etc. As Ryman says, typically of so many contemporary artists: '[t]here is never a question of what to paint, but only how to paint'.[50]

There are a host of post-painterly abstract artists who make the sensuality of surface primary in their works: Brice Marden, for instance, with his post-Johnsian oil and wax panels; Jean Dubuffet and Antoni Tapiès love to crowd their surfaces with mixtures of materials;[51] Anselm Keifer sticks bits of straw onto his oil paintings.[52] There are any number of contemporary painters for whom touch and surface are crucial: Julian Schnabel, Anselm Keifer, Thérèse Oulton, Gillian Ayres and Jennifer Bartlett.

There are many artists who use multiple panels or 3-D paintings that more than rival Frank Stella's recent 'maximalist' 'paintings': Elizabeth Murray, for instance, produced marvellous shaped panels.[53] Sam Gillam creates complexly shaped paintings which, like Stella's constructs, gleefully smash the primacy of the traditional rectangle in painting;[54] Jennifer Bartlett has explored the dynamics of perception and space using multiple panels and rainbow-curved canvases;[55] Robert Mangold explores colour and

---

50 In D. Wheeler, 207.

51 Antoni Tàpies: *Great Painting*, 1958, oil and sand on canvas, 6"6' x 8'7', Guggenheim Museum, New York; Dubuffet: *Run Grass, Jump Pebbles*, 1956, oil on canvas (assemblage), 6'8" x 5'1", private collection, Paris

52 Anselm Keifer: *Margarethe*, 1981, oil and straw on canvas, 9'2" x 12'6", Saatchi Collection, London; *Nürnberg–Festspiel–Weise*, 1981, oil, straw, mixed media on canvas, 9'2" x 12'6", collection; Eli & Edythe L. Broad, Los Angeles; *Wayland's Song (With Wing)*, 1982, oil, emulsion, straw on photo, on canvas with lead.

53 Elizabeth Murray: *Simple Meaning*, 1982, oil on two canvases, 107 x 96in, collection: Jerry & Emily Spiegel, New York; *Fire Cup*, 1982, oil on canvas, each canvas 92 x 82in, Paula Cooper Gallery, New York. See Paul Gardner: "Elizabeth Murray Shapes Up", *Ârt News*, Sept 1984, 47-55; Roberta Smith: *Elizabeth Murray*, Dallas Museum of Art 1987

54 Sam Gillam: *Like Today*, 1985, acrylic on canvas with aluminium construction, 55 x 67 x 4in, Monique Knowlton Gallery, New York

55 Jennifer Bartlett: *Horizon*, 1979, enamel, silkscreen and baked enamel on steel plates, oil on canvas, 20 plates, 1 canvas, 48 x 250in, collection: Martin Sklar, New York. See John Russell: *In the Garden*, Abrams, New York 1982; M. Goldwater et al: *Jennifer Bartlett*, Abbeville Press, New York 1985

architecture in his multi-panelled paintings which often contain a unifying element of drawing;[56] and Judy Pfaff's multi-media installations are riots of colour and materials which out-distance Frank Stella in scale and madness.[57]

Of course, you can extend eroticism in painting to any aspect of it; to colour for instance. Painters who have produced erotically-charged colours in their works include Vincent van Gogh, Henri Matisse, Mark Rothko, Leonardo da Vinci, Rogier van der Weyden and Emil Nolde. Painters such as Helen Frankenthaler rejoice in the exuberance of pure colour.[58] Morris Louis poured paint directly onto the canvas to produce his deeply saturated furls, blotches and curtains of colour (in paintings such as *Aleph, Alpha-Delta* and *Saraband*). Colour has been central to contemporary artists such as Barnett Newman, Clyfford Still, Christopher Le Brun, Howard Hodgkin, Kenneth Noland, Jules Olitski, Joseph Albers, etc.

What this shows, this emphasis on the sensuality of surface, colour and other formal elements of painting, is that painting's eroticism is crucial to its effect. Without this eroticism of colour, surface, texture, shape, pattern and form, painting loses much of its impact. Art historians call this eroticism of form 'beauty', that old Platonic word for all that is desirable. What beauty means is precisely this experience of the eroticism of the painting-as-object. The word beauty too is distinctly feminized in art criticism, for the beauty of a painting is a feminine quality; the painting is thus equivalent to a woman. The more a painting reveals its sensuality, the more beautiful it will be. It is the same when people look at women: women and paintings are thus equated in fine art criticism: the painting is stared at and enjoyed, as is the woman.

The female nude, then, combines the two erotic pleasures, of

56 Robert Mangold: *Four Color Frame Painting no. 1*, acrylic and pencil on canvas, 111 x 105in, collection: Martin Sklar, New York
57 Judy Pfaff: *N.Y.C.–B.Q.E, 1987*, painted steel, plastic laminates, fibreglass and wood, 15 x 35 x 5 feet, Max Protetch Gallery, New York
58 Helen Frankenthaler: *Moveable Blue*, 1973, acrylic on canvas, 5'10" x 20'3", Citizens Fidelity Bank and Trust Company, Louisville; *Nature Abhors a Vacuum*, 1973, acrylic on canvas, 104 x 113in, Andre Emmerich Gallery, New York

art and women, of art and sex. Beauty is thus that neat Platonic term that incorporates many forms of erotic looking or pleasure. The art object is that beautiful thing that gives pleasure, like woman in cultural discourse.

3

CONTEMPORARY ART

Eroticism abounds in contemporary art, where the æsthetic of materialism, of junk, of mass culture, of design and printed reproduction, dominates art. Certain artists have made eroticism their special province, but in highly idiosyncratic ways. TOM WESSELMAN. Tom Wesselman's bland, alienating *Great American Nudes* are distinctly his own: no one else makes images quite like that: those women without eyes or personalities, legs open on beds, lying back, smoking cigarettes, grinning vacuously, or towelling themselves dry in the shower. Wesselman presents a depersonalized, commodity-driven view of eroticism.[59]

ANDY WARHOL. Equally bland, alienating, depersonalized and vacuous, and wittily, intentionally so, of course, is Andy Warhol's art, which adores glamour, particularly stars such as

---

59 Tom Wesselman: *Great American Nude no. 54*, 1964, oil, acrylic and collage on canvas, with assembled sound effects and items, 177 x 215 x 99cm, Museum moderner kunst, Vienna; *Great American Nude no. 98*, 1967, five canvases arranged behind one another in three planes, 250 x 380 x 130cm, Museum Ludwig, Cologne

Marilyn Monroe and Liz Taylor and Elvis Presley. Warhol make icons out of movie and pop stars, so Monroe becomes the ultimate postwar Goddess of Sex, a modern Aphrodite, a modern 'holy whore', as Mary Magdalene, Isis, Venus and Aphrodite were in ancient times. Warhol's blank repetitions of electric chairs, Campbell soup cans, car crashes and movie stars seem to be cleverly ironic commentaries on the hedonism of consumerism, the pleasure of mass culture.[60]

Brilliantly, Andy Warhol brings everything that can be visualized onto the same level. He puts it all in the same place, philosophically as well as physically, on the canvas. He presents everything, from celebrities to violence, from flowers to electric chairs, with the same technique. His painterly approach is 'slipshod, slovenly, average';[61] images are slammed down onto the canvas, yet Warhol knows *precisely* what he is doing. Robert Rosenblum says of Warhol:

> He was the first artist of major significance to sense the realities of reproduction, of commercialisation of art, of commodity, of distribution of information in the 1960s and 70s. He's really the one who killed this definitively. That's an amazing achievement. I think he pinpointed the total change in our times[62]

Andy Warhol, of course, is famously self-deprecatory, always modest, always doing his achievement down. His seemingly deadpan manner applies to eroticism. Discussing his movie *Fuck*, which is absolutely *the* title for any postwar, post-atomic work of art, Warhol said: '[n]o, I don't think it's erotic because we don't show everything and the way we show it, it doesn't look really that sexy.'[63] This is Warhol's stance, to reduce everything to the level of trash, junk, triviality, banality. Warhol debunks every

60 Andy Warhol: *Orange Car Crash 10 Times*, 1963, acrylic and liquitex on canvas, 2 panels, each 332 x 206cm, Museum moderner kunst, Vienna; *Double Silver Disaster*, 1963, acrylic and liquitex silkscreen on canvas, 106.5 x 132cm, J. W. Fröhlich Collection, Stuttgart; *The Twenty-Five Marilyns*, 1962, acrylic and silkscreen on canvas, 205.7 x 169.5cm, Moderna Museet, Stockholm; *Orange Disaster*, 1963, 105 x 81in, collection: Harry N. Abrams, New York
61 Timon Osterwold, 11
62 Robert Rosenblum: "Romanticism and Retrospection", *Art and Design: The New Romantics*, 13
63 quoted in P. & E. Kronhausen, 45

notion of high art, of pretension, even though many think him pretentious, which he is too, even though he is firmly at the centre of high contemporary art.

Andy Warhol is the high priest of contemporary art, of Pop Art, of art that embraces anything and everything. Everything can be included in contemporary art: ashtrays, car crash victims, Coke cans, bland skyscrapers, whatever is around can be used. This is the 'pop æsthetic'.[64]

The artist who throws anything onto the picture plane is Robert Rauschenberg (see his many 'combine' paintings, mixed media extravaganzas).[65] Claes Oldenburg's soft telephones and toilets far out-do Rauschenberg for pure silliness. Oldenburg goes much further than Warhol in questioning the holy notion of 'Art' with a capital 'a'.[66] Contemporary art has to have three dimensions in its specifications, it seems. The picture plane, which had been so scrupulously flat throughout the Renaissance (ignoring the embossed and punched gold), suddenly bursts open in contemporary art. As Clement Greenberg put it: '[p]ictorial space has lost its "inside" and become all "outside".'[67] Of course, some contemporary artists asserted the flatness of the picture plane even more fervently: Morris Louis with his stained, furled canvas, Frank Stella with his black stripes done with housepaint direct onto cotton duck, Mark Rothko with his cloud-like shapes, Agnes Martin with her finely pencilled squares, Sol LeWitt with his spacious wall-drawings, etc. Lucio Fontana, though, destroyed the flatness of the canvas in a phallic, penetrative fashion: he slashed

64 See Bob Colacello: *Holy Terror: Andy Warhol Close Up*, New York 1990; Andy Warhol: *POPism: The Warhol 60s*, New York 1980; Carter Ratcliff: *Andy Warhol*, New York 1983
65 Rauschenberg: *Canyon*, 1959, combine painting, 219.7x 179 x 57.8cm, Sonnabend Gallery, New York; *Odalisque*, 1955-8, wood, material, wire, grass, paper, photographs, metal, stuffed rooster, 4 lightbulbs, 205 x 44 x 44cm, Museum Ludwig, Cologne. See Robert Hughes: "The Arcadian as Utopian", *Time*, 24 Jan 1983, 74, 77; Roni Feinstein: "The Early Work of Robert Rauschenberg: The White Paintings, the Black Paintings, and the Elemental Sculptures", *Arts*, September 1986, 28-37; Charles F. Stuckey: "Reading Rauschenberg", *Art in America*, April 1977, 74-84; Calvin Tomkins: *Off the Wall: Robert Rauschenberg and the Art World of Our Time*, New York 1980
66 Oldenburg: *Soft Toilet*, 1966, vinyl filled with kapok, painted with liquitex, and wood, 132 x 81 x 76.2cm, Whitney Museum of American Art, New York; *Soft Pay-Telephone*, 1963, vinyl filled with kapok, mounted on painted wood, 118.1 x 48.2 x 23cm, Guggenheim Museum, New York
67 Greenberg: *Art and Culture*, Beacon Press, Boston 1961, 134

the canvas.[68] Fontana explained his seemingly violent, nay, pornographic act thus:

> I want to open up space, create a new dimension for art, tie in at the cosmos as it endlessly expands beyond the confining place of the picture. With my innovation of the hole pierced through the canvas in repetitive perforations, I have not attempted to decorate a surface, but, on the contrary, I have tried to break its dimensional limitations. Beyond the perforations a newly gained freedom of interpretation awaits us, but also, and just as inevitably, the end of art.[69]

Everyone apart from the Minimalists, though, was throwing everything they could lay their hands on at the canvas. Typical contemporary works employ a plethora of media and techniques, including wood, plastic, acrylic, oil, pencil, metal, wire, fur, stone, leaves, cotton and glue. There is certainly an element of eroticism in this chaotic use of multiple medias. Contemporary art sometimes looks like that of adults regressed to kids and let loose on a mound of materials. Pop Art in particular is highly energetic in its appropriation of every sort of material.

In many contemporary artists, gesture is crucial, and erotic in its sensuality. It is central to Jackson Pollock's dripped paintings, to Franz Kline's arcane, thick black brushstrokes, to Willem de Kooning's wild expressionism.[70]

It's easy to spot the cases of pornography in contemporary high art. In Allen Jones' fetishized half-naked women who become chairs or the legs of a table. Jones' painted fibreglass women, with their high heels, stockings and elbow-length gloves are pure porn.[71] They are pure fetish-objects, like Hans Bellmer's *Doll,* or Rowlandson's erotic drawings. Lucas Samaras drew a pastel entitled *Lady Being Fucked By a Blue Dog* in 1965. Various Pop artists featured the phallus: Brigid Polk with her *Cock Book,*

68 Lucas Fontana: *Tela tagliata,* c. 1960, private collection
69 Fontana, quoted in Jan Van der Marck, *Lucas Fontana,* catalogue, Walker Art Center Minneapolis 1966
70 Pollock: *Blue Poles,* 1952, enamel, aluminium, glass on canvas, 41 x 106in, collection: Joseph H. Hazen; de Kooning: *Door to the River,* 1960, 203 x 179cm, Whitney Museum, New York; Kline: *Wotan,* 1950, oil, 201 x 150cm, collection: A. I. Sherr, New York
71 Allen Jones: *Table,* 1969, *Chair,* 1969, both painted fibre-glass, leather and hair, life-size, Neue Galerie, Aachen

Claes Oldenburg in his *Capric Monument*, Andy Warhol with his prints from *Blue Movie* and Robert Rauschenberg with his *Carnal Clock*. Tom of Finland, no Pop artist, produced umpteen images of beefy, camp gay men nude or in the ubiquitous gay bar uniform of jeans, leather jacket and cop cap, each guy fitted out with giant genitals.[72]

Images such as Tom Wesselman's 1966 *Nude*, with her legs spread wide and her tongue stuck out in orgasmic ecstasy are obviously pornographic.[73] More problematic are those artworks that try to question accepted codes or values of sexuality, which aim to be sarcastic or ironic, such as Peter Phillips' *Custom Painting*, where the woman (*naked of course*) is fused ironically with sex symbols such as a car, or Pop artist Richard Lindner, with his bizarre images of distorted bodies (horrible misogynist art),[74] in Mel Ramos' very bizarre image of a woman, *naked of course*, posing astride a hippotamus.[75] One is familiar with women straddling phallic cars at automobile shows, but astride a hippotamus? Ramos uses other phallic objects around which his pin-up women drape themselves (spark plugs, bottles, corn cobs, pelicans, gorillas, etc).[76] Ramos' West Coast Pop Art image is painted in the most revolting colours, in the most disgusting style imaginable: like Superrealism with an airbrush. The result is a Pop icon that parodies the female nude tradition in high art. Of his æsthetic intentions, Mel Ramos says:

> I try to celebrate folk heroes and sex queens in a straightforward manner. While their likeness is not faithful, their character is obvious.[77]

72 Tom of Finland: *Sauna-Bar*, c. 1966, Athletic Model Guild, Los Angeles
73 Wesselman: *Nude*, 1966, collection: Victor Lownes, London
74 Lindner: *New York City IV*, 1964, oil on canvas, 5'10" x 5', Hirshhorn Museum and Sculpture Garde, Washington DC
75 Mel Ramos: *Miss Corn Flakes*, 1964, 71 x 59in, collection Kimiko & John Powers, Colorado; *Hippotamus*, 1967, oil on canvas, 180 x 247cm, Saarland Museum, Saarbrücken; Phillips: *Custom Painting no. 5*, 1965, oil on canvas, 172 x 300cm, Galerie Bruno Bischofberger,Zurich
76 Mel Ramos: *Kar Kween*, 1964, oil on canvas, 5 x 4 feet, Hirshhorn Museum and Sculpture Garden, Washington DC
77 quoted in *Six More*, exhibition catalogue, Los Angeles County Museum of Art, 1963

The 'original' Pop Art image, by Richard Hamilton,[78] depicts a muscleman carrying a huge lollipop. The red sphere and stick of the lollipop is a phallus, an image of the phallus which has been reduced to idiocy, to mere candy. Much of Pop Art, and contemporary art, is wildly phallic; that is, inundated with phallic lust, phallic desires, phallic objects (cars, guns, machines), and phallic values (the values of advanced capitalism).

Richard Hamilton's view of idiot culture, the culture of advertizing and consumerism, presents eroticism as just another commodity in the flow of materialism. Beautiful lives can be bought, we are told, by buying the right magazines, going on the right diets, wearing the right clothes, driving the right cars, living in the right areas, in homes decorated in the right way. Pop Art explores the lies and mechanisms of contemporary consumerism in the West. Sex is just a part of this moneyed worldview, something to be sold, as James Dean's or Brad Pitt's sexuality or Scarlett Johansson's or Monica Bellucci's sexuality sells movies. In the contemporary world, money can buy *anything*, even though the Beatles sang *money can't buy you love*. It can't buy you love, but it can buy you new breasts, or a face-lift, or sex. Or, if not love or sex, then the dream of love and sex: dreams of love and sex abound, in websites, magazines, TV shows, movies, car ads, etc. And sex and beauty sell soft drinks, jeans, pop music, Hollywood, clothes, everything. It is a dream, the Great American Dream, the Great Capitalist Dream.

---

78 Richard Hamilton: *Just what is it that makes today's homes so different, so appealing?*, 1956, collage, 26 x 25cm, Kunsthalle Tübingen, Tübingen

4

EROTICISM IN CONTEMPORARY FIGURATIVE ART

Some of the art of the 1960s and 1970s is pretty crude. It was a period when the 1960s permissiveness and un-PC, no-holds-barred attitudes were at their height in popular culture (well, at least in more recent times – but compared to, say, ancient Rome, pretty tame). Painters such as Philip Pearlstein, Johannes Grützke, Lucien Freud and Michael Leonard are the acceptable face of contemporary erotic art.[79] Pearlstein's nudes are 'clean': he shows wrinkles but his figures retain their 'dignity' and 'integrity'. The nude in the work of Leonard, Freud, Pearlstein and Grützke is painted in a detailed, meticulous fashion, so that every portion of the body can be stared at. Blemishes are kept in, as are ugly

---

[79] Philip Pearlstein: *Two Nudes, Bamboo and Linoleum*, 1984, oil on canvas, 96 x 96 in, Hirschl & Adler Modern, New York; Lucien Freud: *Night Portrait*, 1985-6, oil on canvas, 37 x 29in, Hirshhorn Museum and Sculpture Garden, Washington DC; Johannes Grützke: *Three Nude Women*, 1973, oil on canvas, 180 x 250cm, Galerie Brusberg, Hanover; Michael Leonard: *Stooping Bather*, 1980, acrylic on cotton duck, 54.6 x 53.3cm, collection: the artist

poses, but eroticism is suppressed.

Great (i.e., celebrated) contemporary artists, such as Willem de Kooning and Yves Klein, are clearly sexist in their paintings. De Kooning's manic, bug-eyed nudes follow on from the savage expressionism of Pablo Picasso, as do Karel Appel's nudes; the ugly satirical (female) nudes of Larry Rivers or the ironic (Warholian) uses of the mechanics of mass reproduction in Alain Jacquet's images; Klein had women, *nude of course*, drag each other on the floor, covered in paint, while a string quartet played, in his 'body prints' or 'anthropometries' series.[80]

Another American contemporary major artist, Jim Dine, breaks his otherwise rigorous and ironic approach to art to produce drawings such as *A Nurse*, which shows a woman (*naked of course*) objectified sexually. No traditional art critic would call Dine's image 'pornographic', yet it clearly is.[81] There is no escaping porn in contemporary art, it seems. It is everywhere – from the less well-known (in the German sculptor Gustav Seitz's *The Chooser*,[82] where three women stand waiting to be 'chosen' by a man), to the most famous icons of Andy Warhol or David Hockney.

There are many, many lesser-known, unknown and thoroughly amateur artists who produce erotic art. Not just the illustrators of science fiction, dungeons and dragons, horror and sword and sorcery books and magazines and merchandizing, though they can be bad enough, but also many artists who call themselves 'artists', who work in oils, pastels, acrylic, watercolour, ink and the materials of sculpture. These artists produce really horrible art, art that has no æsthetic saving graces. Such as Guillermo Medrano's *Sera in Red*, a picture of a woman stroking

80 Yves Klein: *Making Anthropometries of the Blue Period*, March 9, 1960, New York; Klein: *People Begin to Fly*, 1961, dry blue pigment in synthetic resin on paper on fabric, 8'1" x 13', Menil Collection, Houston; Karel Appel: *La Hollandaise*, 1969, 51 x 38in, Galerie Ariel, Paris; Larry Rivers: *Girlie*, 1970, 30 18in, Marlborough Graphics, New York; Alain Jacquet: *The Rape of Europa*, 1965, 30 x 21in, collection: Heinz Beck, Düsseldorf; Willem de Kooning: *Woman and Bicycle*, 1952-3, oil on canvas, 76 x 49in, Museum of American Art, New York; *Woman I*, 1950-2, 75 x 57in, Museum of Modern Art, New York
81 Jim Dine: *A Nurse*, 1976, etching with watercolour additions, 60 x 50.2cm,
82 Gustav Seitz: *The Chooser*, 1956

her clitoris – clearly derived from Gustave Klimt; or *The Gust of Wind*, by Lothar Fischer, a woman with no arms or heads, her breasts naked and prominent, with her legs apart, and her skirt blowing up, like Marilyn Monroe's;[83] or *Jism* by Tom Swanston, showing a man ejaculating; or Philip Becker's archetypal David Baileyesque 'erotic' photos showing women – *nude, of course* – with cow skulls or plastic bags on their heads; or Michael Riley's *Adam*, an Expressionist-style painting of a man masturbating, clearly derived from Egon Schiele's ithyphallic self-portraits; or van Genderen's *Moonfish*, which depicts a woman's buttocks clad in tights montaged over a sea with an island, as if the woman's ass forms the whole sky; or Ronald Markman's *Rhineoceros*, showing a woman bending over a rhineoceros, echoing Mel Ramos' nude woman on a hippopotamus.[84]

What is surprising about some pornographic 'erotic art', or erotic 'pornographic art', is its lack of humour, its lack of irony, its lack of emotion, and joy, and exuberance, and wildness. Bad erotic art, which tries so hard with the computer mouse, pen and ink or oils to be serious erotic art, fails. True or authentic erotic art, art critics claim, is saved from being pornography or banality by its brilliant technique, or true feeling. But bad erotic art is neither erotic nor art. It is pornography unadorned, while true erotic art (the art of, say, Pablo Picasso, Titian, François Boucher, Egon Schiele or Michelangelo Buonarroti) is all adornment, technique, slickness, glitz, bravura, performance. Awful erotic art reveals the bleak ethics, outlook, and morals of porn, and, by extension, of so much of all art. Bad, ugly, coarse – unrefined erotic art shows how bleak the world of pornography is. And bad erotic art is the stuff of millions of weekend newspaper ads for cars, or billions of fashion spreads in countless magazines, or the costumes and gestures of thousands of movies, or the staple diet of TV soaps, sit

---

83 Lothar Fischer: *The Gust of Wind*, 1967
84 Guilermo Medrano: *Sera in Red*, 1988, oil, 16 x 20in, collection: the artist; Tom Swanston: *Jism*, watercolour, 9 x 6in, collection: the artist; Philip Bekker: *Skull #3*, photograph, 20 x 25in; Michael Riley: *Adam*, acrylic, 24 x 30in, collection: the artist; van Genderen: *Moonfish*, graphite, 9.5 x 11.5in, collection: the artist; Ronald Markman: *Rhineoceros*, pen & ink, 18 x 24in, private collection

coms, dramas, documentaries and newscasts.

Good erotic art, for the critical establishment, has æsthetic sophistication. It is protected, beloved, caressed, controlled, policed and defended by the guardians of culture and art, but from one angle there is no difference between good erotic art and bad erotic art: both are meant to arouse and amuse, like porn.

Some figurative painters, though, have employed figuration with a sense of irony, criticizing notions of gender, power, race, economy and desire. Jonathan Borofsky's *Male Aggression Now Playing Everywhere* is a comment on male violence.[85] It depicts a naked man with a bundle of weaponry thrusting out of his groin: instead of the phallus the viewer sees a car, missile, arrow, club, knife and a gun. It is an image of the male as an ape, an aggressive Neanderthal. Behind the figure, the globe of the Earth is breaking apart. The message is simple: men are fucking up the planet, a familiar battlecry of green politics.

American painter David Salle's images are more problematic. Clearly, Salle, like Eric Fischl, is aiming to be ironic, yet his continual quotes from pornographic magazines produce deeply ambivalent discourses, which implicate author, text and viewer in an economy of pornographic exchange which the irony does not negate. Salle is particularly fond of women bending over, showing off their asses, inviting that type of tupping that's a favourite in porn. Salle's women are anonymous, their faces are turned away from the viewer. They offer their bodies, albeit in parodic contexts, for the pleasure of the (male) viewer.[86]

Eric Fischl also employed the iconography of pornography, and gives it a high art treatment. Fischl's Middle American settings and often child's viewpoint produced deliberately, self-consciously ambivalent images, such as his *Bad Boy*, where a boy has his hand inside a handbag while looking at a woman, *nude of*

85 Jonathan Borofsky: *2,841,778 Male Aggression Now Playing Everywhere*, 1981-3, acrylic on canvas, 110 x 84in, collection: Suzanne & Howard Feldman, New York
86 David Salle: *Saltimbanques*, 1986, acrylic and oil on wood and canvas, 152.4 x 254cm, Mary Boone Gallery, New York; *Making the Bed*, 1985, oil and acrylic on wood and canvas, 304.8 x 248.9cm, collection: Emily & Jerry Spiegel, New York; *Untitled*, 1984, watercolour on paper, 63.5 x 78.7cm, Mary Boone Gallery, New York

349

course, on a bed.[87] The tropes of pubescent sex, œdipal tension, the purse and vulva, etc, are all clear. Ken Kiff reproduces the stereotypical views of women in his *The Feminine as Generous, Frightening and Serene* without, it seems, much of a sense of irony.[88]

Robert Longo also used the imagery of porn, though his multi-media approach makes the irony more obvious, as in his *Still,* for instance.[89] Francis Bacon's few depictions of lovemaking emphasize the brute physicality of bodies clashing together.[90] Bacons' expressionist view of sex is the familiar one of patriarchy: that sex is an aggressive, violent act, a view found in much of Western art and literature.

R.B. KITAJ. R. B. Kitaj produced art that fuses eroticism and politics in an ironic, fantastical way.[91] His art echoed the Expressionists, particular Max Beckmann and George Grosz with their visions of hellish, chaotic urbanscapes, where people and objects whirl together in confusion. Kitaj takes the stereotypical gestures of pornography (voyeurs, white women with black men, lingerie) and manipulates the codes to produce satirical and impassioned comments on modern life. His *The Rise of Fascism* employs the theme of three semi-naked women of traditional art, as used by Pablo Picasso, for instance, or those'modern masters who painted images called *Bathers* (Pierre Renoir, Henri Matisse, Ernst Kirchner).[92] In Kitaj's *The Rise of Fascism,* the pastoral scene turns bleak, and the women are prostitutes, but not the eulogized women of Henri de Toulouse-Lautrec. The old woman in the centre is the figure of fascism, here looking Germanic.

---

87 Fischl: *Bad Boy,* 1981, oil on canvas, 66 x 96in, Saatchi Collection, London
88 Ken Kiff: *The Feminine as Generous, Frightening and Serene,* 1982-3, oil on canvas, 160 x 129.5cm, Nicola Jacobs Gallery
89 Robert Longo: *Still,* 1984, acrylic on silkscreen on wood; charcoal and graphite on dyed paper; oil and copper leaf on hammered oak; oil on hammered lead, 248 x 732cm, private collection
90 Bacon: *Two Figures,* 1953, oil on canvas, 5 x 3'10", private collection
91 See Marco Livingstone: *R. B. Kitaj,* Oxford 1985; John Asberry et al: *R. B. Kitaj,* Hirshorn Museum and Sculpture Garden, Washington, 1983; R. B. Kitaj: *The Human Clay: An Exhibition Selected By R. B. Kitaj,* Hayward Gallery, London 1976
92 R. B. Kitaj: *The Rise of Fascism,* 1975-9, pastel, charcoal & oil on paper, 81 x 158cm, Tate Gallery, London

In R.B. Kitaj's *Communist and Socialist*,[93] the title gives a new slant to an otherwise mundane pornographic image of two people on a bed, *nude of course*, the man lying back with an erection. The message of the picture is that bad sex makes for bad societies, a theorem propounded by some of the modern 'priests' of sexuality, Sigmund Freud, Wilhelm Reich and D.H. Lawrence. *This Knot of Life* shows a white woman on top of a black man, being watched by a furtive voyeur.[94] It is an image of a brothel, that place which is, for Kitaj, 'at the heart of decaying cities'.[95] The brothel is the supreme pornographic fantasy zone, which Kitaj sees as definitely decadent, an erotic wilderness where desires run to nothing, where the rot at the heart of Western life is situated.

Gladys Nilsson has created an ironic commentary on sexual desire in her *Pandemoneum*, which she calls *A Trip-Dick*.[96] Nilsson's painting shows a chaos of desire, as comic-strip figures cavort manically with each other.

Eroticism in photography follows the same æsthetic and moral patterns as those found in painting. There are countless nudes in photography, ranging from high art to porn. Images such as those by US photographer Harry Callahan of his wife Eleanor seem to be distanced and formal, like the pastel nude drawings of Edgar Degas.[97] But the cool approach, of high art photography, as in the art of Degas (who himself used photography), masks the age-old objectification of women.

Many photographic nudes are fetishized or eroticized as in erotica. Those of the famed Surrealist Man Ray, for example, are erotica masquerading as high art,[98] even those images of Ray's which seem to mock gender stereotypes, as in his photograph of Meret Oppenheim.[99]

Erwin Blumenfeld photographed a woman (*naked of course*)

93 Kitaj: *Communist and Socialist*, 1975, pastel, 39 x 57cm, collection: the artist
94 Kitaj: *This Knot of Life*, 1975, pastel, 39 x 57cm, collection: the artist
95 Kitaj, quoted in Tilly, 76
96 Gladys Nilsson: *Pandemoneeum – A Trip Dick*, 1983, water on panel, 129.5 x 257cm, Phyllis Kind Gallery, New York
97 Callahan: *Eleanor, Port Huron*, 1954, 17 x 16.5cm, Museum of Modern Art, New York
98 Man Ray: *Nude*, 1940, solarized photograph
99 Man Ray: *Érotique violée*, photograph, 1933, private collection, Paris

351

with a veil over her body, blurring her face but clearly emphasizing her breasts, echoing the 'wet Tee shirt' photos of contemporary titillation.[100] E.J. Belloq photographed a woman, *nude of course*, wearing stockings and a mask – archetypal fetish items – on a sofa. It seems to be 'Surreal' before the time of the Surrrealists, but in fact it is more porn, pornography dressed up as 'erotica'.[101] Manuel Alvarez Bravo created a reclining nude woman for the cover of a Surrealist magazine. She lies wrapped in bandages, on a rug, with spiky cacti placed around her.[102]

BILL BRANDT. Bill Brandt's famous distorted nudes emphasize the model's sexuality, as do those of other celebrated photographers like André Kertèsz, Edward Weston, Eadweard Muybridge and Brassai, among others.[103] Brandt produced a series of photographs of the female form as a part of the landscape, of the female form *as* landscape. He moved in close and photographed parts of the body – legs, flanks, ears – on a beach, forming a continuum between human and geographical form. The result is woman as landscape, woman as Earth Mother, a Goddess.[104] This sort of photography seems to be innocuous enough. More sinister, and pornographic, are Brandt's 'Surreal' nudes where a woman, *nude of course*, is shown tied up, with her face covered. This is pornography, not 'art photography', though the two are so often kept separate, as with erotic prose and porn.[105]

EDWARD WESTON. Edward Weston is the archetypal American photographer – macho, powerful, fiercely heterosexual, technically precise. He is the Ernest Hemingway, the bulldog of American photography. Like so many painters, his models became his lovers, or his lovers became his models. He followed

100 Blumenfeld: *Wet Veil II*, 1937
101 Belloq: *Nude woman reclining dressed in mask and stockings*, 1911-3, printing-out paper, gold-toned, Victoria & Albert Museum
102 M. A. Bravo: *Good Reputation Sleeping*, 1938, gelatin silver print, Victoria & Albert Museum, London
103 André Kertesz: *Distortion no. 6*, 1933, gelatin silver print, Victoria & Albert Museum; Eadweard Muybridge: plate 425 from *Animal Locomotion*, 1887, photogravure, Victoria & Albert Museum, London
104 Brandt: *Nude*, gelatin silver print, Victoria & Albert Museum, London
105 Brandt: *Nude: Campden Hill, London* 1978, gelatin silver print, Victoria & Albert Museum, London

his passions wherever they took him – to the Mexican desert, through tumultuous love affairs, and to the purism of photographic technique: shooting with a large format camera, using tiny apertures (f256), long exposures (four hours, say, on a rose, or a chopped-up plant, or a sea shell) and contact printing (so that nothing came between the negative and the photographic paper). Weston's nudes are eroticized (in intent, at least): for instance, the famous nude woman lying face down on the sand, or floating in a swimming pool.[106]

Certain photographers have made a particular kind of fetishized, eroticized high art strain of photography, such as Helmut Newton, who depicts half-naked women in bondage and S/M gear and poses (in his *Sleepless Nights* book), or David Bailey, who photographs high heeled shoes stuck in the crotch of knickers (in his *Trouble and Strife* collection of photos). These high art photographs, made by distinguished or famous photographers use the motifs of pornography – the high heeled shoe, stockings, leather, chains, master-and-slave scenarios and introduce them into glossy high fashion contexts. As Karen Myers writes, this form of erotic photography 'has enabled explicit allusions to sexual violence which would not be tolerated within the legal and political constraints which surround mass market 'soft' porn.'[107]

The photography of David Bailey, Helmut Newton, Guy Bourdin and John Hedgecoe features many sadomasochistic motifs, but treated as high art, as well as high camp. The lack of humour or irony, though, is startling. Their form of 'erotic' photography emphasizes surface and style and technique, while employing motifs and situations from pornography. It is indeed curious that images of flagellation, pain, S/M, leather, chains, rubber, and so on, should be printed and widely circulated in glossy high fashion magazines, and the 'artistic' photographic magazines. Karen Myers suggests one reason:

Edward Weston: *Nude*, 1936, gelatin silver print; *Nude floating*, 1939, gelatin silver print, both Victoria & Albert Museum, London
Karen Myers: *Screen*, vol. 23, no. 3/4, 1983, and in Angela McRobbie, ed. *Zoots Suits and Second-hand Dresses: An Anthology of Fashion and Music*, Macmillan 1989, 191

One of the reasons for the exemption of so-called 'Erotica' from legal censorship is its location at the intersection of a number of different visual discourses which continually compete for the interpretation of the image. These are the visual traditions established with fine art, commercial fashion photography and hard-core pornography. The inability easily to classify the erotic photograph lends it enough ambiguity to defy censorship under a current legal system which has established an effective exemption clause for that which is thought to be 'art'.[108]

Robert Mapplethorpe made ironic pictures of the human form, at once celebrating the human body and criticizing it. His photographs are ambivalent depictions of various forms of eroticism – gay, S/M, fetishized, black, lesbian, etc.

A lot of photography beloved of amateur photographers is soft porn, where models are depicted in swimsuits or topless, against coloured backgrounds and the models have glamorous hairstyles and glossy make-up. These pictures are featured on the covers of amateur and practical photography magazines. These magazines are full of copy on photographic techniques, but the examples of the genres of photography they use to illustrate their technical articles – sport, nature, landscape, portrait – are used side-by-side with porn images of women. This's typical of masculine technofetishism.

108 Myers, op.cit., 192

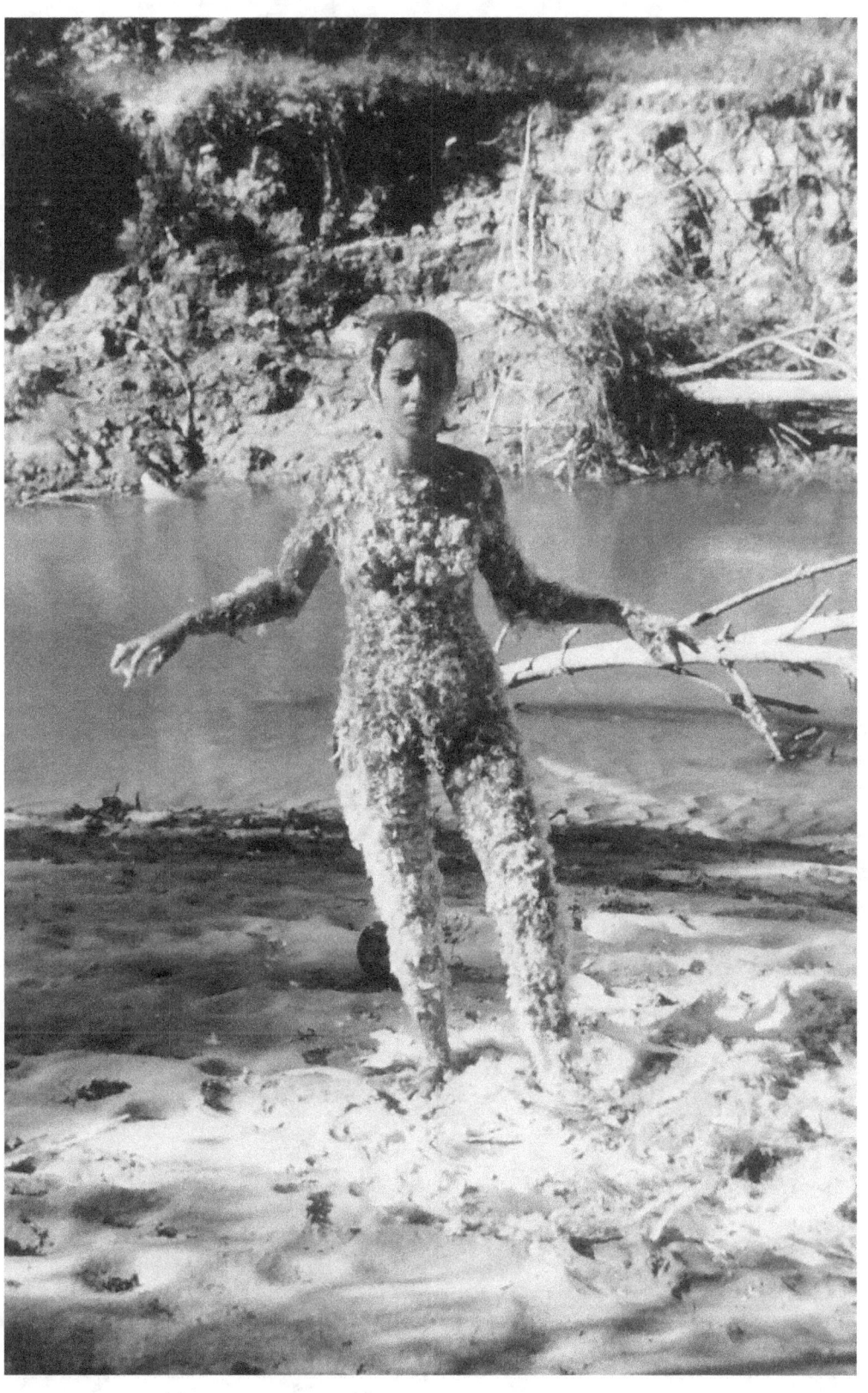

Ana Mendieta, Blood and Feathers, 1974

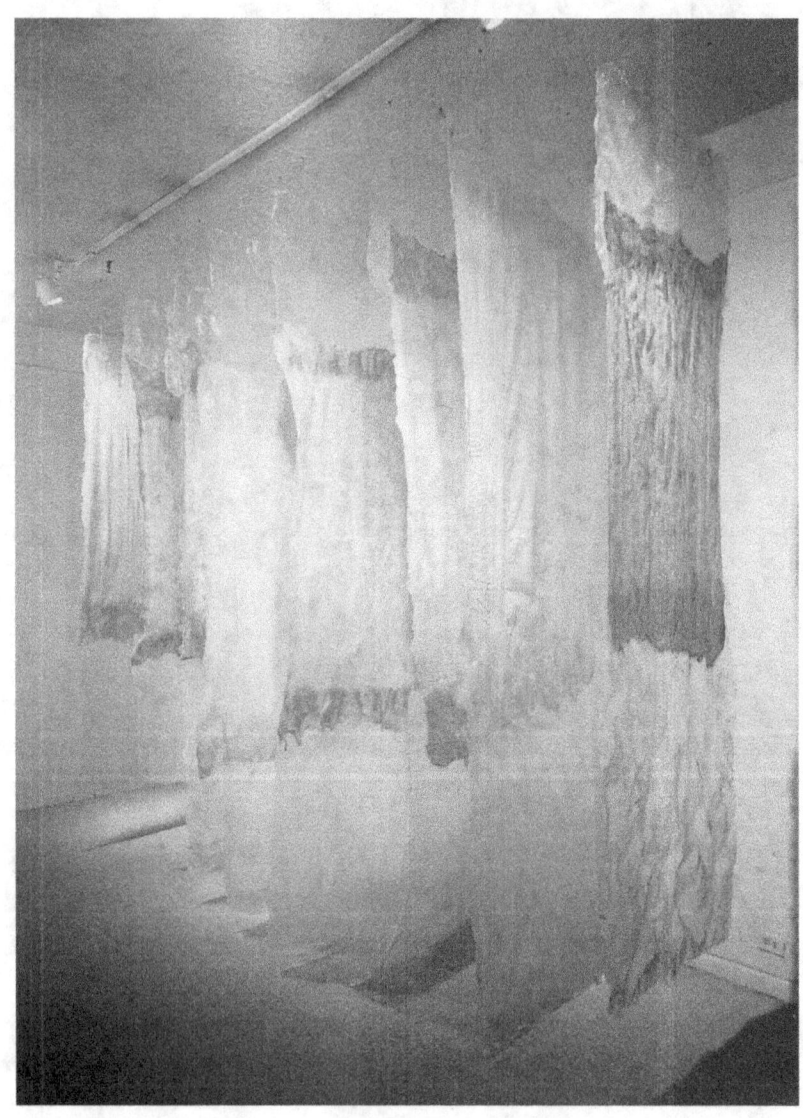

Eva Hesse, Contingent, 1969

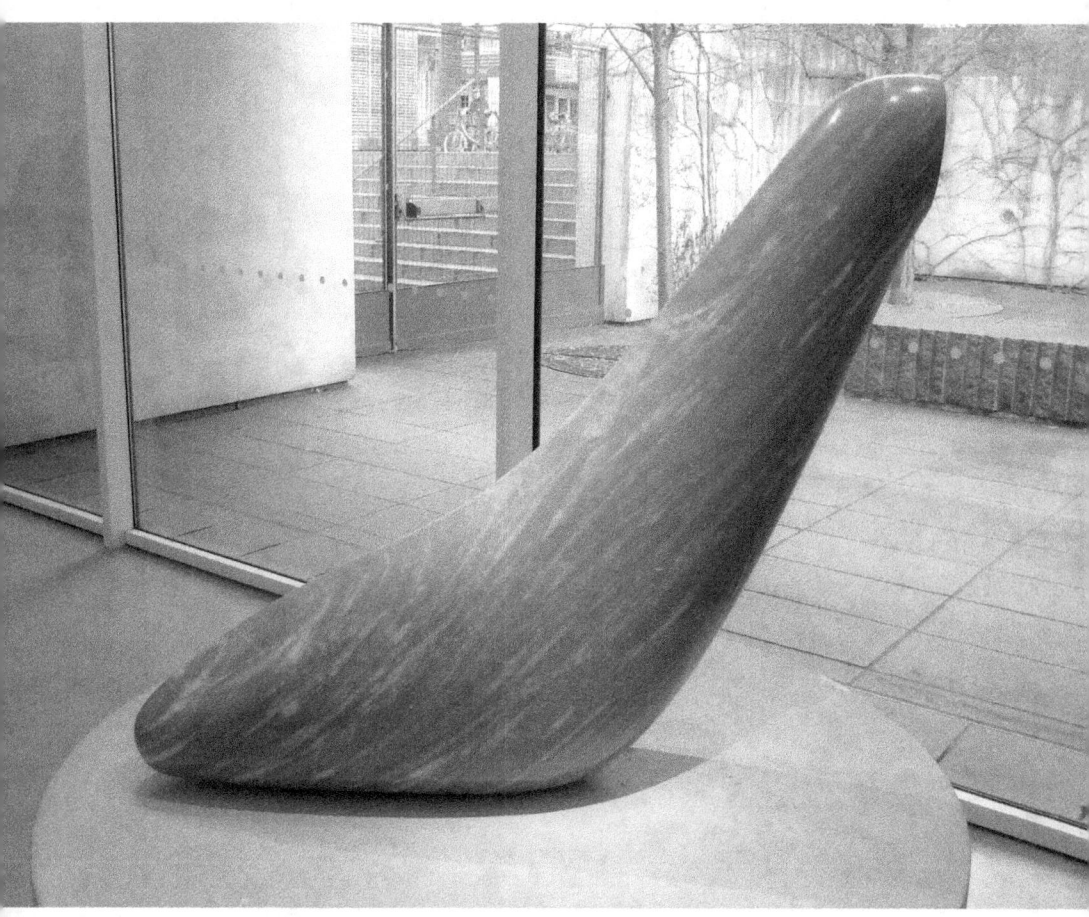

Constantin Brancusi

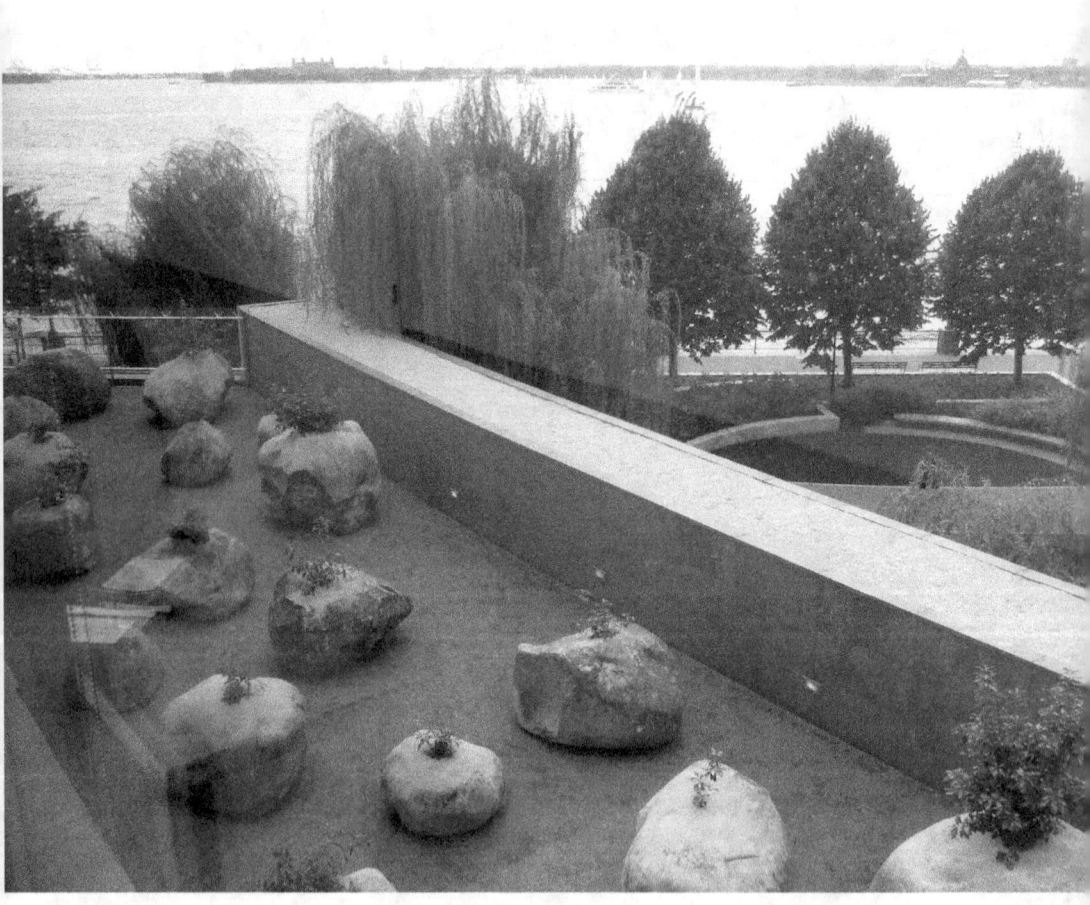

Andy Goldsworthy in New York City

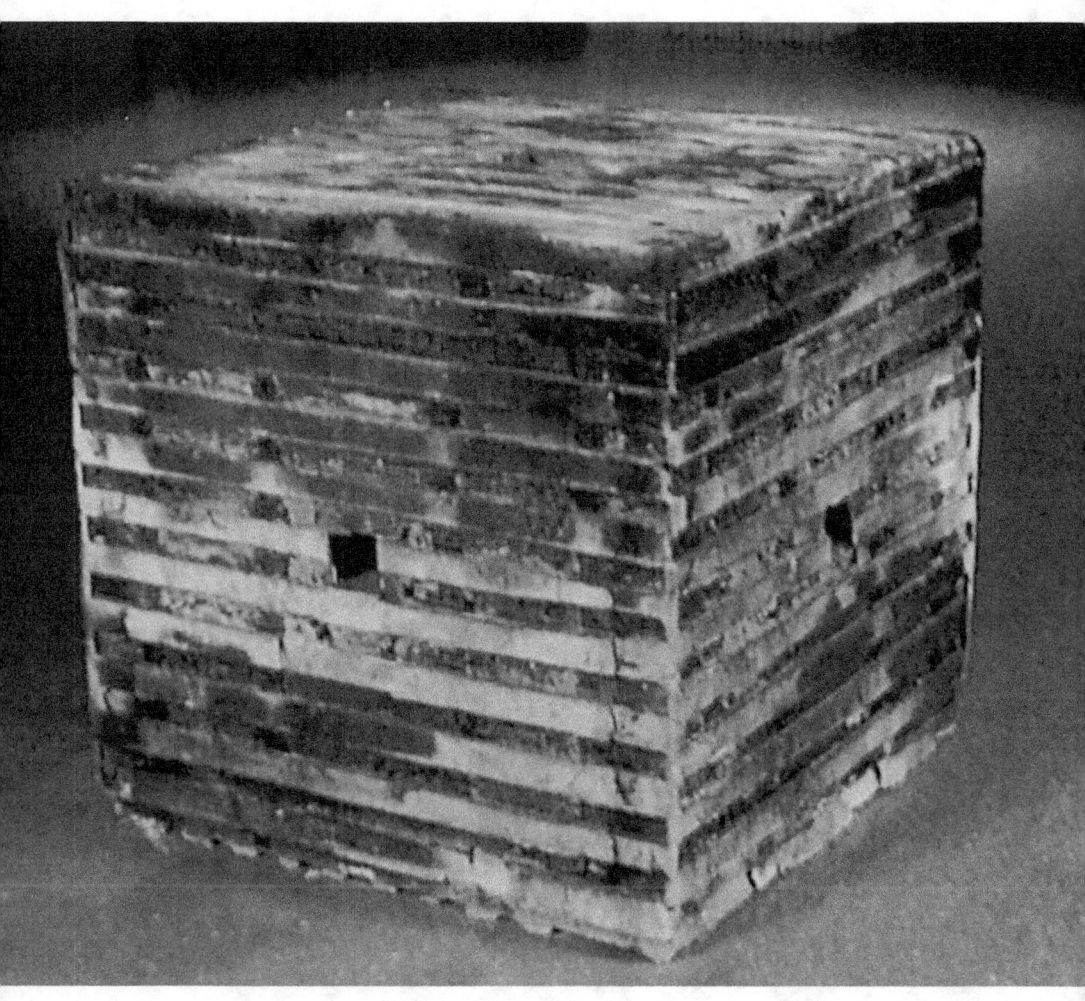

Jackie Winsor, Burnt Piece, 1977

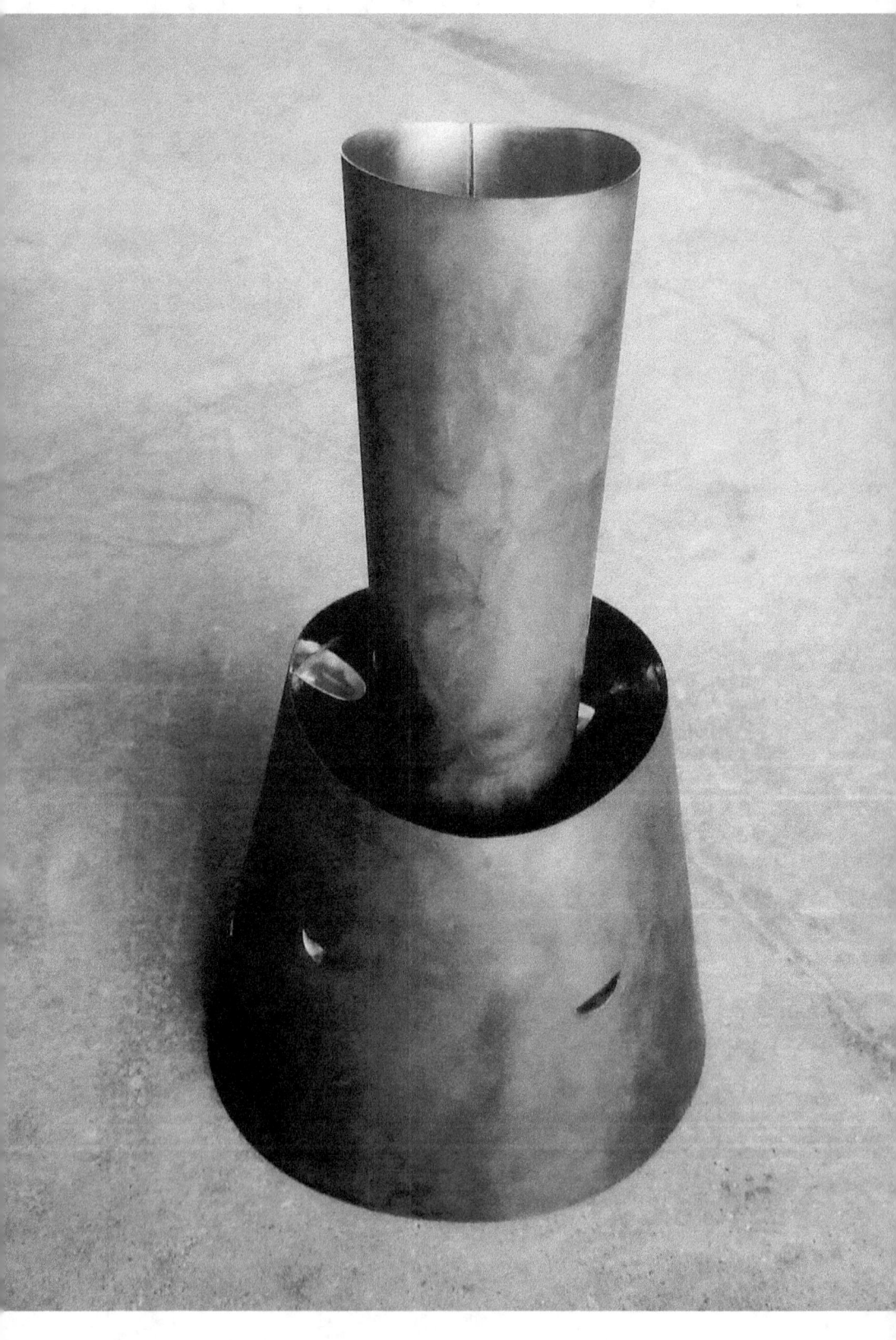

Alison Wilding, Immersion, 1988

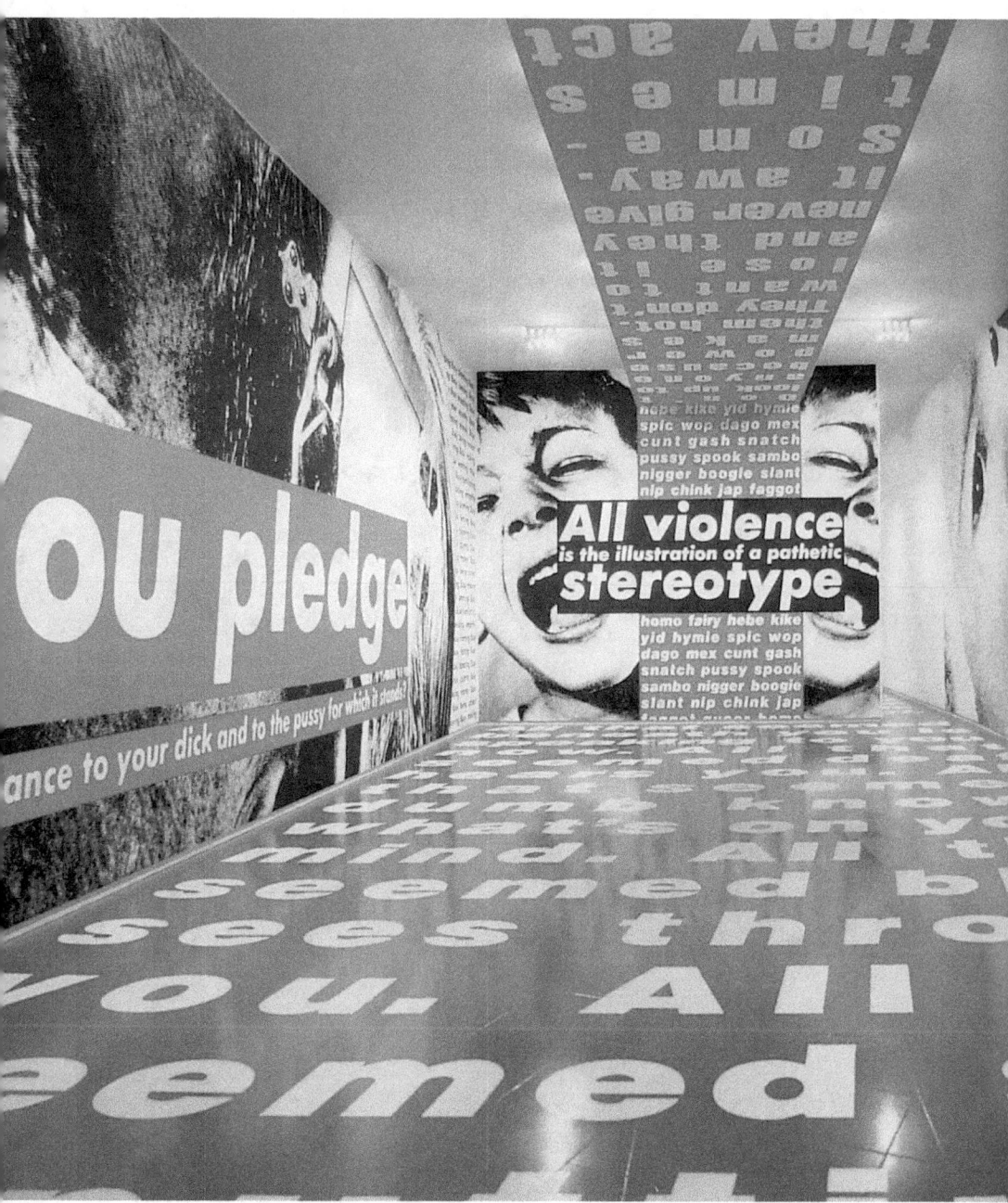

Barbara Kruger, Untitled, 1991

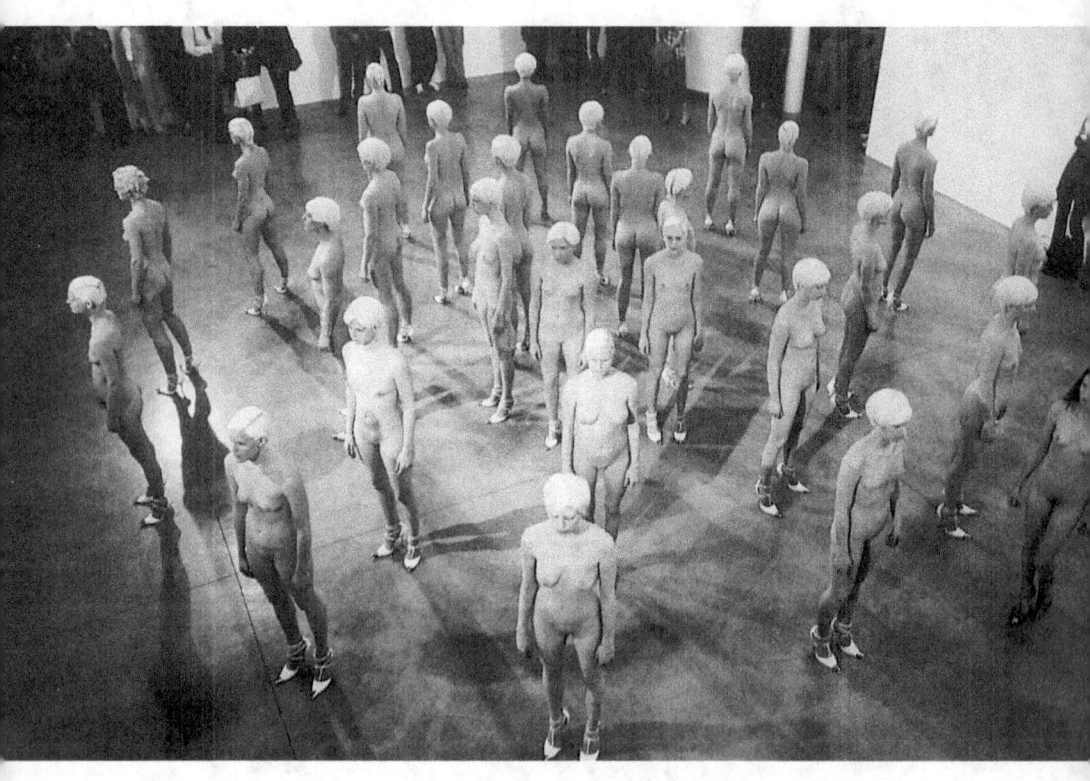

Vanessa Beecroft, VB45.026.ali, 2001

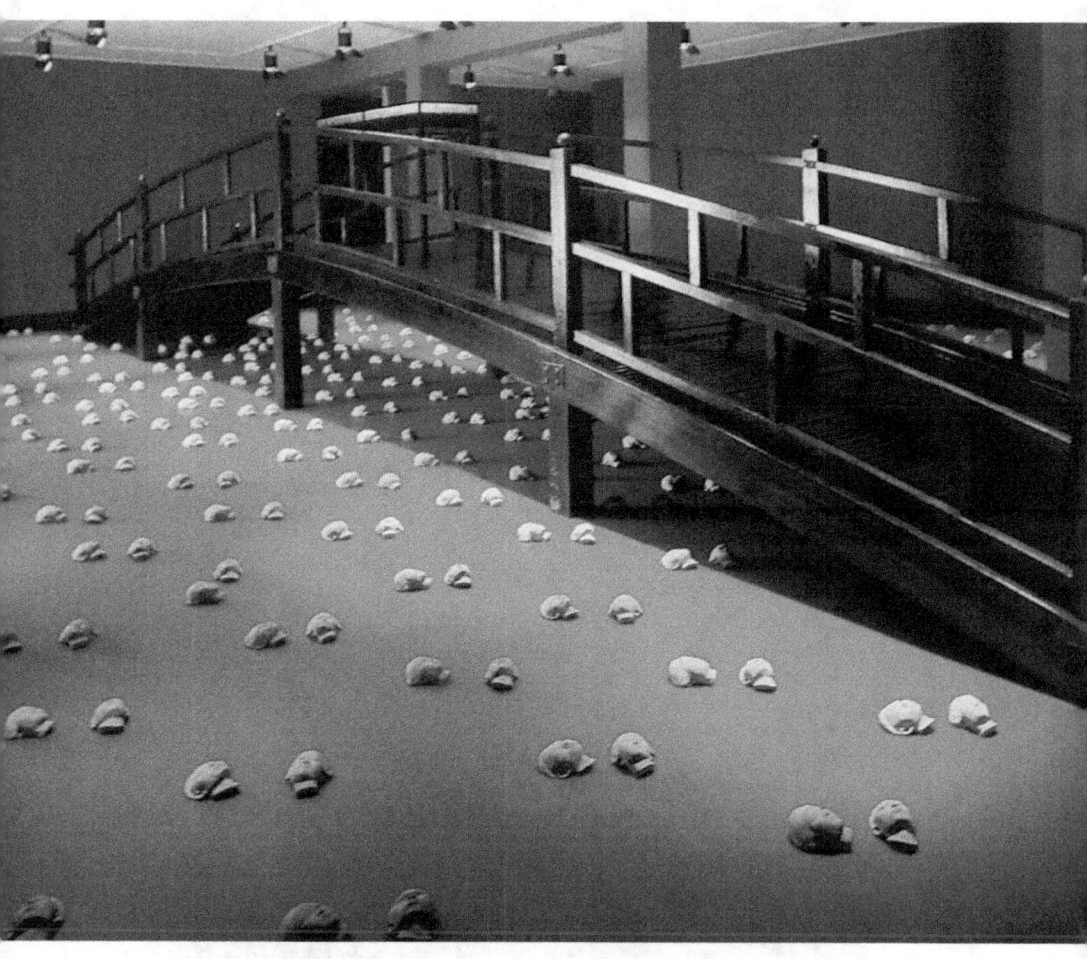

Barbara Bloom, Pictures From the Floating World, 1995

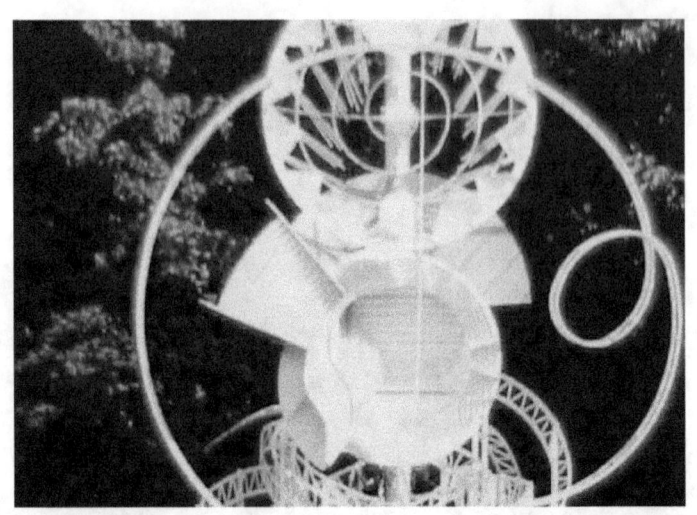

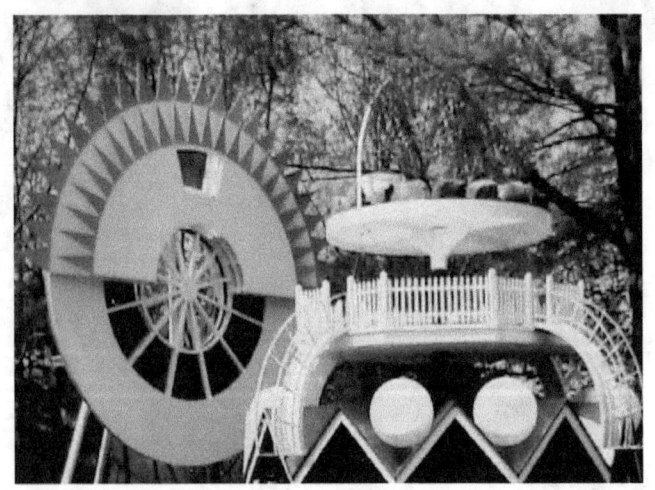

Alice Aycock

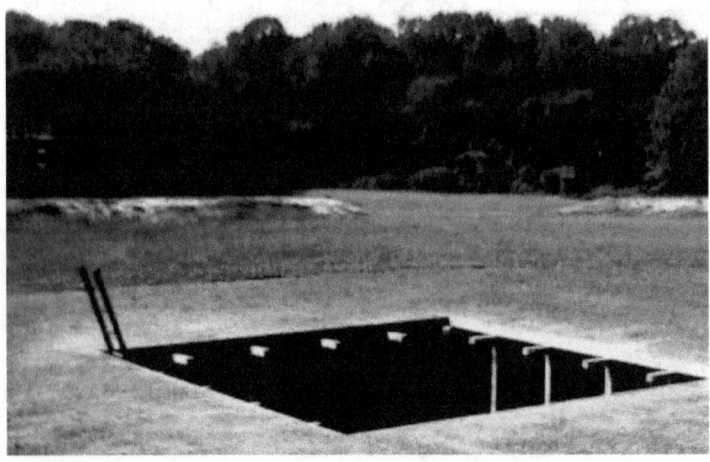

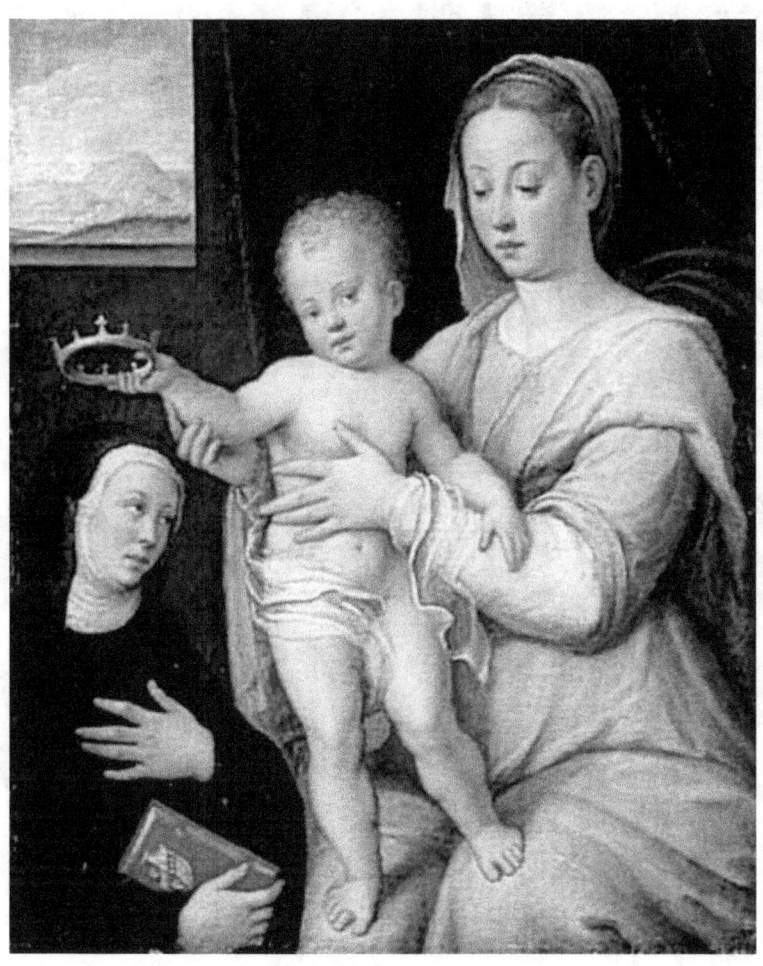

Barbara Longhi, Madonna and Child

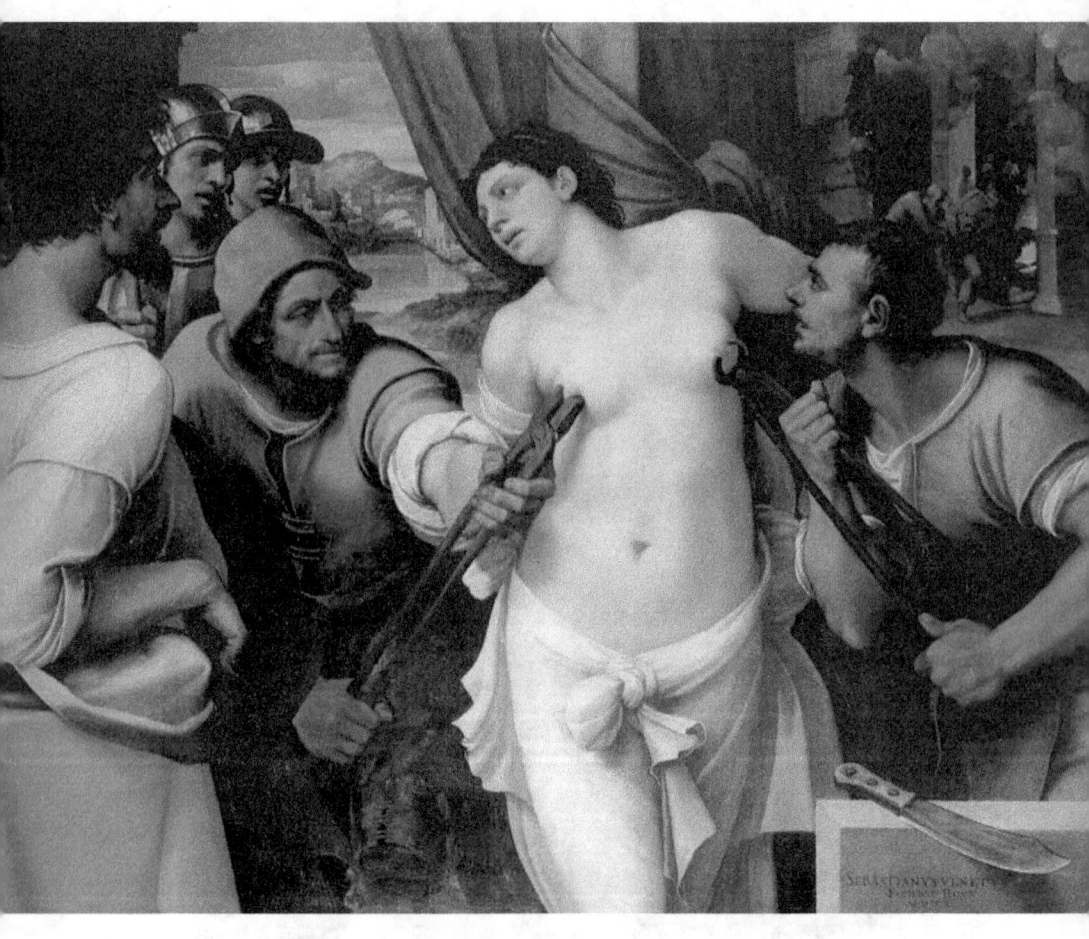

Sebastiano del Piombo, The Martyrdom of St Agatha, 1520,
Pitti Palace, Florence

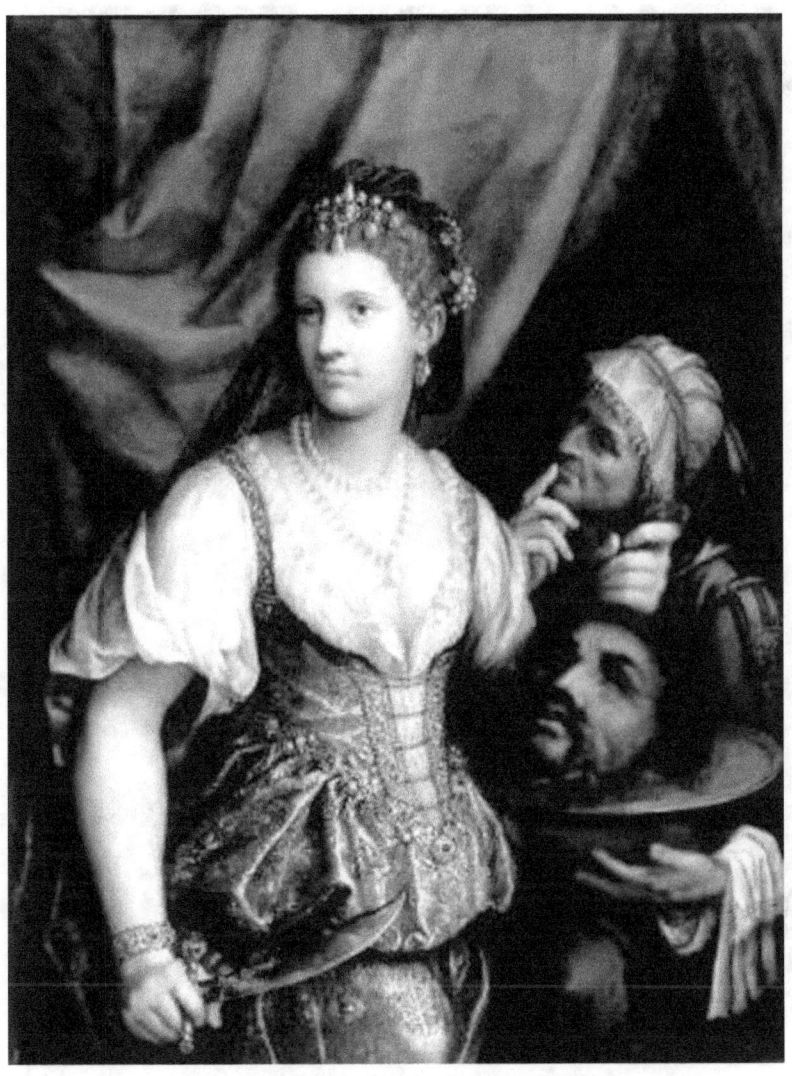

Fede Galizia, Judith with the Head of Holofernes,
Museum of Art, Sarasota, Florida

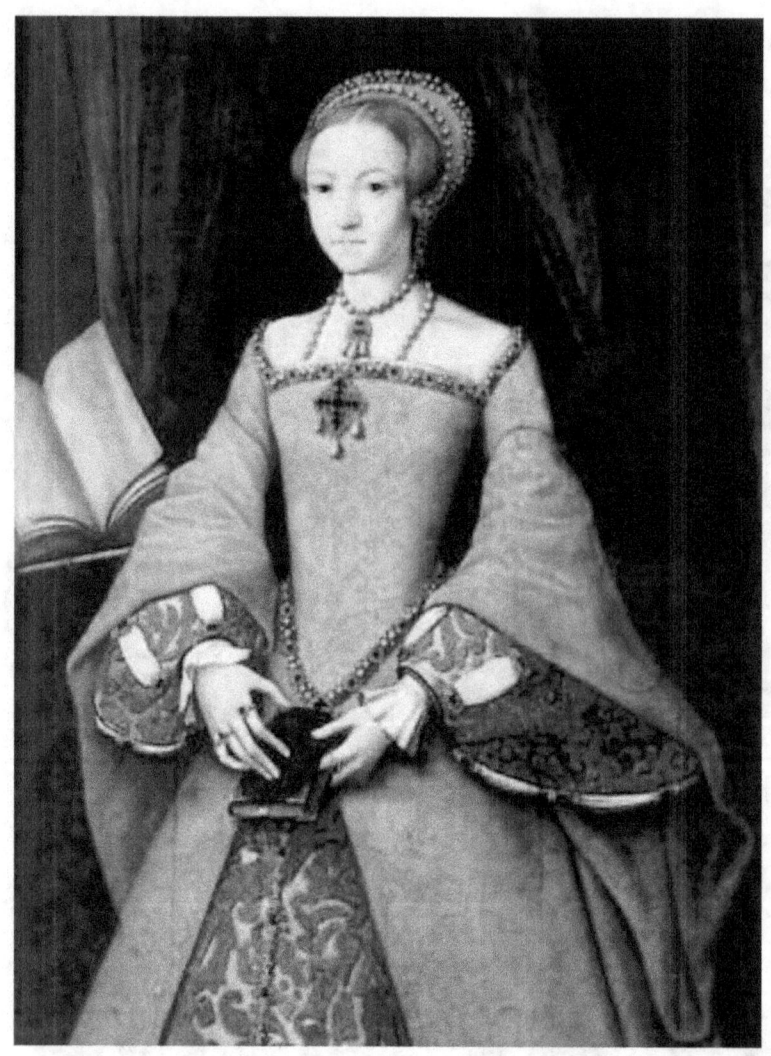
Levina Teerline (a Flemish painter)

Artemisia Gentileshi, Self-Portrait as a Martyr, 1615

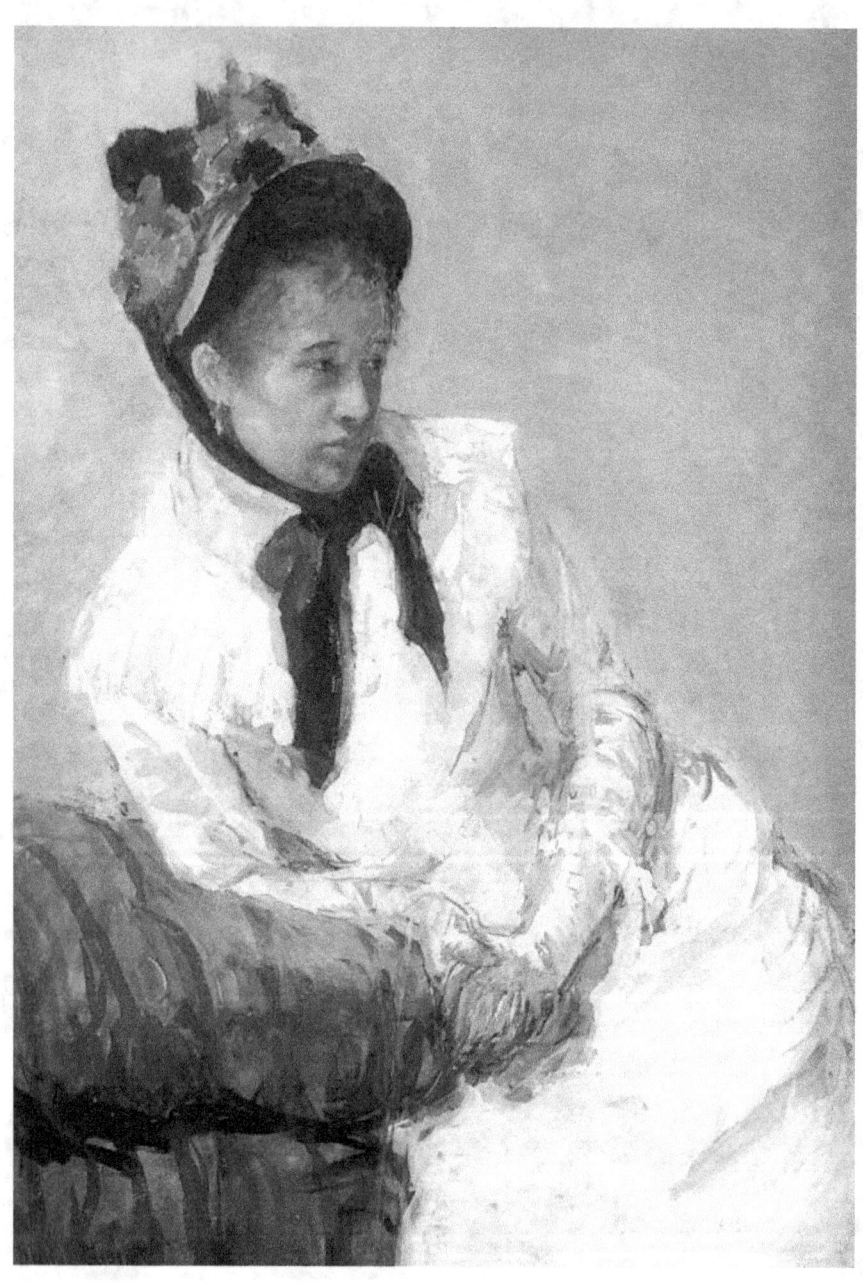

Mary Cassatt, Self-Portrait, 1878,
Metropolitan Museum of Art, New York City

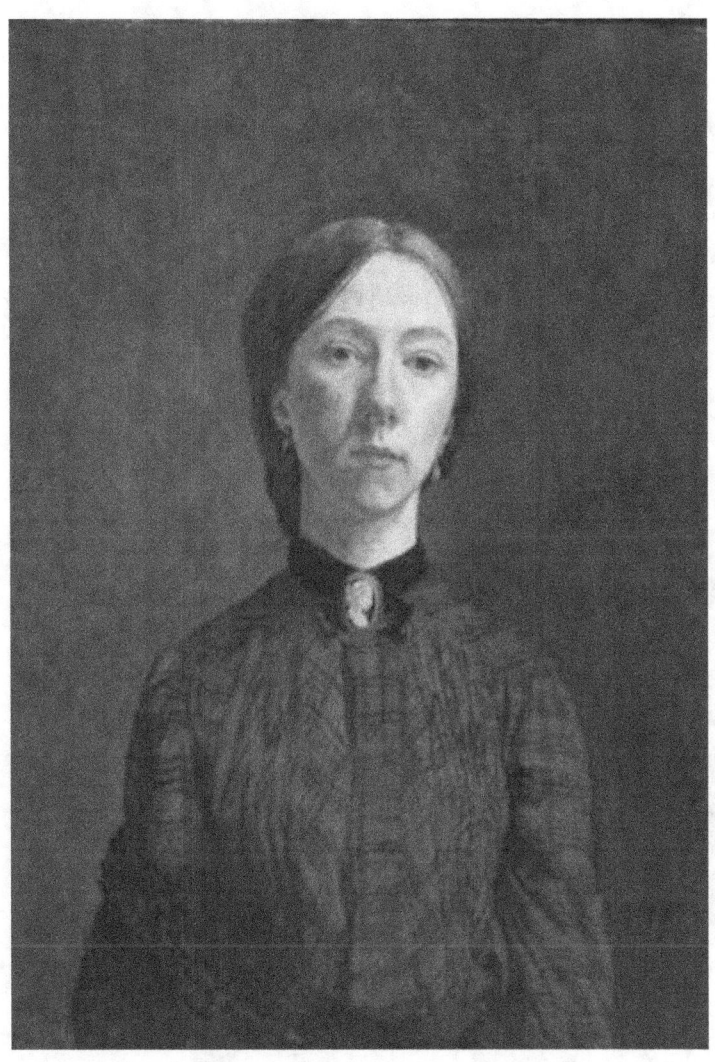

Gwen John, Self-Portrait, National Portrait Gallery, London

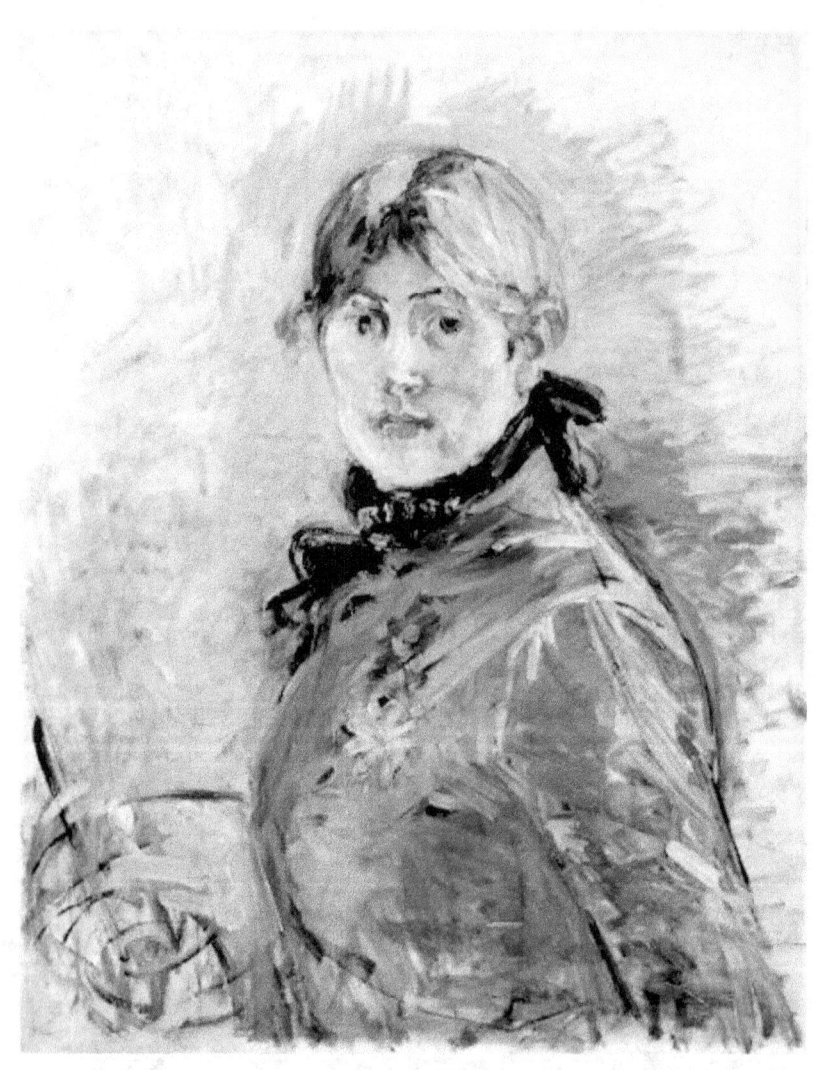

Berthe Morisot, Self-Portrait, 1885

Part Five

SCULPTURE

LAND ART

MINIMAL ART

CONSTANTIN BRANCUSI

WOMEN'S ART

FEMINIST ART

1

SCULPTURE

Sculpture is a three dimensional projection of primitive feeling: touch, texture, size and scale, hardness and warmth, evocation and compulsion to move, live and love.

Barbara Hepworth[1]

Sculpture, of its nature, is object, in the world, in a way in which painting, music, poetry are not.

William Tucker[2]

Sculpture is of course supremely erotic in its sense of surface. Visitors to museums are not allowed to touch sculpture – God forbid that anyone should try to touch Michelangelo's statue of *Dawn* in the Medici tombs in Florence.[3] But sculptures, the fetish object *par excellence, beg* to be touched. So, regardless of what sculpture depicts or represents, it can be seen as erotic. All those surfaces are sensuous: wood, glass, marble, granite, clay, china, bronze. Touching a chunk of unhewn Portland stone is pure

---

1 Hepworth: quoted in A.M. Hammacher: *The Sculpture of Barbara Hepworth*, Abrams, New York 1968, 99

2 Tucker: *The Language of Sculpture*, 107

3 Michelangelo: *Dawn*, 1524-5, Lorenzo Medici tomb, New Sacristy of S. Lorenzo, Florence

pleasure. It is a pleasure that is, perhaps, pre-cultural, pre-institutional, pre-industrial and pre-political. Touching cuts through socio-politico-cultural constructs, such as art, politics, ethnicity, education or war, and goes back to a primal form of being. At the same time, touching re-activates a sense of the past, both personal and societal. As John Keats said, '[t]ouch has a memory'.[4] Sculpture activates this fundamental relation with things. Sculpture renews our contact with the simple but utterly crucial experiences such as touch.

D.H. Lawrence wrote extensively on the importance of touch. In *Lady Chatterley's Lover*, Tommy Dukes yearns for touch: '"[g]ive me the democracy of touch, the resurrection of the body!"' he says (78). In stories such as *You Touched Me* and *The Blind Man*, Lawrence explored the mystery of the direct touch. It was all to do with Lawrence's cult of a new relation with the body, which must be physical, he said.[5] His model for this new sense of touch was Mary Magdalene touching the resurrected Christ,[6] in the *touch me/ touch me not* tension, explored in many Renaissance paintings, most famously, perhaps, by Titian.[7] Lawrence's sense of touch is soft, holy, of softly flowing blood.[8]

Sigmund Freud recognized the power relation exercised in the mere act of touching: '[t]ouching is the first step towards obtaining any sort of control over, or attempting to make use of, a person or object.'[9]

The sense of touch is not crucial to all sculpture, but without it sculpture loses some of its *frisson*, its visceral effect. Painters too explore the eroticism of touch, its tactile element in paintings. Rebecca Purdun paints with her fingers. Her billowy, smeared canvases resound with the vibrancy of the touch of the human

4 Keats, quoted in W. Jackson Bate: "Keats' Style: Evolution toward Qualities of Permanent Value", in Clarence D. Thorpe, ed. *The Major English Romantic Poets: A Symposium in Reappraisal*, Southern Illinois University Press, 1957
5 D.H. Lawrence: *John Thomas and Lady Jane*, Penguin 1973, 265
6 D.H. Lawrence: *The First Lady Chatterley*, Penguin 1973, 85
7 Titian: *Noli me tangere*, c. 1510, 109 x 91cm, National Gallery, London
8 D.H. Lawrence: *Pansies*, in *the Complete Poems*, ed. Vivian de Sola pinto & Warren Roberts, Heinemann 1972, 468, 471
9 Freud: *Toten and Taboo and Other Works*, tr. James Strachey & Anna Freud, *Standard Works*, vol. 13, Hogarth Press 1955, 33-4

hand, the eloquence of the pure gesture.[10] She writes:

> The more you get physically into the paint, you lose, you forget yourself. You become the paint, you become the form, you become the structure.[11]

It is this palpable sense of touch in sculpture that the German poet Rainer Maria Rilke described in his famous poem 'Archaic Torso of Apollo'. Rilke had worked with one of the most erotic of modern sculptors, Auguste Rodin. Rilke's poem lucidly evokes the animal, sexual nature of statues:

> We cannot know his legendary head
> with eyes, like ripening fruit. And yet his torso
> is still suffused with brilliant form inside,
> like a lamp, in which his gaze, now turned to low,
>
> gleams in all its power. Otherwise
> the curved breast could not dazzle you so, nor could
> a smile run through the placid hips and thighs
> to that dark centre where procreation flared.
>
> Otherwise this stone would seem defaced
> beneath the translucent cascade of the shoulders
> and would not glisten like a wild beast's fur:
>
> would not, from all the borders of itself,
> burst like a star: for here there is no place
> that does not see you. You must change your life.[12]

In Rainer Maria Rilke's sinuous sonnet the statue comes alive like an animal, and the stone becomes fur. This is an alarming, arresting transformation, and one that occurs often in modern sculpture – for example, the felt in Dorothea Tanning's sculptures, or the fur in Meret Oppenheim's *Object*, or the wood in Louise

---

10 Rebecca Purdum: *In Threes*, 1985, oil on canvas, 210.2 x 204.5cm,
11 Purdun, in C. Jolles: *Rebecca Purdun: Abstract Painting*, Jack Tilton Gallery, catalogue, 1986
12 in *The Selected Poetry of Rainer Maria Rilke*, tr. Stephen Mitchell, Picador 1987, 61

Bourgeois' works.[13] Bourgeois explores the relations between form and eroticism, volume and psychology, shape and nature. Her forms are nearly always dealing with eroticism – her *Nature Study*, for instance, feature bulbous volumes which are practically her trademark, echoing breasts, clitorises, vulvas, buttocks, heads, hands, knees, tongues, all the parts of the eroticized body.[14]

ALISON WILDING. The works of contemporary sculptors such as Alison Wilding are distinctly erotic. Wilding's *Hemlock III*, for example, is, like her *Blueblack*, a wooden dish containing hemlock, lead, lime and beeswax, hinting at alchemical trans-mutations.[15] The dish with its dangerous substances is a kind of womb, a motif or experience that appears in much of modern sculpture, from Judy Chicago's *Dinner Table* to the womb interiors of Louise Bourgeoise and others. Alison Wilding's sculpture often features two elements, one is often large, the other, small.[16] These two elements are luscious and mysterious, beyond interpretation, though some interpret them as masculine and feminine elements, the twin poles of heterosexuality, which are involved in some arcane dance or dalliance.[17]

Alison Wilding directly embraces the potential for sculpture to be supremely sensual. Her abstract forms hint at alchemical transformations, intimate experiences, investigations of sexuality and the relations between space, imagination, fantasy and the body.[18] Wilding herself stresses the enigmatic nature of her work: '[t]he obverse of making is looking, not telling',[19] and she

13 Louise Bourgeois: *One and Others*, 1955, painted wood, 18 x 20 x 17in, Whitney Museum of American Art, New York. See Deborah Wye: *Louise Bourgeois*, MOMA, New York 1982, Carl R. Baldwin: "Louise Bourgeois: An Iconography of Abstraction", *Art in America*, April 1975, 82-3, Corrinne Robbins: "Louise Bourgeois: Primordial Environments", *Arts Magazine*, June 1976, 81-3, Paul Gardner: "The Discreet Charm of Louise Bourgeois", *Art News*, Feb 1980, 80-86; Robert Storr: *Louise Bourgeois*, Galerie Maeght Lelong, Zurich 1985
14 Bourgeois: *Nature Study*, 1984, bronze, 30 x 19 x 15in, Serpentine Gallery, London
15 Alison Wilding: *Hemlock III*, 1986, lime, hemlock, lead, beeswax, pigment, Karsten Schubert; *Blueblack*, 1984, lime & elm woods, wax, lead, 36 x 28 x 49cm, collection: the artist
16 See Alison Wilding's *Nature: Blue and Gold*, 1984, brass, ash, oil and pigment, 47 x 109 x 22cm, British Council Collection, and *Untitled*, 1980, Arts Council of Great Britain, London; *Locust*, 1983, wood, wax, copper, 208 x 71 x 46cm, collection: the artist
17 See Lynne Cooke: *Alison Wilding*, Arts Council 1985; L. Biggs: *Between Object and Image*, British Council 1986; Wendy Beckett, 116;Terry A. Neff, 43-5
18 Alison Wilding: *Bare*, 1989-90, Newlyn Art Gallery, *Into the Dark*, 1986, limewood, lead and pigment, Newlyn Art Gallery. See also Hilary Gresty: *Bare*, Newlyn Art Gallery 1993
19 Wilding, quoted in Wendy Beckett, 116

emphasizes, as so many artists do, the making of the sculpture: '[t]he making and doing processes... [are] always the mainspring of the work'.[20]

The eroticism of sculpture is everywhere affirmed in high art itself, and in high art cultural criticism. Of course, a lot of this has to do with the eroticism of the nude human form, something that thousands of sculptors have explored and exploited. Renaissance sculptors – Luca della Robbia, Lorenzo Ghiberti, Andrea del Verrocchio, Pietro Lombardo, Michel Colombe – systematically exaggerated the sexuality of the body. Donatello's famous *David*, for instance, is a highly camp, homoerotic boy, an icon of stylized homoeroticism.[21] (A similar eroticization occurs in Verrocchio's *David*, Benvenuto Cellini's *Perseus*, Giovanni da Bologna's *Mercury*.[22])

The Renaissance eroticization of the human form finds its apotheosis in, of course, the art of Michelangelo Buonarroti, in his *Dawn, David*, early and late *Pietàs*, and of course the most volupt-uous of all figurative statues, the *Dying Slave*. The heroic homo-eroticism of Michelangelo's sculpture continues throughout post-Renaissance sculpture. In, for instance, the bombast and mascu-line power of Antonio Canova's *Hercules and Lichas*, or Gian-lorenzo Bernini's *David*.[23]

And there is much homoeroticism in that most sinister of all forms of sculpture, fascist art: in, for instance, Josef Thorak's *Comradeship*, two monumental male nudes with the bodies of he-men, supermen, Nietzschean *Übermensch*, clasping each other by the hand. The statues were commissioned by the Nazi govern-ment.[24] Fascist sculpture typically presents an ascetic, aggressive but banal stance, where eroticism is suppressed but never completely erased, as so much of fascist art depicts naked people.

20 Wilding, quoted in Terry A. Neff, 45
21 Donatello: *David*, c. 1440-2, bronze, Museo Nazionale, Florence
22 Benvenuto Cellini: *Perseus with the Head of Medusa*, 1554, bronze, Loggia dei Lanzi, Florence; Giovanni da Bologna: *Mercury*, 1564, Museo Nazionale, Florence; Andrea del Verrocchio: *David*, c. 1475, bronze, Museo Nazionale, Florence
23 Canova: *Hercules and Lichas*, 1812-5, marble, 138in high, Gallery of Modern Art, Rome; Bernini: *David*, 1623-4, marble, Galleria Borghese, Rome
24 Josef Thorak: *Comradeship*, 1937

See, for the apotheosis of violence and banality, Ferruccio Vecchi's statue of Benito Mussolini.[25]

The eroticism of celebrated statues of the ancient and Classical world, such as the *Venus de Milo*,[26] has been seen by some feminists as another manifestation of patriarchal culture's dismemberment of the female form. So many statues of the ancient world are headless or armless. For feminists, this fragmentation of the female body echoes that of pornography, where women's bodies are cut up, sometimes literally (as in S/M porn, and the porn of amputees). Any number of (mainly male) artists have depicted armless and/ or legless and/ or headless women (Gustave Courbet in his infamous torso of a woman, Eric Gill, Bill Brandt, Edvard Munch in his 'cruel' *Madonna,* etc).[27]

Other heterosexist depictions of people (i.e. women) in contemporary sculpture include Alberto Giacometti's *Spoon Woman*, a view of woman as Earth Mother, a kind of a totemic figure;[28] Gaston Lachaise's *Standing Woman*, one of the smooth, curvy Goddess types, also favoured by Aristide Maillol;[29] Hans Bellmer's bizarre *Dolls*, where the slit of a vulva is where the head would be, and set amidst exaggerated, bulbous forms (American photographer Cindy Sherman took up the Surrealist doll approach);[30] Henri Gaudier-Breska's *Red Stone Dancer*, though it attempts a new way of depicting gesture and posture in space, is still sexist;[31] Elie Nadelman's *Dancer*, like Paul Manship's *Dancer and Gazelles*, and Edgar Degas' *Dancer* sculptures, is also sexist;[32] and Ernst Kirchner's *Standing Nude* is porn masquerading

25 Ferruccio Vechi: *The Empire*, 1939-40
26 *Venus de Milo*, 2nd or 1st centuries BC, Parian marble, Louvre, Paris
27 See Bill Brandt: *Nude: London 1977*, silver gelatin print, Estate of Bill Brandt; Eric Gill: *Life study of a woman*, 1927, pencil, Victoria & Albert Museum; and see Saunders, 75f
28 Giacometti: *Spoon Woman*, 1926, bronze, 57.2in high, Kunsthaus, Zurich
29 Gaston Lachaise: *Standing Woman*, 1912-27, bronze, 70in high, Whitney Museum of American Art, New York
30 Bellmer: *La Poupée,* 1936, painted bronze, 16.8in high, Musée National d'Art Moderne, Paris
31 Henri Gaudier-Breska: *Red Stone Dancer*, 1914, waxed stone, 33.5in high, Tate Gallery, London
32 Degas: *Dancer Putting On Her Stocking*, bronze, 17in high, Metropolitan Museum of Art, New York; Elie Nadelman: *Dancer*, c. 1918, painted wood, 28.5in high, Robert Isaacson Gallery, New York; Paul Manship: *Dancer and Gazelles*, 1916, bronze, 32.2in high, Smithsonian Institute, Washington DC

as art, but then, most of his depictions of women are really porn, as well as art.[33]

CONTEMPORARY SCULPTURE

Contemporary sculpture has out-dazzled painting in many ways. However exciting a painting by, say, Julian Schnabel, Anselm Keifer, Jasper Johns, Robert Longo, Eric Fischl or David Salle may be, sculptures by artists such as Nancy Graves, Rebecca Horn, Robert Morris, Tony Smith, Mark di Suvero, Eva Hesse, Lucas Samaras and Louise Nevelson out-shine the painters.

Contemporary sculpture is, on the whole, really extraordinary. While Renaissance painting may represent the apotheosis of high art, and Greek sculpture may be the height of high sculpture, contemporary sculpture really is startling. Part of the reason is, of course, *scale*. Contemporary artists, of all kinds, have made massive art, sometimes achieving the truly monumental effect beloved of art critics. David Smith's *Wagon I* and his *Cubi* sculptures, for example, are huge, heavy, chunky, truly colossal pieces which dominate their surroundings.[34] Donald Judd wrote: '[t]his scale is one of the most important developments in twentieth century art'.[35] The Abstract Expressionists may still have made 'easel paintings' despite claiming they didn't (Barnett Newman argued on this matter), but they created gigantic paintings. Helen Frankenthaler, Mark Rothko, Franz Kline and Barnett Newman produced huge paintings, which swallow up the spectator when s/he moves close to them. Similarly, contemporary sculptors have made massive works. Artists such as Christo

---

33 Kirchner: *Standing Nude*, 1908-12, wood, painted yellow, 35.5in, Stedelijk Museum, Amsterdam
34 David Smith: *Wagon I*, 1963-4, painted steel, 308.6 x 162.6 x 224.8cm, National Gallery of Scotland
35 Donald Judd, 1975, 200f

built pieces that were 24 miles long.[36]

The bombastic, monumental, massive and brash 3-D art of contemporary sculpture was not made exclusively by male artists. American artist Mary Miss created a 5-acre scale work in Illinois, while Nancy Holt produced gigantic *Sun Tunnels*, 18 foot long pipes that were 9 feet high with many holes punched in the side, to let light in.[37] Helen Escobedo created some huge concrete and steel sculptures which 'attempt to fuse hard-edge geometric forms with nature's organic manifestations', as she puts it. Works such as *Snake* rise impressively from the earth, celebrating the flux and movement of organic forms.[38]

Many of the exalted products of contemporary sculpture, however, have been made by male artists: Donald Judd's 'specific objects', blocks of aluminium and Plexiglass that climb gallery walls,[39] Tony Smith's monumental cubes with their *thereness*, the primacy of presence, not effect,[40] Dan Flavin's mesmeric fluorescent tubes,[41] Sol LeWitt's Conceptual cubes, Richard Serra's huge 'walls' or slabs of steel,[42] and Carl Andre's plates of steel,

36 Christo: *Running Fence*, 1972-6, steelpoles, steel cables, woven nylon, 18ft high, 24.5 miles long, Sonoma & Marin Counties, California
37 Mary Miss: *Field Rotation*, 1981, wood, steel, gravel, earth, 5-acre site, central well 60 ft square and 7 feet deep, Governors' University, Park Forest South, Illinois; Nancy Holt: *Sun Tunnels*, 1973-6, concrete, each pipe 18 ft long, 9ft high, Great Basin Desert, near Lucin, Utah
38 Helen Escobedo: *Snake*, 1980-1, painted steel, 49ft high, National University of Mexico Cultural Centre
39 Donald Judd: *Untitled*, 1968, ten units, each 9 x 40in x 31in, height 14'3", Nelson A. Rockefeller Empire State Plaza Art Collection, New York. See Donald Judd, 1975; William Agee: "Unit, Series, Site: A Judd Lexicon", *Art in America*, May 1975, 40-49; P. Carlson: "Donald Judd's Equivocal Objects", *Art in America*, Jan 1984, 114-8; Donald Kuspit: "Donald Judd", *Artforum*, vol. 23, no. 5, February 1985; Barbara Haskell: *Donald Judd*, Whitney Museum of American Art, New York, 1988; Brydon Smith: *Donald Judd*, National Gallery of Canada, Ottawa 1975
40 Tony Smith: *Die*, 1962, 72 x 72 x 72in, Paula Cooper Gallery, New York. See Lucy Lippard: *Tony Smith*, Thames & Hudson 1972; Gene Baro: "Toward Speculation in Pure Form", *Art International*, Summer 1967, 27-31; E. Greene: "Morphology of Tony Smith's Work", *Artforum*, April 1974, 54-9
41 Dan Flavin: *Untitled (to the "innovator" of Wheeling Peachblow)*, 1968, 96.5 x 96.5 x 5.7in, Museum of Modern Art, New York; *Untitled*, 1976, pink, blue, green fluorescent light, 96in high, Saatchi Collection, London. See Ira Licht: "Dan Flavin", *Artscanada*, Dec 1968, 50-57; William Wilson: "Dan Flavin: Fiat Lux", *Art News*, Jan 1970, 48-51; Jack Burnham: "A Dan Flavin Retrospective in Ottawa", *Artforum*, vol. 8, no. 4, December 1969, 48-55
42 Richard Serra: *Clara-Clara*, 1983, Cor-Ten steel, installation, Jardin des Tuileries, Paris. See Rosalind E. Kraus: "Richard Serra: Sculpture Redrawn", *Artforum*, May 1972, 38-43; Douglas Crimp: "Richard Serra: Sculpture Exceeded", *October*, Fall 1981, 67-78

copper and zinc.[43]

One of the most exciting developments of contemporary sculpture and art is the installation, the taking-over of a whole space or environment – the floor, walls and ceiling, as in Rebecca Horn's *Ballet of the Woodpecker*, a room full of mirrors, or Sylvia Stone's *Crystal Palace*.[44]

WOMEN SCULPTORS

Among women artists, Eva Hesse is particularly powerful. Her artworks hang from ceilings, in rows, made of rubber, latex, cloth, wire, fibreglass, evoking organic forms in ambivalent, sensual ways.[45] Pieces such as *Ingeminate* offer up a mysterious affirmation of life in the form of two coils of cord connected by a long piece of surgical hose. *Sans II*, meanwhile, is a dozen rectangular 'compartments' made from fibreglass which hints at some obscure systematization of flesh and organic form. Hesse wrote: '[i]f I can name the content... it's the total absurdity of life.'[46] Hesse's works haven't dated at all, and remain fresh and inspiring.

Louise Nevelson produced post-Surrealist huge reliefs or

43 Carl Andre: *Lead Piece (144 Lead Plates)*, overall 75 x 144.8 x 145.5in, Museum of Modern Art, New York. See Kenneth Baker: "Andre in Retrospect", *Art in America*, April 1980, 88-94, Diane Waldman: "Holding the Floor", *Art News*, Oct 1970, 60-2, 75-9, Phyllis Tuchman: "Background of a Minimalist: Carl Andre", *Artforum*, March 1978, 29-33; Enno Develing: *Carl Andre*, Gemeentenmeuseum, The Hague 1969
44 Sylvia Stone: *Crystal Palace*, 1971-2, Plexiglass, 6.5 x 14 x 16ft, Andre Emmerich Gallery, New York; Rebecca Horn; *Ballet of the Woodpecker*, 1986-7, room installation with mirrors, small hammers and a painting machine, 330 x 230cm (4 mirrors), 330 x 125cm (4 mirrors), Eric Franck Gallery, Geneva; Red Grooms & Mimi Gross: *The City of Chicago*, 1967, mixed media, c. 12 x 25 x 25ft, Art Institute of Chicago
45 Eva Hesse: *Contingent*, 1969, reinforced fibreglass and latex over cheesecloth, each of 8 units, 9.5-14 x 3-4ft, Australian National Gallery, Caberra; *Aught*, 1968, double sheets of latex rubber, polyethylene plastic inside, 4 units, each 78in high, collection: the artist; *Ice Piece*, 1969, fibreglass and wire, 62 x 1in, Xavier Fourcade Gallery, New York. See Bill Barrette: *Eva Hesse's Sculpture*: Catalogue Raissonné, New York 1989; Rosalind Krauss & Eva Hesse: *Eva Hesse: Sculpture*, Whitechapel Art Gallery 1979; Cindy Nemser: "My Memories of Eva Hesse", *Feminist Art Journal*, Winter 1973, 12-3
46 Cindy Nemser: "An interview with Eva Hesse", *Artforum*, May 1970, 62

structures which are like Cubist or Constructionist altarpieces full of objects, various articles made of wood, all painted in one colour, black, white or gold: chair legs, railings, door knobs.[47] Her sculptures are like magical cupboards, vertical dreamscapes made of boxes stacked on top of each other.

German sculptor Rebecca Horn's works are based on natural forms, but also on movement, dance, time and environments. Horn's wonderful *Peacock Machine* is an exuberant activator of space, one of those pieces that aims for the essence of a natural form and captures it: a peacock's magnificent tail.[48]

In the art of Barbara Hepworth, organic forms are not sexualized, as they are in so many other sculptors. As with Constantin Brancusi, Hepworth's art hovers between subjectivity and objectivity, between natural form and æsthetic abstraction (as in her *Two Forms*, for example.)[49] Like Brancusi, Hepworth maintained that she always returned to nature, and took her inspiration from nature. For her, nature meant the (Cornish) landscape, and the human body. 'We return always to the human form – the human form in landscape', she said.[50] Her sculpture stems from emotion and expression, from feeling: 'I rarely draw what I see – I draw what I feel in my body', she said.[51]

Barbara Hepworth's distinctive forms, with their smooth curves and holes, are clearly sensual objects.[52] Hepworth acknowledged the sensuality of sculptural forms (see the quote, above). In 1969 Elizabeth Catlett took the holed form of Hepworth and suppressed the erotic dimension to produce a political work that celebrated 'the struggle for liberation by black women in this

47 Louise Nevelson: *Royal Tide IV*, 1960, wood, 1 x 14ft, Ludwig Museum, Cologne; *Sky Cathedral – Moon Garden Plus One*, 1957-60, black painted wood, 9.1 x 10.1 x 1.6ft, collection: A. & M. Glimcher, New York
48 Rebecca Horn: *Peacock Machine*, 1982, installation at Documenta 7, Kassel. See Mina Roustayi: "Getting Under the Skin: Rebecca Horn's Sensibility Machines", *Arts*, May 1989, 58-68; Michael Kimmelman: "A Sculptural Circus of Whips and Suspense", *New York Times*, 23 Sept 1988, C29
49 Hepworth: *Two Forms*, 1937, marble, 26in high, private collection
50 Barbara Hepworth: *Pictorial Autobiography*, Praeger, New York, 50-3
51 quoted in Hammacher, op.cit., 98
52 Barbara Hepworth: *Porthmeor: Sea Form*, 1958, bronze, 30.5in high, Hirshhorn Museum and Sculpture Garden, Washington DC; *Pendour*, 1947, painted wood, 10 x 27 x 9in, Hirshhorn Museum and Sculpture Garden, Washington DC, *Forms in Movement*, 1956, Barbara Hepworth Museum and Sculpture Garden, St Ives, Cornwall

country and everywhere'.[53]

German artist Käthe Kollwitz's monumental pieces are heavy with life, heavy with grave feelings, the weight of life on one's shoulders. This emotional gravity is apparent in powerful sculptures such as her *Pietà*, where Christ lays in his mother's lap, as in Sandro Botticelli's *Pietàs*, or those of the Flemish school.[54] Her body encircles the dead Christ, like the *Madonna della Misericordia* of Piero della Francesca. Here, the Mother encircles the Son. The Madonna, though, is brooding on her fate, not just the death of her child, but on the whole meaning of the cycle of events which brought her from being the 'handmaiden of the Lord', as a young woman, to this final, terrible point, with her grown child dead on her lap.

Käthe Kollwitz's *Pietà* is unusual among *Pietàs*, if one thinks of those of Michelangelo Buonarroti, Sandro Botticelli and Rogier van der Weyden, in that instead of gut-wrenching pain and anguish, which is usual in *Pietàs*, Kollwitz depicts a sombre, contemplative Mother, musing up the ravages of time and age. Similar deeply parental feelings are expressed in sculptures such as *Twins* where, again, the mother passionately enfolds her offspring.[55]

American land artist Alice Aycock, one of the very best contemporary women artists around, using science as her muse, has produced some wonderfully fantastical machines, such as *The Angels Continue Turning the Wheels of the Universe,* or or the marvellous, massive piece *The Miraculous Machine in the Garden (Tower of the Winds),* which features 268 antenna and bells ringing in a vacuum.[56] Aycock's works are provocative and inspiring, drawing on childhood emotions, mythology, and remembered spaces. Aycock has explored the fear and fascination of under-ground places, for instance, in many works. Lila Katzen sets alive public spaces with her flowing, curling forms.[57]

53 K. Petersen & J. Wilson, 142.
54 Kollwitz: *Pietà*, 1937, bronze, Staatliche Museen, Berlin
55 Kollwitz: *Twins*, 1935, bronze, Staatliche Museen, Berlin
56 Alice Aycock: *One Thousand and One Nights in the Mansion of Bliss,* 1983, mixed media, private collection; *The Miraculous Machine in the Garden (Tower of the Winds),* 1983, mixed media, 16ft high, private collection
57 Lila Katzen: *Guardian*, 1979, bronze, 35 x 15 x 3ft, private collection, Saudi Collection

LAND ART

Land art (a.k.a. earthworks, earth art and environmental art) has proved to be the more typically phallic and patriarchal of contemporary artistic productions, in terms of second wave feminism.[58] We have already mentioned Christo, who 'wraps' buildings or stretches curtains across valleys or surrounds islands with tarpaulin.[59] Other works of earth art which seem have described as phallic and domineering include Michael Heizer's *Double Negative*, where he took two chunks out of the earth, a gigantic mark on the planet.[60] Heizer's other works include gouging huge holes in the ground and putting great chunks of rock in them.[61]

Walter de Maria made a similarly deep gesture in the earth when he cut a 4.5 mile long scar in the desert in Nevada. The ultimate in ithyphallic, male land art must be Walter de Maria *Vertical Earth Kilometer*. At a cost of $500,000, de Maria sunk a 1-kilometre brass rod into the planet. Nothing can be seen of it except a 2 inch brass disc on the ground.

There's no denying the sensuality and eroticism of land art and earthworks. Walter de Maria filled a gallery with black soil, and the effect is undoubtedly sensual (you can still see it in New York City, At DIA). More spectacular, and just as masculine and phallic in its connotations of male creativity, sperm, fire, power and shamanism is de Maria's *Lightning Field*, a grid of 400 stainless steel poles, each about 20 feet high, set in the New

---

58 See Alan Sonfit, ed. *Art in the Land: A Critical Anthology of Environmental Art*, New York 1983, John Beardsley: *Earthworks and Beyond: Contemporary Art in the Landscape*, New York 1984

59 Christo: *Surrounded Islands, Biscoyne Bay, Greater Miami*, 1980-3, 6 million square feet of polypropylene fabric; *Valley Curtain*, synthetic fabric, 417m long, 1970-2, Grand Canyon, Colorado

60 Michael Heizer: *Double Negative*, 1969-70, 1,500 x 50 x 42 feet, Mormon Mesa, Nevada. See Julia Brown *et al*: *Michael Heizer: Sculpture in Reverse*, Museum of Contemporary Art, Los Angeles 1984, Gregoire Müller: Michael Heizer", *Arts Magazine*, Dec 1969, 42-5

61 Michael Heizer: *Displaced, Replaced Mass*, 1969, Silver Springs, Nevada

Mexico desert.[62] The sheer size of some of the works of land artists is itself visceral and erotic. De Maria's *Lightning Field*, for instance, attracts lightning, and a storm, as anyone knows, is one of the most sensual phenomenon in nature.[63] Many poets have written of the sensuality of the natural world, among them Johann Wolfgang von Goethe, Sylvia Plath, Arthur Rimbaud, and Emily Dickinson. In many poems, Cornish poet Peter Redgrove has written of the eroticism of nature, and especially of thunderstorms. This is from 'The Pale Brows of Lightning':

> And lightning opens its shutter but an instant,
> When it catches you burn like a candle,
> What is that lambent shadow fluttering into the woods
> In its own blue light that illuminates primrose
> The ripped tree's flesh?[64]

Joseph Beuys produced a startling piece entitled *Lightning*: a gigantic chunk of bronze, thin at the top, splaying out towards the bottom, as if he is trying to make manifest the bolt of energy leaping down to the earth.[65]

Robert Smithson's famous *Spiral Jetty* is another monumental earthwork, though the use of the spiral motif has connotations with the ancient symbols of the Goddess.[66] Of his *Spiral Jetty*, Smithson writes:

> As I looked at the site, it reverberated out to the horizons only to suggest an immobile cyclone while flickering light made the entire landscape appear to quake. A dormant earthquake spread into an immense roundness. From that gyrating space emerged the possibility of the Spiral Jetty. No idea, no concepts, no systems, no struct-

---

62 Walter de Maria: *The New York Earth Room*, 1977, 250 cubic yards of earth and earth mix (peat and bark), covering 3,600 square feet to a depth of 22 inches, installation, Dia Art Foundation, New York; *Lighting Field*, 1971-7, 400 stainless steel poles, in a rectangular grid, 16 x 25, spaced 220 feet apart, average pole height 20'7", New Mexico. See David Bourdon: "Walter de Maria: The Singular Experience", *Art International*, 20 Dec 1968, 39-43, 72; Malcolm Winton: "Sculptures That Blow Away", *Ark*, Spring 1970, 18-19; Roberta Smith: "De Maria: elements", *Art in America*, May 1978, 102-5
63 See Peter Redgrove: *The Black Goddess and the Sixth Sense*, Bloomsbury 1987; *The Clypoean Mistress*, Bloodaxe, 1993
64 Peter Redgrove: *The Man Named East and other new poems*, Routledge & Kegan Paul 1985
65 Joseph Beuys: *Lightning*, 1982-5, bronze, Anthony d'Offay Gallery, London
66 See Marija Gimbutas; Monica Sjöo, Shirley Nicholson

388

ures, no abstractions could hold themselves together in the actuality of that phenomenological evidence.[67]

Not all of land art is phallic and bombastic. Richard Long speaks for many British sculptors when he writes:

> In the sixties there was a feeling that art need not be a production line of more objects to fill the world. My interest was in a more thoughtful view of art and nature, making art both visible and invisible, using ideas, walking, stones, tracks, water, time, etc, in a flexible way... It was the antithesis of so-called American "Land Art," where an artist needed money to be an artist, to buy real estate to claim possession of the land, and to wield machinery. True capitalist art.[68]

The circle motif, one of the primæval symbols of eternity, cycles, time, rebirth, etc, is employed throughout the work of Richard Long. Long's circles, made from slate, timber or by walking in a circle, are gentler, more eco-friendly kinds of sculpture.[69] The circle shape itself speaks of organic forms, and, in some religions, speaks of the feminine and the Goddess. Not a few sculptors and land artists have made the circle crucial to their works: Richard Long, Andy Goldsworthy, Robert Morris and Dennis Oppenheim.

American artist Robert Morris has produced gigantic circular works, such as his *Observatory*, which is a huge earthwork recalling the megalithic structures of ancient times, such as Avebury stone circle, while his *Labyrinth* is a maze-size sculpture, the kind of maze one finds in theme parks and country houses, except that Morris' *Labyrinth* uses the ancient pattern of the Cretan labyrinth, itself a motif some see as distinctly feminine, speaking of Goddess mysteries; Robert Smithson's *Closed Mirror Square* is like a Aztec ziggurat, while his *Amarillo Ramp* recalls the gigantic embankments found at Neolithic earthworks such as, in Britain, Maiden Castle, or Iron Age hill forts such as British Camp on the

67 Smithson" "The Spiral Jetty", unpublished MS, quoted in Krauss, 282. See Robert Hobbs: *Robert Smithson: Sculpture*, Cornell University Press, New York 1981
68 Long, quoted in Suzi Gablik: *Has Modernism Failed?*, Thames & Hudson 1984, 44
69

Malvern Hills.[70]

Some artists have produced stone circles which look very much like Stonehenge, such as Nancy Holt's monumental *Stone Enclosure: Rock Rings*.[71] These Minimal sculptures are ambivalently related to ancient monuments, however, as Samuel Wagstaff remarks of Tony Smith's works:

> They are related to early cultures intentionally or through sympathy – menhirs, earth mounds, cairns... [and] to this culture with equal sympathy – smokestacks, gas tanks, dump trucks, poured concrete ramps.[72]

Constantin Brancusi, Richard Long, Bill Woodrow and many sculptors have spoken of the importance of materials in their work, how they learn from their materials, and 'follow' their materials. Tony Cragg speaks of 'works in which I learnt from the materials'.[73]

German artist Wolfgang Laib dusts the earth with pollen, to form an enormous square layer of brilliant yellow.[74] Andy Goldsworthy and Laib collect leaves, berries, pollen, honey and other natural elements and weave sensuous artifacts that are ephemeral and intricate. Dennis Oppenheim worked with snow and circles in his *Annual Rings*, a series of concentric circles that straddle the Canadian/ American border, and with burning circles onto grass in his *Branded Mountain*.[75] Oppenheim made snow one of his primary media in his works of the 1960s, and explored notions of borders, time zones and spaces.

70 Robert Morris: *Observatory*, 1971, earth, grass, wood, steel, granite, diameter c. 300 feet, Oosterlijk Flevoland, Holland; *Labyrinth*, 1974, painted masonite, plywood & two-by-fours, 96 x 360in, Institute of Contemporary Art, University of Pennsylvania, Philadelphia; Robert Smithson: *Closed Mirror Square*, 1969, rock salt, mirrors and glass, Blum Helman Gallery, New York, *Amarillo Ramp*, 1973, red sandstone shale, 1800in diameter, estate of the artist. See also Maurice Berger: *Labyrinths: Robert Morris, Minimalism, and the 1960s*, Harper & Row, New York 1989
71 Nancy Holt: *Stone Enclosure: Rock Rings*, 1977-8, hand-quarried schist, outer ring 40 feet, inner ring 2 feet across, ring walls 10 feet high, Western Washington University, Bellingham
72 quoted in Lucy Lippard: "Tony Smith", *Art International*, Summer 1967, 26
73 quoted in Norbert Lynton, introduction to *Tony Cragg*, Fifth Triennale India, British Council 1982, 2
74 Wolfgang Laib: *Hazelnut Pollen*, Dokumenta 8
75 Dennis Oppenheim: *Annual Rings*, 1968, 150 x 200 feet, Fort Kent, Maine and Clair, New Brunswick; *Branded Mountain*, 1969, 30ft diameter, San Pablo, California

Other intriguing and sensual land artists include the British artist David Nash, who has built a number of 'stoves' and 'hearths', out of natural materials – snow, slate, wood – which then he sets alight.[76] His *Wooden Boulder* is exactly that – a huge, near-spherical chunk of oak. Nash tipped the boulder into a stream near his studio at Blaenau Ffestiniog, Wales. His idea was for the sculpture to make its way to the ocean. Instead, it stayed put in a pool, for a long time, and interacted continually with the environment.[77] Eventually it moved down the stream a number of times. Nash's art is gentle and based firmly in a reverence for nature, and trees and wood in particular.

Crucial in land art is the concept and reality of change, for these works in wood, snow, ice, leaves, water, slate, grass, etc, do not stay. They are not 'permanent', in the way that, say, bronze, marble, steel or stone can be. We have bronze and marble sculptures still looking remarkable from the ancient Graeco-Roman period, and stone figurines from the Palæolithic period. One cannot see how Andy Goldsworthy's leaves could last very long, or Richard Long's clusters of stones on remote mountainsides, which will be blown over. Indeed, ephemerality, transiency and change are key components in land art. As British artist Barry Flanagan writes:

> Truly sculpture is always going on. With proper physical circumstances and the visual invitation, one simply joins in and makes the work... there is a never-ending stream of materials and configurations to be seen, both natural and man-made, that have visual strength but not object or function apart from this. It is as if they existed for just this physical, visual purpose – to be seen.[78]

---

76 David Nash: *Slate Stove*, 1988, Blaenau Ffestiniog, Wales; *Wood Stove*, 1979, Maentwrog, Wales; *Snow Stove*, 1982, Kotoku, Japan. See Alan McPherson: "Interview with David Nash", *Artscribe*, 12, June 1978; Hugh Adams: "The Woodman", *Art and Artists*, 12, April 1979; *Sixty Seasons: David Nash*, Third Eye Centre, Glasgow, 1983; David Nash: "David Nash", *Aspects*, 10, Spring 1980
77 Nash: *Wooden Boulder*, 1978, oak, Maentwrog, Wales
78 quoted in Gene Baro: "Sculpture made visible: Barry Flanagan in discussion with Gene Baro", *Studio International*, 178, 915, October 1969, 122. See Charles Harrison: "Barry Flanagan's sculpture", *Studio International*, 175, 900, May 1968, 266-8; Judith Russi Kirshner: "Barry Flanagan", *Artforum*, 23, 10, Summer 1985, 112

RICHARD LONG

Crucial, too, is the sense and delicacy of touch in land art. Richard Long[79] sprinkles snow in a circle, or smears mud, often from the River Avon near his home in Bristol in England, in huge circles on walls, or he makes marks on grass using his feet. The sense of touch, of gesture and of sensuality is crucial in Richard Long's circles, lines, cairns and routes. Often the touch in Richard Long's art is the foot. The touch of the feet on grass, rock, soil, water, mud. The walk itself is an artistic 'statement' in Richard Long's work. Many of his works are 'walks'. The 'walk' is a mark, a gesture, an interaction of artist and 'material', the 'material' being the world.

There is a historical and human dimension to Richard Long's walks, because his art is always aware of the personal and social history of a place, even when it is a wilderness. 'A walk is just one more layer, a mark laid upon the thousands of other layers of human and geographic history on the surface of the land', explained Long.[80] Long talks in terms of walking as a kind of palimpsest, where one layer is written upon the next (a notion central to Lawrence Durrell's *The Alexandria Quartet*). Long is aware of re-activating history as he walks through landscapes. He walks in time as much as space. His works also emphasize the temporal, historical dimension: for instance, Long will pick up a stone for a mile then drop it, or spend a certain length of time building a sculpture before moving on.

Everywhere the human touch is present in Richard Long's sculpture, as in all sculpture. The shapes might be 'organic' –

79 Richard Long: *Circle in Alaska*, driftwood on the Artic Circle, Bering Strait 1977; *Untitled*, 1987, mud on paper, Anthony d'Offay Gallery, London; *Mountain Lake Powder Snow*, 1985, Lapland. See J. Poinsot: "Richard Long: To Build the Landscape", *Art Press*, Nov 1981, 9-11, Michael Compton: *Some Notes on the Work of Richard Long*, British Council 1976, Gabriella Jeppson: *Richard Long*, Fogg Art Museum, Cambridge, Mass., 1980, Nancy Foote: "Long Walks", *Artforum*, Summer 1980, 42-7, Simon Field: "Touching the Earth", *Art and Artists*, April 1973, 14-19, John T. Paoletti: "Richard Long", *Arts Magazine*, Dec 1982, 3; Richard Long: "Richard Long replies to a critic", *Art Monthly*, 68, July 1983, 20-21; Rudi H. Fuchs: "Memories of Passing: A Note on Richard Long, *Studio International*, 1987, 965, April 1974, 172-3.
80 Long, quoted in Wheeler, 264

circles, spirals, zigzags – but the appearance of Long's sculpture in their wilderness settings is always of some sophisticated (not archaic) human gesture at work.

Like Bruce Chatwin, who also spoke lovingly of walking, wandering, nomads and wildernesses, Richard Long has travelled to some wild places: Lapland, Africa, Australia, Peru, Bolivia, Alaska and the Himalayas. It's easy to see his art as simply pure romanticism, a 'back to the land' art that utterly ignores political, societal, ideological, racial, economic and gender issues. True. His art is not concerned with the urban 'real world' at all. And it looks very odd to see his work in galleries in cities.

Rather, Richard Long's sculpture is deeply poetic, personal, subjective and romantic. It is *all* about a response to nature, about getting into connection with nature, as with Andy Goldsworthy and David Nash. Like Goldsworthy, Long works with his hands too – touches of the hand not to be seen, perhaps, in the walks or the lines of stones amidst rocky valleys – but in the circles of mud smeared on gallery walls.[81] The eroticism of such mud-smeared works is obvious, as is the sensuality of rites such as mud dancing.

The personal details of each sculpture in land art are important, and artists catalogue themselves meticulously. It is curious to visit a Richard Long exhibition and be confronted by lots of large pieces of paper with Long's documentation of his walks or sculptures printed on them. Similarly with Andy Goldsworthy.

Typical is Richard Long's *The Moors Three Circle* of 1982 – a walk in his beloved Southwest British terrain. The whole artwork is a large piece of paper (you can buy it framed or unframed). There are three concentric rings of words, printed in red, which read: *Three miles on Exmoor, two miles on Dartmoor, one mile on Bodmin Moor.* The words are printed in circles clearly to indicate a number of things – the walk itself, on the earth, in circles, and stone circles, and circles in general, as symbols and as Long's

---

81 Long: *Avon Mud Circle*, 1986, installation, Guggenheim Museum, New York

primary motif. The next line, also in red, is the title: *Three Moors, Three Circles*. The next line of type, in black, reads: *A 108 mile walk from Bodmin Moor, to Dartmoor, to Exmoor, walking around three circles along the way*. The next three lines read: *Liskeard to Porlock, Richard Long, England 1982*. That's it. That the whole artwork, a cursory, matter-of-fact description of the walk.

The words on the paper, though, have little if anything to do with the actual experience of walking on England's wild moors, with their sudden rainfalls out of nowhere, their amazingly impenetrable mists, their vast marshes, and their utter solitude. Richard Long's bits of paper are word games which only hint at the reality of walking in wildernesses. They are semiotic games which point towards the powerful nature of Long's 'landscape of the soul'. The 'reality' of Long's work is clearly 'out there', in the world, in the landscape. Yet much of his art is conceptual, fictive, representations of representations. There is much ambivalence in his importing of 'natural' forms and materials into the urban space of the art gallery. The walks themselves are the reality of his art. Everything else is secondary, something for the punters and art critics; something, perhaps, to do on cold Winter evenings in between walks and trips and travels to wildernesses.

The relationship between titles/ documentation and artworks is precarious in land art, because the photography, the document-ation, description of the artwork is often all that remains of it. Richard Long's cairns or lines made by flattening grass will soon be lost. Similarly, Andy Goldsworthy's sculptures of ridges of sand are blown away, the ice melts – but we have the photographs.

Richard Long speaks in poetic, religious terms of his art: 'art should be a religious experience'.[82] Although his sculptures alter the world – no *object* can avoid altering the world – he maintains that he takes his cue from the landscape, instead of imposing on it 'from outside', as it were: 'I use the world as I find it'.[83] Bill

82 quoted in Wheeler, 264
83 Long: *Five, six, pick up sticks/ Seven, eight, lay them straight*, 1980, Anthony d'Offay Gallery, September 1980

Woodrow, a contemporary of Long's, also 'uses' the world as he finds it: he trawls the world for materials with which to make sculptures:

> My choice of objects is dictated, I think in the first instance by what is available, what I come across in the streets, on dumps... What I find more interesting about the work, is that these items are material for me that is found in my environments...[84]

Richard Long's views have something in common with Zen Buddhism, Taoism, shamanism and Western magic.[85] The sculpture and the place are one, in a mystical relationship, as Long points out in his writings:

> The material and the idea are of the place; sculpture and place are one, the same. The place is as far as the eye can see from the sculpture. The place for a sculpture is found by walking. Some works are a succession of particular places along a walk, e.g. *Milestones*. In this work, the walking, the places and the stones all have equal importance.[86]

Richard Long promulgates the *participation mystique* with the earth, with places and atmospheres and organic materials, that the archaic peoples of the world had (and have). It is a pre-institutionalized, pre-pagan and pantheistic rapport with the world, deliberately eschewing dogma, doctrine and manifestos. It is also part, as many commentators have noted, of a British Romantic tradition, that feeling for nature found in the art of William Blake, J.M.W. Turner, Lord Byron, Percy Shelley and John Constable.[87]

---

84 Woodrow, quoted in *Objects and Sculpture*, Institute of Contemporary Arts, 1981, 37
85 See Anne Seymour: "El Estanque de Basho – una nueva perspectiva", in *Piedras Richard Long*, Ministerio de Cultura, Dirección general de Bellas Artes y Archivos and the British Council 1986
86 Long, quoted in Lucie-Smith: *Sculpture Since 1945*, 121
87 See Anne Seymour, op.cit., Suzi Gablik, op.cit.

ANDY GOLDSWORTHY

Andy Goldsworthy (b. 1956) seems to be a particularly gentle and sensitive in his handling of materials: he stitches together leaves to forms lines, often placed in water, or makes circular slabs of snow, or entwines twigs in an arc.[88] He creates a delicate spiral of chestnut leaves, called *Autumn Horn*; he pins bright yellow dandelions on willowherb stalks in a circle, on bluebells; he makes lines and cairns, like Richard Long, of pebbles; he fashions hollow, circular structures, like igloos, from slate, leaves, driftwood and bracken; he makes long wavy ridges in Arizona desert sand; he builds arches, globes, hollow spheres, slabs, spires, spirals and star-shapes out of snow and ice.[89] It's all very impressive. The sculptures made of sticks, for instance, stuck together in an arch, or a line, reflected in the mirror-like water of Derwent Water in Cumbria, are indeed wonderful.[9] Or the globe created from oak leaves in varied states of autumnal decay, superb stuff.[90] Or the globe carved out of snow, and perched amidst some young trees, or the slabs of snow, set up in a line with slits cut in them.[91] Or his most dramatic work, *Touching North*, four circular arches or tunnels made of snow, which is dramatic partly because its location, that space so thoroughly a masculine 'wild zone', the place of macho adventures and courage, the North Pole.[92]

Paul Nesbitt writes of Andy Goldsworthy's art:

88 Andy Goldsworthy: *Japanese maple leaves stitched together to make a floating chain*, 21 November 1987, Ouchiyama-mura, Japan; *Slate Stack*, 1988, Scaur Water Valley, Penpont, Dumfriesshire, Scotland; *Circular stalks in a lake*, 29 April 1987, Yorkshire Sculpture Park
89 Goldsworthy: *Autumn Horn*, Nov 1986, chestnut leaves, Penpont, Dumfriesshire; *Dandelion Flowers*, 1 May 1987, 'flowers pinned to willowherb stalks laid in a ring held above bluebells with forked sticks', Yorkshire Sculpture Park, West Bretton; *Line and Carin* 31 May & 1 June 1985, pebbles, St Abbs, the Borders; [*Cairns*], made of plane leaves, 19 Oct 1988, Castres, France, slate, Summer 1987, Stonewood, Dumfriesshire, bracken, 13 February 1988, Borrowdale, Cumbria, driftwood, 29 November 1987, Kinagashima-cho, Japan; [*Waves of Sand*], 21 Nov 1989, 'fine dry sand', Arizona; *Ice Arch*, 1-2 Dec 1982, Brough, Cumbria; *Stacked Ice*, 28 Dec 1985, Hampstead Heath
90 [*Oak Globe*], 15 September 1985, branches and oak leaves, Jenny Noble's Gill, Dumfriesshire
91 Goldsworthy: *Slits cut into frozen snow*, 12 February 1988, Blencathra, Cumbria; *Snowball in Trees*, February 1980, Robert Hall Wood, Lancashire
92 Goldsworthy: *Touching North*, 24 April 1989, North Pole

Throughout these works the dominant theme is one of working with nature, to reveal nature itself – physical, chemical and biological. Goldsworthy uses nature's materials – rock, water (snow and ice, rain and mist), earth and the plants and animals which inhabit these; he uses nature's properties – structure, shape, form and colour; he uses nature's forces which together create, alter and animate those materials and properties – forces of light, heat, wind and gravity.[93]

Andy Goldsworthy's ethics are those of Richard Long, David Nash and other British land artists: a mystical feeling for the landscape, expressed by an exquisite sensitivity of *touch*, that all-important component in the eroticism of sculpture:

Movement, change, light, growth and decay are the lifeblood of nature, the energies that I try to tap through my work, I need the shock of touch, the resistance of place, materials and weather, the earth as my source.[94]

Andy Goldsworthy says, like Barry Flanagan, Richard Long and any number of sculptors, that the personal touch, of the hand on materials, is crucial:

The work itself determines the nature of its making. I enjoy the freedom of just using my hands and 'found' tools – a sharp stone, the quill of a feather, thorns. I am not playing the primitive. I use my hands because this is the best way to do most of my work.

Andy Goldsworthy's sculptures are marked by a number of elements familiar in land art: transience, domination, penetration, circular forms (globes, circles, spirals, snakes, cones) and nature mysticism. The ephemerality of the pieces, for instance, is a key component. Snow and ice will melt away, leaves will disintegrate, stones will be blown over. Each Goldsworthy sculpture has a date printed with its title. Not just a year, as in the usual artwork, but a specific day. Thus, one of his best pieces, the delicious poppy covered boulder, has the title: *Poppy petals wrapped around a boulder*

93 Paul Nesbitt: "A Landscape touched by Gold", in Graham Hughes: *Arts Review: Yearbook 1990*, Arts Review Magazine 1990, 49
94 Goldsworthy: *Andy Goldsworthy*, Viking 1990, no page numbers. All Goldsworthy's quotes are from this edition.

held with water (Sibobre, France, June 6, 1989). The petal-covered rock, with its brilliant red colour, nestles in some mossy boulders, looking very much like one of Constantin Brancusi's 'cosmic eggs'.

Andy Goldsworthy speaks of '[r]hythms, cycles, seasons in nature working at different speeds'.[95] Each date records a particular day (September 24, 1982, December 30, 1987, February 9, 1981, March 11, 1984, October 19, 1988); each day has its own weather, atmosphere and events, which are important for the artist.

Andy Goldsworthy says he is not against long-term art, as some people might think from contemplating his transient sculptures:

> That art should be permanent or impermanent is not the issue. Transience in my work reflects what I find in nature and should not be confused with an attitude towards art generally. I have never been against the well-made or long-lasting.

Domination and *penetration* are familiar terms describing patri-archal actions or constructions or ideologies used by feminists. Is Andy Goldsworthy, seemingly so delicate in his touches, dominating nature? He doesn't think so:

> By working large, I am not trying to dominate nature. If people feel small in relation to a work, they should not assume that there is an intention to make nature itself small.

Yet, clearly, Goldsworthy, and Long – and the American land artists (Heizer, de Maria, Smithson, Simonds, Christo, Aycock) – do dominate nature. Robert Smithson's *Spiral Jetty* or Michael Heizer's gigantic *Double Negative* will probably be around for a long time, unless someone destroys them. Goldsworthy's stone pieces, too, like Long's, may indeed stay around for a while. There is a sense of gloating when Goldsworthy says '[f]ourteen years ago I made a line of stones in Morecambe Bay. It is still

95 Goldsworthy: *Touching North*, Fabian Carlsson Gallery, London 1989

398

there, buried under the sand, unseen. All my work still exists, in some form.' Daring not to change or affect nature, land artists do just that, all the time. They 'interact' with nature, but their 'interactions', however small scale, can't help changing nature.

Andy Goldsworthy, like Long, Heizer, de Maria and Smithson, has made some huge pieces, such as the long 'snake' and the 'pool' or maze, in Country Durham, England large works of the late 1980s which take up a lot of space, and certainly dominate the surrounding landscape.[96] In a forest, Goldsworthy, helped by students and friends, created another snake-like sculpture out of pine trees, pinned together to form a huge structure weaving between the trees.[97] At Storm King in upstate New York, Goldsworthy built a very long stone wall. Goldsworthy's large-scale works, like Long's or Heizer's or de Maria's, are monumental works, which sprawl across the landscape.

Mysticism is emphasized in Andy Goldsworthy's writing. Goldsworthy's æsthetics are those of a neo-pagan, shamanic, pantheistic, nature worshipping kind, the sort of beliefs that some pagans people call Goddess worship. Goldsworthy speaks of the earth's energies and atmospheres. Goldsworthy writes:

> The energy and space around a material are as important as the energy and space within. The weather – rain, sun, snow, hail, mist, calm – is that external space made visible. When I touch a rock, I am touching and working the space around it.

This talk of earth energies recalls the 'dragon lines' or *feng shui* of Chinese geomancy. The spiral and snake employed by so many land artists down the ages (in ancient Peru, or on the doors of Neolithic tombs, or in the Mid-West of America), is associated with the Goddess and with the energies of life. The circles and spirals of Goldsworthy, Nash, Smithson and Long are clearly those of the Goddess, the ancient Earth Mother.

Land artists often use circular forms, which hide the

96 *Leadgate and Lambton Earthworks*, 1989, County Durham
97 *Snow and Wind Damaged Pine Trees*, Spring 1985, Grizedale forest

aggression of their gestures. The spiral or circle is a kind, organic, even gentle shape, seemingly in tune with earth energies. Circular structures (igloos, huts, stone circles, tombs, earthworks, pools) seem to be in harmony with nature, echoing the circle shapes of the planet itself, or suns, eyes, blood cells, orifices, orbits. The circular structures speak of primitive, archaic more authentic ethics. There is, then, not only a mystical side to land art, to the art of Goldsworthy, Long, Nash, Smithson and de Maria, but also a nostalgic element (nostalgia is a key element in any religion). Looking *back* to the land, the earth and land artists also look *back* to a former, even ancient era which was, patently, better (but never existed: but it *should* have existed). This is the hidden subtext in the writings of the land artists, this nostalgia for the better times of archaic cultures.

CONTEMPORARY SCULPTURE

Much of contemporary sculpture has been thoroughly traditional, and patriarchal, in its orientation and expression. Take Henry Moore, one of the most celebrated of Western sculptors. His nudes, though, are no different from the conventional 'female nude lying down', found in so much of high art from the Renaissance onwards.[98] Contemporary figurative sculpture has rarely escaped the usual confines of patriarchal art. David Smith's bronze sculpture *The Rape* depicts a woman being raped by a canon, a phallic gun which climbs over her.[99] It is meant to be a savage and ironic comment on violation, but it isn't really, as with Aristide Maillol's relief of a man assaulting a woman, entitled –

---

98 Henry Moore: *Reclining Figure*, 1945-6, elmwood, 75in long, collection: Humana Corp, Louisville; *Three Piece Reclining Figure: Draped*, 1975, bronze, 14ft 8in long, Henry Moore Foundation
99 David Smith: *The Rape*, 1945, bronze, 9 x 5.75 x 3.5in, private collection

what else? – *Desire*.[100] Edward Kienholz's quasi-Surrealist *Back Seat of a '38 Dodge* is a re-assembled car with all manner of bits added to it and inside it – hey! – two people get freaky.[101]

But when sexuality is addressed, contemporary sculptors have rarely been ironic. Usually, the norms of oppositions of male/ female, active/ passive, culture/ nature, good/ evil are enshrined. The great or celebrated names in contemporary sculpture – Alberto Giacometti, Henry Moore, David Smith, David Hare, Eduardo Chillida, Pablo Picasso, Isamu Noguchi, Mark Di Suvero, Jean Tinguely – rarely tackled notions of sexuality in major works of sculpture. When Picasso incorporates eroticism, it is invariably heterosexist, as in his *Bust* with its gigantic breasts, echoing the "Stone Venuses" of prehistory.[102] The great works of contemporary sculpture – David Smith's *Cubi XXVII*, Alexander Calder's mobiles, Richard Serra's chunks of metal and John Chamberlain's squashed cars – seem to eschew issues of sexuality.[103] Not much of mainstream or 'malestream' contemporary sculpture concerns itself with eroticism, although certainly there is eroticism in Tony Cragg's steel vessels, for instance, or Anne and Patrick Poirier's long, elegant *Archæological Model*.[104] Tony Cragg has spoken of having 'an erotic response to the external world', something which, it seems, all artists have, or have to have, to be truly great artists.[105]

In the figures of realist or hyperrealist sculpture we see people frozen in often bizarre attitudes and poses, as in Duane Hanson's

---

100 Aristide Maillol: *Desire*, 1903-5, lead relief, Musée Nationale d'Art Moderne, Paris
101 Edward Kienholz: *Back Seat of a '38 Dodge*, 1964, the Kleiner Foundation, Los Angeles
102 Picasso: *Bust of a Woman*, 1932, bronze, 25.1in high, estate of the artist
103 David Smith: *Cubi XXVII*, 1965, stainless steel, 9.2ft high, Guggenheim Museum, New York; Alexander Calder: *Red Flock*, c. 1949, hanging mobile, metal, 2.8 x 5.5ft, Phillips Collection, Washington DC; John Chamberlain: *Toy*, 1961, welded auto parts and plastic, 4 x 3.1 x 2.6ft, Art Institute, Chicago; Richard Serra: *Prop*, 1968, 96in high, sheet 60 x 60in, Whitney Museum of Art, New York
104 Tony Cragg: *Instinctive Reactions*, 1987, cast steel, 8 x 21 x 15ft, Lisson Gallery, London; Anne & Patrick Poirier: *Archæological Model*, 1986, Bath International Festival. See Terry A. Neff: *A Quiet Revolution: British Sculpture Since 1965*, London 1967; Ben Jones: "A New Wave in Sculpture: A Survey of recent work by ten younger sculptors", *Artscribe*, 8, September 1977, 16; Lisa Ponti: "Tony Cragg", *Domus*, 611, Nov 1980, 50-51; Isabelle Lamaître: "Interview with Tony Cragg", *Artefactum*, 2, Dec 1985, 7-11; Germano Celant: "Tony Cragg and Industrial Platonism", *Artforum*, 20, 3, Nov 1981, 40-46
105 Tony Cragg, quoted in Wheeler, 324

The Tourists and other works.[106] Hanson's figures are vicious and ironic, while George Segal's figures explore the alienation of modern life. Anthony Donaldson has produced a truly horrible *Girl Sculpture*, a plastic red and gold model of a woman – *naked, of course* – set in a 'streamlined' mould, rather like those 3-D logos beloved of entertainment organizations, where the letters are drawn in exaggerated perspective.[107]

John De Andrea also explored 'the resignation, emptiness and loneliness'[108] of contemporary life, that emotional territory of Middle America that Raymond Carver so successfully explored in his short stories. But De Andrea's nudes turn out to be just as pornographic as other high art nudes.[109] Take his *Reclining Woman*,[110] which is a Superrealist version of the high art reclining nude, a life-size and seemingly life-like rendition of a person. There are differences of æsthetic approaches in the Superrealist plastic doll-woman and the female nude of high art sculpture, but, essentially, both are works of pornography, and De Andrea's work is no different than sculptures such as Fritz Klimsch's *Eros*, a woman posing in voluptuous fashion, arms behind her head, hips thrown to one side, a pin-up sculpted nude.[111] Reg Butler's bronzes of women – *naked, of course* – are 'exquisitely crafted', to use terms typical of art criticism,[112] but in fact turn out to be very sexist representations of women.[113]

George Sugarman's flowing sculptures tend towards eroticism, with their twisting, entwined forms painted in red, white, green and yellow.[114] Lucas Samaras's artworks were the

106 Duane Hanson: *The Tourists*, 1970, polyster resin, polychrome glass fibre, National Gallery of Scotland, Edinburgh; *Bunny*, 1970, fibreglass, life-size, O.K. Harris Gallery, New York
107 Anthony Donaldson: *Girl Sculpture "Red 'n' Gold"*, 1970, 75 x 448cm, Rowan Gallery, London
108 John De Andrea, quoted in Le Normand-Romain, 241
109 John De Andrea: *Couple*, 1971, acrylic on polyester and hair, man 5.7ft high, woman 5.1ft high, Musée d'Art Moderne, Paris
110 John De Andrea: *Reclining Woman*, 1970, life-size, David Bermant Collection
111 Fritz Klimsch: *Eos*, 1904
112 Edward Lucie-Smith: *Sculpture since 1945*, 33
113 Reg Butler: *Girl on Red Base*, 1968-72, painted bronze, 32 x 43 x 63.5in, Pierre Matisse Gallery, New York
114 George Sugarman: *Bardana*, 1962-3, polychromed woof, 8 x 12 x 5.1ft, Galerie Renée Ziegler, Zurich

flipside of Sugarman's sensual forms. Samaras deliberately subverted the eroticism of sculpture by furnishing his sculptures and assemblages with pins, nails, razor blades, knives and scissors, as in his bitter *Book 4*, which is stuffed with knives, nails and razor blades.[115] For Samaras, as for so many (male) artists from Dante Alighieri through the Marquis de Sade to Georges Bataille, sex (pleasure) is intermixed with death, or, as Samaras puts it: 'I cannot separate beauty from pain.'[116]

SCULPTURE IN BRITAIN

I'm fed up with objects on pedestals. I'd like to break down the graspability of sculpture. Sculpture is terrifically tangible, but a painting, however concrete, is partly in the realm of illusion.

Anthony Caro[117]

British sculptors, those of St Martin's School of Art, the 'New Generation', the 'new sculpture' and others, benefitted from the openness and freedom of American sculpture. 'America made me see that there are no barriers and no regulations', wrote Anthony Caro, the influential British sculptor (ib). According to William Tucker, postwar or 'modern', post-Cubist sculpture 'could be made from anything, about anything.'[118] Caro described a mood that was common in the æsthetics of the 1960s, in painting as much as in sculpture, the idea that sculpture should not be on pedestals, but on the floor; that there are no barriers.

The big (and little) patriarchal statements in British sculpture include: Anthony Caro's welded steel constructions, which are

---

115 Lucas Samaras: *Book 4*, 1962, 5.5 x 8.8 x 11.5in, Museum of Modern Art, New York
116 quoted in Diane Waldman: "Samaras", *Art News*, Oct 1966, 56
117 Anthony Caro: in Lawrence Alloway: "Interview with Anthony Caro", *Gazette*, 1, 1961, 1
118 William Tucker: "An Essay on Sculpture", *Studio International*, 177, 907, January 1969, 13

abstract but also emotional, such as *Early One Morning* • Philip King's flamboyant steel and fibreglass pieces, such as his *Genghis Khan*, which speak of a direct apprehension of the object in itself, in the manner of Constantin Brancusi and Frank Stella's art • Tony Cragg's coloured spreads of found objects arranged in lines on the floor (such as his *New Stones*), which are works of found objects, all manner of objects, each given the same status, in a non-hierarchical fashion, laid out on the floor • William Tucker's hard-edged and organic forms, which aim for maximum 'visibility' and physicality • Stephen Cox's Kleinian, post-Renaissance reliefs • and Tim Scott's segments of circles in glass, perspex and acrylic sheets.

Anish Kapoor's erotic, mysterious painted objects, which are bizarre yet wholly believable departures from natural forms – a pitted surface like that of a blackcurrant, interfolding petals like those of a rose, multi-part spirals, cones made of shapes like the folds in robes – but most startling about Kapoor's forms are their colours, powdery blues, lemon yellow and scarlet, at once seductive and unreal, simultaneously, like all sculpture, inviting touch and repelling it, perhaps by being indifferent to it.

Bill Woodrow's wonderful remaking and remingling of everyday found objects – a post-industrial sculpture with a lot of humour – for instance, structures such as flowers of branches sprouting from the smashed car door of a Porsche 928, and *A Passing Car, A Caring Word*, another car door, this time fixed against a decayed double bed base, with a cross on the floor made by tearing the bed's cloth, while in front of the car door is a 'microphone' on a stand, connected by a ribbon of steel torn from the door, with a gun connected to the door, lying on the floor; the resulting sculpture is a meditation, perhaps on violence, oppression, and death.

Barry Flanagan's witty, seemingly naïve semi-figurative works, such as his bronze hares, or his *Soprano*, which is a bronze bird, mouth wide open, singing like an operatic diva, with a gilded arrow through her breast. Tim Head's *State of the Art* is a collection of phallic objects, stacked up like a Louis Nevelson wall sculpture: Head placed a host of dildoes and vibrators next to electronic calculators, model aircraft, tape players, computers, computer games, deodorants, hair sprays, all the panoply of consumerist items. And David Nash's environmentally-friendly interactions with nature are some of the most intriguing of recent explorations of the natural world in art.[119]

119 Anish Kapoor: *Six Secret Objects*, 1983, mixed media, 115 x 425 x 60cm, Lissom Gallery, London; Stephen Cox: *The Fiery Kind*, 1982-3, marble, 100 x 110cm, British Council, London; Anthony Caro: *Early One Morning*, 1962, painted metal, 114 x 244 x 132in, Tate Gallery, London; Philip King: *Genghis Khan*, 1963, fibreglass and plastic with steel support, 41 x 56.5 x 34.5in, Tate Gallery, London; Tony Cragg: *New Stones*, 1982, Marian Goodman Gallery, New York; Tim Scott: *Quinquereme* 1966, Tate Gallery; Richard Deacon: *Turning a Blind Eye no. 2*, 1984-5, High Museum of Art, Atlanta, Georgia; Bill Woodrow: *Winter Jacket*, 1986, mixed media, collection: Anne MacDonald Walker, San Francisco; Barry Flanagan: *Soprano*, 1981, bronze, 80 x 66 x 57cm, Arts Council of Great Britain; Tim Head: *State of the Art*, 1984, colour photograph, 183 x 274cm, collection: the artist; David Nash: *Fletched Over Ash Dome*, 1977, Caény-Coed, Maentwrog, Wales

2

CONSTANTIN BRANCUSI

Constantin Brancusi may well be the most erotic of all sculptors. He is more erotic than Michelangelo, Gianlorenzo Bernini, Antonio Canova, Donatello, Auguste Rodin, Eric Gill, Louise Bourgeois and Judy Chicago. For me, and for some other commentators, Constantin Brancusi is the key sculptor of the modern period – not Auguste Rodin, Henry Moore, Pablo Picasso, Barbara Hepworth or others.[120] Brancusi is diametrically opposed, æsthetically, to Rodin, and quite different from Naum Gabo; his art has some affinities with Henri Gaudier-Breska – it is interesting to compare Gaudier-Breska's heavy, gaunt *Standing Birds* with Brancusi's slim *Birds in Space* series.[121]

Constantin Brancusi's eroticism stems from his superb forms,

120 Friedrich Teja Bach: *Brancusi*, Du Mont, Cologne 1987; Barbu Brezianu: *Brancusi: A Retrospective Exhibition*, Muzeul de Arta R.S.R, Bucharest, 1970; Petry Comarnescu, Mircea Eliade & Constantin Noica: *Brancusi, Introduction Témoignages*, Arted, Paris 1982; Sidney Geist: *Brancusi: A Study of the Sculpture*, Hacker, New York 1983, also *Brancusi: The Sculpture and Drawings*, Harry N. Abrams, New York 1975; Pontus Hulten, Natalia Dumitresco & Alexandre Istrati: *Brancusi*, Harry N. Abrams, New York 1987; David N. Lewis: *Constantin Brancusi*, St Martin's Press, New York 1974; William Tucker: *Early Modern Sculpture: Rodin, Degas, Matisse, Brancusi, Picasso, Gonzalez*, Oxford University Press, New York 1974
121 Gaudier-Breska: *Standing Birds*, 1914, Museum of Modern Art, New York; Brancusi: *Bird in Space*, or *Yellow Bird*, 1923-4, yellow marble, 45.8in high, base; one marble, one oak and two limestone sections, 57.2in high, Philadelphia Museum of Art

which are delicious in their form, shape, texture and feel. Brancusi develops all the erotic formal aspects of sculpture to their extreme. He reduces organic, natural forms to 'essences'. Yet he maintained that his sculpture was not abstract. Wassily Kandinsky said that abstraction = realism,[122] and this is true of Brancusi, who vigorously stressed the realism of his works:

> They are imbeciles who call my work abstract; that which they call abstract is the most realist, because what is real is not the exterior form but the idea, the essence of things.[123]

It is a quest for things, for things-in-themselves, as Existential philosophers such as Jean-Paul Sartre and Martin Heidegger put it, the 'thingness' of Rainer Maria Rilke. The 'things' are organic forms, not abstract ideas or abstruse conceptualizations. As Henry Moore wrote, a 'sculptor is a person obsessed with the form and shape of things... the shape of anything and everything.'[124] Though Constantin Brancusi denies the urge towards abstraction, he founds his sculpture on the abstractions of Platonism. It is Plato's ideal philosophy that influences much of Brancusi's sculpture. Plato's notion of Ideal Forms and essences excited Brancusi. Reducing his art further and further, Brancusi aimed to get as close as possible to the 'essence of the thing'. It is a process of Neoplatonic purification, as Dorothy Adlow noted when she visited his studio in 1925:

> Brancusi has purified his sculpture of every attracting feature. He has swept out of his plan every motive that might distract him or the observer from what he considers the central idea... He has tried to make of his sculpture a working philosophy. He calls it the philosophy of Plato.[125]

There is a parallel to this purification in poets and novelists.

122 Wassily Kandinsky: "On the Problem of Form", *Der Blaue Reiter*, R. Piper, Munich 1912, and in Chipp, 162
123 Brancusi, in "Propos de Brancusi", *Prisme des Arts*, Paris, no. 12, May 1957, 6
124 in Philip James & Henry Moore: *Henry Moore on Sculpture*, Viking Press, New York 1971, 60
125 Dorothy Adlow: "Brancusi", *Drawing and Design*, 2 Feb 1927, 37f

French writers, such as Stendhal, Gustave Flaubert, André Gide and (honorary Frenchman) Samuel Beckett spoke of wanting to clear away all the garbage that gets in the way of purity of expression. Beckett, for instance, steadily pared away his language, moving from the relatively conventional novel forms of books such as *Mercier and Camier* through the reduced vocabulary and syntax of *The Unnameable Trilogy* to the severely reduced poesie of *Company* and *Still*. For some artists, nothing must get in the way of expression of the idea or emotion. As Dorothy Adlow wrote:

> It is the *idea* that should be related, that is all. Everything else is superfluous... Brancusi is not satisfied with the things of the moment, he looks out for what is true of all time.

So many major modern artist have admired Constantin Brancusi: Amedeo Modigliani, Frank Stella, Donald Judd, Carl Andre, Barbara Hepworth, Henry Moore and Andy Goldsworthy. Simplicity, as Brancusi and many artists have said, was the key: but it is a mystical simplicity, that arises out of the sculpture's materials: '[s]implicitly is not an objective in art, but one achieves simplicity despite oneself by entering into the real sense of things.'[126]

For Mircea Eliade, the historian of religion (and a fellow Romanian), Constantin Brancusi's talent was one of 'interiorization', a mythic descent simultaneously into himself, into his personal and national past, and into mythic forms. The endpoint of Brancusi's quest for the 'essence of things' was a mystical sculpture. Although he declined to talk in religious terms of his art, it is distinctly mystical. Some of Brancusi's statements admit to a mystical solidarity with materials and sculptures:

> I am no longer of this world. I am far from myself, I am no longer a part of my own person. I am within the essence of things

---

126 Brancusi: "Résponses de Brancusi; Aphorismes; Histoire de brigands", *This Quarter*, 1, no. 1, Paris 1925

themselves.[127]

Constantin Brancusi's goal of mythic interiorization have affinities with Martin Heidegger's notion of Being and presence, with James Joyce's idea of the æsthetic 'epiphany' of authentic art, with Lawrence Durrell's poetic concept of the heraldic 'sigil' or signature of a thing, and with *sammadassana* of Zen Buddhism. D.T. Suzuki writes: '[s]eeing is experiencing, seeing things in their states of suchness (*tathata*) or is-ness. Buddha's whole philosophy comes from this "seeing", this experiencing.'[128]

Constantin Brancusi speaks of a similar mystical 'seeing', where the viewer of his sculptures see not simply beautiful surfaces, but essences. He wrote:

> What is real is not the external form, but the essence of things. Starting from this truth it is impossible for anyone to express anything luscious and real by imitating its exterior surface.[129]

Constantin Brancusi starts with the essence, and ends up with those severely reduced but open forms – the birds, heads, fish, eggs, lovers and columns.

Searching for the essence, Constantin Brancusi nevertheless bases his art on natural forms, on elemental forms. The material that makes the sculpture itself helps in the quest for the essence of things. The final form of the sculpture is, Brancusi believes, somehow buried in the material, whether it is stone, marble, wood or bronze. Brancusi has a *participation mystique* with his sculpture's materials, much as primitive or prehistoric societies had a *participation mystique* with nature and the earth. Each material has its own feel, tensions, problems. Somehow, the material 'renders up' the final form. 'Each material has its own life,' Brancusi says.[130] The 'essence' must be brought out by the

127 quoted in David Lewis: *Constantin Brancusi*, Wittenborn, New York 1937, 43
128 Suzuki: *The Basics of Buddhist Philosophy*, Allen & Unwin 1957, quoted in Richard Woods, ed., *Understanding Mysticism*, Athlone Press 1980, 126
129 quoted in *Brancusi*, catalogue, Brummer Gallery, New York 1926
130 Brancusi, quoted in Dorothy Dudley: "Brancusi", *Dial*, 82, February 1927, 124

artist, as Brancusi said:

The natural element in sculpture means allegorical thinking, symbol, sacredness or the search for essences hidden in the material and not the photographic reproduction of external appearances.[131]

Constantin Brancusi's sculptures bear out how successful he was in pursuing the Holy Grail of Platonic purity and mystical essence. His career was one whole quest for the essence of form. 'Everything I do is a seeking after form,' he remarked in 1949.[132]

When one contemplates his works, they seem to be so *right*, so spot on in their depiction of their subject. Thus, the sculptures based on fishes, birds, heads, cocks, seals, capture the 'essence' of their subject so brilliantly.[133] Barbara Hepworth, one of many sculptors who found Constantin Brancusi an inspiration, wrote of her 1932 visit to Brancusi's Paris studio:

In Brancusi's studio I encountered the miraculous feeling of eternity mixed with beloved stone and stone dust... The simplicity and dignity of the artist; the inspiration of the dedicated workshop with great millstones used as bases for classical forms; inches of accumulated dust and chips on the floor; the whole great studio filled with soaring forms and still, quiet forms, all in a state of perfection in purpose and loving execution, whether they were in marble, brass or wood – all this filled me with a sense of humility hitherto unknown to me.[134]

Constantin Brancusi's sculptures entitled *Fish*, in marble or bronze, are such gorgeous objects, with their sleek bodies. They are supremely erotic sculptures, not least because they aim to be

131 Brancusi, in Petre Pandrea: "The Laws of Craiova", *Portraits and Controversies*, Bucharest, Romania 1946, vol. 1, 120
132 quoted in Russell Warren Howe: "The Man Who Doesn't Like Michelangelo", *Apollo*, 49, May 1949, 124
133 Brancusi: *Fish*, 1932, white marble, 5.3 x 16.8 x 1.1in, base, a mirror, diameter 17in, on oak, 24in high, Philadelphia Museum of Art; *Fish*, 1924, polished bronze, 5 x 16.5 x 1.8in, based, a polished steel disk, diameter 19.6in, Museum of Fine Arts, Boston; *The Cock*, 1935, polished bronze, 40.8in high, base of stone & wood sections, 76.1in, Brancusi studio, Musée National d'Art Moderne, Paris; *Golden Bird*, 1919, polished bronze, 38in high, base of stone and wood, 48.1in, Arts Club of Chicago; *The Seal*, 1943, blue-grey marble, 43.8in high, Musée National d'Art, Paris; *Head of a Woman*, 1910-c. 1925, white marble, 11.2in, private collection
134 Barbara Hepworth: *Barbara Hepworth, Carvings and Drawings*, Lund Humphries 1952

the mystic essence of animals that swim in the sea. The erotic aspects of fish, as many artists have long known, are linked symbolically to the fecund oceans, the ocean being, quite literally, the womb of life on earth. Brancusi in his *Fish* sculptures aimed to capture what it was that was special about fish. He said:

> When you see a fish, you do not think of its scales, do you? You think of its speed, its floating, flashing body seen through water... I've tried to express just that... I want just the flash of its spirit.[135]

The *Fish* sculptures are often set on mirrors, perhaps to hint at water. The circular mirrors, like all circular forms in Constantin Brancusi's art, hint at cosmic dimensions, representing the Great Round of existence, the cosmos itself, and the spherical forms from which all life comes: the circular ocean, cells, wombs, hearts, planets. The 1926 work *Fish* is set on an elaborate base.[136] The importance of the base upon which sculpture rests is crucial for Brancusi. His bases are very distinctive, setting him instantly apart from all other sculptors. The Brancusi base is and is not part of the sculpture.

Constantin Brancusi's forms leap out at you, how they make their presence felt immediately when surrounded by all manner of other works. Brancusi's work is, as William Tucker writes, 'the antithesis of Rodin's – private, silent, withdrawn, morally neutral' (131). Despite being 'private, silent, withdrawn, morally neutral', Brancusi's sculptures have immense authority and presence. As Tucker argues, it is precisely this intimacy ('interiority', as Mircea Eliade calls it) that makes Brancusi's works so powerful (131-2).

There are inherent paradoxes in Constantin Brancusi's æsthetics. For example, Platonism emphasizes the 'idea' or 'essence'. Yet these 'essences' or 'ideas' must be manifested in flesh and blood bodies and organic forms. Platonism could not reconcile these two things – spirit and flesh – successfully, and neither could Christianity, even after two thousand years of

135 Brancusi, in Malvina Hoffman: *Sculpture Inside and Out*, Norton, New York 1939, 52
136 Brancusi: *Fish*, 1926, polish bronze, 5in, private collection

hacking away at the problem. For, while Constantin Brancusi emphasizes 'essence', what we see in his sculptures are highly polished, highly worked surfaces, an emphasis on beautiful surfaces, on smoothness and sleekness. Brancusi's sculptures, like those of the Minimalists Donald Judd or Robert Morris or Carl Andre, are smooth and slick. Roughness, where it appears, as in the stone bases and pedestals, is similarly worked and carved, integrated stylishly into the design. Even as they exalt idealism and essence, then, Brancusi's sculptures are caught up in all kinds of problems to do with expression, manifestation, formalism, material and intention.

There is, for instance, an intrinsic sexism in Constantin Brancusi's treatment of male and female, masculine and feminine forms. His *Torso of a Young Woman III* is, typically, a softly rounded volume, like a vase, recalling the eternal and mythical association of women with vessels, of women as something to be filled. [137]

Constantin Brancusi's *Torso of a Young Woman* is supremely stereotypical, sexist. The male *Torso*, on the other hand, is, as you might expect, phallically upright. Indeed, it looks like a phallus. [138] Interestingly, however, Brancusi claimed that '[n]ude men in sculpture are not as beautiful as toads.' [139] Further sexism occurs in Brancusi's *Adam and Eve*, where people are reduced to – hey – genitals, once again. So Eve is a mouth and vagina, and Adam is a phallus and testicles. [140]

Constantin Brancusi's sculptures of women turn out to be as sexist as any portraits of depictions of the female (nude) body by artists such as Henri Matisse, Peter Rubens, J.A.D. Ingres, Pablo Picasso, etc. Brancusi's *Madame Pogany* and *Princess X* are the usual rounded, feminine forms, while works such as *The White*

137 Brancusi: *Torso of a Young Woman III*, 1925, onyx, 10.4in, Musée National d'Art Moderne, Paris
138 Brancusi: *Torso of a Young Man*, after 1924, bronze, 18.4 x 12 x 6.7in, Cleveland Museum of Art
139 Brancusi, quoted in *This Quarter*, op.cit.
140 Brancusi: *Adam and Eve*, 1916-21, chestnut and oak, 89in high, base of limestone, 5.2in, Guggenheim, New York

Negress and *Blond Negress* have dubious racist connotations.[141]

When Constantin Brancusi exhibited the curved bronze *Princess X* in 1920, Pablo Picasso – or was it Henri Matisse? – said 'Voici, le phallus!' Indeed, *Princess X* does look phallic, and it is featured on the cover of a survey of erotic art (see Peter Webb). But the art object, sculpted, painted or otherwise, is a kind of displaced phallus, a fetish object turned into high culture. The art object is that item made to provide pleasure. Most of sculpture is designed and crafted as a 'beautiful' object, to use that key word of Platonic philosophy. Sculptures are 'The Beautiful'. Sculptures are 'beauty' concretized, eroticism made into bronze, marble and stone.

The history of sculpture is the history of anal/ oral/ genital touches of pleasure, self-reflexive gestures where artists touch objects physically and, later, viewers drink them up visually, forbidden by the ropes of museums and guards to actually touch the sculpture itself. The sculpted object is indeed the erotic object *par excellence* in art. It is the phallus endlessly caressed by the eyes, in Lacanian, scopic, scopophillic, voyeuristic pleasure. As Julia Kristeva says, 'isn't art the fetish *par excellence,* one that badly camouflages its archeology?'[142]

Constantin Brancusi produced a number of sculptures that are pure phalluses, seen from one, religious, viewpoint. In Hindu culture, there is a holy object called Savayambhu, meaning the 'self-originated', a phallic emblem of cosmic energy. They are egg-shaped stones which are worshipped in Indian religion. They are the cosmic phallus, the *lingam*, and are associated with the World Egg or Cosmic Egg.[143] The Eggs of Brahman or Svayambhu *lingams* are phallic energy associated with cosmic/ religious energies solidified into stone. Typically seven inches long, these Hindu phallic stones are very much like the human penis.

141 Brancusi: *Madame Pogany III*, 1939, white marble, 17.8in high, Philadelphia Museum of Art; *Princess X*, 1916, polished bronze, 23 x 16.5 x 9in high, base of stone, 7.2in high, Philadelphia Musem of Art; *The White Negress*, 1923, white marble, 19in high, base of marble, 6.4in high, Philadelphia Museum of Art; *Blond Negress II*, 1933, polished bronze, 15.8in high, base of marble and limestone and two wood sections, 55.5in high, MOMA, New York
142 Kristeva: *Revolution in Poetic Language*, tr. Margaret Walker, in *The Kristeva Reader*, 115
143 See Philip Ransom: *The Art of Tantra*, Thames & Hudson 1973, 193-7

Indeed, as Philip Ransom noted, the cosmic egg-stones have 'surface-divisions' that imitate those 'on the actual male penis'.[144]

Constantin Brancusi's own cosmic eggs are given a clearly mytho-religious dimension, apparent not only in their supremely beautiful and erotic forms, but also in their titles: *Beginning of the World, The First Cry* and *The Newborn*.[145] Sculptures such as *The First Cry* and *The Newborn* connect human birth with the birth of the cosmos, in a mythic, sensual volume. For the egg shape is obvious, as, like *The Kiss*, it looks towards a fundamental sense of life, where life begins, in the biology of cells and eggs. Indeed, Constantin Brancusi painted a version of his *The Kiss* on a real egg.[146] The lovers embracing on the egg pulls together any number of erotic and cosmic dimensions, from the egg-shape of genitals (womb, clitoris, testes, glans) to the Platonic two-in-oneness symbolized by two yokes in one egg, to the womb of the universe, the cells at the heart of organic life.

Constantin Brancusi's most famous sculpture is probably the *Birds in Space* series. The many – 28 or so – *Birds in Space* sculptures are the manifestations of an artistic, spiritual quest for the essence of flight.[147] 'All my life I've been looking for one thing, the essence of flight... What a marvellous thing flight is', Constantin Brancusi commented.[148] Each *Bird in Space* sculpture is a slender, upright form, a mythic striving for the sky, for ascension, for space.

Constantin Brancusi's success of embodying the essence of

---

144 in ib., 194; *Egg of Brahman*, Benares, age unknown, stone, 7in high; *Egg of Brahman*, Benares, age unknown, stone, 7 in high

145 Brancusi: *Beginning of the World*, c. 1920, marble, 7,2 x 10.25 x 6.5in, polished metal disc, 19.75in, diam., base: stone, 22.5in high, Dallas Museum of Art; *The First Cry*, 1917, polished bronze, 6.75 x 10.2in, Art Gallery of Ontario; *The Newborn*, 1915, white marble, 6 x 8.5in,

Philadelphia Museum of Art

146 Brancusi: *The Kiss*, date unknown, paint on an egg, the Lydia & Harry L. Winston Collection

147 Brancusi: *Bird in Space*, 1941, polished bronze, 76.2in high, Musée National d'Art Moderne, Paris; *Bird in Space*, 1925, white marble, 71in high, base: stone and wood sections, 64.5in high, National Gallery of Art, Washington DC; *Bird in Space*, 1931-6, black marble, 76.2in high, base: marble and sandstone sections, 53.25in high, Australian National Gallery, Canberra

148 Brancusi, in Carola Giedin-Welcker: *Constantin Brancusi*, George Braziller, New York 1959, 220. See Sidney Geist: "The Birds", *Artforum*, 9, November 1970, 74-82; Athena Tacha Spear: *Brancusi's Birds*, New York University Press, New York 1969

flight in sculpture is all the more startling, Mircea Eliade says, because he used 'the very archetype of *heaviness*, that ultimate form of "matter" – stone.'[149]

Constantin Brancusi's *Birds in Space* dispense with feathers and, typically for Brancusi, go for the essence of flight, symbolized and actualized by that slender, curving shape. The *Birds in Space* sculptures are a stretching-up to the infinite. Brancusi spoke of a desire to extend the surfaces of his sculptures to infinity:

> In bad form... the surfaces and planes all come to an end. They finished themselves within the mass. I think the true form out to suggest infinity. The surfaces ought to look as though they went on forever, as though they proceeded out from the mass into some perfect and complete existence.[150]

The *Birds in Space* aim to be infinity-reaching sculpture, works that arch out into the 'open', into the 'beyond'. The endpoint of Constantin Brancusi's artistic search was his *Endless Column* of 1937, a monumental structure at Tîrgu-Jiu,[151] which Brancusi called 'a stairway to heaven'.[152] The column, variously entitled *Column of Endless Remembrance, Infinite Column, The Column of Endless Memory* and *The Column of Endless Gratitude,* soars into space, literally and metaphorically, mythically and spiritually.

It is, like the *Birds in Space,* a monument of magical, shamanic flight, a sculpture of pure ascension, which is pure desire. You don't need to have any time for Sigmund Freud to see the phallic aspects of such towers, totem poles, minarets and columns. Brancusi's *Endless Column* and *Birds in Space* sculptures can be seen in Freudian, genital terms as phallic erections.

The shaman's dance, trance and magical journey have erotic,

149 Eliade: *Ordeal*, op.cit., 201
150 Brancusi, in Adeline L. Atwater: "A Recluse of Modern Art", *New York Herald Tribune Magazine,* 12 January 1930, 12
151 Brancusi: *Endless Column,* 1937-8, cast iron, 96.2ft x 35.4 x 35.4in, Tirgu-Jiu, Romania; Stefan Georgescu-Gorjan: "The Genesis of the 'Column Without End', *Revue roumaine d'histoire de l'art*, Bucharest, no. 2, 1964, 279-93
152 Brancusi, quoted in Barbu Brezianu: *Brancusi in Romania*, Editura Academiei R.S.R., Bucharest, Romantia, 1976, 134

phallic components. The shaman climbs up the World Tree, itself another phallic symbol, a manifestation of phallic power. Further, dreaming, which is the key state of shamanism, for the shaman is the one who can dream magically, is associated with phallic energy, as Sigmund Freud noted: during REM sleep erections occur (what men refer to as their 'morning glory', a penis rising like the sun rising), and women are similarly aroused.

All these things are caught up in Constantin Brancusi's sculptures of flight: shamanism, Cosmic Trees, phallic columns, erections, patriarchal power, and religious/ mythic rebirth. Brancusi's most erotic sculpture was one of his early pieces, which turned up in different forms: *The Kiss*.[153] Unlike Auguste Rodin's *tour-de-force* depiction of erotic passion,[154] Brancusi's *The Kiss* is a 'primitive', non-naturalistic square block of stone, very far indeed from the art of Michelangelo Buonarroti, Gianlorenzo Bernini or Auguste Rodin. For Brancusi *The Kiss* was his 'road to Damascus', a key work.[155]

Much of Auguste Rodin's art pivots around eroticism. Rodin produced drawings of women masturbating, which influenced Gustav Klimt's images of masturbating women.[156] Rodin's *Oceanides*, like his *Gates of Hell*, depicts lovers entwining in a series of fluid lines and sensuous forms.[157] Rodin's depictions of *The Kiss* centre around the voluptuousness of eroticism, on the beauty of bodies clasped together in complex poses. Rodin's *The Kiss* is the height of modern figurative sculpture, Michelangelo made heterosexually erotic. Other sculptors produced similarly sensuous, entwined *Kisses*, with the man always on top, always bearing down onto the woman, always enveloping, always controlling the kiss (in M.L. Bégine's *The Embrace*, J. Dalou's *The Kiss*, Edvard Munch's *The Kiss*, Klimt's *The Kiss*, F. Voulot's *The*

153 Brancusi: *The Kiss*, 1907-8, stone, 11in high, Museum of Art, Craiova, Romania; *The Kiss II*, c. 1908, stone, 12.5in high, private collection. See Sidney Geist: *Brancusi: The Kiss*, Harper & Row, New York 1978
154 Rodin: *The Kiss*, 1886, marble, Musée Rodin, Paris
155 quoted in H.P. Roche: "L'Enterrement de Brancusi", *Homage de la Sculpture à Brancusi*, Paris, 1957, 26f
156 Rodin: *Reclining Female Nude*, c. 1900, pencil, 12.2 x 8in, Musée Rodin, France
157 Rodin: *Océanides*, 1905, marble, 22in high, Musée Rodin, Paris

Kiss, *Pablo* Picasso's *The Embrace*, William Zorach's *The Embrace* and E. Derré's *La Grotte d'Amour*).[158]

The different versions of *The Kiss* aim to depict the intimate erotic experience of lovemaking, symbolized by a kiss. The two people – male and female, of course – are shown kissing face-on, their bodies fused together.

Constantin Brancusi's *The Kiss* is distinctly gendered, with many details that describe the man and the woman not apparent from just a glance. The hair, for instance, is parted on the woman but pulled back on the man; the man's hands are on her shoulders, while hers are pressed against the back of his head; the woman is clearly sexualized by her breasts, as ever in masculine art; the eyes and lips (there are no ears) seem to be the same, though the man is shorter than the woman. In subtle ways, Brancusi delineated the psychology of his male and female figures. They are at once flawed individual and generalized (idealized) archetypes.

The variations on *The Kiss* (Constantin Brancusi regarded them all as one work) reveal interesting departures from that first, Craiova *The Kiss*. The 1908 Diamond *The Kiss* is much rougher, in its grey limestone, with the strokes of the chisel still visible, but the eyes bulge, with those heavily-lined eyelids. These eyes became so enlarged in the later works they filled up the face until, in the late columns, all you can see is the great orbs of the eyes, fused together, in *The Gate of the Kiss* and *Column of the Kiss*.[159]

These late *Kisses*, the column and the gate, are monumental versions of the Platonic *syzygy*, the Platonic soul union, but erotic and cosmological versions. The 'eyes' are biological 'cells', as Constantin Brancusi explained. They are the basic form of life, the

---

158 E. Derré: *La Grotte d'Amour*, 1905; Jules Dalou: *The Kiss*, Giraudon; M.L. Béguine: *The Embrace*, 1906; Edvard Munch: *The Kiss*, 1895, private collection; Picasso: *The Embrace*, 1900; F. Vaoulot: *The Kiss*, 1905; William Zorach: *The Embrace*, 1933, bronze, 66in high, collection the Zorach children
159 Brancusi: *The Gate of the Kiss*, 1937-8, banpotoc travertine, 17ft 3.5in x 21ft 7.2in x 6ft 6in, Tirgu Jiu, Romania; *Column of the Kiss*, c. 1933, plaster, 18in high, Musée National d'Art Moderne, Paris. See Sidney Geist: "The centrality of the Gate", *Artforum*, 12, October 1973, 70-78

5454545454545454

organic cell, from which all life grows. These 'eyes' are also circles, and in *The Column of the Kiss* and *The Gate of the Kiss*, Constantin Brancusi uses the circle as the prime symbol of life. He cuts it in two, and so those two semi-circles become the perfect symbol of the Platonic souls finding their 'other half'. Circles split in two also have sexual associations, hinting at the genitals of men and women. The bisected circle can be, if you like, labia, or testes, or glans, etc. Brancusi explained the meaning of the 'eyes':

> What is left behind when you are no more? It is the memory of the eyes, of your looks that imparted love for man and people. These figures are a representation of the amalgamation of man and woman through love.[160]

It is worth noting, too, that above the pillars of *The Gate of the Kiss* are forty couples inscribed on the surface of the massive lintel. These couples are copulating, they are drawn like the full-length bodies on the Montparnasse *The Kiss,* where legs and arms entwine in a Tantric lovemaking. Constantin Brancusi's *The Gate of the Kiss* is thus an epic, monumental poem to erotic, human love, love made cosmic and mythic. The tenderness that writers such as D.H. Lawrence, William Shakespeare, Sappho, and André Gide thought of as essential in love is there in Brancusi's *Kissing Gate*, but made vast and monolithic.

In Constantin Brancusi's vision of the supreme erotic moment, the *unio mystica* as Catholic mystics and theologians call it, the two figures are clasped together so tightly nothing gets between them. It is a pure fusion of body and soul: their eyes touch, their faces touch, their mouths touch, their bodies touch.

Constantin Brancusi's *The Kiss* motif has been influential, though not, perhaps, as influential as the *Birds in Space*, the eggs and heads, or the *Endless Column*. Barry Flanagan has produced a sculpture of erotic figures carved into a chunk of square stone that directly recalls Brancusi's *The Kiss*.[161]

---

160 Brancusi, quoted in Barbu Brezianu: *Brancusi in Romania*, op. Cit., 143
161 Flanagan: *Tantric Figures*, 1973, collection: E.J. Power, London

418

Constantin Brancusi's lovers recall the figures in Tantric art, where couples are shown erotically entwined with each other. In Oriental sex yoga and erotic literature, couples are depicted in a series of poses, which demonstrate how the cosmic energies, *yin* and *yang* or *Shiva* and *Shakti* fuse together in an erotic-religious embrace. Brancusi's *The Kiss* makes the ephemeral nature of eroticism permanent: it is carved not in marble or bronze, but in stone, which gives the work a heavy, earthy, durable feel.

The Kiss is a sculpture that is meant to represent by its solid mass a timeless erotic union. *The Kiss* is nothing less than a representation of one of the central acts of humanity – making love. It is a cosmic vision of togetherness, a vision that goes down to the fundamental, organic levels of life. Constantin Brancusi used the image of two halves melding into one in his monuments at Tirgu Jiu. Asking the American sculptor Malvina Hoffman what she thought of the columns, she said: 'I see the forms of two cells that meet and create life. The beginning of life... through love. Am I right?' Brancusi replied,

> Yes, you are... and these columns are the result of years of searching. First came this group of two interlaced, seated figures in stone... then the symbol of the egg, then the thought grew into this gateway to a beyond.[162]

---

162 M. Hoffman: *Sculpture Inside and Out*, New York 1939, 53

3

WOMEN'S ART, FEMINIST ART, WOMEN ARTISTS

Many feminists and art commentators have studied the history of women's art and women artists. Where are the great women painters, feminists ask, the artists who can stand alongside Édouard Manet, Michelangelo Buonarroti, Sandro Botticelli and Peter Paul Rubens? So feminists have been discovering, rediscovering, excavating and rewriting the past of art history. It turns out there have been many, many brilliant women artists: Artemisia Gentileschi, Sofonisba Anguissola, Gwen John, Mary Cassatt, Berthe Morisot, Suzanne Valadon, Käthe Kollwitz, Frida Kahlo, Paula Modersohn-Becker, Ch'en Shu, Barbara Longhi, Natalia Goncharova, Gabriele Münter, Dorothea Lange, Julia Margaret Cameron, Harriet Hosmer, Ma Shou-Chen, Anna Bilinska, Elisabeth Vigée-Lebrun, Françoise Duparc, Rosalba Carriera, Angelica Kauffmann, Georgia O'Keeffe, Diane Arbus, Judith Leyster, Sonia Delaunay, Kuan Tao-Sheng, Ts'ao Miao-Ch'ing, Clara Peeters, Catharina van Hemessen, and a host of contemporary artists: Miriam Schapiro, Leonor Fini, Niki de Saint-Phalle, Judy Chicago, Mary Beth Edelson, Barbara Hepworth, Helen Frankenthaler, Cindy Sherman, Jennifer Bartlett, Elizabeth Catlett, Alison Wilding, Barbara Kruger, Mary Duffy, Jo Spence, Lyn Malcolm, Agnes Martin, Elizabeth Murray, Judy Rifka, Louise Bourgeois, Nancy Graves, Katherine Porter, Susan Rothenberg, Eva Hesse, Louise Nevelson, Lynda Benglis, Lee Bontecou, Sherrie Levine, Rebecca Horn, Magdalena Abakanowicz, Ana Mendieta, Judy Pfaff, Pat Steir, Catherine Murphy, and Audrey Flack.

Many images made by women artists have become widely celebrated: Artemisia Gentileschi's marvellous *Judiths*, and her luminous *Self-Portrait*; Käthe Kollwitz's emotionally-charged sculptures; Georgia O'Keeffe's vulva-shaped flowers; Barbara Hepworth's holed stone and metal forms; Mary Cassatt's independent form of Impressionism; Elisabeth Vigée-Lebrun's royal portraits, and so on. These works by women, though, are still not as highly regarded by the art world as, say, Jasper Johns' *American Flag* or Eugène Delacroix's *Sardanapale*.

One of the problems that feminists have addressed with regard to women's art is: can there be a truly female or feminine or women's art? Is art made by women (women's art) ever completely free of patriarchal influences, structures, forms? Can there be a women's art that exists in its own female space, away from patriarchy and masculinist ideas and experiences? Julia Kristeva is pessimistic on this contentious issue. For her, there has been no 'female writing' thus far in our culture. She says:

> If we confine ourselves to the *radical* nature of what is today called 'writing', that is, if we submit meaning and the speaking subject in language to a radical examination and then reconstitute them in a more polyvalent than fragile manner, there is nothing in either past or recent publications by women that permits us to claim that a specifically female writing exists.[163]

---

163 "A partir de *Polylogue*", interview with Françoise van Rossum-Guyon, *Revue des sciences humaines*, vol. XLIV, no. 168, tr. Seán Hand, Oct-Dec 2977, 495f

For Hélène Cixous, most writing, by men or women, is masculine. She writes:

> Most women are like this; they do someone else's – man's – writing, and in their innocence sustain it and give it voice, and end up producing writing that's in effect masculine.[164]

The notion of '*écriture féminine*' of French feminists Luce Irigaray and Hélène Cixous is much discussed in feminist literary criticism.[165] It is rejected by Monique Wittig. Wittig also rejects the notion of terms such as 'man' and 'woman'. For her, 'woman' is a historical, political, ideological and cultural construct. She writes that "woman' has meaning only in heterosexual systems of thought and heterosexual economic systems'.[166] (Camille Paglia, one of the more outspoken of (American) feminist critics, is not so optimistic about female artists).[167]

The discussion of women's art and women artists is, though, many feminists feel, crucial to feminism. After all, *we know what male artists are like,* and we are utterly familiar with male art. We are surrounded, embedded, drenched by patriarchal art and culture, by male-orientated, even if not specifically male-*made*, culture. Male projections, often onto women, have become dogma. Masculinist fear of the body, and sexuality, have been projected onto women, so that the vagina becomes a hell hole, the 'gateway to Hell'. As Luce Irigaray remarked: men's '*fantasies lay down the*

---

164 Cixous: "Castration or Decapitation?", *Signs*, 7, 1, 52
165 Arleen B. Dallery: "The politics (the body: *écriture féminine*", in Alison M. Jaggar & Susan R. Bordo, eds. *Gender/Body/Knowledge: feminist reconstruction of being and knowing*, Rutgers University Press, New Brunswick, 1989; Deborah Cameron: *The Feminist Critique of Language*, Routledge 1990; Jan Montefiore: *Feminism and Poetry: Language, Experience, Identity in Women's Writing*, Pandora 1987; Andrea Nye: "The voice of the serpent: French feminism and the philosophy of language", in Ann Garry & Marilyn Pearsal, eds. *Women, Knowledge and Reality: explorations in feminist philosophy*, Unwin Hyman 1989
166 Wittig: "The Straight Mind, *Feminist Issues*, I:1, 110
167 'One of the many lies of women's studies is that European art history was written by white males and that feminism has conclusively rewritten that history by discovering and restoring major female artists excluded from the pantheon by patriarchal conspiracy. But European art history was not just written but created by white males. We may lament the limitations placed on women's training and professional access in the past, but what is done cannot be undone. The last 20 years of scholarship have brought many forgotten women artists to attention, but too often their presentation has been marred by anachronistic feminist rhetoric: feminism has not found a single major female painter or sculptor to add to the canon. (Camille Paglia: "New Sexism for women", *The Guardian*, 30 September 30, 1993).

law.[168]

Feminists have, rightly, a lot to complain about. Look at any art history book: nearly all the names, either of artists or critics, are male. Books such as *Techniques of the World's Great Painters* are typical. *All* the fifty painters featured in this book are male. Published in 1980, i.e. in the age of second wave feminism, around the time of Griselda Pollock and Rozsika Parker's book *Old Mistresses: Woman, Art and Ideology* and Karen Petersen and J.J. Wilson's study *Women Artists* were published, books such as *Techniques of the World's Great Painters* should have known better.

There are hundreds of art books which feature the same roll-call of male artists: in Robert Goldwater and Marco Treves' anthology *Artists on Art From the 14th to the 20th Century*, there are no women artists in amongst the quotes from one hundred and forty-one male artists.

The litany of holy male artists includes: Giotto, Duccio, Jan van Eyck, Piero della Francesca, Leonardo da Vinci, Hieronymous Bosch, Titian, Caravaggio, El Greco, Diego Velásquez, Peter Rubens, Rembrandt van Rijn, Jan Vermeer, J.A.D. Ingres, Eugène Delacroix, J.M.W. Turner, Jean Millet, Gustave Courbet, Édouard Manet, Claude Monet, Pierre Renoir, Edgar Degas, Vincent van Gogh, Edvard Munch, Paul Cézanne, Paul Gauguin, Henri Matisse, Pablo Picasso, Wassily Kandinsky, Pierre Bonnard, Edward Hopper, Salvador Dali, Paul Klee, Piet Mondrian, Max Ernst, Jackson Pollock, Jasper Johns, Frank Stella, Roy Lichenstein, and David Hockney. These are the Great Names of Art. They form a religion of art, a cult which decisively excludes women and the female voice. High art is distinctly a male preserve, an area presided over and fiercely guarded by men and male ideology.

Of course, the reasons why there are so few exalted women artists in the art world are many and complex, having to do with economy, power, politics, law, ideology, sexuality, identity, etc. The guardians of high art are also male: the critics and reviewers. The celebrated critics have always been male: Vasari, Bruce

---

168 Luce Irigaray: *Parler n'est jamais neutre*, tr. David Macey, in *The Irigaray Reader*, 94

Berenson, Jacob Burckhardt, Kenneth Clark, John Ruskin, Walter Pater, Friedrich Nietzsche, Leon Battista Alberti, and Benvenuto Cellini, going back to Plato and Aristotle.

Is there a true women's art? Is there feminist art? What is the relation of feminist to masculinist art? Does feminist art have to be made by women? These questions go to the heart of feminist and feminist cultural criticism. Feminist art is not simply all women's art, all women's 'experience' in art, of art, some feminists state: '[f]eminist art is not the same as any art which emphasizes women's experience.'[169]

There are many feminists who advocate the exaltation of all manner of women artists, who argue for a women's art based on women artists, who want viewers to look at women artists. There are other feminists who deny the primacy of the author, who say that the work – the text – is primary, who deny the transparency of the text. Toril Moi and many other feminists have questioned the humanist notion of realism or authenticity where a text is seen to reflect the actual experience of the one who created it. Humanist criticism sees a direct relation between author and text, assuming that the artwork is a 'direct expression' of the artist's experience. Artists, however, know that very often the artwork ends up being far away from what they intended to 'express' or 'communicate'.

The artwork, whether painting, sculpture, magazine, book, dance, performance, etc – is not a 'person' or an individual, but a series of gestures, surfaces, motions, materials, signs, and so on. The link between artist/ author and artwork/ text is often very tenuous. As Toril Moi commented:

> When the text no longer offers an individual grasped as the transcendental origin of language and experience, humanist feminism must lay down its arms. (*Sexual/ Textual Politics*, 80)

The artwork, then, is a set of words, signs, symbols, materials, codes, colours, gestures, etc. It is not a direct extension of the artist,

---

169 Michele Barrett: "Feminism and the Definition of Cultural Politics", *Feminism, Culture and Politics*, ed. Rosalind Brunt & Caroline Rowan, and in Eagleton, ed., 163

even though it is manufactured by and from her body, however indirectly. When the text is primary, the notion of an artist/author dies. Roland Barthes remarked:

> Once the Author is removed, the claim to decipher a text becomes quite futile. To give a text an Author is to impose a limit on that text, to furnish it with a final signified, to close the writing.[170]

There is no final and definitive reading of any text, then, but only endless openness, endless permutations of readings, which shift continually, dependent upon a variety of factors, among them: politics, ideology, identity, power, economy, class, race, sex, etc.

There are many problems, then, in creating a philosophy of feminist criticism, in looking at women authors and artists, in producing a tradition of feminine art. Many feminist critics have addressed the matter of women's or feminist art.[171] Focusing on women artists – Jane Austen, Emily Brontë, George Eliot, Emily Dickinson, Virginia Woolf and Gertrude Stein in writing, or Artemisia Gentileschi, Mary Cassatt, Gwen John, Berthe Morisot, Georgia O'Keeffe, Käthe Kollwitz and Susan Valadon among visual artists – is absolutely crucial.

But what is the relation of the feminine qualities of the woman artist to her work? Is not all art, of any kind, produced *within* patriarchal culture? Is it possible to make art that is utterly outside of patriarchy? Is the female tradition of women artists simply patriarchal art made by women? If men, or masculine culture, has

---

170 Barthes: *Image Music Text*, tr. Stephen Heath, Fontana 1977, 147

171 See H. Robinson, ed. *Visibly Female: feminism and art today*, Camden Press 1987; J.P.Stanley & S.J. Wolfe: "Toward a feminist æsthetic", *Chrysalis*, no. 6, 57-71; P. Palmer: *Contemporary Women's Fiction: narrative practice and feminist theory*, Harvester Wheatsheaf 1989; L. Nochlin: "Why are there no great women artists?", in V. Gornick & B. Moran, eds. *Women in Sexist Society*, 1971; R. Betterton, ed. *Looking On: Images of femininity in the visual arts and media*, Pandora Press 1987; D. Butturuff & E.L. Epstein, eds. *Women's Language and Style*, University of Akron, Akron 1978; Griselda Pollock: "A Politics of Art or an Aesthetics for Women?", *Feminist Art News*, 1981, no. 5; Maggie Humm: *Feminist Criticism: Women as Contemporary Critics*, Harvester 1986; Barbara Smith: *Toward a Black Feminist Criticism*, Crossing Press, New York 1980; I.J. Nicholson, ed. *Feminism/Postmodernism*, Routledge 1990; C. Belsey & J. Moore: *The Feminist Reader: Essays in the Politics of Literary Criticism*, Macmillan 1989; Gisela Ecker: *Feminist Aesthetics*, Women's Press 1985; Susan Santoro: *Towards a New Expression*, Rome 1974

defined everything in culture, how can there by a truly feminine art'? These are important questions, that require much debate and analysis.

Feminist art, then, aims to question all manner of notions of æsthetics, attitudes, assumptions, traditions, representations, meanings and mythologies. Feminist æsthetics aims to rewrite, recreate, re-work received, established notions of art. Feminist art remakes art from the foundations upwards. It seems to be an impossible task, but it has to be attempted. As Giselda Ecker wrote: '[w]e have to be aware of the paradox that there cannot be any certainty about what is feminine in art but that we have to go looking out for it.'[172]

It is crucial to make art, to write, to create, as every feminist, of whatever political belief, agrees. You must write, because otherwise you get written. If you don't write, someone else will 'write' you. You'll be written over, written out, edited, selected, controlled, censored, cut up, packaged, suffocated. All feminists agree that, whatever one believes, and whatever one desires, whether emotionally, politically, or socially, writing and creating are absolutely essential. As Hélène Cixous stated in "The Laugh of the Medusa", her highly influential essay of the mid-1970s:

> And why don't you write? Write! Writing is for you, you are for you; your body is yours... Write, let no one hold you back, let nothing stop you... Women should break out of the snare of silence...[173]

You can 'read' creatively, if you don't write. Much of feminist theory is based on 'reading' texts as a woman, a feminist, a lesbian. If the author is 'dead', and the text is primary, then deeply engaging with texts is crucial. Hence the importance, too, of feminist æsthetic and philosophic criticism, which aims to interpret all manner of texts. The reader, at least, is 'real'. The reader, it would seem, is truly flesh and blood, not a linguistic abstraction. Even here, though, some feminists dispute the reality

---

172 Gisela Ecker: *Feminist Aesthetics,* Women's Press 1985
173 Cixous: "The Laugh of the Medusa", in Marks, 246-7, 251

or authenticity of the body, for the body, like education or desire or the family, is culturally and socially conditioned. That is, there is no such thing as a 'pure' reality, a 'pure' experience, a 'pure' response to a text, a response that is not modulated by all manner of social, societal, familial, psychological, political, ideological and cultural influences.

In feminism, the scenario is not simply a woman and a book, existing completely separately from everything else, in some utopian place. No, there is so much that gets in the way of the seemingly 'innocent' or 'pure' exchange between a woman and an artwork, a person and a text. But the personal response is crucial, and alive. Reading can be, in itself, radical and trans-formative.

Creating a feminist æsthetics means writing and re-writing language, art, culture, notions of knowledge and ontology, of identity and politics, all manner of things. For Julia Kristeva, there is no 'other place' in language, for, as the philosopher Ludwig Wittgenstein said, the world we live in is a world circumscribed by language. In effect, language 'writes' the world: to go beyond it is the quest for the wild zone, the utterly Other Place. For Kristeva, revolution must occur *within* symbolic (that is, patriarchal) language.[174] Women's writing or art becomes a literature of absence, of negative capability, revealing by what it does not reveal, forever outside yet also inside patriarchal discourse. As the Marxist-Feminist Literature Collective write:

> Women, who are speaking subjects but partially excluded from culture, find modes of expression which the hegemonic discourse cannot integrate. Whereas the eruptive word cannot make the culturally inaccessible, it can surely speak its absence.[175]

Julia Kristeva asks questions which are central to feminist æsthetics and women's art. Will there be a visionary feminism

174 See Julia Kristeva: *Desire in Language* and *Révolution du language poétique*, Seuil, Paris 1974
175 Marxist-Feminist Literature Collective: "Women's Writing: *Jane Eyre, Shirley, Villette, Aurora Leigh*", in Francis Barker *et al*, eds. *1848: The Sociology of Literature*, in Eagleton, ed. *Feminist Literary Theory: A Reader*, 197

which takes women's art (French feminists use the term 'writing' to cover cultural/ creative activities) into a new era?

> Or is it [Kristeva comments], on the contrary and as avant-garde feminists hope, that having started with the idea of difference, feminism will be able to break free of its belief in woman, her power, her writing, so as to channel this demand for difference into each and every element of the female whole, and, finally, to bring out the singularity of each woman, and beyond this, her multiplicities, her plural languages, beyond the horizon, beyond sight, beyond faith itself?[176]

Julia Kristeva is very positive, though, despite her insistence on absence. She is uncompromising; in her essay "Freud and Love" she says she believes in the 'notion of emptiness, which is at the heart of the human psyche'.[177] Yet she is optimistic, too. Her philosophy is founded on absence, yet she often writes of the possibility that a wild zone or otherness has been neglected, that there maybe a nighttime space, of the unconscious, of magic or otherness. In *Women's Time* Kristeva asks more questions:

> Is it because, faced with social norms, literature reveals a certain knowledge and sometimes the truth itself about an otherwise repressed nocturnal, secret and unconscious universe? Because it thus redoubles the social contract by exposing the unsaid, the uncanny?[178]

Language is central to the creation of a feminist æsthetics. Women are denied the place to really *speak*, as many feminists note. Luce Irigaray commented:

> When a girl begins to talk, she is already unable to speak of/ to herself. Being exiled in man's speech, she is already unable to auto-affect. Man's language separates her from her mother and from other women, and she speaks it without speaking in it.[179]

Mary Daly has written exuberantly of creating a new

176 Kristeva: *Women's Time*, in *The Kristeva Reader*, 208
177 Kristeva: *Histoires d'amour*, Denoël, Paris, 1983, and in *The Kristeva Reader*, 242
178 Kristeva: *The Kristeva Reader*, 207
179 Irigaray: "The poverty of psychoanalysis", *The Irigaray Reader*, 101

language, and her books – *Pure Lust, Gyn/Ecology, Webster's First New Intergalactic Wickedary of the English Language* – are full of energetic incantations of a new women's language:

> Our call of the wild is a call to dispossess our Selves of the shrouds, the winding sheets of words. We eject, banish, dispose the possessing language – spoken and written words, body language, architectural language, technological language, the language of symbols and of institutional structures – by inspiriting our Selves. The Sister Selves are the only Selves who can bond together and conquest beyond, before, beneath, and around the seductive pseudowords.[180]

So far in our history, men have done most of the 'speaking', or male-made culture has. Language itself, as Dale Spender noted, seems to be 'man-made'.[181] And everybody knows somebody who speaks as the person (the male) does in Xavière Gauthier's essay:

> the frightful masculine fashion of speaking always surprises me. Speaking in order to be right – how ridiculous! In fact, to put someone else in the wrong. Speaking to nail the listener's trap shut. Speaking to put her in her place: man's language, man's rod.[182]

It is not a simple act of substituting feminism for masculinism, women for men, female for male. Griselda Pollock wrote:

> Feminism in culture cannot be reduced to substituting *women's* for men's subjectivities in an otherwise unchanged notion of art as self-expression. It is not, therefore, the fact that activities or representations are undertaken by *women* which renders them feminist. Their feminism is crucially a matter of *effect*. To be feminist at all work must be conceived within the framework of a structural, economic, political and ideological critique of the power relations of society and with a commitment to collective action for their radical transformation.[183]

---

180 Mary Daly: *Gyn/Ecology*, 345
181 Dale Spender: *Man-Made Language*, Routledge & Kegan Paul 1985, 12
182 Gauthier: "Why Witches?", in *Sorcières*, 1, 1976, in Marks, 200
183 Griselda Pollock: "Feminism and Modernism", in Rozsika Parker & Griselda Pollock, eds. *Framing Feminism: Art and the Women's Movement 1970-1985*, Pandora 1987

The question we keep returning to is: can there be a female of feminine wild zone, an utterly non-patriarchal, non-male space? If it is true, as Andrea Dworkin maintains, that '[m]en have defined the parameters of every subject',[184] how can there be an extra-masculinist place? For Julia Kristeva, the problem is not one, as in the feminism of Hélène Cixous and Luce Irigaray, of essence, but of positionality, a question of discourse and viewpoint, rather than biology and essentialism.

The problems stem, partly, from accepting and using systems and approaches of criticism, philosophy, psychology and politics that are male-made or masculinist. It's all very well, feminists comment, using the vulva or womb as a powerful image of the feminine, as artists such as Judy Chicago has done in many works (one of Chicago's ceramic pieces is entitled *The Cunt as Temple, Tomb, Cave and Flower*),[185] but this very notion plays into the hands of men and patriarchal attitudes, which so often reduce women to sex objects, so that the body becomes mere 'cunt'.[186]

And a female artist such as Nancy Grossman, who employs the imagery of bondage, S/M and fetish porn, seems to be wholly phallic and patriarchal. Her images depict cult, kitsch gear, such as leather, zips, straps, chains, and guns in erotic contexts.[187] Her views on art are patriarchal and phallic, those of the Marquis de Sade, Charles Baudelaire, Georges Bataille, Wilhelm Reich, and Henry Miller: she wishes to get rid of taboos: 'to have a head and no feelings, to have a vagina and not fill it, to have a penis and not stick it in – that is not living.'[188]

How is it possible, though, to employ strategic, radical, political and specifically feminist approaches to criticism, philosophy, psychology and politics, when the means and structures

184 Andrea Dworkin; *Pornography*, 7
185 Judy Chicago: *The Dinner Party*, 1975-9; *The Cunt as Temple, Tomb, Cave and Flower*, c. 1974, china pencil on porcelain, collection; the artist; *Female Rejection Drawing*, 1974, coloured pencil on paper, 30 x 40in, collection: the artist; *Earth Birth*, from *The Birth Project*, 1982-3, sprayed fabric paint and quilting, 152 x 365cm, ACA Gallery, New York
186 See Lisa Tickner: "The Body Politic: Female Sexuality and Women Artists since 1970", *Art History*, 1:2, June 1978, 236-51; also Lynda Nead: *The Female Nude*, 65f
187 Nancy Grossman: *Figure*, 1970, ink on paper, 45.5. x 34.5in, Princeton Art Museum, Princeton
188 Nancy Grossman, quoted in Tilly, 74

and approaches available are shot through with masculinist notions? As Elaine Showalter says:

> One of the problems of the feminist critique is that it is male-orientated. If we study stereotypes of women, the sexism of male critics, and the limited roles women play in literary history, we are not learning what women have felt and experienced, but only what men have thought women should be.[189]

If there really is no non-patriarchal culture space, then feminism is going to end up somewhat limited in its scope and depth, and limited in its effects. Perhaps. If there is no true female wild zone, a place which is strange, terrifying, ecstatic and truly beyond men or, rather, beyond male culture, this is a depressing thought. As Toril Moi remarked in *Sexual/Textual Politics*:

> If there is no space uncontaminated by patriarchy from which women can speak, it follows that we really don't need a fulcrum at all: there is simply nowhere else to go. (81)

Of course, it might be utopian to think there is a truly non-patriarchal, non-male place. But, after all, men have their own wild zone, their thoroughly male/ masculinist space. Why not women too?

Some of the problems of feminist poetics, and of feminism in general, is the constant reference to patriarchy and masculinist experiences and ideas. If men and patriarchy are always the measure of all things, the results will always be limited, some feminists claim. That is, being female is simply being 'not-male'. Being feminist always means being non- or anti -masculinist. As Luce Irigaray puts it: '[b]eing a woman is equated with not being a man.' (*Je, to, Nous*, 71) This cannot be the case. It's not right to use men/ masculinity/ patriarchy as a guide or measure for feminist æsthetics and criticism. Because everything said will be referenced to men and male constructions. Far better to speak of

189 Elaine Showalter: "Towards a feminist poetics", in Mary Jacobus, ed. *Women and Writing and Writing About Women*, Croom Helm 1979, 27

difference, to state that women's creations, experiences and ideas are not the other side of the ontological coin from men's; they are different. Instead of saying all things female or feminine are simply the counterpart or companion, or opposite, of all things male and masculine, it is, perhaps, more fruitful to say all things female and feminine are *different* from all things male and masculine. Of course, a mythology or economy of *difference* has its problems, as commentators acknowledge,[190] but it does free feminists up from always referring to men, masculinity and patriarchy.

The notion of difference is controversial in feminist philosophy. There is cultural, psychological, political and emotional difference, but most problematic is sexual and biological difference, the culture of difference based in sexuality and the body.

The figure of the lesbian and the culture of lesbianism becomes central to some approaches of feminism, because the lesbian stands outside of patriarchy, even as she is defined by heterosexuality and patriarchy. Men cannot control lesbian culture in the same way they can control heterosexual culture. As Alice, Gordon, Debbie and Mary say: '[l]esbians, by loving women and not men, pose a direct threat to the very basis of male supremacy.'[191] Feminism and lesbian culture can lead to separatism, where patriarchy is avoided – not only culturally, but physically. Janet Dixon writes that '[s]eparatism is to feminism what fundamentalism is to Christianity.'[192] The extreme of separatism is the creation of an all-woman state, a utopian female and feminine space. Utopian, separatist or lesbian, feminism, then, looks towards a radical and revolutionary transformation of the world. The opposers of radical separatism claim it is fascistic and racist, in its destruction of all things built, written and

---

190 See Teresa de Lauretis: "The essence of the triangle or, taking the risk of essentialism seriously", *differences*, 1 (2), 1989, 3-37; Domna C. Stanton: "Difference on Trial: a critique of the maternal metaphor in Cixous, Irigaray and Kristeva", in Nancy K. Miller, eds. *The Poetics of Gender*, Columbia University Press, 1986, 157-82; Rosi Braidotti: "The ethics of sexual difference: the case of Foucault and Irigaray", in *Australian Feminist Studies*, 3, 1986, 1-13
191 Alice, Gordon, Debbie and Mary: "Separatism", in Sarah Lucia Hoagland& Julia Penelope, eds. *For Lesbians Only: A Separatist Anthology*, Onlywomen Press 1988, 31-40
192 Janet Dixon: "Separatism", *Spare Rib*, 192 (1988), 6

produced by men.

Lesbian culture seeks to get beyond patriarchy, and lesbian-orientated art is perhaps one way of producing non-patriarchal art. As Monique Wittig says of the lesbian: '[l]esbian is the only concept that I know of which is beyond the categories of sex (man and woman)'.[193]

Other feminist critics have said that lesbianism is not a culture that exists truly outside of patriarchy. In fact, says Elizabeth Kee, 'lesbian as an attack on hetero-relations, takes (its) place within the structure of the institution of heterosexuality. The lesbian is born of/ in it.'[194] Defined by heterosexual patriarchy, lesbianism may be limited in its potential for radically transforming society, say some feminists. The movement totally away from patriarchal culture is all the more urgent, then, if the radical forms of feminism, lesbianism and separatism are to be realized.[195]

---

193 Monique Wittig: "One is not born a woman", in Hoagland, op.cit., 440
194 Meese, in Karla Jay and Joanna Glasgow: *Lesbian Texts and Contexts: Radical Revisions*, New York University Press, New York 1990, 82
195 See Bonnie Zimmerman, and Sonya Andermahr's essays in Sally Munt, 4, 133, 151; Sally Miller Gearhart: *The Wanderground*, Persephone Press, Watertown 1978; Joanna Russ: *The Female Man*, Women's Press, 1976; S. Rowbotham: *Beyond the Fragments: Feminism and the Making of Socialism*, Merlin 1979; Adrienne Rich: "Toward a woman-centred university", in *On Lies, Secrets and Silence*, Novotony, New York 1979 and "Compulsory heterosexuality and lesbian existence", *Signs*, vol. 5, no. 4, 631-660; C. Moraga & G. Amzaldue, eds. *This Bridge Called my Back: Writings by Radical Women of Color*, Persephone Press, Watertown 1981; Jill Johnston: *Lesbian Nation: The Feminist Solution*, Simon & Shuster, New York 1974; Radicalesbians: "The woman-identified woman", in A. Koedt, ed. *Radical Feminism*, Quadrangle, New York 1973.

4

CONTEMPORARY FEMINIST AND WOMEN'S ART

There are many brilliant women artists working at the moment. Most of the feminist art being produced is by women. Male artists have only made tentative steps in producing art that radically questions or rewrites patriarchal attitudes, values, ideas, experiences or laws. Much of feminist or women's art celebrates the feminine, what is special to femininity or womanhood, the being of woman and women.

One aspect of feminist or women's art is embodied by the figure of the Goddess, the ancient and primæval Great Mother of all, celebrated then – and now – as Isis, Ishtar, Demeter, Kali, etc. The Goddess is now variously interpreted as fact, experience, idea, æsthetic, cult, religion, pagan emblem and many other things by women artists. There are a host of artists who have made what we might call Goddess art, art that employs the figure of the Goddess as an embodiment of female being or experience: Judy Chicago, Mary Beth Edelson, Miriam Schapiro, Niki de

Saint-Phalle, Louis Bourgeois, and Helen Chadwick. Mary Beth Edelson engaged in the resurgence of the Goddess, in her *Great Goddess* series.[196] Edelson has also produced a piece on menstruation, entitled, appropriately, *Blood Mysteries*.[197] In a piece of performance art, Catherine Elwes sat in an enclosed studio space and menstruated.[198] Judy Chicago looked to the flowers of Georgia O'Keeffe, which, she said, 'stand for femininity'.[199]

The Goddess is a symbol and experience of a new spiritual consciousness that also embraces eroticism. Catholic feminists, such as Meinrad Craighead, have spoken of the need for Christians to embrace eroticism as well as spirituality.[200] Sutra Biswas depicts women as incarnations of the Goddess Kali, who beheads men.[201]

Feminist artists and writers have been putting the erotic dimension back into the Goddess, after thousands of years of desexed deities such as the Virgin Mary. Images such as Piero della Francesca's *Madonna del Parto* are taken up by feminists because here is a depiction of a pregnant Goddess.[202] Goddess art is full of images of menstruation, pregnancy, childbirth, all those things termed by some 'women's mysteries'.

NIKI DE SAINT-PHALLE. Niki de Saint-Phalle has produced exuberant Goddesses, such as her *Black Venus*, or her marvellous *Pink Childbirth*, a Great Mother Goddess made from dolls, toys, tissues and various items collected together like a totem of the prehistoric world, while Saint-Phalle's *Un Ensemble de "Les Nanas"* is an effervescent – and multicoloured – representation of female

196 Mary Beth Edelson: *Great Goddess Series*, 1975, collection: the artist
197 Edelson: *Blood Mysteries*, 1973, drawing, 91 x 57 in, collection: the artist
198 Catherine Elwes: "Floating femininity: a look at performance art by women:, in S. Kent & J. Morreau, eds. *Women's Images of Men*, Pandora Press, 1985, 182
199 quoted in Lucy Lippard, 219. See also Lucy Lippard: "Dinner Party", *Art in America*, April 1980, 122
200 See Mary Giles, ed. *The Feminist Mystic*, Crossroad, 1982
201 Sutapa Biswas, interview with Yasmin Kureishi, *Spare Rib*, no. 173, December 1986;
202 Piero della Francesca: *Madonna del Parto*, c. 1450-5, fresco, 260 x 203cm, Cemetery Chapel, Monterchi, Arezzo

forms, dancing, cavorting, balancing,[203]

British artist Helen Chadwick has made a *Madonna and Child* image with a female Christ Child, complete with labia, placenta and birthcord.[204] US artist Lynda Benglis appeared in *Artforum* in 1974 nude, holding a giant phallus between her legs.[205] Louis Bourgeois, one of the grand dames of contemporary art, has investigated the female form in many works, using, as so many feminist artists have done, the female body as the site of feminist explorations.[206] Feminist artists have rewritten, recreated, reviewed the female body. Many feminist artists have used their own bodies as artworks, challenging radically traditional notions of fine and art criticism.

CINDY SHERMAN. Cindy Sherman's photographs investigate the female body, often naked, in ever more complex and ironic ways. Her richly coloured photographs quote from films and create narratives which hover between fear and desire, clarity and ambivalence. Sherman (a favourite with art critics) takes the bland furniture and gestures of life and imbues them with a narrative strangeness that engages the spectator in an exploration of æsthetic expectation, identity, perception and tradition. Cindy Sherman has also used a Hans Bellmer-like doll, or plastic parts of the (female) body in ironic ways, in works that are, typically, titled *Untitled*.[207]

Feminist artists are using the body to explore political, erotic, pornographic, æsthetic and philosophical discourses. As Lisa

203 Niki de Saint-Phalle: *Black Venus*, 1967, painted polyester, 110 x 35 x 24in, Whitney Museum of Art, New York; *Pink Childbirth*, 1964, painted relief, 86.24in high, Moderner Museet, Stockholm; *Un Ensemble de "Les Nanas"*, 1965, Archives Galerie Alexandre Iolas, New York. See David Bourdon *et al*: *Niki de Saint-Phalle: Fantastic Vision*, Nassau County Musem of Fine Art, Rosyln, New York 1987; Jean-Yves Mock: *Niki de Saint-Phalle: Exposition Retrospective*, CGP 1980
204 Helen Chadwick: *One Flesh*, 1986, photocopies, 160 x 107cm, Victoria & Albert Museum, London
205 Benglis: *Self-portrait*, 1974, advert in *Artforum*
206 Louis Bourgeois: *Fragile Goddess*, c. 1970, clay, 10in high, Robert Miller Gallery, New York; *Femme Couteau*, 1982, black marble, 14 x 77.5 x 20.3cm, Robert Miller Gallery, New York
207 Cindy Sherman: *Untitled*, 1985, two colour photographs, both 72.5 x 49.5in; and see Laura Mulvey: "A Phantasmagoria of the Female Body: The Work of Cindy Sherman", *New Left Review*, 188, July/August 1991, 136-150; P. Schjeldahl: *Cindy Sherman*, Pantheon Books 1984

Tickner writes: '[l]iving *in* a female body is different from looking *at* it, as a man.'[208] The female nude, for so long the model and image and object of lust in so many high art paintings, has usurped the power relation between artist and art object, and between artwork and spectator. The woman is no longer content to be looked at and lusted after: she is making her own art, employing her body in a radical, challenging way. The 'Old Master/ *Playboy* tradition', as Tickner calls it, has been smashed. Feminists and feminist artists must make sure that the 'Old Master/ *Playboy* tradition' never assumes dominance again.[209]

Feminist body and performance art is a way of repossessing the body, sexuality, identity and power, it is a way of 'rewriting the body'. It can be an act of transgression and subversion, which usurps the power relation between spectator and artwork, so that the (male) viewer's 'cloak of invisibility has been stripped away and his spectatorship becomes an issue within the work', as Catherine Elwes puts it.[210]

Displaying the female body, though, can also make it available for being appropriated by men, as some feminists have cautioned.[211] Women artists have to make sure they are not titillating their audience in that way so familiar in pornography. The issues raised by feminist body and performance art are many and complex, basically pivoting around whether body art is truly subversive, or whether it plays into the grasping hands of patriarchy.[212] As the Editorial Collective of *Questions féminists* write, 'it is also dangerous to place the body at the centre of a

---

208 Lisa Tickner: "Body Politic", op.cit., 239
209 See T. Gouma-Peterson & P. Matthews: "The feminist critique of art history", *The Art Bulletin*, LXIX, 1987, 326-57
210 Elwes, op.cit., 172
211 See Lynda Nead, 67; Lucy Lippard: "The Pain and Pleasures of Rebirth: European and American Women's Body Art", in *From the Center*, op.cit., 125
212 See Henry M. Sayre: *The Object of Performance: the American Avant-garde Since 1970*, University of Chicago Press 1989; Sally Potter: "Our Shows", *About Time: Video, Performance and Installation by 21 Women Artists*, ICA, 1980; Jeannie Forte: "Women's Performance Art: Feminism and Postmodernism", *Theatre Journal*, 40:2, May 1988, 217-35; Elinor Fuchs: "Staging the Obscene Body", *The Drama Review*, 33:1, Spring 1989, 33-58; Janet Wolff: "Reinstating Corporeality: Feminism and Body Politics", *Feminine Sentences: Essays on women and culture*, Polity Press, Cambridge 1990; Claudette Johnson: "Issues Surrounding the Representation of the Naked Body of a Woman", *Feminist Art News*, 3:8, 1991

search for female identity.'[213]

American artist Carole Schneemann pulled a scroll from her vagina and reads from it.[214] China Kumari Berman made 'body prints'. Karen Finley poured 'a can of yams over her naked buttocks'; she was described as 'a frightening and rare presence',[215] in her *Cut Off Balls* she castrated Wall Street bankers.[216] Mary Duffy displayed her disabled body in performance and photographic sequences;[217] Jo Spence photographed the 'unhealthy and aging female body'.[218]

NANCY GRAVES. Among non-figurative, abstract or partially-figurative artists, people such as Nancy Graves are absolutely astonishing, with her superb multi-media constructions.[219] Graves' skeletal, fossil-like works combine fantasy and natural forms in 'one exuberantly open-form, polychrome, freestanding construction after another' (Daniel Wheeler, 303).

THÉRÈSE OULTON. Painters such as Thérèse Oulton are as sensuous and powerful in their technique and subjects as any male painter. Oulton's canvases are as luscious and romantic as

213 "Variations on Common Themes", *Question féministes,* no. 1, November 1977, quoted in Marks, 218
214 See Carolee Schneemann: *Interior Scroll,* 1975; *More than Meat Joy: Complete Performance Works and Selected Writings,* ed. Bruce MacPherson, Documentext, New York 1979
215 C. Carr: "Unspeakable Practices, Unnatural Acts", *Village Voice,* 24 June 1986
216 See Anthony Adler: "Dangerous Woman: Karen Finley", *Chicago Reader,* 26 October 1990; Richard Lacayo: "Talented Toiletmouth", *Time,* 4 June 1990; Miranda Joseph: "Further Finley", *The Drama Review,* Winter 1990, 13; Kay Larson: "Censor Deprivation", *New York,* 6 August 1990; Catherine Schuler: "Spectator Response and Comprehensions: The Problems of Karen Finley's *Constant State of Desire*", *The Drama Review,* Spring 1990, 131-145; Clive Barnes: "Finley's Fury", *New York Post,* 24 July 1990; Tim Page: "Karen Finley's Tantrum, Amid Chocolate", *New York Newsday,* 24 July 1990
217 Mary Duffy: *Cutting the Ties that Bind,* 1987; *Stories of a Body,* 1990. See Hilary Robinson: "The Subtle Abyss: Sexuality and Body Image in contemporary Feminist Art", unpublished dissertation, RCA 1987; Mary Duffy: "Cutting the Ties that Bind", *Feminist Art News,* 2:10, 1989, 6-7; and "Redressing the Balance", *Feminist Art News,* 3:8, 1991
218 Jo Spence and Tim Sheard: *Narratives of Dis-ease.* See Jo Spence: *Putting Myself in the Picture: A Political, Personal and Photographic Autobiography,* Camden Press 1986; Patricia Holland, Jo Spence and Simon Watney, eds. *Photography/Politics: Two,* Commedia 1986; Darcy Grimaldo Grigsby: "Dilemmas of Visibility: Contemporary Women Artists' Representations of Female Bodies", *Michigan Quarterly Review,* XXIX: 4, Autumn 1990, 584-618
219 Nancy Graves: *Zaga,* 1983, cast bronze with polychrome chemical patination, 6' x 4'1" x 2'8", Nelson-Atkins Museum of Art, Kansas City; *Cantileve,* 1983, bronze with polychrome patina, 999 x 67 x 55in, M. Knoedler & Co, New York. See Avis Berman: "Nancy Graves", *Art News,* Feb 1986, 57-64; Debra Bricker Balken and Linda Nochlin: *Nancy Graves: Painting, Sculpture, Drawing 1980-5,* Vassar College Art Gallery, Poughkeepsie, 1986; E.A. Carmean et al: *The Sculpture of Nancy Graves,* Fort Worth 1987; Amy Fine Collins and Bradley Collins: "The Sum of the Parts [Nancy Graves]", *Art in America,* 1988, 113-8; L. Cathcart: *Nancy Graves: A Survey 1969-1980,* Albright-Knox Gallery, catalogue, 1981

anything by, say, Titan, Diego Velásquez or Caravaggio. Oulton's *Spinner*, painted in 1986, is a voluptuous, abstract creation, recalling the energetic gestures of the Expressionists and the Abstract Expressionists, while the colours, which melt from earth and ochre to white and pale, cerulean blue, recall landscape painters such as J.M.W. Turner, John Constable and Thomas Girtin.[220]

The surfaces of Thérèse Oulton's canvases – *Voice, The Heart of the Matter, In Fidelity, Countenance, The Passions, Mortal Coil* and *Space for Leda* – are extraordinarily sumptuous.[221] 'Oulton's work has a 'strong but non-specific erotic power,' writes Wendy Beckett (82), while John Griffiths describes Oulton's work thus:

> Highly textured 'wild' landscapes of the emotions, painted on a grand scale which suggest possible figurative images only to subvert the meanings suggested by the intrusion of quasi-abstract forms without obvious significance. Above all a sense of mystery and openness of spirit emerges underpinned by a strange, new, unlocated sense of landscape.[222]

And, as with the art of William Turner, her textures are always moving, never fixed. But, for all its surface sensuality, its iridescent but shadowy hues, Thérèse Oulton's work is religious, with spiritual goals. As with Turner, Oulton's canvases hint at a radiance busting out from behind shadows and darkness, as in her *Old Gold*,[223] which, like so many of Oulton's paintings, features a sense of overarching structures, perhaps something of the sky or a mountainscape, as it might be in one of Turners' boiling, stormy seas, or a storm in the Alps. In Oulton's work such direct connections are hinted at but not made dogmatic. Her abstraction hovers between hints of figuration and post-painterly

220 Thérèse Oulton: *Spinner*, 1986, oil on canvas, 234 x 213.5cm, private collection. See Gidal Lampert: *Thérèse Oulton Fools' Gold*, Gimpel Fils, catalogue, 1984; S. Morgan: *Thérèse Oulton: Skin Deep*, Galerie Thomas, Munich, 1986;
221 Thérèse Oulton: *Mortal Coil*, 1984, oil; *In Fidelity*, 1987, oil; *Countenance*, 1986, oil, all Marlborough Fine Art Gallery, London; *Voice*, 1984, oil on canvas, 92 x 84in, private collection; *Space for Leda*, 1983, oil on canvas, 269 x 228.5cm, collection: the artist
222 John Griffths: "New Romantic Artists", in Papadakis: *The New Romantics*, 60
223 T. Oulton: *Old Gold*, 1984, oil on canvas, 205.7 x 259.1cm, Frankel Collection, Philadelphia

abstraction. A sense of mystery is always retained, that spiritual openness which renders her art so exciting. Critics call it 'romantic', and certainly it describes an area as far away as possible from the so-called 'real world' of socialist realistic, political, issue-based art.

If you have doubts about there being any great or powerful women painters about, painters who can more than look good when set against Julian Schnabel, Robert Longo, Eric Fischl, Gerard Richter, David Salle, Jeff Koons and Francesco Clemente – then look at Thérèse Oulton's work. If you want luscious sensuality in art, or a metaphysical, transcendent dimension, or rigorous formalism, or explorative abstraction, then you don't need to go to the revered modern masters of contemporary art (David Hockney, R.B. Kitaj, Sol LeWitt, Sean Scully, Frank Stella, Jasper Johns, Robert Rauschenberg and Andy Warhol). You can find it aplenty in the work of women artists such as Oulton, Nancy Graves, Jennifer Bartlett, Niki de Saint-Phalle, Mary Beth Edelson, Helen Frankenthaler, Elizabeth Cartlett, Alison Wilding, Barbara Kruger, Lynn Malcolm, Agnes Martin, Elizabeth Murray, Judy Rifka, Katherine Porter, Susan Rothenberg, Eva Hesse, Lee Bontecou, Rebecca Horn, Magdalena Abakanowicz, Judy Pfaff and Pat Steir.

LYNDA BENGLIS. Lynda Benglis has produced three dimensional works which develop the ironic objects of Claes Oldenburg, such as in her wonderful, twisted *Aldebaran*.[224] Edward Lucie-Smith writes of Lynda Benglis thus:

> Oldenburg's drooping flaccid forms become emblems of impotence. Benglis's rosettes are successors to an earlier group of sculptures in the shape of giant dildoes or penises. If we read what she is doing in the context supplied by Oldenburg's work, she still seems to be concerned with sexual issues – her comment is no longer one about men's fears of female aggression, but about women's need to adorn and at the same time 'cheapen' themselves, because they live in a man's world. (*American Art Now*, 57)

---

224 Lynda Benglis: *Aldebaran*, 1983, bronze, zinc, copper, aluminium, 167.5 x 134.5cm, Paula Cooper Gallery, New York

The photographer Robert Mapplethorpe produced many pictures of penises: a penis on a pedestal, a black man's penis hanging out of a polyester suit, and so on.[225] These images were heavily contextualized as part of a homoerotic discourse. Women artists, such as Benglis have taken the phallus and put it into ironic, satirical contexts.

JUDITH BERNSTEIN. Judith Bernstein produced thirty-foot high phallic drawings in the late 1960s, entitled *Phallic Screws*. Of these gigantic phalluses, Laurie Anderson wrote: '[t]he scale of Bernstein's seven new drawings, *Phallic Screws*, made Claes Oldenburg look like a miniaturist.'[226] Bernstein's aim was to appropriate some of the power of the phallus, an impossible goal to achieve for some feminists. Bernstein wrote: 'I feel the phallus has stood for power for so many centuries, and I feel that we women want to be part of that power.'[227] Bernstein's other pieces include *Supercock* (Superman with a penis twice as big as his body), and *Union Jack-Off Series* (flags with penises).

LEONOR FINI. The women Surrealists have been celebrated by some feminists and art critics as a crucial element not only in male/ patriarchal Surrealism, but also in high art generally. There are some startling women artists who made Surrealist art, or art that has affinities with André Breton, Marcel Duchamp, Yves Tangy, René Magritte, Salvador Dali, Max Ernst, Man Ray and the other oh so wonderful Surrealists. Leonor Fini created exquisite dream scenes,[228] such as *Red Vision*, which may be about the menstrual cycle: a white girl (ovulation, domesticity) meets in an empty room a floating red girl (menstruation, wildness); or her *Compositions with Figures on a Terrace*, where extraordinary women, dressed fabulously, stare off into space; or her highly potent *Chthonian Divinity Watching Over the Sleep of a Young Man*, where the woman, a dark sphinx behind the young Adonis, is

225 R. Mapplethorpe: *Man in Polyester Suit*, 1980, photograph, Estate of Robert Mapplethorpe
226 L. Anderson: "Judith Bernstein (AIR)", *Art News*, December 1973, 94
227 J. Bernstein in Jeanie Weiffenback: "Interview with Judith Bernstein", *Criss-Cross Art Communications*, January 1977, 228
228 See Xavière Gauthier: *Léonor Fini*, Paris 1973; Constantin Jelenski: *Léonor Fini*, Lausanne 1972; *Léonor Fini*, Galleria Civica d'Arte Moderna, Ferrara 1983; Silvio Gaggi: "Léonor Fini: A Mythology of the Feminine", *Art International*, 23, Sept 1979, 34-38

clearly a Black Goddess of marvellous eroticism.[229]

LEONORA CARRINGTON. Like Leonor Fini, Leonora Carrington paints the clean, empty rooms of the unconscious, populated by bizarre items, bizarre partly for their juxta-positioning with other objects,[230] such as in her *Self-Portrait*.[231] DOROTHEA TANNING. Dorothea Tanning, for so long known simply as 'the wife of a famous artist' (Max Ernst), which has been (and is) the fate of so many women artists, also painted fantastic dreamscapes.[232] She paints places where shapes merge into shapes in flowing streams of energy, such as in her visionary *Guardian Angels*, or where young women, again, as in the art of Fini and Carrington, with long, wild hair, encounter gigantic yellow sun-flowers on mysterious hotel landings, as in *Die Kleine Nachtmusik*.[233]

REMEDIOS VARO. For strangeness, the images of women Surrealists far surpass those of most male artists. This is not only because the women's images are not so well known – indeed, are hardly featured in many art history books – but because they are actually far stranger. Take the work of Remedios Varo, who, again, like Fini, Carrington and Tanning, creates the rooms of dreams, spacious spaces that haunt the viewer with their extraordinary perspectives and contents.[234]

In Remedios Varo's *Creation of the Birds* we see a bird woman (a female shaman) making birds with the aid of the light of a distant star focused through a prism, a machine which looks like

229 Leonor Fini: *Red Vision*, 1984, oil on canvas, 17.2 x 20.6in, private collection; *Chthonian Divinity Watching Over the Sleep of a Young Man*, 1947, oil on canvas, 13 x 21.8in, private collection; *Composition with Figures on a Terrace*, 1939, oil on canvas, 38.8 x 31.2in, collection: Edward James Foundation, Sussex
230 See Juan Garcia Ponce & Leonora Carrington: *Leonora Carrington*, Mexico City 1974; Edward James, intr, *Leonora Carrington*, Center for Inter-American Relations, New York 1975; Gloria Orenstein: "Leonora Carrington's Visionary Art for the New Age", *Chrysalis*, 4, 1978, 65-77
231 L. Carrington: *Self-Portrait*, 1936-7, oil on canvas, 25.5 x 32in, Pierre Matisse Gallery, New York
232 See Gilles Plazy: *Dorothea Tanning*, Paris 1969; Dorothea Tanning: *Abyss*; *Dorothea Tanning*: Exposition Retrospective, Knokke-le-Zoute, Casino Communale 1977
233 Dorothea Tanning: *Eine Kleine Nachtmusik*, 1946, oil on canvas, 16.2 x 24in, private collection; *Guardian Angels*, 1946, oil on canvas, 48 x 55in, New Orleans Museum of Art, New Orleans
234 See Octavio Paz & Roger Callois: *Remedios Varo*, Mexico City 1973; Édouard Jaguer: *Remedios Varo*, Paris 1980; *Remedios Varo*, Museo de Arte Moderno, Mexico City 1983

two eggs on top of each that dispenses paint, and a paint brush
connected to a violin. The painting fuses the magic of light, music
and colour in an alchemical fantasy of creation, as in *Harmony*,
where a poet, aided by supernatural Muses, composes art on a
luminous, three dimensional musical stave.[235] Remedios Varo's
paintings are based on an alchemical view of the world, where all
things are related in a holistic continuum. Janet Kaplan wrote:

> Varo believed in magic. She had an animistic faith in the power of
> objects and in the interrelatedness of plant, animal, human, and
> mechanical worlds.[236]

FRIDA KAHLO. The most celebrated female Surrealist is
Frida Kahlo (1907-54), whose amazing self-portraits with their
cutaway images of her body, are among the most ruthless
explorations of sexuality in modern high art.[237] Kahlo's *The Broken
Column*, *The Two Friday*, and the astonishing *My Birth*, investigate
forms of (female) suffering, the relation of sexuality to violence,
sexuality to self-image, sexuality to emotions (hatred, self-
loathing, insecurity, rage).[238]

For Andrea Dworkin, Frida Kahlo is 'the great painter of
primal female pain' whose 'paintings are the most vivid
renderings by any woman of the female screwed, gashed,
wounded', who, married to Diego Rivera, the Mexican artist,
'painted what it was like being fucked by him'.[239] Dworkin
quotes Diego Rivera's testament of his relationship with Kahlo:
'[i]f I loved a woman, the more I loved her, the more I wanted to
hurt her. Frida was only the most obvious victim of this

235 Remedios Varo: *Creation of the Birds*, 1958, oil on masonite, 20.6 x 24.6in, private
collection; *Harmony*, 1956, oil on masonite, 30 x 37in, private collection
236 J. Kaplan: "Remedios Varo: Voyages and Visions:, *Woman's Art Journal*, 1, no. 2, Autumn
1980/ Winter 1981, 13
237 See Hayden Herrera: *Frida: A Biography of Frida Kahlo*, Harper & Row, New York 1983;
"Frida Kahlo: Her Life, Her Art", *Artforum*, 14, May 1976, 38-4; Gloria Orenstein: "Frida
Kahlo: Painting For Miracles", *Feminist Art Journal*, Autumn 1973, 7-9; Terry Smith: "From the
Margins: Modernity and the Case of Frida Kahlo", *Block*, 8, 1983, 14;
238 Frida Kahlo: *My Birth*, oil on sheet metal, 12.2 x 14in, collection: Edgar J. Kaufmann, New
York; *The Broken Column*, 1944, oil on masonite, 15.8 x 12.2in, colection: Dolores Olmedo,
Mexico City; *The Two Fridas*, 1939, oil on canvas, 67 x 67in, Museo de Arte Moderno, Mexico
City
239 Andrea Dworkin: *Intercourse*, 211-2

disgusting trait.'[240] For Dworkin, as for many feminists, Kahlo's paintings are the astonishing record of a woman's incredibly painful relationship with a man:

> She painted the suffering, enraged; she created an iconography of the *chingada* [literally the "screwed one"] that was resistance, not pornography; knowing herself to be the screwed one, she made an art of passionate rebellion that shows the pain of inferiority delivered into your body – the violence of the contempt... Kahlo paints the woman vividly wounded, dripping blood; in one, *A Few Small Nips*, painted in 1935, a naked woman (except for one sock and one shoe) is on a bed, gashed all over; she is alive, wide-eyed, her body animated in curves and subtle, living contortion; a man stands upright next to the bed, he is fully dressed, even wearing a hat, and he holds a knife in his hand; he is aloof, indifferent, blank; and the blood in blotches and smears is all over her body and spreads out over the walls and over the floor in spots and smears even past the boundaries of the canvas to the frame. Kahlo shows the unspeakable pain of being *alive* and female, penetrated like this.[241]

Frida Kahlo's art is that of an outsider, someone who inhabits the edges of society, a place that is perhaps the feminist wild zone. As Whitney Chadwick wrote: '[w]hen it came to sharing in the collective mythology of Surrealism, women experienced themselves as outsiders.'[242] Leonor Fini saw herself as that archetypal female outsider, Lilith, the mythic witch of Western religion: 'I know that I belong with the idea of Lilith, the anti-Eve, and that my universe is that of the spirit.'[243]

ANA MENDIETA. Ana Mendieta covered herself in mud (while *nude, of course*) and stood against a tree (for *The Tree of Life* series, 1977, made in Old Man's Creek, Iowa), a combination of Goddess art, performance art and environmental art. In *The Tree of Life* series, Mendieta left the outline of her body in leaves on a tree trunk. In the *Silueta* series (1979), Mendieta imprinted her body in the snow in Amana, Iowa, and in mud on a riverbank, or set the form on fire in the earth, or made a silhouette from

240 Rivera, quoted in Hayden Herrera: *Frida*, op.cit., 183
241 Dworkin: *Intercourse*, 212, 223
242 Whitney Chadwick, *Women Artists and the Surrealist Movement*, 129
243 Léonor Fini, quoted in Xavière Gauthier: *Léonor Fini*, op.cit., 74

flowers.

Ana Mendieta's performances echo other land and installation art, such as Andy Goldsworthy's rain and snow 'body prints'. However, Mendieta's art has an undisguised ideological, spiritual and ecological agenda; some of Mendieta's works are explicit performance explorations of rapes, and Mendieta was also exploring her Cuban and Latin American heritage.

In some pieces Ana Mendieta remodelled the entrance of a cave and a ravine into her Goddess shape. She also buried herself under turf – a literal Earth-Goddess mound, and had herself photographed in an ancient Mexican stone grave.[244] Mendieta also lit fires in sculptures (such as *Volcano*, 1979), like Chris Drury and David Nash, and lit candles and fireworks in the shape of a woman.

ITHEL COLQUHOUN. Looking at Surrealist concepts of eroticism from the alienated viewpoint of the female Surrealist artist, Ithel Colquhoun painted some ironic parodies of Surrealist sexuality, such as her *The Pine Family*, which depicts three male torsos made of pine logs, each with the penis lopped off.[245] Colquhoun's painting sends up Freudian psychoanalysis and the grotesque notion of castration.

But while Frida Kahlo creates a powerful and idiosyncratic art, completely her own world, there were women Surrealists who produced disappointing art, art which did not veer from the patriarchal norms of masculine art. Nusch Éluard's collages, for instance, replay patriarchal views of women without much irony.[246]

Land artists, such as Beverly Pepper or Nancy Holt, might also be seen as producing Goddess-orientated art. BEVERLY PEPPER. Pepper's large, curving mirrored slabs of wood buried in sandy beaches might be seen as a type of Earth Mother art, art

244 See L. Lippard, 1983, 49.
245 Ithell Colquhoun: *The Pine Family*, 1941, oil on canvas, 18 x 20in, private collection. See *Ithell Colquhoun*, Leva Gallery, London 1974 Dawn Ades: "Notes on Two Women Surrealist Painters: Eileen Agar and Ithell Colquhoun", *Oxford Art Journal*, 3, no. 1, April 1980
246 Nusch Éluard: *Photo-Collages*, c. 1935, photo-collage postcard, 5.4 x 3.5in, collection: Timothy Baum, New York. See Nusch Éluard: *Collage Dreams*, Nadada Editions, New York 1978

which worships and works with the earth, rather than, as in some of male land art, cutting or penetrating it, phallically (like Michael Heizer, Robert Smithson and Walter de Maria).[247]

NANCY HOLT. Nancy Holt's art is more obviously comparable with the male earth artists, with its large, heavy landscaping gestures (such as her *Dark Star Park*).[248] The globes and pools of water, though, are traditional feminine volumes, here given a new, monumental turn. Holt has explored cosmo-logical and astronomical associations in her art, her works linking Earth with the heavens.

MIRIAM SCHAPIRO. Miriam Schapiro has taken up materials branded feminine by patriarchy (cotton, taffeta, burlap, wool, sequins, buttons, thread), and has created artworks (she calls them 'femmages') that deal with notions of the home, feminist iconography, abstraction and the æsthetics of 'Pattern and Decoration'.[249] Schapiro says: 'I wanted to explore and express a part of my life which I had always dismissed – my homemaking, my nesting'.[250]

A number of male artists have explored traditionally feminine notions of pattern, decoration and colour, among them Robert Zakanitch, Lucas Samaras, Robert Kushner, Rodney Ripps, Kim MacConnel, Frank Stella and Ned Smyth. The male-made pieces, such as by Rodney Ripps,[251] occasionally approach the flamboyance and intricacy of artworks made by women, such as by Joyce Kozloff or Valerie Jaudon.[252] The traditional women's arts and crafts of textiles, pattern, sewing, decoration, pottery, etc, are bound up with the economies of labour, race, class, identity, patriarchy, politics and finance. They are modes of production and

247 Beverly Pepper: *Sand Dunes*, 1985, Mylar over wood, approximately 100ft long, temporary installation for the Atlantic Center for the Arts, New Smyrna Beach, Florida
248 Nancy Holt: *Dark Star Park*, 1979-84, concrete, steel, water, earth, 0.67 of an acre, Rosslyn, Virginia
249 Miriam Schapiro: *Heartland*, 1985, acrylic, fabric and glitter on canvas, 7.1 x 7.8ft, Bernice Steinbaum Gallery, New York
250 quoted in D. Wheeler, 285
251 Rodney Ripps: *Gay Princess*, 1980, oil, wax and cloth on wood, 52 x 51 x 8in, Holly Solomon Gallery, New York
252 Valerie Jaudon: *Caile*, 1985, oil on canvas, 48 x 40in, Sidney James Gallery, New York; Joyce Kozloff: *New England Decorative Arts*, 1985, tile mural, 8 x 83 feet overall, Harvard Square subway station, Cambridge, Mass.

art that are regarded as secondary by patriarchal culture, not as high art, such as painting or sculpture. Feminist artists, then, have to tackle not only the images of themselves, whether of patriarchy, the body, or whatever, but also the *production* of the images. The economics of artistic production are embedded with patriarchal slants, just as much as the images themselves.

As Catherine King writes, '[m]edia associated with 'male-stream' codes, like bronze, marble, or oil, have been regarded with suspicion' by women artists.[253] The piece of textiles, the decorative tile, the pot, then, are objects that in the patriarchal system speak of their second-rate mode of production. To make a pot, tile or blanket and to hold it up as a serious artwork, like a painting or a sculpture, the feminist artist has to grapple with the scorn of high art critics, who demean such work (and not all high art critics are male).

The field of sculpture is just one area in which women artists often far excel male artists. Ultimately, of course, gender has nothing to do with making good art – or good erotica; it's just that men have done most of the talking so far in the history of art. So let's hear from women for a change.

253 Catherine King: "Feminist Arts", in Frances Bonner *et al*, eds., 185

Bibliography

W.C. Agee: *Don Judd*, Whitney Museum of American Art, New York, NY, 1968

—. "Unit, Series, Site: A Judd Lexicon", *Art in America*, May, 1975

—. *The Sculpture of Donald Judd*, Art Museum of South Texas, Corpus Christi, TX, 1977

C. Andre. "Frank Stella: Preface to Stripe Painting", in Miller, 1959

—. "An Interview with Carl Andre", Phyllis Tuchman, *Artforum*, 8, 10, June, 1970

—. *Carl Andre, Sculpture, 1958-1974*, Kunsthalle, Bern, 1975

—. "Object v Phenomenon", *Sculpture Today*, The International Sculpture Center, Toronto, 1978

—. *Carl Andre: Sculpture*, State University of New York Press, Albany, NY, 1984

—. *Carl-Andre: works on land*, Exhibitions International, 2001

D. Anfam: *Abstract Expressionism*, Thames & Hudson, London, 1990

E. de Antonio & M. Tuchman: *Painters Painting*, Abbeville Press, New York, NY, 1984

C.G. Argan: *The Renaissance*, Thames & Hudson, London, 1969

I. Armstrong, ed. *New Feminist Discourses: Critical Essays on Theories and Texts*, Routledge, London, 1992

K. Armstrong: *The Gospel According to Woman; Christianity's Creation of the Sex War in the West*, Pan, London, 1987

G. Ashe: *The Virgin: Mary's Cult and the Re-emergence of the Goddess*, Arkana, London, 1987

D. Ashton. *Modern American Sculpture*, Abrams, New York, NY, 1968

—. *American Art Since 1945*, Thames & Hudson, London, 1982

A. Assiter: *Althusser and Feminism*, Pluto Press, London, 1990

—. & A. Carol, eds. *Bad Girls and Dirty Pictures: The Challenge to Reclaim*

Feminism, Pluto Press, London, 1993:

J. Atkins: *Sex in Literature,* volume 2: *The Classical Experience of the Sexual Impulse,* Calder & Boyars, London, 1973

P. Bade: *Femme Fatale: Images of evil and fascinating women,* Ash & Grant 1979

E. Baker: "Judd the Obscure", *Art News,* 67, 2, 1968

K. Baker. "Andre in Retrospect", *Art in America,* Apl, 1980a

—. "Reckoning with Notation: The Drawings of Pollock, Newman, and Louis", *Artforum,* 18, 10, Summer, 1980b

—. *Minimalism: Art of Circumstance,* Abbeville, New York, NY, 1988

S. Bann: *Brice Marden: Paintings, Drawings, Etchings 1975-80,* Stedelijk Museum, Amsterdam 1981

A. Barnstone & W. Barnstone, eds. *A Book of Women Poets: From Antiquity to Now,* Schocken Books, New York, NY, 1980

G. Bataille: *Literature and Evil,* tr. A. Hamilton, Calder, London, 1973

G. Battock, ed. *Minimal Art: A Critical anthology,* Studio Vista, London, 1969

M. Baxandall: *Painting and Experience in 15th Century Italy,* Oxford University Press 1988

—. *Patterns of Intention: On the Historical Explanation of Pictures,* Yale University Press 1985

G. Bazin: *A Concise History of World Sculpture,* David & Charles, Newton Abbot 1981

J. Beardsley. *Probing the Earth: Contemporary Land Projects,* Smithsonian Press, Washington, 1977

—. *Earthworks and Beyond: Contemporary Art in the Landscape,* Abbeville Press, New York, NY, 1984

J. Beck: *Italian Renaissance Painting,* Harper & Row, New York, NY, 1981

E. Begg: *The Cult of the Black Virgin,* Routledge, London, 1985

D. Belgrad. *The Culture of Spontaneity: Improvisation and the Arts in Postwar America,* University of Chicago Press, Chicago, IL, 1998

C. Belsey: *Critical Practice,* Routledge, London, 1980

N. Bennett: *The British Art Show: Old Allegiances and New Directions 1979-1984,* Orbis, London, 1984

B. Berenson: *The Italian Painters of the Renaissance,* Phaidon, London, 1952

—. *Looking at Pictures with Bernard Berenson,* selected by Hann Kiel, Abrahams, New York, NY, 1974

M. Berger: *Labyrinths: Robert Morris, Minimalism and the 1960s,* Harper & Row, New York, NY, 1989

P. Berger: *The Goddess Obscured,* Robert Hale, London, 1988

B. Bernard: *The Queen of Heaven: A Selection of Painting the Virgin from the Twelfth to the Eighteenth Centuries,* Macdonald/ Orbis, London, 1987

—. *The Bible and Its Painters,* Orbis, London, 1983

L. Bersani: *A Future For Astynanax*, Boyars, London, 1978

C. Bertelli: *Piero della Francesca*, Yale University Press, New Haven 1992

A. Bertram: *Piero della Francesca*, Studio Publications, London, 1949

F. Bonner *et al*, eds. *Imagining Women Cultural Representations and Gender*, Polity Press, Cambridge 1992

S. Botticelli: *The Complete Paintings of Botticelli*, Granada, London, 1980

G. Boudaille: *Expressionists*, Alpine Fine Arts Collection, London, 1976

P. Bourdieu: *Distinction: A Social Critique of the Judgment of Taste*, tr. R. Nice, Routledge & Kegan Paul London, 1984

D. Bourdon. "The Razed Sites of Carl Andre", *Artforum*, 5, 2, Oct, 1966

—. "Walter de Maria: The Singular Experience", *Art International*, 20 Dec, 1968

— "The Mini-Conceptual Age", *Village Voice*, 17 Oct, 1974

—. *Carl Andre: Sculpture, 1959-1977*, Jaap Rietman, New York, NY, 1978

S. Bramly: *Leonardo: The Artist and the Man*, Michael Joseph 1992

A. Brahama: *Italian Renaissance Painters of the Sixteenth Century*, National Gallery 1985

J. Bremmer, ed. *From Sappho to de Sade: Moments in the History of Sexuality*, Routledge, London, 1989

R. Briffault: *The Mothers: A Study of the Origins of Sentiments and Institutions*, Allen & Unwin, 3 vols, London, 1927

H. Brinker: *Zen in the Art of Painting*, Routledge & Kegan Paul, London, 1987

S. Brown: *Religious Painting*, Phaidon, London, 1979

J. Burckhardt: *The Altarpiece in Renaissance Italy*, Phaidon, London, 1988

T. Burckhardt: *Sacred Art in East and West*, Perennial Book, Middlesex 1967

J. Burnham: *Beyond Modern Sculpture*, George Braziller, New York, NY, 1968

R. Cafritz *et al. Places of Delight: The Pastoral Landscape*, Weidenfeld & Nicolson, London, 1989

N. & E. Calas. *Icons and Image of the Sixties*, Dutton, New York, NY, 1971

R. Calder: *Leonardo and The Age of the Eye*, Heinemann 1970

D. Cameron, ed. *The Feminist Critique of Language: A Reader*, Routledge, London, 1990

J. Campbell: *The Power of Myth*, with Bill Moyers, ed. Betty Sue Flowers, Doubleday, New York, NY, 1988

—. *The Hero With a Thousand Faces*, Paladin, London, 1988

—. *An Open Life*, Larson Publications, New York, NY, 1988

—. *Myths To Live By*, Paladin, London, 1985

—. *The Hero's Journey: Joseph Campbell on his Life and Work*, ed. Phil Cousineau, Harper & Row, San Francisco 1990

M. P. Carroll: *The Cult of the Virgin Mary*, Princeton University Press, NJ 1986

W. Chadwick: *Women, Art, and Society*, Thames & Hudson, London, 1990

—. *Women Artists and the Surrealist Movement*, Thames & Hudson, London, 1991

A. Chastel: *Art of the Italian Renaissance*, tr. P. & L. Murray, Alpine Fine Arts Collection, London, 1985

—. *The Studios and Styles of the Renaissance, Italy 1460-1500*, tr. Griffin, Thames & Hudson, London, 1966

G. Chester & J. Dickey, ed. *Feminism and Censorship: The Current Debate*, Prism Press, Bridport, Dorset 1988

L. Chester, ed. *Deep Down: New Sensual Writing By Women*, Faber, London, 1987

T. Chetwyd: *A Dictionary of Symbols*, Collins, London, 1982

H.B. Chipp, ed. *Theories of Modern Art*, University Press of California, Los Angeles, 1968

J.E. Cirlot: *A Dictionary of Symbols*, Routledge, London, 1981

H. Cixous & C. Clément: *The Newly Born Woman*, tr. B. Wing, Manchester University Press 1986

K. Clark: *Landscape into Art*, Reader's Union, London, 1965

—. *Piero della Francesca*, Phaidon, London, 1969

—. *Rembrandt and the Italian Renaissance*, John Murray, London, 1969

B. Cole: *The Renaissance Artist at Work*, John Murray, London, 1983

F. Colpitt: *Minimal Art: The Critical Perspective*, University of Washington Press, Seattle, 1990

J.C. Cooper: *The Aquarian Dictionary of Festivals*, Aquarian Press, Northants 1990

—. *An Illustrated Dictionary of Traditional Symbols*, Thames & Hudson, London, 1978

—. *Fairy Tales*, Aquarian Press, Northants 1983

P. Courthion: *Flemish Painting*, Thames & Hudson, London, 1958

M. Craig-Martin: *Minimalism*, Tate Gallery, Liverpool 1989

M. Crichton: *Jasper Johns*, Thames & Hudson, London, 1977

P. Crowther. "Barnett Newman and the Sublime", *Oxford Art Journal*, 7, 2, 1984

—. ed. *The Contemporary Sublime*, *Art & Design*, 40, 1995

G. Cunningham: *The New Woman and the Victorian Novel*, Macmillan, London, 1978

M. Dabrowski: *Contrasts of Form: Geometric Abstract Art 1910-80*, MOMA, New York, NY, 1985

M. Daly: *Pure Lust: Elemental Feminist Philosophy*, Women's Press, London, 1984

—. *Gyn/Ecology: The Metaethics of Radical Feminism*, Women's Press, London, 1979

—. *Beyond God the Father*, Women's Press, London, 1985

J. Daval: *History of Abstract Painting*, Art Data 1989

H. Davies *et al. Blurring the Boundaries: Installation Art 1969-1996*, Museum of Contemporary Art, San Diego, CA, 1997

R. Davies & T. Knipe, eds. *A Sense of Place: Sculpture in Landscape*, London, 1984

K. Davis *et al*, eds. *Coming to Power, Writings and Graphics on Lesbian S/M*, Alyson Publications, Boston 1983

M. Davies: *Rogier van der Weyden*, Phaidon, London, 1972

A. Dempsey. *Styles, Schools Movements*, Thames & Hudson, London, 2002

J. De Mul. *Romantic Desire in (Post)Modern Art and Philosophy*, State University of New York Press, Albany, NY, 1999

N. de Oliveira *et al*. *Installation Art*, Thames & Hudson, London, 1994

—. *et al*, eds. *Installation Art in the New Millennium*, Thames & Hudson,London, 2003

E. Develing. *Carl Andre*, Gemeentenmeuseum, The Hague, 1969

—. & L. Lippard. *Minimal Art*, Stadtische Kunsthalle, Dusseldorf, 1969

J. Dollimore & A. Sinfield, eds. *Political Shakespeare*, Manchester University Press 1985

J. Drakakis, ed. *Alternative Shakespeares*, Routledge, London, 1988

L. Dresen-Coenders, ed. *Saints and She-Devils: Images of Women in the 15th and 16th Centuries*, Rubicon Press 1987

W. Dube: *The Expressionists*, Thames & Hudson, London, 1972

S.C. Dubin: *Arresting Images: Impolitic Art and Uncivil Actions*, Routledge, London, 1992

G. Duby & M. Perrot: *Power and Beauty: Images of Women in Art*, Tauris Parke Books,

M. Duffy: *The Erotic World of Faery*, Cardinal/ Sphere, London, 1989

L. Durrell: *The Durrell-Miller Letters 1935-80*, ed. Ian MacNiven, Faber, London, 1988

—. *Spirit of Place*, Faber, London, 1971

A. Dworkin. *Women-Hating*, Dutton, New York, 1974

—. *Mercy*, Arrow, London, 1990

—. *Intercourse*, Arrow, London, 1988

—. *Pornography: Men Possessing Women*, Women's Press, London, 1984

—. *Our Blood*, Harper & Row, New York, NY, 1976

—. *Right-Wing Women: The Politics of Domesticated Females*, Women's Press, London, 1978

M. Eagleton, ed. *Feminist Literary Criticism*, Longman, London, 1991

—. ed. *Feminist Literary Theory: A Reader*, Blackwell 1986

H. Eisenstein: *Contemporary Feminist Thought*, Unwin Paperbacks, London, 1984

C. Eisler: *Early Netherlandish Painting: The Thyssen-Bornemisza Collection*, Sotheby's Publications, London, 1989

D. Elger: *Expressionism: A Revolution in German Art*, Benedikt Taschen, Köln 1991

M. Eliade: *Ordeal by Labyrinth,* University of Chicago Press 1984

—. *A History of Religious Ideas,* I, Collins, London, 1979

—. *Patterns in Comparative Religion,* Sheed & Ward, London, 1958

—. *Symbolism, the Sacred and the Arts,* Crossroad, New York, NY, 1985

—. *Myths, Dreams and Mysteries,* Harper & Row, New York, NY, 1975

—. *Shamanism: Archaic Techniques of Ecstasy,* Princeton University Press, 1972

—. *From Primitives to Zen: A Sourcebook,* Collins, London, 1977

A. Elsen: *Modern European Sculpture 1918-45,* New York, NY, 1979

J. Evans, ed. *The Flowering of the Middle Ages,* Thames & Hudson, London, 1966

J. Evola: *The Metaphysics of Sex,* East-West Publications, London, 1985

G.T. Faggin: *The Complete Paintings of the Van Eycks,* Weidenfeld & Nicolson, London, 1970

Feminist Review, eds. *Sexuality: A Reader,* Virago, London, 1987

G. Ferguson: *Signs and Symbols in Christian Art,* Oxford University Press 1961

J. Ferguson: *An Illustrated Encyclopaedia of Mysticism,* Thames & Hudson, London, 1976

P. Fingesten: *The Eclipse of Symbolism,* University Press of California 1970

J. Fletcher & A. Benjamin, ed; *Abjection, Melancholia and Love: the Work of Julia Kristeva,* Routledge, London, 1990

S. Foley. *Unitary Forms: Minimal Structures by Carl Andre, Donald Judd, J. McCracken, Tony Smith,* Museum of Modern Art, San Francisco, CA, 1970

M. Foucault: *The History of Sexuality,* Penguin, London, 1981

—. *The Use of Pleasure: The History of Sexuality,* vol. 2, Penguin, London, 1987

C. Franklin, ed. *Erotic Art by Living Artists,* Directors Guild Publishers, Renaissance, California 1988

F. Frascina *et al,* eds. *Modern Art and Modernism: A Critical Anthology,* Paul Chapman, 1988

J.G. Frazer: *The Golden Bough,* abridged edition, Macmillan, London, 1922/59

S.J. Freedberg: *Painting of the High Renaissance in Rome and Florence,* Harper & Row, New York, NY, 1972

S. Freud: *Leonardo da Vinci,* tr. A. Tyson, Penguin, London, 1963

M. Fried. "New York Letter", *Art International,* 8, 3, Apl, 1964

—. *Three American Painters: Kenneth Noland, Jules Olitski, Frank Stella,* Fogg Art Museum, Harvard University, Cambridge, MA, 1965

—. "Shape as Form: Frank Stella's New Paintings", *Artforum,* 5, 3, Nov, 1966

—. "Art and Objecthood", *Artforum,* 5, Summer, 1967

—. *Morris Louis,* Abrams, New York, NY, 1970

M.J. Friedlander: *From Van Eyck to Bruegel*, Phaidon, London, 1969

M. Friedman. "Robert Morris: Polemics and Cubes", *Art International*, 10, 10, Dec, 1966

—. *14 Sculptors*, Walker Art Center, Minneapolis, MN, 1969

E. Fry. *Alice Aycock*, University of South Florida Art Galleries, Tampa, FL, 1981

—. "The Poetic Machines of Alice Aycock", *Portfolio*, Nov, 1981

—. *et al. Robert Morris*, Museum of Contemporary Art, Chicago, IL, 1986

R.H. Fuchs: *Richard Long*, Thames & Hudson, London, 1986

E. Gadon: *The Once and Future Goddess*, Aquarian Press 1990

N. Garavaghlia: *The Complete Paintings of Mantegna*, Weidenfeld & Nicholson, London, 1971

Fred Gettings: *The Hidden Art: A Study of the Occult Symbolism in Art*, Studio Vista, London, 1978

M. Ghyka: *The Geometry of Art and Life*, Sheed & Ward, New York, NY, 1946

P. Gibson & R. Gibson, ed. *Dirty Looks: Women, Pornography, Power*, British Film Institute, London, 1993

M. Gimbutas: *The Language of the Goddess*, Thames & Hudson, London, 1989

C. Ginzburg: *The Enigma of Piero: Piero della Francesca, The Baptism, The Arezzo Cycle, The Flagellation*, Verso, London, 1985

T. Godfrey. *Conceptual Art*, Phaidon, London, 1998

R. Goffen: *Giovanni Bellini*, Yale University Press, New Haven 1989

R. Goldwater & M. Treves, eds. *Artists on Art*, John Murray, London, 1975

E.H. Gombrich: *Norm and Form: Studies in the Renaissance I*, Phaidon, London, 1985

—. *Symbolic Images, Renaissance Studies II*, Phaidon, London, 1985

E. Goodheart: *Desire and Its Discontents*, Columbia University Press, New York, NY, 1991

M. Gooding & W. Furlong. *Song of the Earth*, Thames and Hudson, 2002

E.C. Goossen: *The Art of the Real: USA 1948-1968*, MOMA, New York, NY, 1968

C. Gould: *Leonardo: The Artist and the Non-Artist*, Weidenfeld & Nicholson, London, 1975

C. Greenberg: *Art and Culture*, Beacon Press, Boston 1961

—. *Post Painterly Abstraction*, Los Angeles County Museum of Art, New York, NY, 1964

G. Greer: *The Obstacle Race: The Fortunes of Women Painters and Their Work*, Secker & Warburg, London, 1979; Picador, London, 1981

S. Griffin: *Pornography and Silence: Culture's Revenge Against Nature*, Women's Press, London, 1981

J. Hale: *Italian Renaissance Painting*, Phaidon, London, 1977

J. Hall: *A Dictionary of Subjects and Symbols in Art*, John Murray, London, 1984

F.C. Happold, ed. *Mysticism*, Penguin, London, 1970

M. Esther Harding: *Women's Mysteries*, Rider, London, 1989

F. Hartt: *History of Italian Renaissance Art: Painting, Sculpture, Architecture*, Thames & Hudson, London, 1987

—. *Sandro Botticelli*, Collins, London, 1954

B. Haskell: *BLAM! The Explosion of Pop, Minimalism, and Performance, 1958-64*, Whitney Museum of American Art, New York, NY, 1984

N.G. Heller: *Women Artists: An Illustrated History*, Virago, London, 1987

T. Hess: *Barnett Newman*, Walker, New York, NY, 1969

M. Hester: *Lewd Women and Wicked Witches: A Study of the Dynamics of Male Domination*, Routledge, London, 1992

J. Hobhouse: *The Bride Stripped Bare: The Artist and the Nude in the Twentieth Century*, Cape, London, 1988

R. Hobbs: *Robert Smithson: Sculpture*, Cornell University Press, Ithaca, New York, NY, 1981

D. Holbrook, ed. *The Case Against Pornography*, Tom Stacey, 1972

A. Hollander: *Seeing Through Clothes*, Viking Press, New York, NY, 1980

K. Honnef: *Contemporary Art*, Benedikt Taschen, Cologne 1988

H. E. Hugo, ed. *The Portable Romantic Reader*, Viking Press, New York, NY, 1957

M. Humm: *Feminisms: A Reader*, Harvester Wheatsheaf, 1992

—. ed. *The Dictionary of Feminist Theory*, Harvester Wheatsheaf 1989

S. Hunter, ed. *An American Renaissance: Painting and Sculpture Since 1940*, Abbeville Press, New York, NY, 1986

—. *American Art of the 20th Century*, Thames & Hudson, London, 1973

L. Irigaray: *The Irigaray Reader,* ed. M. Whitford, Blackwell, Oxford 1991

—. *Je, tu, nous: Toward a Culture of Difference*, tr. A. Martin, Routledge, London, 1993

M. Jacobs: *A Guide to European Painting*, David & Charles 1980

—. *Mythological Painting*, Phaidon 1979

W. Januszczak, ed. *Techniques of the World's Great Painters*, Phaidon, London, 1980

E.H. Johnson: *American Artists on Art from 1940 to 1980*, Harper & Row, New York, NY, 1982

D. Judd. "Frank Stella", *Arts Magazine*, 36, Sept, 1962

—. "In the Galleries", *Arts Magazine*, 37, 10, Sept, 1963

—. "Local History", *Arts Yearbook 7*, 1964

—. "Black, White and Gray", *Arts Magazine*, 38, 6, Mch, 1964

—. "Specific Objects", *Arts Yearbook*, 8, Art Digest, New York, NY, 1965

—. "Barnett Newman", *Studio International*, 179, 919, Feb, 1970

—. *Complete Writings, 1959-1975*, Nova Scotia College of Art and Design, Halifax, Canada, 1975

455

—. *Complete Writings, 1975-1986*, Van Abbemuseum, Netherlands, 1987

P. Julian: *Dreamers of Decadence: Symbolist Painters of the 1890s*, tr. R. Baldick, Pall Mall Press, London, 1971

C.G. Jung: *Memories, Dreams, Reflections*, Collins, London, 1967

S. Kappeler: *The Pornography of Representation*, Polity Press, Cambridge 1986

J. Kastner, ed. *Land and Environmental Art*, Phaidon, London, 1998

B. Kawin: *How Movies Work*, Macmillan, New York, NY, 1987

D. Kelder: *Pageant of the Renaissance*, Pall Mall Press, London, 1969

J.A. Kestner: *Mythology and Misogyny: The Social Discourse of Nineteenth-Century British Classical-Subject Painting*, University of Wisconsin Press, Madison 1989

D. Kinsley: *The Goddess's Mirror: Visions of the Divine From East and West*, State University of New York Press 1989

C. Knight: *Art of the Sixties and Seventies: The Panza Collection*, Rizzoli, New York, NY, 1987

C. Kramarae & P.A. Treichler, eds. *A Feminist Dictionary*, Pandora Press, London, 1987

R.E. Krauss. *Passages in Modern Sculpture,* Thames & Hudson, London, 1977

—. "Sculpture in the Expanded Field", *October*, 8, Spring 1978

—. *et al. Robert Morris*, Abrams, New York, NY, 1994

J. Kristeva: *The Kristeva Reader*, ed. Toril Moi, Blackwell 1986

—. *Desire in Language: A Semiotic Approach to Literature and Art*, ed. L. Roudiez, tr. T. Gora *et al*, Blackwell 1982

W. La Barre: *The Ghost Dance*, Allen & Unwin, London, 1972

—. *Muelos*, Columbia University Press, New York, NY, 1985

J. Lacan and the *Ecole Freudienne: Feminine Sexuality*, eds. J. Mitchell and J. Rose, Macmillan, London, 1982

M. Laski: *Ecstasy*, Cresset Press 1961

D.H. Lawrence: *Study of Thomas Hardy and Other Essays*, ed. B. Steele, Cambridge University Press 1985

—. *A Selection from Phoenix*, ed. A.A.H. Inglis, Penguin, London, 1971

—. *Selected Essays*, Penguin, London, 1950

—. *Lady Chatterley's Lover*, Penguin, London, 1960

—. *Phoenix*, Heinemann, London, 1956

—. *Phoenix II*, Heinemann, London, 1968

A. Le Normand-Romain *et al. Sculpture: The Adventure of Modern Sculpture in the Nineteenth and Twentieth Centuries*, Skira, Geneva, 1986

C. Lenz *et al*, eds. *The Woman's Part: Feminist Criticism of Shakespeare*, University of Illinois Press, Urbana 1980

L. da Vinci: *The Drawings of Leonardo da Vinci*, introduction A.E. Popham, Cape, London, 1964

—. *The Complete Paintings*, introduction by L.D. Ettinger, Weidenfeld & Nicolson, London, 1969

—. *Selections from the Notebooks*, Oxford University Press 1952

M. Levey:*High Renaissance*, Penguin, London, 1975

—. *Early Renaissance*, Penguin, London, 1967

M. Levy: *Drawing and Sculpture*, Adams & Dart, Bath, Somerset 1970

F. Licht: *Sculpture, 19th and 20th Centuries*, Michael Joseph, London, 1967

R.R. Linden *et al*, eds. *Against Sadomasochism*, Frog in the Well, East Palo Alto, California, 1982

L. Lippard: *From the Center: feminist essays on women's art*, Dutton, New York, NY, 1976

—. *Six Years: The Dematerialization of the Art Object from 1966 to 1972*, Praeger, New York, NY, 1973

—. *Ad Reinhardt*, Abrahams, New York, NY, 1981

C. Lloyd: *Fra Angelico*, Phaidon, London, 1979

—. *A Picture History of Art*, Phaidon, London, 1979

E. Lucie-Smith: *Symbolist Art*, Thames & Hudson, London, 1972

—. *Sculpture Since 1945*, Phaidon, London, 1987

—. *Sexuality in Western Art*, Thames & Hudson, London, 1991

F. MacCarthy: *Eric Gill*, Faber, London, 1989

E. Male: *The Gothic Image*, Collins, London, 1961

J. van der Marck. *Wrapped Museum*, Museum of Contemporary Art, Chicago, IL, 1969

B. Marden: *Paintings, Drawings and Prints 1975-1980*, ed. Nicholas Serota, Whitechapel Art Gallery, London, 1987

E. Marks & I. de Courtivron, eds. *New French Feminisms: an Anthology*, Harvester Wheatsheaf 1981

K.B. MacFarlane: *Hans Memling*, Clarendon Press 1971

D. Mayhall: *The Minimal Tradition*, The Aldrich Museum of Contemporary Art, Ridgefield, CT, 1979

D. McKinney. *Yves Klein, Brice Marden, Sigmar Polke*, Hirschl & Alder Modern, New York, NY, 1989

R. McMullen: *Mona Lisa: The Picture and the Myth*, Macmillan, London, 1975

K. McShine: *Primary Structures*, Jewish Museum, New York, NY, 1966

G. Meaney: *(Un)Like Subjects: Women, Theory, Fiction*, Routledge, London, 1993

J.C.J. Metford: *Dictionary of Christian Lore and Legend*, Thames & Hudson, London, 1983

Michelangelo: *The Complete Paintings*, Granada, London, 1980

D.C. Miller, ed. *Sixteen Americans*, MOMA, New York, NY, 1959

M. Miller. *The Garden as an Art*, State University of New York Press, Albany, 1993

K. Millett: *Sexual Politics*, Doubleday, New York, NY, 1970

C. Millett. "De Kooning, Newman, Rothko: des bâtards", *Art Press International*, 26, Mch, 1979

E. Mitsch: *The Art of Egon Schiele*, Phaidon 1975

T. Moi: *Sexual/ Textual Politics: Feminist Literary Theory*, Routledge, London, 1988

—. ed. *French Feminist Thought: A Reader*, Blackwell, Oxford 1987

R. Morgan: *The Word of a Woman: Selected Prose 1968-1992*, Virago, London, 1993

A. Moszynska: *Abstract Art*, Thames & Hudson, London, 1990

J.-E. Muller: *Velasquez*, Thames Hudson, London, 1976

E. Mullins: *The Painted Witch: Female Body, Male Art*, Secker & Warburg, London, 1985

L. Mulvey: *Visual and Other Pleasures*, Macmillan, London, 1989

S. Munt, ed. *New Lesbian Criticism: Literary and Cultural Readings*, Harvester Wheatsheaf, London, 1992

P. & L. Murray: *The Penguin Dictionary of Art and Artists*, Penguin, London, 1976

L. Murray: *High Renaissance*, Thames & Hudson, London, 1977

L. Nead: *Female Nude: Art, Obscenity and Sexuality*, Routledge, London, 1992

T. A. Neff, ed. *A Quiet Revolution: British Sculpture Since 1965*, Thames & Hudson, London, 1987

C. Nemser. "An interview with Eva Hesse", *Artforum*, May, 1970

—. "My Memories of Eva Hesse", *Feminist Art Journal*, Winter, 1973

E. Neumann: *The Great Mother*, Princeton University Press, NJ 1972

S. Nicholson, ed. *The Goddess Re-awakening: The Goddess Principle Today*, Theosophical Publishing House, New York, NY, 1989

S. Nodelman: *Marden, Novros, Rothko: Painting in the Age of Actuality*, Institute for the Arts, Rice University, Houston 1978

Onlywomen, eds. *Love your Enemy?*, Onlywomen Press 1981

P. Osborne, ed. *Conceptual Art*, Phaidon, London, 2002

R. Otto: *The Idea of the Holy*, Oxford University Press, Oxford, 1958

E. Panofsky: *Studies in Iconology*, Harper & Row, New York, NY, 1972

—. *Early Netherlandish Painting*, Harvard University Press, Mass., 1953

A.C. Papadakis, ed. *British and American Art: The Uneasy Dialectic, Art & Design*, 3, 9/1, Academy Group, London, 1987

—. ed. *Abstract Art and the Rediscovery of the Spiritual, Art & Design*, 3, 5/6, Academy Group, London, 1987

—. ed. *The New Romantics, Art & Design*, 4, 11/12, Academy Group, London, 1988

—. *et al*, eds. *New Art*, Academy Group, London, 1991

R. Parker & G. Pollock. *Old Mistresses: Women, Art an Ideology*, Routledge & Kegan Paul, London, 1981

G. Parrinder: *Mysticism in the World's Religions*, Sheldon Press, London,

1976

W. Pater: *The Renaissance*, Oxford University Press 1980

M. Payne: *Reading Theory: An Introduction to Lacan, Derrida, and Kristeva*, Blackwell 1993

R. Payne: *Leonardo da Vinci*, Robert Hale, London, 1979

K. Petersen & J.J. Wilson: *Women Artists: Recognition and Reappraisal from the Early Middle Ages to the Twentieth Century* Women's Press, London, 1978

R. Pincus-Witten. "Systematic Painting", *Artforum*, 5, 3, Nov, 1966

—. "Ryman, Marden, Manzoni: Theory, Sensibility, Mediation", *Artforum*, 10, 10, June, 1972

—. "Sol LeWitt", *Artforum*, 11, 6, Feb, 1973

—. *Postminimalism*, Out of London, New York, NY, 1977

M. Phillipson: *Painting, Language and Modernity*, Routledge, London, 1978

G. Picon: *Surrealists and Surrealism 1919-1939*, Skira/Macmillan, London, 1983

P. della Francesca: *The Complete Paintings of Piero della Francesca*, intr. P. Murray, notes by P. de Vecchi, Penguin, London, 1985

M. Poirier. "Color-coded Mysteries", *ARTnews*, Jan, 1985

—. & J. Necol: "The '60s in Abstract Painting: 13 Statements...Brice Marden", *Art in America*, Oct, 1983

G. Pollock: *Vision and Difference: femininity, feminism and histories of art*, Routledge, London, 1988

J. Pope-Hennessy: *Fra Angelico*, Phaidon, Oxford, 1974

M. Praz: *The Romantic Agony*, tr. Davidson, Oxford University Press 1933

S. Prokopoff: *A Romantic Minimalism*, Institute of Contemporary Art, Philadelphia, PA, 1967

C. Ratcliff: *In the Realm of the Monochrome*, Renaissance Society, University of Chicago, Chicago, IL, 1979

P. Rawson: *The Art of Tantra*, Thames & Hudson, London, 1973

P. Redgrove & P. Shuttle. *The Wise Wound: Menstruation and Everywoman*, Paladin, London, 1986

—. *The Black Goddess and the Sixth Sense*, Bloomsbury, London, 1987

B. Redhead: *The Inspiration of Landscape: Artists in National Parks*, Phaidon 1989

H.J. Reiger, ed. *The Spiritual Image in Modern Art*, Theosophical Publishing House, Wheaton, Illinois 1987

A. Reinhardt: *Art as Art: The Selected Writings of Ad Reinhardt*, University of California Press, Berkeley, 1991

C. Riley II. *Color Codes: Modern Theories in Color in Philosophy, Painting and Architecture, Literature, Music and Psychology*, University Press of New England, Hanover, NH, 1995

C. Robins. "Object, Structure or Sculpture: Where Are We?", *Arts Magazine*, 40, 9, 1966

—. "Empty Paintings", *SoHo Weekly News*, 22 Apl, 1976

—. *The Pluralist Era: American Art, 1968-1981*, Harper & Row, New York, NY, 1984

F. Roh: *German Art in the Twentieth Century: Painting, Sculpture, Architecture*, Thames & Hudson, London, 1968

B. Rose. "ABC Art", *Art in America*, 53, 5, Nov, 1965

—. *A New Aesthetic*, Washington Gallery of Modern Art, Washington DC, 1967

—. *American Art Since 1900*, Thames & Hudson, London, 1967

—. *American Painting*, Skira/Rizzoli International, New York, NY, 1986

H. Rosenberg. *The De-Definition of Art*, Horizon Press, New York, NY, 1972

—. *Barnett Newman*, Abrams, New York, NY, 1978/1994

—. *The Tradition of the New*, Da Capo Press, New York, NY, 1994

R. Rosenblum. "Frank Stella: Five Years of Variations on an Irreducible Theme", *Artforum*, 3, 6, Mch, 1965

—. *Frank Stella*, Penguin, London, 1971

—. "Notes on Sol LeWitt", in Legg, 1978

—. *Modern Painting and the Northern Romantic Tradition*, Thames & Hudson, London, 1978

—. *Jasper Johns' Paintings and Sculptures, 1954-1974*, Ann Arbor, Michigan, MI, 1985

—. "Romanticism and Retrospective: An Interview with Robert Rosenblum", in Papadakis, 1988

M. Roskill: *What is Art History?*, Thames & Hudson, London, 1976

L. Rubin. *Frank Stella Paintings: 1958-1965*, New York, NY, 1986

W. S. Rubin. *Frank Stella*, New York Graphic Society, Greenwich, CT., 1970

—. *Frank Stella: 1970-1987*, Museum of Modern Art, New York, NY, 1987

J. Ruskin: *Works*, ed. E.T. Cook & A. Wedderburn, 39 vols, Allen, London, 1903-12

B. Russell: *A History of Western Philosophy*, Allen & Unwin, London, 1971

—. *Why I am Not a Christian*, Allen & Unwin, London, 1963

—. *Bertrand Russell's Best*, Allen & Unwin, London, 1971

M. Ryan, ed. *Gravity and Grace: The Changing Condition of Sculpture, 1965-1975*, Hayward Gallery, London, 1993

K. Sagar: *A D.H. Lawrence Handbook*, Manchester University Press 1982

I. Sandler. "The New Cool-Art", *Art in America*, 53, 1, Feb, 1967

—. *The Triumph of American Painting*, Harper & Row, New York, NY, 1970

—. *American Art of the 1960s*, Harper & Row, New York, NY, 1988

—. *Art of the Postmodern Era: From the 1960s to the Early 1990s*, Harper-Collins, London, 1997

J.P. Sartre: *Being and Nothingness*, tr. H. Barnes, Methuen, London, 1969

G. Saunders. *The Nude: a new perspective*, Herbert Press, London, 1989

E. Schiele: *I, Eternal Child: Paintings and Poems*, tr. A. Hollo, Grove Press, New York, NY, 1985

P. Schjeldahl: *Art in Our Time The Saatchi Collection*, Lund Humphries, London, 1984

A. Schopenhauer: *Essays and Aphorisms*, Penguin, London, 1970

E. Sedgwick: *Between Men: English Literature and Male Homosexual Desire*, Columbia University Press, New York, NY, 1985

P. Selz. *German Expressionist Painting*, University of California Press, Berkely, CA, 1974

—. *Art in Our Times: A Pictorial History 1890-1980*, Thames & Hudson, London, 1982

E. Shanes. *Constantin Brancusi*, Abbeville, New York, NY, 1989

D. Shapiro & C. Shapiro, eds. *Abstraction Expressionism: A Critical Record*, Cambridge University Press 1990

L. Shearer: *Brice Marden*, Guggenheim Museum, New York, NY, 1975

R. Sherry: *Studying Women's Writings: An Introduction*, Edward Arnold, London, 1988

E. Showalter, ed. *The New Feminist Criticism*, Virago, London, 1986

—. ed. *Speaking of Gender*, Routledge, London, 1989

—. *Sexual Anarchy: Gender and Culture at the* Fin de Siècle, Virago, London, 1992

P. Sims. *From Minimalism to Expressionism*, New York, NY, 1963

H. Singerman, ed. *Individuals: A Selected History of Contemporary Art, 1945-1986*, Museum of Contemporary Art, Los Angeles, CA, 1986

M. Sjöo & B. Mor: *The Great Cosmic Mother*, Harper & Row, San Francisco 1987

H. J. Smagula. *Currents: Contemporary Directions in the Visual Arts*, Prentice-Hall, Englewood Cliffs, NJ, 1983

A. Smith: *Early Netherlandish and German Painting*, National Gallery, London, 1985

B. Smith. *Fluorescent Light, etc, from Dan Flavin*, National Gallery of Canada, Ottawa, 1969

—. *Donald Judd*, National Gallery of Canada, Ottawa, 1975

D. Smith. *Sculpture and Drawings*, ed. J. Merkert, Prestel-Verlag, Munich, 1986

R. Smith. "Sol LeWitt", *Artforum*, Jan, 1975

—. "Review", *Artforum*, Dec, 1975

—. "De Maria: Elements", *Art in America*, May, 1978

R. Smithson. "Entropy and the New Monuments", *Artforum*, 4, 10, June, 1966

—. "A Museum of Language in the Vicinity of Art", *Art International*, 12, 3, Mch, 1968

—. *The Writings of Robert Smithson*, ed. N. Holt, New York University Press, New York, NY, 1979

—. *Robert Smithson*, ed. J. Flam, University of California Press, Berkeley, CA, 1996

T. Sokolowski *et al. Robert Morris*, New York University Press, New York, NY, 1989

N. Spector: *Robert Ryman*, Whitechapel Art Gallery 1977

S. Spencer: *Mysticism in World Religion*, Penguin, London, 1963

D. Spender: *The Writing or the Sex? why you don't have to read women's writing to know it's no good*, Pergamon Press, New York, NY, 1989

W. Spies. *The Running Fence Project, Christo*, Abrams, New York, NY, 1977

N. Stangos, ed. *Concepts of Modern Art*, Thames & Hudson, London, 1981

F. Stella. *Working Space*, Harvard University Press, Cambridge, MA, 1986

—. *Frank Stella*, Madrid, 1995

K. Stiles & P. Selz, eds. *Theories & Documents of Contemporary Art: A Sourcebook of Artists' Writings*, University of California Press, Berkeley, CA, 1996

V.I. Stoichita: *Leonardo da Vinci*, Abbey Library, London, 1978

P. Streider: *Dürer: Paintings, Prints, Drawings*, F. Muller, London, 1982

E. Suderburg, ed. *Space, Site, Intervention*, University of Minnesota Press, Minneapolis, MN, 2000

S. Rubin Suleiman, ed. *The Female Body in Western Culture: Contemporary Perspectives*, Harvard University Press, Cambridge, Mass., 1986

J. Taylor *et al. Robert Rauschenberg*, Smithsonian Institute, Washington, 1976

A. Tilly: *Erotic Drawings*, Phaidon 1986

W. Thompson: *The Time Falling Bodies Take to Light: Mythology, Sexuality and the Origins of Culture*, St Martins Press, New York, NY, 19811

L.T. Topsfield: *Troubadours and Love*, Cambridge University Press 1975

P. Trevor-Roper: *The world blunted through sight: An inquiry into the influence of defective vision on art and character*, Thames & Hudson, London, 1970

E. Tsai. *Robert Smithson Unearthed*, Columbia University Press, New York, NY, 1991

M. Tuchman. *American Sculpture of the Sixties*, Los Angeles County Museum of Art, 1967

—. *The New York School*, Thames & Hudson, London, 1971

—. *The Spiritual in Art: Abstract Painting 1880-1985*, Los Angeles County Museum of Art/ Abbeville Press, New York, NY, 1986

P. Tuchman. "Minimalism and Critical Response", *Artforum*, 15, 9, May, 1977

—. "Background of a Minimalist: Carl Andre", *Artforum*, Mch, 1978

M. Tucker. *Robert Morris*, New York, NY, 1970

W. Tucker. *The Language of Sculpture*, Thames & Hudson, London, 1974

N. Usherwood: *The Bible in 20th Century Art*, Pagoda Books 1987

M. Valency: *In Praise of Love: An Introduction to the Love-Poetry of the Renaissance*, Macmillan, New York, NY, 1961

K. Varnedoe: *Vienna 1900: Art, Architecture & Design*, Museum of Modern Art, New York, NY, 1986

L. Venturi: *Renaissance Painting, from Leonardo to Dürer*, Skira/ Macmillan 1979

—. *Italian Paintings*, Zwemmer, London, 1950

—. *Botticelli*, Phaidon 1964

P. Vergo: *Art in Vienna: 1898-1918: Klimt, Kokoschka, Schiele and Their Contemporaries*, Phaidon 1975

P. Vogt: *Contemporary Painting*, Abrahams, New York, NY, 1981

G. de Vries, ed. *On Art: Artists' Writings on the Changed Notion of Art After, 1965*, Cologne, 1974

A.M. Wagner. *Three Artists (Three Women): Modernism and the Art of Hesse, Krasner and O'Keeffe*, University of California Press, Berkeley, 1996

D. Waldman: *Mark Rothko*, Thames & Hudson, London, 1978

B. Walker: *Body Magic*, Paladin, London, 1979

—. *Tantrism: Its Secret Principles and Practices*, Aquarian Press, Wellingborough 1982

M. Warner: *Alone Of All Her Sex: The Myth and Cult of the Virgin Mary*, Picador, London, 1985

—. *Monuments and Maidens*, Weidenfeld & Nicholson, London, 1985

A. Watts: *The Myth and Ritual of Christianity*, Thames & Hudson, London, 1983

V. Wayne, ed. *The Matter of Difference: Materialist Feminist Criticism of Shakespeare*, Harvester Wheatsheaf 1991

P. Webb: *The Erotic Arts*, Secker & Warburg, London, 1983

D. Wheeler: *Art Since Mid-Century: 1945 to the Present*, Thames & Hudson, London, 1991

J. White: *The Birth and Rebirth of Pictorial Space*, Faber, London, 1957/87

F. Whitford: *Egon Schiele*, Thames & Hudson, London, 1981

E. C. Whitmont: *Return of the Goddess*, Routledge, London, 1987

L. Williams: *Hard Core*: Powe*r, Pleasure, and the 'Frenzy of the visible'*, Pandora, London, 1990

R. Williams: *Marxism and Literature*, Oxford University Press 1971

C. Wilson: *The Sexual Misfits: A Study of Sexual Outsiders*, Collins, London, 1989

P. Lamborn Wilson: *Angels*, Thames & Hudson, London, 1980

H. Wolfflin: *Classic Art*, Phaidon 1952/80

G. Woods *et al*, eds. *Art Without Boundaries*, Thames & Hudson, London, 1972

M. Wudram: *Art of the Renaissance*, Weidenfeld & Nicolson, London, 1985

M. Yorke: *Eric Gill: Man of Flesh and Spirit*, Constable, London, 1981

www.ingramcontent.com/pod-product-compliance
Lightning Source LLC
Chambersburg PA
CBHW072010230526
45468CB00021B/1176